Lecture Notes in Artificial Intelligence   4455

Edited by J. G. Carbonell and J. Siekmann

Subseries of Lecture Notes in Computer Science

T0216602

Stephen Muggleton   Ramon Otero
Alireza Tamaddoni-Nezhad (Eds.)

Inductive
Logic Programming

16th International Conference, ILP 2006
Santiago de Compostela, Spain, August 24-27, 2006
Revised Selected Papers

 Springer

Series Editors

Jaime G. Carbonell, Carnegie Mellon University, Pittsburgh, PA, USA
Jörg Siekmann, University of Saarland, Saarbrücken, Germany

Volume Editors

Stephen Muggleton
Alireza Tamaddoni-Nezhad
Imperial College London
Department of Computing
180 Queen's Gate, London SW7 2AZ, UK
E-mail: {shm,atn}@doc.ic.ac.uk

Ramon Otero
University of Corunna
Department of Computer Science
15071 Coruna, Spain
E-mail: otero@udc.es

Library of Congress Control Number: 2007931449

CR Subject Classification (1998): I.2.3, I.2.6, I.2, D.1.6, F.4.1

LNCS Sublibrary: SL 7 – Artificial Intelligence

ISSN   0302-9743
ISBN-10   3-540-73846-0 Springer Berlin Heidelberg New York
ISBN-13   978-3-540-73846-6 Springer Berlin Heidelberg New York

Springer is a part of Springer Science+Business Media

springer.com

© Springer-Verlag Berlin Heidelberg 2007
Printed in Germany

Typesetting: Camera-ready by author, data conversion by Scientific Publishing Services, Chennai, India
Printed on acid-free paper   SPIN: 12097890   06/3180   5 4 3 2 1 0

Preface

The inherent dangers of change are often summed up in the misquoted Chinese curse "May you live in interesting times." The submission procedure for the 16th International Conference of Inductive Logic Programming (ILP 2006) was a radical (hopefully interesting but not cursed) departure from previous years. Submissions were requested in two phases. The first phase involved submission of short papers (three pages) which were then presented at the conference and included in a short papers proceedings. In the second phase, reviewers selected papers for long paper submission (15 pages maximum). These were then assessed by the same reviewers, who then decided which papers to include in the journal special issue and proceedings. In the first phase there were a record 77 papers, compared to the usual 20 or so long papers of previous years. Each paper was reviewed by three reviewers. Out of these, 71 contributors were invited to submit long papers. Out of the long paper submissions, 7 were selected for the *Machine Learning Journal* special issue and 27 were accepted for the proceedings. In addition, two papers were nominated by Program Committee referees for the applications prize and two for the theory prize. The papers represent the diversity and vitality in present ILP research including ILP theory, implementations, search and phase transition, distributed and large-scale learning, probabilistic ILP, biological applications, natural language learning and planning and action learning.

ILP 2006 was held in Santiago de Compostela under the auspices of the University of Corunna and the University of Santiago de Compostela. The annual meeting of ILP researchers acts as the premier forum for presenting the latest work in the field. In addition to the many technical paper presentations, the invited talks this year were given by some of the most distinguished names in artificial intelligence research, namely, Vladimir Lifschitz, John McCarthy, Stuart Russell, Bart Selman and Ehud Shapiro.

We gratefully acknowledge support of the PASCAL network of excellence, the Spanish National Commissions of Science and Technology, the Galicia-Spain Secretary of R&D, the University of Corunna, Imperial College London, the University of Santiago de Compostela, the Spanish Association of AI and the *Machine Learning Journal*. Finally we would like to thank the many individuals involved in the preparation of the conference. These include the Journal Special Issue organizer (Simon Colton), the Local Chair (David Losada), the Local Organizers (Jorge Gonzalez and Miguel Varela) as well as Bridget Gundry, who organized and distributed the conference poster.

March 2007

Stephen Muggleton
Ramon Otero
Alireza Tamaddoni-Nezhad

Organization

Organizing Committee

Program Chair:	Stephen Muggleton (Imperial College, UK)
Program Chair:	Ramon Otero (University of Corunna, Spain)
Special Issue Organizer:	Simon Colton (Imperial College, UK)
Proceedings Organizer:	Alireza Tamaddoni-Nezhad (Imperial College, UK)
Local Organization Chair:	David Losada (University of Santiago, Spain)
Local Organizer:	Jorge Gonzalez (University of Corunna, Spain)
Local Organizer:	Miguel Varela (University of Corunna, Spain)

Program Committee

Hendrik Blockeel, Belgium
Rui Camacho, Portugal
James Cussens, UK
Luc Dehaspe, Belgium
Luc De Raedt, Germany
Saso Dzeroski, Slovenia
Floriana Esposito, Italy
Peter Flach, UK
Tamas Horvath, Germany
Katsumi Inoue, Japan
Andreas Karwath, Germany
Roni Khardon, USA
Joerg-Uwe Kietz, Switzerland
Ross King, UK
Stefan Kramer, Germany
Nada Lavrac, Slovenia
Francesca Lisi, Italy
John Lloyd, Australia
Donato Malerba, Italy
Stephen Muggleton, UK

Ramon Otero, Spain
David Page, USA
Bernhard Pfahringer, New Zealand
Jan Ramon, Belgium
Celine Rouveirol, France
Michele Sebag, France
Jude Shavlik, USA
Takayoshi Shoudai, Japan
Arno Siebes, Netherlands
Ashwin Srinivasan, India
Tomoyuki Uchida, Japan
Lyle Ungar, USA
Christel Vrain, France
Stefan Wrobel, Germany
Akihiro Yamamoto, Japan
Mohammed Zaki, USA
Gerson Zaverucha, Brazil
Filip Zelezny, Czech Republic
Jean-Daniel Zucker, France

Invited Speakers

Vladimir Lifschitz	University of Texas at Austin, USA
John McCarthy	Stanford University, USA
Stuart Russell	University of California at Berkeley, USA
Bart Selman	Cornell University, USA
Ehud Shapiro	Weizmann Institute, Israel

Sponsoring Institutions

PASCAL European Network of Excellence
Consellería de Innovación, Industria e Comercio, Xunta de Galicia
Consellería de Educación e Ordenación Universitaria, Xunta de Galicia
Universidade da Coruña
Imperial College London
Universidade de Santiago de Compostela
Asociación Española de Inteligencia Artificial (AEPIA)
Machine Learning Journal

Additional Referees

Annalisa Appice
Gilles Bisson
Janez Brank
Damjan Demsar
Aloisio De Pina
Nicola Di Mauro
Anton Dries
Stefano Ferilli
Kristian Kersting
Jiri Klema
Yoshiaki Okubo

Aline Paes
Andrea Passerini
Joel Plisson
Chiaki Sakama
Vitor Santos Costa
Leander Schietgat
Ivica Slavkov
Jan Struyf
Anneleen Van Assche
Takeaki Uno

Table of Contents

Invited Papers

Special Issue Extended Abstracts

Research Papers

Actions, Causation and Logic Programming

Vladimir Lifschitz

Department of Computer Sciences
University of Texas at Austin, USA

Reasoning about changes caused by the execution of actions has long been at the center of attention of researchers in the area of logic-based AI. Logical properties of causal dependencies turned out to be similar to properties of rules in logic programs. This fact allows us to apply methods of logic programming to computational problems related to action and change. Ideas of answer set programming, based on the concept of a stable model, turned out to be particularly useful. In the past they have been applied primarily to the problem of plan generation. There is now increasing interest also in using logic programming for learning action descriptions.

S. Muggleton, R. Otero, and A. Tamaddoni-Nezhad (Eds.): ILP 2006, LNAI 4455, p. 1, 2007.
© Springer-Verlag Berlin Heidelberg 2007

Challenges to Machine Learning: Relations Between Reality and Appearance

John McCarthy

Stanford University, USA

Abstract. Machine learning research, e.g. as described in [4], has as its goal the discovery of relations among observations, i.e. appearances. This is inadequate for science, because there is a reality behind appearance, e.g. material objects are built up from atoms. Atoms are just as real as dogs, only harder to observe, and the atomic theory arose long before there was any idea of how big atoms were. This article discusses how atoms were discovered, as an example of discovering the reality behind appearance. We also present an example of the three-dimensional reality behind a two-dimensional appearance, and how that reality is inferred by people and might be inferred by computer programs. Unfortunately, it is necessary to discuss the philosophy of appearance and reality, because the mistaken philosophy of taking the world (or particular phenomena) as a structure of sense data has been harmful in artificial intelligence and machine learning research, just as behaviorism and logical positivism harmed psychology.

1 Introduction

Apology: My knowledge of of machine learning research is no more recent than Tom Mitchell's book [4]. Its chapters describe, except for inductive logic programming, programs solely aimed at classifying appearances.

We live in a complicated world that existed for billions of years before there were humans, and our sense organs give us limited opportunities to observe it directly. Four centuries of science tell us that we and the objects we perceive are built in a complicated way from atoms and, below atoms, quarks. Maybe there is something below quarks.

Science, since 1700, is far better established than any kind of philosophy. Bad philosophy, proposing to base research entirely on appearances, has stunted AI, just as behaviorism stunted psychology for many decades.

Here's the philosophy in a nutshell. As emphasized by Descartes, all a human's information comes through the senses. Therefore, it is tempting to try to base science on relations among sense data and relations between actions that may be performed and subsequent sense data. [6] is an important source for this approach. Unfortunately for this approach, humans and our environment are complicated structures built of vastly smaller objects that our senses do not directly observe. Science had to discover atoms.

Besides the fundamental realities behind appearance studied by science, there are hidden every day realities—the three dimensional reality behind two

S. Muggleton, R. Otero, and A. Tamaddoni-Nezhad (Eds.): ILP 2006, LNAI 4455, pp. 2–9, 2007.

dimensional images, hidden surfaces, objects in boxes, people's names, what people really think of us.

Human common sense also reasons in terms of the realities that give rise to the appearances our senses provide us. Thus young babies have some initial knowledge of the permanence of physical objects. This initial knowledge seems not to be expressed in terms of particular senses. Blind babies have it too, and so do babies whose sense of touch is compromised by lack of arms. See [7] for experiments related to initial knowledge.

Perhaps if your philosophy rejects the notion of reality as a fundamental concept, you'll accept a notion of *relative reality* appropriate for the design and debugging of robots. Thus the robot needs to be designed to determine this relative reality from the appearance given by its inputs.

We'll discuss:

Dalton's atomic theory as a discovery of the reality behind appearance.

A simple problem involving changeable two dimensional appearances and a three dimensional reality.

Some formulas relating appearance and reality in particular cases.

What can one know about a three dimensional object and how to represent this knowledge.

The use of touch in finding the shape of an object.

How scientific study and the use of instruments extends what can be learned from the senses. Thus a doctor's training involving dissection of cadavers enables him to determine something about the liver by palpation.

2   Elements, Atoms, and Molecules

Some scientific discoveries like Galileo's $s = \frac{1}{2}gt2$ involve discovering the relations between known entities. Patrick Langley's Bacon program [1] did that.

John Dalton's postulation of atoms and molecules made up of fixed numbers of atoms of two or more kinds was much more creative and will be harder to make computers do. That's the reason for this section of the paper.

The ancient ideas of Democritus and Lucretius that matter was made up from atoms had no important or even testable consequences. Dalton's did.

Giving each kind of atom its own atomic mass explained the complicated ratios of masses in a compound as representing small numbers of atoms in a molecule. Thus a sodium chloride (NaCl) molecule would have one atom of each of its elements. Water came out as H_2O.

The simplest forms of the atomic theory were inaccurate. [Thus early 19th century chemists didn't soon realize that the hydrogen and oxygen molecules are H_2 and O_2 and not just H and O.] Computers also need to be able to propose theories adventurously and fix their inaccuracies later later.

Only the relative masses of atoms could be proposed in Dalton's time. The first actual way of estimating these masses was made by Maxwell and Boltzmann about 60 years after Dalton's proposal. They realized that the coefficients of viscosity, heat conductivity, and diffusion of gases as explained by the kinetic theory of gases depended on the actual sizes of molecules.

The last important scientific holdout against the reality of atoms, the chemist Wilhelm Ostwald, was convinced by Einstein's 1905 quantitative explanation of Brownian motion as caused by liquid molecules striking a suspended object. The philosopher Ernst Mach was unconvinced.

Long after the reality of atoms was accepted in science, it was still believed that individual atoms could not be observed. The first actual pictures of atoms in the 1990s were a big surprise. Now quarks are accepted as real although an actual picture of a proton showing the quarks would be even more surprising and seems quite unlikely, because the quarks move too fast.

Philosophical point: Atoms cannot be regarded as just an explanation of the observations that led Dalton to propose them. Maxwell and Boltzmann used the notion to explain entirely different observations, and modern explanations of atoms are not at all based on the law of combining proportions. In short, atoms were discovered, not invented.

Reality is usually more stable than appearance, i.e. changes more slowly. Formulas giving the effects of events (including actions) are almost always written in terms of reality. Getting reality from appearance is an *inverse problem*. Geologists, oil companies, and astronomers are faced with inverse problems. Their solution is intellectually difficult and computationally intensive. Human-level AI systems will also have to be able to infer reality from appearances related to them in complex ways.

3   Elements, Atoms, Molecules - Formulas

Most likely, it is still too hard to make programs that will discover elements, atoms, and molecules. Let's therefore try to write logical sentences that will introduce these concepts to a knowledge base that has no ideas of them.

We assume that the notions of a body being composed of parts and of mass have already been formalized, but the idea of atom has not. The ideas of bodies being disjoint is also assumed to be formalized.

The following formulas approximate a fragment of high school chemistry and should be somewhat *elaboration tolerant* [2], e.g. should admit additional information about the structure of molecules. The situation argument s is included only to point out that material bodies change in chemical reactions.

$$Body(b, s) \rightarrow (\exists u \subset Molecules(b, s))(\forall y \in u)(Molecule(y) \wedge Part(y, b)),$$

$$y1 \in Molecules(b, s) \wedge y2 \in Molecules(b, s) \wedge y1 \neq y2 \rightarrow Disjoint(y1, y2),$$

$$Part(x, b, s) \rightarrow (\exists y \in Molecules(b, s))\neg Disjoint(y, x),$$

$$Body(b, s) \rightarrow Mass(b, s) = \sum_{x \in Molecules(b,s)} Mass(x, s).$$

$$(1)$$

$Water(b, s) \wedge x \in Molecules(b, s)$
$\rightarrow (\exists h1 \; h2 \; o)(Atoms(x) = \{h1, h2, o\} \wedge h1 \neq h2$
$\wedge HydrogenAtom(h1) \wedge HydrogenAtom(h2) \wedge OxygenAtom(o)),$

$Salt(b, s) \wedge x \in Molecules(b, s)$
$\rightarrow (\exists na \; cl)(Atoms(x) = \{na, cl\} \wedge SodiumAtom(na) \wedge ChlorineAtom(cl)).$

$$(2)$$

$$Molecule(x) \rightarrow Mass(x) = \sum_{y \in Atoms(x)} Mass(y),$$

$$HydrogenAtom(y) \rightarrow Mass(y) = 1.0,$$
$$OxygenAtom(y) \rightarrow Mass(y) = 16.0,$$
$$SodiumAtom(y) \rightarrow Mass(y) = 23.0,$$
$$ChlorineAtom(y) \rightarrow Mass(y) = 35.5.$$

$$(3)$$

4 Appearance and Reality

Reality is usually more stable than appearance, i.e. changes more slowly. Formulas giving the effects of events (including actions) are almost always written in terms of reality. Getting reality from appearance is an *inverse problem*. Geologists, oil companies, and astronomers are faced with inverse problems. Their solution is intellectually difficult and computationally intensive.

The formulas that follow will need a situation or time argument once we consider changing appearances.

5 Another Start on Three Dimensional Objects

How can we best express what a human can know and a robot should know about a three dimensional object? We start from a standard kind of object with particular types of objects and individual objects defined by successive approximations.

I propose starting with a rectangular parallelopiped, which we'll abbreviate *rppd*. An object is an rppd modified by dimension information, shape modifications, attached objects, information about its internal structure, location information, folding information, information about surfaces, physical information like mass. Perhaps one should start even more simply with just a size, a ball too large to be included in the object and too small to include it.

My small Swiss army knife is an rppd, 5cm by 2cm by 1.5cm, rounded in the width dimension at each end. Its largest surface has a smooth plastic surface texture, and its other surfaces are metallic with stripes parallel to the long axis, i.e. the backs of the blades. This description should suffice to find the knife in my pocket and get it out, even though it says nothing about the blades.

Consider a baby and a doll of the same size. Each may be described as an rppd with attached rppds in appropriate places for the arms, legs, and head. The most obvious and significant differences come in a texture, motion, and family relationships.

We begin with a little bit about touch rather than with vision. Imagine putting one's hand into one's pocket in order to take out one of the objects.

$$Touching(Side(1), x) \wedge PocketKnife1(x, Jmc) \rightarrow Feels(Texture17),$$

$$(4)$$

$$Texture(Side(PocketKnife1)) = Texture17$$

For now we needn't say anything about $Texture17$ except that it is distinguishable from other textures. Textures for touch have similarities to and differences from textures for vision. Both are very scale dependent.

Touch differs from vision in that the information is usually more partial, e.g. one can pickup a new object without getting a full image of its shape. One can get more information about an object by feeling it more.

I made a small informal experiment in which subjects were asked to draw an object that they could feel inside a paper bag but could not see. The quality of the drawing was about the same as the subject could make when he was allowed to see.

6   A Puzzle About Inferring Reality from Appearance

Here's the appearance. The puzzle is: What is the reality behind the appearance? Clicking on the < and > signs is how one experiments.

Alas, figures in published proceedings are still not dynamic. To experiment with this puzzle, go to http://www-formal.stanford.edu/jmc/appearance.html.

The reality is three dimensional, while the appearance is two dimensional.

Those who implement display know that computing appearance is difficult. Those who do computer vision know that inverting the relation is even more difficult.

The appearance in the puzzle is a genuine appearance. The reality behind the appearance is rather abstract. Thus the bodies have no thickness or mass. This doesn't seem to bother people; we're used to abstractions.

We use concepts like like *solid body, behind, part of, length*, etc.

The first step in solving the version given in the above url is to realize that partial surfaces of objects are displayed as strings of letters and that the actions move the strings. One also must realize that some surfaces are hidden behind others but can be displayed by moving the objects by clicking on the tabs. Forming wrong initial hypotheses can make the puzzle very difficult.

Some of the relevant concepts may be learned by babies from experience, as Locke proposed. However, there is good evidence that many of them, e.g. *solid body* and *behind* were learned by evolution and are built into human and most animal infants.

The quickest and most articulate human solution was by Donald Michie. Stephen Muggleton and Ramon Otero [5] have solved a simplified version of the puzzle using inductive logic programming.

7   Formulas for Appearance and Actions in the Puzzle

We introduce positions. There is a string of 13 positions. Bodies are also represented by strings of squares of length appropriate to the body. $Content(sq)$ is either a color or a letter depending on the version of the puzzle.

$$
\begin{aligned}
& Body(b) \wedge sq \in b \wedge Location(sq, s) = pos \\
& \wedge (\forall b' \neq b)((\exists sq' \in b')(Location(sq', s) = pos \\
& \rightarrow Higher(b, b'))) \\
& \rightarrow Appearance(pos, s) = Content(sq).
\end{aligned}
\tag{5}
$$

$$
\begin{aligned}
& Body(b) \wedge sq \in b \wedge Location(sq, s) = pos \\
& \wedge (\forall b' \neq b)((\exists sq' \in b')(Location(sq', s) = pos \\
& \rightarrow Higher(b, b'))) \\
& \rightarrow (\forall sq' \in b)(Location(sq', Result(ClickCW(pos), s)) \\
& = CWloc(Location(sq', s))) \\
& \wedge (\forall b' \notin b)(Location(sq', Result(ClickCW(pos), s)) \\
& = Location(sq', s)).
\end{aligned}
\tag{6}
$$

Here's the formula for the effect of counter-clockwise motion.

$$
\begin{aligned}
& Body(b) \wedge sq \in b \wedge Location(sq, s) = pos \\
& \wedge (\forall b' \neq b)((\exists sq' \in b')(Location(sq', s) = pos \\
& \rightarrow Higher(b, b'))) \\
& \rightarrow (\forall sq' \in b)(Location(sq', Result(ClickCCW(pos), s)) \\
& = CCWloc(Location(sq', s))) \\
& \wedge (\forall b' \notin b)(Location(sq', Result(ClickCCW(pos), s)) \\
& = Location(sq', s)).
\end{aligned}
\tag{7}
$$

The last parts of the last two formulas tell what doesn't change.

These formulas give the appearance as a function of the reality and also tell how the reality is changed by the allowed actions. There can't be a formula giving how the appearance changes that only involves the present appearance, because an action may make a position visible that was previously invisible. Even taking into account past appearances will only work if the previous actions have uncovered all of the surfaces.

8   How Should a Computer Discover the Reality?

A point of view common (and maybe dominant) in the machine learning community is that the computer should solve the problem from scratch, e.g. inventing *body* and *behind* as needed. It is not dominant in the computer vision community.

Our opinion, and that of the knowledge representation community, is that it is better to provide computer programs with common sense concepts, suitably formalized. There is some success, but the formalisms tend to be limited in the contexts in which they apply. I think, but won't argue here, that formalizing *context* itself is a necessary step.

Here are two sample formulas relevant to the version of the puzzle presented at ILP2006 in which the objects were colored rather than displayed as strings of letters. These formulas are still too specialized to be put in a *knowledge base* of common sense.

$$Color\text{-}Appearance(scene, x, s) = Color(Highest(scene, x, s)) \qquad (8)$$

$$Behind(b2, b1, s) \wedge Opaque(b1) \rightarrow \neg Visible(b2, s). \qquad (9)$$

Solving the puzzle involves inferring formulas like

$$
\begin{aligned}
&Body(b) \wedge Present(b, Scene) \equiv b \in \{B1, B2, B3, B4\}, \\
&Color(B1) = Blue \wedge Color(B2) = Orange \wedge Color(B3) = Green \\
&\quad \wedge Color(B4) = Red, \\
&Length(B1) = 6 \wedge Length(B2) = 8, \text{etc.}, \\
&Higher(B1, B2) \wedge Higher(B2, B3) \wedge Higher(B3, B4), \\
&Higher(B4, Background) \wedge Length(Background) = 13.
\end{aligned}
\qquad (10)
$$

9   Limitations of Our Treatment and Remarks

Actions are the converse of observations. The relations between the muscle movements of an action and its effects in the world are analogous to the relations between appearance and reality. One thinks in terms of the effects. Evidence: (1) A person's handwriting style on the blackboard is the same as that of his writing on paper, even though the muscle movements are entirely different. (2) A person can sign his name with his foot on the floor or with his nose in chalk dust on the blackboard. Thus the monitoring is in terms of effect rather than it terms of muscle movements.

The lengths and colors of the bodies are assumed not dependent of the situation. Human language tolerates *elaborations* such as actions that affect color better than do present AI formalisms.

The ideas of the last two sections about what knowledge should be given to the program have benefited from discussions with Stephen Muggleton and Ramon Otero.

Similar considerations to those of this paper are discussed in connection with what I call *phenomenal data mining* [3], the point being that one is interested in the relations among phenomena in the world and not in the relations among the assertions in a database. Successful phenomenal data mining will require large knowledge bases of facts about the world and so will systems good at inferring reality from experience.

Confession: I have been thinking about inferring reality from experience separately from phenomenal data mining. They are really the same problem.

We haven't considered entities extended in time. These include histories and more abstract entities like tunes. The telling of a joke is another example.

References

1. Simon, H.A., Bradshaw, G.L., Zytkow, J.M., Langley, P.: Scientific Discovery: Computational Explorations of the Creative Processes. MIT Press, Cambridge (1987)
2. McCarthy, J.: Elaboration tolerance (1999), web only as
   http://www-formal.stanford.edu/jmc/elaboration.html
3. McCarthy, J.: Phenomenal data mining. Communications of the ACM (August 2000), http://www-formal.stanford.edu/jmc/phenomenal.html
4. Mitchell, T.: Machine Learning. McGraw-Hill, New York (1997)
5. Muggleton, S.H., Otero, R.: On McCarthy's appearance and reality problem. In: Short Paper Proceedings of the 16th International Conference on Inductive Logic Programming, University of Corunna (2006)
6. Russell, B.: On the notion of cause. Proceedings of the Aristotelian Society 13, 1–26 (1913)
7. Spelke, E.: Initial knowledge: six suggestions. Cognition 50, 431–445 (1994)

First-Order Probabilistic Languages: Into the Unknown

Brian Milch[1] and Stuart Russell[2]

[1] Computer Science and AI Laboratory
Massachusetts Institute of Technology
32 Vassar St. Room 32-G480
Cambridge, MA 02139, USA
`milch@csail.mit.edu`
[2] Computer Science Division
University of California at Berkeley
Berkeley, CA 94720-1776, USA
`russell@cs.berkeley.edu`

Abstract. This paper surveys *first-order probabilistic languages* (FOPLs), which combine the expressive power of first-order logic with a probabilistic treatment of uncertainty. We provide a taxonomy that helps make sense of the profusion of FOPLs that have been proposed over the past fifteen years. We also emphasize the importance of representing uncertainty not just about the attributes and relations of a fixed set of objects, but also about what objects exist. This leads us to *Bayesian logic*, or *BLOG*, a language for defining probabilistic models with unknown objects. We give a brief overview of BLOG syntax and semantics, and emphasize some of the design decisions that distinguish it from other languages. Finally, we consider the challenge of constructing FOPL models automatically from data.

1 Introduction

Many real-world tasks, from identifying objects in images to extracting facts about people from text documents, require probabilistic reasoning about many related objects. These tasks often require weighing competing pieces of evidence, so some form of probabilistic reasoning is necessary. However, the number of random variables needed to describe such a scenario grows with the number of objects. Thus, *propositional* probabilistic languages such as Bayesian networks (BNs) — which describe a fixed set of random variables, and specify dependencies and probability distributions for each variable individually — are insufficient.

To represent probabilistic models for such tasks, we need *first-order probabilistic languages* (FOPLs): probabilistic modeling languages that can model large families of random variables compactly by abstracting over objects. A significant number of FOPLs have been proposed over the last fifteen years or so. In Section 2, we organize many of the proposed languages into a taxonomy, attempting to clarify the major ways in which they differ from one another. An important

S. Muggleton, R. Otero, and A. Tamaddoni-Nezhad (Eds.): ILP 2006, LNAI 4455, pp. 10–24, 2007.

desideratum for FOPLs is the ability to represent uncertainty about the number of objects that exist and the correspondence between observations and underlying objects. In Section 3, we focus on a FOPL that we developed with this goal in mind: *Bayesian logic*, or BLOG [13]. In addition to discussing its syntax and semantics, we highlight some of BLOG's distinctive design features.

Section 4 turns to the question of learning FOPL models. Parameter estimation for FOPL models is well-understood, and there has been considerable work on learning the dependency structure of such models. However, an even more challenging problem remains open: how to automatically hypothesize new functions or predicates, or even new types of objects, to explain the data.

2   A Taxonomy of FOPLs

2.1   Outcome Spaces

The most basic way in which certain FOPLs differ from others is in their outcome spaces: that is, the sets of outcomes to which they assign probabilities. In most FOPLs, the outcome space is a set of *relational structures*, which specify a set of objects and some relations (or functions) on these objects. To make this idea more concrete, consider the following pedagogical example:

Example 1. Suppose we are given a list of papers that have been submitted to a conference over several years. Each paper is either accepted or not accepted. We are also given a list of researchers, which includes the primary author of each paper. Suppose that each researcher can be classified as brilliant or not brilliant, and the probability that a paper is accepted depends on whether its primary author is brilliant or not. Given the authorship and acceptance status of certain papers, we would like to predict which other papers will be accepted.

A relational structure for Example 1 specifies a set of papers, a set of researchers, a unary predicate Accepted that applies to papers, a unary predicate Brilliant that applies to researchers, and a function PrimaryAuthor that maps papers to researchers. Depending on the what aspects of the scenario are known in advance, the outcomes may share some *relational skeleton* [3]: for instance, they may all have the same sets of objects and the same PrimaryAuthor function.

One reason for the diversity of FOPLs is that different communities talk about relational structures in different ways. In logic, a relational structure is a logical model structure: a domain of discourse plus an interpretation of a logical language over that domain. Exanples of FOPLs that define distributions over logical model structures include Halpern's logic of probability on possible worlds [5], relational Bayesian networks (RBNs) [7], PRISM [34], Markov logic [33] and BLOG [13]. Relational structures can also be thought of as instances of a relational database schema. This view has led to a distinct set of FOPLs, including probabilistic relational models (PRMs) [10,3] and relational Markov networks (RMNs) [36].

The statistics community thinks of possible outcomes in yet another way: as instantiations of a set of random variables. The statistical analogue of a unary

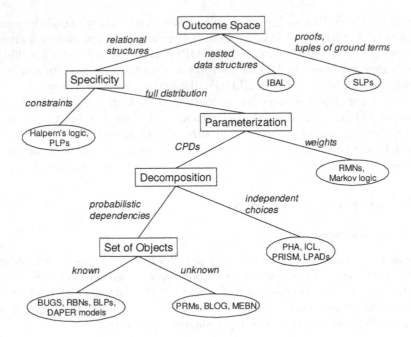

Fig. 1. A taxonomy of first-order probabilistic languages

predicate Accepted is a family of binary-valued random variables A_i, indexed by natural numbers i that represent papers. Similarly, the function PrimaryAuthor can be represented as an indexed family of random variables P_i, whose values are natural numbers representing researchers. Thus, instantiations of a set of random variables can represent relational structures. Indexed families of random variables are a basic modeling element in the BUGS system [37], where they are represented graphically using "plates" that contain co-indexed nodes.

There are two well-known FOPLs whose possible outcomes are not relational structures in the sense we have defined. One is stochastic logic programs (SLPs) [17]. An SLP defines a distribution over proofs from a given logic program. If a particular goal predicate R is specified, then an SLP also defines a distribution over tuples of logical terms: the probability of a tuple $(t_1, \ldots, t_k)$ is the sum of the probabilities of proofs of $R(t_1, \ldots, t_k)$. SLPs are useful for defining distributions over objects that can be encoded as terms, such as strings or trees; they can also emulate more standard FOPLs [31]. The other prominent FOPL with a unique outcome space is IBAL [26], a programming language that allows stochastic choices. An IBAL program defines a distribution over *environments* that map symbols to values. These values may be individual symbols, like the values of variables in a BN; but they may also be other environments, or even functions.

This analysis defines the top level of the taxonomy shown in Figure 1. In the rest of the paper, we will focus on languages that define probability distributions over relational structures.

2.2   Specificity

Among the FOPLs that define distributions over relational structures, the first distinction we can draw is between languages that fully define a distribution, and those that only impose constraints on a distribution. As an example of the latter type, Halpern's logic of probability on possible worlds [5] allows statements such as $\forall x\, P(\mathsf{Brilliant}(x)) = 0.3$. Such statements just specify particular marginal probabilities: in general, they do not fully define a distribution. Probabilistic logic programs (PLPs) [21] are essentially a version of Halpern's language restricted to Horn clauses, although one can obtain a full distribution from a PLP by finding the maximum entropy distribution consistent with the PLP's constraints [12]. The FOPLs that we will discuss from here on all define probability distributions completely, just as BNs and Markov networks do.

2.3   Conditional Probabilities Versus Weights

In the propositional realm, Bayesian networks are directed models that specify a conditional probability distribution (CPD) for each variable given some parent variables, whereas *Markov networks* are undirected models that use weights to define the relative probabilities of instantiations. This distinction carries over to the first-order case. The CPD-based or directed FOPLs include BUGS [37], PRISM [34], PRMs [10], Bayesian logic programs (BLPs) [8], and BLOG [13]. The principal weight-based or undirected formalisms are relational Markov networks [36] and Markov logic [33].

To understand the trade-offs between directed and undirected representations, consider a directed FOPL model for Example 1 with the following CPDs:

Brilliant(r) ∼	True	False
	0.2	0.8

Accepted(p) ∼ Brilliant(PrimaryAuthor(p))	Accepted(p) True	Accepted(p) False
True	0.8	0.2
False	0.3	0.7

If the relational skeleton contains just one paper Pub1 and just one researcher Res1, with PrimaryAuthor(Pub1) = Res1, then this model defines the BN in Figure 2(a). If there are two papers by Res1, we get the BN in Figure 2(b).

This directed model has several attractive properties. First, the parameters have clear interpretations as prior and conditional probabilities, and can be

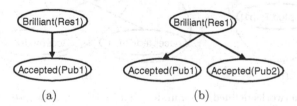

(a)   (b)

Fig. 2. BNs defined by a directed FOPL model whose relational skeleton includes (a) one paper, or (b) two papers

estimated from fully observed data using elementary formulas. Even more importantly, the parameters are *modular*: they reflect causal processes that apply regardless of the relational skeleton. Thus, if we estimate the parameters using only examples with one paper per researcher, we will get the same CPDs that we would get from examples with two papers per researcher. We can also exploit a related modularity property when performing inference: rather than doing inference on the whole BN defined by the FOPL model, it suffices to use the subgraph consisting of the query and evidence nodes and their ancestors [22].

The drawback of directed models is that they must not have any cycles. This requirement is especially burdensome in FOPLs, because we must ensure that the probability model is acyclic for every relational skeleton in some class. Also, certain properties of relations are difficult to describe without creating cycles: for instance, it is not easy to specify that for all people a and b, if $\mathsf{Likes}(a, b)$ is true than $\mathsf{Likes}(b, a)$ is probably true as well.

Undirected models, on the other hand, have no acyclicity constraints. An undirected model is defined by *potential functions* that assign weights to instantiations based on some subsets of the random variables. The weight of an instantiation is the product of the weights assigned by all the potentials; these weights are then normalized to yield a probability distribution. In the first-order case, a model specifies *potential function templates* that apply to all sets of variables that satisfy certain conditions. For instance, in Example 1, we can include a potential template that applies to $\mathsf{Brilliant}(r)$ for every researcher r, and another template that applies to $\{\mathsf{Brilliant}(r), \mathsf{Accepted}(p)\}$ for all pairs (r, p) such that $\mathsf{PrimaryAuthor}(p) = r$. Figure 3 shows the Markov networks that result when these templates are applied to relational skeletons with one or two papers.

This undirected FOPL model can reproduce the distributions defined by our directed model above: we can simply set the potential on $\mathsf{Brilliant}(r)$ equal to the CPD for $\mathsf{Brilliant}(r)$, and the potential on $\{\mathsf{Brilliant}(r), \mathsf{Accepted}(p)\}$ to the CPD for $\mathsf{Accepted}(p)$. However, suppose we estimate our parameters solely on examples with one paper per researcher (recall that this caused no problems in the directed

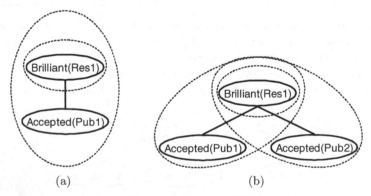

(a)   (b)

Fig. 3. Markov networks defined by an undirected FOPL model whose relational skeleton includes (a) one paper, or (b) two papers. Dotted ovals indicate sets of variables that are in the domain of the same potential function.

case). Our learning algorithm may arrive at the following parameterization for the network in Figure 3(a), defining the same joint distribution as the CPD-like parameterization:

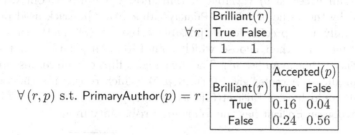

$\forall r :$

Brilliant(r)	
True	False
1	1

$\forall (r, p)$ s.t. PrimaryAuthor(p) $= r$:

	Accepted(p)	
Brilliant(r)	True	False
True	0.16	0.04
False	0.24	0.56

The meanings of the parameters in these potential templates are no longer so obvious. The potential on Brilliant(r) is all 1's, but the marginal distribution on Brilliant(Res1) in Figure 3(a) still ends up being $(0.2, 0.8)$. This is because the event Brilliant(Res1) = True receives a total weight of $0.16 + 0.04 = 0.2$ in the potential over $\{$Brilliant(Res1), Accepted(Pub1)$\}$. This coupling between potentials means that maximum-likelihood parameters for Markov networks cannot be found with simple formulas: one must use a gradient-based optimization algorithm [33].

Now consider what happens if we apply the undirected probability model above to the two-paper network in Figure 3(b). Then the template for pairs (r, p) such that PrimaryAuthor(p) $= r$ applies twice, and the marginal distribution on Brilliant(Res1) ends up being proportional to $(0.2^2, 0.8^2)$, which normalizes to about $(0.06, 0.94)$. If the actual probability that a researcher is brilliant is 0.2, then these parameters are sub-optimal: we would not learn them if we had instances with two papers in our training set.[1] Thus, unlike in the directed case, we need to ensure that the relational skeletons in our training set reflect the diversity of relational skeletons that we may encounter in test data.

2.4   Independent Choices Versus Probabilistic Dependencies

The category of CPD-based languages for defining complete distributions over relational structures is still quite large. However, one of the languages we have mentioned, namely PRISM [34], stands out from the rest in that it represents only deterministic dependencies and independent random choices. That is, each variable either has no parents, or has a deterministic CPD. Other FOPLs that take this approach include probabilistic Horn abduction [27], independent choice logic [28] and logic programs with annotated disjunctions (LPADs) [39].[2]

---

[1] The problem actually gets worse if we eliminate the apparently redundant potential template on Brilliant(r): then there is no parameterization that yields the desired distribution for all relational skeletons.

[2] In LPADs, the independent choices do not set the values of ground atoms directly; instead, there is one choice for each ground disjunctive clause, and this choice determines which element of the clause's head will be entailed by the clause's body.

It may not be immediately obvious how independent choices could suffice to represent all the randomness in a probabilistic model. First, consider the directed model that we defined in the previous section for Example 1. To sample a value for an Accepted(p) variable in that model, we flip a coin with a bias determined by the value of Brilliant(PrimaryAuthor(p)). The trick used in PRISM is, conceptually, to flip coins for all possible values of Brilliant(PrimaryAuthor(p)) ahead of time, and then choose which coin flip to use based on the actual value of Brilliant(PrimaryAuthor(p)). The initial coin flips can be represented by an auxiliary predicate Accepted_given_Brilliant(p, b), which represents the value that Accepted(p) would have if Brilliant(PrimaryAuthor(p)) were equal to b. The predicate Accepted_given_Brilliant has the following probability model:

$$\text{Accepted\_given\_Brilliant}(p, \text{True}) \sim \begin{array}{|cc|} \hline \text{True} & \text{False} \\ \hline 0.8 & 0.2 \\ \hline \end{array}$$

$$\text{Accepted\_given\_Brilliant}(p, \text{False}) \sim \begin{array}{|cc|} \hline \text{True} & \text{False} \\ \hline 0.3 & 0.7 \\ \hline \end{array}$$

Now the probability model for Accepted is deterministic (note that we are treating Brilliant here as a Boolean function, yielding values in {True, False}):

$$\text{Accepted}(p) = \text{Accepted\_given\_Brilliant}(p, \text{Brilliant}(\text{PrimaryAuthor}(p)))$$

The advantage of this technique is that it completely separates the logical and probabilistic parts of the language. This separation can be exploited to obtain efficient algorithms for certain tasks [35]. However, this decomposition often makes the representation considerably less intuitive.

2.5   Known Versus Unknown Objects

The last distinction in our taxonomy regards whether a language requires the set of objects to be specified in the relational skeleton, or allows the set of objects to be unknown. To motivate our discussion of unknown objects, consider the following example, based on our earlier work on citation matching [24].

Example 2. Suppose we are given a set of citation strings extracted from the "References" sections of online papers. These citations use a variety of different formats; they use initials and abbreviations in different places; and they contain typographical errors. The task is to reconstruct a database of publications and researchers who are referred to in the citations. This database should contain just one record for each publication and each researcher, including all the true attributes of these entities that can be inferred from the citations.

In this example, the sets of publications and researchers that underlie the citations are not known in advance. Furthermore, we do not know which citations refer to which publications, or which substrings of citations refer to which researchers. If Cit1 and Cit2 are two citations and PubCited is a function that maps citations to the publications they refer to, then the ground terms PubCited(Cit1) and PubCited(Cit2) may or may not denote the same object.

Most FOPLs assume that the objects are in one-to-one correspondence with a given set of constant symbols, or with the ground terms of the language. The CPD-based FOPLs that make such assumptions include BUGS [37] (where the objects correspond to specified sets of natural numbers), RBNs [7], BLPs [8], and directed acyclic probabilistic entity-relationship (DAPER) models [6]. One can model unknown objects to some extent in these languages by adding an Exists predicate, but one still has to specify all the objects that could exist, and craft the probability models so that objects for which Exists is false cannot serve as values for functions or have any probabilistic influence on other objects.

There are three prominent languages that make unknown objects a fundamental part of their semantics. One of these is PRMs, which allow uncertainty about the number of objects that stand in a given relation to an existing object (*e.g.*, papers written by a researcher) [10], about whether there exists an object that stands in certain relations to several other objects (*e.g.*, a role for a given actor in a given movie) [4], and about the total number of objects of a given type [24]. However, PRMs do not have a unified syntax that supports all these types of uncertainty. The language of multi-entity Bayesian networks (MEBN) [11] does have a consistent syntax, and incorporates Exists variables as part of its semantics. But MEBN still requires the modeler to list all objects that might exist. The third language that supports unknown objects is BLOG, which we discuss in the next section.

3   Bayesian Logic (BLOG)

In this section we give an informal overview of Bayesian logic (BLOG) [13], a language that facilitates defining probability distributions over relational structures with varying sets of objects. In fact, BLOG's design makes it an attractive choice even for scenarios that do not involve unknown objects.

3.1   Syntax

A BLOG model defines a probability distribution over model structures of a typed first-order language. To this end, the model defines a typed first-order language for a particular scenario; specifies certain nonrandom aspects of the scenario; and specifies a probability model for the remaining aspects. The probability model can be thought of as describing a generative process for constructing a possible world. This process has two kinds of steps: steps that set the value of a function[3] on some objects, and steps that add new objects to the world.

Figure 4 gives a complete BLOG model for Example 2. We will begin by walking through the generative process defined by this model; then we will discuss the syntax in more detail. Line 1 of Figure 4 says that there are three types of objects in this scenario; then line 2 asserts that four citations are guaranteed to exist. Line 3 begins the random part of the generative process: a random number

---

[3] We treat predicates as Boolean functions.

```
1 type Res; type Pub; type Cit;

2 guaranteed Cit Cit1, Cit2, Cit3, Cit4;

3 #Res ~ NumResearchersPrior;
4 random String Name(Res r) ~ NamePrior;

5 #Pub ~ NumPublicationsPrior;
6 random String Title(Pub p) ~ TitlePrior;
7 random NaturalNum NumAuthors(Pub p) ~ NumAuthorsPrior;
8 random Res NthAuthor(Pub p, NaturalNum n)
9     if (n < NumAuthors(p)) then ~ Uniform({Res r});

10 random Pub PubCited(Cit c) ~ Uniform({Pub p});
11 random String Text(Cit c)
12    ~ FormatModel(Title(PubCited(c)),
13                  {n, Name(NthAuthor(PubCited(c), n)) for
14                  NaturalNum n : n < NumAuthors(PubCited(c))});
```

Fig. 4. A BLOG model for citation matching

of researchers are added to the world, with this number being sampled according to NumResearchersPrior. Then, for each researcher r, a name is sampled from NamePrior. Line 5 adds a random number of publications to the world. For each publication, the title and the number of authors are sampled from appropriate priors (lines 6–7). Then for each publication p and each number $n < \text{NumAuthors}(p)$, a researcher is sampled uniformly at random to serve as the nth author of p. In line 10 we get to the model for citations: for each citation c, the publication cited is sampled uniformly from the set of publications. Finally, the text of each citation is sampled according to a format model that conditions on the title of the cited paper and the names of its authors.

The syntax in Figure 4 may seem complicated, but in fact it can be explained fairly simply. A BLOG model is a series of statements, each ending with a semicolon. The three statements in line 1 are *type declarations*; a BLOG model can also include *function declarations* that specify the type signatures of functions (these are necessary if we use a function before we define its probability model). Line 2 is a *guaranteed object statement* that asserts the existence of a set of distinct objects, and assigns a constant symbol to each one. Along with *nonrandom function definitions*, which do not appear in this model, guaranteed object statements define a relational skeleton. The probabilistic portion of the model consists of *number statements*, which describe steps where objects are added to the world, and *dependency statements*, which describe how values are assigned to functions. These six types of statements constitute the full syntax of BLOG.

Dependency statements and number statements have a rich syntax of their own. A BLOG model must contain exactly one dependency statement for each random function. If f is a function with return type τ_0 and argument types $\tau_1, \ldots, \tau_k$, then a dependency statement for f has the following general form:

```
random τ₀ f(τ₁ x₁, . . . , τₖ xₖ)
    if cond₁ then  ~  cpd₁(a₁,₁, . . . , a₁,ₘ₁)
    elseif cond₂ then  ~  cpd₂(a₂,₁, . . . , a₂,ₘ₂)
        ⋮
    else  ~  cpdₙ(aₙ,₁, . . . , aₙ,ₘₙ);
```

The conditions $cond_1, \ldots, cond_{n-1}$ are arbitrary first-order formulas that can use the variables $x_1, \ldots, x_k$. The *elementary CPDs* $cpd_1, \ldots, cpd_n$ can be thought of as functions that take in a list of arguments $a_1, \ldots, a_m$ and return a probability distribution over objects of f's return type. More technically, they are the names of Java classes that implement a certain interface. The arguments a can be logical terms, such as Title(PubCited(c)); *set expressions*, such as {Pub p} or {Pub p : Venue(p) = ILP}; or *tuple multiset expressions*, such as the one in lines 13–14, which defines a multiset of pairs consisting of an author number and a name.

Obviously, not all the dependency statements in Figure 4 have this full-fledged if-then-else form: we allow a number of abbreviations. The expression "if $cond_1$ then" can be omitted if $cond_1$ is simply True. Also, if a statement contains some non-trivial conditions but omits the else clause, then the function gets a default value of null when none of the conditions are satisfied. This default convention is exploited in line 9.

The number statements in Figure 4 are very simple, but in general, they can have the same syntax as dependency statements. The only difference is that the expression "random τ_0 $f(\tau_1 x_1, \ldots, \tau_k x_k)$" is replaced with #$\tau$, where τ is the type of object being generated.[4] Thus, the number of objects that exist can depend on other variables.

3.2   Semantics

We have given an intuitive semantics for BLOG in terms of a random process that generates possible worlds. However, BLOG also has a more formal, declarative semantics [13]. A BLOG model defines a set of *basic random variables*: a *number variable* for each number statement, and a *function application variable* for each random function and each tuple of arguments that exist in any possible world. The distribution defined by a BLOG model can be represented as a *contingent Bayesian network* (CBN) [14] over these basic variables.

A CBN is a directed graphical model in which the edges are labeled with conditions that specify when they are active. For example, Figure 5 shows a CBN for a simplified version of the citation model from Figure 4. Note that the node Text(Cit1) has infinitely many parents, because it may depend on the title of any publication. Most treatments of Bayesian networks do not provide well-definedness results for networks that contain infinite parent sets. However, the edge labels in Figure 5 allow us to see that at most two edges into Text(Cit1)

---

[4] In fact, BLOG supports more complex number statements to model scenarios where objects generate other objects [13].

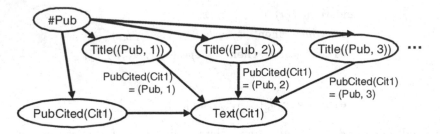

Fig. 5. A contingent Bayesian network for a simplified version of the BLOG model in Figure 4. This simplified model has just one citation and does not include researchers.

can be active in any single outcome: one edge from PubCited(Cit1), and one edge from Title(p) where p = PubCited(Cit1). It turns out that one can obtain stronger well-definedness results for CBNs than for standard BNs — well-defined CBNs can even contain cycles, as long as some edges on each cycle have mutually contradictory labels [14]. In [13], we build on these results to give conditions under which a BLOG model is guaranteed to define a unique probability distribution over possible worlds.

3.3   Design Features

Distributions over function values. A dependency statement in BLOG can define a probability distribution for a function, such as NthAuthor or PubCited. By contrast, many FOPLs — including PRISM [34], relational Bayesian networks [7], DAPER models [6], and Markov logic [33] — only express uncertainty about the values of predicates. In a purely logical context, this limitation might be innocuous: one can simply write PubCited(c, p) rather than PubCited(c) = p. However, using a predicate to represent a *random* functional relationship yields an unnecessarily complicated probability model. Instead of a single object-valued random variable PubCited(Cit1), one ends up with many binary random variables PubCited(Cit1, p) — and all these binary variables are mutually dependent, because exactly one of them must have the value True.

Explicit aggregation. In BLOG, we allow our elementary CPDs to take multisets as arguments. This eliminates the need for separate "combination functions", as used, for example, in BLPs [8]: the burden of aggregation is now on the CPDs.

Contingent dependencies. Dependency statements make a clear distinction between the values that are passed into elementary CPDs, and the logical formulas in "if" statements and set expressions, which determine what CPD to apply and what values to pass into it. This contrasts with the situation in BLPs [8], where any logical atom that is included in a clause to govern when the clause applies is also passed into the CPD for the head variable. Also, unlike in the probabilistic knowledge bases of Ngo and Haddaway [22] or the logical BNs of Fierens *et al.* [2], the conditions that govern dependencies in a BLOG model do not have to be nonrandom.

The contingent dependency structure that a BLOG model makes explicit can be exploited in sampling-based algorithms for approximate inference [14,15]. The basic insight is that algorithms such as likelihood weighting or Markov chain Monte Carlo only need to instantiate variables that are *context-specifically relevant* for the query: that is, variables that are known to be relevant given the other instantiated variables. Crucially, it is not necessary to instantiate all the variables that *might* be relevant for a query in some circumstances — this would be an infinite set if the query were about Text(Cit1) in Figure 5.

4   Learning in FOPLs

4.1   Parameters

Parameter estimation for FOPLs is well understood: the goal is to find parameters that maximize the likelihood of the data, or that have maximal *a posteriori* probability given the data and some Bayesian prior. As we noted in Section 2.3, parameter estimation tends to be computationally straightforward in directed models with complete data. For undirected models, and for directed models with unobserved variables, parameter estimation becomes computationally difficult as the number of random variables increases. However, this difficulty is common to all large probabilistic models, not just models defined by FOPLs.

4.2   Dependency Structure

Learning the dependency structure of FOPL models, on the other hand, raises issues that do not arise in the propositional case. In a Bayesian network, the dependency structure can be represented simply as a list of parents for each variable. But in a FOPL, we need a first-order representation of each variable's parent set. For instance, in Example 1, we need to learn that for all papers p, Accepted(p) depends on Brilliant(PrimaryAuthor(p)). Also, a variable often depends on a whole class of parents in a symmetrical way. In Example 1, if we take multiple authors into account by adding a predicate HasAuthor(p, r), then Accepted(p) might depend on some *aggregation function* of the variables {Brilliant(r) : HasAuthor(p, r)}, such as their average value, or the number that have the value True.

A well-known paper by Friedman *et al.* [3] introduces a method for learning the structure of a probabilistic relational model. In that work, a parent set is represented as a set of attribute chains, and parents that are reachable by the same attribute chain are aggregated together using one of a pre-defined library of aggregation functions. However, there are many other kinds of structures that we would like to be able to learn (and that are expressible in BLOG): for example, a variable may depend on different sets of parents in different contexts, or the parents may be selected using criteria other than single slot chains (*e.g.*, in Figure 4, Text(c) depends on those variables Name(NthAuthor(PubCited(c), n)) for $n <$ NumAuthors(PubCited(c))). Also, aggregation functions might be constructed from more primitive components rather than being chosen from a library.

There has been significant work on learning more complex selection and aggregation rules for estimating the conditional distribution of a single variable [30,20,25,38]. However, there does not seem to be any work so far on using these sophisticated techniques to learn directed, acyclic FOPL models for multiple variables (although they have been used to learn cyclic directed models called *dependency networks* [19]). There has been other work on structure learning for stochastic logic programs [18] and for Markov logic [9], building on inductive logic programming techniques for searching over logical formulas. We are interested in developing structure learning algorithms for BLOG models; this line of work might begin with restricted versions of the BLOG dependency statement syntax.

4.3 Functions and Types

Algorithms that learn the dependency structure of FOPL models typically assume that the functions, predicates, and object types are given. But as John McCarthy pointed out in his invited talk at ILP 2006, hypothesizing new objects and relations to explain observed data is a fundamental part of human learning. For instance, it would be useful to hypothesize a binary predicate on researchers, which might be called $\mathsf{Colleagues}(r_1, r_2)$, to explain how researchers co-occur in author lists. There has been considerable work in the inductive logic programming literature on *predicate invention* [16], but it is not yet clear how to generalize it to the probabilistic case. Inventing a new random function (or predicate) in a FOPL model corresponds to discovering a whole family of hidden variables. The task of discovering hidden variables in Bayesian networks has been investigated by Elidan and Friedman [1]; recently, Revoredo *et al.* [32] have taken some steps toward applying these ideas to BLPs.

It may also be possible to improve probabilistic models by automatically hypothesizing new types of objects. For example, to explain recurring substrings that come after the titles in citations, a system might hypothesize objects that could be called conferences. One simple form of type invention that has already been implemented involves clustering some observed objects, and treating the clusters as a new type of object [29]. In this case, the hypothesized type plays a predetermined role in the probabilistic model; in the general case, we would like a system to discover what roles need to be filled. Otero and Muggleton [23] sketch a learning algorithm for purely logical models that addresses this problem.

5 Conclusion

First-order probabilistic languages combine a principled treatment of uncertainty with the ability to describe large models formally and concisely. We hope the taxonomy of FOPLs given in this paper will make the wide landscape of proposed languages less daunting, and help researchers choose the most appropriate FOPL for a given application. This paper has highlighted two major areas of FOPL research: the development of languages such as BLOG, which support reasoning about the unknown objects that underlie a particular data set; and some preliminary work on discovering initially unknown predicates and object types that can be used to build more accurate and parsimonious models. In both of these areas, FOPL research is moving "into the unknown".

References

[1] Elidan, G., Friedman, N.: Learning hidden variable networks: The information bottleneck approach. JMLR 6, 81–127 (2005)

[2] Fierens, D., Blockeel, H., Bruynooghe, M., Ramon, J.: Logical Bayesian networks and their relation to other probabilistic logical models. In: Kramer, S., Pfahringer, B. (eds.) ILP 2005. LNCS (LNAI), vol. 3625, Springer, Heidelberg (2005)

[3] Friedman, N., Getoor, L., Koller, D., Pfeffer, A.: Learning probabilistic relational models. In: Proc. 16th IJCAI, pp. 1300–1307 (1999)

[4] Getoor, L., Friedman, N., Koller, D., Taskar, B.: Learning probabilistic models of relational structure. In: Proc. 18th ICML, pp. 170–177 (2001)

[5] Halpern, J.Y.: An analysis of first-order logics of probability. Artificial Intelligence 46, 311–350 (1990)

[6] Heckerman, D., Meek, C., Koller, D.: Probabilistic models for relational data. Technical Report MSR-TR-2004-30, Microsoft Research (2004)

[7] Jaeger, M.: Relational Bayesian networks. In: Proc. 13th UAI, pp. 266–273 (1997)

[8] Kersting, K., Raedt, L.D.: Adaptive Bayesian logic programs. In: Rouveirol, C., Sebag, M. (eds.) ILP 2001. LNCS (LNAI), vol. 2157, Springer, Heidelberg (2001)

[9] Kok, S., Domingos, P.: Learning the structure of Markov logic networks. In: Proc. 22nd ICML, pp. 441–448 (2005)

[10] Koller, D., Pfeffer, A.: Probabilistic frame-based systems. In: Proc. 15th AAAI, pp. 580–587 (1998)

[11] Laskey, K.B., da Costa, P.C.G.: Of starships and Klingons: First-order Bayesian logic for the 23rd century. In: Proc. 21st UAI, pp. 346–353 (2005)

[12] Lukasiewicz, T., Kern-Isberner, G.: Probabilistic logic programming under maximum entropy. In: Hunter, A., Parsons, S. (eds.) ECSQARU 1999. LNCS (LNAI), vol. 1638, pp. 279–292. Springer, Heidelberg (1999)

[13] Milch, B., Marthi, B., Russell, S., Sontag, D., Ong, D.L., Kolobov, A.: BLOG: Probabilistic models with unknown objects. In: Proc. 19th IJCAI (2005)

[14] Milch, B., Marthi, B., Sontag, D., Russell, S., Ong, D.L., Kolobov, A.: Approximate inference for infinite contingent Bayesian networks. In: Proc. 10th AISTATS (2005)

[15] Milch, B., Russell, S.: General-purpose MCMC inference over relational structures. In: Proc. 22nd UAI, pp. 349–358 (2006)

[16] Muggleton, S., Buntine, W.: Machine invention of first-order predicates by inverting resolution. In: Proc. 5th ICML, pp. 339–352 (1988)

[17] Muggleton, S.H.: Stochastic logic programs. In: De Raedt, L. (ed.) Advances in Inductive Logic Programming, pp. 254–264. IOS Press, Amsterdam (1996)

[18] Muggleton, S.H.: Learning structure and parameters of stochastic logic programs. Electronic Trans. on AI 6 (2002)

[19] J.,, Neville, D.J.: Dependency networks for relational data. In: Proc. 4th IEEE Int'l Conf. on Data Mining, IEEE Computer Society Press, Los Alamitos (2004)

[20] Neville, J., Jensen, D., Friedland, L., Hay, M.: Learning relational probability trees. In: Proc. 9th KDD (2003)

[21] Ng, R.T., Subrahmanian, V.S.: Probabilistic logic programming. Information and Computation 101(2), 150–201 (1992)

[22] Ngo, L., Haddawy, P.: Answering queries from context-sensitive probabilistic knowledge bases. Theoretical Comp. Sci. 171(1–2), 147–177 (1997)

[23] Otero, R., Muggleton, S.: On McCarthy's appearance and reality problem. In: ILP '06: Short Papers (2006)

[24] Pasula, H., Marthi, B., Milch, B., Russell, S., Shpitser, I.: Identity uncertainty and citation matching. In: NIPS 15, MIT Press, Cambridge, MA (2003)

[25] Perlich, C., Provost, F.: Aggregation-based feature invention and relational concept classes. In: Proc. 9th KDD (2003)

[26] Pfeffer, A.: IBAL: A probabilistic rational programming language. In: Proc. 17th IJCAI (2001)

[27] Poole, D.: Probabilistic Horn abduction and Bayesian networks. Artificial Intelligence 64(1), 81–129 (1993)

[28] Poole, D.: The Independent Choice Logic for modelling multiple agents under uncertainty. Artificial Intelligence 94(1–2), 5–56 (1997)

[29] Popescul, A., Ungar, L.H.: Cluster-based concept invention for statistical relational learning. In: Proc. 10th KDD (2004)

[30] Popescul, A., Ungar, L.H., Lawrence, S., Pennock, D.M.: Statistical relational learning for document mining. In: Proc. 3rd IEEE Int'l Conf. on Data Mining, pp. 275–282. IEEE Computer Society Press, Los Alamitos (2003)

[31] Puech, A., Muggleton, S.: A comparison of stochastic logic programs and Bayesian logic programs. In: IJCAI Workshop on Learning Statistical Models from Relational Data (2003)

[32] Revoredo, V.K., Paes, A., Zaverucha, G., Costa, S.: Combining predicate invention and revision of probabilistic FOL theories. In: ILP '06: Short Papers (2006)

[33] Richardson, M., Domingos, P.: Markov logic networks. MLJ 62, 107–136 (2006)

[34] Sato, T., Kameya, Y.: PRISM: A symbolic–statistical modeling language. In: Proc. 15th IJCAI, pp. 1330–1335 (1997)

[35] Sato, T., Kameya, Y.: Parameter learning of logic programs for symbolic–statistical modeling. JAIR 15, 391–454 (2001)

[36] Taskar, B., Abbeel, P., Koller, D.: Discriminative probabilistic models for relational data. In: Proc. 18th UAI, pp. 485–492 (2002)

[37] Thomas, A., Spiegelhalter, D., Gilks, W.: BUGS: A program to perform Bayesian inference using Gibbs sampling. In: Bernardo, J., Berger, J., Dawid, A., Smith, A. (eds.) Bayesian Statistics 4, Oxford Univ. Press, Oxford (1992)

[38] Van Assche, A., Vens, C., Blockeel, H., Džeroski, S.: First order random forests: Learning relational classifiers with complex aggregates. MLJ 64, 149–182 (2006)

[39] Vennekens, J., Verbaeten, S., Bruynooghe, M.: Logic programs with annotated disjunctions. In: Demoen, B., Lifschitz, V. (eds.) ICLP 2004. LNCS, vol. 3132, pp. 431–445. Springer, Heidelberg (2004)

Integration of Learning and Reasoning Techniques

Bart Selman

Cornell University, USA

Since the early days of AI, automated reasoning has been a rather elusive goal. In fact, up till the early nineties, general inference beyond hundred variable problems appeared infeasible. Over the last decade, we have witness a qualitative change in the field: current reasoning engines can handle problems with over a million variables and several millions of constraints. I will discuss what led to such a dramatic scale-up, and how progress in reasoning technology has opened up a range of new applications in AI and computer science in general. I will also discuss initial progress on the use of learning techniques in reasoning engines and the remaining challenges for obtaining a true integration of learning and reasoning.

S. Muggleton, R. Otero, and A. Tamaddoni-Nezhad (Eds.): ILP 2006, LNAI 4455, p. 25, 2007.
© Springer-Verlag Berlin Heidelberg 2007

Injecting Life with Computers

Ehud Shapiro

Weizmann Institute, Israel

Although electronic computers are the only "computer species" we are accustomed to, the mathematical notion of a programmable computer has nothing to do with wires and logic gates. In fact, Alan Turing's notional computer, which marked in 1936 the birth of modern computer science and still stands at its heart, has greater similarity to natural biomolecular machines such as the ribosome and polymerases than to electronic computers. Recently, a new "computer species" made of biological molecules has emerged. These simple molecular computers inspired by the Turing machine, of which a trillion can fit into a microliter, do not compete with electronic computers in solving complex computational problems; their potential lies elsewhere. Their molecular scale and their ability to interact directly with the biochemical environment in which they operate suggest that in the future they may be the basis of a new kind of "smart drugs": molecular devices equipped with the medical knowledge to perform disease diagnosis and therapy inside the living body. They would detect and diagnose molecular disease symptoms and, when necessary, administer the requisite drug molecules to the cell, tissue or organ in which they operate. In the talk we review this new research direction and report on preliminary steps carried out in our lab towards realizing its vision.

S. Muggleton, R. Otero, and A. Tamaddoni-Nezhad (Eds.): ILP 2006, LNAI 4455, p. 26, 2007.

On the Connection Between the Phase Transition of the Covering Test and the Learning Success Rate

Erick Alphonse and Aomar Osmani

LIPN-CNRS UMR 7030, Université Paris 13, France

1   Introduction

To investigate the impact of the occurrence of a phase transition (PT) in the covering test on the learning success rate, systematic experiments with several learning algorithms have been conducted on a large set of artificially generated problems by Botta et al. [3]. The authors generated a set of 451 problems by choosing each target concept according to its location in the (m, L) plane with respect to the PT. The "yes", "no" and "pt" regions are uniformly visited by varying (m,L) pairs without replacement (m ranges in [5,30] and L ranges in [12,40]). One important conclusion of their work is that the occurrence of a PT in the covering test is a general problem for all learning algorithms: the PT is viewed as an attractor for the heuristic search of any learning algorithms, which are bound to find a concept definition in the PT. Moreover, for all tested learners, there exists a failure region, starting from the "pt" region to the beginning of the "no" region, where the learnt theories are seemingly randomly constructed, with no better predictive accuracy than random guessing.

We note however that only generate-and-test (GT) learning algorithms have been investigated in this work and that this conclusion has to be qualified in the case of data-driven learning algorithms. In the GT paradigm, refinements are only based on the structure of the hypothesis space, independently of the learning data. Therefore, for a given hypothesis, GT algorithms have to deal with many refinements that are not relevant with respect to the discrimination task. On the contrary, data-driven strategies allow to rely on the training data to prune irrelevant branches of the refinement graph before relying on the evaluation function and may overcome the problem of plateaus. Notably, building on the pioneering work of Winston on near-miss examples [4], we show that, on the same set of problems as [3], a top-down data-driven (TDD) strategy can cross any plateau and reach the target concept whenever near-misses are supplied in the training set, whereas these near-misses do not change the plateau profile and do not guide a GT strategy. We conclude that the location of the target concept with respect to the phase transition alone is not a reliable indication of the learning problem difficulty, as previously thought.

S. Muggleton, R. Otero, and A. Tamaddoni-Nezhad (Eds.): ILP 2006, LNAI 4455, pp. 27–29, 2007.
© Springer-Verlag Berlin Heidelberg 2007

2   Experiments

For that purpose, we re-use the set of learning problems proposed in [3]. Notably, we run additional experiments of FOIL on these problems with new settings where the hypothesis space is set so that the value of a given evaluation function can be directly read from the coverage probability of a hypothesis, as in figure 1. Although our conclusion on the ability of a generate-and-test approach in this setting differs from [3], these new experiments allow us to better compare the behaviour of the generate-and-test and data-driven approaches when facing plateaus in the evaluation function.

We ran FOIL on problems on $m = 5$ and $m = 10$ lines and on the upper-right corner problems ranging from $L \in [24, 39]$ on the $m = 18$ line and from $m \in [18, 29]$ on the $L = 24$ line. We also sampled some other problems without any difference in the results. On all these problems, FOIL is unable to find any good approximation of the target concepts, being in the "yes", "no" or "pt" regions.

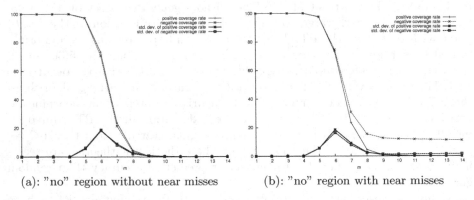

(a): "no" region without near misses   (b): "no" region with near misses

Fig. 1. Coverage rates and plateau profiles for representative problems in the "no" region with and without near misses

To show why, we plot for a problem the coverage rate of the positive and the negative examples as well as their standard deviation, depending on the size m of the hypothesis, averaged over 1000 randomly and uniformly drawn hypotheses. A plateau is materialised by a standard deviation of the coverage rates of the examples close to 0. For instance, on the $(14, 28)$ problem (figure 1 (a)), whatever the evaluation function is, the top-down learner will see hypotheses up to 4 literals long of equal value, or equivalently, it has to cross a plateau of width 4 before being able to use the evaluation function to discriminate between hypotheses.

In [1], we show how we can add near-misses to those problems in such a way that the plateaus are unchanged whereas they guide a top-down data-driven algorithm to the target concept without search in the hypothesis space. Again, on all these problems, FOIL is unable to find any good approximation of the target concepts, being in the "yes", "no" or "pt" regions. The plateau profile does not change (see figure 1 (b)) and a TGT learner cannot take advantage of the addition of the most informative negative examples. The opposite behaviour is exhibited by the TDD learner PROPAL which, by construction, solves all the problems being in the "yes", "pt" or "no" region. The learner makes the most of the learning data by exploiting the information provided by the most specific negative examples only and therefore use only the near-misses to guide its search. Note that as the branching factor is reduced to one thanks to the near-misses, the target concept is exactly identified each time as opposed to evaluating the quality of the approximation on a test set as for FOIL.

3   Conclusion

Plateau phenomenon problems have been studied recently in the phase transition framework and an important work has been done on identifying the criteria of success of learning algorithms [3]. The conclusion drawn from this work was that the location of the target concept with respect to the PT of the covering test was conclusive of the difficulty of the learning problems. A failure region was identified for all the tested learners. We performed additional experiments that strengthen this result. When the top-down search is conducted in the hypothesis space that exhibits a PT in its covering test, the "yes" region acts as a plateau for the heuristic search. This is the pathological case of heuristic search, whether complete or not, as the plateau must be crossed without being able to differentiate between refinements. In such a case, the greedy TGT learner, FOIL, cannot solve any of the problems. We showed however that this criterion alone is not reliable. As a main result, we showed that a TDD learning algorithm [2], supplied with near-miss examples was able to solve all problems, although the near-miss examples are still non-informative for GT algorithms. The plateau phenomena exhibited in the PT framework is a pathological case of the GT learners as they only rely on an evaluation function to guide their search, but it is not a reliable complexity measure for data-driven learners.

References

1. Alphonse, E., Osmani, A.: On the connection between the phase transition of the covering test and the learning success rate. Journal of Machine Learning, submitted (2007)
2. Alphonse, E., Rouveirol, C.: Extension of the top-down data-driven strategy to ILP. In: Etalle, S., Truszczyński, M. (eds.) ICLP 2006. LNCS, vol. 4079, Springer, Heidelberg (2006)
3. Botta, M., Giordana, A., Saitta, L., Sebag, M.: Relational learning as search in a critical region. Journal of Machine Learning Research 4, 431–463 (2003)
4. Winston, P.H.: Learning structural descriptions form examples. In: Winston, P.H. (ed.) The Psychology of Computer Vision, pp. 157–209. McGraw-Hill, New York (1975)

Revising Probabilistic Prolog Programs

Luc De Raedt, Kristian Kersting, Angelika Kimmig, Kate Revoredo*,
and Hannu Toivonen**

Inst. f. Informatik, Universität Freiburg, Georges-Köhler-Allee 079, D-79110 Freiburg
Dep. Computerwetenschappen, K.U.Leuven, Celestijnenlaan 200A, B-3001 Leuven
{luc.deraedt,angelika.kimmig}@cs.kuleuven.be,
hannu.toivonen@cs.helsinki.fi,
{kersting,revoredo}@informatik.uni-freiburg.de

Abstract. The ProbLog (probabilistic prolog) language has been introduced in [1], where various algorithms have been developed for solving
and approximating ProbLog queries. Here, we define and study the problem of revising ProbLog theories from examples.

1 ProbLog: Probabilistic Prolog

A ProbLog program consists – as Prolog – of a set of definite clauses. However,
in ProbLog every clause c_i is labeled with the probability p_i that it is true.

Example 1. Within bibliographic data analysis, the similarity structure among
items can improve information retrieval results. Consider a collection of papers
$\{a, b, c, d\}$ and some pairwise similarities similar(a, b), e.g., based on key word
analysis. Two items X and Y are related(X, Y) if they are similar (such as a and
c) or if X is similar to some item Z which is related to Y. Uncertainty in the data
and in the inference can elegantly be represented by the attached probabilities:

1.0 : related(X, Y) : −similar(X, Y).
0.8 : related(X, Y) : −similar(X, Z), related(Z, Y).
0.9 : similar(a, c). 0.9 : similar(c, b). 0.6 : similar(c, d). 0.7 : similar(d, b).

A ProbLog program $T = \{p_1 : c_1, \cdots, p_n : c_n\}$ now defines a probability distribution over logic programs $L \subseteq L_T = \{c_1, \cdots, c_n\}$ in the following way:

$$P(L|T) = \prod_{c_i \in L} p_i \prod_{c_i \in L_T \setminus L} (1 - p_i).$$

Unlike in Prolog, where one is typically interested in determining whether a query
succeeds or fails, in ProbLog one is interested in computing the probability that
it succeeds. The *success probability* $P(q|T)$ of a query q in a ProbLog program
T is defined by $P(q|T) = \sum_{L \subseteq L_T} P(q, L|T) = \sum_{L \subseteq L_T} P(q|L) \cdot P(L|T)$ with

$$P(q|L) = \begin{cases} 1 & \exists \theta : L \models q\theta \\ 0 & \text{otherwise.} \end{cases}$$

---

* Financially supported by Brazilian Research Council, CNPq - Brazil.
** Also at University of Helsinki, Finland; supported by the Humboldt foundation.

S. Muggleton, R. Otero, and A. Tamaddoni-Nezhad (Eds.): ILP 2006, LNAI 4455, pp. 30–33, 2007.

In other words, the success probability of query q corresponds to the probability that the query q has a proof, given the distribution over logic programs.

Example 2. There are two proofs of related(c, b), obtained using either the base case and one fact, or the recursive case and two facts. One way of computing the total probability is to disjoin the proofs first and then sum their probabilities. For instance, by excluding similar(c, b) in the formula for the second proof the probability of related(c, b) is obtained by $1.0 \cdot 0.9 + 0.8 \cdot 0.6 \cdot 0.7 \cdot (1 - 0.9) = 0.9336$. Similar, the probability of related(a, b) is 0.67824.

Reference [1] proposes and evaluates various algorithms for computing and approximating the success probability of ProbLog queries, whose evaluation is computationally hard. This problem is tackled by employing a reduction to the computation of the probability of a monotone DNF formula and the use of binary decision diagrams (BDDs). ProbLog is applied to biological network analysis problems. Other interesting application areas are hypertext and web mining, communication networks, and related domains.

2 Revising ProbLog Theories

Large ProbLog theories can be obtained automatically in many of the domains mentioned above, e.g., by statistical similarity, relevance or link analysis. Unfortunately, large theories are hard to utilize, both computationally and by end users, and there is need to revise them to smaller ones. Furthermore, new information can often improve the quality of an initial ProbLog theory, and also guide in reducing its size. For instance in our bibliographic example, user feedback might have revealed that items a, b and c, d are related but d, b are actually not. Thus, the initial theory in Example 1 should be revised.

The present paper introduces the revision problem for ProbLog theories:

Definition 1. Given *a ProbLog theory S (a set of ProbLog clauses), a set of positive and negative examples P and N in the form of ground goals, a constant $k \in \mathbb{N}$,* **find** *a theory $T \subseteq S$ of size at most k (i.e. $|T| \leq k$) that maximizes the likelihood $L(E|T) = \prod_{e \in E} L(e|T)$ of examples $E = P \cup N$ where*

$$L(e|T) = \begin{cases} P(e|T) & \text{if } e \in P \\ 1 - P(e|T) & \text{if } e \in N \end{cases} \tag{1}$$

In the ProbLog theory revision problem, we are interested in finding a small number of clauses from T that maximizes the likelihood of the data. Here a ProbLog theory T is used to determine a relative class distribution: it gives the probability $P(e|T)$ that any given example e is positive. (This is subtly different from specifying the distribution of (positive) examples.) The examples are assumed to be mutually independent, so the total likelihood is obtained as a simple product. For an optimal ProbLog theory T, the probability of the positives is as close to 1 as possible, and for the negatives as close to 0 as possible. However, because we want to allow misclassifications, but with a high cost, in order to avoid overfitting, to effectively handle noisy data, and to obtain smaller theories, one has to slightly redefine $P(e|T)$ in Equation (1), for instance as

$$\hat{P}(e|T) = \max\left(\min[1 - \epsilon, P(e|T)], \epsilon\right) \text{ for some } \epsilon > 0.$$

This avoids the possibility that the likelihood function becomes 0, e.g., when a positive example is not covered by the theory at all.

It is now instructive to look at specific instances of this problem:

- $k > |S|$: find the maximum likelihood theory. Closely corresponds to traditional theory revision in ILP; however, in the current ProbLog setting, only deletions of clauses are allowed as operations on the theory.
- $k < |S|$: theory compression.
- $k < |S|$ and $|N| = 0$: find the k clauses from S that contribute the most to the success probabilities of the positives.

3   The ProbLog Theory Revision Algorithm

The ProbLog theory revision algorithm performs a *greedy* search in the space of subsets of S. In each step, the algorithm finds the clause whose deletion results in the best likelihood score, and then deletes it. This process is continued until both $|T| \leq k$ *and* deleting further clauses does not improve the likelihood.

Example 3. Reconsider Example 1 and assume that the user feedback revealed one positive example related(a, b), and one negative example related(c, b). With $\epsilon = 0.05$, their initial likelihood is 0.045. The greedy approach first deletes 0.9 : similar(c, b) and thereby increases the likelihood to 0.2008. The probability of the positive example related(a, b) is now 0.3024 (was 0.67824), and that of the negative example related(c, b) is 0.336 (was 0.9336).

An important computational optimization is that the BDDs are reused. Their costly construction has to be done only once in the very first iteration; later on only the truth values of variables in the existing BDD are manipulated.

Experimental results on revising a large, real-world ProbLog theory for link mining are promising and appear in the longer version of this paper.

4   Conclusion

We have introduced a new type of theory revision problem involving probabilistic theories and sketched an algorithm for solving it. The problem setting is related to probabilistic ILP approaches such as Sato's PRISM and Muggleton's SLPs, which – if at all – have focused on learning theories from scratch. Only Revoredo *et al.* considered revision of BLPs. The revision problem as introduced here is closely related to the traditional ILP one but employs probabilistic principles to guide the search. Furthermore, by using the constant k it is possible to influence the degree of compression that is desired. An important question for further research is concerned with allowing for other operations than deletions of clauses.

Reference

1. De Raedt, L., Kimmig, A., Toivonen, H.: ProbLog: A probabilistic Prolog and its application in link discovery. In: Proceedings of 20th International Joint Conference on Artificial Intelligence, pp. 2468–2473 (2007)

Inductive Logic Programming for Gene Regulation Prediction

Sebastian Fröhler and Stefan Kramer

Technische Universität München, Institut für Informatik
Boltzmannstr. 3, 85748 Garching bei München, Germany
kramer@in.tum.de, s@froehler.info

1 Introduction and Background

One of the central goals in computational and systems biology is to understand the mechanisms of gene transcriptional regulation on a system-wide level. The efforts are often based on high-throughput genomic data of model organisms such as S. cerevisiae. The goal of this work is to learn a model of gene regulation predicting under which conditions genes are up- or down-regulated. Our starting point is the model of Middendorf *et al.* [1], where the presence of transcription factor binding sites (motifs) in the gene's regulatory region and the expression levels of regulators (e.g., transcription factors or protein kinases) are used to predict gene regulation. It is clear that in this formulation, important information related to gene regulation is missing, for instance due to post-translational modifications. Thus, information integration could be extremely useful to fill in and take into account various missing pieces of information related to gene regulation.

Uncovering the multi-relational nature of the problem, we first rephrased it in a logic-oriented framework and defined predicates for various interdependent pieces of information (see below). A logic-oriented representation enables the integration of various data sources: genome-wide cDNA microarray data, motif profile data from regulatory sequences and more. In particular, it is easy to take into account information that might, in any way, be related to gene regulation, for instance, protein-protein interactions and functional categorizations. Given the data in a logical representation, we can apply a variety of algorithms and systems for learning classification and regression models in logic, mostly developed in the field of inductive logic programming (ILP). We chose the Tilde system [2] for learning logical decision trees, since it is known to perform well in terms of runtimes and error rates.

2 Data and Representation

The approach is tested on the S. cerevisiae data by Gasch *et al.* [3]. As stated above, the goal is to learn a prediction model for the regulatory response of genes under different environmental conditions. In the following, we briefly present the predicates/relations in our logical formulation of the problem. In its most basic version, we have three different predicates, gene(GeneId, CondId, Level),

S. Muggleton, R. Otero, and A. Tamaddoni-Nezhad (Eds.): ILP 2006, LNAI 4455, pp. 34–36, 2007.

hasTFBS(GeneId, BsId), and expression(RegId, CondId, RegLevel).gene
(GeneId, CondId, Level) gives the expression level for each gene under a specific experimental condition. As in the study by Middendorf *et al.*, gene expression is discretized and mapped onto three distinct values +1 (up-regulated), 0,
and -1 (down-regulated). The learning task is to predict the expression level for
a given gene under a certain condition, given some background information (see
below). The dataset contains information about 1,411 genes, 173 experimental
conditions, and 54,183 instances. The relation hasTFBS(GeneId, BsId) holds
information about the binding sites for each gene found in its regulatory region,
taken from the TRANSFAC database. The regulatory region of each gene is
represented as a vector containing the binding sites for this gene.

Thus, we are able to identify subsets of genes according to binding motifs, which are assumed to share regulation behavior. The relation expression
(RegId, CondId, RegLevel) gives the expression levels of regulators (e.g., transcription factors or protein kinases) under certain experimental conditions. In
our representation, the regulators are a subset of all genes. In the experiments
described in this paper, we used a set of 53 different regulators. The goal of
the application is to predict the expression level for a given gene under a given
condition (predicate gene(GeneId, CondId, Level)), in terms of the predicates hasTFBS(GeneId, BsId) and expression(RegId, CondId, RegLevel).
With these predicates, the problem posed by Middendorf *et al.* is translated into
first-order predicate logic, amenable for logical approaches to machine learning. Additionally to the two basic predicates, we enrich the representation with
further predicates:

- assignedToFuncat(GeneId, FunCatId), containing all annotated FunCat
  [4] terms for gene GeneId and all parent FunCat terms of this term,
- hasPPI(GeneId, GeneId), containing binary protein-protein interactions
  from the MIPS database [5] for each gene whose expression state is to be
  predicted, and hasTFPPI(RegId, RegId) containing binary protein-protein
  interactions of the regulators themselves.

3   Summary of Experimental Results and Conclusion

In Table 1, a summary of our experimental results with single, bagged and
boosted Tilde decision trees can be found. In the first row, the baseline accuracy
of 54.7% indicates that the models clearly improve upon random guessing. The
second row shows the reference result by Middendorf *et al.* [1], where alternating decision trees (ADTs) were applied to a propositional version of the basic
data (without the additional predicates). We included the results both with and
without the use of FunCat terms. Since the predicates related to protein-protein
interactions are not frequently used in the trees, we omitted them altogether in
the experiments presented here. Given the same information, boosted decision
trees are on par with ADTs (another boosting technique), whereas FunCat terms
substantially improve the performance, both in predictive accuracy and compact-
ness. Moreover, it is possible to extract the functional categories affected by the

Table 1. Summary of experimental results: data (with/without FunCat), model, runtime (in s), predictive accuracy (in %), sensitivity, specificity, area under ROC curve (AUC) and number of nodes in tree(s)

Data	Model	Runtime	Acc.	Sens.	Spec.	AUC	# Nodes
all	baseline	——	54.7	0.0	100.0	*50.0*	0
wo funcat	ADTs [1]	——	88.5	—	—	—	—
all	single Tilde tree	185	85.1	87.1	83.5	92.8	186
all	10x bagging	951	85.1	87.3	83.4	93.0	1,201
wo funcat	10x bagging	921	80.6	78.6	82.4	88.7	1,388
all	10x boosting	2,658	91.2	91.2	91.3	97.7	2,491
wo funcat	10x boosting	2,052	88.4	87.6	89.1	96.3	2,620

experimental conditions, together with important transcription factor binding sites and transcription factors for these categories from the induced trees. For a detailed description of the data and a qualitative discussion of the results, we have to refer to the long version of the paper [6].

Summing up, we propose a systems biology application of ILP, where the goal is to predict the regulation of a gene under a certain condition from binding site information, the state of regulators, and additional information. We believe that decoding the regulation mechanisms of genes is an exciting new application of learning in logic, requiring data integration from various sources and potentially contributing to a better understanding on a system level.

References

1. Middendorf, M., Kundaje, A., Wiggins, C., Freund, Y., Leslie, C.: Predicting genetic regulatory response using classification. Bioinformatics 20(suppl_1), 232–240 (2004)
2. Blockeel, H., Raedt, L.D.: Top-down induction of first-order logical decision trees. Artificial Intelligence 101(1-2), 285–297 (1998)
3. Gasch, A.P., Spellman, P.T., Kao, C.M., Carmel-Harel, O., Eisen, M.B., Storz, G., Botstein, D., Brown, P.O.: Genomic Expression Programs in the Response of Yeast Cells to Environmental Changes. Mol.Biol.Cell 11(12), 4241–4257 (2000)
4. Ruepp, A., Zollner, A., Maier, D., Albermann, K., Hani, J., Mokrejs, M., Tetko, I., Guldener, U., Mannhaupt, G., Munsterkotter, M., Mewes, H.W.: The FunCat, a functional annotation scheme for systematic classification of proteins from whole genomes. Nucl. Acids Res. 32(18), 5539–5545 (2004)
5. Mewes, H., Albermann, K., Heumann, K., Liebl, S., Pfeiffer, F.: MIPS: a database for protein sequences, homology data and yeast genome information. Nucl. Acids Res. 25(1), 28–30 (1997)
6. Frö hler, S., Kramer, S.: Inductive logic programming for gene regulation prediction. Machine Learning (to appear)

QG/GA: A Stochastic Search for Progol

Stephen Muggleton and Alireza Tamaddoni-Nezhad

Department of Computing, Imperial College, London
{shm,atn}@doc.ic.ac.uk

Abstract. A search approach is presented, based on a novel algorithm called QG (Quick Generalisation). QG carries out a random-restart stochastic bottom-up search which efficiently generates a consistent clause on the fringe of the refinement graph search without needing to explore the graph in detail. We use a Genetic Algorithm (GA) to evolve and re-combine clauses generated by QG. Initial experiments with QG/GA indicate that this approach can be more efficient than standard refinement-graph searches, while generating similar or better solutions.

1 Introduction

There is a long-standing and increasing interest in stochastic search methods in Inductive Logic Programming (ILP) [4]. Stochastic methods have been explored both for clause evaluation (e.g. [5]) and for searching the space of candidate clauses (e.g. [6]). Most search techniques within ILP are based on clause refinement. Such searches are typically time-consuming, requiring the testing of a large number of inconsistent clauses. For example, it can be shown [3] that on a range of learning problems around 96% of the clauses considered by Progol are inconsistent. The low average density of consistent clauses motivates an investigation in this paper into a novel algorithm called QG (Quick Generalisation).

2 QG Algorithm

The following definitions are used to describe the QG algorithm in Figure 1.

Definition 1 (Progol refinement setting). *Let $S = \langle B, \mathcal{E}, \mathcal{L}, \succeq \rangle$ be Progol's ILP setting as defined in [2]. Let $\mathcal{E} = \langle \mathcal{E}^+, \mathcal{E}^- \rangle$ consist of a set of positive and negative examples (ground unit clauses) respectively. The "top" clause, denoted by $\triangle$, is the maximal$_\succeq$ element in $\mathcal{L}$. The "bottom" clause, denoted by $\bigtriangledown_{e,S}$, is the least$_{\succeq, \mathcal{L}}$ element such that $B, \bigtriangledown_{e,S} \models e$. Refinement of clause C, denoted by $\rho_{e,S}(C)$, is the set of maximal$_{\succeq, \mathcal{L}}$ clauses D such that $C \succ D \succeq \bigtriangledown_{e,S}$.*

Definition 2 (S-consistency). *Given $S = \langle B, \mathcal{E}, \mathcal{L}, \succeq \rangle$, $e \in \mathcal{E}$ and $\triangle \succeq C \succeq \bigtriangledown_{e,S}$ we say that C is S-consistent iff $B, \mathcal{E}, C$ is satisfiable.*

Definition 3 (Head-connectness). *A definite clause $h \leftarrow b_1, .., b_n$ is said to be head-connected if and only if each body atom b_i contains at least one variable found either in h or in a body atom b_j, where $1 \leq j < i$.*

S. Muggleton, R. Otero, and A. Tamaddoni-Nezhad (Eds.): ILP 2006, LNAI 4455, pp. 37–39, 2007.

Quick Generalisation (QG) algorithm
Input: Bottom clause $\triangledown_{e,S}$ and setting S
R is a random head-connected permutation of $\triangledown_{e,S}$
Output: Reduce R wrt S
Reduce algorithm
Input: Clause $C = h \leftarrow b_1, ..b_n$ and setting S
Res is C
While there is an unseen cutoff atom b_i in the body of Res
For b_i find minimal support set $S_i = \{b'_1, .., b'_m\} \subseteq \{b_1, .., b_{i+1}\}$
such that $h \leftarrow S_i, b_i$ is head-connected
Res is $h \leftarrow S_i, b_i, S_{i-1}$
where S_{i-1} is $b_1, .., b_{i-1}$ with S_i removed
Repeat
Output: Reduced clause Res

Fig. 1. Quick Generalisation (QG) algorithm

Definition 4 (Minimal support set). *Let $h \leftarrow B$ be a definite clause and B be a set of atoms. $S \subseteq B$ is a minimal support set for b from B iff $h \leftarrow S, b$ is head-connected and there does not exist a set $S' \subset S$ for which $h \leftarrow S', b$ is head-connected.*

Definition 5 (Fringe). *Clause C is in Fringe(e,S) iff it is head-connected and for every D it is the case that $C \in \rho_{e,S}(D)$ implies D is not S-consistent.*

Definition 6 (Profile and cutoff atom). *Let $C = h \leftarrow b_1, \ldots b_n$ be a definite clause and B be background knowledge. $E_i \subseteq \mathcal{E}^-$ is the ith negative profile of C, where $E_i = \{e : \exists \theta, e = h\theta, B \models (b_1, \ldots, b_i)\theta\}$. b_i is the cutoff atom iff i is the least value such that $E_i = \emptyset$.*

The QG algorithm (Figure 1) works by randomly permuting the given clause body and then applying to the result the deterministic "Reduce" algorithm. The result is a randomly constructed "fringe" clause (see Definition 5).

3   QG and QG/GA in Progol

The QG algorithm described in the previous sections can be used for efficiently sampling from consistent clauses. A simple integration of QG in Progol can be realised by replacing Progol's A^* search by a QG sampling mechanism which returns the clause with highest positive compression from a sample of consistent clauses. Clauses generated by the simple QG sampling mechanism lack diversity and also it is very likely that the optimal solution is not among them. We also examine a more advanced setting in which a Genetic Algorithm (GA) is used to evolve and re-combine clauses generated by QG. In this setting QG is used to seed a population of clauses processed by the GA. The GA-ILP setting used in the present study is similar to the one described in [7]. In the present study, the occurrences of literals from the bottom clause are directly encoded as bit strings (as described as further work in [7]). In a long version of this paper [3] QG and QG/GA have been tested on a range of problems. These include a set of problems from [1] with varying concept sizes (i.e. $m6.l12$ to $m16.l12$). Table 1

Table 1. Predictive accuracies and learning times for different search algorithms on a set of learning problems with varying concept sizes from 6 to 16. Density of consistent clauses is taken as being the proportion of consistent clauses in the A^* search $(Cs(\%))$.

m	A^*			QG		GA		QG/GA	
	$Cs(\%)$	$A(\%)$	$T(s)$	$A(\%)$	$T(s)$	$A(\%)$	$T(s)$	$A(\%)$	$T(s)$
6	31.71	98	3.22	99.5	3.89	99.5	5.83	99.5	10.32
7	3.36	99.5	633.16	99.5	45.11	99.5	12.99	99.5	86.51
8	1.05	100	1416.55	100	175.03	100	13.92	100	169.55
10	0.0015	97.5	25852.80	99	242.22	95.5	74.68	99	1064.22
11	0.36	80	37593.20	91	774.02	99	30.37	99.5	110.15
14	0	50	128314.00	69	4583.25	79.5	529.67	88.5	1184.76
16	4×10^{-6}	59	55687.44	77.5	4793.01	74	297.93	89.5	4945.20

shows predictive accuracies and average learning and testing times for different algorithms. According to this table, in most cases QG has found a solution with a similar or better accuracy than the A^* search in significantly less time. These results also suggest that we can get a better predictive accuracy by combining QG and GA (e.g. for $m = 14$ and $m = 16$). According to the table, the efficiency and accuracy advantages of QG and QG/GA are more evident when the density of consistent clauses $(Cs\%)$ is low.

4 Conclusions

In this paper we presented a search approach based on a novel algorithm called QG (Quick Generalisation). Initial experiments indicate that when the proportion of consistent clauses is small, QG and QG/GA are more efficient than standard refinement-graph searches, while still generating the same (or similar) solutions in most cases. The QG can be easily adopted for any ILP system which uses a bottom clause or a template for generating the hypotheses. These include ILP systems which use some form of Inverse Entailment.

References

1. Botta, M., Giordana, A., Saitta, L., Sebag, M.: Relational learning as search in a critical region. J. Mach. Learn. Res. 4, 431–463 (2003)
2. Muggleton, S.: Inverse entailment and Progol. New Gen. Comp. 13, 245–286 (1995)
3. Muggleton, S., Tamaddoni-Nezhad, A.: QG/GA: A stochastic search for Progol. Machine Learning Journal (to appear)
4. Page, D., Srinivasan, A.: ILP: a short look back and a longer look forward. J. Mach. Learn. Res. 4, 415–430 (2003)
5. Sebag, M., Rouveirol, C.: Resource-bounded relational reasoning: Induction and deduction through stochastic matching. Machine Learning Journal 38, 43–65 (2000)
6. Srinivasan, A.: A study of two probabilistic methods for searching large spaces with ILP. Technical Report PRG-TR-16-00, Oxford Univ. Comp. Lab (2000)
7. Tamaddoni-Nezhad, A., Muggleton, S.H.: A genetic algorithms approach to ILP. In: Matwin, S., Sammut, C. (eds.) ILP 2002. LNCS (LNAI), vol. 2583, pp. 285–300. Springer, Heidelberg (2003)

Generalized Ordering-Search for Learning Directed Probabilistic Logical Models

Jan Ramon, Tom Croonenborghs, Daan Fierens, Hendrik Blockeel,
and Maurice Bruynooghe

K.U.Leuven, Dept. of Computer Science, Celestijnenlaan 200A, 3001 Heverlee, Belgium
{Jan.Ramon,Tom.Croonenborghs,Daan.Fierens,
Hendrik.Blockeel,Maurice.Bruynooghe}@cs.kuleuven.be

Abstract. Recently, there has been an increasing interest in directed probabilistic logical models and a variety of languages for describing such models has been proposed. Although many authors provide high-level arguments to show that in principle models in their language can be learned from data, most of the proposed learning algorithms have not yet been studied in detail. We introduce an algorithm, generalized ordering-search, to learn both structure and conditional probability distributions (CPDs) of directed probabilistic logical models. The algorithm upgrades the ordering-search algorithm for Bayesian networks. We use relational probability trees as a representation for the CPDs. We present experiments on blocks world domains, a gene domain and the Cora dataset.

1 Introduction

An important class of probabilistic logical models are directed models that are relational extensions of Bayesian networks. A variety of languages for describing such models has been proposed: Probabilistic Relational Models (PRMs) [4], Bayesian Logic Programs (BLPs) [5], Logical Bayesian Networks [2] and many others. Although most authors describe high-level algorithms to learn models in their language or provide arguments to show that such algorithms can be developed, there are still many problems that have not been studied in detail. One such problem is how to deal with recursive dependencies. Consider for example the blocks world [1]: we have a set of blocks that can be stacked on top of each other, the $on/2$ predicate is used to represent a certain state. Obviously some (recursive) dependencies hold between all the different $on/2$ facts. In undirected models one could state that each $on/2$ fact depends on all other $on/2$ facts, but in directed models this is not allowed since it would lead to cycles. Hence, learning a directed probabilistic logical model of the blocks world is a challenging problem.

In this paper we introduce an algorithm, generalized ordering-search, to learn both structure and conditional probability distributions of directed probabilistic logical models. Our algorithm is based on the ordering-search algorithm of Teyssier and Koller [8] for learning propositional Bayesian networks. Our contribution is that we upgrade this algorithm to the relational case and investigate the use of relational probability trees [3,6] as compact and interpretable models of conditional probability distributions (CPDs). We will use the terminology of Logical Bayesian Networks (LBNs) [2] but our discussion applies equally to other directed probabilistic logical models such as PRMs and BLPs. More details can be found in the full paper [7].

S. Muggleton, R. Otero, and A. Tamaddoni-Nezhad (Eds.): ILP 2006, LNAI 4455, pp. 40–42, 2007.

2 Generalized Ordering-Search

When learning directed models one of the main problems is to avoid cycles. For propositional Bayesian networks (BNs) this can be done by assuming a causal ordering on the set of random variables (RVs). Given such an ordering, we can learn for each RV X a probability tree [3] that identifies which of the preceding RVs are most relevant for X (these will be X's parents in the BN), and specifies how they influence X (the CPD). However, we usually do not know the optimal ordering. One solution is to do hill-climbing through the space of all orderings and in each step apply the above procedure to learn a BN, until an accurate BN is encountered. This is known as *ordering-search* [8].

Ordering-search cannot be applied directly to the relational case for two reasons. First, we cannot simply learn a separate CPD for each ground RV because we want our model to generalize over the domain (set of constants), i.e. the model should be on the predicate-level instead of on the ground-level. Second, we do not want to learn the optimal ordering on the set of ground RVs but rather a model of this ordering that generalizes over the domain.

To deal with the above two problems, we adapt the original ordering-search algorithm in two ways. First, instead of learning a separate CPD for each RV, we learn for each probabilistic predicate a single so-called *generalized conditional probability function (GCPF)*. Basically, a GCPF for a predicate p is a function that takes as input any set of RVs (the possible parents) plus a target RV T built from p and that returns a set of parents for T as well as a CPD for T given these parents. Second, instead of searching through the space of orderings until a good ordering is found, we now search through the space of orderings only to collect information about the likelihood of different orderings (using the learned GCPFs) and afterwards we use this information to learn a model of the optimal ordering. Note that an ordering on the RVs together with an appropriate set of GCPFs fully specifies an LBN. We now briefly explain the two steps of our algorithm in more detail.

In the first step we learn for each probabilistic predicate a GCPF under the form of a logical probability tree [3,6]. Let $\mathcal{R}$ denote the set of all ground RVs. More precisely, for each predicate p we learn a tree $\mathcal{T}_{gcpf}$ such that for any target $T \in \mathcal{R}$ built from p, any assignment v_T to T, any set $\mathcal{E} \subseteq \mathcal{R}$ of known evidence RVs and any assignment $v_{\mathcal{E}}$ to the RVs in $\mathcal{E}$, $\mathcal{T}_{gcpf}(T, v_T, \mathcal{E}, v_{\mathcal{E}}, \mathcal{R}) = \hat{P}(T = v_T \mid \mathcal{E} = v_{\mathcal{E}})$ expresses the probability that T has value v_T given the values of all RVs in $\mathcal{E}$. To learn such a tree we first generate training data by sampling data from random orderings (i.e. randomly selecting T and $\mathcal{E}$) and then apply the TILDE system adapted to learn probability trees [3] on this dataset. The final result of this step is a set of GCPFs that can be used together with any ordering to determine an LBN.

In the second step we learn a model of the optimal ordering. Concretely, we use TILDE to learn a logical decision tree that specifies for any pair of RVs their best ordering. The training data for this regression tree is generated by searching through the space of orderings and computing for each considered ordering the difference in likelihood when swapping two adjacent RVs in this ordering (this difference in likelihood is the target of the regression). To compute the likelihood of an ordering we use the GCPFs of the previous step. Using the obtained regression tree we can determine the optimal ordering for any pair of RVs and hence indirectly also for any number of RVs. This optimal ordering together with the GCPFs fully determines an LBN.

3   Experiments

We evaluated our approach on four datasets: a simple artificial dataset about the inheritance of genes, two datasets derived from relational reinforcement learning experiments on the blocks world [1] and the Cora dataset. We compared the results of generalized ordering search with the results obtained when learning CPDs for a given expert ordering and for a random ordering.

The main conclusion from our experiments is that generalized ordering-search succeeds in learning an ordering that performs approximately equally well (in terms of likelihood) as the expert orderings and considerably better than random orderings. Also, the complexity (size) of the learned CPDs for generalized ordering search is similar to that for the expert orderings and smaller than for random orderings.

Acknowledgements

TC and DF are supported by the Institute for the Promotion of Innovation by Science and Technology in Flanders (IWT Vlaanderen). JR and HB are post-doctoral fellows of the Fund for Scientific Research (FWO) of Flanders.

References

1. Croonenborghs, T., Ramon, J., Blockeel, H., Bruynooghe, M.: Online learning and exploiting relational models in reinforcement learning. In: Proceedings of the 20th International Joint Conference on Artificial Intelligence (2007)
2. Fierens, D., Blockeel, H., Bruynooghe, M., Ramon, J.: Logical Bayesian networks and their relation to other probabilistic logical models. In: Kramer, S., Pfahringer, B. (eds.) ILP 2005. LNCS (LNAI), vol. 3625, pp. 121–135. Springer, Heidelberg (2005)
3. Fierens, D., Ramon, J., Blockeel, H., Bruynooghe, M.: A comparison of approaches for learning probability trees. In: Gama, J., Camacho, R., Brazdil, P.B., Jorge, A.M., Torgo, L. (eds.) ECML 2005. LNCS (LNAI), vol. 3720, pp. 556–563. Springer, Heidelberg (2005)
4. Getoor, L., Friedman, N., Koller, D., Pfeffer, A.: Learning Probabilistic Relational Models. In: Dzeroski, S., Lavrac, N. (eds.) Relational Data Mining, pp. 307–334. Springer, Heidelberg (2001)
5. Kersting, K., De Raedt, L.: Towards combining inductive logic programming and Bayesian networks. In: Rouveirol, C., Sebag, M. (eds.) ILP 2001. LNCS (LNAI), vol. 2157, pp. 118–131. Springer, Heidelberg (2001)
6. Neville, J., Jensen, D.: Dependency networks for relational data. In: Proceedings of the 4th IEEE International Conference on Data Mining (2004)
7. Ramon, J., Croonenborghs, T., Fierens, D., Blockeel, H., Bruynooghe, M.: Generalized ordering-search for learning directed probabilistic logical models. Machine Learning (special issue ILP'06), 2007 Conditionally accepted
8. Teyssier, M., Koller, D.: Ordering-based search: A simple and effective algorithm for learning Bayesian networks. In: Proceedings of the Twenty-first Conference on Uncertainty in AI (UAI), pp. 584–590 (2005)

ALLPAD: Approximate Learning of Logic Programs with Annotated Disjunctions

Fabrizio Riguzzi

Dipartimento di Ingegneria, Università di Ferrara, Via Saragat 1
44100 Ferrara, Italy
fabrizio.riguzzi@unife.it

Abstract. In this paper we present the system ALLPAD for learning Logic Programs with Annotated Disjunctions (LPADs). ALLPAD modifies the previous system LLPAD in order to tackle real world learning problems more effectively. This is achieved by looking for an approximate solution rather than a perfect one. ALLPAD has been tested on the problem of classifying proteins according to their tertiary structure and the results compare favorably with most other approaches.

1 Introduction

Logic Programs with Annotated Disjunctions [1] are a relatively new formalism for representing probabilistic information in logic programming. They have been recognized as one of the simplest and most expressive languages that combine logic and probability [2].

In [3] the definition of a learning problem for LPADs has been proposed together with an algorithm for solving it called LLPAD. However, LLPAD does not work well on non-toy problems because it relies on the exact solution of a large constraint satisfaction problem. On real world problems such a solution may not exist or may be too expensive to find. Therefore in this paper we propose the system ALLPAD (Approximate Learning of Logic Programs with Annotated Disjunctions) that modifies LLPAD in order to be able to solve real world problems by looking for a solution that "approximately" satisfies the learning problem.

2 ALLPAD

ALLPAD learns ground LPADs in five phases. The first and the third are the same as those of LLPAD. The second and the fourth modify those of LLPAD and the fifth one is new.

In the first and second phases ALLPAD looks respectively for definite and disjunctive clauses that satisfy a number of constraints reported in [3]. In the third phase the disjunctive clauses found in the second phase are annotated with probabilities by exploiting theorem 1 of [3].

In the fourth phase ALLPAD solves an optimization problem in which a subset of the found disjunctive clauses is selected so that the resulting program assigns

S. Muggleton, R. Otero, and A. Tamaddoni-Nezhad (Eds.): ILP 2006, LNAI 4455, pp. 43–45, 2007.

to the input interpretations a probability that is as close as possible to the one given. This is done by exploiting theorem 2 of [3]. Since the optimization problem can be expressed as a linear problem, we can use mixed-integer programming (MIP) techniques. If no perfect solution exists, a non zero optimum will be found.

However, the optimization problem is NP-hard and thus solvable only for small instances. To overcome this problem, we exploit the possibility of setting a time limit offered by many MIP packages. In this way, ALLPAD looks for the best solution given the available time.

To make sure that an admissible solution will be found within the time limits, the complete search in the space of bodies performed by LLPAD in the second phase is given up for an incomplete search strategy, beam search. The heuristic to be used for ranking bodies is the sum of the probabilities of the interpretations where the body is true. This heuristic ensures that the clauses that apply only to a small number of improbable interpretations are discarded and the dimension of the optimization problem is reduced.

In the fifth phase, the definite clauses not mutually exclusive with the selected disjunctive clauses are removed.

3   Experiments

ALLPAD was applied to the problem of predicting the tertiary structure of proteins by classifying them into one of the SCOP classes [4]. Each protein is described by a sequence of secondary structure elements. The elements are either of the form *he(Type,Length,Position)* or of the form *st(Orientation,Length,Position)*. The last argument is an ordinal number indicating the position in the sequence.

The dataset available [5] (kindly provided by Kristian Kersting) has the following distribution of examples into classes (class,examples): (fold1, 721), (fold2, 360), (fold23, 274), (fold37, 441), (fold55, 290).

ALLPAD can be used for classification as other probabilistic model learners: a model is learned for each class and an example is assigned the class whose model gives the highest probability to the example.

In order to learn an LPAD that describes a class, the interpretations given as input to the system are annotated each with the same probability given by 1 over the total number of interpretations in the training set.

Proteins are modeled with LPADs as stochastic processes: the structure at position p is predicted on the basis of the structures in a number of previous positions. To this purpose, ALLPAD learns programs containing rules having all the possible structures with position equal to p in the head and a conjunction of structures in the body with positions belonging to the set $S(p, k) = \{p-1, p-2, \ldots, p-k\}$ for a given k.

Since the constraint solving phase finds only an approximate solution, the theories learned are tested in an approximate way: if for a sequence position no learned rule is applicable, the marginal probability of the atom in the class is used.

The accuracy of the learned LPAD is compared with the accuracy of a naïve Bayes classifier obtained in the following way: the approximate testing procedure is applied by using for all positions the marginal probability in the class.

Two experiments were performed using 10-fold cross validation.

In both experiments we used Xpress-Optimizer by Dash Optimization for solving the MIP problem. The time limit has been set to 1 hour for each class in the first experiment and to 100 minutes for each class in the second experiment.

The other important parameters are: the value of k (the number of previous positions to consider), set to 4; the size of the beam, set to 100, and the maximum number of bodies to be explored for each clause template, which has been set to 100 in the first experiment and to 125 in the second experiment. The experiments have been performed on a PC with an Athlon XP 2600+ processor at 2138 Mhz, 1GB of RAM and Windows 2000.

In the two experiments ALLPAD reached respectively an average accuracy of 85.14% and of 85.67%, while the naïve Bayes approach reached an average accuracy of 82.79%. A cross-validated paired two-tailed t test was performed for comparing the accuracy of ALLPAD to that of naïve Bayes and the null hypothesis of equivalence can be rejected with 98.3% probability for the first experiment and with 98.6% probability for the second experiment.

The results available in the literature regarding accuracy on datasets in the same domain are: 74% in [5], 83.6% in [6], 76% and 73% in [7] and 92.96% in [8]. The results of ALLPAD compare favorably with all results apart from the last one, even if the system is not specifically tailored to learning sequences.

References

1. Vennekens, J., Verbaeten, S., Bruynooghe, M.: Logic programs with annotated disjunctions. In: Demoen, B., Lifschitz, V. (eds.) ICLP 2004. LNCS, vol. 3132, Springer, Heidelberg (2004)
2. Blockeel, H.: Probabilistic logical models for mendel's experiments: An exercise. In: Camacho, R., King, R., Srinivasan, A. (eds.) ILP 2004. LNCS (LNAI), vol. 3194, Springer, Heidelberg (2004)
3. Riguzzi, F.: Learning logic programs with annotated disjunctions. In: Camacho, R., King, R., Srinivasan, A. (eds.) ILP 2004. LNCS (LNAI), vol. 3194, pp. 270–287. Springer, Heidelberg (2004)
4. Turcotte, M., Muggleton, S., Sternberg, M.J.E.: The effect of relational background knowledge on learning of protein three-dimensional fold signatures. Machine Learning 43(1/2), 81–95 (2001)
5. Kersting, K., Raiko, T., Kramer, S., De Raedt, L.: Towards discovering structural signatures of protein folds based on logical hidden markov models. In: Pacific Symposium on Biocomputing, pp. 192–203 (2003)
6. Kersting, K., Gärtner, T.: Fisher kernels for logical sequences. In: Boulicaut, J.-F., Esposito, F., Giannotti, F., Pedreschi, D. (eds.) ECML 2004. LNCS (LNAI), vol. 3201, pp. 205–216. Springer, Heidelberg (2004)
7. Kersting, K., De Raedt, L., Raiko, T.: Logical hidden markov models. Journal of Artificial Intelligence Research 25, 425–456 (2006)
8. Gutmann, B., Kersting, K.: TildeCRF: Conditional random fields for logical sequences. In: Fürnkranz, J., Scheffer, T., Spiliopoulou, M. (eds.) ECML 2006. LNCS (LNAI), vol. 4212, Springer, Heidelberg (2006)

Margin-Based First-Order Rule Learning

Ulrich Rückert and Stefan Kramer

Institut für Informatik/I12, Technische Universität München, Boltzmannstr. 3,
D-85748 Garching b. München, Germany
{rueckert,kramer}@in.tum.de

1 Introduction and Motivation

Learning sets of first-order rules has a long tradition in machine learning and inductive logic programming. While most traditional systems follow a separate-and-conquer approach, many modern systems are based on statistical considerations, such as ensemble theory, large margin classification or graphical models. In this work, we frame relational learning as a statistical *classification* problem and apply tools and concepts from statistical learning theory to design a new statistical first-order rule learning system. The system's design is motivated by the goal of finding theoretically well-founded answers to some of the greatest challenges faced by first-order learning systems. First, using strict binary-valued logic as a representation language is known to be suboptimal for noisy, imprecise or uncertain data and background knowledge as frequently encountered in practice. As in many other state-of-the-art rule learning approaches [1], we therefore assign weights to the rules. In this way, a rule set represents a linear classifier and one can optimize *margin-based* optimization criteria, essentially reducing the misclassification error on noisy data. Since we aim at comprehensible models, we employ margins without the kernel trick. Second, the problem of finding a hypothesis that explains the training set is known to be NP-hard even for the simplest possible classifiers, from propositional monomials to linear classifiers. To avoid the computational complexity of optimizing the empirical training error directly, we use a feasible margin-based relaxation, *margin minus variance* (MMV), as introduced recently for propositional domains [2]. MMV minimization is linear in the number of instances and therefore well-suited for large datasets. Third, in multi-relational learning settings, one can formulate almost arbitrarily complex queries or clauses, to describe a training or test instance. Thus, there is a potentially unlimited number of features that can be used for classification and overfitting avoidance should be of great importance. We derived an error bound based on MMV, giving us a theoretically sound stopping criterion controlling the number of rules in a weighted rule set. The rule generation process is based on traditional first-order rule refinement and declarative language bias. It is possible to choose from a variety of search strategies, from a predefined order of clauses to rearranging the order based on the weights attached to clauses in the model so far. The system is implemented as a stand-alone tool integrating a Prolog engine.

S. Muggleton, R. Otero, and A. Tamaddoni-Nezhad (Eds.): ILP 2006, LNAI 4455, pp. 46–48, 2007.

2   First-Order Rule Learning as Model Selection

In order to give a more formal definition of the setting, we assume that the instances are drawn i.i.d. according to a fixed but unknown distribution D. D ranges over $\mathcal{X} \times \mathcal{Y}$, where $\mathcal{X}$ is the set of all possible instances (i.e., sets of tuples from several relations), and $\mathcal{Y} := \{-1, 1\}$ contain the target labels. A sample $X = \{x_1, \ldots, x_m\}$ of size m is drawn. Furthermore, we assume we already have a (possibly infinite) repository of first-order rules $R = \{r_1, r_2, \ldots\}$, where a rule $r_j : \mathcal{X} \to [-1, 1]$ assigns either -1 or 1 to each instance. A rule can depend on any arbitrary number of relations. The rules are enumerated from a language bias declaration according to some chosen search strategy. Let $x_i(j)$ denote the result of the application of rule j on instance x_i. If we consider only the first n rules, we can represent the ith instance by the vector of rule values $x_i := (x_i(1), x_i(2), \ldots, x_i(n))^T$. Likewise, a weighted rule set can be given by a weight vector $w \in [-1, 1]^n$. An individual rule set q assigns class label $\operatorname{sgn}(w^T x_i)$. Note that the weight vector defines a hyperplane separating $[-1; 1]^n$ into two half-spaces so that rule sets in our setting are related to linear classifiers and perceptrons. Since the usual approach of optimizing the empirical error is computationally infeasible and prone to overfitting, we are optimizing a related quantity, the mean margin minus the variance of the margin (*margin minus variance – MMV* [2]). This is motivated by the observation that ideally one would want to maximize the average distance from the separating hyperplane to the training instances and to minimize the sample variance of these distances. More formally: given an instance (x, y) let $\mu_w(x, y) := w^T x \cdot y$ denote the *margin*. The margin is positive, if the instance is correctly classified by q and negative otherwise. Then, the *empirical margin* is $\hat{\mu}_w := \frac{1}{m} \sum_{i=1}^{m} \mu_w(x_i, y_i)$ and the *empirical variance* is $\hat{\sigma}_w := \frac{1}{m-1} \sum_{i=1}^{m} (\mu_w(x_i, y_i) - \hat{\mu}_w)^2$. Using this notation, one can look for weight vectors w that maximize $\hat{\mu}_w - \hat{\sigma}_w$ subject to the constraint that $\|w\|_p = 1$. With $p = 1$, most weights are set to zero, thus, the rule sets tend to be small. Greater values of p (typically values > 1 and ≤ 2) distribute the weights more evenly among the rules. MMV maximization is a quadratic optimization problem and can be solved in time linear in the number of instances.

The success of this algorithm obviously depends to a large degree on the choice of the rule repository, and, in particular, on its size. If the repository is too small, the algorithm will most likely underfit, if it is too large, it will overfit. To overcome this dilemma we start with a small repository, then iteratively increase its size. We calculate the optimal MMV weight vector for each size and use a concentration inequality [2] to gain an estimate of the structural risk, i.e. the risk of overfitting. The best repository is the one which minimizes the sum of empirical and structural risk. Ideally, the rules that are generated during this iterative procedure should be as informative as possible about the prediction task. Since rules that are generated early are less likely to be pruned away by the structural risk estimation procedure, the user should adjust rule generation to build assumedly informative rules first. This provides an easy, but powerful way of providing uncertain and imprecise background knowledge for a particular learning task. The rules are generated from typical language bias declarations including types and modes of variables as well as conjunctions of literals. The system starts with a set of basic rules and repeatedly applies refinement operators to obtain new rules from existing rules. The operators add a literal or conjunction of literals to an existing rules to create a new one, or combine two existing rules disjunctively.

Depending on the way new rules are generated, the method can be categorized as genuine relational learning or propositionalization scheme. In particular, the system can be configured to generate new rules depending on their coverage (for instance, filtered by some minimum coverage), depending on the diversity of coverage, depending on the class and depending on the rules so far. For instance, more sophisticated operators are able to filter new rules having a high mutual information with respect to an existing rule. The system provides plug-ins to incorporate different representation languages, such as a module for evaluating mathematical terms, graphs or a whole Prolog engine.

3   Summary of Experimental Results and Conclusion

We performed three series of experiments: In a first batch on the mutagenesis data, we evaluated the sensitivity of the method on variations of the parameters and determined default settings. In particular, it turned out that the performance with p set to one is consistently worse than with $p > 1$. This is an indication that many different structural features contribute equally to the performance of the classifier. Another finding is that the performance does not degrade as more and more rules are added. In other words, overfitting does not seem to occur too easily. In a second batch of experiments on seven small molecule datasets, we showed that margin-based rule learning performs favorably compared to margin-based ILP approaches using kernels. In our third batch, variants of propositionalization and relational learning are tested on the task of bioavailability prediction. To investigate the "feature efficiency" of those variants, we plot the training set and test set accuracies against the number of rules added.

In summary, we propose relational rule learning based on margins. The new approach optimizes the mean margin minus its variance. Error bounds can be derived to obtain a theoretically sound stopping criterion. Overall, MMV optimization seems to be a useful new learning scheme that can be adapted to various data types via plug-ins, and can be adjusted to the noise level via parameters. As the optimization is linear in the number of instances, it should also scale up well for the analysis of larger datasets.

References

1. Friedman, J., Bogdan, E.: Popescu. Predictive learning via rule ensembles. Technical report, Stanford University (2005)
2. Rückert, U., Kramer, S.: A statistical approach to rule learning. In: Machine Learning. Proceedings of the 23rd International Conf., ACM Press, New York (2006)

Extension of the Top-Down Data-Driven Strategy to ILP

Erick Alphonse and Céline Rouveirol

LIPN-CNRS UMR 7030, Université Paris 13, France
{alphonse,rouveirol}@lipn.univ-paris13.fr

Abstract. Several upgrades of Attribute-Value learning to Inductive Logic Programming have been proposed and used successfully. However, the Top-Down Data-Driven strategy, popularised by the AQ family, has not yet been transferred to ILP: if the idea of reducing the hypothesis space by covering a seed example is utilised with systems like PRO-GOL, Aleph or MIO, these systems do not benefit from the associated data-driven specialisation operator. This operator is given an incorrect hypothesis h and a covered negative example e and outputs a set of hypotheses more specific than h and correct wrt e. This refinement operator is very valuable considering heuristic search problems ILP systems may encounter when crossing plateaus in relational search spaces. In this paper, we present the data-driven strategy of AQ, in terms of a lgg-based change of representation of negative examples given a positive *seed* example, and show how it can be extended to ILP. We evaluate a basic implementation of AQ in the system PROPAL on a number of benchmark ILP datasets.

1 Introduction

In Inductive Logic Programming (ILP), various learning strategies from Attribute-Value (AV) learning have been adapted: to name a few, top-down induction of decision trees in the TILDE system [4], top-down induction of rules in the systems FOIL [28], PROGOL [24], Aleph [35] and MIO [26]. Bottom-up data-driven algorithms, based on the *least-general-generalisation* (*lgg*) operator (also known as *most-specific generalisation*) have also been implemented (see [17] for the main results). However, the Top-down Data-Driven (TDD) strategy has very few incarnations and is not used in ILP. Its emblem is the family of AV systems AQ [22]. The search is top-down in the space of hypotheses more general than or equal to a particular example which is named in this context a *seed example*. If the idea of reducing the hypothesis space by covering a seed example is utilised with systems like PROGOL, Aleph or MIO, these systems do not benefit from the associated TDD operator. They address the learning problem within the generate-and-test paradigm (computing refinements based on the structure of the search space only) : they have to deal with many refinements, for a given hypothesis, that are not relevant with respect to the discrimination task. The TDD operator is the dual of the *lgg* operator in the sense that, given

S. Muggleton, R. Otero, and A. Tamaddoni-Nezhad (Eds.): ILP 2006, LNAI 4455, pp. 49–63, 2007.
© Springer-Verlag Berlin Heidelberg 2007

an incorrect hypothesis h and a covered negative example e, it outputs a set of hypotheses more specific than h and correct with respect to e. This refinement operator is described in [22] as a set of *extension-against* rules for computing refinements of boolean attributes, numerical attributes, nominal as well as hierarchical ones. For example, a rule for using a boolean attribute att for refining an incorrect hypothesis is:

If $att = val$ in the seed and $att \neq val$ in a covered negative example then $att = val$ is a valid refinement

Relying on the training set allows a TDD strategy to have a branching factor which is necessarily smaller than or equal to the branching factor of a generate-and-test strategy searching in the same hypothesis space. This makes this strategy very appealing for ILP which is known to be prone to important plateau phenomena in heuristic search (see e.g. [13,2]). As a special case and as advocated by Winston [39] (see also [34]), a TDD learning algorithm can take advantage of negative examples that differ from positive examples by only one attribute, the so-called *near-misses*, to reduce the branching factor to 1 during the heuristic search. Ultimately, a TDD algorithm learning from a dataset provided with all near-misses of the target concept would converge to the concept without search, generating only one refinement each step.

In the rest of the paper, we present the TDD strategy of the AQ system in terms of a *lgg*-based change of representation of negative examples given a positive *seed* example. After applying this representation change, the instance space and the hypothesis space are merged into a simpler hypothesis space, and learning can rely on an algebraic formalisation of AQ's extension against rules. The second contribution of the paper concerns the implementation of the TDD in relational languages as complex as Datalog with negation and constrained variables, which is complete for OI-subsumption [1]. We propose a formalisation of the problem of computing the set of "nearest-miss" *lggs* between two relational examples, which is at the core of the TDD strategy, as a Weighted Constraint Satisfaction Problem [8]. In the last part of the paper, we present an implementation of the basic AQ strategy as given by Clark and Niblett [5] (often referred as AQR) in PROPAL and we evaluate it on a number of ILP benchmark datasets. Although this version of PROPAL does not include any noise-handling mechanism, its performance is quite competitive with respect to state of the art ILP generate-and-test systems.

2 Change of Representation of Learning Data in the TDD Strategy

2.1 Top-Down Data Driven Strategy

The AQ system [22] is a top-down covering learning algorithm. AQ's outer loop is a classical covering algorithm that iterates while some positive examples are still uncovered. Its inner-loop randomly selects an uncovered positive example, the *seed example*, denoted as s in the rest of the paper. AQ then performs a top-down data driven beam search to build a set of maximal and correct generalisations of s, given the set of negative examples. For a given negative example e^-, if a candidate hypothesis h in the beam covers e^-, h is minimally specialised in order to reject it, while still covering s. Throughout the paper, E^+ and E^- denote the set of positive and negative examples of the learning problem, $\mathcal{L}_h$ denotes the hypothesis space, $\succeq$ the coverage relation between a hypothesis of $\mathcal{L}_h$ and an example, $\geq_h$ the partial order between hypotheses of $\mathcal{L}_h$ (generality relationship). $\mathcal{L}_s \subseteq \mathcal{L}_h$ is the space of generalisations of the seed s. The TDD operator can be formally defined as follows.

Definition 1 (TDD operator). *Let* $s \in E^+, h \in \mathcal{L}_s, e^- \in E^-, \rho_s(h, e^-) = \{h' \in \mathcal{L}_s \mid h \geq_h h' \text{ and } h' \not\succeq e^-\}$

This operator can be seen as the dual of the *lgg* operator [27]: given an incorrect hypothesis h and a covered negative example e^-, it outputs a set of maximally general hypotheses more specific than h and correct with respect to e^-, with the additional constraint that each of these specialisations of h should still cover s.

The fact that each minimal specialisation of h should cover a seed example amounts to map the initial search space of the learning algorithm onto the space of generalisations of the seed example. Looking for a hypothesis of $\mathcal{L}_h$ that both covers s and rejects e^- can be equivalently performed by looking for a generalisation of s that rejects $lgg(s, e^-)$. By definition of the *lgg* [27], we have $h \succeq s \wedge h \succeq e^- \Leftrightarrow h \geq_h lgg(s, e^-)$. Equivalently, by contraposition, we have $h \not\succeq s \vee h \not\succeq e^- \Leftrightarrow h \not\geq_h lgg(s, e^-)$. As the TDD strategy is biased towards generating hypotheses that cover s, $h \not\succeq e^- \Leftrightarrow h \not\geq_h lgg(s, e^-)$.

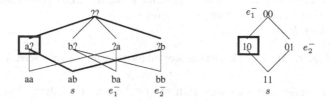

Fig. 1. Bias of $\mathcal{L}_h$ towards the covering of a positive example

This *lgg*-based representation change transforms the initial learning problem $(E, \succeq, \geq_h, \mathcal{L}_h)$ into a new learning problem $(E_s, \geq_h, \geq_h, \mathcal{L}_s)$, E_s being the new set of examples where each example $e \in E$ is reformulated into $lgg(s, e)$. In this new problem, the instance space and the hypothesis space are merged, as illustrated in figure 1 for a simple AV learning problem. The leftmost part of figure 1 shows three training instances, described in terms of two AV attributes. In the initial search space, each of the involved attributes has domain $\{a, b, ?\}$, where '?' denotes any value in the domain, meaning this attribute should be dropped from the hypothesis. The three initial examples s, e_1^- and e_2^- are each mapped in the new search space $\mathcal{L}_s$ (right part of figure 1), here the power-set of the seed example. By definition, s is mapped to the lower bound of $\mathcal{L}_s$, e_1^- is mapped to the top node of $\mathcal{L}_s$ $'00'$ ($lgg(s, e_1^-) = '??' \geq_h 'ab'$) and e_2^- is mapped to $'01'$ ($lgg(s, e_2^-) = '?b' \geq_h 'ab'$).

This reformulation is interesting, because it shows that the so-called "extension-against" rules correspond to an algebraic resolution of the learning problem in a boolean lattice[1] and have broader applications than attribute-value learning as long as the generalisation space of the seed is isomorphic to a boolean lattice as shown in figure 1. In the rest of the paper, we will refer to the TDD refinement operator instead of the "extension-against" rules to point that we take into account the *lggs* of the negative examples directly in the generalisation space of the seed. It is therefore possible to reformulate the specialisation step of AQ as shown in the algorithm of figure 2.

FindBestRule(s, E^-, E^+)
   $G := \{\top\}$ *% top element of $\mathcal{L}_h$*
   $BestRule := \emptyset$
   While $G \neq \emptyset$
     $G' := \emptyset$
    For each $g \in G$
     $G := G \setminus g$
     If g is correct and $score(g, E^+) \geq score(BestRule, E^+)$ **Then**
      $BestRule := g$
     Else
      % computation of the nearest-miss
      $NM := g$ *% by definition $g \geq_h NM$*
      For each $e^- \in E^-$
       If $lgg(s, e^-)$ nearer-miss than NM **Then** $NM := lgg(s, e^-)$
      $G' := G' \cup \rho_s(g, NM)$ *% specialisation using the TDD refinement operator*
    $G := k$ best hypotheses from G' *% beam search*
   Return *BestRule*

Fig. 2. AQ's specialisation loop algorithm for a given seed s

In order to make the specialisation step efficient, the algorithm makes the most of the partial ordering of negative examples to handle most informative negative examples only. First of all, only most specific negative examples in E_s are useful: in the toy example of figure 1, e_2^- is more specific than e_1^- so rejecting e_2^- also rejects e_1^-. In this simple example, there is only one candidate solution obtained by applying once the TDD operator: hypothesis $'10'$ in the boolean space, corresponding to the hypothesis $'a?'$ in the initial search space. If several most specific negative examples are available at that step, which are incomparable by definition, we give preference to the one that is closer to s than

---

[1] The "extension-against" rules are actually more general and can consider distributive lattices as the product of a boolean lattice with interval lattices and chains whenever numerical and hierarchical attributes are involved [1]. In the present work, we use the product of boolean and interval lattices but in this section, we only discuss the logical part.

any other negative examples as it yields the smallest branching factor for ρ_s (see e.g. [34,5]). We name it the *nearest-miss* and we define it as a most specific element with respect to a total pre-order named *nearer-miss*. It is reflexive, transitive, total, but not antisymmetric.

Definition 2 (nearer-miss). *Let $s \in \mathcal{L}_h$ be the seed example, $x, y \in \mathcal{L}_s$, the distance $d(s, y)$ be the number of attributes' values that differ between s and y. x is nearer-miss than y iff $(x \leq_h y) \vee (y \nleq_h x \wedge d(s, x) \leq d(s, y))$. It is a total pre-order on the elements of $\mathcal{L}_s$. A least element (most specific) with respect to this total pre-order is a nearest-miss.*

The nearer-miss pre-order induces an equivalence relation between elements of $\mathcal{L}_s$ which are incomparable under $\geq_h$ and at the same distance from the seed. Note that we define the nearer-miss relation as a linear extension of the partial order $\geq_h$ to deal with redundancy in E_s, such that the nearest-miss is necessarily a most specific element of E_s wrt $\geq_h$. This is necessary when we deal with numerical attributes. For example, if we have only one numerical attribute a and a seed $a = 1$ and two negative examples $a = 2$ and $a = 3$ reformulated as $a \in [1, 2]$ and $a \in [1, 3]$, although both negative examples are at a distance of 1 from the seed, $a \in [1, 2]$ is nearer-miss than $a \in [1, 3]$ as it is more specific and its rejection will reject the other negative example.

On figure 1, it can be seen that the maximal branching factor of a top-down generate-and-test operator is 4 without the seed bias, and 2 when only considering specialisations covering s. The branching factor of the TDD operator is 1, as the *lgg* of e_2^- with s is actually a Winston's near-miss. Note that even in the worst case (only far-misses are provided, i.e. negative examples that maximally differ from the seed example), the branching factor of the TDD operator cannot exceed the one of the top-down generate-and-test operator biased to cover a seed example. We now will go on to discuss the extension of the TDD strategy to ILP.

3   Extension of the TDD Strategy to ILP

The TDD strategy, which is biased towards covering a seed example, relies on the reformulation of each negative example e^- as its *lgg* with the seed. The strength of the strategy is that the instance space is merged into the hypothesis space which forms a simple boolean lattice (or a product of a boolean lattice and interval lattices in the case of numerical learning). In this lattice, the TDD refinement operator can efficiently discriminate the negative examples as explained in the previous section. Our approach to upgrade this TDD strategy to ILP consists in working in a seed generalisation space with the same algebraic structure and then computing *lggs* between the negative examples and the seed in such a space. Such algebraic structures can be obtained in relational languages, although with the cost of increased complexity, and sometimes incompleteness.

In this work, we target languages as expressive as non-recursive Datalog clauses with negation [21]. In order to deal with numerical data, we add constraint variables to the language (see e.g. [32]) and classically set their generalisation language to the lattice of convex intervals for numerical variables [22].

A substantial number of works have been done on computing *lggs* in restrictions of first-order logic under several partial orders [27,14,17,12]. One particularly interesting partial order is the *Object Identity* (OI) subsumption. It is stronger than the well-known θ-subsumption, because matching substitutions are limited to be injective, that is, each variable has to be bound to a different object. It has been shown in [38,10] that a Datalog space lower-bounded by a null element (the seed here) under OI-subsumption is isomorphic to a boolean lattice: the set of generalisations of a clause is its power set (up to a variable renaming) and the complete generalisation operator is the dropping-literal rule. An important corollary is that the TDD strategy is complete under OI-subsumption. However, as noted for example in [14,18], the generalisation of two examples is not unique, as opposed to AV learning, and computing their least general generalisation will yield several *lggs*, as shown in figure 3.

$$
\begin{aligned}
s: \quad west(T) &\leftarrow car(T, V_1), rectangular(V_1),\\
&\quad car(T, V_2), \#wheels(V_2, 2),\\
&\quad car(T, V_3), \neg roof(V_3), short(V_3), circular(V_3).\\
e^-: \quad west(T') &\leftarrow car(T', V_1'), \neg roof(V_1'), rectangular(V_1'),\\
&\quad car(T', V_2'), \neg roof(V_2'), \#wheels(V_2', 3), circular(V_2'),\\
&\quad car(T', V_3'), triangular(V_3'), short(V_3').
\end{aligned}
$$

Fig. 3. A train-like problem with a positive example s and a negative example e^-

This figure describes a toy relational learning problem inspired by the Michalski's trains. The semantic is classical: s is a train having three cars, one is rectangular, the other has two wheels and the last one does not have a roof, is short and circular. Using s as a seed example, it is equivalent to consider the new learning problem where all *lggs* between the seed and the negative examples have to be rejected in the generalisation space of s. This new problem is given in figure 4 as well as its propositional encoding, given the OI-subsumption order.

In fact, any partial order can be used within the TDD strategy, like θ-subsumption, as soon as the generalisation space of the seed example is limited to a boolean lattice for the logical part (the logical part of a clause excludes literals with numerical variables). This is at the expense of completeness, as it is known that the space of generalisation under θ-subsumption is infinite even in Datalog [27] and that no ideal refinement exists for this partial order [37]. Various restrictions in generate-and-test approaches have been proposed to define operational restrictions of θ-subsumption, the most usual one consisting in restricting the generalisation space of the clause to its power-set (see e.g. [24,35]), which exactly corresponds to the applicability condition of the TDD strategy. Let us now provide an example that illustrates this *lgg-based* representation change as well as a sketch of the algorithm to compute these *lggs*.

$$e_1^- : west(T) \leftarrow car(T, V_1),$$
$$car(T, V_2), \#wheels(V_2, [2, 3]),$$
$$car(T, V_3), \neg roof(V_3).$$
$$e_2^- : west(T) \leftarrow car(T, V_1), rectangular(V_1),$$
$$car(T, V_2),$$
$$car(T, V_3), \neg roof(V_3), circular(V_3).$$
$$e_3^- : west(T) \leftarrow car(T, V_1), rectangular(V_1),$$
$$car(T, V_2), \#wheels(V_2, [2, 3])$$
$$car(T, V_3), short(V_3).$$

s	$car(T,V_1)$	$rec(V_1)$	$car(T,V_2)$	$\#w(V_2,N)$	N	$car(T,V_3)$	$\neg roof(V_3)$	$short(V_3)$	$cir(V_3)$
e_1^-	1	0	1	1	[2,3]	1	1	0	0
e_2^-	1	1	1	0	-	1	1	0	1
e_3^-	1	1	1	1	[2,3]	1	0	1	0

Fig. 4. A train-like problem and its reformulation with s as seed example, with OI-subsumption as partial ordering on the relational search space

3.1 Example

In order to exemplify the approach, let us solve the learning problem presented in figure 3. This problem is reformulated by replacing e^- by the three clauses resulting from the computation of $lgg(s, e^-)$ as shown in figure 4. For instance, e_2^- in figure 4 represents the lgg obtained with the matching substitution $\{V_1/V_1', V_2/V_3', V_3/V_2'\}$ between s and e^- of figure 3. The learning algorithm is that of figure 2. In this example, we instantiate the beam size k to 2. The candidate literals to refine the top clause produced by the rejection of the first negative example e_1^- are:

$$\{rectangular(V1); N \in (-\infty, 3); short(V_3); circular(V_3)\}$$

Those produced by the second negative example e_2^- are:

$$\{\#wheels(V_2, N); short(V_3)\}$$

Note that the examples e_1^-, e_2^- and e_3^- are incomparable with respect to $\geq_h$, but according to algorithm of figure 2, we chose to reject e_2^- first, as e_2^- is nearer-miss than both e_1^- and e_3^-. Specialising G against e_2^- produces only two refinements, which corresponds to the size of the beam. Selecting nearest-miss examples has the advantage that the algorithm relies as little as possible on the evaluation function to select the best refinements of the current hypothesis. G specialises into two hypotheses with the addition of the literal $\#wheels(V_2, N)$ and the literal $short(V_3)$. The most general specialisation of G is produced by adding all the literals necessary to get linked hypotheses.[2] The following new bound is obtained:

---

[2] The discriminant literal selected by the TDD strategy do not necessarily produce a connected clause. We assume in this example and in this work that adding the literals to produce linked clauses, such as $car(T, V_2)$ and $car(T, V_3)$, is simple.

$$G = \{ \ west(T) \leftarrow car(T, V_2), \#wheels(V_2, N);$$
$$west(T) \leftarrow car(T, V_3), short(V_3)\}$$

We now take each hypothesis in G and check for their correctness. None of them are correct and both cover the nearest-miss e_3^-. After another specialisation step, we obtain the new G bound:

$$G = \{ \ \mathbf{west(T)} \leftarrow \mathbf{car(T, V_2)}, \#\mathbf{wheels(V_2, N)}, \mathbf{N} \in (-\infty, \mathbf{3});$$
$$west(T) \leftarrow car(T, V_2), \#wheels(V_2, N), car(T, V_3), circ(V_3);$$
$$\mathbf{west(T)} \leftarrow \mathbf{car(T, V_2)}, \#\mathbf{wheels(V_2, N)}, \mathbf{car(T, V_3)}, \neg\mathbf{roof(V_3)};$$
$$west(T) \leftarrow car(T, V_3), short(V_3),$$
$$car(T, V_2), \#wheels(V_2, N), N \in (-\infty, 3);$$
$$west(T) \leftarrow car(T, V_3), short(V_3), circular(V_3);$$
$$west(T) \leftarrow car(T, V_3), short(V_3), \neg roof(V_3)\}$$

Let us now assume that the evaluation function selects the two hypotheses in boldface in the previous list: the first hypothesis is correct and is a candidate solution. The second one is incorrect (it covers e_1^-) and will in turn be specialised. Finally, after specialising and pruning G, we obtain at the end of this refinement step:

$$G = \{ \ west(T) \leftarrow car(T, V_2), \#wheels(V_2, N), N \in (-\infty, 3);$$
$$west(T) \leftarrow car(T, V1), rectangular(V1), car(T, V_2), \#wheels(V_2, N),$$
$$car(T, V_3), \neg roof(V_3)\}$$

After three refinement steps, we have a subset of all correct hypotheses with respect to the initial relational example e^-. We can notice that the second hypothesis has six literals which would have required six refinement steps with a generate-and-test approach *a la* FOIL or PROGOL.

3.2   Computation of a Nearest-Miss of the Seed from a Negative Example

At the core of algorithm of figure 2 is the computation of nearest-miss examples among *lggs* between the seed and the negative examples. In this section, we show that their computation is equivalent to the resolution of Weighted Constraint Satisfaction Problems. After recalling the main results on computation of *lggs* under OI, we extend them to handle constraint variables and give an example of encoding for the learning example given above.

A complete algorithm to compute all *lggs* under OI-subsumption has been proposed by [18,12]. This algorithm is based on the observation that these *lggs* are maximally incomparable substructures embedded into Plotkin's *lgg*. Both works propose a graph encoding of the problem such that computing *lggs* under OI-subsumption amounts to extract all incomparable maximal cliques in the graph. We build upon their result but provide some simplifications and an extension of the algorithm to handle constraint variables. First, let us note that not all *lggs* are needed to solve the problem as shown in the algorithm of figure 2:

i) only those more specific than the hypotheses in the current G bound are necessary; ii) only the nearest-miss lgg is used for the current specialisation step (see section 2). The problem is then to compute the maximum-clique, that is the largest maximal one, in the corresponding graph. Second, it can be seen that their graph formulation is the consistency graph of a Constraint Satisfaction Problem (CSP). This equivalence between the CSP and the clique problem on the CSP consistency graph is well-known [15,30]. The CSP formulation is more natural as it is equivalent to the one used for computing the covering test in ILP [9]. Therefore, finding the nearest-miss lgg between a seed and a negative example corresponds to finding the largest subset of variables in s which admits a consistent variable assignment.

This formulation needs to be adapted for handling constraint variables. To take that information into account, we need to add a valuation structure to the CSP which is known in the literature as a Weighted CSP. Weighted CSP (WCSP) extends the CSP framework by associating costs to tuples. These costs give preferences among partial assignments. The usual task is to find a complete consistent assignment with minimum cost, which is NP-hard. Informally, to compute a nearest-miss, we define a cost as the number of literals and constraint variables' values of the seed example that are not matched onto the negative example. Concerning the numerical literal $\#wheels(V_2, 2)$ in the seed, there are three options: either there is an exactly matching literal in the negative example, the associated cost is then 0. If there is a literal of the form $\#wheels(V_2, N)$ with $N \neq 2$ in the negative example, the cost is 1^3. Finally, it may also be the case that the literal is unmatched, in that case the cost is 2.

Due to lack of space, we refer to [8,7] for a detailed description of WCSPs and the associated algorithms. Here, we briefly give the definition of a Weighted CSP and illustrate the encoding of the problem of nearest-miss computation of figure 3.

Definition 3 (Weighted CSP). *A binary WCSP is a tuple (k, X, D, C). X and D are the variables and domains as in classical CSP. C is a set of cost functions. A binary constraint C_{ij} assigns costs to assignments of variables i and j, ranging from 0 to k. A unary constraint C_i assigns costs to assignments of variable i, ranging from 0 to k. The cost of a tuple t, noted $cost(t)$, is the sum of all its associated costs. When a constraint C assigns a cost greater than or equal to k to a tuple t ($cost(t) \geq k$), it means that C forbids t, otherwise t is allowed by C, with the corresponding cost. A tuple is consistent if $cost(t) < k$.*

For computing the nearest-miss of the seed example s from the example e^- (see figure 3), we have the corresponding WCSP, omitting the head literal for convenience:

---

[3] This way of handling cost does not take into account partial ordering between numerical values in the negative examples and this has to be handled through postprocessing.

Variables	Domains
$car(T, V_1)$	$1 : nm$ **$0 : \mathbf{car(T', V_1')}$** $0 : car(T', V_2')$ $0 : car(T', V_3')$
$rectangular(V_1)$	$1 : nm$ $\qquad\qquad\qquad$ **$0 : \mathbf{rectangular(V_1')}$**
$car(T, V_2)$	$1 : nm$ $0 : car(T', V_1')$ $0 : car(T', V_2')$ **$0 : \mathbf{car(T', V_3')}$**
$\#wheels(V_2, 2)$	**$2 : \mathbf{nm}$** $\qquad\qquad$ $1 : \#wheels(V_2', 3)$
$car(T, V_3)$	$1 : nm$ $0 : car(T', V_1')$ **$0 : \mathbf{car(T', V_2')}$** $0 : car(T', V_3')$
$\neg roof(V_3)$	$1 : nm$ $\quad$ $0 : \neg roof(V_1')$ $\quad$ **$0 : \mathbf{\neg roof(V_2')}$**
$short(V_3)$	**$1 : \mathbf{nm}$** $\qquad\qquad$ $0 : short(V_3')$
$circular(V_3)$	$1 : nm$ $\qquad\qquad$ **$0 : \mathbf{circular(V_2')}$**

Literals of the seed s (i.e., the variables of the WCSP) are shown in the first column of the table. For each literal of s, we describe candidate matching literals in e^-, i.e., the domains of the WCSP variables. Matching a literal corresponds to satisfying a unary constraint. To each literal of e^-, we associate the corresponding unary cost of matching it. In order to account for unmatched seed literals, we use an additional value nm for *not matched*, which indicates that the seed literal is not matched and does not belong to the *lgg*. For instance, if the literal $short(V_3)$ is unmatched, this will have a cost of 1. The binary costs (not shown here) are the same as for a CSP encoding of the subsumption test: they define that a pair of matchings is compatible to ensure that the solution tuple is a *lgg* of the seed and the negative example. To each matched literal of the seed, we associate a substitution θ_i. A pair (θ_i, θ_j) is compatible iff the substitution $\theta_i.\theta_j$ is a valid substitution under the partial order considered. The corresponding cost is zero or k otherwise. The solution of the WCSP which leads to construct e_2^- is outlined in boldface in the table, this solution has cost 3. e_2^- is among the solutions of lowest cost and is used to compute $(west(T) \leftarrow car(T, V_2), \#wheels(V_2, N))$. The computation of the next nearest-miss more specific than this hypothesis is computed by removing the nm values from the domain of the two literals $car(T, V_2)$ and $\#wheels(V_2, N)$, thus forcing them to be part of the nearest-miss.

4 Related Works

A first version of the PROPAL algorithm has been presented in [3], where the link between the TDD strategy and PROPAL was not made and no formalisation was proposed. Moreover, the algorithm could not deal with numerical data. It was also presented as a propositionalisation system and we plan to further investigate in the future the link between propositionalisation and computation of *lggs* between examples and a seed.

A first comparison has to be made with the learning systems PROGOL, Aleph and MIO. As we said, they use the same search space as PROPAL, by the mean of a seed example, but are rooted in the generate-and-test paradigm and do not use the TDD strategy. They have to deal with many refinements during the search that are not relevant with respect to the discrimination task.

A related approach to our system is the system STILL [33]. STILL is a propositionalisation system [19] which upgrades the attribute-value learning algorithm

DiVS [31]. DiVS makes use of the extension-against rules of Michalski in the following manner. For each example e (positive and negative) DiVS builds $G(e)$, the bound G covering e and rejecting all the negative examples with respect to its class by applying the extension-against rules. Each $G(e)$ votes to classify unseen examples. The upgrade of DiVS to ILP is done through the use of the propositionalisation technique in an indeterminate language prior to learning [40,32]: all matchings between a seed example and the examples to reformulate are computed and rewritten as attribute-value vectors. To avoid the exponential space requirement of propositionalisation in an indeterminate hypothesis space, the authors perform a sampling of k vectors in the matching space (k a user-supplied parameter). As the propositionalisation technique of STILL randomly selects matchings and is applied before learning, STILL does not benefit from the TDD strategy that focuses on *lggs* between the seed examples and the informative negative examples. As a consequence, STILL mostly extracts irrelevant vectors for the discrimination task as only the ones corresponding to *nearest-miss lggs* are relevant in the case of the TDD strategy (section 2). Therefore STILL, being a randomised polynomial-time algorithm, cannot ensure to output a correct theory with respect to the learning data. However, STILL has been shown to be successful on the "mutagenesis" dataset (B_2 and B_3 only, see section 5) with some parameters inherited from DiVS.

5 Experiments

The TDD strategy implemented in PROPAL to run the experiments detailed below is the same as AQ's presented figure 2. PROPAL conducts a beam search in the hypothesis space, guided by the Laplace function[4]. The default beam size is fixed to 5. We extended this basic algorithm to handle missing values in constraint variables (or attributes) with the same technique as AQ's [23] and Ripper's [6]: all tests involving the constraint variable V are defined to fail on examples for which the value of V is missing.

To solve the WCSPs, PROPAL's implementation of nearest-miss extraction relies on the state-of-the-art complete algorithm Toolbar[5] [8]. We have used in the experiments the default parameters of Toolbar. However, we set the timer of Toolbar to 60 seconds to keep computation of a nearest-miss within a reasonable amount of time. This is usually needed for the one or two last seeds of problems like "mutagenesis", that can be quite large compared to the other positive examples. When the time limit is reached, Toolbar returns the best solution (i.e., the most specific negative example) found so far. As shown in [3], this approximation degrades the heuristic search by increasing the branching factor but still ensures the correctness of the output theory.

We validate our implementation of the TDD strategy in ILP by comparing PROPAL's performances with the ILP systems FOIL, PROGOL, STILL and

---

[4] The Laplace function is defined as $\frac{p+1}{p+n+2}$, with p and n the number of positive and negative examples covered by the hypothesis.

[5] http://carlit.toulouse.inra.fr/cgi-bin/awki.cgi/ToolBarIntro

TILDE on the "mutagenesis" datasets [36]. The "mutagenesis" dataset used is *regression-friendly* with the 4 versions of background knowledge (from B_1 to B_4). We made additional comparisons with the two propositionalisation systems RSD and RELAGGS, on the "KRK illegal chess position" [25] datasets and two learning problems extracted from the PKDD99 financial challenge by [20]. The two last problems involve learning to classify bank loans into profitable and non-profitable loans. For the last three problems, we performed a 10-fold cross-validation averaged over 10 runs as in [20]. For the "mutagenesis" dataset, we followed the protocol described in [36].

On the "mutagenesis" datasets, the results for FOIL and PROGOL have been taken from [36], for TILDE from [4] and for STILL from [33]. On the "KRK illegal position" and the two tasks from PKDD99, the results are taken from [20]. When several values of parameters were tried for these systems, we chose their best results. As noted in [29], this can produce an optimistic bias in favour of the other algorithms compared to PROPAL, which is run on all datasets with a standard size of beam of 5. This is the only parameter of PROPAL for now as we recall that no noise-coping strategy has been implemented.

Table 1. Accuracy in % of learnt theories by PROGOL, FOIL, TILDE, STILL, RSD, RELAGGS and PROPAL on the "mutagenesis", "KRK" and "loans" datasets, and time for PROPAL to output the theories

	$B1$	$B2$	$B3$	$B4$	KRK.illegal	Loan (AvB)	Loan (ACvBD)
PROGOL	76	81	83	88	n.a.	45.7	n.a.
FOIL	-	75.8	83	86	97.2	-	87.3
TILDE	75	79	85	86	75.1	-	n.a.
STILL	-	86.5	88.8	-	-	-	-
RELAGGS	-	-	-	-	72.3	88	94.1
RSD	-	-	-	-	76.2	n.a.	n.a.
PROPAL	85.5	86.7	88.2	85.1	100	84,4	85,19
Time (s.)	3692	60698	40949	8274	179	117	564

Table 1 summarises the results. The symbol "-" indicates that the result is not available or that the experiments have been done with a different protocol. The symbol "n.a." indicates that the learner exhausted the time limit of 2 days of computation on at least one of the fold as reported in [20].

We can see from table 1 that PROPAL's performance is competitive with the state-of-the-art generate-and-test approaches which use sophisticated heuristic search and pruning techniques. On B_1, which is the hardest domain for learning in the "mutagenesis" domain, PROPAL performed as well as the other systems with B_3, which uses expert attributes; the performance on B_1, B_2 and B_3 are among the best reported. We see a lower performance on the richest domain B_4, where descriptions of higher-level structures that appear in a molecule are added. This over-fitting may be explained by the large increase in the size of the hypothesis space, as PROPAL does not restrict the search space beyond the choice of a seed example, and the fact that no noise-coping strategies are implemented.

The "KRK" dataset is a good example where the TDD strategy pays off: the dataset provides a lot of near-misses (the branching factor being often reduced to 1) and it can be considered noise-free. The result largely improves those of the propositionalisation systems and of TILDE.

Another example of a good performance of PROPAL is on the "Loan" datasets, which is advocated in [20] as representative of large datasets where current ILP systems do not perform well: on "loanAvB", PROGOL has an accuracy below 50% and RSD cannot solve at least one fold after two days of computation; on "loanACvDB", they run out of time, as well as TILDE and only FOIL performs well on it. RELAGGS [20] performs best with 88% and 94.1% respectively. PROPAL is able to solve the two problems quickly with rather good performance comparatively.

6 Conclusion

We have studied in this paper the TDD strategy, popularised by the AQ family, in the context of ILP. We made a link between AQ, Winston's work on near-misses and a change of representation of the negative examples through *lggs* computed with a seed example. This *lgg*-based reformulation merges the instance space and the search space into a simpler learning space, where the learning problem can be solved algebraically. This formalisation allowed us to propose a simple extension of the TDD strategy to ILP in languages as expressive as non-recursive Datalog clauses with negation. The TDD strategy offers a theoretical advantage over generate-and-test systems such as PROGOL, Aleph and MIO, by making it possible to prune irrelevant branches of the refinement graph by using most relevant negative examples. The extraction of nearest-miss examples through a *lgg*-based reformulation has been formalised as a Weighted CSP, allowing a flexible implementation of the AQR strategy within PROPAL using a state-of-the-art WCSP solver, Toolbar. This implementation, which does not include any noise-handling mechanism, has been shown to be competitive with generate-and-test FOL learners and propositionalisation systems. However, it is known that data-driven strategies are more prone to noise issues than their generate-and-test counterparts. We plan to further validate the approach by studying the impact of noise. In particular, we plan to investigate the works in this domain proposed for the AQ system [16] and for rule learning [11]. Secondly, now that the mechanism for extracting nearest-miss examples has been implemented within Toolbar, we plan study the impact of various propagation mechanisms and various approximation strategies on PROPAL's running time and performance.

Acknowledgements

We are very grateful to H. Soldano for the numerous discussions on the Top-Down Data-Driven strategy and its relevance to ILP, and to A. Osmani for sharing with us his many insights concerning WCSP. We also would like to thank Mark-André Krogel for providing the "loan" datasets and for helping us with the experiments. Finally, we thank Christophe Caron of the MIG-INRA group and the LRI-UMR8623, for providing us access to their computational resources.

References

1. Alphonse, E.: Macro-opérateurs et Sélection Relationnelle en Programmation Logique Inductive: théorie et algorithmes. PhD thesis, Université Paris-Sud (2003)
2. Alphonse, E., Osmani, A.: On the connection between the phase transition of the covering test and the learning success rate. In: Proc. 16th Conf. of Inductive Logic Programming (2006)
3. Alphonse, E., Rouveirol, C.: Lazy propositionalization for relational learning. In: Proc. ECAI'2000, pp. 256–260. IOS Press, Amsterdam (2000)
4. Blockeel, H., De Raedt, L.: Top-down induction of first order decision trees. Artificial Intelligence 101, 285–297 (1998)
5. Clark, P., Niblett, T.: The CN2 induction algorithm. Machine Learning 3, 261–283 (1989)
6. Cohen, W.W.: Fast effective rule induction. In: Proc. 12th ICML, pp. 115–123. Morgan Kaufmann, San Francisco (1995)
7. de Givry, S., Larrosa, J., Meseguer, P., Schiex, T.: Solving Max-SAT as weighted CSP. In: Rossi, F. (ed.) CP 2003. LNCS, vol. 2833, pp. 363–376. Springer, Heidelberg (2003)
8. de Givry, S., Zytnicki, M., Heras, F., Larrosa, J.: Existential arc consistency: Getting closer to full arc consistency in weighted CSP. In: Proc. of IJCAI-05 (2005)
9. Eisinger, N.: Subsumption and connection graphs. In: Proc. of IJCAI'81, pp. 480–486. William Kaufmann (1981)
10. Esposito, F., Laterza, A., Malerba, D., Semeraro, G.: Refinement of Datalog programs. In: Proc. of the MLnet Familiarization Workshop on ILP for KDD, pp. 73–94 (1996)
11. Fürnkranz, J.: Pruning methods for rule learning algorithms. In: Proc. 4th Int. Workshop on ILP, pp. 321–336 (1994)
12. Geibel, P., Wysotzki, F.: A Logical Framework for Graph Theoretical Decision Tree Learning. In: Proc. ILP'97 (1997)
13. Giordana, A., Saitta, L., Sebag, M., Botta, M.: Analyzing relational learning in the phase transition framework. In: Proc. ICML, pp. 311–318 (2000)
14. Haussler, D.: Learning conjunctive concepts in structural domains. Machine Learning 4(1), 7–40 (1989)
15. Jagota, A.: Constraint satisfaction and maximum clique. In: Working Notes, AAAI Spring Symposium on AI and NP-hard Problems, pp. 92–97 (1993)
16. Kaufman, K.A., Michalski, R.S.: Learning from inconsistent and noisy data: The AQ18 approach. In: Proc. of the Eleventh ISMIS, pp. 411–419 (1999)
17. Kietz, J.-U.: A comparative study of structural most specific generalisations used in machine learning. In: Proc. Third Workshop on ILP, pp. 149–164 (1993)
18. Kietz, J.-U.: Some computational lower bounds for the computational complexity of inductive logic programmming. In: Proc. 6th ECML, Vienna, Austria (1993)
19. Kramer, S., Lavrac, N., Flach, P.: Propositionalization approaches to relational data mining. In: Dzeroski, S., Lavrac, N. (eds.) Relational Data Mining, pp. 262–291. Springer, Heidelberg (2001)

20. Krogel, M.: On Propositionalization for Knowledge Discovery in Relational Databases. PhD thesis, Univ. Magdeburg (2005)
21. Lloyd, J.W.: Foundations of Logic Programming, 2nd edn. Springer, Berlin (1987)
22. Michalski, R.S.: A theory and methodology of inductive learning. Machine Learning: An Artificial Intelligence Approach I, 83–134 (1983)
23. Michalski, R.S., Wojtusiak, J.: Reasoning with meta-values in AQ learning. Technical report, George Mason University (2006)
24. Muggleton, S.: Inverse entailment and PROGOL. New Generation Computing 13, 245–286 (1995)
25. Muggleton, S.H., Bain, M., Hayes-Michie, J., Michie, D.: An experimental comparison of human and machine learning formalisms. In: Proc. 6th IWML, San Mateo, CA, pp. 113–118. Morgan Kaufmann, San Francisco (1989)
26. Castillo, L.P., Wrobel, S.: On the stability of example-driven learning systems: A case study in multirelational learning. In: Coello Coello, C.A., de Albornoz, Á., Sucar, L.E., Battistutti, O.C. (eds.) MICAI 2002. LNCS (LNAI), vol. 2313, pp. 321–330. Springer, Heidelberg (2002)
27. Plotkin, G.: A note on inductive generalization. In: Machine Intelligence, vol. 5, Edinburgh University Press, Edinburgh (1970)
28. Quinlan, J.R.: Learning logical definitions from relations. Machine Learning 5(3), 239–266 (1990)
29. Scheffer, T., Herbrich, R.: Unbiased assessment of learning algorithms. In: Proc. Int. Joint Conf. on Artificial Intelligence (IJCAI'97), pp. 798–803 (1997)
30. Scheffer, T., Herbrich, R., Wysotzki, F.: Efficient θ-subsumption based on graph algorithms. In: Inductive Logic Programming. LNCS, vol. 1314, pp. 312–329. Springer, Heidelberg (1997)
31. Sebag, M.: Delaying the choice of bias: a disjunctive version space approach. In: Proc. 13th ICML, pp. 444–452 (1996)
32. Sebag, M., Rouveirol, C.: Constraint inductive logic programming. In: Advances In Inductive Logic Programming, pp. 277–294. IOS Press, Amsterdam (1996)
33. Sebag, M., Rouveirol, C.: Resource-bounded relational reasoning: Induction and deduction through stochastic matching. Machine Learning 38(1/2), 41–62 (2000)
34. Smith, B.D., Rosenbloom, P.S.: Incremental non-backtracking focusing: A polynomially bounded generalization algorithm for version spaces. In: Proc. 8th AAAI, pp. 848–853 (1990)
35. Srinivasan, A.: A learning engine for proposing hypotheses (Aleph) (1999)
36. Srinivasan, A., Muggleton, S., King, R.D.: Comparing the use of background knowledge by inductive logic programming systems. In: De Raedt, L. (ed.) Proc. of the 5th ILP Workshop, pp. 199–230. Scientific Report, K.U.Leuven (1995)
37. van der Laag, P.R.J., Nienhuys-Cheng, S-H.: Existence and nonexistence of complete refinement operators. In: Bergadano, F., De Raedt, L. (eds.) Machine Learning: ECML-94. LNCS, vol. 784, pp. 307–322. Springer, Heidelberg (1994)
38. VanLehn, K.: Efficient specialization of relational concepts. Machine Learning 4, 99–106 (1989)
39. Winston, P.H.: Learning structural descriptions form examples. In: Winston, P.H. (ed.) The Psychology of Computer Vision, pp. 157–209. McGraw-Hill, New York (1975)
40. Zucker, J.-D., Ganascia, J.-G.: Selective reformulation of examples in concept learning. In: Proc. 11th ICML, pp. 352–360 (1994)

Extracting Requirements from Scenarios with ILP

Dalal Alrajeh[1], Oliver Ray[1,2], Alessandra Russo[1], and Sebastian Uchitel[1,3]

[1] Imperial College London
{da04,or,ar3,su2}@doc.ic.ac.uk
[2] University of Cyprus
oliver@cs.ucy.ac.cy
[3] University of Buenos Aires/CONICET
s.uchitel@dc.uba.ar

Abstract. Requirements Engineering involves the *elicitation* of high-level stakeholder goals and their *refinement* into operational system requirements. A key difficulty is that stakeholders typically convey their goals indirectly through intuitive narrative-style scenarios of desirable and undesirable system behaviour, whereas goal refinement methods usually require goals to be expressed declaratively using, for instance, a temporal logic. Currently, the extraction of formal requirements from scenario-based descriptions is a tedious and error-prone process that would benefit from automated tool support. We present an ILP methodology for inferring requirements from a set of scenarios and an initial but incomplete requirements specification. The approach is based on translating the specification and scenarios into an event-based logic programming formalism and using a non-monotonic ILP system to learn a set of missing event preconditions. The contribution of this paper is a novel application of ILP to requirements engineering that also demonstrate the need for non-monotonic learning.

1 Introduction

Requirements Engineering refers to all aspects of the software development life-cycle concerned with identifying, analysing and documenting stakeholder requirements [2]. Several approaches have been developed to assist Requirements Engineers in the refinement of high-level goals into operational requirements [12,13] declaratively expressed in a temporal logic [16]. The use of a temporal formalism enables the deployment of automated analysis and refinement tools, but is not directly accessible to most stakeholders with a less technical background. In practice, stakeholders prefer to convey their goals through more intuitive narrative-style scenarios of desirable and undesirable system behaviour [30]. Because scenarios are inherently *partial* descriptions that leave requirements implicitly defined, it is necessary to synthesise a declarative requirements specification that admits the desired behaviours while rejecting the undesired ones. Currently, the extraction of declarative requirements from scenario-based

S. Muggleton, R. Otero, and A. Tamaddoni-Nezhad (Eds.): ILP 2006, LNAI 4455, pp. 64–78, 2007.

descriptions is a tedious and error-prone process that relies on the manual efforts of an experienced engineer and would benefit from automated tool support.

This paper presents an ILP approach for extracting requirements from example scenarios and a partial requirements specification. Scenarios represent examples of desirable and undesirable system behaviour over time while the requirements specification captures our initial but incomplete background knowledge of the envisioned system and its environment. The task is to complete the specification by learning a set of missing requirements that cover all of the desirable scenarios, but none of the undesirable ones. We show how this task can be naturally represented as a non-monotonic ILP problem in which the partial requirements specification provides the background knowledge and the scenarios comprise the positive and negative examples. In particular, we show how the initial specification and scenarios can be translated into an ILP representation based on the Event Calculus [8,17]. Because this representation makes essential use of negation in formalising the effects and non-effects of actions, the resulting learning problem is inherently non-monotonic. We show that, under the *stable model* [4] semantics for logic programs with negation, the stable models of the transformed program correspond to the temporal models of the original specification. We show that stable models of the program correspond to the temporal models of the original specification. We then use a non-monotonic ILP system, called XHAIL [24,25], to generalise the scenarios with respect to the initial specification. For the purposes of illustration, we restrict the language bias of XHAIL so as to compute a specific form of missing requirements, called *event preconditions*, which state that a certain event may not happen under some particular conditions.

The paper is organised as follows. Section 2 presents some background material on Linear Temporal Logic (LTL) and the Event Calculus (EC). Section 3 describes the main features of our approach. Section 4 provides an illustrative case study involving a Mine Pump controller. We conclude with a summary and remarks about related and future work.

2   Background

Several logic-based formalisms have been used for representing requirements specifications [5,10,27]. Among these, the Event Calculus (EC) [8] is particularly well suited to logic programming approaches like ILP. Moreover, its explicit representation of time and domain specific axioms makes EC an ideal formalism for representing and reasoning about a wide class of event-driven systems. Although EC has been successfully used as a "back-end" computational formalism [27] it is not a mainstream representation because it necessitates familiarity with logic programming. By contrast, Linear Temporal Logic (LTL) [16] is very widely used by software engineers for specifying system goals and properties. In this paper we propose a method for translating between LTL and EC descriptions in order to enable the use of ILP techniques in Requirements Engineering. In the rest of this section we briefly recall the syntax and semantics of these formalisms.

2.1   Linear Temporal Logic

The language of LTL includes a set of propositions P, the Boolean connectives ($\neg, \wedge, \vee$ and $\rightarrow$) and the temporal operators $\bigcirc$ (*next*), $\square$ (*always*), $\Diamond$ (*eventually*), U (*strong until*) and W (*weak until*). Well-formed formulae are constructed in the standard way. We use $(\neg)$ a to refer to either the atom a or the negation $\neg\, a$ of that atom. Also, we use $\bigcirc^i$ to denote i consecutive applications of the $\bigcirc$ operator. We assume P is partitioned into two sets P_e and P_f denoting *event* and *fluent* propositions, respectively. The truth or falsity of an LTL formulae is specified relative to a graph-based structure called a *Labelled Transition System* (LTS) [15,6].

Definition 1. *A labelled transition system (LTS) is a tuple $\langle S, E, \rightarrow, s_0 \rangle$ where S is a non-empty set of states, E is a non-empty set of events, $\rightarrow\ \subseteq S \times E \times S$ is a labelled transition relation, and s_0 is the initial state. A transition $(s, e, s') \in\ \rightarrow$ from a state s to a new state s' labelled by e is denoted graphically as $s \xrightarrow{e} s'$. A path in an LTS is a sequence of states and transitions, from the initial state, of the form $\sigma = s_0 \xrightarrow{e_1} s_1, \ldots$ where $e_i \in E$ is said to be at position i in σ and s_i is said to be the ith state in σ.*

As formalised in Definition 2 below, an LTL model is a pair $\langle T, V \rangle$ consisting of an LTS, T, and a valuation function, V, that assigns to each fluent proposition an arbitrary set of states in paths of T. The events are not specified in V as their truth is implicitly determined by the transitions in T. This is formalised in Definition 3, which defines the satisfaction of an LTL formula ϕ with respect to a path σ in the LTS T.

Definition 2. *Given an LTL language with propositions $P = P_e \cup P_f$ an LTL model is a pair $\langle T, V \rangle$ where T is an LTS with events P_e and V is a valuation function $V : P_f \Rightarrow 2^A$, where $A = \{(\sigma, i) \mid \sigma$ path in T and i position in $\sigma\}$.*

The satisfiability of an LTL formula is defined with respect to positions (or states) in a given path σ. A formula ϕ is said to be true at position i in a path σ, denoted $\sigma, i \models \phi$ iff it is true at the s_i state in the path σ.

Definition 3. *Given an LTL language with propositions $P = P_e \cup P_f$, an LTL model $\langle T, V \rangle$ and a path σ in T, the satisfaction of an LTL formula ϕ at a position $i \geq 0$ of the path σ is defined inductively as follows:*

- $\sigma, 0 \not\models e$ *for any event proposition* $e \in P_e$
- $\sigma, i \models e$ *iff* e *is at position* i $(i \geq 1)$ *in the path* σ, *where* $e \in P_e$
- $\sigma, i \models f$ *iff* $(\sigma, i) \in V(f)$, *where* $f \in P_f$
- $\sigma, i \models \neg\phi$ *iff* $\sigma, i \not\models \phi$
- $\sigma, i \models \phi \wedge \psi$ *iff* $\sigma, i \models \phi$ *and* $\sigma, i \models \psi$
- $\sigma, i \models \phi \vee \psi$ *iff* $\sigma, i \models \phi$ *or* $\sigma, i \models \psi$
- $\sigma, i \models \bigcirc\phi$ *iff* $\sigma, i+1 \models \phi$
- $\sigma, i \models \square\phi$ *iff* $\forall j \geq i.\ \sigma, j \models \phi$
- $\sigma, i \models \Diamond\phi$ *iff* $\exists j \geq i.\ \sigma, j \models \phi$

$- \ \sigma, i \models \phi \ U \ \psi \ \text{iff} \ \exists j \geq i. \ \sigma, j \models \psi \ \text{and} \ \forall i \leq k < j. \ \sigma, k \models \phi$

$- \ \sigma, i \models \phi \ W \ \psi \ \text{iff} \ \sigma, i \models \Box \phi \ \text{or} \ \sigma, i \models \phi \ U \ \psi$

An LTL formula ϕ is said to be *satisfied in a path* σ if it is satisfied at the initial position, i.e. $\sigma, 0 \models \phi$. Similarly, a set of formulae Γ is said to be satisfied in a path σ if each formula $\psi \in \Gamma$ is satisfied in the path σ.

Definition 4. *Let* Γ *be a set of LTL formulae and* ϕ *be an LTL formula. Let* $M = \langle T, V \rangle$ *be an LTL model. The formula* ϕ *is said to be entailed by* Γ *under* M, *written* $\Gamma \models_M \phi$, *iff* ϕ *is satisfied in each path* σ *of* T *that satisfies* Γ.

2.2 Event Calculus

The Event Calculus (EC) is a widely-used logic programming formalism for reasoning about actions and time [29]. The standard definition of an EC language includes three sorts of terms: *event* terms, *fluent* terms, and *time* terms. The latter are represented by the non-negative integers $0, 1, 2, \ldots$, while the events and fluents are chosen according to the domain being modelled. In this paper, we assume an additional sort representing *scenarios*. The EC ontology includes the basic predicates *happens*, *initiates*, *terminates* and *holdsAt*. The atomic formula *happens*(e, t, s) indicates that event e occurs at time-point t in a given scenario s, while *initiates*(e, f, t, s) (resp. *terminates*(a, f, t, s)) means that, in a given scenario s, if event e were to occur at time t, it would cause fluent f to be true (resp. false) immediately afterwards. The predicate *holdsAt*(f, t, s) indicates that fluent f is true at time-point t in a given scenario s. The formalism also includes an auxiliary predicate *clipped*(t_1, f, t_2, s) which means that, in a given scenario s, an event occurs which terminates f between times t_1 and t_2. Events correspond to actions which can be performed, while fluents correspond to time-varying Boolean properties. The interactions between the EC predicates are governed by a set of domain-independent core axioms shown below[1].

$$clipped(T_1, F, T_2, S) \leftarrow happens(E, T, S), \\ terminates(E, F, T, S), T_1 \leq T < T_2. \tag{1}$$

$$holdsAt(F, T_2, S) \leftarrow happens(E, T_1, S), initiates(E, F, T_1, S), \\ T_1 < T_2, not \ clipped(T_1, F, T_2, S). \tag{2}$$

$$holdsAt(F, T, S) \leftarrow initially(F, S), not \ clipped(0, F, T, S). \tag{3}$$

$$happens(E, T, S) \leftarrow attempt(E, T, S), not \ impossible(E, T, S). \tag{4}$$

These axioms formalise the commonsense law of inertia which states that, in any scenario S, a fluent that has been initiated by an event occurrence continues

---

[1] The EC axioms used here are identical to those in [17] apart from the extra argument S for representing scenarios and the predicate *impossible* for capturing preconditions.

to hold until a terminating event occurs and vice versa. To allow the representation of preconditions, we say that an event E happens at a time point T if it is attempted and is not impossible[2]. Information about which events affect which fluents is provided by domain-dependent axioms for the predicates *initiates* and *terminates*, together with information about which fluents are initially true and which events are attempted in given system behaviours.

EC theories are *normal logic programs* - i.e. a set of clauses of the form $A \leftarrow B_1, \ldots, B_n, not\ C_1, \ldots, not\ C_m$ where A is the *head atom*, B_i are *positive body literals*, and $not\ C_j$ are *negative body literals*. Their semantics is given by the standard *stable model* semantics [4]. In general, a *model I* of a program Π is a set of ground atoms such that, for each ground instance G of a clause in Π, I satisfies the head of G whenever it satisfies the body. A model I is *minimal* if it does not strictly include any other model. Definite programs (i.e. programs with no negative body literals) always have a unique minimal model. Normal programs may have instead one, none, or several minimal models. It is usual to identify a certain subset of these models, called *stable models*, as the possible meanings of the program. Given a normal program Π, the definite program Π^I is the program obtained from the ground instances of Π by removing all clauses with a negative literal that is not satisfied in Π and removing negative literals from the remaining clauses. Clearly Π^I is a definite logic program and as such has a unique minimal (Herbrand) model M_{Π^I}. A model I of a program Π is *stable* if it is equal to M_{Π^I}.

Definition 5. *A model I of Π is a* stable model *if $I = M_{\Pi^I}$ where Π^I is the definite program $\Pi^I = \{A \leftarrow B_1, \ldots, B_n \mid A \leftarrow B_1, \ldots, B_n, not\ C_1, \ldots, not\ C_m$ is the ground instance of a clause in Π and I does not satisfy any of the $C_j\}$.*

3   The Approach

In this section we show how ILP can be used to extend an incomplete requirements specification using information from given scenarios. We formalise the learning problem in terms of LTL specifications and scenarios, and show how these can be soundly translated into a non-monotonic ILP problem using an EC formalisation to extend the specification in order to cover the given scenarios.

3.1   Problem Description

Our aim is to develop an approach for extending an incomplete requirements specification with a particular type of requirement called event preconditions by using information inferred from desirable and undesirable user scenarios. In order to formalise this task we need to state precisely what we mean by a requirements specification and by a desirable or undesirable scenario and we need

---

[2] Alternative formalisations of event preconditions have been proposed in EC [17]. The one adopted here captures the intuition that $impossible(E, T, S)$ means the event E could not actually occur at time point T.

to define what it means for a specification to cover a set of such scenarios. To do this, we assume an LTL language with fluents P_f and events P_e in which each fluent $f \in P_f$ is associated with two disjoint sets I_f and T_f of initiating and terminating events $e \in P_e$. For convenience we use the notation E_I^f to represent the disjunction $\bigvee_{e \in I_f} e$ of f-initiating events, and E_T^f for the disjunction $\bigvee_{e \in T_f} e$ of f-terminating events. We also use the notation S_0 to represent the set of fluents $f \in P_f$ that are true in the initial system state s_0. We now define requirements specifications and scenarios as LTL theories containing formulae of the forms defined below.

As formalised in Definition 6, a requirements specification consists of a set of *initial state axioms* (5,6) stating which fluents are initially true and false; *persistence axioms* (7,8) formalising the commonsense law of inertia that any fluent will remain true (resp. false) until a terminating (resp. initiating) event occurs that causes it to flip state; *change axioms* (9,10), stating that, for any fluent $f \in P_f$, the occurrence of any initiating (resp. terminating) event will cause f to become true (resp. false); and a set of *event precondition axioms* (11) which disallow any models that include transitions of the form $s_k \xrightarrow{e} s_{k+1}$ for any state s_k that satisfies a certain conjunction of fluent literals $\bigwedge_{0 \leq i \leq n}(\neg) f_i$.

Definition 6. *A requirements specification is an LTL theory consisting of*

- *two* initial state axioms

$$\bigwedge_{f_i \in S_0} f_i \qquad (5)$$

$$\bigwedge_{f_j \in P_f - S_0} \neg f_j \qquad (6)$$

- *two* persistence axioms *for each fluent* $f \in P_f$

$$\Box(f \rightarrow f \; W \, E_T^f) \qquad (7)$$

$$\Box(\neg f \rightarrow \neg f \; W \, E_I^f) \qquad (8)$$

- *two* change axioms *for each fluent* $f \in P_f$

$$\Box(E_I^f \rightarrow f) \qquad (9)$$

$$\Box(E_T^f \rightarrow \neg f) \qquad (10)$$

- *a set of* event precondition axioms *of the form*

$$\Box(\bigwedge_{0 \leq i \leq n}(\neg) f_i \rightarrow \bigcirc \neg e) \qquad (11)$$

As formalised below, a scenario is a formula stating a sequence of occurrences of events $\langle e_1, \ldots, e_m \rangle$.

Definition 7. *A scenario is an LTL formula of the form*

$$\bigwedge_{1 \leq i \leq m} \bigcirc^i e_i \qquad (12)$$

Note that the definition above assumes one event to be true per point position. A *desirable scenario* is a scenario that may occur while an *undesirable scenario* is a sequence of events that should never occur.

Using Definition 7, we can now formalise our learning task. Given an initial specification *Spec* together with a set of undesirable scenarios *Und* and desirable scenarios *Des*, our aim is to learn a set of event precondition axioms *Pre* that, when added to *Spec*, entails the negation of each undesirable scenario and is consistent with each desirable scenario. As formalised in Definition 8, the first condition states that, in any model of *Spec* ∪ *Pre*, there is no path which produces any undesirable scenario in *Und*, while the second condition states that, in any model of *Spec* ∪ *Pre*, there is always a path corresponding to each desirable scenario in *Des*. Any set of event precondition axioms that satisfy these two properties is said be a *correct extension* of a requirements specification with respect to the given scenarios.

Definition 8. *Let* Spec *be a requirements specification,* Des *be a set of desirable scenarios, and* Und *be a set of undesirable scenarios. A set* Pre *of event precondition axioms is a* correct extension *of* Spec *with respect to* Des *and* Und *iff*

- $Spec \cup Pre \models_M \neg P_u$,   *for each undesirable scenario* $P_u \in Und$
- $Spec \cup Pre \not\models_M \neg P_d$,   *for each desirable scenario* $P_d \in Des$

3.2   Translating LTL into EC

To apply ILP to the task of learning correct extensions, a methodology is now defined for translating LTL specifications and scenarios of the form defined above into EC normal logic programs. The EC language is obtained very simply from the LTL formulae: one fluent (resp. event) term is introduced to represent each fluent f (resp. event e) in P_f (resp. P_e); time points are represented by the non-negative integers 0, 1, 2, ...; one scenario term is introduced to represent each desirable (resp. undesirable) scenario $P_d \in Des$ (resp. $P_u \in Und$). Relative to this language, the EC translation of a requirements specification is defined as follows.

Definition 9. *Let* Spec *be a requirements specification. The EC translation* $\tau(Spec)$ *of* Spec *is the EC program* Π *constructed as follows:*

- *add to* Π *one fact* $initially(f_i, S)$ *for each fluent* f_i *in an initial state axiom of the form* $\bigwedge_{f_i \in S_0} f_i$.

- *add to* Π *one fact* $initiates(e, f, T, S)$ *for each* f*-initiating event* $e \in E_I^f$ *in a change axiom of the form* $\square(E_I^f \rightarrow f)$.

- *add to* Π *one fact* $terminates(e, f, T, S)$ *for each* f*-terminating event* $e \in E_T^f$ *in a change axiom of the form* $\square(E_T^f \rightarrow \neg f)$.

– add to Π one rule $impossible(e, T, S) \leftarrow \bigwedge_{0 \leq i \leq k}(not)holdsAt(f_i, T, S)$ for each event precondition axiom of the form $\Box(\bigwedge_{0 \leq i \leq k}(\neg)f_i \rightarrow \bigcirc \neg e)$.

Note that the negative initial state axiom (6) and the persistence axioms (7) and (8) are all implicitly captured by stable model interpretation of the EC core axioms (which are incorporated into the translation of scenarios in Definition 10 below). Note also that the effect of the temporal operator $\Box$ is captured by implicit universal quantification on the time variable T appearing in the *initiates* and *terminates* facts. As shown in Theorem 1, the translation τ is sound in the sense that for any path σ in any model of *Spec* there is a corresponding narrative of events *Nar* such that the program $\Pi = \tau(Spec) \cup Nar$ has a stable model that satisfies the same fluent and event formulae as σ.

Theorem 1. *Let Spec be a requirements specification with LTL model $\langle T, V \rangle$ such that any path in T satisfies Spec at position 0. Let σ be a path in T of the form $s_0 \xrightarrow{e_1} s_1, \ldots, s_{n-1} \xrightarrow{e_n} s_n$, and let Nar be the set of facts of the form $attempt(e_i, i-1, \sigma)$ for each event e_i in σ. Let Π be the EC logic program $\Pi = \tau(Spec) \cup Nar$ with stable model I. Then, for any fluent f and position i, we have $\sigma, i \models f$ iff $holdsAt(f, i, \sigma)$ is true in I; and, for any event e and position i, we have $\sigma, i \models e$ iff $happens(e, i-1, \sigma)$ is true in I.*

The function τ translates an LTL requirements specification into an ILP theory. It now remains to specify a corresponding translation from scenarios to ILP examples. As formalised in Definition 10 below, scenarios contribute facts to the background theory as well as to the examples. Specifically, each scenario produces a set of example literals of the form $(not)happens(e, t, s)$ and a set of background facts of the form $attempt(e, t, s)$. The translation of the undesirable scenarios depends on the event for which the precondition axiom is to be learned. In what follows, it is assumed that preconditions are to be learned for the last event of each undesirable scenario. Consequently, each undesirable scenario produces a sequence of facts stating that certain events do happen followed by one fact stating that some particular event does not happen immediately afterwards. Each desirable scenario simply states that a certain sequence of events does happen.

Definition 10. *Let Spec be a requirements specification, and Des and Und be sets of desirable and undesirable scenarios respectively. The EC translation $\tau(Spec, Des, Und)$ is the pair (B, E) of EC programs constructed as follows:*

– *for each undesirable scenario $P_u = \bigwedge_{1 \leq i \leq n} \bigcirc^i e_i$ in Und*
  - *add to E $n-1$ facts $happens(e_i, i-1, u)$ with $1 \leq i < n$*
  - *add to E 1 fact $not\ happens(e_n, n-1, u)$*
  - *add to B n facts $attempts(e_i, i-1, u)$ with $1 \leq i \leq n$*
– *for each desirable scenario $P_d = \bigwedge_{1 \leq i \leq m} \bigcirc^i e_i$ in Des*
  - *add to E m facts $happens(e_i, i-1, d)$ with $1 \leq i \leq m$*
  - *add to B m facts $attempts(e_i, i-1, u)$ with $1 \leq i \leq m$*
– *add to B all of the facts and rules in $\tau(Spec)$*
– *add to B the 4 EC core axioms (1)-(4).*

3.3   Computation of Event Precondition Axioms Using XHAIL

Given an initial specification *Spec* and sets of desirable and undesirable scenarios *Des* and *Und*, the translation τ defined above can be used to generate a normal ILP theory B and examples E (such that $\tau(Spec, Des, Und) = (B, E)$). For any set *Pre* of event precondition axioms, τ can also be used to generate a set H of normal clauses of the form (13) below (such that $\tau(Pre) = H$).

$$impossible(e, T, S) \leftarrow \bigwedge_{0 \leq j \leq n} (not)\ holdsAt(f_j, T, S) \tag{13}$$

Moreover, it follows from Theorem 1 that *Pre* is a correct extension of *Spec* with respect to *Des* and *Und* iff $B \cup H \models E$ under the stable model view of $\models$. Hence, the task of computing correct extensions can be reduced to a non-monotonic ILP problem in the sense of [28] where the hypothesis space is the set of all clauses of the form (13) above.

The computation of such preconditions is performed by the non-monotonic ILP system XHAIL [25], which uses an abductive engine to implement a three-phase Hybrid Abductive Inductive Learning (HAIL) approach [24]. This approach is based on constructing and generalising a preliminary ground hypothesis K, called a *Kernel Set* of B and E, which can be regarded as a non-monotonic multi-clause generalisation of the well-known *Bottom Set* concept used in several Progol-based ILP systems [20]. As in these monotonic ILP systems, the construction of the Kernel Set is heavily guided by language and search bias, and its main purpose is to bound the ILP hypothesis space.

The XHAIL language and search bias mechanisms are based upon the tried-and-tested notions of mode declarations and compression as used for example in Progol [20]. Intuitively, the compression heuristic favours the inference of theories containing the fewest number of literals and is motivated by the scientific principle of Ocam's razer (which roughly speaking, means choose the simplest hypothesis that fits the data). Mode declarations on the other hand provide a convenient mechanism for specifying which predicates may appear in the heads and bodies of hypothesis clauses and for controlling the placement and linking of constants and variables within those clauses [20].

As formalised in [20] mode declarations are of two types *head* and *body* declarations. To learn formulae of the form (13) above, one head mode declaration is needed $modeh(*, impossible(\#event, +time, +scenario))$ to allow atoms of the form impossible(e,T,S) to appear in the heads of H. Two body mode declarations are also needed, $modeb(*, holdsAt(\#fluent, +time, +scenario))$ and $modeb(*, not\ holdsAt(\#fluent, +time, +scenario))$, to allow literals of the form $holdsAt(f, T, S)$ and $not\ holdsAt(f, T, S)$ to appear in the bodies of H. The symbols $\#, +, -$ are called *placemarkers* and are replaced by constants, input and output variables, respectively.

As explained in [25], the hypothesis H is computed in three stages: first the head atoms Δ of the Kernel Set K are obtained abductively, then the body literals of K are obtained by deduction, and finally K is inductively generalised to give H. To exploit a close correspondence between negation and abduction,

XHAIL performs all three phases by translating them into an Abductive Logic Programming (ALP) [7] formalism and using an efficient extension [26] of the Kakas-Mancarella proof procedure [7] to solve each subproblem in turn.

The first phase of the XHAIL proof procedure returns a minimal set of ground atoms Δ that entail all of the examples E when added to the theory B. This done by simply querying the examples E against the theory B. The abducible atoms are defined as the well-typed ground instances of any head declarations. To avoid any unsoundness caused by the non-monotonicity of the EC axioms, an incremental cover set approach is not used; instead XHAIL generalises all of the examples at once.

The second phase of the procedure computes a ground Kernel Set K of B and E by making each abduced atom $\alpha \in \Delta$ into the head of a clause and saturating it with a set of ground body literals entailed by B. This is done using a non-monotonic generalisation of the Progol saturation procedure [20]. In order to compute the deductive consequences of B, XHAIL employs the Eshgi-Kowalski transformation for implementing negation through abduction [3]. In effect, negative literals $not(a)$ are treated as positive abducibles a^* subject to the implicit integrity constraints $a \rightarrow \neg a^*$ and $a^* \rightarrow \neg a$.

The third phase, returns a hypothesis H that subsumes K and entails E with respect to B. Two transforms prepare the ALP system for this task. First, all input and output terms in K are replaced by variables. Then, each body literal λ_i^j at position i in the j-th clause of K is replaced by the atom $try(i, j, [X_1, \ldots, X_k])$, where $X_1, \ldots, X_k$ are the variables added to that clause, and the two clauses $try(i, j, [X_1, \ldots, X_k]) \leftarrow not(use(i, j))$ and $try(i, j, [X_1, \ldots, X_k]) \leftarrow use(i, j), \lambda_i^j$ are added to K. Applying an ALP procedure to the resulting theory $B \cup K$ with goal E and abducible $use/2$ gives a set of atoms $S = \bigwedge use(i, j)$ indicating which literals λ_i^j should be kept in H.

Soundness of XHAIL with respect to the stable model semantics follows from the soundness of the Kakas-Mancarella ALP procedure and the fact that H is equivalent to the theory $K \cup S$ computed in the inductive phase of the XHAIL procedure and which, by definition, entails the examples. Strictly speaking, XHAIL implements the partial stable model semantics, but since the EC programs generated by τ are categorical in the sense of [28], the two semantics coincide in this particular application. As illustrated by the case study in the next section, XHAIL can therefore be used to compute correct extensions of a partial specification and scenarios via the translation function τ.

4   Case Study: A Mine Pump Control System

This section shows an application of the learning approach proposed in this paper on a real event-driven system, namely the Mine Pump Control System fully described in [9]. This is a system that is supposed to monitor and control water levels in a mine, so to avoid the risk of flood. It is composed of a pump for pumping mine-water up to the surface. The pump works automatically, controlled by water-level sensors: detection of a high-level water causes the pump to run until low-level is indicated. For safety reasons, the pump must not run if the percentage of methane in the mine exceeds a certain critical limit.

An initial partial requirement specification *Spec* is given, written in an LTL language with fluent propositions $P_f = \{pumpOn, criticalMethane, highWater\}$ and event propositions $P_e = \{turnPumpOn, turnPumpOff, signalCriticalMethane, signalNotCriticalMethane, signalHighWater, signalNotHighWater\}$. The specifications includes information about the initial state of the system, persistence axioms, and change axioms formalised as follows:

$$(\neg criticalMethane \wedge \neg pumpOn \wedge \neg highWater) \tag{14}$$

$$\Box(criticalMethane \rightarrow (criticalMethane \ W \ signalNotCriticalMethane)) \tag{15}$$

$$\Box(\neg criticalMethane \rightarrow (\neg criticalMethane \ W \ signalCriticalMethane)) \tag{16}$$

$$\Box(pumpOn \rightarrow (pumpOn \ W \ turnPumpOff)) \tag{17}$$

$$\Box(\neg pumpOn \rightarrow (\neg pumpOn \ W \ turnPumpOn)) \tag{18}$$

$$\Box(highWater \rightarrow (highWater \ W \ signalNotHighWater)) \tag{19}$$

$$\Box(\neg highWater \rightarrow (\neg highWater \ W \ signalHighWater)) \tag{20}$$

$$\Box(signalCriticalMethane \rightarrow criticalMethane) \tag{21}$$

$$\Box(signalNotCriticalMethane \rightarrow \neg criticalMethane) \tag{22}$$

$$\Box(signalHighWater \rightarrow highWater) \tag{23}$$

$$\Box(signalNotHighWater \rightarrow \neg highWater) \tag{24}$$

$$\Box(turnPumpOn \rightarrow pumpOn) \tag{25}$$

$$\Box(turnPumpOff \rightarrow \neg pumpOn) \tag{26}$$

Equation (14) defines the initial state of the system, equations (15)–(20) specify the persistence axioms, and equations (21)–(26) define the change axioms. Together with the informal description the case study includes undesirable and desirable scenarios which have been formalised as follows:

$$P_u = (\bigcirc signalCriticalMethane \wedge \bigcirc^2 signalNotCriticalMethane \wedge \\ \bigcirc^3 signalCriticalMethane \wedge \bigcirc^4 turnPumpOn) \tag{27}$$

$$P_{d1} = (\ \bigcirc signalCriticalMethane \ \wedge \bigcirc^2 signalHighWater \ \wedge \\ \bigcirc^3 signalNotCriticalMethane \ \wedge \bigcirc^4 turnPumpOn \ \wedge \\ \bigcirc^5 signalCriticalMethane \wedge \bigcirc^6 turnPumpOff) \tag{28}$$

$$P_{d2} = (\bigcirc signalHighWater \wedge \bigcirc^2 turnPumpOn \ \wedge \\ \bigcirc^3 signalNotHighWater \wedge \bigcirc^4 turnPumpOff \wedge \\ \bigcirc^5 signalHighWater \wedge \bigcirc^6 turnPumpOn) \tag{29}$$

Applying the translation τ to the specification and scenarios above results in an ILP theory B composed of the EC core axioms and the following clauses:

initiates(signalCriticalMethane,criticalMethane,T,S).
terminates(signalNotCriticalMethane,criticalMethane,T,S).
initiates(signalHighWater,highWater,T,S).
terminates(signalNotHighWater,highWater,T,S).
initiates(turnPumpOn,pumpOn,T,S).
terminates(turnPumpOff,pumpOn,T,S).

attempt(signalCriticalMethane,0,u).
attempt(signalNotCriticalMethane,1,u).
attempt(signalCriticalMethane,2,u).
attempt(turnPumpOn,3,u).

attempt(signalHighWater,0,dp1).
attempt(turnPumpOn,1,dp1).
attempt(signalNotHighWater,2,dp1).
attempt(turnPumpOff,3,dp1).

attempt(signalCriticalMethane,0,dp2).
attempt(signalHighWater,1,dp2).
attempt(signalNotCriticalMethane,2,dp2).
attempt(turnPumpOn,3,dp2).
attempt(signalCriticalMethane,4,dp2).
attempt(turnPumpOff,5,dp2).

In addition, the translation produces the following set of ILP examples E:

happens(signalCriticalMethane,0,u).
happens(signalNotCriticalMethane,1,u).
happens(signalCriticalMethane,2,u).
not happens(turnPumpOn,3,u).

happens(signalHighWater,0,dp1).
happens(turnPumpOn,1,dp1).
happens(signalNotHighWater,2,dp1).
happens(turnPumpOff,3,dp1).

happens(signalCriticalMethane,0,dp2).
happens(signalHighWater,1,dp2).
happens(signalNotCriticalMethane,2,dp2).
happens(turnPumpOn,3,dp2).
happens(signalCriticalMethane,4,dp2).
happens(turnPumpOff,5,dp2).

Applying XHAIL to B and E yields a single abductive explanation

$$\Delta = \{impossible(turnPumpOn, 3, u)\} \tag{30}$$

This results in a single Kernel Set containing one clause

$$K = \{impossible(turnPumpOn, 3, u) \leftarrow holdsAt(criticalMethane, 3, u),$$
$$not\ holdsAt(pumpOn, 3, u), not\ holdsAt(highWater, 3, u)\} \tag{31}$$

which gives two maximally compressive inductive generalisations

$$H_1 = \{impossible(turnPumpOn, T, S) \leftarrow holdsAt(criticalMethane, T, S)\} \tag{32}$$

$$H_2 = \{impossible(turnPumpOn, T, S) \leftarrow not\ holdsAt(highWater, T, S)\} \tag{33}$$

that correspond to the two correct LTL event precondition axioms

$$Pre_1 = \Box(criticalMethane \rightarrow \bigcirc \neg turnPumpOn) \tag{34}$$

$$Pre_2 = \Box(\neg highWater \rightarrow \bigcirc \neg turnPumpOn) \tag{35}$$

5   Conclusion, Related and Future Work

This paper describes a methodology for using ILP to extend a partial requirements specification with event preconditions extracted from user scenarios. The proposed approach works in two stages whereby the initial specification and scenarios are first translated from an LTL model into an EC representation so that a nonmonotonic ILP system can then be used to learn the missing requirements. By exploiting the semantic relationship between the LTL and EC, we thereby provide a sound ILP computational "back-end" to a temporal formalism familiar to Requirements Engineers.

Our approach is closely related to that of [11], where an inductive method is proposed for inferring high-level goal assertion from positive and negative scenarios provided by stakeholders. Scenarios are incrementally generalised by (a) conjoining new assertions with those obtained from previous scenarios and (b) merging assertions through pattern matching on common antecedent prefixes. Compared to [11], our ILP-based approach has the advantage of incorporating background knowledge into the learning process and producing more compact and comprehensible hypotheses. Moreover, by making *happens* abducible, our approach can be applied to scenarios missing events while [11] cannot.

The method proposed in this paper builds upon earlier work in [19] and [18] in which the ILP systems Progol5 and Alecto were applied to the learning of domain specific EC axioms. Like XHAIL, these procedures employ an abductive reasoning module to enable the learning of predicates distinct from those in the examples — an ability that is clearly required in this application. However, unlike XHAIL, they do not have a well-defined semantics for non-definite programs and their handling of negation is rather limited [25]. In fact, the inability of Progol5 and Alecto to reason abductively through nested negations means that neither of these systems can solve the case study presented in this paper.

Some related approaches for inferring action theories from examples are presented in [14], [21] and more recently in [23], which reduce learning in the

Situation Calculus to a monotonic ILP framework. These approaches work by pre- and post- processing the inputs and outputs of a conventional Horn Clause ILP system. This technique is very efficient, but is not as general as our own approach. An alternative method for nonmonotonic ILP under the stable model semantics is proposed in [28], but cannot be used in our case study because it assumes the target predicate is the same as the examples. [28] also includes a thorough review of previous work on nonmonotonic ILP. A more recent technique is proposed in [22] that uses a combination of SAT solvers and Horn ILP to perform induction under the stable model semantics.

Although the approach presented in this paper has been tailored for the learning of event preconditions, it can also learn other types of requirements such as triggers and post-conditions of the form $\Box(\bigwedge_{0 \leq i \leq k} f_i \rightarrow \bigcirc e)$ and $\Box(e \rightarrow \bigwedge_{0 \leq j \leq h} f_j)$ respectively. In principle, this can be achieved by changing the language bias appropriately; but it remains to test the efficiency of the approach when learning more general forms of requirements and when processing larger case studies. In this paper we also assumed that scenarios are provided by stakeholders. However, scenarios could also be automatically generated from desirable system properties via model-checking [1]. We therefore intend to investigate the integration of ILP and model checking techniques in order to find new ways of increasing the flexibility and efficiency of the approach.

Acknowledgments. This work is funded by the Philip Leverhulme Trust and the Saudi Arabian Ministry of Higher Education.

References

1. Alrajeh, D., Russo, A., Uchitel, S.: Inferring operational requirements from goal models and scenarios using inductive systems. In: Proc. 5th Int. Workshop on Scenarios and State Machines (2006)
2. Dardenne, A., Lamsweerde, A.v., Fickas, S.: Goal-directed requirements acquisition. Science of Computer Programming 20 (1), 3–50 (1993)
3. Eshghi, K., Kowalski, R.A.: Abduction compared with negation by failure. In: Levi, G., Martelli, M. (eds.) Proc. of the 6th Int. Conf. on Logic Programming, pp. 234–254 (1989)
4. Gelfond, M., Lifschitz, V.: The stable model semantics for logic programming. In: Kowalski, R.A., Bowen, K. (eds.) Proc. of the 5th Int. Conf. on Logic Programming, pp. 1070–1080. MIT Press, Cambridge (1988)
5. Giannakopoulou, D., Magee, J.: Fluent model checking for event-based systems. In: Proc. 11th ACM SIGSOFT Symp. on Foundations Software Engineering, ACM Press, New York (2003)
6. Huth, M., Ryan, M.D.: Logic in Computer Science: Modelling and Reasoning about systems. Cambridge University Press, Cambridge (2000)
7. Kakas, A.C., Kowalski, R.A., Toni, F.: Abductive Logic Programming. Journal of Logic and Computation 2(6), 719–770 (1992)
8. Kowalski, R.A., Sergot, M.: A logic-based calculus of events. New generation computing 4(1), 67–95 (1986)
9. Kramer, J., Magee, J., Sloman, M.: Conic: An integrated approach to distributed computer control systems. In: IEE Proc., Part E 130, pp. 1–10 (January 1983)

10. Lamsweerde, A.V.: Goal-oriented requirements engineering: A guided tour. In: Proc. 5th IEEE Int. Symp. on Requirements Engineering, pp. 249–263. IEEE Computer Society Press, Los Alamitos (2001)
11. Lamsweerde, A.V., Willemet, L.: Inferring declarative requirements specifications from operational scenarios. IEEE Trans. on Software Engineering 24(12), 1089–1114 (1998)
12. Letier, E., Kramer, J., Magee, J., Uchitel, S.: Deriving event-based transitions systems from goal-oriented requirements models. Technical Report 2006/2, Imperial College London (2005)
13. Letier, E., Lamsweerde, A.V.: Deriving operational software specifications from system goals. In: Proc. 10th ACM SIGSOFT Symp. on Foundations of Software Engineering, pp. 119–128. ACM Press, New York (2002)
14. Lorenzo, D.: Learning non-monotonic Logic Programs to Reason about Actions and Change. PhD thesis, University of Coruna (2001)
15. Magee, J., Kramer, J.: Concurrency: State Models and Java Programs. John Wiley and Sons, Chichester (1999)
16. Manna, Z., Pnueli, A.: The Temporal Logic of Reactive and Concurrent Systems. Springer, Heidelberg (1992)
17. Miller, R., Shanahan, M.: Some alternative formulation of event calculus. Computer Science: Computational Logic: Logic programming and Beyond 2408 (2002)
18. Moyle, S.: An investigation into Theory Completion Techniques in ILP. PhD thesis, University of Oxford (2000)
19. Moyle, S., Muggleton, S.: Learning programs in the event calculus. In: Proc. 7th Int. Workshop on ILP (1997)
20. Muggleton, S.H.: Inverse Entailment and Progol. New Generation Computing, Special issue on Inductive Logic Programming 13(3-4), 245–286 (1995)
21. Otero, R.: Embracing causality in inducing the effects of actions. In: Proc. 10th Conf. of the Spanish Assoc. for AI (2004)
22. Otero, R., Gonzalez, J.: Iaction: a system for induction under non-horn programs with stable models. In: Dumke, R.R., Abran, A. (eds.) IWSM 2000. LNCS, vol. 2006, Springer, Heidelberg (2001)
23. Otero, R., Varela, M.: Iaction: a system for learning action descriptions for planning. In: Dumke, R.R., Abran, A. (eds.) IWSM 2000. LNCS, vol. 2006, Springer, Heidelberg (2001)
24. Ray, O.: Hybrid Abductive-Inductive Learning. PhD thesis, Imperial College London (2005)
25. Ray, O.: Using abduction for induction of normal logic programs. In: Proc. of the ECAI'06 Workshop on Abduction and Induction in AI and Scientific Modelling, pp. 28–31 (2006)
26. Ray, O., Kakas, A.: Prologica: a practical system for abductive logic programming. In: Dix, J., Hunter, A. (eds.) 11th International Workshop on Non-monotonic Reasoning. IFL Technical Report Series, pp. 304–312 (2006)
27. Russo, A., Miller, R., Nuseibeh, B., Kramer, J.: An abductive approach for analysing event-based requirements specifications. In: Stuckey, P.J. (ed.) ICLP 2002. LNCS, vol. 2401, pp. 22–37. Springer, Heidelberg (2002)
28. Sakama, C.: Induction from answer sets in non-monotonic logic programs. ACM Trans. on Computational Logic 6(2), 203–231 (2005)
29. Shanahan, M.P.: Solving the Frame Problem. MIT Press, Cambridge (1997)
30. Sutcliffe, A., Maiden, N.A.M., Minocha, S., Manuel, D.: Supporting scenario-based requirements engineering. IEEE Trans. on Software Engineering 24, 1072–1088 (1998)

Learning Recursive Patterns for Biomedical Information Extraction

Margherita Berardi and Donato Malerba

Dipartimento di Informatica, Università degli Studi di Bari
via Orabona, 4 - 70126 Bari - Italy
{berardi,malerba}@di.uniba.it

Abstract. Information in text form remains a greatly unexploited source of biological information. Information Extraction (IE) techniques are necessary to map this information into structured representations that allow facts relating domain-relevant entities to be automatically recognized. In biomedical IE tasks, extracting patterns that model implicit relations among entities is particularly important since biological systems intrinsically involve interactions among several entities. In this paper, we resort to an Inductive Logic Programming (ILP) approach for the discovery of mutual recursive patterns from text. Mutual recursion allows dependencies among entities to be explored in data and extraction models to be applied in a context-sensitive mode. In particular, IE models are discovered in form of classification rules encoding the conditions to fill a pre-defined information template. An application to a real-world dataset composed by publications selected to support biologists in the task of automatic annotation of a genomic database is reported.

1 Introduction

The last decade has witnessed an unexampled expansion of biomedical data and related literature. Advances of genome sequencing techniques have led to an overwhelming increase in the number of publications about discovered genes, proteins and their roles in biological processes. The ability to survey this literature and extract relevant pieces of information is crucial for researchers in biomedicine. However, finding explicit entities (e.g., a protein or a kinase) and facts (e.g., phosphorylation and interaction relationships) in unstructured text is a time consuming and boring task because of the size of available resources, data sparseness and continuous updating of published material. Information Extraction (IE) is the process of mapping unstructured text into structured form, such as knowledge bases or databases, by filling predefined templates of information describing objects of interest and facts about them. This motivates the interest of IE and text mining practitioners toward the biomedical field [24,15].

In a machine learning perspective, IE can be tackled as a classification task, where classification models composed by rules or patterns encoding the conditions to fill a given slot of a template of interest are learned from a set of annotated texts (i.e., examples of filled templates) [21]. Natural language research

S. Muggleton, R. Otero, and A. Tamaddoni-Nezhad (Eds.): ILP 2006, LNAI 4455, pp. 79–93, 2007.
© Springer-Verlag Berlin Heidelberg 2007

has widely made use of statistical techniques (e.g., hidden Markov models and probabilistic context-free grammars) because of their robustness and wide coverage peculiarities. However, these techniques cannot properly cope with the level of semantic interpretation. Moreover, they discover linguistically impoverished models which are difficult to interpret and extend [20]. To solve these problems, logic-based approaches, such as those developed in ILP, can be employed. Indeed, they make encoding easy for natural language statements reported both in training data and in the background knowledge [10], and they learn logical theories that can be easily interpreted and revised [10]. Moreover, IE tasks can be naturally framed in the ILP relational setting where data have a relational structure and examples can be related to each other.

Several papers on ILP approaches to learning rule-based models from logical representations of texts are reported in the literature [1,11,16,13,4]. However, only some of them face problems of IE from biomedical texts [5,14], despite the fact that biomedical IE is considered a major application area where ILP may converge [7]. Difficulties are due to the complexity of the biomedical language which is characterized by inconsistent naming conventions, i.e. ambiguities occurring when the same term denotes more than one semantic class (e.g., p53 is used to specify both a gene and a protein) or when many terms lead to the same semantic class (abbreviations, acronym variations). Further problems derive from the continuous creation of new biological terms or evolutions of the same biological object (e.g., genes are renamed once their function is known). The use of non standard grammatical structures as well as domain-specific jargon represent another source of complexity. All these issues make the preparation of training data really difficult. On the other hand, a number of controlled vocabularies, lexicons and ontologies which can be exploited both in the data processing and reasoning steps are available. This further motivates an ILP approach which can naturally handle such a background knowledge.

In the IE literature, there are two main tasks, namely *named entity recognition* and *multi-slot extraction* (or *template filling*). The former aims to identify peculiar objects of interest (the *named entities*), such as the pathology associated to a mutation or the substitution that causes a mutation. The latter looks for conceptual relationships between named entities, such as the genetic mutation associated to both a pathology and a substitution (template *mutation(⟨pathology⟩, ⟨substitution⟩)*).

A multi-slot extraction task, which is generally based on the results of a named entity recognition task, can be simplified if tagging of named entities is, in its turn, performed by considering some conceptual dependencies implicitly defined at either the syntactic or structural level (e.g., the type of mutation is normally reported after the corresponding substitution). These conceptual dependencies are particularly evident in biomedical domain, since biological systems intrinsically involve relations among several entities (e.g., genes and proteins interacting in regulation networks). Therefore, in this paper, we propose to learn tagging models in the form of *recursive logical theories* which can naturally represent conceptual dependencies between named entities.

The paper is organized as follows. In the following section, we describe the biomedical information extraction problem employed as case study in this work, namely the annotation of a genomic database. Both the data preprocessing techniques and the representation employed for training examples and background knowledge are reported in Section 3. In Section 4, the ILP learning algorithm used to learn recursive logical theories is briefly described. Results obtained on a real-world dataset composed by publications concerning studies on mitochondrial pathologies are reported in Section 5. Finally, some conclusions are drawn in Section 6.

2   The Information Extraction Problem

The application we are addressing concerns the annotation of some resources stored in HmtDB[1], a database of variability and clinical data associated to mitochondrial pathological phenotypes [2]. Currently, HmtDB stores data from healthy subjects while variability and clinical data are manually extracted from published literature. A peculiarity of this fragment of the scientific literature is that biomedical documents are organized according to a regular section structure (composed by Abstract, Introduction, Methods, Results and Discussion) and that often biologists already know which part of the documents may contain a certain kind of information. This suggests to conduct the IE process in a local way to pre-categorized sections of interest [3]. Indeed, selecting relevant portions of text is a prerequisite step for IE, since the lack of robustness and data sparseness makes IE methods inapplicable to large corpora and irrelevant documents. In this application, selected publications concern mitochondrial mutations and biologists are interested in automating the identification of occurrences of specific biological objects (i.e., mitochondrial mutations) and their features (i.e., type, position, involved nucleotides, expressing locus, related pathology) as well as the particular method and experimental setting (i.e., dimension, age, sex, nationality of the sample) reported in the publication.

Let us consider the following example of a text fragment of the collection:

Cytoplasts from two unrelated patients with MELAS (mitochondrial
myopathy, encephalopathy, lactic acidosis, and strokelike episodes)
harboring an A-*G transition at nucleotide position 3243 in the
tRNALeU(UUR) gene of the mitochondrial genome were fused with human
cells lacking endogenous mitochondrial DNA (mtDNA)

Here MELAS is an instance of the *pathology* associated to the mutation under study, A-*G is an instance of the *substitution* that causes the mutation, transition is the *type* of the mutation, 3243 is the *position* in the DNA where the mutation occurs, and tRNALeU(UUR) is the *locus* associated to the mutation.

Two examples of clauses used for the annotation of the named entities *type* and *substitution* are the following:

---

[1] http://www.hmtdb.uniba.it/

```
substitution(X) ← follows(Y,X), type(Y).
type(X) ← distance(X,Y,3), position(Y),
  word_between(X,Y,''nucleotide position'').
```

Their interpretation is straightforward. The first clause states that a token X is labeled as *substitution* (i.e., which nucleotide is substituted by which other, A in G in the example text) if it is followed by a token Y which has been labeled as mutation *type* (transition). The second clause states that X is labeled as mutation *type* (transition) if it is three words far from a token Y that has been labeled as mutation *position* (3243) and there is an intermediate word nucleotide position.

It should be noted that in the above example, the first clause expresses a dependency between the annotation classes *type* and *substitution* of the same template of interest (mutation). As previously clarified, learning classification models which express these dependencies might lead to more accurate models, which reflect some co-occurrence of named entities in the text. Furthermore, when automated annotation is performed, context-sensitive recognition of named entities is possible thanks to learned models which reflect dependencies among annotation classes. However, discovering such concept dependencies poses additional problems for inductive learning. A brief description of an ILP learning algorithm that provides a solution to these problems is reported in Section 4.

3   Data Preparation

The dataset is composed by a set of manually annotated pre-categorized texts. Annotated texts are preprocessed by means of natural language facilities provided in the GATE (General Architecture for Text Engineering) system [6]. We exploit the ANNIE (A Nearly-New IE system) component which contains finite-state algorithms and the JAPE (a Java Annotation Patterns Engine) language which is also a finite-state transduction engine to recognize regular expressions. By means of ANNIE we perform tokenization, sentence splitting, part-of-speech tagging, general purpose named-entity recognition (e.g., persons, locations, organizations), and mapping into dictionaries.

We use both predefined dictionaries available with ANNIE (e.g., organization names, job title, geographical locations, dates, etc.) and domain-specific dictionaries that categorize biological entities such as diseases, enzymes, genes, and so on. General domain dictionaries are used to disambiguate some terms (e.g., places and geographical locations are useful to recognize terms about the ethnic origin of the diseased sample). Domain-specific dictionaries are flat dictionaries of canonical forms and variants of names that are peculiar of mitochondrial genetics. They include lists of names about diseases, genes, methods of analysis, nucleic acids, enzymes, and so on. They are exploited to reduce heterogeneity of data and to perform syntactic and semantic normalization such as a rough resolution of acronyms which in this domain are one of the sources of redundancy and ambiguity. For instance, recognizing that "myopathy, encephalopathy, lactic acidosis, and stroke-like episodes" and "mitochondrial encephalomyopathy lactic acidosis and strokelike episodes" are two variants of the same mitochondrial disease widely known by its acronym "MELAS" is possible when a disease dictionary is used.

JAPE grammars have been defined to identify appositions occurring in texts as well as some numeric and alphanumeric strings which are frequent in this domain. Finally, stopwords (e.g., articles, adverbs, and prepositions) are removed and stemming is performed by means of Porter's algorithm for English texts [22].

3.1 Data Representation

In this work the analysis units are sentences, which are, in their turn, composed of tokens. Each sentence or token is given a unique identifier (in the context of an abstract) based on its ordering within the given text. The relational representation of a sentence is described in terms of properties of occurring tokens and relations between them.

Properties, which are represented by unary descriptors, express statistical (e.g., token frequency), lexical (e.g., alphanumeric, capitalized token), structural (e.g., structure of complex tokens such as alphanumeric strings, abbreviations, acronyms, hyphenated tokens), syntactical (e.g., singular/plural proper/ not proper nouns, base/conjugated verbs) and domain-specific knowledge (e.g., an entity belonging to a dictionary). More precisely, the predicate class specifies the category of the described text (i.e., abstract, methods, results, etc.) and expresses information on the localization of annotations in documents. The predicate word_to_string maps an identifier to the corresponding stemmed token, word_frequency expresses the relative frequency of a token in the given text, type_of refers to morphological features and takes values in the set {allcaps, mixedcaps, upperinitial, numeric, percentage, alphanumeric, real_number}. Parts-of-speech are encoded by the predicate type_pos, while semantics is added by the word_category predicate.

Relations express structural properties such as the composition of sentences in passages of text and tokens in chunks or directly in sentences. Indeed, the following binary descriptors have been defined: part_of, which list tokens composing a sentence, and follows, which relates a token to its direct successor. Complex tokens (e.g., A-*G) are described by several predicates: the s_part_of relation on component tokens, the first and last predicates which define the first and second part of an hyphenated token respectively, the length predicate defining the length of component tokens, and some predicates (e.g., middle_is_char, first_is_numeric) defining the morphological nature of an alphanumeric string. Another form of relational knowledge concerns domain dictionaries and expresses the distance between two categorized tokens in the context of a sentence (distance_word_category).

In this work, we focus on the template *mutation*, which is composed of the following slots: *position* (i.e., position in the DNA where the mutation occurs), *type* (i.e., type of the mutation: insertion, deletion, translation, substitution, etc.), *type_position* (i.e., pieces of the DNA involved in the mutation and relative position in the DNA), *locus* (gene involved in the mutation), and *substitution* (i.e., type of substitution: which nucleotide is substituted by which other).

For the training data, only sentences containing at least a positive example of *position*, *type*, *type_position*, *locus* and *substitution* are considered. Henceforth, they are called *target sentences*. No relation between target sentences is currently considered, that is, the extraction of named entities remains local to sentences. An example of relational description generated for the target sentence reported in Section 2 is the following:[2]

```
annotation(3)=no_tag, ... annotation(7)=pathology,
annotation(8)=no_tag, ... annotation(13)=substitution,
annotation(14)=type, annotation(15)=no_tag, ...,
annotation(17)=position, annotation(18)=locus, ...,
annotation(30)=no_tag ←
class(2)=abstract, part_of(2,3)=true, ..., part_of(2,30)=true,
word_to_string(3)=cytoplast, ..., word_to_string(13)=a-*g,
s_part_of(13,31)=true, s_part_of(13,32)=true, first(13)=a,
last(13)=t, lenght(13)=4, single_char(31)=true,
single_char(32)=true, type_of(31)=allcaps, type_of(32)=allcaps,
word_to_string(14)=transition, ..., word_to_string(30)=cell,
type_of(3)=upperinitial, ..., type_of(29)=alphanumeric,
type_pos(3)=nnp, ..., type_pos(30)=nns, word_frequency(3)=1,
..., word_frequency(30)=2, word_category(7)=disease, ...,
word_category(9)=disease, ..., word_category(28)=nucleic_acid,
distance_word_category(7,9)=2, ..., distance_word_category(27,28)=1,
follows(3,4)=true, follows(4,5)=true, ..., follows(29,30)=true
```

The constant 2 denotes the sentence described in this clause, which belongs to an abstract of the collection, while the constants 3, 4, ..., 30 denote identifiers of tokens which are described in the body of the clause.

3.2 Background Knowledge

The background knowledge includes a transitive definition of the relation of "indirect successor":

```
tfollows(X,Y)=true ← follows(X,Y)=true
tfollows(X,Y)=true ← follows(X,Z)=true, tfollows(Z,Y)=true
```

as well as a number of clauses that express the synonymy between (stemmed) biological terms such as:

```
word_to_string(X)=transit ← word_to_string(X)=transversion
word_to_string(X)=substitut ← word_to_string(X)=replac
```

---

[2] Here, the first-order literals $p(X, Y)$ and $\neg p(X, Y)$ will be represented as $f_p(X, Y)=true$ and $f_p(X, Y)=false$, respectively, where f_p is the function symbol associated to the predicate p. This means that we deal with *classical negation*, $\neg$, but not with *negation by failure*, *not* [17].

The learning system used in this work makes the automated change of representation possible for training examples. This form of abstraction is very useful for tuning the representation of the training examples without acting on the procedures developed for text pre-processing. In this work, the following predicates are intensionally defined in the background knowledge:

```
char_number_char(X)=true ← first_is_char(X)=true,
    middle_is_numeric(X)=true, last_is_char(X)=true
number_char_char(X)=true ← first_is_numeric(X)=true,
    middle_is_char(X)=true, last_is_char(X)=true
char_char_number(X)=true ← first_is_char(X)=true,
    middle_is_char(X)=true, last_is_numeric(X)=true
```

They can appear in the body of learned clauses, while predicates on the morphological nature of alphanumeric strings (e.g., first_is_char, middle_is_char, etc.) cannot.

Finally, a typified form of both direct and transitive successor relations is also introduced. Some examples are reported in the following:

```
follows_string_jj(Y)=Z ←
    word_to_string(X)=Z, follows(X,Y)=true, type_pos(Y)=jj
follows_nn_string(X)=Z ←
    type_pos(X)=nn, follows(X,Y)=true, word_to_string(Y)=Z
tfollows_vb_nn(X,Y)=true ←
    type_pos(X)=vb, tfollows(X,Y)=true, type_pos(Y)=nn
tfollows_jj_nn(X,Y)=true ←
```

The first two clauses express the direct successor relations between a generic string and an adjective or a noun, while the last two clauses specify the transitive successor relations for verb-noun and adjective-noun pairs, respectively.

4   Learning Recursive Patterns

Tagging rules for automated entity extraction are automatically learned in the form of recursive logical theories which can naturally represent conceptual dependencies between named entities. Indeed multiple predicate learning (or multiple concept learning) and recursive theory learning are two faces of the same coin. In this application, each concept plays the role of an annotation class (i.e., template slot) and each textual object can be associated with at most one concept, i.e., concepts are considered mutually exclusive. The system used in this learning problem is ATRE[3] [18] which solves the following learning problem:

Given
- a set of concepts $K_1, K_2, \ldots, K_r$ to be learned,
- a set of observations O described in a language $\mathcal{L}_O$,
- a background knowledge BK described in a language $\mathcal{L}_{BK}$,

---

[3] http://www.di.uniba.it/~malerba/software/atre

- a language of hypotheses $\mathcal{L}_H$ that defines the space of hypotheses S_H
- a user's preference criterion PC,

Find
a (possibly recursive) logical theory $T \in S_H$, defining the concepts $K_1, K_2, \ldots,$ K_r, such that T is complete and consistent with respect to the set of observations O and satisfies the preference criterion PC.

Both the language of hypotheses $\mathcal{L}_H$ and the language of background knowledge $\mathcal{L}_{BK}$ are limited to linked, range-restricted definite clauses [8]. Observations are represented as ground multiple-head clauses, called *objects*, which have a conjunction of literals in the head. Each object is associated with a unique object identifier (OID). The notion of multiple-head clauses in ATRE adapts the notion of *interpretation*, which is common to many relational data mining systems for efficiency reasons [9]. ATRE distinguishes objects from *examples*, which are described as pairs $\langle L, OID \rangle$, where L is a literal in the head of the object identified by OID. Examples can be considered *positive* or *negative*, according to the concept to be learned. For instance $\langle annotation(x10)=locus,$ $O_1 \rangle$ is a positive example of the concept annotation(X)=locus and a negative example of the concept annotation(X)=type. Actually, in this work, the set of concepts to be learned is defined by means of a set of literals of the type annotation(X)=annotation_class. No clause is generated for the concept annotation(X)=no_tag.

At the high-level ATRE implements a *sequential covering* algorithm [19]. A recursive theory T is built iteratively, starting from an empty theory T_0, and then adding a new clause at each iteration. In this way we obtain a sequence of theories:

$$T_0 = \emptyset, T_1, \ldots, T_i, T_{i+1}, \ldots, T_n = T$$

such that $T_{i+1} = T_i \cup \{C\}$ for some clause C and $LHM(T_i) \subseteq LHM(T_{i+1})$, where $LHM(T)$ denotes the least Herbrand model of a theory T. Let $pos(LHM(T))$ and $neg(LHM(T))$ be the number of positive and negative examples in $LHM(T)$, respectively. If we guarantee that:

1. $pos(LHM(T_i)) < pos(LHM(T_{i+1}))$, for each $i \in \{0, 1, \ldots, n-1\}$ and
2. $neg(LHM(T_i)) = 0$, for each $i \in \{0, 1, \ldots, n\}$,

then, after a finite number of iterations, a theory T, which is complete and consistent, is built. The first condition is guaranteed by selecting a positive example (or *seed*) $e^+ \notin LHM(T_i)$ of a concept K_j to be learned, and then by looking for a clause C, if any, such that $e^+ \in LHM(T_i \cup \{C\})$ (i.e., $pos(LHM(T_i \cup \{C\})) > pos(LHM(T_i))$). The second condition is more difficult to guarantee since the addition of a locally consistent clause C to a theory T_i does not preserve consistency of $T_i \cup \{C\}$ (non-monotonicity of the normal ILP setting). The approach followed in ATRE consists of simple syntactic changes in T_i, which eventually creates new *layers* [18].

The automated discovery of dependencies between concepts $K_1, K_2, \ldots, K_r$ is based on a variant of the sequential covering learning strategy, which is traditionally adopted by single concept learning systems that generate clauses with the same literal in the head at each iteration. In multiple concept learning, clauses generated at each iteration may refer to different concepts. In addition, the body of the clause generated at the i-th iteration may involve any concept $K_1, K_2, \ldots, K_r$ for which at least a clause has been added to the theory partially learned in previous iterations. In this way, dependencies between concepts can be generated.

At each iteration of the main loop of the sequential covering algorithm, clauses for distinct concepts are generated, and then one of them is picked. Since the generation of a clause depends on a seed, several seeds have to be chosen (if any, at least one seed per concept to be learned). Therefore, the search space is a forest of as many search-trees as the number of chosen seeds. Each search-tree is rooted with a unit clause and ordered by the generalization model adopted in ATRE (*generalized implication* [18]). The forest can be processed in parallel by as many concurrent tasks as the number of search-trees. Each task traverses the specialization hierarchy top-down through a sequential covering strategy, but synchronizes traversal with the other tasks at each level. Search proceeds toward deeper and deeper levels of the specialization hierarchies until at least a user-defined number of consistent clauses is found. Task synchronization is performed after that all "relevant" clauses at the same depth have been examined. A supervisor task decides whether the search should carry on or not on the basis of the results returned by the concurrent tasks. When the search is stopped, the supervisor selects the "best" consistent clause according to the user's preference criterion. This search strategy provides us with a solution to the problem of *interleaving* the induction of distinct concept definitions.

Actually, several special-purpose techniques have been designed specifically for the inductive synthesis of recursive logic theories. They are overviewed in [12]. As observed by Flener and Yilmaz, they are all non-incremental, i.e., the training examples are input all-at-once, therefore, the distinction of bottom-up versus top-down induction[4] does not really apply to them. Incremental techniques do not seem to be a promising research avenue for recursive theory learning (or, equivalently, for multiple concept learning), because they are often very sensitive to the ordering of the examples, which is not really adequate considering the fragile nature of recursive theories.

5   Experiments

We considered a data set of seventy-four papers concerning mithocondrial mutations selected for the annotation of HmtDB[5]. We considered the abstract of each paper and 228 target sentences out of 581 sentences. The total number of annotated tokens is 362, that is, 1.58 tokens per target sentence and 4.89 per

---

[4] In the bottom-up (top-down) approach the theory monotonically evolve from the maximally specific one (the maximally general one).

[5] The data set is available at
http://www.di.uniba.it/~malerba/software/atre/index.htm#Exp9

abstract. They correspond to about 9.3% of the total number of tokens that are described in the data set. The remaining tokens, that is 3004, are considered as *no tagged* tokens (i.e., as negative examples for all concepts to be learned).

The dataset is clearly imbalanced. However, it should be noted that the learning strategy implemented in ATRE is not affected by imbalanced data, since the goal is not to maximize the accuracy [23] but to generate consistent theories. Other systems that suffer from this problem may prove unsuitable for the task at hand, since they generate trivial classifiers.

Performances are evaluated by means of a 6-fold cross-validation, that is, the set of seventy-four abstracts is firstly divided into six folds (see Table 1), and then, for every fold, ATRE is trained on the remaining folds and tested on the hold-out fold. Results have been evaluated along several criteria. For each concept, we computed both the number of omission and commission errors and the value of precision and recall. *Omission* errors occur when annotations of tokens are missed, while *commission* errors occur when wrong annotations are "recommended" by some clause. The omission measure is reported as the ratio of the number of omission errors and the number of positive examples, while the commission measure as the ratio of the number of commission errors and the total number of examples. The *recall* measure is computed as the ratio of positive examples correctly annotated (i.e., true positives) and the sum of true positives and false negatives (i.e., omission errors). The *precision* measure is computed as the ratio of true positives and the sum of true positives and false positives (i.e., commission errors). Experimental results are reported in Table 2 for each fold. No omission error is reported for *type_position* when the third fold is held-out because there are no positive examples to test on.

Table 1. Distribution of examples per folds

Fold	# sentences	# locus	# position	# substitution	# type	# type_position	# no_tag	# literals in body
1	36	16	12	4	8	12	452	2424
2	40	27	13	2	5	4	546	2552
3	40	22	14	6	17	0	510	3098
4	34	16	6	5	17	23	517	3260
5	39	24	15	8	8	19	485	3083
6	27	14	6	2	6	31	494	3199
Total	228	119	66	27	61	89	3004	17793

The high variability among folds is mainly due to a heterogeneous distribution of examples that leads to different degrees of data sparseness. However, the percentage of commission errors is very low with respect to the percentage of omission errors (the system misses annotations rather than suggesting wrong annotations) independently of the fold. This means that learned rules are quite specific. By considering the complexity of learned theories (see Table 3), coverage rate can explain recall values. Best performances are obtained on the *substitution* class for which the system learns a more general and accurate

Table 2. Experimental results (percentage values): Average number and standard deviation of omission errors over positive ex., commission errors over negative ex., precision and recall

Fold	locus omiss.	locus comm.	position omiss.	position comm.	substitution omiss.	substitution comm.	type omiss.	type comm.	type_position omiss.	type_position comm.
1	68.750	0.205	83.333	0.203	75	0	25	0.202	91.667	0.203
2	70.370	0.516	61.538	0.168	100	0	20	0.332	100	0
3	54.545	0.548	21.429	0	66.667	0	29.412	0.181	–	0.351
4	43.750	0.176	50	1.038	60	0.345	17.647	0	82.609	1.070
5	41.667	0.562	20	0.184	100	0.727	62.500	0.545	73.684	0.372
6	85.714	3.154	50	0	100	0	33.333	0.366	77.419	0.575
Avg	60.799	0.860	47.717	0.266	83.611	0.179	31.315	0.271	–	0.428
St.D.	17.155	1.137	24.205	0.389	18.572	0.302	16.340	0.187	–	0.368
	Avg	St.D.	Avg	St.D.	Avg	St.D.	Avg	St.D.	Avg	St.D.
Prec.	77.305	18.387	81.355	25.258	87.778	19.052	65.972	23.632	74.009	37.073
Rec.	67.093	20.916	50.596	23.130	89.167	17.440	31.315	16.340	–	–

Table 3. Complexity of the learned theories: number of positive examples over number of learned clauses per concept and average values

Fold	locus	position	substitution	type	type_position
1	16/35	12/23	4/3	8/34	12/15
2	27/30	13/23	2/2	5/2	4/17
3	22/34	14/20	6/1	17/30	0/16
4	16/32	6/19	5/2	17/26	23/13
5	24/27	15/17	8/2	8/27	19/14
6	14/36	6/24	2/2	6/22	31/11
Avg	0.63	0.54	2.64	0.37	1.16

theory. Indeed, examples of this class are the most homogeneous and the pre-processing module is able to produce discriminative descriptions. Conversely, worst performances of the system are related to the *type* class for which the lowest value of coverage rate is reported. Some low recall values and overfitted theories are due to the preprocessing module which is not completely apt to manage the variety of morpho-syntactic variations on the same term that affect this application domain. By scanning the learned theories, we observe that for some annotation classes, namely *locus* and *type_position*, many clauses do take into account only lexical information specified by the predicate *word_to_string*. Actually, learning tasks for these two classes appear to be intrinsically more complex since we observe the highest percentage of commission errors despite the the highest percentage of positive examples available. As regards the percentage of omission errors, we notice that while it is positively correlated to the number of discovered clauses, it results uncorrelated to the number of positive examples.

We adopt the same experimental setting to run the system by disabling the search for recursive definitions in the space of clauses. In this experiment, the

90   M. Berardi and D. Malerba

system explores a specialization hierarchy for one concept at a time and learned theories are independently generated. Results are reported in Table 4. By comparing precision and recall values observed in the two experiments, we conclude that recursive theory learning improves performances for both *locus* and *type* classes, while it does not affect the results for the *position* and the *substitution* classes. This observation justifies the computational effort spent for learning recursive theories in this IE task.

Table 4. Experimental results obtained by disabling recursion (percentage values): Average number and standard deviation of omission errors over positive ex., commission errors over negative ex., precision and recall

Fold	locus		position		substitution		type		type_position	
	omiss.	comm.	omiss.	comm.	omiss.	comm.	omiss.	comm.	omiss.	comm.
1	75	0.205	83.33	0.203	75	0	75	0.202	100	0.203
2	59.26	0.516	61.54	0.168	100	0	80	0.332	100	0
3	63.64	0.731	21.43	0	66.67	0	35.29	0.181	–	0.351
4	62.50	0.880	50.00	1.038	60	0.345	29.41	0	91.30	0.891
5	41.67	0.562	20	0.184	100	0.727	62.50	0.545	63.16	0
6	64.29	2.597	50.00	0	100	0	50	0.366	64.52	0.575
Avg	61.058	0.915	47.717	0.266	83.611	0.179	55.368	0.271	–	0.337
St.D.	20.729	0.187	24.205	0.389	18.572	0.302	10.888	0.855	–	0.349
	Avg	St.D.	Avg	St.D.	Avg	St.D.	Avg	St.D.	Avg	St.D.
Prec.	72.836	18.568	81.355	25.258	87.778	19.052	76.766	16.041	76.672	38.299
Rec.	61.058	10.888	50.596	23.130	89.167	17.440	55.368	20.729	–	–

For the sake of completeness, some clauses learned by ATRE have been analyzed. Some of them follow:

```
annotation(X1)=type_position ← char_number_char(X1)=true
annotation(X1)=type_position ← tfollows_string_nn(X2)=trnaser,
    type_of(X1)=alphanumeric
annotation(X1)=position ← follows(X2,X1)=true,
    type_of(X1)=numeric, follows(X1,X3)=true,
    word_category(X3)=gene, word_to_string(X2)=position
```

The first clause states that X1 is labeled as *type_position* if it is an alphanumeric token composed by a char, a number and another char. This is one of the first clauses that ATRE adds to the learned theory and covers many examples. Actually, information on *type_position* of a mutation are tokens such as *A1262G*, that means that *A* is substituted by *G* at position 1262 of the DNA. The second clause concerns the same concept and it states that X1 is labeled as *type_position* if it is an alphanumeric token which is followed by the string **trnaser**. This matches patterns where *type_position* information occurs in the neighborhood of gene names (e.g., **trnaser**). The third clause states that X1 is labeled as *position* if it is a numeric token which succeeds the token "position" and precedes a token of the "gene" category. This clause captures patterns like "an A-to-G mutation at *position 3426 (tRNALeu)*".

Meaningful dependencies have been also discovered such as the following:

```
annotation(X1)=type ← follows(X1,X2)=true,
   word_frequency(X2) ∈ [8..140],
   follows(X3,X1)=true, annotation(X3)=substitution
```

It states that $X1$ is annotated as *type* if it precedes a frequent token and succeeds another token which has been annotated as *substitution*. Another example of discovered concept dependency is the following:

```
annotation(X1)=position ← follows(X2,X1)=true
   annotation(X2)=substitution, follows(X3,X1)=true,
   follows(X1,X4)=true, word_frequency(X4) ∈ [6..6],
   annotation(X3)=type, follows(X1,X5)=true,
   annotation(X5)=locus, word_frequency(X1) ∈ [1..2]
```

This clause states that $X1$ is annotated as *position* if it succeeds two tokens which have been annotated as *type* and *substitution*, respectively. Moreover it precedes a token occurring about 6 times in the abstract and that is followed by a *locus* annotation. Finally, $X1$ is quite infrequent in the abstract. It matches text portions like the following: "a G-to-A (X2) transition (X3) at nucleotide pair 14459 (X1), changed a moderately conserved alanine to a valine at NADH (X4) dehydrogenase subunit 6 (ND6) (X6) residue 72".

6   Conclusions

ILP provides appropriate computational solutions for problems posed by biomedical IE thanks to its adequacy to work with first-order logic representations of texts and to its suitability to take advantage of the abundant domain knowledge. *Template filling* tasks appear to be especially challenging for ILP, since they raise problems that are peculiar of link-learning tasks, where examples, in addition to their inherent relational structure, present relations to other examples [14]. Intuitively, template filling operations can be simplified when tagging of named entities is performed by considering some conceptual dependencies implicitly defined among entities of the same template. In this paper, we have proposed an application of recursive theory learning to a real-world IE task on the biomedical literature. Recursive patterns are discovered by inducing mutually dependent definitions of concepts by means of the ILP system ATRE. This system allows us to discover meaningful patterns among biomedical entities of interest. Results obtained on a limited number of documents show that high performances are obtained when descriptions of examples are safe from inconsistencies due to morpho-syntactic variations that are not completely handled by the preprocessing module. Moreover, results show that when learned theories can express mutual dependencies between concepts tagging performances improves.

As future work, further experiments on some recently made available biomedical datasets for ILP [7] will be conducted. We also plan to examine benefits of discovering template slot dependencies in reconstructing records of a complete template filling task. Finally, the application of a transductive framework [25] is worth to be investigated because of the high disproportion between the number of labeled documents and that of unlabeled documents available in IE tasks.

Acknowledgments

This work has been funded by the IBM Faculty Award 2004 received from IBM Corporation to promote collaborative research on "Knowledge Discovery Technologies for the development of a Gene and SNPs filtering engine". The authors would like to thank Prof. Marcella Attimonelli for her assistance in the use of HmtDB and Antonio Varlaro for his support in the use of the system ATRE.

References

1. Aitken, J.S.: Learning information extraction rules: An inductive logic programming approach. In: Proceedings of the 15th European Conference on Artificial Intelligence, pp. 355–359 (2002)
2. Attimonelli, M., Accetturo, M., Santamaria, M., Lascaro, D., Scioscia, G., Pappada, G., Tommaseo-Ponzetta, M., Torroni, A.: Hmtdb, a human mitochondrial genomic resource based on variability studies supporting population genetics and biomedical research. BMC Bioinformatics 1(6) (2005)
3. Berardi, M., Ceci, M., Malerba, D.: A hybrid strategy for knowledge extraction from biomedical documents. In: ICDAR workshop on "Neural Networks and Learning in Document Analysis and Recognition", Seoul, Korea (2005)
4. Califf, M.E., Mooney, R.J.: Relational learning of pattern-match rules for information extraction. In: AAAI '99/IAAI '99, pp. 328–334. American Association for Artificial Intelligence (1999)
5. Craven, M., Kumlien, J.: Constructing biological knowledge bases by extracting information from text sources. In: Proceedings of the Seventh International Conference on Intelligent Systems for Molecular Biology, pp. 77–86. AAAI Press, Stanford (1999)
6. Cunningham, H., Maynard, D., Bontcheva, K., Tablan, V.: Gate: A framework and graphical development environment for robust nlp tools and application. In: Proc. of the 40th Anniversary Meeting of the Association for Computational Linguistics (ACL'02), Philadelphia, USA (2002)
7. Cussens, J., Nedellec, C(ed.): Proceedings of the 4th ICML Workshop on Learning Language in Logic (LLL05), Bonn, Germany (2005)
8. Cussens, J., Nedellec, C. (ed.): In: Proceedings of the 4th ICML Workshop on Learning Language in Logic (LLL05), Bonn, Germany (2005)
9. Džeroski, S., Lavrač, N.: Relational Data Mining. Springer-Verlag, Heidelberg (2001)
10. Dzeroski, S., Cussens, J., Manandhar, S.: An introduction to inductive logic programming and learning language in logic. In: Cussens, J., Džeroski, S. (eds.) Learning Language in Logic. LNCS (LNAI), vol. 1925, pp. 3–35. Springer, Heidelberg (2000)

11. Ferilli, S., Fanizzi, N., Semeraro, G.: Learning logic models for automated text categorization. In: Esposito, F. (ed.) AI*IA 2001: Advances in Artificial Intelligence. LNCS (LNAI), vol. 2175, pp. 81–86. Springer, Heidelberg (2001)
12. Flener, P., Yilmaz, S.: Inductive synthesis of recursive logic programs: achievements and prospects. Journal of Logic Programming, Special Issue on Synthesis, Transformation, and Analysis 41(2-3), 141–195 (1999)
13. Freitag, D.: Toward general-purpose learning for information extraction. In: Proceedings. of the 17th int. conf. on Computational linguistics, pp. 404–408, Morristown, NJ, USA, Association for Computational Linguistics (1998)
14. Goadrich, M., Oliphant, L., Shavlik, J.W.: Learning ensembles of first-order clauses for recall-precision curves: A case study in biomedical information extraction. In: Proceedings of the Fourteenth International Conference on Inductive Logic Programming, pp. 98–115 (2004)
15. Hirschman, L., Yeh, A., Blaschke, C., Valencia, A.: Overview of biocreative: critical assessment of information extraction for biology. Bioinformatics 6 (2005)
16. Junker, M., Sintek, M., Rink, M.: Learning for text categorization and information extraction with ilp. In: Learning Language in Logic, pp. 247–258 (1999)
17. Lloyd, J.W.: Foundations of Logic Programming, 2nd edn. Springer-Verlag, Heidelberg (1987)
18. Malerba, D.: Learning recursive theories in the normal ilp setting. Fundamenta Informaticae 57(1), 39–77 (2003)
19. Mitchell, T.M.: Machine Learning. McGraw-Hill, New York (1997)
20. Mooney, R.: Learning for semantic interpretation: Scaling up without dumbing down. In: Cussens, J. (ed.) Proc. of the 1st Workshop on Learning Language in Logic, Bled, Slovenia, pp. 7–15 (1999),
    citeseer.ist.psu.edu/mooney99learning.html
21. Loveland, D.W. (ed.): Machine Learning for Information Extraction in Genomics - State of the art and perspectives. LNCS, vol. 138. Springer, Heidelberg (1982)
22. Porter, M.F.: Readings in information retrieval, chapter An algorithm for suffix stripping, pp. 313–316 (1997)
23. Provost, F.: Learning with imbalanced data sets (invited paper). In: Proc. of AAAI'2000 Workshop on Imbalanced Data Sets (2000)
24. Shatkay, H., Feldman, R.: Mining the biomedical literature in the genomic era: an overview. Journal of Computational Biology 10, 821–855 (2003)
25. Vapnik, V.: Statistical Learning Theory. Wiley, New York (1998)

Towards Learning Non-recursive LPADs by Transforming Them into Bayesian Networks

Hendrik Blockeel and Wannes Meert

Katholieke Universiteit Leuven, Department of Computer Science
Celestijnenlaan 200A, 3001 Leuven, Belgium

Abstract. Logic programs with annotated disjunctions, or LPADs, are an elegant knowledge representation formalism that can be used to combine first order logical and probabilistic inference. While LPADs can be written manually, one can also consider the question of how to learn them from data. Methods for learning restricted classes of LPADs have been proposed before, but the problem of learning any kind of LPADs was still open. In this paper, we describe a reduction of non-recursive LPADs with a finite Herbrand universe to Bayesian networks. This reduction makes it possible to learn such LPADs using standard learning techniques for Bayesian networks. Thus the class of learnable LPADs is extended.

1 Introduction

Logic programs with annotated disjunctions, LPADs for short, have been introduced by Vennekens, Verbaeten and Bruynooghe (2004) as a knowledge representation formalism that can be used to combine probabilistic and logic inference. It is a simple and elegant formalism: LPADs are easy to write and interpret, and have formally defined semantics. But while Vennekens et al. define the syntax and semantics of LPADs and illustrate their broad applicability, they do not discuss learning in this framework. Yet learning LPADs is of interest: because LPADs express explicitly the causal structure of stochastic processes, learning them amounts to explicitating this causal structure from observations. It is well known that Bayesian networks, for instance, do not exhibit this property: edges in a Bayesian network do not necessarily indicate a causal relationship.

Riguzzi (2004) proposes an algorithm for learning LPADs. However, only a subclass of LPADs can be learned with his method, and Riguzzi does not discuss whether the subclass is semantically equivalent to the class of all LPADs, that is, whether for each LPAD a semantically equivalent LPAD in the subclass exists.

In this paper we introduce two novel subclasses of LPADs: 1-compliant LPADs and CP-compliant LPADs. We show that each LPAD can be rewritten as a semantically equivalent 1-compliant LPAD; that each 1-compliant LPAD is CP-compliant; and that there is a transformation from (non-recursive, finite-universe) CP-compliant LPADs to Bayesian networks that preserves the LPADs semantics and includes a one-to-one mapping between the LPAD parameters and the Bayesian net parameters.

S. Muggleton, R. Otero, and A. Tamaddoni-Nezhad (Eds.): ILP 2006, LNAI 4455, pp. 94–108, 2007.

As a consequence, the many advanced techniques for learning Bayesian networks (both parameters and structure) can be exploited for learning a broad class of LPADs. This class includes LPADs that were not previously learnable.

In the following, we first give the intuitions behind the method (Section 2). Then we treat it more formally: we recall several definitions from the original LPAD paper in Section 3, introduce CP-compliant LPADs in Section 4, and discuss the transformation of LPADs into CP-compliant LPADs in Section 5. In Section 6 we discuss the transformation to Bayesian networks. We briefly discuss learning in Section 7 and wrap up in Section 8.

Note that this work focuses on a specific formal relationship between LPADs and Bayesian networks that can be exploited for learning LPADs. There is no experimental study of learning techniques. Obviously, through the proposed reduction, many well-studied techniques for learning Bayesian networks become available for learning LPADs. Which of these work best in this specific context is a subject for later work.

2   Intuitions

An LPAD can be seen as a set of if-then-rules, where each rule has several possible conclusions, each of which has a certain probability assigned to it. The rule makes exactly one of the conclusions true with the associated probability. For instance,

$$(heads(C) : 0.5) \vee (tails(C) : 0.5) \leftarrow cointoss(C)$$

expresses that if we toss a coin and call the result C, C is heads or tails each with 50% probability.

While in principle the probabilities in the head add up to one, it is possible to write a rule where the sum is less than one; there is then an implicit, anonymous, proposition that is made true with the remaining probability. Thus,

$$(result(C, 6) : 0.167) \leftarrow dieroll(C)$$

expresses that a die roll has 16.7% probability to result in a six. There is then an 83.3% probability to have some other result, but we are not interested in what those other results are.

Multiple rules in an LPAD may lead to the same conclusions. Take, for instance, the following logic program

$$wet \leftarrow gone\_swimming$$
$$wet \leftarrow rain$$

which expresses that if I have gone swimming or if it is raining, my hair is wet.

If we assume that the rules do not hold in 100% of the cases, for instance, I dry my hair immediately after swimming in 30% of the cases, and I use an umbrella when it is raining in 60% of the cases, then we could indicate this as:

$$wet : 0.7 \leftarrow gone\_swimming$$
$$wet : 0.4 \leftarrow rain$$

The numbers associated with *wet* now indicate the probability that the event mentioned in the rule body causes my hair to get wet. We will use the convention that when the probability is 1, it may be omitted. The LPAD rule is then equivalent to a regular logic programming clause.

It is part of the semantics of LPADs (see Section 3) that each rule *independently of all other rules* makes one of its head atoms true when triggered. LPADs are therefore particularly suitable for describing models that contain a number of independent stochastic events or causal processes [4]. Consequently, learning LPADs amounts to discovering the causal structure of possibly complex processes.

It may be tempting to interpret the numbers as the conditional probability of *wet* given the body, e.g., $Pr(wet|rain) = 0.4$. However, this would be incorrect. The conditional probability that my hair is wet, given that it is raining, is higher than 0.4, because there is a second possible cause for my hair getting wet, namely the swimming. To compute this conditional probability, we need information on the probability that I have gone swimming. For instance, with

wet : 0.7 ← *gone_swimming*
wet : 0.4 ← *rain*
gone_swimming : 0.1.
rain : 0.3.

we can say that $Pr(wet|rain) = 0.4 + 0.1 * 0.7 * 0.6 = 0.442$: the rain causes my hair to get wet with probability 0.4 but there is also a probability of 0.1 that I have gone swimming, and hence a probability of 0.1*0.7*0.6 that my hair is wet not because of the rain but because of swimming.

Thus, for head atoms that occur in multiple rules, the relationship between the mentioned probabilities and conditional probabilities is somewhat complex. But it is not unintuitive. The meaning of the probabilities mentioned in the rules is quite simple: they reflect the probability that the body *causes* the head to become true. This is different from the conditional probability that the head is true given the body, but among the two, *the former is the more natural one to express*. Indeed, the former is local knowledge: we can estimate the probability that *rain* causes *wet* without considering any other possible causes for *wet*. To estimate $Pr(wet|rain)$, we need global knowledge: we need to know all possible causes for *wet*, the probability of them occurring, and how they interact with *rain*.

Arguing that the probabilities in the rules are unintuitive when they do not reflect conditional probabilities, some researchers have proposed to focus on LPADs where all probabilities are conditional probabilities. Let us call such LPADs *CP-compliant* LPADs (CP for conditional probabilities). Riguzzi [3] proves that, when in an LPAD any two rules sharing head atoms have mutually exclusive bodies (i.e., there exist no interpretations for which both bodies are true; we call such an LPAD *ME-compliant*), then it is CP-compliant. Exploiting this property, Riguzzi proposes a learning algorithm for ME-compliant LPADs.

The above example shows that non-ME-compliant LPADs are by no means far-fetched; they may express knowledge in a straightforward and interpretable way. For that reason, limiting ourselves to ME-compliant LPADs seems undesirable.

In this paper we show that *any* LPAD, ME-compliant or not, can be rewritten into a CP-compliant LPAD. If this LPAD is non-recursive and has a finite Herbrand universe, it can in turn be translated into a Bayesian network[1] in which the conditional probability tables contain exactly the conditional probabilities occurring in the CP-compliant LPAD. As a consequence, if we can learn such Bayesian networks, we have a method for learning any non-recursive LPAD with a finite Herbrand universe.

The conversion from LPAD to CP-compliant LPAD goes as follows. To avoid that head atoms occur in the head of multiple rules, we annotate them with an index that uniquely identifies their rule. To preserve the semantics, we add regular logic programming clauses (or, LPAD rules with one head atom with annotation 1) defining the original predicates in terms of the indexed predicates. Thus, the LPAD

$$wet : 0.7 \leftarrow gone\_swimming$$
$$wet : 0.4 \leftarrow rain$$

is turned into the semantically equivalent LPAD

$$wet_1 : 0.7 \leftarrow gone\_swimming$$
$$wet_2 : 0.4 \leftarrow rain$$
$$wet \leftarrow wet_1$$
$$wet \leftarrow wet_2$$

LPADs resulting from this conversion have the property that head atoms can only be shared by multiple rules if their annotation is 1; we call such LPADs 1-compliant. We prove in this paper that the conversion preserves the LPAD's semantics and that all 1-compliant LPADS are CP-compliant.

A non-recursive CP-compliant LPAD can be converted into a Bayesian network as follows. First, the LPAD is grounded; from now on we refer only to the ground LPAD. The Bayesian network will have one variable for each atom in the ground LPAD, *except the indexed atoms*: since all atoms with index i are mutually exclusive, we can represent them with a single variable C_i instead of introducing a separate boolean variable for each of them. C_i takes on value j if rule i selects its j'th head atom, and 0 if no listed atom is selected. For each C_i we then have one node in the Bayesian network, which has as parent nodes the body atoms of rule i, and its CPD reflects that $C_i = j$ with the corresponding probability if all body literals are true, and $C_i = 0$ otherwise. The original head atoms are also nodes in the Bayesian network: if h occurs as the j'th head atom of rule i, then h has C_i as a parent and its CPD reflects that h is true whenever $C_i = j$.

The CP-compliant LPAD just mentioned is shown as a Bayesian network in Fig. 1.

---

[1] A recursive LPAD would give rise to cycles in the Bayesian network, which are not allowed. An infinite Herbrand universe would give rise to an infinite Bayesian net.

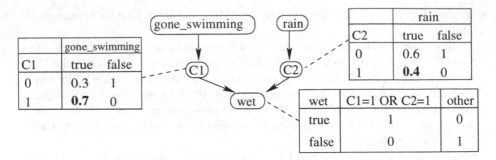

Fig. 1. A Bayesian network corresponding to our example CP-compliant LPAD. The probabilities in boldface are those occurring explicitly in the LPAD.

In the remainder of this text, we define the transformation more formally, show that it always yields CP-compliant (though not ME-compliant) LPADs, and show how to construct from a CP-compliant LPAD a semantically equivalent Bayesian network. Learning (non-recursive, finite-universe) LPADs will thus be formally reduced to learning Bayesian networks, for which many techniques already exist.

3   LPADs: Syntax and Semantics

We start with a brief overview of the syntax and semantics of LPADs, as given by Vennekens et al. [5]. We assume familiarity with standard logic programming terminology (atoms, literals, Herbrand universe, Herbrand base, variable substitutions, groundings, etc.). See Lloyd [1] for an introduction on this.

An LPAD consists of a set of rules of the following form:

$$(h_1 : \alpha_1) \vee (h_2 : \alpha_2) \vee \ldots \vee (h_n : \alpha_n) \leftarrow b_1, b_2, \ldots, b_m.$$

with h_i atoms and b_i literals in the logical sense, all $\alpha_i \in [0, 1]$, and $\sum_{i=1}^{n} \alpha_i = 1$. We call the set of all $(h_i : \alpha_i)$ the head of the rule c, denoted $head(c)$, and the set of all b_i the body, denoted $body(c)$. If the head contains only one atom $h : 1$, we may write it as h.

The semantics of an LPAD is defined using its grounding. We denote the set of all ground LPADs with $\mathcal{P}_\mathcal{G}$. Given an LPAD P, $\mathcal{I}_P$ is the set of all Herbrand interpretations of P. The Herbrand base of P is denoted H_P. The semantics of an LPAD is defined as a probability distribution on $\mathcal{I}_P$, as follows.

Definition 1. *Let $P \in \mathcal{P}_\mathcal{G}$. An admissible probability distribution π on $\mathcal{I}_P$ is a mapping from $\mathcal{I}_P$ to $[0, 1]$ such that $\sum_{I \in \mathcal{I}_P} \pi(I) = 1$.*

Definition 2. *Let $P \in \mathcal{P}_\mathcal{G}$. A selection σ is a function that selects one pair $(h : \alpha)$ from each rule of P, i.e., $\sigma : P \to (H_P \times [0, 1])$ such that for each $c \in P$, $\sigma(c) \in head(c)$. With $\sigma(c) = h : \alpha$, we also write $\sigma_{atom} = h$ and $\sigma_{prob} = \alpha$. The set of all selections σ is denoted by $\mathcal{S}_P$.*

Definition 3. *Let $P \in \mathcal{P}_\mathcal{G}$ and $\sigma \in \mathcal{S}_P$. The instance P_σ chosen by σ is defined as $P_\sigma = \{\sigma_{atom}(c) \leftarrow body(c) | c \in P\}$.*

Definition 4. *Let $P \in \mathcal{P}_\mathcal{G}$ and $\sigma \in \mathcal{S}_P$. The probability of σ is*

$$C_\sigma = \prod_{c \in P} \sigma_{prob}(c).$$

This definition of the probability of a selection implies that the selection of a head atom in one rule is stochastically independent from the selection of head atoms in all other rules.

The following definition defines the LPADs to which we can give meaning:

Definition 5. *An LPAD P is sound iff for each $\sigma \in \mathcal{S}_P$, the well founded model of P_σ, denoted $WFM(P_\sigma)$, is two-valued.*

Since we only consider two-valued well-founded models, we can represent the well-founded model as a single interpretation. We will use this convention in the remainder of the paper.

Given an interpretation I, we denote the set of all $\sigma \in \mathcal{S}_P$ for which $WFM(P_\sigma) = I$ as $\mathcal{S}_P^I$. The semantics of a sound LPAD is then defined as follows.

Definition 6. *Let $P \in \mathcal{P}_\mathcal{G}$ be a sound LPAD. For each of its interpretations $I \in \mathcal{I}_P$, the probability $\pi_P^*(I)$ assigned by P to I is the sum of the probabilities of all selections that lead to I, i.e.,*

$$\pi_P^*(I) = \sum_{\sigma \in \mathcal{S}_P^I} C_\sigma.$$

Vennekens et al. [5] prove that if P is a sound LPAD in $\mathcal{P}_\mathcal{G}$, then π_P^* is an admissible probability distribution over $\mathcal{I}_P$. This defines the semantics of any sound LPAD.

We next recall the definition of the probability of a logic formula, again from Vennekens et al.

Definition 7. *For any logic formula ϕ, the set of Herbrand models of ϕ is denoted and defined as*

$$\mathcal{I}_P^\phi = \{I \in \mathcal{I}_P | I \models \phi\}.$$

Definition 8. *Let P be a sound LPAD in $\mathcal{P}_\mathcal{G}$. The probability of ϕ according to P, denoted $\pi_P^*(\phi)$, is defined as*

$$\pi_P^*(\phi) = \sum_{I \in \mathcal{I}_P^\phi} \pi_P^*(I).$$

We add the notion of conditional probability:

Definition 9. *Let P be a sound LPAD in $\mathcal{P}_\mathcal{G}$. The conditional probability of ϕ given ψ, according to P, is denoted and defined as*

$$\pi_P^*(\phi|\psi) = \pi_P^*(\phi \wedge \psi)/\pi_P^*(\psi)$$

if $\pi_P^*(\psi) > 0$ (and undefined otherwise).

When P is clear from the context, we will often denote $\pi_P^*(\phi)$ as $Pr(\phi)$ and $\pi_P^*(\phi|\psi)$ as $Pr(\phi|\psi)$.

As said before, one should take care not to interpret α_i $Pr(h_i|B)$, the conditional probability of h_i given the body B. However, LPADs generally do have the property that $Pr(h_i|B) \geq \alpha_i$ [5].

4   CP-Compliant LPADs

Riguzzi [3] presents a learning algorithm for a subclass of LPADs, which we will refer to as ME-compliant LPADs. The definition is as follows.

Definition 10 (ME-compliant LPADs). *An ME-compliant LPAD is an LPAD in which for each two rules $H_1 \leftarrow B_1$ and $H_2 \leftarrow B_2$ it holds that (a) H_1 and H_2 do not share any atoms, or (b) B_1 and B_2 are mutually exclusive.*

Under these conditions, it holds for each annotated head atom $h_i : \alpha_i$ in a rule that $Pr(h_i|B) = \alpha_i$ with B the body of the rule. We call LPADs fulfilling this property CP-compliant.

Definition 11 (CP-compliant LPADs). *A CP-compliant LPAD is an LPAD in which for each rule $H \leftarrow B$ it holds that $\forall (h_i : \alpha_i) \in H : Pr(h_i|B) = \alpha_i$.*

CP-compliance is important because conditional probabilities can easily be estimated from data: if an LPAD is CP-compliant, then its parameters can be estimated equally easily. This property is exploited by Riguzzi to learn the α_i parameters of ME-compliant LPADs from data.

Now we introduce a different subclass of LPADs, which (as we shall prove) also has the property that all parameters to be estimated are conditional probabilities. We call this subclass 1-compliant LPADs. The name refers to the property that each head atom either occurs only in the head of a single rule, or its annotation is 1 in all the heads where it occurs.

Definition 12 (1-compliant LPADs). *A 1-compliant LPAD is an LPAD in which for each atom h that occurs in the head of a rule, it holds that either h occurs in only one rule (i.e., it cannot be unified with any atom in the head of any other rule), or it always occurs with an annotation of 1.*

1-compliant LPADs are of the same form as the transformed LPAD we mentioned in our intuitive treatment.

In the syntactic sense, our CP-compliant LPADs are neither a subclass nor a superclass of Riguzzi's ME-compliant LPADs. Riguzzi allows several rules to share head atoms as long as their bodies are mutually exclusive, which is generally not allowed in CP-compliant LPADs. On the other hand, we allow rules to share head atoms even if their bodies are not mutually exclusive, as long as the probabilities of these atoms are one.

Riguzzi shows that ME-compliant LPADs are CP-compliant. We now show that 1-compliant LPADs are CP-compliant.

Table 1. Algorithm for transforming LPADs into CP-compliant LPADs

> **function** Transform(P: LPAD) **returns** CP-compliant LPAD
> $P' := \emptyset$
>   **for each** rule $(h_{i1} : \alpha_{i1} \vee \ldots \vee h_{in_i} : \alpha_{in_i} \leftarrow B_i) \in P$:
>   let h'_{ij} be h_{ij} with its predicate name p changed into p_i
> $P' := P' \cup \{h'_{ij} : \alpha_{i1} \vee \ldots \vee h'_{in_i} : \alpha_{in_i} \leftarrow B_i\}$
> $P' := P' \cup \bigcup_{j=1}^{n_i} \{h_{ij} \leftarrow h'_{ij}\}$
>   **return** P'

Theorem 1. *In a 1-compliant LPAD, for each rule of the form* $h_1 : \alpha_1 \vee \ldots \vee h_n : \alpha_n \leftarrow B$, $Pr(h_i|B) = \alpha_i$. *That is, each* α_i *can be interpreted as the conditional probability that its atom is true, given that the rule body is true.*

Proof. According to the definition of a 1-compliant LPAD, for each $h_i : \alpha_i$ in a rule head with body B, it holds that either (a) h_i does not occur in any other rule heads, or (b) $\alpha_i = 1$.

Case (a): $Pr(h_i|B) = \alpha_i$ follows from Riguzzi's proof of Theorem 1 [3]. While the theorem states that for any rule, $\alpha_i = Pr(h_i|B)$ if all the rules (in the whole LPAD) sharing head atoms have mutually exclusive bodies, the proof in fact just exploits the mutual exclusion property for the rule for which the equality is proven. Case (a) implies this property.

Case (b): We know from the definition of LPADs and their semantics that $\alpha_i \leq Pr(h_i|B) \leq 1$. If $\alpha_i = 1$, this implies $Pr(h_i|B) = \alpha_i$.

5   Transforming LPADs to 1-Compliant LPADs

An algorithm for transforming LPADs into 1-compliant LPADs is shown in Table 1. The algorithm just adds an index i to the predicate names of all the head atoms of each rule c_i, and adds rules stating that the original (unindexed) version of the atom must be true if its indexed version is true.

Example 1. Consider the following LPAD:

$$(a : 0.5) \vee (b : 0.5) \leftarrow c$$
$$(b : 0.2) \vee (c : 0.8) \leftarrow d$$

The i-th rule is transformed by just adding an index i to each atom in the head:

$$(a_1 : 0.5) \vee (b_1 : 0.5) \leftarrow c$$
$$(b_2 : 0.2) \vee (c_2 : 0.8) \leftarrow d$$

and the following rules are added:

$$a \leftarrow a_1$$
$$b \leftarrow b_1$$
$$b \leftarrow b_2$$
$$c \leftarrow c_2$$

Theorem 2. *The transformation yields a 1-compliant LPAD.*

Proof. The resulting program consists of two types of rules: rules with indexed atoms in the head (type 1 rules) and rules with original atoms in the head (type 2 rules). A type 1 rule cannot share a head atom with any other rule: not with a type 2 rule because it has only indexed atoms in the head (and type 2 rules contain only original atoms), and not with other type 1 rules because the indexes differ. Only type 2 rules can therefore share head atoms, but they all have a single head atom with annotation 1. Consequently, the conditions for 1-compliance are fulfilled.

We now prove that the transformation preserves the semantics of the LPAD, in the sense that any logic formula ϕ defined over the original LPAD has the same probability according to the transformed LPAD.

Theorem 3. *Let $P \in \mathcal{P}_\mathcal{G}$ be a sound LPAD, and let P' be the transformed version of P. For each formula ϕ defined over P,*

$$\pi_P^*(\phi) = \pi_{P'}^*(\phi)$$

Proof. First, we expand the left hand side of the equation:

$$\pi_P^*(\phi) = \sum_{I \in \mathcal{I}_P^\phi} \sum_{\sigma \in \mathcal{S}_P^I} \prod_{r \in P} \sigma_{prob}(r)$$

Define $\mathcal{S}_P^\phi$ as the set of all selections σ for which $WFM(P_\sigma) \models \phi$; that is, $\mathcal{S}_P^\phi = \bigcup \{\mathcal{S}_P^I | I \models \phi\}$. We can then shorten the above expression to

$$\pi_P^*(\phi) = \sum_{\sigma \in \mathcal{S}_P^\phi} \prod_{r \in P} \sigma_{prob}(r)$$

Similarly, for the right hand side we have

$$\pi_{P'}^*(\phi) = \sum_{\sigma \in \mathcal{S}_{P'}^\phi} \prod_{r \in P'} \sigma_{prob}(r)$$

So we need to prove

$$\sum_{\sigma \in \mathcal{S}_P^\phi} \prod_{r \in P} \sigma_{prob}(r) = \sum_{\sigma \in \mathcal{S}_{P'}^\phi} \prod_{r \in P'} \sigma_{prob}(r) \tag{1}$$

We can define a one-to-one correspondence between $\mathcal{S}_P$ and $\mathcal{S}_{P'}$ as follows. Let $\sigma \in \mathcal{S}_P$ and $\sigma' \in \mathcal{S}_{P'}$ be such that

$$\sigma(P) = \{(h_{1s_1} : \alpha_{1s_1}), \ldots, (h_{ms_m} : \alpha_{ms_m})\}$$

$$\sigma'(P') = \left\{ (h'_{1s_1} : \alpha_{1s_1}), \ldots, (h'_{ms_m} : \alpha_{ms_m}), \bigcup_{i=1}^{m} \bigcup_{j=1}^{n_i} \{h_{ij}\} \right\}$$

$(a : 0.3) \vee (b : 0.4) \vee (c : 0.3) \leftarrow B_1$	$(a_1 : 0.3) \vee (b_1 : 0.4) \vee (c_1 : 0.3) \leftarrow B_1$
$(a : 0.1) \vee (d : 0.5) \vee (e : 0.1) \leftarrow B_2$	$(a_2 : 0.1) \vee (d_2 : 0.5) \vee (e_2 : 0.1) \leftarrow B_2$
$(d : 0.5) \vee (f : 0.5) \leftarrow B_3$	$(d_3 : 0.5) \vee (f_3 : 0.5) \leftarrow B_3$
	$\underline{a} \leftarrow a_1$
	$\underline{a} \leftarrow a_2$
	$\underline{b} \leftarrow b_1$
	$\underline{c} \leftarrow c_1$
	$\underline{d} \leftarrow d_2$
	$\underline{d} \leftarrow d_3$
	$\underline{e} \leftarrow e_2$
	$\underline{f} \leftarrow f_3$

Fig. 2. An illustration of the one-to-one correspondence between selections in P and in P'. For the program P to the left, the 1-compliant version P' is shown to the right. For each selection σ for P there is precisely one selection σ' for P' according to the defined correspondence, and they have the properties that the probabilities of σ and σ' are equal and WFM($P'_{\sigma'}$) restricted to H_P equals WFM(P_σ).

where m is the number of rules, n_i is the number of head atoms in rule i and $s_i \in [1, n_i]$. This is clearly a one-to-one correspondence because both σ and σ' map one-to-one to a vector $(s_1, s_2, \ldots, s_m)$. Fig. 2 illustrates this correspondence more graphically.

To prove Equation 1, it suffices to show that (1) this one-to-one-correspondence carries over to $\mathcal{S}_P^\phi$ and $\mathcal{S}_{P'}^\phi$, that is, $\sigma \in \mathcal{S}_P^\phi \Leftrightarrow \sigma' \in \mathcal{S}_{P'}^\phi$, and (2) the probabilities associated with corresponding selections are the same.

(1) We need to prove $\sigma \in \mathcal{S}_P^\phi \Rightarrow \sigma' \in \mathcal{S}_{P'}^\phi$ and $\sigma \notin \mathcal{S}_P^\phi \Rightarrow \sigma' \notin \mathcal{S}_{P'}^\phi$. But since $\sigma \notin \mathcal{S}_P^\phi$ is equivalent to $\sigma \in \mathcal{S}_P^{\neg\phi}$, it suffices to prove that the first implication holds for any formula ϕ.

So assume $\sigma \in \mathcal{S}_P^\phi$; this implies there is an I such that $\sigma \in \mathcal{S}_P^I$ and $I \models \phi$. Now define $I' = I \cup \{h'_{ij} | h_{ij} \in \sigma_{atom}(P)\}$. We will prove that (1a) $\sigma' \in S_{P'}(I')$ and (1b) $I' \models \phi$; from this follows $\sigma' \in \mathcal{S}_{P'}^\phi$.

(1a) σ' is defined in such a way that P_σ contains $h_{ij} \leftarrow B_i$ if and only if $P'_{\sigma'}$ contains the clauses $\{h_{ij} \leftarrow h'_{ij}, h'_{ij} \leftarrow B_i\}$. Thus, whenever h_{ij} can be derived in P_σ, it can be derived in $P'_{\sigma'}$, and vice versa. In addition, whenever h_{ij} can be derived in P_σ, h'_{ij} can be derived in $P'_{\sigma'}$. This proves that $WFM(P_\sigma) = I$ if and only if $WFM(P'_{\sigma'}) = I'$, in other words, $\sigma \in \mathcal{S}_P^I \Leftrightarrow \sigma' \in S_{P'}(I')$.

(1b) The formula ϕ refers only to original (non-indexed) predicates. Since I', restricted to non-indexed predicates, equals I, $I' \models \phi$ if and only if $I \models \phi$.

This proves the one-to-one correspondence between $\mathcal{S}_P^\phi$ and $\mathcal{S}_{P'}^\phi$.

(2) If we multiply all the σ_{prob} as defined by σ and σ' we get:

$$\prod_{r \in P} \sigma_{prob}(r) = \alpha_{1s_1} \ldots \alpha_{ms_m}$$

$$\prod_{r \in P'} \sigma'_{prob}(r) = \alpha_{1s_1} \ldots \alpha_{ms_m} \cdot \underbrace{1 \ldots 1}_{\sum_{i=1}^m n_i \text{ times}}$$

Thus the probability of σ and σ' is the same. This concludes the proof.

Corollary 1. *Any LPAD can be transformed into a 1-compliant, and therefore CP-compliant, LPAD.*

Corollary 2. *ME-compliant LPADs can be transformed into 1-compliant LPADs.*

6   A Reduction to Bayesian Networks

We now turn to the transformation of a 1-compliant LPAD into a Bayesian network. From here on we assume LPADs to be non-recursive and have a finite Herbrand universe.

First, the LPAD needs to be grounded. From here one, when we refer to the LPAD, we mean the ground LPAD.

The nodes in the Bayesian network are the original LPAD atoms (which become boolean variables) as well as so-called choice variables C_i (which are included instead of the indexed atoms, as explained before). Each C_i takes integer values in the interval $[0, n_i]$ where n_i is the number of head atoms of LPAD rule i. When $C_i = j$, this means the j'th atom of rule i has been selected. $C_i = 0$ will be used to denote that no listed head atom was selected, which may be either because the rule body is false, or because an anonymous atom was selected.

The conditional probability distribution (CPD) of each C_i has a very simple structure, represented by the following function:

$P(C_i = j | \text{all parents true}) = \alpha_j$, for all $j > 0$
$P(C_i = 0 | \text{all parents true}) = 1 - \sum_j \alpha_j$
$P(C_i = 0 | \text{not all parents true}) = 1$
$P(C_i = j | \text{not all parents true}) = 0$, for all $j > 0$

The CPD of a non-choice variable always expresses a logical or, since the second part of our LPAD is essentially a standard logic program. For instance, in the example, b is true if $C_1 = 2$ or $C_2 = 1$. This can be represented with a simple CPD function:

$P(h_i = true | \text{all parents false}) = 0$
$P(h_i = true | \text{not all parents false}) = 1$

(the probabilities for $h_i = false$ are the complements).

Example 2. For the LPAD of Example 1, which in 1-compliant form became

$a_1 : 0.5 \vee b_1 : 0.5 \leftarrow c$
$b_2 : 0.2 \vee c_2 : 0.8 \leftarrow d$
$a \leftarrow a_1$
$b \leftarrow b_1$
$b \leftarrow b_2$
$c \leftarrow c_2,$

the corresponding Bayesian net is shown in Fig.3.

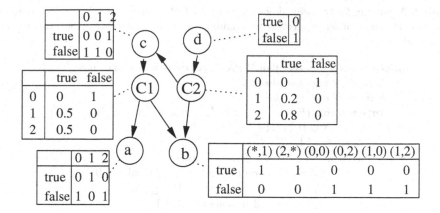

Fig. 3. Bayesian net corresponding to the example LPAD

The algorithm to produce a Bayesian net from a 1-compliant LPAD is shown in Table 2.

Thus, given an LPAD with certain parameters, it can be transformed into a Bayesian network with a specific structure, consisting of two kinds of variables: atom variables and choice variables. The CPD's for the atom variables have a fixed structure that is independent of the probabilities in the LPAD; they always express a logical or. The CPD's for the choice variables have a fixed structure and contain only 0's, 1's, and the LPAD probabilities α_{ij}.

7 Perspectives on Learning LPADs

The previous sections contain the main contribution of the paper. In the following we briefly discuss the perspectives on learning LPADs that our results entail.

7.1 Learning the Parameters of an LPAD

Given an LPAD with unknown values for the probabilities, we can learn these probabilities using the following approach: (1) ground the LPAD; (2) reduce the ground LPAD to a Bayesian net, as outlined above; (3) learn the CPDs of the Bayesian net, taking into account constraints on these CPDs; (4) map these CPDs onto the LPAD probabilities.

Our previous discussion leaves only step 3 to be discussed. First, note that the Bayesian net contains unobserved variables: indeed, none of the C_i are observed in the data. There are well-known procedures for parameter estimation in such Bayesian nets, e.g., EM-MAP [2].

Second, we want the CPDs that are being learned to have a specific structure. As explained before, the CPDs of the atom variables are fixed (they express a logical "or"). In the CPDs of the choice variables C_i, only one row of values is to be learned, the other rows contain 0 and 1. To learn these CPDs, it suffices to

Table 2. Algorithm for transforming non-recursive CP-compliant LPADs into Bayesian networks. By convention, h_{ij} refers to original atoms in this description, and h'_{ij} to indexed atoms.

> **function** BN(P: 1-compliant LPAD) **returns** a Bayesian net
> $\quad N := \emptyset$ // *nodes of the BN*
> $\quad E := \emptyset$ // *edges of the BN*
> $\quad$ **for each** rule $(h'_{i1} : \alpha_{i1} \vee \ldots \vee h'_{in_i} : \alpha_{in_i} \leftarrow b_{i1}, \ldots, b_{im_i}) \in P$:
> $\quad\quad N := N \cup \{C_i\} \cup \bigcup_j \{b_{ij}\}$
> $\quad\quad E := E \cup \bigcup_j \{(b_{ij}, C_i)\}$
> $\quad\quad$ associate with C_i a CPD as follows:
> $\quad\quad\quad P(C_i = j | \text{all parents true}) = \alpha_{ij}$, for all $j > 0$
> $\quad\quad\quad P(C_i = 0 | \text{all parents true}) = 1 - \sum_j \alpha_{ij}$
> $\quad\quad\quad P(C_i = 0 | \text{not all parents true}) = 1$
> $\quad\quad\quad P(C_i = j | \text{not all parents true}) = 0$, for all $j > 0$
> $\quad$ **for each** clause $(h_{ij} \leftarrow h'_{ij}) \in P$:
> $\quad\quad N := N \cup \{h_{ij}\}$
> $\quad\quad E := E \cup \bigcup_j \{(C_i, h_{ij})\}$
> $\quad$ **for each** $l \in N$ that is not a C_i:
> $\quad\quad$ associate with l a CPD as follows:
> $\quad\quad\quad C := \bigvee_{ij:(l \leftarrow h'_{ij}) \in P} C_i = j$
> $\quad\quad\quad P(l = true | C) = 1$
> $\quad\quad\quad P(l = false | C) = 0$
> $\quad\quad\quad P(l = true | \neg C) = 0$
> $\quad\quad\quad P(l = false | \neg C) = 1$
> $\quad$ **return** (N, E, CPD)

initialize the 0 and 1 elements with their right value: the Bayesian update rule can only update values strictly between 0 and 1.

Finally, note that when grounding an LPAD, a single rule is typically transformed in a set of rules, all with the same α parameters. These α's occur in multiple places in the Bayesian net. When learning the parameters of the Bayesian net, we need to take into account that all the parameters corresponding to one α must have the same value. This can be done by forcing these parameters to be their average after each iteration of the EM algorithm.

7.2   Learning Both Structure and Parameters of an LPAD

We consider the following task: given a set of predicates, learn an LPAD that may contain any of these predicates. This involves a search over possible LPAD structures, which can be done either in LPAD space or in Bayesian net (BN) space. Typically, a greedy algorithm such as the ones below would be used:

LPAD := $\emptyset$	BN := initial Bayesian net
while LPAD is not good enough:	**while** BN is not good enough:
$\quad S :=$ refinements(LPAD)	$\quad S :=$ refinements(BN)
$\quad$ LPAD := argmax$_{L \in S}$ eval(L)	$\quad$ BN := argmax$_{L \in S}$ eval(L)
return LPAD	**return** LPAD(BN)

In LPAD space, a refinement operator similar to Riguzzi's [3] could be used for the search, though alternatives can be explored. In BN space, since Bayesian nets corresponding to LPADs are a subset of all possible Bayesian nets, one needs to ensure that the Bayesian net returned maps to a valid LPAD. To this aim, the refinement operator can be redefined so that only LPAD-compatible Bayesian nets are generated.

The *eval* function is typically based on the likelihood of the data given the candidate model. Computing this involves (in LPAD space) grounding the candidate LPAD and transforming it into a Bayesian network; then (in both cases) estimating the parameters of the network and computing the likelihood.

Some experiments with a first implementation of the above described parameter and structure learning approaches, which space restrictions prevent us from detailing here, indicate that at least learning small LPADs such as the ones shown in this paper is quite feasible, and suggest that the repeated conversion of LPADs into Bayesian nets may make the LPAD search much slower than the BN search. We plan a more detailed experimental comparison of the approaches as future work.

8 Conclusions

The main contribution of this paper is the definition of a reduction of non-recursive finite-universe LPADs to Bayesian networks. This reduction is defined in two steps: in a first step, an LPAD is transformed into a so-called 1-compliant LPAD. In a second step, the latter is transformed into a Bayesian network.

The reduction provides some novel insights regarding the meaning of the α parameters in an LPAD. In particular, we have shown that while the probabilities in LPADs cannot generally be interpreted as conditional probabilities within the universe of atoms occurring in the LPAD, it is always possible to transform the LPAD into another LPAD where this property does hold.

The reduction also offers several perspectives with respect to learning LPADs. First, the only existing methods for learning LPADs, up till now, handled only a restricted type of LPADs, so-called ME-compliant LPADs. Using the reduction proposed here, that restriction is lifted. Second, the reduction makes the extensive expertise on learning Bayesian networks available for learning LPADs.

In future work we intend to have a closer look at the many existing methods for learning Bayesian networks, and evaluate how suitable these approaches are from the point of view of learning LPADs (i.e., how well they work in the presence of constraints on the parameters that are being learned).

Our reduction still leaves open the question of how to learn recursive LPADs. One approach may be based on translating the LPAD to an undirected graphical model, removing the problem that cycles are not allowed. Another approach would be to abandon the reductionist approach and develop an algorithm specifically for learning LPADs. Both approaches will be investigated in the future.

Acknowledgements

H.B. is a post-doctoral fellow of the Fund for Scientific Research of Flanders (FWO-Vlaanderen). Research supported by the Flemish Institute for the Promotion of Innovation by Science and Technology in Flanders (IWT-Vlaanderen) and project GOA/2003/08 (B0516) on Inductive Knowledge Bases. The authors thank Kristian Kersting, Jan Ramon, Joost Vennekens and Maurice Bruynooghe for their valuable inputs.

References

1. Lloyd, J.W.: Foundations of Logic Programming, 2nd edn. Springer, Heidelberg (1987)
2. Neapolitan, R.: Learning Bayesian Networks. Prentice Hall, Upper Saddle River, NJ, USA (2003)
3. Riguzzi, F.: Learning logic programs with annotated disjunctions. In: Camacho, R., King, R., Srinivasan, A. (eds.) ILP 2004. LNCS (LNAI), vol. 3194, pp. 270–287. Springer, Heidelberg (2004)
4. Vennekens, J., Denecker, M., Bruynooghe, M.: Extending the role of causality in probabilistic modeling. In: Proceedings of the 11th International Workshop on Non-monotonic Reasoning, pp. 183–190 (2006)
5. Vennekens, J., Verbaeten, S., Bruynooghe, M.: Logic programs with annotated disjunctions. In: Demoen, B., Lifschitz, V. (eds.) ICLP 2004. LNCS, vol. 3132, pp. 431–445. Springer, Heidelberg (2004)

Multi-class Prediction Using Stochastic Logic Programs

Jianzhong Chen[1], Lawrence Kelley[2], Stephen Muggleton[1], and Michael Sternberg[2]

[1] Department of Computing, Imperial College London, London SW7 2AZ, UK
{cjz,shm}@doc.ic.ac.uk
[2] Department of Biological Sciences, Imperial College London, London SW7 2AZ, UK
{l.a.kelley,m.sternberg}@imperial.ac.uk

Abstract. In this paper, we present a probabilistic method of dealing with multi-class classification using Stochastic Logic Programs (SLPs), a Probabilistic Inductive Logic Programming (PILP) framework that integrates probability, logic representation and learning. Multi-class prediction attempts to classify an observed datum or example into its proper classification given that it has been tested to have multiple predictions. We apply an SLP parameter estimation algorithm to a previous study in the protein fold prediction area and a multi-class classification working example, in which logic programs have been learned by Inductive Logic Programming (ILP) and a large number of multiple predictions have been detected. On the basis of several experiments, we demonstrate that PILP approaches (eg. SLPs) have advantages for solving multi-class prediction problems with the help of learned probabilities. In addition, we show that SLPs outperform ILP plus majority class predictor in both predictive accuracy and result interpretability.

1 Introduction

Multi-class classification is a central problem in machine learning, as applications that require a discrimination among several classes are ubiquitous [1]. We consider the problem of multi-class prediction/classification[1] using Probabilistic Inductive Logic Programming (PILP) approaches [2]. A conventional Inductive Logic Programming (ILP) program is given with a training data set consisting of examples belonging to $N > 2$ different classes, and the goal is to construct a method that, given a new unlabeled datum, will correctly predict the class to which the datum belongs[2].

The motivation comes from an existing multiple prediction problem detected in a previous protein fold prediction study [3], where a number of proteins can be predicted to belong to more than one protein fold but in fact each of them should have only one unique prediction. This is called the 'False Positive' problem in binary classification [4], where in practice many examples show positive on more than one class which leads to

---

[1] It is also called multiclass prediction, multiple classification or multi-classification in some references.

[2] We distinguish the case where each datum is required to belong to a single class from the other case where a given example is allowed to be a member of more than one class simultaneously. The former case of requirement is assumed in our framework, where multiple predictions have been detected due to some reasons in practice and the goal is to solve the uncertainty from the observations so that a single prediction could be made correctly for each datum.

S. Muggleton, R. Otero, and A. Tamaddoni-Nezhad (Eds.): ILP 2006, LNAI 4455, pp. 109–124, 2007.

ambiguous prediction results. Another example can be taken from the animal classification program (Table 2), in which one can easily detect, using the given background knowledge, that a bat is predicted to be a member of both mammal and bird classes, and a dolphin is predicted to belong to both mammal and fish classes. Multi-class classification/prediction discussed in this paper aims to find ways to solve these multiple prediction problems and make correct decisions, so that a protein has only one correct fold prediction, and a bat and a dolphin can be predicted only in mammal class.

While binary classification [4,5], which classifies the members of a given set of objects into two groups on the basis of whether they have some property or not, is well understood, multi-class classification requires extra techneques. Most of the current multi-class classification techniques are developed in the discriminative classification methods, including decision trees, kernel methods, support vector machine and neural networks. Some of them extend the binary classification algorithms to handle multi-class problems directly, such as decision trees, regression, discriminant analysis, etc [5,6]. The others build multi-class methods on the basic binary classification methods, such as one-versus-others, pairwise classification, all-versus-all, error-correcting output coding, etc [1,4,7,8]. There has also been some work on the combination of these methods with probabilistic modeling [8,9]. The above approaches have limited relevance to ILP-based classifiers, as most of them are based on regularization, modeling the decision boundaries or evaluating several binary classification methods. In logic-based classification methods , such as ILP, majority voting is often used to solve the multiple prediction problems, however the performance depends on the empirical distribution and the (im)balance feature of data.

To solve the multiple prediction uncertainty that naturally exists in the ILP classifiers, we use PILP techniques, which aim at integrating three underlying constituents: statistical learning and probabilistic reasoning within logical or relational knowledge representations [2]. There have been increasing number of attempts to use PILP methods in practical settings recently [10,11]. In this paper, we present applications of Stochastic Logic Programs (SLPs) [12], one of the existing PILP frameworks, to learn probabilistic logic programs that help to solve the multi-class prediction problem detected in a protein fold prediction study and a working example. We apply a comparative experimental strategy to demonstrate our method in which SLPs are learned from the existing ILP programs and training data, and then the results, including the predictive accuracy and interpretability, are compared between SLP predictors against ILP plus majority class predictors.

2   Motivation

2.1   Biological Motivation

Protein fold prediction is one of the major unsolved problems in modern molecular biology. Given the amino acid sequence of a protein, the aim is to predict the corresponding three-dimensional structure or local fold [13]. It has been proved that determining actual structure of a protein is hard. It is a good idea to predict the structure and machine learning methods are useful. A major event in the area is the well-known Comparative Assessment of protein Structure Prediction (CASP) competition and CAFASP2 [13].

Table 1. Ratio of examples with multiple predictions in the previous study

all-α class	all-β class	α/β class	$\alpha + \beta$ class	overall
30/77=38.96%	34/116=29.31%	67/115=58.26%	23/73=31.51%	154/381=40.42%

A variety of machine learning approaches have been successful, such as decision trees [7], support vector machines [4,7] and kernel methods [14,15], neural networks [4], hidden Markov models [10,11], ILP [3,16,17], etc. ILP is useful as it can learn explainable logic rules from examples with the help of relational background knowledge. Multi-class protein fold prediction has been investigated in [4,7,11].

An experimental study of applying ILP to automatically and systematically discover the structural signatures of protein folds and functions has been explored in [3]. The rules derived by ILP from observation and encoded principles are readily interpreted in terms of concepts used by biology experts. For 20 populated folds in SCOP database [18], 59 logical rules were found by ILP system Progol [19]. With the same experiments, the effect of relational background knowledge on learning protein three-dimensional fold signatures has also been addressed in [16]. However, there exists a problem of multiple predictions unsolved in the previous study, ie. a number of protein domains have been predicted to belong to more than one of 20 protein folds or can be explained by rules across multiple folds. In fact, only one protein fold prediction is expected for each protein. We have investigated that, in the previous study, about 40% of the examples have been involved in the problem (Table 1). For example, the worst case we have found is where protein domain 'd1xyzb_' is given to be in fold 'β/α (TIM)-barrel', however it has been tested to have up to four fold predictions - 'β/α (TIM)-barrel', 'NAD(P)-binding Rossmann-fold domains', 'α/β-Hydrolases' and 'Periplasmic binding protein-like II'.

One of the main reasons for the false positive problem [4] is that the decision boundary between ILP rules can be naturally overlapped due to the complex nature of protein folding, the quality and noise of acquired background knowledge and data, etc. From biology point of view, our study is motivated by finding ways to solve the multiple prediction problem so that, deriving the ILP program and data from the previous study, only one unique fold prediction can be discovered for each protein domain.

2.2   Machine Learning Motivation

From machine learning point of view, solving the above problem requires us to deal with *multi-class prediction* rather than the *binary classification* approach[3] used in the original study. Generally speaking, binary classification can be used to predict whether an example belong to a class or not, whereas multi-class prediction can classify an example into one class from multiple ambiguous predictions based on some given 'ranking' or 'leveraging' mechanism. Precisely, a *binary predictor* defines a function f that maps an example e and a class label cl to a binary set, ie. $f : (e, cl) \mapsto \{yes, no\}$; and

---

[3] When there are multiple classes and the class labels are assumed to be independent, a conventional ILP classifier actually provides a set of binary classifiers, each of which is used to distinguish whether or not an example is in a certain class.

Table 2. A working example: multi-class animal classification program

Prob.	Logic rules	Comments
0.195:	class(mammal,A) :- has_milk(A).	%classification rules
0.205:	class(mammal,A) :- animal_running(A).	%A is in 'mammal' class
0.222:	class(bird,A) :- animal_flying(A).	%A is in 'bird' class
0.189:	class(fish,A) :- has_gills(A).	%A is in 'fish' class
0.189:	class(fish,A) :- habitat(A,water),has_covering(A,none),has_legs(A,0).	
0.433:	animal_running(A) :- hemeothermic(A),habitat(A,land), has_legs(A,4).	% *extensional* background knowledge
0.567:	animal_running(A) :- hemeothermic(A),habitat(A,caves).	
0.6:	animal_flying(A) :- hemeothermic(A),habitat(A,air), has_covering(A,feathers),has_legs(A,2).	
0.4:	animal_flying(A) :- hemeothermic(A),habitat(A,air), has_covering(A,hair),has_legs(A,2).	
	animal(bat).has_milk(bat).hemeothermic(bat).habitat(bat,air). habitat(bat,caves).has_covering(bat,hair).has_legs(bat,2).	% *intensional* background knowledge
	animal(dolphin).has_milk(dolphin).hemeothermic(dolphin). habitat(dolphin,water).has_covering(dolphin,none).has_legs(dolphin,0).······	
	class(mammal,bat).class(mammal,dolphin).······	% data,examples

a *multi-class predictor* defines a function g that maps an example e and a set of class labels $\{cl_1, \ldots, cl_m\}$ to one class label $cl_i \in \{cl_1, \ldots, cl_m\}$ with some ranking mechanism r_i, ie. $g : \{(e, cl_1), \ldots, (e, cl_m)\} \mapsto (e, cl_i, r_i), m > 1, 1 \leq i \leq m$. Multi-class predictor is more useful for unlabeled/unseen data classification. In majority voting, the ranking mechanism is the class size, ie. the number of predicted examples of a class. In PILP approaches, the class-conditional probabilities are computed for each example e as the ranking mechanism, which specify a distribution of the prediction probabilities of e over multiple classes.

The work is also motivated by the applications of PILP approaches. PILP extends ILP to explicitly deal with uncertainty and has an advantage over ILP because it can provide additional knowledge by building probabilistic models for the observations. We apply SLPs, a well-known PILP framework, to the existing ILP programs that use binary classification. Probabilities will be machine learned by applying an SLP parameter estimation algorithm based on the given ILP rules, (positive) examples and background knowledge. By comparing the performance of multi-class prediction using SLPs against non-probability approaches, eg. ILP plus majority voting, we aim to demonstrate some showcases where PILP approaches outperform ILP methods in some applications.

2.3 A Working Example

An artificially generated working example is defined and processed in order to clarify the problem of multi-class prediction and to demonstrate our method. It also shows that multiple prediction problem may naturally happen in logic-based classifiers due to the overlapping among logic clauses.

The so-called *multi-class animal classification* example starts from a logic program illustrated in Table 2, which contains a set of logic rules learned using ILP and can be used to classify animals into three classes, ie. mammal, bird or fish. The program was learned from an artificial data set with 10% of noise and 30% of multiple prediction examples. An example of multiple predictions can be gained by testing that a bat belongs to both mammal and bird classes, or a dolphin is predicted to be in both mammal and fish classes. An example of SLP is also listed in Table 2 in which probabilities are estimated for some rules from data.

3 Background

3.1 Protein Fold Prediction

Protein structures can be described at various levels of abstraction [17]. The *primary structure* refers to the sequence of amino acids. The *secondary structure* is local ordered structure brought about via hydrogen bonding and the most common secondary structure elements in proteins are the α-helices and the β-strands, while the intervening region are called loops or coils. The *tertiary structure* is the global folding of a single polypeptide chain. A particular sequence of amino acids folds into a specific compact three-dimensional or tertiary/quaternary structure from which the exact location of every atom can be deduced. In this level of abstraction, *protein folds* are defined to represent a high-level description of the three-dimensional structures found in amino acid sequences and are our targets of discovery.

The "Holy Grail" of molecular biology is to devise a method that would predict the three-dimensional structure from the knowledge of the sequence alone [16]. The problem is often broken down into two sub-tasks: *secondary structure prediction* which aims to map each residue to one of the three types (helix, strand and coil); and *protein fold classification* whose aim is the docking of the secondary structure elements to form the compact three-dimensional structure. We concentrate on protein fold prediction that would predict protein folds from the knowledge of protein domains based on the famous SCOP classification scheme [18]. The scheme is a classification done manually by the experts on protein structure and facilitates the understanding of protein structure which can be served as a starting point for machine learning experiments. Table 3 illustrates the hierarchy of protein structures we are using. A *domain* is the building block of the classification; a *fold* represents a classification for a group of protein domains. At the top level, a *class* is used to group folds based on the overall distribution of their secondary structure elements.

In our study, we have been using the above classification scheme to design the experiments. The data are a set of (positive) examples in protein domain level associated with known protein fold classification for training and test purpose. The background knowledge are a set of domain knowledge for representing the structural and inter-relational information of the domains. The learned ILP rules derived from the previous study stand for the prediction knowledge discovered from the data with the help of background knowledge in protein fold level. The learned SLP probabilities associated with rules and background knowledge represent the probabilistic distributions or statistical frequencies of the protein fold predictions that can be used as the ranking mechanism for solving multiple prediction problem.

Table 3. protein structure classification scheme

Level	Description	Examples
CLASS	folds are grouped into classes based on the overall distribution of their secondary structure elements.	all-α α/β
FOLD	proteins that share the same core secondary structures and the same interconnections.	Globins Cytokines
superfamily	a group of families.	
family	a group of domains.	
DOMAIN	a structure or substructure that is considered to be folded independently; small proteins have a single domain, and for larger ones, a domain is a substructure.	d1scta_ d1xyzb_

3.2   Stochastic Logic Programs

Stochastic logic programs (SLPs) [12] have been chosen as the PILP framework in the study as SLPs provide a natural way in associating probabilities with logical rules. SLPs were introduced originally as a way of lifting stochastic grammars to the level of first-order logic programs. SLPs were considered as a generalization of hidden Markov models and stochastic context-free grammars. SLPs have later been used to define distributions for sampling within inductive logic programming (ILP). It is clear that SLPs provide a way of probabilistic logic representations and make ILP become better at inducing models that represent uncertainty.

Syntactically, an SLP S is a definite logic program, where each clause C is a first-order range-restricted definite clause and some of the definite clauses are labelled/ parameterised with non-negative numbers, $l : C$. S is said to be a *pure* SLP if all clauses have parameters, as opposed to an *impure* SLP if not all clauses have labels. The subset S_q of clauses in S whose head share the same predicate symbol q is called the definition of q. For each definition S_q, we use π_q to denote the sum of the labels of the clauses in S_q. S is *normalised* if $\pi_q = 1$ for each q and *unnormalised* otherwise. Till now, the definition does not show SLPs represent probability distributions, as each label can be any non-negative number and there is no constraints for the parameters of unnormalised SLPs. For our interest, SLPs are restricted to define probability distributions over logic clauses, where each l is set to be a number in the interval [0,1] and, for each S_q, π_q must be at most 1. In this case, a normalised SLP is also called a *complete* SLP, as opposed to a *incomplete* SLP for unnormalised one. In a pure normalised/complete SLP, each choice for a clause C has a parameter attached and the parameters sum to one, so they can therefore be interpreted as probabilities. Pure normalised/complete SLPs are defined such that each parameter l denotes the probability that C is the next clause used in a derivation given that its head C^+ has the correct predicate symbol. Impure SLPs are useful to define logic programs containing both probabilistic and deterministic rules, as shown in this paper. Unnormalised SLPs can conveniently be used to represent other existing probabilistic models, such as Bayesian nets.

Semantically, SLPs have been used to define probability distributions for sampling within ILP [12]. Generally speacking, an SLP S has a *distributional semantics* [20], that is one which assigns a probability distribution to the atoms of each predicate in the

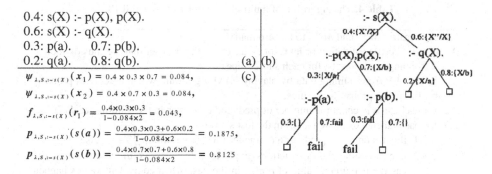

$$\psi_{\lambda,S,:-s(x)}(x_1) = 0.4 \times 0.3 \times 0.7 = 0.084,$$

$$\psi_{\lambda,S,:-s(x)}(x_2) = 0.4 \times 0.7 \times 0.3 = 0.084,$$

$$f_{\lambda,S,:-s(x)}(r_1) = \frac{0.4 \times 0.3 \times 0.3}{1 - 0.084 \times 2} = 0.043,$$

$$p_{\lambda,S,:-s(x)}(s(a)) = \frac{0.4 \times 0.3 \times 0.3 + 0.6 \times 0.2}{1 - 0.084 \times 2} = 0.1875,$$

$$p_{\lambda,S,:-s(x)}(s(b)) = \frac{0.4 \times 0.7 \times 0.7 + 0.6 \times 0.8}{1 - 0.084 \times 2} = 0.8125$$

Fig. 1. (a)an example of SLP S (adapted from [21]); (b)a stochastic SLD-tree for S with goal :-s(X), including 6 derivations in which 4 are refutations (end with □) and 2 are fail derivations; (c)probability distributions defined in S for the two fail derivations x_1 and x_2, for the leftmost refutation r_1, and for the two atoms $s(a)$ and $s(b)$, respectively.

Herbrand base of the clauses in S. The probabilities are assigned to ground atoms in terms of their proofs according to a stochastic SLD-resolution process which employs a stochastic selection rule based on the values of the probability labels. Furthermore, some quantitative results are shown in [21], in which an SLP S with parameter $\lambda = \log l$ together with a goal G defines up to three related distributions in the stochastic SLD-tree of G: $\psi_{\lambda,S,G}(x)$, $f_{\lambda,S,G}(r)$ and $p_{\lambda,S,G}(y)$, defined over derivations $\{x\}$, refutations $\{r\}$ and atoms $\{y\}$, respectively. An example is illustrated in Fig. 1, in which the example SLP S defines a distribution $\{0.1875, 0.8125\}$ over the sample space $\{s(a), s(b)\}$. It is important to understand that SLPs do not define distributions over possible worlds, i.e., $p_{\lambda,S,G}(y)$ defines a distribution over atoms, not over the truth values of atoms.

There are two tasks for learning SLPs. Parameter estimation aims to learn the parameters from observations assuming that the underlying logic program is fixed. *Failure-Adjusted Maximization* (FAM) [21] is a parameter estimation algorithm for pure normalised SLPs. Structure learning tries to learn both logic program and parameters from data. Although some fundamental work have been done for SLP structure learning [20,22], it is still an open hard problem in the area which requires one to solve almost all the existing difficulties in ILP learning. In this paper, we apply the two-phase SLP learning method developed in [20] to solve multi-class protein fold predication problem, in which SLP structure has been learned by some ILP learning system and SLP parameters will then be estimated by playing with FAM to the learned ILP program.

4   Multi-class Prediction Using SLPs

Our method of multi-class prediction using SLPs is illustrated as an algorithm in Table 4. As shown in Table 2, an SLP for multi-class prediction is an impure SLP that has a hierarchical structure, consisting of a set of probabilistic *classification/prediction rules*, a set of probabilistic clauses for *extensional background knowledge*, and a set of non-probabilistic clauses for *intensional background knowledge*. Probabilities are

Table 4. The algorithm of multi-class prediction using SLPs

---

1. Initialize matrix M^{ILP} and M^{SLP} to be zero matrix;
2. Apply n-fold cross validation or leave-one-out test to the data set that are thus divided into n (training,test) subsets; for each subset repeat
   2.1. Learn SLP from training data by playing FAM algorithm, which associates probabilities to the probabilistic rules;
   2.2. for each class cl count the number of predicted examples in the training set $d(cl)$;
   2.3. for each labeled example (e, cl_i) in the test set do
      2.3.1. if e has only one prediction cl_j then set $M_{ij}^{\text{ILP}} + +$ and $M_{ij}^{\text{SLP}} + +$; else
      2.3.2. in all possible class predictions, apply majority class voting to choose cl_j that has the maximum value of $d(cl)$; (in the case when equivalent values happen, cl_j is randomly chosen from the set)
      2.3.3. for each possible class prediction cl, apply the learned SLP to compute the prediction probability of e in cl, $p(e \mid cl, \lambda, S)$;
      2.3.4. choose cl_k that has the maximum value of $p(e \mid cl_k, \lambda, S)$;
      2.3.5. set $M_{ij}^{\text{ILP}} + +$ and $M_{ik}^{\text{SLP}} + +$;
3. Compute predictive accuracies pa^{ILP} and pa^{SLP} bases on M^{ILP} and M^{SLP};
4. Learn the final SLP from the whole data set.

---

parameter-estimated by FAM algorithm (step 2.1). FAM is designed to deal with SLP parameter learning from incomplete or ambiguous data in which the atoms in the data have more than one refutation that can yield them. It is an adjustment to the standard EM algorithm where the adjustment is explicitly expressed in terms of failure derivation. The key step in the algorithm is the computation of $\psi_{\lambda^h}[\nu_i|y]$, the expected frequency for clause C_i given the observed data y and the current parameter estimate λ^h

$$\psi_{\lambda^h}[\nu_i|y] = \sum_{k=1}^{t-1} N_k \psi_{\lambda^h}[\nu_i|y_k] + N(Z_{\lambda^h}^{-1} - 1)\psi_{\lambda^h}[\nu_i|fail],$$

where ν_i counts times C_i appeared in some derivation, N_k is the number of times datum y_k occurred in the observed data, $N = \sum_k N_k$ is the number of observed data, $\psi_{\lambda^h}[\nu_i|y_k]$ is the expected number of times C_i was used in refutations yielding y_k, $\psi_{\lambda^h}[\nu_i|fail]$ denotes the expected contribution of C_i to failed derivations, and Z_{λ^h} is the probability of success. Therefore, the first part corresponds to refutations while the second term to failed derivations. Broadly speaking, the equation gathers together the contributions of a particular clause C_i to derivations against the program, the current parameters and the data. FAM can be used to estimate the parameters for normalized impure SLP in which some rules are set to be probabilistic and others are pure logical rules.

Given an example e and a set of predictions $\{cl_1, \ldots, cl_N\}$ for e, a FAM-learned SLP defines a distribution over the predictions, ie. $\{p(e \mid cl_1, \lambda, S), \ldots, p(e \mid cl_N, \lambda, S)\}$. Each $p(e \mid cl_n, \lambda, S)$ denotes a class-conditional prediction probability of e in class cl_n and can be computed (step 2.3.3) as

$$p(e \mid cl_n, \lambda, S) = p_{\lambda, S, :-\text{class}(cl_n, e)}(\text{class}(cl_n, e)) = \frac{\sum_{i=1}^{M_n} \prod_{j=1}^{M_i} l_j^{\nu_j(r_i)}}{\sum_{k=1}^{N} p(e \mid cl_k, \lambda, S)}$$

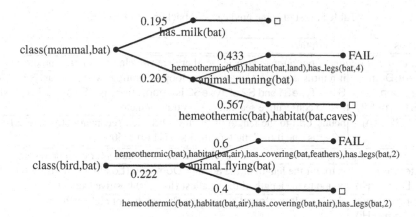

Fig. 2. Stochastic SLD-trees for goals class(mammal,bat) and class(bird,bat)

in its stochastic SLD-tree given S and goal :-class(cl_n, e), where r_i is the i-th refutation that satisfies e, M_n denotes the total number of refutations of e in cl_n, l_j is the probability of clause C_j, $v_j(r_i)$ is the number of times C_j has been used in r_i, and M_i denotes the number of clauses occurred in r_i. Because impure SLPs are allowed, some clauses are unparameterised in a derivation. We apply the 'equivalence class' feature developed in [21] to deal with the case where an unparameterised clause, with probability 1, either succeeds or fails in a derivation (exclusively). Two stochastic SLD-trees for the animal classification working example are illustrated in Fig. 2, from which we have $p(\text{bat} \mid \text{mammal}, \lambda, S) = \frac{0.195+0.205\times0.567}{0.3112+0.0888} = 0.778$ and $p(\text{bat} \mid \text{bird}, \lambda, S) = \frac{0.222\times0.4}{0.3112+0.0888} = 0.222$ given the SLP presented in Table 2. They thus define a distribution over {class(mammal,bat),class(bird,bat)}, the two predictions of bat.

In the algorithm, two multi-class confusion matrixes are built in a n-fold cross validation or leave-one-out test in order to evaluate the corresponding predictive accuracies. We informally define a multi-class confusion matrix to be an integer square matrix $M_{(m+1)\times(m+1)}$ for m known classes[4], in which an arbitrary element M_{ij}, $1 \le i, j \le (m+1)$, will be increased by 1 if a labeled example taken from class cl_i is predicted to be in class cl_j (or in class cl_{m+1} if no prediction). The overall predictive accuracy based on the multi-class confusion matrix can then be computed by $pa = \frac{\sum_{i=1}^{m+1} M_{ii}}{\sum_{i,j=1}^{m+1} M_{ij}}$ (step 3). Two matrixes with the predictive accuracies for the working example are shown as follows

$$M_{4\times4}^{\text{ILP}} = \begin{pmatrix} 16 & 0 & 2 & 0 \\ 2 & 10 & 0 & 0 \\ 2 & 0 & 17 & 1 \\ 0 & 0 & 0 & 0 \end{pmatrix}, pa^{\text{ILP}} = 86 \pm 4.9\%; \quad M_{4\times4}^{\text{SLP}} = \begin{pmatrix} 18 & 0 & 0 & 0 \\ 2 & 10 & 0 & 0 \\ 2 & 0 & 17 & 1 \\ 0 & 0 & 0 & 0 \end{pmatrix}, pa^{\text{SLP}} = 90 \pm 4.2\%.$$

---

[4] The $(m + 1)$-th column is set to be an 'unknown' class, where an example in some cases fails to be predicted in any of m known classes.

Table 5. List of some predicates of background knowledge

Predicates	Description
extensional relational background knowledge, there are two clauses for each predicate	
adjacent(Dom, S1,S2,Loop, TypeS1,TypeS2)	it returns true if the length of the loop separating two secondary structures S1 of TypeS1 and S2 of TypeS2 is Loop; otherwise, S1 and S2 are bound to two consecutive secondary structure elements.
coil(S1,S2,Len)	bound Len to the length of the loop between secondary structure S1 and S2 or is true if the length of the loop is Len ± 50%.
extensional global background knowledge, there are two clauses for each predicate	
len_interval (Lo=<Dom=<Hi)	is true if the length of the domain Dom is in [Lo,Hi]; otherwise, Lo (Hi) is bound to the length of the smallest (longest) positive example.
nb_alpha_interval (Lo=<Dom=<Hi)	similar to len_interval but process the number of alpha helices.
nb_beta_interval (Lo=<Dom=<Hi)	similar to len_interval but process the number of beta helices.
intensional local background knowledge, there is one clause for each predicate	
unit_len(S,Cst)	is true if the length of the secondary structure S is Cst, the values for Cst are very_lo, lo, hi and very_hi.
unit_aveh(S,Cst)	similar to unit_len but process the average hydrophobicity.
unit_hmom(S,Cst)	similar to unit_len but process the hydrophobic moment.
has_pro(S)	is true if S contains a proline amino acid.

5   Experiments

A set of scientific experiments[5] are designed to demonstrate and evaluate our methods.

5.1   Hypotheses to Be Tested

The **null hypotheses** to be empirically investigated in the study are as follows,

- PILP approaches based on highly expressive probabilistic logic learning frameworks, eg. SLPs, **do not** outperform any conventional ILP methods on the multiclass prediction showcase.
- For a given logic program with multiple predictions/classifications and a corresponding data set, provision of probabilities **does not** increase predictive accuracy compared with non-probabilistic approaches such as majority class predictor.
- Probabilistic knowledge learned by PILP approaches **does not** produce improved explanatory insight.

5.2   Materials and Inputs

In terms of ILP, the input materials consist of an ILP logic program that has multiple prediction problem and a corresponding data set. An example can be found in Table 2

---

[5] Details of the experiments can be found at
http://www.doc.ic.ac.uk/~cjz/research

Table 6. Description of the experiments

Experiment	Data set and description
1	protein fold prediction, 59 learned ILP rules and 381 protein domains; learning SLP from uniform initial parameters, ie. each parameterised clause with definition S_q is initially set to have a probability $\frac{1}{|S_q|}$
2	protein fold prediction, 59 learned ILP rules and 381 protein domains; learning SLP from random initial parameters
3	animal classification, 18 examples of mammal class, 12 of bird class and 20 of fish class; predicted class size in order: mammal $\geq$ fish > bird
4	animal classification, 17 examples of mammal class, 17 of bird class and 16 of fish class; predicted class size in order: bird $\geq$ mammal > fish
5	animal classification, 14 examples of mammal class, 18 of bird class and 18 of fish class; predicted class size in order: bird $\geq$ fish > mammal

Table 7. Comparison of predictive accuracies for experiment 1 (overall and by four protein classes), 3, 4 and 5

Experiment	1 (overall)	3	4	5
SLP predictor	71.39±2.32%	90±4.24%	90±4.24%	90±4.24%
majority class predictor	64.57±2.45%	86±4.91%	84±5.18%	68±6.60%
Significance of Difference	0.021	0.269	0.185	0.003

Experiment 1 by protein class	all-α class	all-β class	α/β class	$\alpha+\beta$ class
SLP predictor	76.62±4.82%	81.03±3.64%	51.30±4.66%	82.19±4.48%
majority class predictor	71.43±5.15%	69.83±4.26%	44.35±4.63%	80.82±4.61%

for the multi-class animal classification and 50 artificial examples are provided. In protein fold prediction, a data set of 381 protein domains together with known protein folds, based on SCOP classification, is provided in Prolog format, for example,

    fold('Globin-like',d1scta_).   fold('beta/alpha (TIM)-barrel', d1xyzb_).

Background knowledge are used to represent the three-dimensional structure information of the examples, eg.

    dom_t(d1scta_). len(d1scta_, 150). nb_alpha(d1scta_,6). nb_beta(d1scta_,0).

Three types of domain background knowledge are further distinguished (Table 5) – *relational knowledge* introduce relationships between secondary structure elements and their properties; *global knowledge* encode global characteristics of protein folds, specifically, the number of residues and the number of secondary structures; and *local knowledge* state local information of a single protein element. Some predicates are designed to be intensional, while others are extensional that are generated from intensional knowledge. In addition, 59 prediction *rules* learned by ILP system Progol [19] over 20 populated protein folds have been derived from the original study, eg.

    fold('Globin-like',A) :- adjacent(A,B,C,1,h,h), has_pro(C).
    fold('beta/alpha (TIM)-barrel',A) :- adjacent(A,B,C,4,h,e), unit_len(B,hi).

5.3   Methods and Results

The method presented in Table 4 has been applied to both multi-class protein fold prediction with a 5-fold cross validation test and multi-class animal classification working example with a leave-one-out test. In order to empirically test the pre-set hypotheses, five sub-experiments (Table 6) are designed and evaluated, each of which has an SLP predictor as well as a majority class predictor. The first two experiments are used to test the convergence property of FAM, while the other three are designed to investigate the influence of empirical data distribution on the performance of the two predictors. Main results of the predictive accuracy for the experiments are shown in Table 7. In summary, SLP predictors outperform majority class predictors in predictive accuracy in all five experiments. The result of protein fold prediction experiment 1 shows a promising improvement in the overall predictive accuracy that is 71.39% achieved by SLP predictor against 64.57% by non-probabilistic majority class predictor, and the difference of the predictive accuracies (ie. the probability of the second null hypothesis in section 5.1) is significant at the 0.021 level. Experiment 3, 4 and 5 imply that the majority class predictors are dependent on the predicted class size of each class, ie. the number of examples predicted in that class, which is further dependent on the empirical data distribution, ie. the ratio of the number of examples provided in the training data set (Table 6). We can see that the predicted class size of mammal class plays a key role on the predictive accuracy, eg. the accuracy is 86% when it has the largest class size in experiment 3, whereas the accuracy decreases to 68% in the worst case when it has the smallest class size in experiment 5.

5.4   Interpretability

Probabilities not only increase predictive accuracy but also improve the interpretability of the learned programs. These are demonstrated by interpreting Fig. 3 as follows, in which the probabilities are learned from the whole data set for all five experiments.

Fig. 3(a) – The probabilities demonstrate the ranking or importance information of the prediction rules in each protein fold; the values exactly match the power rules selected in [3] that was determined by recall, however different recall thresholds have to be manually set for different folds, whereas the probabilities can be automatically learned; by comparing the results between experiment 1 and 2, which are shown in the two legends, we claim that the initial parameter settings have no effect on the learning results, ie. the FAM algorithm converges with any normalised initial parameters.

Fig. 3(b) – The fold probabilities, that are computed by summing up corresponding rule probabilities and shown in the first legend, indicate the popularity of different protein folds, which has been agreed by the biologists (the second and fourth authors of the paper); they tend towards empirical data distribution that is shown in the other legend.

Fig. 3(c) – Probabilities have been learned for the extensional background knowledge (Table 5), each of which has two clauses shown in two legends; it is one of the advantages of PILP to learn the probabilities for extensional background knowledge in addition to those for the prediction rules that might be simply estimated from or tend to converge to the empirical data distribution; these probabilities play the key roles in the computation of prediction probabilities for examples (section 4).

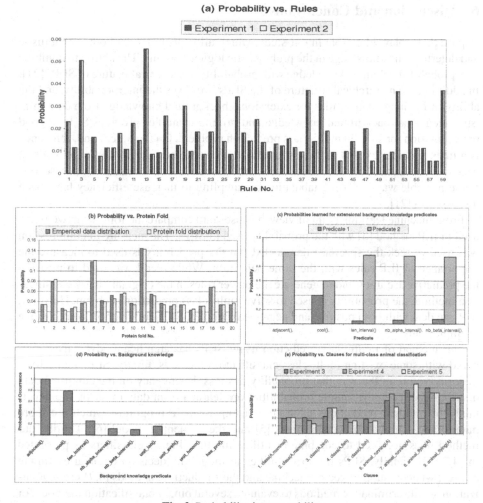

Fig. 3. Probability interpretability

Fig. 3(d) – The probabilities shown are summed up from all 59 probabilistic rules by counting the frequencies of use of particular extensional background knowledge: relational > global > local; it is clear to find that relational knowledge are far more frequently used and occurred than the other two; the finding reenforces the conclusions in [3] - different predicates play different roles in defining protein fold signatures, but the predicate coil() has been found to have a higher frequency of use as relational knowledge in our study than that in [3], where it was treated as global knowledge.

Fig. 3(e) – The probabilities of probabilistic clauses in the animal working example (Fig. 2) are illustrated by the three legends for experiments 3, 4 and 5, respectively; the values are slightly changed by providing data sets with different empirical distributions, which result in the SLP predictors having the same predictive accuracy in the three experiments (Table 7); in contrast, the predictive accuracies of majority class predictors are dependent on the empirical data distribution and the predicted class sizes.

6 Discussion and Conclusions

Impure SLPs play a key role in our study, which allow us to model both probabilistic and deterministic knowledge in the probabilistic logic programs. The ability to combine non-probabilistic domain knowledge with probabilities is a central feature of SLPs [21]. In addition, the hierarchical structure of the SLPs improves the interpretability, and the ability of learning probabilities for extensional background knowledge from deterministic intensional background knowledge and ground examples provides SLPs a good representation for solving multi-class prediction problem. On the other hand, efficiency is a main problem existed in the current FAM algorithm, especially for large SLPs. It needs at least seven CPU days for experiment 1 to run five iterations at a Linux server! Some possible ways of using tabulation or sampling to increase efficiency have been discussed in [21].

From machine learning point of view, it is useful to compare the following two terms used in ILP method [3] with the probability used in SLPs. The measure of compression was used to seek the specific rules in ILP, but the probability is used to measure the importance of ILP rules with the same definition. While recall was used to measure the predictive accuracy and to generate the power rules in the original binary classification method, the probability is used to solve multi-class prediction problem. However, ILP can deal with both positive and negative examples, SLPs are learned from positive examples only.

Our method of multi-class prediction using SLPs has significant advantages compared with some existing multi-class classification methods. Firstly, SLPs outperform majority voting in the way that probability has less dependency on the empirical data distribution. Secondly, sample probabilities are learned from data to tackle the uncertainty of multiple predictions naturally existing in logic programs, which are more natural and sound than decision trees [5] and the sequential model [6]. Thirdly, our method does not need to combine or utilize multiple binary classifiers as presented in [4,7,8,9]. Finally, SLPs use probabilities to model the decision boundaries among classes, whereas support vector machine and their reduction methods [4,7] use regularization and discriminative methods to evaluate several binary classification methods for stochastic voting and usually result in reduced accuracy and efficiency.

The same protein folding data set or similar sets have been applied as a benchmark by some other machine learning methods. Improved logic rules have been learned using ILP in [17], in which the multiple predictions have been effectively reduced by rearranging background knowledge. Logical hidden Mardov models, another PILP framework, are applied in [11] to deal with multi-class protein fold prediction by representing the secondary structure of protein domains as logical sequences; the work increases predictive efficiency and accuracy by reducing the problem representation complexity. Conditional random fields [10] provide another PILP approach to deal with multi-class protein fold classification using logical sequence method. A novel kernel method on Prolog proof trees for binary protein fold prediction has been studied in [15] which provides higher overall accuracy compared with Progol. Even with the same data set, it is not straightforward to compete the results gained by these methods with those shown in this paper due to our specific research motivation and target, which aims to solve multi-class prediction problem by learning SLPs on the basis of the existing ILP programs and data, while the other methods apply their own binary or multi-class classification solutions to the data without deriving the ILP programs. As our future work, resolving rule conflicts with double induction [23] and using Area Under the Curve (AUC) [24] rather than predictive accuracy for performance evaluation will be considered.

In conclusion, the null hypotheses we have set in experiments were rejected on the basis of the results. Overall we conclude that PILP approaches (eg. SLPs) have demonstrable advantages for solving multi-class prediction problem and SLPs have outperformed ILP plus majority class predictor in both predictive accuracy and result interpretability.

Acknowledgements

The authors would like to acknowledge the support of the EC Sixth Framework Project "Application of Probabilistic Inductive Logic Programming II (APrIL II)" (Grant Ref: FP-508861).

References

1. Har-Peled, S., Roth, D, Zimak, D.: Constraint Classification: a New Approach to Multiclass Classification and Ranking. In: Proc. of the Inter. Conf. on Algorithmic Learning Theory, pp. 365–379 (2002)
2. De Raedt, L., Dietterich, T., Getoor, L., Muggleton, S.H.: Probabilistic, Logical and Relational Learning - Towards a Synthesis. Dagstuhl Seminar Proceedings 05051.(2006)
3. Turcotte, M., Muggleton, S.H., Sternberg, M.J.E.: Automated Discovery of Structural Signatures of Protein Fold and Function. J. Mol. Biol. 306, 591–605 (2001)
4. Ding, C.H.Q., Dubchak, I.: Multi-class Protein Fold Recognition Using Support Vector Machines and Neural Networks. Bioinformatics 17(4), 349–358 (2001)
5. Mitchell, T.M.: Machine Learning. McGraw Hill, New York (1997)
6. Even-Zohar, Y., Roth, D.: A Sequential Model for Multi Class Classification. In: Proc. of the Conf. on Empirical Methods for Natural Language Processing (EMNLP), pp. 10–19 (2001)
7. Tan, A.C., Giltert, D., Deville, Y.: Multi-class Protein Fold Classification Using a New Ensemble Machine Learning Approach. In: Inter. Conf. on Genome Informatics, GIW (2003)
8. Wu, T.-F., Lin, C.-J., Weng, R.C.: Probability Estimates for Multi-class Classification by Pairwise Coupling. JMLR 5, 975–1005 (2004)
9. Yukinawa, N., Oba, S., Kato, K., Taniguchi, K., Iwao-Koizumi, K., Tamaki, Y., Noguchi, S., Ishii, S.: A Multi-class Predictor Based on a Probabilistic Model: Application to Gene Expression Profiling-based Diagnosis of Thyroid Tumors. BMC Genomes 7, 190 (2006)
10. Gutmann, B., Kersting, K.: TildeCRF: Conditional Random Fields for Logical Sequences. In: Fürnkranz, J., Scheffer, T., Spiliopoulou, M. (eds.) ECML 2006. LNCS (LNAI), vol. 4212, pp. 18–22. Springer, Heidelberg (2006)
11. Kersting, K., De Raedt, L., Raiko, T.: Logical Hidden Markov Models. JAIR. 25, 425–456 (2006)
12. Muggleton, S.H.: Stochastic Logic Programs. In: De Raedt, L. (eds.) Advances in Inductive Logic Programming, pp. 254–264 (1996)
13. Moult, J.: Rigorous Performance Evaluation in Protein Structure Modeling and Implications for Computational Biology. Phil. Trans. R. Soc. B 361, 453–458 (2006)

14. Kersting, K., Gartner, T.: Fisher Kernels for Logical Sequences. In: Boulicaut, J.-F., Esposito, F., Giannotti, F., Pedreschi, D. (eds.) ECML 2004. LNCS (LNAI), vol. 3201, pp. 205–216. Springer, Heidelberg (2004)
15. Passerini, A., Frasconi, P., De Raedt, L.: Kernels on Prolog Proof Trees: Statistical Learning in the ILP Setting. JMLR 7, 307–342 (2006)
16. Turcotte, M., Muggleton, S.H., Sternberg, M.J.E.: The Effect of Relational Background Knowledge on Learning of Protein Three-Dimensional Fold Signature. Machine Learning 43(1-2), 81–95 (2001)
17. Cootes, A.P., Muggleton, S.H., Sternberg, M.J.E.: The Automatic Discovery of Structural Principles Describing Protein Fold Space. J. Mol. Biol. 330, 839–850 (2003)
18. Brenner, S.E., Chothia, C., Hubbard, T.J., Murzin, A.G.: Understanding protein structure: using SCOP for fold interpretation. Methods in Enzymology 266, 635–643 (1996)
19. Muggleton, S.H., Firth, J.: CProgol4.4: a Tutorial Introduction. In: Džeroski, S., Lavrač, N. (eds.) Relational Data Mining, pp. 160–188 (2001)
20. Muggleton, S.H.: Learning Stochastic Logic Programs. Electronic Transactions in Artificial Intelligence. 5(041) (2000)
21. Cussens, J.: Parameter Estimation in Stochastic Logic Programs. Machine Learning 44(3), 245–271 (2001)
22. Muggleton, S.H.: Learning Structure and Parameters of Stochastic Logic Programs. Electronic Transactions in Artificial Intelligence, 6 (2002)
23. Lindgren, T., Boström, H.: Resolving Rule Conflicts with Double Induction. Intell. Data Anal. 8(5), 457–468 (2004)
24. Hand, D.J., Till, R.J.: A Simple Generalisation of the Area Under the ROC Curve for Multiple Class Classification Problems. Machine Learning 45(2), 171–186 (2001)

Structuring Natural Language Data by Learning Rewriting Rules

Guillaume Cleuziou, Lionel Martin, and Christel Vrain

LIFO, Laboratoire d'Informatique Fondamentale d'Orléans
Rue Léonard de Vinci B.P. 6759
45067 Orléans cedex2 - France
{Guillaume.Cleuziou,Lionel.Martin,Christel.Vrain}@univ-orleans.fr

Abstract. The discovery of relationships between concepts is a crucial point in ontology learning (OL). In most cases, OL is achieved from a collection of domain-specific texts, describing the concepts of the domain and their relationships. A natural way to represent the description associated to a particular text is to use a structured term (or tree). We present a method for learning transformation rules, rewriting natural language texts into trees, where the input examples are couples (*text, tree*). The learning process produces an ordered set of rules such that, applying these rules to a *text* gives the corresponding *tree*.

1 Introduction

The work presented in this paper has been motivated by a French project (ACI Biotim http://www-rocq.inria.fr/imedia/biotim/) in the field of Biodiversity. The task we address aims at semi-automatically building an ontology of the domain from corpora describing flora.

The term *ontology* has various definitions in various domains. From a practical point of view, an ontology can be defined as a quadruple $O = (C, R, A, Top)$ where C is a set of concepts, R is a set of relations, A is a set of axioms and Top is the highest-level concept [SB03]. The set R contains relations between concepts, as for example, the binary relation *partof* relating the concepts *hand* and *human*. Usually we distinguish taxonomic and non-taxonomic relations: taxonomic relations are used to organize information with generalization/specialization (or hyponymy) relationships in a "ISA hierarchy"; non-taxonomic relations are any other relations such as synonymy, meronymy, antonymy, attribute-of, possession, causality, ...

Ontology learning refers to extracting one of these elements from input data. This task has been addressed in several research areas. Ontology learning systems extract their knowledge from different types of sources, such as structured data (databases, existing ontologies, ...) or semi-structured data (dictionaries, XML documents, ...). One of the problems is to learn from unstructured data

S. Muggleton, R. Otero, and A. Tamaddoni-Nezhad (Eds.): ILP 2006, LNAI 4455, pp. 125–138, 2007.
© Springer-Verlag Berlin Heidelberg 2007

(domain-specific natural language texts). A quite natural formalism for structuring texts is first-order logics (usually logic programs), thus allowing the use of Inductive Logic Programming for different tasks, as for instance Text Categorization, Information Extraction or Parser Acquisition [Coh95, JSR99, Moo96]. This usually leads to a two-step process: a syntactic analysis of the texts, followed by the learning task. Nevertheless, in our application, the corpora is specific (long descriptions of flore without verbs) making difficult the use of classical syntactic parsers. For instance, the following example is the beginning of the description of the plant called "Pulchranthus variegatus":

> " *Subshrubs or shrubs, 0.5-2 m tall. Stems terete with red, exfoliating bark. Leaves: petioles 3-13 mm long; blades elliptic-lanceolate, 13-26 × 5-9 cm, glabrous, the apex acuminate-cuspidate. Inflorescences terminal, racemes or panicles, 4-15 cm long, green, the flowers 2-many per node; peduncle 10-15 mm long; bracts small, narrowly triangular, 2.5-3 x 0.5 mm; pedicels lacking to short, 1.5 mm long; bracteoles 1.5-2 mm long. ...*"

This text describes different concepts (stem, bark, leaf, ...) and various relations: part-of relations (bark is a part of a stem, flower is a part of inflorescences, ...) and attribute-value relations (stem is terete, bark is red, petiole is 3-13 mm long...).

All this information can be represented into a tree (term), the leaves (constants) are elements of the text. For example, the term

> *partOf(desc(stem, terete), desc(bark, [red, exfoliating]))*

could be a representation of information associated with the sentence *"Stems terete with red, exfoliating bark"*. The detailed formal language used in our work is presented in Section 3.

Given a set of sentences and their corresponding terms (manually built), our goal is to produce a set of rules able to rewrite a sentence into a term. The corpora shows that in many cases, some simple regular structures can be automatically discovered, these structures are based on the punctuation and the syntactical categories of words. For example, when a noun is immediately followed by an adjective, then the adjective describes the noun; when two descriptions are separated by ",", or ", *with*", then the second description is about a concept which is a part of the concept of the first description. This short example also shows that a preprocessing step is required: the initial text is transformed into a list of elements (words, punctuation), each element is tagged, using a part-of-speech (POS) tagger; this preprocessing is done in most existing ontology learners.

Some works have already adressed this task: [MPS02] proposes a survey of methods relying either on statistics or predefined patterns, [SM06] is based on cooccurrences with verb phrases, [Yam01] uses a n-grams representation and [Ait02] uses ILP techniques to characterize specific relations. [Bri93] proposes a transformation-based approach for parsing text into binary trees.

Our approach can be compared with [Hea92] which proposes to use a pattern-based approach to extract hyponymy/hyperonymy relations from texts. [Hea92] proposes to use patterns like for instance :

$$NP_0 \ such \ as \ \{NP_1, NP_2..., (and/or)\} \ NP_n$$

to infer that $hyponymy(NP_0, NP_i)$ for $i = 1..n$. In Hasti [SB04], patterns are also used for building ontology. In these works, the user has to define the patterns. The particularity of our approach is that we propose to learn such rules automatically, from a set of examples. In [Bos00], transfer rules are learned in a bi-lingual translation perspective: rules are produced from pairs of structured terms. These rules are mainly based on the structure of both terms, i.e. on the non-terminal symbols occurring in each term. In our approach, rules are learned from pairs $(sentence, term)$ where the sentence is a list of (tagged) words, i.e. a term which is not sufficiently structured to apply the approach of [Bos00].

For this reason, our method can be applied to any type of relation. The learning process presented in this paper is simple: it is an iterative method, from the inner structure to the outer structure, building new examples for each iteration. We propose a divide and conquer approach guided by the structure and based on a least general generalization principle, applied independently on different parts of couples $(sentence, term)$. In that sense, this work is a preliminary one, and we plane to explore deeply the search space, taking into account the sequential aspect of the data. From an ILP perspective, this point is a challenging problem.

2   Introductive Example

To introduce the learning problem, let us consider the three following sentences:

s_1:   *"Stems terete to quadrangular, with swollen nodes"*
s_2:   *"Bracts imbricate, the margins toothed"*
s_3:   *"Corolla curved, the lobes subequal to dimorphic"*

We propose to associate to each sentence a term (or tree), representing information which can help to build an ontology. For example, the first sentence presents two concepts (stem and node), where node is a part of stem; these concepts are described by:

- stems are terete to quadrangular,thus introducing a range of values
- nodes are swollen

In order to represent this information, we can associate to the sentence s_1 the following term:

$term_1$:   *partOf(desc(stem, range(terete, quadrangular)), desc(swollen, node))*

In the same way, we can produce $term_2$ and $term_3$ from sentences s_2 and s_3. We have chosen here very similar examples to introduce the learning process and so the corresponding terms are very similar. These terms are represented by the following trees:

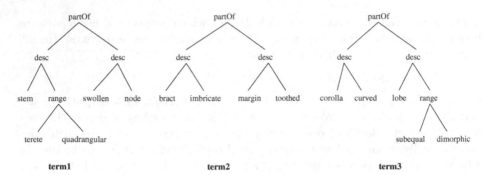

term1   term2   term3

Our goal is to build rules such that, applying them on a sentence builds the corresponding term. The rewriting process is based on the grammatical categories of elements in sentences, so we need a mapping from the set of elements in a sentence to a set of possible tags. We use TreeTagger [Tre] to perform this mapping and the possible tags are those proposed by TreeTagger : **nn** (noun, common singular), **jj** (adjective, general), **vvn** (verb, past participle), ..., a detailed list is proposed in [Tre]. We have added the tag **pct** for punctuation.

Then a sentence can be viewed as a list of terms; the previous examples s_1, s_2 and s_3 are respectively represented by the lists $list_1$, $list_2$ and $list_3$:

$list_1$: [nn(stem),jj(terete),to(to),jj(quadrangular),pct(virg),in(with), jj(swollen),nn(node)]

$list_2$: [nn(bract),jj(imbricate),pct(virg),dt(the),nn(margin),vvn(toothed)]

$list_3$: [nn(corolla),vvn(curved),pct(virg),dt(the),nn(lobe),jj(subequal), to(to),jj(dimorphic)]

The goal is then to learn rules, rewriting such lists into the corresponding terms. The input of the process is a set of couples ($list_i$, $term_i$), and we propose to learn these rules by a generalization process. However, the terms are usually too much different to be generalized. For this reason, we consider all their sub-terms with their corresponding subtrees in the generalization process: this requires to be able to extract the sub-list associated to a sub-term, this point is detailed in Section 3.2.

In our example, we can get for instance the two following couples (sub-list, sub-term):

([jj(terete),to(to),jj(quadrangular)], range(terete, quadrangular))

and

([jj(subequal),to(to),jj(dimorphic)], range(subequal, dimorphic))

which can be generalized into

([jj(X),to(to),jj(Y)], range(X, Y))   (rule 1)

The last couple can be considered as a rule, producing a term from a list of terms (we propose in the following section a detailed definition of rewriting rules). Then, applying such a rule to a list of terms consists in replacing a part of the list matching the left-hand side of the rule by the corresponding right-hand side.

Such a rule will have to be applied to lists of terms such as $list_1$. So, it will be necessary to decompose such a list into 3 lists l_1, l' and l_2 such that l' matches with the left-hand list of the rule and then, l' is replaced by the right-hand term of the rule. For the example $list_1$, a possible decomposition is

$l_1 = [$ nn(stem)$]$,
$l' = [$jj(terete),to(to),jj(quadrangular) $]$
$l_2 = [$ pct(virg),in(with), jj(swollen),nn(node)$]$

and applying the rule 1 to $list_1$ gives the list:

$list'_1$: [nn(stem),range(terete, quadrangular),pct(virg),in(with),
        jj(swollen),nn(node)]

In the next section, we introduce special symbols $\diamond_i$ instead of variables $X, Y, \ldots$. Then, the right-hand term of the rule 1 will be written $range(\diamond_1, \diamond_2)$ and we will have to extract the a sub-list from l' (in our example $[terete, quadrangular]$) such that symbols $\diamond_1$ and $\diamond_2$ are replaced by the terms belonging to this sub-list.

We can notice that, applying the previous rule to any list from the initial lists $list_1$, $list_2$ or $list_3$, produces only expected sub-terms. Conversely, the rule

$([$nn(X),jj(Y) $],$ desc(X, Y))

could also be considered but it produces some unexpected terms since it can be applied to the sub-list [nn(stem),jj(terete)] of the sentence s_1, producing the term $desc(stem, terete)$ which is not a sub-term of $term_1$. For this reason, this rule is not acceptable at this level (in this paper, we require that rules are 100% correct).

Once an acceptable rule is produced, we propose to apply it to all the sublists of the positive examples: if we apply the previous rule to the couple $(list_1, term_1)$, we obtain the couple

([nn(stem),range(terete,quadrangular),pct(virg),in(with),jj(swollen),
        nn(node)], $term_1$)

Then we get a new set of positive examples and we propose to continue this process until either all the couples have the form $([term], term)$ or no more rule can be learned. In our example, we can expect that, after learning and applying some rules, $list_1$, $list_2$ and $list_3$ will be rewritten respectively into

$list'_1$: [desc(stem,range(terete,quadrangular)),
            pct(virg),in(with), desc(swollen,node)]
$list'_2$: [desc(bract,imbricate),
            pct(virg),dt(the), desc(margin,toothed)]
$list'_3$: [desc(corolla,curved),
            pct(virg),dt(the), desc(lobe, range(subequal, dimorphic))]

These terms are similar in their structure but in order to generalize the examples $(list'_1, term_1)$, $(list'_2, term_2)$, $(list'_3, term_3)$, we have to introduce a more general form of rewriting rules, generalizing the three previous examples allowing either "*the*" or "*with*" between two descriptions in a rule producing a *partOf* term. These problems also arise with the following example:

([nn(bract),**jj**(imbricate)], desc(bract, imbricate))

and

([nn(margin),**vvn**(toothed)], desc(margin, toothed))

where two different tags are possible for the second word.

This process is formally detailed in the following sections.

3   Definitions and Languages Specification

As mentioned in the previous section, the examples used by the learning method are couples (*list*, *term*) where *list* is a list of term. In this section we introduce some definitions and we present the language specifications used in our application, for both terms in the initial lists of terms and terms representing intended information to extract.

3.1   Terms and Lists

We first recall some definitions and notations for terms and lists, see [CDG+97] for more details.

A regular tree language is defined by a ranked alphabet $(\mathcal{F}, arity)$ where $\mathcal{F}$ is a finite set of symbols and $arity$ a function from $\mathcal{F}$ to $\mathbb{N}$, which indicates the arity of a symbol. Given a set of variables $\mathcal{X}$, terms are inductively defined by: a symbol of arity 0 is a term, a variable of $\mathcal{X}$ is a term, if f is a symbol of arity n and $t_1, ..., t_n$ are terms, then $f(t_1, ..., t_n)$ is a term. For any $i \in [1..n]$, t_i is a sub-term of $f(t_1, ..., t_n)$ and any sub-term of t_i is a sub-term of $f(t_1, ..., t_n)$. Given a term $t = f(t_1, ..., t_n)$, we define $top(t) = f$.

A context is a term $C[\diamond]$ containing a special variable $\diamond$ which occurs just once in that term, it marks an empty place. Throughout, the substitution of $\diamond$ by a term u is written $C[u]$.

Lists are usually terms build with a 2-ary symbol (*cons*) and a 0-ary symbol (ϵ). In this paper, lists of terms are written with square brackets in order to distinguish terms from lists of terms.

Given n terms $t_1, ..., t_n$, the list containing $t_1, ..., t_n$ is denoted by $[t_1, ..., t_n]$, n is the size of l. Let l be the list $[t_1, ..., t_n]$, $l(i)$ denotes the i-th term t_i. The concatenation of two lists $l_1 = [a_1, ..., a_n]$ and $l_2 = [b_1, ..., b_p]$ is written $l_1.l_2 = [a_1, ..., a_n, b_1, ...b_p]$.

3.2   Definitions and Notations

Let l be the list $[t_1, ..., t_n]$, a *sub-list* of l is a list $[l(i_1), ..., l(i_k)]$ with $i_1 < i_2 < ... < i_k$. We write $S_k(l)$ the set of sub-lists of l with size k, and $S_*(l)$ the set of sub-lists of l of any size.

Given a list $l = [t_1, ..., t_n]$, the list l' is a *part of the list* l if l can be written as a concatenation $l = l_1.l'.l_2$ (l_1 and l_2 are lists possibly empty). In this case, l' is a sub-list of l that can be written $l' = [l(i), l(i+1), ..., l(i+k)]$.

◇ **Definition : k-context.** A *k-context* is a term $C[[\diamond_1, ..., \diamond_k]]$ containing k special variables $\diamond_1, ..., \diamond_k$ which occur just once in that term, each one marks an empty place. Given a list of terms $l = [t_1, ..., t_k]$, the substitution of each $\diamond_i$ by the term t_i is written $C[l] = C[[t_1, ..., t_k]]$. The special variable $\diamond_i$ appears to the right-hand side of $\diamond_j$ iff $i > j$

Given a couple (l, t) (l is a list of terms and t is a term), the role of a k-context is to express that the term t can be obtained from a k-context $C[[\diamond_1, ..., \diamond_k]]$ and a sub-list $l_k \in S_k(l)$ such that $t = C[l_k]$. To learn rewriting rules, we have to find k-contexts that are common to different couples.

For instance, let us consider a couple (l, t) with $l = [a, b, c, d]$ and $t = f(b, h(d))$. If we consider the 2-context $C[[\diamond_1, \diamond_2]] = f(\diamond_1, h(\diamond_2))$, we can extract the sub-list $l' = [b, d]$ from l such that $t = C[l']$. Let us notice that another possible context is for instance the 1-context $C'[[\diamond_1]] = f(b, h(\diamond_1))$ with the sub-list $l'' = [d]$, such that $t = C'[l'']$.

Since for a couple (l, t) t is a possible 0-context, we propose a more restrictive definition:

◇ **Definition : k-skeleton.** A *k-skeleton* is a k-context $sk_k = C[[\diamond_1, ..., \diamond_k]]$ such that there are no other 0-ary symbols in sk_k than the $\diamond_i$. A term t is a *skeleton* if there exists k such that t is a k-skeleton (such a value k is unique).

For example, $f(a, g(\diamond_1, \diamond_2))$ is a 2-context but is not a 2-skeleton. On the other hand, $f(\diamond_1, g(\diamond_2, \diamond_3))$ is a 3-skeleton.

In the following, rewriting rules are obtained from skeletons. This choice has been made in order to ensure that the information associated to term are all contained in the initial sentence. In a more general process, we could consider k-contexts to learn rewriting rules.

◇ **Definition : consistency.** A couple (l, t) (l is a list of terms and t is a term) is said to be *consistent* if there exists a unique couple (sk, sl) such that sk is a skeleton $C[[\diamond_1, ..., \diamond_k]]$, $sl \in S_k(l)$ and $C[sl] = t$.

The consistency condition for (l, t) ensures that the term t can be obtained from a skeleton and a sub-list of l. It ensures also that there exists only one way to obtain t from a skeleton and a sub-list. Then, the uniqueness of the skeleton and the sub-list allow to denote by $skel(l, t)$ and $sub(l, t)$ the associated skeleton and sub-list of a consistent couple (l, t).

The consistency condition is not necessary in a general rewriting-rule framework. It is required in the method presented here in order to reduce the search space for learning rules. In order to ensure the consistency condition:

- we can require that the order of words occurring in a term is the same that the order of words in the associated sentence,
- we can also require that each word occurring in a term occurs exactly one time in the associated sentence.

3.3 Rewriting Rule

A rewriting rule allows to replace a part of a list of terms, by a new term, containing some terms of the list of sub-terms. This replacement is made under some conditions that are specified in the rule. For this reason, we propose the following general and formal definition:

$\diamond$ **Definition : Rewriting rule.** A *rewriting rule* is defined by an integer k and a triple $(Cond, Ext, T)$ that expresses how to apply it on a list l decomposed into three sub-lists $l = l_1.l'.l2$,

- $Cond$ is a condition which has to be satisfied by $(l_1, l', l2)$,
- Ext specifies conditions on sub-lits l'' with size k that can be extracted from l'. $Ext(l')$ denotes the set of sub-lists that can be extracted from l' by applying Ext
- $T = C[[\diamond_1, ..., \diamond_k]]$ is a k-context.

This definition is very general. It will be illustrated in Section 4, after having defined a first order language.

Given a list of terms l, to apply a rewriting rule $r = (Cond, Ext, T)$, we first need to search for a decomposition $l = l_1.l'.l_2$ such that the condition $Cond$ is satisfied for $(l_1, l', l2)$. Then, given $l'' \in Ext(l')$, the list $l_1.[C[l'']].l_2$ can be produced from l, by applying r.

In this general context, given a list of terms l and a rewriting rule r, applying r to l may produces different results; we note the set of results $r(l)$. In the same way, we note $r^2(l) = \{r(l')|l' \in r(l)\}$, and so on. We note $r^*(l)$ the set $r^n(l)$ such that the rule r cannot be applied to any element of $r^n(l)$, if it exists.

The previous definition is very general, we do not propose a precise formalism to express conditions and extraction methods. In the next section, we detail a specific form of rule.

3.4 Languages Specification

We specify here the language used in our experiments. Examples are couples $(list, term)$ associated to a sentence. In such couples, $list$ is a list of terms and $term$ represents information to extract from the sentence.

Initially, the list of terms is built from the elements in the sentence, associated to their corresponding syntactical tag. As mentioned above, TreeTagger has been used for the tagging task. The language for terms in the initial lists of terms is then specified as follows:

- all the syntactical elements (words, punctuations) are 0-ary symbols,
- any tag is a 1-ary symbol.

We have used the tagset proposed in the original English parameter files given with TreeTagger [Tre]. We have added a specific tag "dimension" for expression such as "$2 - 4 \times 2.5\ cm$".

Concerning the right-hand part of the examples, the language used has to represent conceptual information associated to a sentence, mainly the concepts, the attributes and values, and the "part of" relations. Moreover, some symbols have been introduced to handle lists.

We chose to use a detailed language; the symbols are (the arity is specified behind /) :

n/1: the argument of this symbol is a concept,

attr/1: the argument is an attribute,

val/1: the argument is a value,

prec/1: the argument is a precision (mainly expressed by adverbs),

att/3: this symbol allows to build an attribute/value association; the arguments are an attribute, a value and a precision. We always put 3 arguments, even when some information is missing in the sentence. In this case, we use the 0-ary symbol *e*. For example, "mostly pilose" is represented by the term *att(prec(mostly), val(pilose), attr(e))*, the attribute is not indicated.

latt/2: this symbol is used for lists of attribute/value associations, the first argument is made with the symbol *att* and the second is a list of attribute/value associations or *e*. We have chosen to systematically use this symbol, even for a single attribute/value association.

range/2: allows to express range of values; this symbol may appear as an argument of *val*,

disj_jj/2: express a disjunction of values (conjunction of values are expressed with lists),

nj/2: this symbol is used for some noun-adjective association, such as "lower lobe" *(nj(lower, n(lobe)))*, "posterior lip" *(nj(posterior, n(lip)))*, ...

rj/2: this symbol is used when a value is associated to an adverb, such as "mostly triangular" *(rj(mostly, triangular))* or "slightly emarginate" *(rj(slightly , emarginate))*, ...

desc/2: this symbol allows to express that a list of attributes/values describes a particular part of the plant. The arguments are a concept and a list of attributes/values,

partOf/2: this symbol expresses a "part of" relation; it has two arguments, one corresponding to a concept (build with symbols *n* or *desc*) and one corresponding to a precision,

conj_nn/2: this symbol expresses conjunctions of concepts, it is used when different part-of relations are described in a sentence.

These symbols are illustrated on the following example: the initial sentence is:

"Corolla tubular to funnelform, +/- arcuate , 2-lipped , mostly pilose, usually red, the posterior lip entire or slightly emarginate, the anterior lip 3-lobed"

and the associated term is:

partOf(
   desc(n(corolla),
      latt(att(val(range(tubular,funnelform)), attr(e), prec(e)),

$latt(att(prec(+/-), val(arcuate), attr(e)),$
$latt(att(val(2\text{-}lipped), attr(e), prec(e)),$
$latt(att(prec(mostly),val(pilose), attr(e)),$
$latt(att(prec(usually),val(red), attr(e)), e)))))),$
$conj\_nn($
$desc(nj(posterior,n(lip)),$
$latt(att(val(disj\_jj(entire,rj(slightly,emarginate))),$
$attr(e), prec(e)),e)),$
$desc(nj(anterior,n(lip)),$
$latt(att(val(3\text{-}lobed), attr(e), prec(e)),e))),$
$prec(e))$

4 Learning Method

As mentioned above, we propose to learn from an initial set of couples $\mathcal{C}_0 = \{(list_i^0, term_i)\}$. We require that any initial couple is consistent.

Once a rule r has been learned, it is applied to any list $list_i^0$, if possible, giving new examples $\mathcal{C}_1 = \{(list_i^1, term_i)\}$, where $list_i^1$ is obtained by applying r to $list_i^0$ as many times as possible, otherwise $list_i^1 = list_i^0$. Then, this process is repeated to define $\mathcal{C}_2$ from $\mathcal{C}_1$, ...

In our framework, when a learned rule r is applied to a list l, we require $r^*(l)$ to exist and to be a singleton. This means that if there are different ways to apply r to a list l, the way r is applied has no importance and any way to apply r leads to the same result. In practice, such rules, if generated, will cover negative examples and therefore are rejected by the learning process; this is realized due to the definition of negative examples.

Moreover, the form of the learned rules ensures that any $\mathcal{C}_m$ contains only consistent examples.

For learning a rule, the idea is to use any subterm and their corresponding list of terms as positive examples. Then, at any step, the set of examples used in the learning process has to be defined from $\mathcal{C}_n = \{(list_i^n, term_i)\}$.

4.1 Positive and Negative Examples

Given a set of couples $\mathcal{C}_n = \{(list_i^n, term_i)\}$, we define the set of positive examples E_n^+ as the set of couple (l_i^k, t_i^k) such that t_i^k is a subterm of $term_i$ and l_i^k is the corresponding part of the list $list_i^n$. In order to automatically build E_n^+ from $\mathcal{C}_n$, this definition requires a function that maps any subterm to the corresponding part of the list. Given a couple $(list_i^n, term_i)$ and a subterm t_i^k from $term_i$, since the couple is consistent, there exists a unique skeleton $sk = C[[\diamond_1, ..., \diamond_k]]$, and a unique sub-list $sl \in S_k(list_i^n)$ such that $C[sl] = term_i$. Then, there exists a sub-term $sk' = C'[[\diamond_j, ..., \diamond_{j+p}]]$ of sk, and the corresponding sub-list sl' such that $t_i^k = C'[sl']$. The sub-list sl' can be written $[list_i^n(j_1), list_i^n(j_2), ..., list_i^n(j_s)]$, we propose to choose $l_i^k = [list_i^n(j_1), list_i^n(j_1+1), ..., list_i^n(j_s)]$, which is the shortest part of list associated to t_i^k.

An example (l_i^k, t_i^k) is said to be *covered* by a rule r if $r(l_i^k)$ is unique and $r(l_i^k) = [t_i^k]$.

From the set of positive examples, we propose to define the set of negative examples E_n^- as the set of couples (l_i^-, t_i^-) such that l_i^- is a part of a list of l_j^k for $(l_j^k, t_j^k) \in E_n^+$ and $(l_i^-, t_i^-) \notin E_n^+$ (any term t_i^- such that $(l_i^-, t_i^-) \notin E_n^+$ can be chosen). The set of negative examples is then infinite, and in practice it is not generated. To ensure that no negative example is covered, it is sufficient to test whether each time a rule r can be applied on $list_i^n$, $(list_i^n, term_i) \in C_n$, the term produced by the rule is a subterm of $term_i$.

4.2   Form of the Learned Rules

As mentioned above, a rewriting rule is a triple $(Cond, Ext, T)$, where T is a k-skeleton. We propose to write a rule (associated to a k-skeleton T) as :

$r = [list_0, (\Diamond_1, Symb_1), list_1, \ldots (\Diamond_n, Symb_n), list_n] \rightarrow T$

where: $list_i$ is a list of list of terms and $Symb_i$ is a list of symbols

We have to specify $Cond$ and Ext from this representation. Let l_1, l' and l_2, be lists of terms, $Cond$ is satisfied by $(l_1, l', l2)$ if l' can be written

$l' = ll_0.[t_1].ll_1.[t_2].ll_2. \ldots .[t_k].ll_k$

with $ll_i \in list_i$ and $top(t_i) \in Symb_i$. In this case, $[t_1, ..., t_k]$ belongs to $Ext(l')$.

In this representation of a rule, $list_i$ corresponds to the list of possible separators between terms occurring in the list and in the term. Let us notice that when the condition is satisfied for $(l_1, l', l2)$, it does not depend on l_1 nor l_2. In this context, the condition does not depend on the context of the list to be replaced.

Consider the following examples $(list_1, term_1)$ and $(list_2, term_2)$:

$list_1 = [dt(the), nn(stem), in(with), nn(anther), jj(2 - locular)]$
$term_1 = partOf(stem, desc(anther, 2 - locular)$
$list_2 = [nn(bract), pct(virg), dt(the), nn(margin), vvn(toothed)]$
$term_1 = partOf(bract, desc(margin, toothed)$

they are covered by the following rule:

$r = [[[dt(the)], [], (\Diamond_1, [nn]), [[in(with)], [pct(virg), dt(the)]], (\Diamond_2, [nn]),$
$\quad\quad [[]], (\Diamond_3, [jj, vvn]), [[]]] \rightarrow partOf(\Diamond_1, desc(\Diamond_2, \Diamond_3))$

The construction of this rule is illustrated in the following table:

	lst_1	lst_2	$\rightarrow r$
l_0	[dt(the)]	[]	[[dt(the)], []]
t_1	nn(stem)	nn(bract)	$\Diamond_1 = nn(...)$
l_1	[in(with)]	[pct(virg),dt(the)]	[[in(with)], [pct(virg),dt(the)]]
t_2	nn(anther)	nn(margin)	$\Diamond_2 = nn(...)$
l_2	[]	[]	[[]]
t_3	jj(2-locular)	vvn(toothed)	$\Diamond_3 = jj(...)$ or $vvn(...)$
l_3	[]	[]	[[]]

4.3   The Search Space

Given a set of positive examples E_i^+ (and the associated set of negative examples E_i^-), the goal is to find a rule covering some positive examples and covering no negative ones, in a "divide-and-conquer" way. In this paper, we propose a simplified method, based on a decomposition of the set E_i^+ into a partition $G_1, \ldots, G_n$, where examples with the same skeleton are in the same group.

A rule is built by generalizing examples of a group. Given a group G_i and the associated skeleton $C[[\diamond_1, ..., \diamond_k]]$, it is possible to write:

$$G_i = \{ll_0^j.[\diamond_1^j].ll_1^j.[\diamond_2^j]. \ldots .[\diamond_k^j].ll_k^j\}, \; j = 1..|G_i|.$$

since examples are consistent (in the previous notation, we just write $\diamond_p^j$ in the term l, where the terms of $sub(l,t)$ occur, for an example (l,t) of the group). Then, we propose to build the rule:

$$r = [list_0, (\diamond_1, Symb_1), list_1, \ldots (\diamond_k, Symb_k), list_k] \to C[[\diamond_1, ..., \diamond_k]].$$

where $list_p = \cup_{j=1..|G_i|} ll_p^j$, $p = 0..k$, and $Symb_p = \cup_{j=1..|G_i|} top(\diamond_p^j)$, $p = 1..k$.

If a rule covers a negative example, it is rejected. The search starts with groups for which the associated skeleton has the lowest depth.

4.4 Learning Process

Our learning process differs from the usual divide-and-conquer methods: each time a rule is learned, t is applied on the set of positive examples. Each rule is then built from a particular set of positive examples. This choice is motivated by the general process of the transformation of a text into a term: rules are applied in the same order they are learned. When a rule is applied, some rules may have been applied before, then, when we start learning a rule, the rules previously learned have to be applied.

Formally, let r_i be the rule learned from E_i^+ (starting by r_0). We define $E_{i+1}^+ = r_i^*(E_i^+) = \{(r_i^*(list^+), term^+)|(list^+, term^+) \in E_i^+\}$.

The learning process stops when each example $(list^+, term^+) \in E_n^+$ is such that $list^+ = [term^+]$, or when any new rule covers some negative examples.

5 Experiments and Conclusion

This approach has been applied in the field of botany, using a corpus on vascular plants of central French Guiana. We have used the description of 5 plants, corresponding to 54 texts, and producing 1115 initial positive examples. The method produces 49 rules covering 81,3% of the positive examples.

The preliminary results are very promising since many improvements can be done: we have used a simplified method for learning a rule; some of the uncovered positive examples could have been covered by splitting some of the groups G_j or by exploring in more details the search space. It could also be interesting to consider the context of the examples: some ambiguous cases could be solved by including in the rule, the category of elements preceding and following the examples. As mentioned above, we will focus in further works on the learning task: we proposed in this paper a least general generalization approach, learning more complex rules is an interesting ILP perspective.

Moreover, in some cases, the rules cannot be based only on categories of elements. Consider the examples *"corolla glandular, mauve or white"* and *"corolla blue, mauve or white"*. In the first case, the disjunction concerns the words "mauve" and "white", in the second case it concerns the 3 colors. This situation could be treated by using additional information or by producing rules allowing different possible transformations from the same text.

References

[Ait02]   Aitken, J.S.: Learning Information Extraction Rules: An Inductive Logic Programming approach. In: Proceedings of the 15th European Conference on Artificial Intelligence, pp. 355–359 (2002), http://citeseer.ist.psu.edu/586553.html

[Bos00]   Boström, H.: Induction of recursive transfer rules. In: Cussens, J., Džeroski, S. (eds.) Learning Language in Logic. LNCS (LNAI), vol. 1925, pp. 237–246. Springer, Heidelberg (2000)

[Bri93]   Brill, E.: Automatic grammar induction and parsing free text: A transformation-based approach. In: Meeting of the Association for Computational Linguistics, pp. 259–265 (1993)

[CDG+97]   Comon, H., Dauchet, M., Gilleron, R., Jacquemard, F., Lugiez, D., Tison, S., Tommasi, M.: Tree automata techniques and applications (1997) (release October, 1rst 2002) Available on: http://www.grappa.univ-lille3.fr/tata

[Coh95]   Cohen, W.W.: Learning to classify English text with ILP methods. In: De Raedt, L. (ed.) ILP95, pp. 3–24. DEPTCW (1995)

[Hea92]   Hearst, M.A.: Automatic acquisition of hyponyms from large text corpora. In: Proceedings of the Fourteenth International Conference on Computational Linguistics, pp. 539–545, Nantes, France (July 1992)

[JSR99]   Junker, M., Sintek, M., Rinck, M.: Learning for text categorization and information extraction with ILP. In: Cussens, J. (ed.) Proceedings of the 1st Workshop on Learning Language in Logic, pp. 84–93, Bled, Slovenia (1999)

[Moo96]   Mooney, R.J.: Inductive logic programming for natural language processing. In: Inductive Logic Programming. LNCS, vol. 1314, pp. 3–24. Springer, Heidelberg (1997)

[MPS02]   Maedche, A., Pekar, V., Staab, S.: Ontology learning part one - on discovering taxonomic relations from the web. In: Zhong, N. (ed.) Web Intelligence, Springer, Heidelberg (2002)

[SB03]   Shamsfard, M., Barforoush, A.: The state of the art in ontology learning: a framework for comparison. Knowl. Eng. Rev. 18(4), 293–316 (2003)

[SB04]   Shamsfard, M., Barforoush, A.: Learning ontologies from natural language texts. Int. J. Hum.-Comput. Stud. 60(1), 17–63 (2004)

[SM06]   Sanchez, D., Moreno, A.: Discovering non-taxonomic relations from the Web. In: Corchado, E., Yin, H., Botti, V., Fyfe, C. (eds.) IDEAL 2006. LNCS, vol. 4224, Springer, Heidelberg (2006)

[Tre]   TC Projetc TreeTagger: http://www.ims.uni-stuttgart.de/projekte/corplex/TreeTagger/DecisionTreeTagger.html

[Yam01]   Yamaguchi, T.: Acquiring conceptual relationships from domain-specific texts. In: Proceedings of the Second Workshop on Ontology Learning OL 2001, Seattle, USA (2001)

A   An Example of Flore Description: ANISACANTHUS

*Branching herbs or subshrubs. Stems covered with brown or gray exfoliating bark.
Leaves: petioles present or absent; blades linear to lanceolate, cystoliths present.
Inflorescences spicate, racemose, or paniculate, the flowers secund or opposite,
borne singly or several at inflorescence node; bracts and bracteoles mostly triangular to linear, usually caducous. Flowers: calyx 3-5-lobed, the lobes triangular
to linear; corolla tubular to funnelform, arcuate, 2-lipped, mostly pilose, usually
red, the posterior lip entire or slightly emarginate, the anterior lip 3-lobed; sta-
mens 2, the anthers 2-locular, subequal, not mucronate or appendaged. Capsules
subpyriform, slightly beaked. Seeds 2-4, homomorphic, flattened, each supported
by curved retinaculum.*

B   Positive Examples Corresponding to the Firt Two Sentences

ex([vvg(branching),nn(herbs),cc(or),nn(subshrubs)],
    disj_nn(desc(latt(att(val(branching), attr(e), prec(e)), e), n(herbs)),
    n(subshrubs))).

ex([nn(stems),vvn(covered),in(with),jj(brown),cc(or),jj(gray),
    vvg(exfoliating),nn(bark)],
    partOf(n(stems),desc(latt(att(val(disj_jj(brown, gray)), attr(e), prec(e)),
    latt(att(val(exfoliating), attr(e), prec(e)), e)), n(bark)))).

C   Examples of Learned Rules

rule 1: [[[[]], ($\diamond_1$, [nn]), [[cc(and)]], ($\diamond_2$, [nn]), [[]]],
        conj_nn($\diamond_1$, $\diamond_2$)]
for example applied to "bracts and bracteoles"

rule 2: [[[[]], w($\diamond_1$, [dim]), [[]], w($\diamond_2$, [rb, nn, jj]), [[]]],
        att(val($\diamond_1$, $\diamond_2$, prec(e)))]
for example applied to "6-8 cm long", "15mm diam", ...

rule 3: [[[[]], ($\diamond_1$, [vv, jj]), [[pct(virg)]], ($\diamond_2$, [jj]), [[pct(virg), cc(or)]],
            ($\diamond_3$, [vvg, jj]), [[]]],
        disj_jj($\diamond_1$, disj_jj($\diamond_2$, $\diamond_3$))]
for example applied to "spicate, racemose, or paniculate".

rule 4: [[[[]], ($\diamond_1$, [range, jj]), [[pct(virg)]], ($\diamond_2$, [att]), [[]]],
        latt(att(val($\diamond_1$), attr(e), prec(e)), latt($\diamond_2$, e))]

for example applied to "triangular to linear, usually caducous". Let us notice
that this rule is learned after some rules have been learned and applied to examples: a first rule has produced the term *range(triangular, linear)*, a second rule
has produced the term *att(prec(usually), val(caducous), attr(e))* from "usually
caducous".

An Efficient Algorithm for Computing
Kernel Function Defined with Anti-unification

Koichiro Doi[1], Tetsuya Yamashita[2], and Akihiro Yamamoto[1]

[1] Graduate School of Informatics, Kyoto University,
Yoshida-honmachi, Sakyo-ku, Kyoto 606-8501, Japan
{doi, akihiro}@i.kyoto-u.ac.jp
[2] Graduate School of Information Science, Nara Institute Science and Technology,
8916-5 Takayama-cho, Ikoma-shi, Nara 630-0101, Japan
tetsuya-y@is.naist.ac.jp

Abstract. In this paper, we give an algorithm for computing the value of the kernel function K_{TERM}, which takes a pair of terms in first-order logic as its inputs, and facilitates Support Vector Machines classifying terms in a higher dimension space. The value of $K_{TERM}(s, t)$ is given as the total number of terms which subsume both s and t. The algorithm presented in the paper computes $K_{TERM}(s, t)$ without enumerating all such terms. We also implement the algorithm and present some experimental examples of classification of first-order terms with K_{TERM}. Furthermore, we also propose the concept of intentional kernels as a generalization of K_{TERM}.

1 Introduction

The Support Vector Machine (SVM, for short) technique combined with kernel functions is now attracting much attention in Machine Learning. Kernel functions were originally investigated for classifying numeric data with non-linear separating functions. Recently kernel functions have been developed for structured data, such as strings and trees. The aim of this research is to apply the SVM technique to data represented in first-order formula or logic programs. In the present paper we introduce a kernel function K_{TERM} for data in the form of first-order terms and give an efficient algorithm to compute the function.

The kernel function K_{TERM} is a natural extension of the DNF kernel and the monotone-DNF kernel, which are developed for Boolean data by Khardon et al. [6] and Sadohara[10][11]. We analyzed the two kernels and showed that they are based on anti-unification [9] (least common anti-instance, least general generalization) of monomials of Boolean formulae[12]. The kernel K_{TERM} is designed on anti-unification of two first-order terms. More precisely, K_{TERM} is given as the total number of terms which subsume the anti-unification of the arguments. In this study we also propose a general concept *intensional kernel* and show that K_{TERM} as well as the DNF kernel and the monotone-DNF kernel are instances of intentional kernels.

S. Muggleton, R. Otero, and A. Tamaddoni-Nezhad (Eds.): ILP 2006, LNAI 4455, pp. 139–153, 2007.
© Springer-Verlag Berlin Heidelberg 2007

Several kernels have been proposed for logical formulae. Gärtner et al. [3] have presented a kernel function for higher-order terms. The kernel is defined with the complexity of the structure of higher-order terms. The structure is obtained by traversing the terms in a top-down manner. The kernel K_{TERM} is different from the kernel on the point that our kernel considers the number of terms subsuming two terms. Muggleton et al. [7] have presented a kernel function for SVILP (Support Vector Inductive Logic Programming). Their kernel function is based on the subsumption relation for definite clauses, and similar to ours. However, they have not shown any clear algorithm for their kernel function. We propose an algorithm for K_{TERM}.

This paper is organized as follows. In Section 2 we give the definition of the kernel function K_{TERM}. In Section 3 we give an algorithm computing K_{TERM}. In Section 4 we show validity and some other properties of K_{TERM}. In Section 5 we give some experimental examples about K_{TERM}. We conclude our discussion with introducing the concept of intensional kernels and comparing it to the convolution kernel in Section 6.

2   Kernel Function K_{TERM}

We follow the standard terminology and notations in Logic Programming, Inductive Logic Programming, Support Vector Machines, and kernels. For more detailed definitions and results readers should refer some textbooks in these areas (e.g., [1,8]).

Let $\mathcal{X}$ be a set, and $\mathbf{B}$ be the set $\{-1, 1\}$. We call $\mathcal{X}$ an *input space*. A *training example* is a pair $(x, E(x)) \in X \times \mathbf{B}$ where X is a finite subset of $\mathcal{X}$, and $E : X \longrightarrow \mathbf{B}$. We call the function E a *training function*. The element x is called a *positive example* if $E(x) = 1$ and is *negative* if $E(x) = -1$.

The SVM technique with kernel functions is aimed at finding a total function $F : \mathcal{X} \longrightarrow \mathbf{B}$ such that $F(x) = E(x)$ for every training example $(x, E(x))$. The function F is called a *separating function* for E. The original form of the SVM technique can be applied in the case that $\mathcal{X} = \mathbf{R}^d$ and F is a linear function using the dot product. When non-linear separating functions are needed or when $\mathcal{X}$ is not identical to $\mathbf{R}^d$ for any $d \geq 1$, a function $\phi : \mathcal{X} \longrightarrow \mathbf{R}^d$ for some d is introduced in order to apply the SVM technique. To such cases SVMs can be applied without using the definition of ϕ but with the function

$$K(x, y) = \phi(x) \cdot \phi(y).$$

The function K is called a *kernel function* or (a *kernel*, for short).

The kernel K_{TERM} is designed for learning in the cases when the input space is the set of first-order terms. In order to define the input space formally, we refer the subsumption relation of terms. We say a term t *subsumes* another s and write $t \succeq s$ if $s = t\theta$ for a substitution θ. The relation $\succeq$ is called the *subsumption relation*. The subsumption relation is a partial order. Two terms t and s are *variants* of each other if $t \succeq s$ and $s \succeq t$. With $\mathcal{T}$ we represent the set of terms where all variants of every term t are regarded as the same one. We

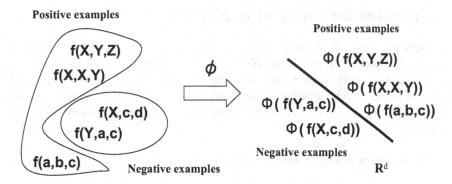

Fig. 1. Illustration of learning in a high dimension feature space $\mathbf{R}^d$

remove singleton variables from $\mathcal{T}$ in order to make it easy to apply K_{TERM} to the domain of atomic formulae. Figure 1 shows brief explanation of learning with SVM technique. Every positive and negative example is represented as a first-order term in $\mathcal{T}$. In this paper we follow the Prolog style notation. That is, every function and constant is represented by a small letter, and every variable is represented by a capital letter.

The kernel K_{TERM} is the one for a mapping $\phi_{TERM} : \mathcal{T} \longrightarrow \mathbf{R}^\infty$ defined as

$$\phi_{TERM}(t) = (\phi^1_{TERM}(t), \phi^2_{TERM}(t), \ldots),$$

where

$$\phi^i_{TERM}(t) = \begin{cases} 1 & (\text{if } s_i \succeq t), \\ 0 & (\text{otherwise}) \end{cases}$$

and $\sigma = s_1, s_2, \ldots$ is the list of terms in which does not include any variants or any singleton variable, that is, the enumeration of $\mathcal{T}$. Note that $\phi^i_{TERM}(t) = 1$ for only finitely many i's. This means that the domain of any training function E is mapped to a subset in $\mathbf{R}^d$ for some d, and therefore we can apply the SVM technique in $\mathbf{R}^d$. So we can define the kernel K_{TERM} as

$$K_{TERM}(s, t) = \phi_{TERM}(s) \cdot \phi_{TERM}(t),$$

which returns a finite value for any t and s.

An interesting property of K_{TERM} is that it is characterized with the anti-unification of s and t. Let $lca(s, t)$ be the *anti-unification* (also sometimes called the *least common anti-instances* or the *least general generalization*) [9] and $size(u)$ be the number of terms which subsume a term u without the term of a singleton variable.

Proposition 1 ([12]). *For every pair of terms s and t,*

$$K_{TERM}(s, t) = size(lca(s, t)). \tag{1}$$

If the root function symbols of s and t are different, $K_{TERM}(s, t) = 0$.

3   Algorithm for Computing K_{TERM}

This section shows an efficient algorithm for computing the kernel function K_{TERM}. For obtaining the value $K_{TERM}(s,t)$, we need two algorithms: one is for computing anti-unification u of s and t, and the other is for the total number of terms which subsume u (see Equation (1)). Since the former is shown by Plotkin[9] (see also [8]), the latter is all that we have to present here. The algorithm is named *TermSize*.

3.1   Basic Terminology and Notation

We introduce terminology and notation needed for explaining our algorithm.

Definition 1 (Types of substitutions). We classify substitutions for a variable X in a term u into the following three: A *function substitution* takes the form of $\{X := f(V_1, \ldots, V_n)\}$ where f is a function symbol and $V_1, \ldots, V_n$ are mutually distinct variables not occurring in u. A *constant substitution* takes the form of $\{X := c\}$ for a constant c. A *variable unification* takes the form of $\{X := Y\}$ where Y is another variable occurring in u. For a substitution θ in either of the three classes, the variable X is denoted by $dom(\theta)$.

It is known that the subsumption relation makes the set $\mathcal{T}$ be a complete lattice, which we call the *subsumption lattice*.

Definition 2. For a term u whose root function symbol is f, the *most general term* for u, denoted by $mgt(u)$ is defined as the term $f(V_1, \ldots, V_n)$ where $V_1, \ldots, V_n$ are mutually distinct variables.

Definition 3. For a term t and u, $lat(u, t)$ denotes the sub-lattice of the subsumption lattice whose maximal element is t and minimal element is u.

Example 1. In Fig. 2, we illustrate the lattice $lat(f(g(X,a), h(a)), f(X,Y))$. Note that $f(X,Y) = mgt(f(g(X,a), h(a)))$. In the figure, every thick line expresses a function substitution, and every thin line expresses a constant substitution or a variable unification.

Definition 4. The *occurrence* of a subterm s in a term t, denoted by $Oc(s,t)$, is defined by using a sequence $i_1.i_2. \ldots .i_n$ of natural numbers as follows:

1. The occurrence of the term t is Λ, an empty sequence.
2. If the occurrence of a subterm of the form $f(t_1, \ldots, t_m)$ is α, then the occurrence of t_i is $\alpha.i$.

For a sequence o of natural numbers t/o denotes the subterm of t whose occurrences is o.

Definition 5. For a term t, $var(t)$ denotes the set of all variables occurring in t. Note that even if a variable X occurs twice in t, X occurs only once in $var(t)$. For a term t, $con(t)$ denotes the set of all constants occurring in t.

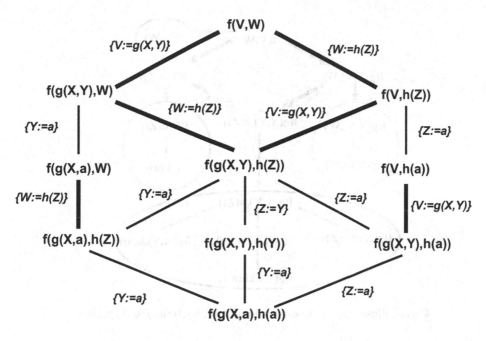

Fig. 2. Subsumption lattice with the minimum element $f(g(X,a),h(a))$

Definition 6. A *linear term* is a term in which no variable occurs more than twice. A *constant-free* term is a term which contains no constants.

Definition 7. Let f be a function with n arguments. Then $t_{f,c,n}$ and $t_{f,V,n}$ mutually denote the term $f(c,\ldots,c)$ and $f(V,\ldots,V)$, where c is a constant and V is a variable. We sometimes omit the n of $t_{f,c,n}$ and $t_{f,V,n}$ if it is clear from the context.

3.2 Outline of *TermSize*

We explain the outline of our algorithm *TermSize*. The algorithm consists of two phases, *Enum* and *TermOp*. This construction is based on the following proposition.

Proposition 2. *For every t subsuming u, there is a sequence $\theta_1, \theta_2, \ldots, \theta_n$ of substitutions and a number N $(1 \leq N \leq n)$ such that*

1. *$t = mgt(u)\theta_1\theta_2\cdots\theta_n$,*
2. *every θ_i for $1 \leq i \leq N$ is a function substitution, and*
3. *every θ_i for $N+1 \leq i \leq n$ is a constant substitution or variable unification.*

The term $mgt(u)\theta_1\theta_2\cdots\theta_N$ is linear and constant-free. Moreover, if t is linear and constant-free, we find such a sequence that $N = n$.

The first phase of *TermSize* is named *Enum*. In the phase, from the input u of the algorithm, $mgt(u)$ is generated and function substitutions are applied to it in

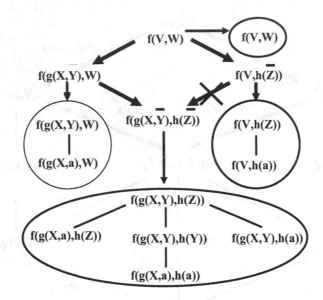

Fig. 3. Illustration of Computation Enum for term $f(g(X, a), h(a))$

order to generate terms subsuming u. From the proposition above, every generated term is linear and constant free. For avoiding redundancy in the generation we use the refinement of the above proposition.

Proposition 3. *Let t and u be linear and constant-free terms such that $t \succeq u$. Then there is a sequence $\theta_1, \theta_2, \ldots, \theta_N$ of function substitutions such that the sequence*

$$Oc(dom(\theta_1), t), Oc(dom(\theta_2), t\theta_1), \ldots, Oc(dom(\theta_N), t\theta_1 \cdots \theta_{N-1})$$

keeps the lexicographic order in sequences of integers, and $u = t\theta_1 \cdots \theta_N$.

The second phase *TermOp* is computing the number of terms obtained by applying variable unifications and constant substitutions to each term generated in *Enum*. Its implementation with dynamic programming is explained later.

Example 2. Figure 3 shows how to work the algorithms *TermSize*. The phase *Enum* the function substitutions represented with thick arrows are applied to $mgt(t)$ but other function substitutions are not applied. Each of the circles indicates the sub-lattices which is obtained by applying constant substitutions and variables unifications to a linear term generated in *Enum*. The number of terms computed by *TermOp* is same as the number of nodes of subsumption lattice in Fig. 2.

3.3   Foundations of Designing *TermOp*

Let t be a linear term subsuming u, $set(u, t)$ denote the set of all terms subsuming u and generated by constant substitutions and variable unifications for

t, $subsize(u,t)$ be the number of elements in $set(u,t)$. The phase $TermOp$ is for computing $subsize(u,t)$. The elements in $set(u,t)$ form a lattice with the subsumption relation.

Proposition 4. *The lattice $set(u,t)$ has a minimum element.*

Theorem 1. *Let $s_1, \ldots, s_k$ be the list of all terms generated by repeated application of function substitutions to $mgt(u)$. $(s_i \neq s_j)$ Then it holds that*

$$size(u) = \sum_{i=1}^{k} subsize(u, s_i).$$

Proof. Because $s_i \neq s_j$ and both of s_i and s_j are obtained only by applications of function substitutions to $mgt(u)$, we cannot obtain s_i by applying constant substitutions and variable unifications. Then the theorem holds from Proposition 2 and the definition of $set(u, s_i)$.

Now we explain how to compute $subsize(u, s_i)$ in the theorem above. Let m_i be the minimum element of the lattice $set(u, s_i)$. Note that s_i is a linear term from Proposition 2. The number of distinct variables and constants in m_i is important for computation of $subsize(u, s_i)$.

Theorem 2. *Let s be a term obtained by applying function subsumptions to $mgt(u)$, and m_i be the minimum element in the lattice $set(u, s_i)$. For every $c \in con(m_i)$ let τ_c be the number of occurrences of c in m_i. For every $V \in var(m_i)$ let η_V be the number of occurrences of V in m_i. Then it holds that*

$$subsize(u, s) = \prod_{c \in con(m_i)} size(t_{f,c,\tau_c}) \prod_{V \in var(m_i)} size(t_{f,V,\eta_V}).$$

Proof. We must treat substitutions to symbols which are same variables or constants in m_i simultaneously, because we must consider variants by variable unification. On the other hand, substitutions to symbols which are different variables or constants in m_i can be treated independently because we need not consider variable unification. Therefore, we compute the number of terms with substitutions for every $V \in var(m_i)$ or every $c \in con(m_i)$, and product these numbers of terms for every variable in $var(m_i)$ or every constant in $con(m_i)$. For every computation of the number of the terms with substitutions for every variable in $var(m_i)$ (or every constant in $con(m_i)$), we can ignore functions in s_i. We can use t_{f,c,τ_c} or t_{f,V,η_V} instead of the original term in the computation.

The most important point in this theorem is that we have to treat substitutions for variables are same variables or constants in u because we must consider variants by variable unification. Therefore, what we have to do is computing $size(t_{f,c,n})$ and $size(t_{f,V,n})$. However, as explained below, $size(t_{f,c,n})$ can be reduced to $size(t_{f,V,n})$, and we consider only computing $size(t_{f,V,n})$.

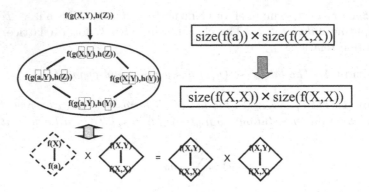

Fig. 4. Counting terms for constant substitution and variable unification

Theorem 3. *For every function f with arity n, we prepare a new function f' with arity $n+1$. Then it holds that*

$$size(t_{f,c,n}) = size(t_{f',V,n+1}).$$

Proof. We transform every term in $lat(t_{f,c,n}, mgt(t_{f,c,n}))$ into a term in $lat(t_{f,V_{n+1},n+1}, mgt(t_{f,V_{n+1},n+1}))$ by adding one argument V_{n+1} to f and replacing c with V_{n+1}. This transformation is one-to-one, and therefore, it holds that $size(t_{f,c,n}) = size(t_{f,V,n+1})$.

Example 3. Figure 4 shows computing $subsize(f(g(a,Y),h(Y)),f(g(X,Y),h(Z)))$ according to Theorem 2 and 3. The minimum element of $set(f(g(a,Y),h(Y)), f(g(X,Y),h(Z)))$ is $f(g(a,Y),h(Y)$. For $u = f(g(a,Y),h(Y))$, the constant occurring in u is a and variable occurring in u is Y. Therefore, it holds that

$$
\begin{aligned}
&subsize(f(g(a,Y),h(Y)), f(g(X,Y),h(Z))) \\
&= size(f(a)) \times size(f(X,X)) && \text{(by Theorem 2)} \\
&= size(f(X,X)) \times size(f(X,X)) && \text{(by Theorem 3)} \\
&= 2 \times 2 = 4.
\end{aligned}
$$

Computing $size(t_{f,V,n})$ is based on counting terms with n variables. Let us consider the process of classifying n variables into l classes. We intend that all of the variables in one class is unified and that with this variable unification a term with l distinct variables at n occurrences is generated.

Proposition 5. *Let $g_l(n)$ be the number of terms with n occurrences of variables and l classes of variables. Then it holds that*

$$size(t_{f,V,n}) = \sum_{l=1}^{n} g_l(n).$$

Proof. Directly from the definition of $g_l(n)$.

In other words, $g_l(n)$ is the number of terms generated by applying variable unifications $n - l$ times to $mgt(t_{f,V,n})$. We explain an example of ad hoc computation of $size(t_{f,V,n})$.

Example 4. We consider computation of $size(t_{f,V,4})$. The combinations of a number of occurrences of variables is as follows: $\{4, 0, 0, 0\}$ for one variable, $\{3, 1, 0, 0\}$ and $\{2, 2, 0, 0\}$ for two variables, $\{2, 1, 1, 0\}$ for three variables, and $\{1, 1, 1, 1\}$ for four variables. Therefore, $g_1(4) = \frac{4!}{4!} = 1$, $g_2(4) = \frac{4!}{3!1!} + \frac{4!}{2!2!2!} = 7$, $g_3(4) = \frac{4!}{2!1!1!2!} = 6$, $g_4(4) = \frac{4!}{1!1!1!4!} = 1$, and $size(t_{f,V,4}) = \sum_{l=1}^{4} g_l(4) = 15$.

As is shown in Example 4, if we can compute $g_l(n)$ by enumerating all combinations of variables, the computation time of $g_l(n)$ is exponential time for n. However, $g_l(n)$ satisfies a recursive equation in the next theorem, and therefore, can be computed in $O(n^2)$ time.

Theorem 4. *Let $g_l(n)$ be the number of such terms of the form $f(V_1, V_2, \ldots, V_n)$ that the n variables are classified into l classes. Then $g_l(n)$ satisfies*

$$
g_l(n) = \begin{cases}
l \times g_l(n-1) + g_{l-1}(n-1) & (n \geq l > 1), \\
1 & (n \geq l = 1), \\
0 & (l > n \geq 1).
\end{cases}
$$

Proof. The case that the n variables in $f(V_1, V_2, \ldots, V_n)$ are classified into l classes are separated into two disjoint subcases. The first subcase is that $l - 1$ classes of variables are in $V_1, \ldots, V_{n-1}$. Assignment of the variable V_n is lth class of variables which is not assigned to $V_1, \ldots, V_{n-1}$. The second subcase is that l classes of variables are in $V_1, \ldots, V_{n-1}$. Assignments of the variable V_n are l classes assigned to $V_1, \ldots, V_{n-1}$. This proves the theorem.

Proposition 5 and Theorem 4 show that $size(t_{f,V,n})$ is the Bell number, and can be computed by using the Stirling number of the second kind.

3.4   Implementation of the Algorithms

We show the program lists of *TermSize* and *Enum* in Fig. 8. We explain the preprocessing phases for *TermOp*, *SearchSame* and *MakeNode*. *SearchSame* enumerates subterms of term u, and outputs the set of occurrences for each subterm. *MakeNode* computes the maximum number M of occurrences of same subterms, and saves $size(t_{f,V,1}), \ldots, size(t_{f,V,M})$ in an array *Node*.

The dynamic programming with the recursive equation in Theorem 4 can compute $size(t_{f,V,n})$ in $O(n^2)$ time. *TermOp* is computed in $O(n^2)$ time because the computation of $subsize(u, s_i)$ is projection of $size(t_{f,V,n})$. However, the total computational time is exponential because exponential size of terms for functions are generated in *Enum*. If the number of functions is small, we can compute K_{TERM} efficiently.

4   Properties of K_{TERM}

This section shows some properties of the kernel K_{TERM}.

Theorem 5. K_{TERM} *satisfies symmetric positive definiteness;* $K_{TERM}(s,t) = K_{TERM}(t,s)$ *for any terms* s, t, *and* $\sum_{i,j} c_i K_{TERM}(x_i, x_j) c_j \geq 0$ *for all* c_i.

Proof. Since $lca(s,t) = lca(t,s)$, it holds that $K_{TERM}(s,t) = K_{TERM}(t,s)$. The fact that K_{TERM} is positive definite is shown as

$$\sum_{i,j} c_i K_{TERM}(x_i, x_j) c_j = \sum_{i,j} c_i c_j \phi_{TERM}(x_i) \cdot \phi_{TERM}(x_j)$$

$$= \sum_i c_i \phi_{TERM}(x_i) \cdot \sum_j c_j \phi_{TERM}(x_j)$$

$$= (\sum_i c_i \phi_{TERM}(x_i))^2$$

$$\geq 0.$$

We show K_{TERM} is a good kernel according the criteria introduced in [2].

Theorem 6 (Completeness). *For any* t, s *and* $s' \in \mathcal{T}$, *if* $K_{TERM}(s,t) = K_{TERM}(s',t)$ *then* $s = s'$. *That is, if all the values of kernel functions are same, inputs are also same.*

Proof. Assuming that $s \neq s'$, we prove $K_{TERM}(s,t) \neq K_{TERM}(s',t)$ for some t. In the case that $s \succeq s'$ and $s \neq s'$, $lca(s,s') = s$ is a proper general term for s', and by letting $t = s'$, we get $K_{TERM}(s,s') < K_{TERM}(s',s')$. If $s \not\succeq s'$, $lca(s,s')$ is a term properly more general than s. Then $K_{TERM}(s,s) < K_{TERM}(s,s') (= size(lca(s,s')))$ and this means that we can let $t = s$ for the conclusion.

Theorem 7 (Correctness). *Let* C *be the set of all concepts. There exist* $\alpha_i \in R, s_i \in \mathcal{T}$, *and* $\theta \in R$ *such that, for* $c \in C$ *and* $s \in \mathcal{T}$, $\sum_i \alpha_i K_{TERM}(s_i, s) \geq \theta$ *is equivalent to* $c(s)$.

This theorem shows that we can identify all concepts with appropriate positive and negative examples. The theorem is proved by the next lemma.

Lemma 1. *There exists a separating function for all positive and negative data in a space according to* $\phi_{TERM}(t)$. *Each dimension corresponds to a term.*

Proof. First, we prove that n given examples compose $n-1$ dimensional simplex in the space according to $\phi_{TERM}(t)$ by an inductive method. We consider the subsumption lattice of the n examples, and to add examples sorted by topological sort. Then, one example composes a point (0 dimensional simplex). Next we assume that i examples compose $i-1$ dimensional simplex, and add the $(i+1)$th example. Because examples are sorted by topological sort, the $(i+1)$th example does not subsume the previous i examples. Therefore, the value of dimension according to the $(i+1)$th example is 1 for only the $(i+1)$th example. This dimension is 0 for the previous i examples. Therefore $i+1$ examples compose i dimensional plane, that is, a simplex.

  If n examples are vertices of an $n-1$ dimensional simplex, all subsets of vertices are faces of simplex. Therefore, we can construct linear separating functions for all combinations of positive and negative examples.

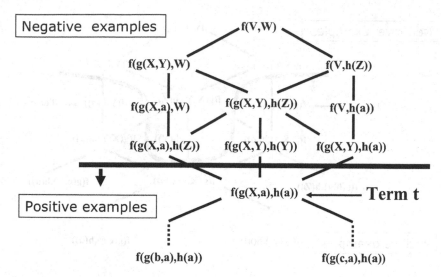

Fig. 5. An example which shows the logical concept "x is subsumed by t ($t = f(g(X, a), h(a))$)"

An example of functions defined with K_{TERM} is $sub_t(x) = K_{TERM}(x, t)$. The value of $sub_t(x)$ satisfies that

$$sub_t(x) \begin{cases} = size(t) \text{ (if } t \succeq x\text{)}, \\ < size(t) \text{ (otherwise)}. \end{cases}$$

The function classifies terms x according to whether or not $t \succeq x$, and this means that $sub_t(x)$ defines the concept $C(t) = \{x \in \mathcal{T} \mid t \succeq x\}$. This concept is very simple defined with a singleton term, and is natural for K_{TERM}.

5   Experimental Examples

We show some experimental results of our kernel function K_{TERM} with some small number of training examples. We have implemented our algorithm as the original kernel function for SVM^{light}[5].

Example 5. For learning a logical concept $C(t)$ with the case $t = f(g(X, a), h(a))$. We compute the separating function $f_1(x)$ with the following training examples (Figure 5):

Positive. $f(g(X, a), h(a))$, $f(g(b, a), h(a))$, $f(g(c, a), h(a))$.
Negative. $f(V, W)$, $f(g(X, Y), W)$, $f(V, h(Z))$, $f(g(X, a), W)$, $f(g(X, Y),$
$h(Z))$, $f(V, h(a))$, $f(g(X, a), h(Z))$, $f(g(X, Y), h(Y))$, $f(g(X, Y), h(a))$.

The obtained separating function is

$$f_1(x) \simeq 1.666\, K_{TERM}\, (f(g(X, a), h(a)), x) - 0.333 K_{TERM}(f(g(X, a), h(Z)), x)$$
$$-0.333\, K_{TERM}\, (f(g(X, Y), h(a)), x) - 1.666.$$

where $f_1(x) \geq 0 \Leftrightarrow F(x) = 1$.

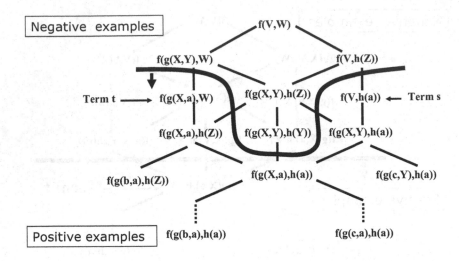

Fig. 6. An example which shows the logical concept "x is subsumed by t or s ($t = f(g(X,a),W)$), $s = f(V,h(a))$)"

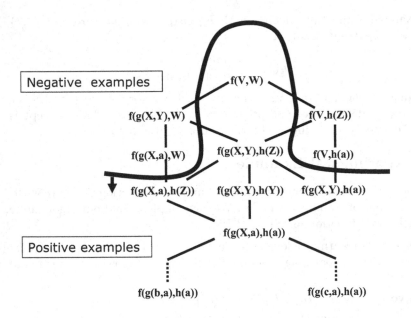

Fig. 7. An example which shows learning a more complex concept

Example 6. For learning a logical concept $M(t,s) = C(t) \cup C(s)$ with the case $t = f(g(X,a),W)$, $s = f(V,h(a))$. We prepare the following training examples (Figure 6):

Algorithm   *TermSize*;
input: term u;
output: $size(u)$;
begin
    /* σ : Sequence of sets of occurrence of subterms in u;
    $Node$: Array for $size(t_{f,v,n})$; */
    $\sigma := SearchSame(u)$;
    $Node := MakeNode(\sigma)$;
    $n := Enum(u, \sigma, Node)$;
    return n
end;

Procedure   *Enum*;
input: term u, line σ, array $Node$;
output: $size(u)$;
begin
    /* function $Right(u, \beta)$: Output the occurrence of a variable
    which is located in the right of all functions and β in u.
    If no such occurrence exists output 'end' ;
    function $Row(u, \alpha, s_{k+1})$: Add a term to s_{k+1} which is
    obtained by applying a function substitution at α in u;
    function $Term(s_k)$: The number of terms in s_k;
    function $Ref(s_k, i)$: The ith term in s_k; */
    $k := 0$; $n := 0$; $s_k :=$ an empty sequence;
    Add the most general term of u into s_k;
    while s_k is not empty **do**
        $s_{k+1} :=$empty;
        for $i = 1$ **to** $Term(s_k)$ **do**
            $n := n + TermOp(Ref(s_k, i), \sigma, Node)$;
            $\alpha := Right(Ref(s_k, i), \Lambda)$;
            while α is not 'end' **do**
                $Row(Ref(s_k, i), \alpha, s_{k+1})$;
                $\beta := \alpha$;
                $\alpha := Right(Ref(s_k, i), \beta)$;
            end while;
        $k := k + 1$;
    end while;
  return n;
end;

Fig. 8. Algorithms *TermSize* and *Enum*

Positive. $f(g(X, a), W)$, $f(g(X, a), h(Z))$, $f(g(X, Y), h(a))$, $f(g(X, a), h(a))$,
   $f(g(b, a), h(a))$, $f(g(c, a), h(a))$, $f(V, h(a))$.
Negative. $f(V, W)$, $f(g(X, Y), W)$, $f(V, h(Z))$, $f(g(X, Y), h(Z))$,
   $f(g(X, Y), h(Y))$.

The obtained separating function is

$$f_2(x) \simeq 2.000\, K_{TERM}\, (f(g(X, a), W), x) + 2.000 K_{TERM}(f(V, h(a)), x)$$
$$+6.661\, K_{TERM}\, (f(g(X, a), h(Z)), x) - 8.882 K_{TERM}(f(V, W), x)$$
$$-2.000\, K_{TERM}\, (f(V, h(Z)), x)$$
$$-2.000\, K_{TERM}\, (f(g(X, Y), h(Z)), x) - 1.$$

Example 7. Figure 7 shows learning a more complex concept.

Positive. $f(V, W)$, $f(g(X, Y), h(Z))$, $f(g(X, a), h(a))$, $f(g(b, a), h(a))$,
   $f(g(c, a), h(a))$, $f(g(X, a), h(Z))$, $f(g(X, Y), h(Y))$, $f(g(X, Y), h(a))$.
Negative. $f(g(X, Y), W)$, $f(V, h(Z))$, $f(g(X, a), W)$, $f(V, h(a))$.

The separating function is

$$f_3(x) \simeq 8\, K_{TERM}\, (f(V, W), x) + 4 K_{TERM}(f(g(X, Y), h(Z)), x)$$
$$-6\, K_{TERM}\, (f(g(X, Y), W), x) - 6 K_{TERM}(f(V, h(Z)), x) + 1.$$

6   Concluding Remarks

The basic idea of K_{TERM} can be generalized for the space where every feature is an element of a partially ordered set. Let x, y be elements in a partially ordered set. We call a kernel function defined with the set $E(x, y) = \{z | z \succeq x, z \succeq y\}$ an *intentional kernel* because $a \succeq b$ can be interpreted as "a explains b". For K_{TERM}, the partially ordered set is T and $K_{TERM} = \#(E(x, y))$.

Both of the DNF kernel and the monotone DNF kernel are other examples of intentional kernels. The kernels are defined by mapping every Boolean vector into the space each coordinate of which is a monomial of propositional variables. We can define the subsumption relation for monomials in the similar way of defining the subsumption relation of first-order terms[12]. By using the subsumption relation, the kernel, for example, is represented as $K_{DNF}(x, y) = \sharp(E(x, y)) - 1$.

At last we compare K_{TERM} with the convolution kernel for trees defined by Haussler [4]. The tree kernel pays attention to the sub-structure of trees, and does not have any logical aspect. In contract, K_{TERM} gives logical interpretation of the data through anti-unification. The subsumption relation has the logical meaning and K_{TERM} maps the meaning to numbers. Therefore, we can apply the basic concept of K_{TERM} to definite clauses or other logical formulae[7].

References

1. Cristianini, N., Shawe-Taylor, J.: An Introduction to Support Vector Machines and other kernel-based learning methods. Cambridge University Press, Cambridge (2000)
2. Gärtner, T.: A survey of kernel for structured data. SIGKDD Explorations 5(1), 268–275 (2003)
3. Gärtner, T., Lloyd, J.W., Flach, P.A.: Kernels and distances for structured data. Machine Learning 57(3), 205–232 (2004)
4. Haussler, D.: Convolution kernels on discrete structures. Technical report, University of California - Santa Cruz (1999)
5. Joachims, T.: Making large-scale support vector machine learning practical. In: Schölkopf, B., Burges, C., Smola, A. (eds.) Advances in Kernel Methods: Support Vector Machines, pp. 169–184. MIT Press, Cambridge (1998)
6. Khardon, R., Roth, D., Servedio, R.: Efficiency versus convergence of boolean kernels for on-line learning. Advances in Neural Information Processing Systems 14, 423–430 (2002)
7. Muggleton, S., Lodhi, H., Amini, A., Sternberg, M.J.E.: Support vector inductive logic programming. In: Proceedings of the Eighth International Conference on Discovery Science, pp. 163–175 (2005)
8. Nienhuys-Cheng, S.-H., de Wolf, R.: Foundations of Inductive Logic Programming. Springer, Heidelberg (1997)
9. Plotkin, G.D.: A note on inductive generalization. Machine Intelligence 5, 153–163 (1970)
10. Sadohara, K.: Learning of boolean functions using support vector machine. In: Proceedings of the 12th International Conference on Algorithmic Learning Theory, pp. 106–118 (2001)
11. Sadohara, K.: On a capacity control using boolean functions. In: Proceedings of the 2002 IEEE International Conference on Data Mining, pp. 410–417 (2002)
12. Yamamoto, A., Tanaka, T.: Kernel functions for first-order terms based on anti-unification. SIG-FPAI-A503, JSAI, pp. 75–79 (2005)

Towards Automating Simulation-Based Design Verification Using ILP

Kerstin Eder, Peter Flach, and Hsiou-Wen Hsueh

Department of Computer Science, University of Bristol
MVB, Woodland Road, Bristol BS8 1UB, UK
Kerstin.Eder@bristol.ac.uk, Peter.Flach@bristol.ac.uk,
hsueh@cs.bris.ac.uk

Abstract. Increasing the productivity of simulation-based semiconductor design verification is one of the urgent challenges identified in the International Technology Roadmap for Semiconductors. The most difficult aspect is the generation of stimulus for functional coverage closure. This paper introduces a new Coverage-Directed test Generation (CDG) feedback loop which applies Inductive Logic Programming (ILP) to selected tests and coverage data to induce rules that can be used to automatically direct stimulus generation towards outstanding coverage. The case study documented in this paper shows a significant reduction of simulation time when ILP-based CDG is compared to random test generation. This is an exciting and promising new application area for ILP.

1 Introduction

ILP has been used to support scientific discovery and knowledge synthesis in a wide range of practical domains [19] such as protein structure prediction, mutagenicity prediction and pharmacophore discovery. Even the very process of scientific hypothesis generation and experimentation has been automated using ILP-based learning in a closed loop environment [12]. The main advantage of ILP over propositional learning is the expressive power resulting from a first-order representation. This allows learning results to be represented in a declarative format which is comprehensible to domain experts, without losing the ability to automatically process the learning results.

This paper aims to introduce the reader to a promising new application area for ILP, namely simulation-based semiconductor design verification, and demonstrates the potential that ILP has to offer in the context of functional coverage closure.

Verification of industrial designs still relies heavily on simulation; it can take up to 70% of the entire design effort [1]. Traditionally, design verification environments are based on a testbench [3] which is the code used to generate a valid input sequence to a design, called a test, drive this test into the design and then observe and check the design's response. Simulators are used to execute testbenches. The increasing complexity of real-world semiconductor designs makes exhaustive simulation prohibitive; in most cases the sun would burn out before even a fraction of the test cases can be simulated [20]. In reality, tight time-to-market constraints force verification engineers to be selective with respect to the tests they run to gain confidence in the functional correctness of a design. The verification plan specifies the scenarios that must be verified

S. Muggleton, R. Otero, and A. Tamaddoni-Nezhad (Eds.): ILP 2006, LNAI 4455, pp. 154–168, 2007.

before a design can be manufactured. It is the task of the verification engineers to create tests that fully cover these scenarios, often within a very short timeframe.

Recent advances in simulation-based verification have established coverage-driven verification methodologies which are essentially feedback loops that automate a large part of the simulation-based verification process. A pseudo-random stimulus generator at the front-end generates valid input stimulus according to a set of parameters or constraints, called directives, which bias test generation towards the scenarios of interest to verification. At the back-end a coverage analysis tool collects and analyses the coverage obtained from running these tests to check the effectiveness of the directives and to identify coverage closure targets such as rarely covered events as well as coverage holes. Coverage results are used to help engineers focus the next round of stimulus generation on these coverage targets.

Generating stimulus to increase functional coverage is a key challenge in simulation-based verification. Closing a functional coverage model is by no means trivial in complex industrial designs. For example, in state-of-the-art microprocessors, the subtle effects of issuing multiple instructions, out-of-order execution and aggressive pipelining can make it very difficult if not impossible to see what sequence of instructions to drive in order to reach a specific functional coverage scenario (coverage task). This is particularly difficult when the signals involved in the specification of the functional coverage task are related to micro-architectural features of the design.

In practice up to 90% of coverage tasks can be reached via *biased pseudo-random tests* which are automatically generated based on a set of user-defined directives. However, even supplying the directives requires significant engineering skill and is often only accomplished through many trial-and-error runs. At the end engineers resort to writing *directed tests* by hand aiming to cover the missing cases. Consequently as much as 90% of a verification team's time and resources can be spent on closing the remaining 10% coverage manually. Figure 1 shows the typical long flat-tailed curve when plotting the coverage rate achieved by random simulation (y-axis) against the number of simulation runs (x-axis). The data for this figure originates from our case study and is representative for many industrial verification projects. It clearly shows that the number of simulations necessary to obtain the last few coverage tasks is excessive in comparison to the number of simulations needed to get most of the coverage. This is one reason why verification has become the dominant cost in the design process and many verification projects run over time and budget. Verification, if not done properly, can cost a company its reputation and potentially put people at serious risk. If it takes too long the product will miss its market window which results in loss or significant decrease of the market share (and hence profits). The latest version of the International Technology Roadmap for Semiconductors [1] calls for more *automation* in the process of functional coverage closure to reach verification targets faster and with less engineering effort.

The most demanding aspect regarding full automation of the existing coverage-driven feedback loops is the *automatic* generation of the directives for functional coverage closure. Coverage-directed stimulus generation (CDG) techniques [18] aim to achieve exactly this. Feedback-based CDG integrates machine learning into the feedback loop (which is depicted in Fig.2) in order to automatically generate new directives that bias stimulus generation towards producing tests which target specific coverage

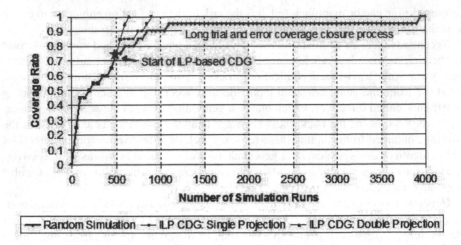

Fig. 1. Coverage progress for random simulation compared to ILP-based CDG

tasks. Machine learning techniques employed in this context include Bayesian networks, evolutionary techniques such as genetic algorithms and genetic programming as well as Markov chains. The underlying assumption is that the learning mechanism can identify, from existing tests and coverage, how best to bias stimulus generation such that the resulting tests can reach outstanding coverage tasks. As a result, the curve in Fig.1 should climb significantly faster than random simulation thus saving a large number of simulation runs and hence verification effort.

In contrast to other machine learning applications where the measure of success is achieving a very high accuracy of the learning output resulting in a large lift when comparing system performance with and without learning, this application is slightly different in that the number of examples to learn from is variable and depends on when the learning is kicked off during simulation. ¿From a machine learning viewpoint, the later in the simulation phase learning is started the more examples are available, hence a higher accuracy can be expected. Conversely, the earlier learning is started the fewer examples are available, resulting in a lower accuracy. From a verification viewpoint, however, the earlier the curve starts to *climb faster than random simulation* the more verification effort can be saved.[1] These two conflicting interests need to be traded off carefully with the verification interests dominating in this context. For example, the lift achieved in our case study, although in machine learning terms not impressive, was good enough to save a significant number of simulations as shown in the two steeper curves in Fig.1.

This paper introduces a novel CDG technique based on an inductive machine learning method that discovers relational information from structured data. Inductive Logic Programming (ILP) is applied to tests and their related coverage in order to induce

---

[1] Finding the best starting point for learning is a challenging optimisation problem which requires further research. A second experiment in which learning commenced after 400 simulations produced curves that climbed much slower than the two steep ILP-based CDG curves in Fig.1 (but still faster than random simulation).

general rules which describe the characteristics of these tests. The resulting rules can be used directly as directives, to obtain tests that are structurally similar to the examples presented to the learning system. Coverage closure can be automated by applying rule learning to clusters of a target coverage task and combining the resulting rules to obtain directives for test generation. As the tests and associated coverage are supplied to the ILP system in a declarative representation, the induced rules are also declarative and in principle human readable. This gives engineers an insight into the knowledge discovered by the ILP system and is also an excellent basis for automatic translation of these rules into test generation directives.

A case study demonstrates the fundamental principles of ILP-based CDG in two steps. The first step evaluates the consistency and reliability of the generated directives for existing coverage in a rediscovery experiment. The second step documents the results of the application of a novel cluster-based coverage closure method.

This paper is organised as follows. Section 2 reviews coverage models and existing CDG approaches. Section 3 introduces the fundamental principles of ILP-based directive generation. The experimental framework and results of our case study are presented in Section 4. Further research and conclusions are discussed in Section 5.

2 Background

This section reviews coverage models and existing CDG approaches.

2.1 Coverage Models

To measure the coverage of simulation test suites, coverage models are generally classified into *structural* and *functional*. Structural coverage is focused on measuring which parts of the design source code have been exercised during simulation at various levels of detail ranging from statement down to expression coverage. Structural coverage helps verification engineers to see which code parts have not been verified. It is inherently weak, however, in determining whether the design is functionally correct.

The most tricky bugs to find often reside in functional *corner cases* of the design which involve multi-cycle scenarios and high degrees of concurrency. To ensure these are covered during verification, experienced engineers define functional coverage models based on the specification, the design and often also the implementation. This makes functional coverage models inherently user-defined and application-specific [22]. Designing meaningful functional coverage models requires significant design knowledge, experience and engineering skill.

One way of specifying a functional coverage model is outlined in [13]. Their models contain a semantic description (story) detailing the purpose of the verification task, the list of attributes mentioned in the story, the set of all possible values (domain) for each attribute and a list of restrictions on the permitted combinations in the Cartesian product, or cross-product, of the attribute domains. The overall size of the coverage space associated with such a functional coverage model is the product of all domain cardinalities. The elements in the cross-product of the attribute domains are referred to as *coverage tasks*. Each coverage task can be represented as an n-tuple of values

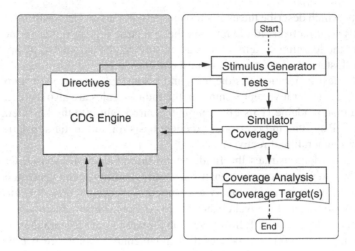

Fig. 2. CDG feedback loop

from the attribute domains, where n is the number of attributes in the coverage model. The restrictions identify which coverage tasks are legal and hence need to be covered during verification. Uncovered legal tasks are referred to as *coverage holes*. The process of constructing tests to cover a hole is called *coverage closure*. In this paper we mean cross-product based coverage models when referring to functional coverage.

2.2 Feedback-Based Coverage-Directed Test Generation

Coverage-Directed test Generation (CDG) is a technique that aims to automate the generation of simulation stimulus based on coverage information [18]. There are two main approaches towards CDG: one is by construction using formal methods and the other is based on feedback. The approach introduced here can be classified as a novel feedback-based CDG technique with a CDG engine that embeds Inductive Logic Programming.

The feedback-based CDG framework [8] is shown in Fig.2. It is built around a state-of-the-art testbench automation environment that contains a stimulus generator, a simulator and coverage analysis. Coverage targets are identified and the coverage analysis results are then fed into the CDG engine together with existing tests and coverage data to generate directives that bias the random stimulus generator towards achieving the target coverage tasks. The CDG engine can be realized with different techniques.

Early approaches [21] focused mainly on genetic algorithms (GAs) that learn specific test cases, such as sequences of assembly code instructions, directly. This required an explicit encoding of the target instructions within the representation on which the GAs worked. Results were application-specific and lacked generality. In [4] another GA for automatic bias generation is presented. This approach generates biases for an industrial instruction stream generator. Its main drawbacks are the architecture-specific encoding of the representation on which the GA works. The approach has also been transferred to a hierarchical test generation framework to target statement and path coverage [24].

A more flexible Genetic Programming (GP) technique that generates machine code test programs for design verification, called μGP, was developed in [6]. It directs test generation towards maximising code coverage with the goal to generate a set of test programs that achieves maximum statement coverage. The test sets generated with μGP are smaller and yield higher statement coverage than randomly generated tests [7]. The approach requires a syntactical description of the microprocessor's assembly language in the form of an instruction library. The internal representation on which the μGP core works is generic and test programs can be generated for any given instruction library. The main limitation is that the approach only targets structural, *i.e.* code-based, coverage models, rather than functional coverage models based on cross-products, which in practice are far more difficult to close.

In [9,5] a coverage-directed test generation approach based on Bayesian networks is presented. It models the relationship between the test directives and coverage tasks via a Bayesian network, where general knowledge regarding the design's operation taken from a domain expert is encoded in the network structure. This approach targets cross-product functional coverage models and has resulted in a significantly improved coverage rate achieved in a shorter time frame. An advantage of the approach is that it can discover diverse directives that all target the same coverage task. However, the design and training of an appropriate Bayesian network is required; this includes the identification of the network structure that models the joint probability distribution based on the directives to the test generator, the coverage model, as well as expert domain knowledge. In practice, very few if any verification engineers have these skills.

An approach based on Markov models that contain user-specified templates for instruction sequence generation has been developed in [23]. The Markov model's parameters are adjusted to settings that stress certain activities of interest to verification through an iterative design-activity directed feedback loop. A simple Markov model was extended by introducing a cache and some dependency variables to propagate directive dependencies further than one step. This approach approximates the correlation of directive parameters over several instructions. However, it is weak in controlling the actual distance of dependency.

In summary, although existing feedback-based CDG approaches achieve promising results, they have shortcomings which have so far prevented them from being widely used for functional coverage closure. The major limiting factors are the requirement of specialised encodings or models on which the algorithms work, the need for non-verification expertise to set up and maintain the environment, or the use of coverage models other than functional coverage.

3   ILP-Based Coverage-Directed Stimulus Generation

The directive generation approach introduced here differs from existing feedback-based CDG approaches by its use of inductive learning from examples, in particular Inductive Logic Programming (ILP), in the CDG engine. ILP [14] is a declarative inductive learning method. It requires a set of factual examples E and some relational background knowledge B. ILP will find a single (or multiple) hypothesis H in terms of the relations given in B such that (ideally) every positive example in E is covered by H and no negative example in E is covered. In this context B, E and H are represented as definite logic programs [15]. The next section provides a more detailed introduction regarding the application of ILP within a CDG framework.

3.1 Method to Learn Rules for Test Generation

To learn rules suitable for test generation, the examples E for ILP learning are the tests, which are initially randomly generated, together with their respective coverage data. Using a first-order logic concept description language each test can automatically be translated into a relational representation of a sequence of instructions together with a test identifier and the coverage data associated with this test by analogy with the encoding of Michalski-style trains in [16]. The background knowledge B describes the general structure of these tests and relationships between test components such as register use, re-occurrence of registers, e.g. as destination or source, specific sequences of instructions, relative distance between dependencies, instruction classes etc. The learning task is to find hypotheses H which represent general rules describing the characteristics of a test to target a given coverage task. Provided there are enough instances to learn from, at the end of the learning process the ILP system returns a set of rules containing at least one rule for each coverage task presented to the system.

The learning task described above produces a set of rules which give rise to directives that can be used to generate tests structurally similar to the original examples.[2] These tests achieve the same amount of coverage as was originally obtained, but with increased accuracy, a smaller number of tests and hence far fewer simulation runs than with biased-random generation alone.[3] In addition, the rules give insight into the structure of the existing test suite and can thus be used to analyse test diversity.

To construct tests that reach coverage holes the learning task needs to be changed to find rules for *coverage clusters* which share a degree of similarity with the target coverage hole. The underlying assumption here is that the *directive* to target the coverage hole shares a degree of similarity with the directives used to approach similar coverage tasks. Learning is most effective when the selected clusters have a high coverage rate. Existing coverage data clustering techniques which can in principle be applied for ILP-based coverage closure are discussed in [13]. The rules returned by the learning system for each cluster are then combined to form a directive to target the coverage hole. This technique can also be used to generate tests that increase the coverage rate of rarely covered tasks via a different execution path compared to existing tests.

---

[2] Note that the learning output is not, as in traditional machine learning applications, used for the *classification* of tests into those which do or don't reach a given coverage task, but instead for the automatic *construction* of tests to target a given coverage task, which is achieved by generating tests that satisfy the constraints imposed by the rules in the learning output.

[3] From discussions with engineers we learned that this can already be valuable in practice, e.g. for rediscovering directives when subtle changes to the design turn out to have a major effect on the coverage of tests, often rendering existing test suites completely invalid. Because these test suites have been generated with an iterative adjustment to the directives, and the history has been lost, automatically rediscovering the directives would save engineering effort.

3.2 Integrating ILP into the CDG Framework

The entire CDG feedback loop with ILP-based learning is shown in Fig.3. Input to the ILP system, such as tests and associated coverage as well as coverage targets, is sourced directly from the data existing within the standard verification flow. In practice, the background knowledge can be provided in pre-defined application-class spe-

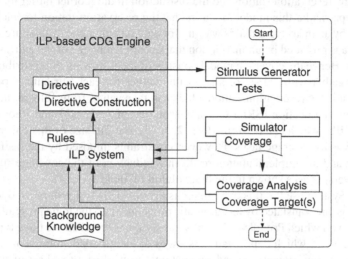

Fig. 3. CDG feedback loop with ILP-based CDG engine

cific libraries. Alternatively, to make background knowledge acquisition more flexible and user-friendly, a domain-specific template-based declarative input language could be designed for verification engineers, which is automatically translated into the first-order logic representation used for ILP-based learning. Defining the background knowledge requires as much expertise as is necessary to efficiently use the features of a state-of-the-art test generation environment such as [2].

The ILP system returns a set of rules for selected coverage tasks or clusters. The final directive construction stage combines these rules to obtain directives that target the coverage holes or rarely covered tasks selected for closure.

4 Preliminary Study

This section demonstrates the key aspects of the ILP-based CDG technique on an example microprocessor Design Under Verification (DUV).

4.1 Experimental Setup

The DUV is a five-stage pipelined Superscalar DLX [11] with four independent execution units: Branch Resolve Unit (BRU), Arithmetic Logic Unit (ALU), Multiply Divide Unit (MDU), and Load Store Unit (LSU). At the entrance of each execution unit, *i.e.*

between the decode and the execution stage, is a buffer pipeline register, called Reservation Station, which is used when the data for an instruction is not yet available to enable the processor to fetch the next instruction. The processor uses a Reorder Buffer, which is a ring buffer with five entries, to ensure in-order-termination of instructions.

The functional coverage model evaluates the utilisation of the reservation station of the Superscalar DLX in conjunction with data dependencies between the instruction waiting in the reservation station and the instruction in the reorder buffer that provides the data. In particular this model monitors that the reservation station for each pipeline unit is used by an instruction that is waiting for data on either one of its source registers, and this data is provided by an instruction that occupies any one of the entries in the reorder buffer. Hence the coverage model consists of the following three attributes which are listed together with the set of all possible values for each attribute: Pipeline Unit (PU) of the utilised reservation station which can take values from {alu, mdu, lsu, bru}, Source Register Location (SRL) which can be one of {rs1, rs2} and Reorder Buffer Location (RBL) which can be from {0, 1, 2, 3, 4}. The full size of this coverage space is 4 x 2 x 5 = 40 coverage tasks. However, constraints imposed by the instruction set architecture and the implementation result in a reduction of the coverage space to the 20 legal coverage tasks shown in the first column of Table 1.

The ILP System used in this experiment is Progol [17]. Test programs together with their coverage are translated by an automatic procedure into the logic programming language Prolog on which Progol works. This translation is based on the three types `task`, `test` and `instr` which define valid instances of identifiers denoting coverage tasks, tests, *i.e.* instruction sequences, and instructions, as well as a fixed set of mnemonics denoting opcodes and a set of register identifiers. The sequence of instructions is then described using the following set of relations:

```
cover(task,test_id).
has_instruction(test_id,instr_id).
is_followed_by(instr_id,instr_id).
instr_has_opcode(instr_id,mnemonic).
instr_has_rs1(instr_id,reg).
instr_has_rs2(instr_id,reg).
instr_has_rd(instr_id,reg).
```

A translation of a test program fragment that contains three instructions and covers task (alu,rs1,3) is given in Fig.4.

The background knowledge provides Progol with an important aid in the learning process because Progol searches for hypotheses by generalising an example in terms of the background relations. An example of such a relation is given below. The relation `same_rd_rs1_d1(I1,I2)` specifies under which conditions the destination register of an instruction `I1` is being reused as first source register by the instruction `I2` which immediately, *i.e.* in distance `d1`, follows `I1`.

```
same_rd_rs1_d1(I1,I2) :-
    is_followed_by(I1,I2),
    instr_has_rd(I1,R),
    instr_has_rs1(I2,R).
```

A set of 161 relations similar to the one above has been used as background knowledge for the experiments.

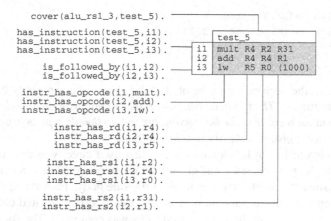

```
cover(alu_rs1_3,test_5).

has_instruction(test_5,i1).
has_instruction(test_5,i2).
has_instruction(test_5,i3).

is_followed_by(i1,i2).
is_followed_by(i2,i3).

instr_has_opcode(i1,mult).
instr_has_opcode(i2,add).
instr_has_opcode(i3,lw).

instr_has_rd(i1,r4).
instr_has_rd(i2,r4).
instr_has_rd(i3,r5).

instr_has_rs1(i1,r2).
instr_has_rs1(i2,r4).
instr_has_rs1(i3,r0).

instr_has_rs2(i1,r31).
instr_has_rs2(i2,r1).
```

Fig. 4. Test program fragment and corresponding Prolog representation

Because Progol uses mode-directed inverse entailment to guide the process of generalisation from examples, a set of mode declarations needs to be provided for the relations which are used in the learning process. The mode declarations constrain the search, and essentially establish a structural template for the output rules. A total number of 156 mode declarations constrained the ILP search space in the two experiments carried out. Representative examples are given below.

```
modeh: cover(#task,+test)
modeb: has_instruction(+test,-instr)
modeb: has_opcode(+instr,#opcode)
modeb: same_rd_rs1_d1(+instr,-instr)
modeb: same_rd_rs2_d1(+instr,-instr)
```

4.2 Rules for Existing Tests and Coverage

The first part of the experiment aims to show that, given a set of pseudo-randomly generated tests together with their coverage, and under the assumption that there are enough tests to learn from for each coverage task, it is possible to induce rules that correctly characterise the features of tests to target the achieved coverage. Successful completion of this experiment confirms the correctness of a fundamental principle of ILP-based CDG. It also validates the actual ILP setup including the data encoding and shows whether the background knowledge is fit for purpose. This initial step can be compared to the rediscovery step described in [10].

The learning was started with the test data available after 500 simulation runs, when the pseudo-randomly generated tests covered 15 of the 20 coverage tasks which equates to an overall coverage rate of 75%. Only 57 out of the 500 randomly generated tests were successful in adding to coverage. The number of successful tests for each coverage task is given in the second column of Table 1. The total number of induced rules after ILP learning is summed up in the third column.

To give the reader an example of the learning output, below is one rule which shows the characteristics of tests that reached coverage task (alu,rs1,2).

```
cover(alu_rs1_2,Test_ID) :-
    has_instruction(Test_ID,I1),
    has_instruction(Test_ID,I2),
    instr_has_opcode(I2,alu),
    same_rd_rs1_d1(I1,I2).
```

Note that due to the declarative nature of ILP, the above rule can easily be translated into natural language: *"The test must contain an instruction with an opcode of alu type, and the destination register of the instruction preceding the alu type instruction is used as the first source register by the alu type instruction."*

The rules obtained from ILP-learning were then used directly as directives for test generation, *i.e.* the test generator was given the task to generate a sequence of instructions that satisfied the constraints contained in the rule body. To evaluate the accuracy of the resulting tests, the average number of successful tests generated either pseudo-randomly or on the basis of the ILP induced rules was compared. The fourth and fifth column of Table 1 contain these numbers which are now termed the *hit rate*. For example, the hit rate of the ILP-based directive for the coverage task (alu,rs1,0) given in Table 1 is 15%, which means on average 15 out of 100 tests generated to satisfy the rule body also covered the task in the rule head. In comparison, when the tests are generated without specific constraints on average 14 out of 1000 tests reached that coverage task. From the results we computed the lift[4] which is shown in the last column of Table 1.

The results show a significant lift (of more than 8) for seven out of the twelve coverage tasks for which rule learning was successful. No rules were generated for (mdu,rs1,0), (mdu,rs1,2), and (mdu,rs1,3), because rule learning is a generalisation process which only works well when there are two or more instances to learn from. For the two coverage tasks (alu,rs2,2) and (mdu,rs1,4) tests generated from the directives obtained after rule learning perform worse. The tests used as examples for learning these two cases show orthogonal aspects in that they represent completely different approaches to reach the same coverage task. For this reason the ILP system did not find a rule that accurately generalised the given tests. The problems encountered can be resolved in practice by increasing the number of examples to learn from. In the majority of cases, however, the results show that the ILP system has successfully generalised the patterns in the existing tests and that test generation from the induced rules gives a higher hit rate.

4.3   Rules for Conceptually New Tests

The second part of the experiment aims to generate directives that target the remaining five coverage holes by learning from related coverage clusters. A simple syntax-based clustering technique which is easily automated is projection [13]. Given a target tuple (coverage task) in a coverage space, projection replaces one or more of the attribute values in the target tuple by a wildcard. In this experiment two types of projection were used. Single projection aggregates successful tests from one dimension of the coverage task, leaving two values in the tuple, *e.g.* (alu,rs1,*). Similarly, double projection aggregates tests from two dimensions, leaving only one value in each tuple, *e.g.* (alu,*,*).

---

[4] The lift was computed as the ratio of the hit rate of tests generated based on the ILP induced directives over the hit rate of tests generated pseudo-randomly.

Table 1. Coverage and learning results after 500 simulation runs

Coverage Task (PU,SRL,RBL)	Covered by Tests	Number of Rules	Random Hit Rate	ILP Hit Rate	Lift
(alu,rs2,4)	2	2	0.4%	7%	17.5
(alu,rs2,1)	4	4	0.8%	13%	16.25
(alu,rs2,3)	4	3	0.8%	13%	16.25
(alu,rs1,1)	4	2	0.8%	12%	15.00
(alu,rs1,4)	7	5	1.4%	17%	12.14
(alu,rs1,0)	7	4	1.4%	15%	10.71
(alu,rs1,2)	8	4	1.6%	13%	8.13
(alu,rs2,0)	3	1	0.6%	1%	1.67
(alu,rs1,3)	8	5	1.6%	2%	1.25
(bru,rs1,2)	2	1	0.4%	0.4%	1
(mdu,rs1,4)	2	1	0.4%	0.1%	0.25
(alu,rs2,2)	3	2	0.6%	0.1%	0.17
(mdu,rs1,0)	1	-	0.2%	-	-
(mdu,rs1,2)	1	-	0.2%	-	-
(mdu,rs1,3)	1	-	0.2%	-	-
(mdu,rs1,1)	0	-	0%	-	-
(bru,rs1,0)	0	-	0%	-	-
(bru,rs1,1)	0	-	0%	-	-
(bru,rs1,3)	0	-	0%	-	-
(bru,rs1,4)	0	-	0%	-	-
Total	57	34	-	-	-

The learning was again started with the test data available after 500 simulation runs. For each coverage hole a set of rules was collected from first applying single and then double projection to the data before learning was performed. Test generation directives were then constructed manually from these sets of rules by simply conjunctively combining rule bodies and resolving conflicts via the introduction of disjunctions which are interpreted as random choice during test generation. A remaining challenge is to fully automate this process of directive construction.

The same method was applied to the five rarely covered tasks from the first part of the experiment to see whether coverage could be increased. Table 2 shows the results obtained after test generation from the so constructed directives for the five coverage holes in the upper half and the five rarely covered tasks in the lower half.

It is encouraging to see that all hit rates have increased significantly for both the coverage holes and the previously rarely covered tasks. Interestingly, in this experiment double projection performs better than single projection for coverage hole closure. This might indicate that, as more dimensions are projected out, more instances are supplied to the ILP system to learn from, which in turn induces rules that give rise to directives with higher accuracy. On the other hand single projection outperforms double projection for the previously rarely covered tasks. This might indicate that when tests that reach the target coverage tasks do exist, double projection introduces more noise into the rules than single projection. Further research is needed to better understand these results.

Table 2. Results for coverage holes (top half) and rarely covered tasks (bottom half)

Coverage Task (PU,SRL,RBL)	Random Hit Rate after		ILP Hit Rate with Single Projection	Lift	ILP Hit Rate with Double Projection	Lift
	500 Random Tests	5000 Random Tests				
(mdu,rs1,1)	-	0.32%	1.00%	3.13	4.13%	12.91
(bru,rs1,0)	-	0.08%	1.00%	12.50	2.38%	29.75
(bru,rs1,1)	-	0.18%	1.00%	5.56	3.63%	20.17
(bru,rs1,3)	-	0.22%	4.00%	18.18	6.38%	29.00
(bru,rs1,4)	-	0.06%	0.50%	8.33	1.86%	31.00
(alu,rs2,2)	0.60%	0.56%	10.00%	17.86	8.33%	14.88
(mdu,rs1,0)	0.20%	0.16%	2.00%	12.50	1.50%	9.38
(mdu,rs1,2)	0.20%	0.20%	9.00%	45.00	5.00%	25
(mdu,rs1,3)	0.20%	0.28%	1.67%	5.96	6.75%	24.1
(mdu,rs1,4)	0.40%	0.30%	2.00%	6.67	2.50%	8.33

Figure 1 from the Introduction section compares the coverage progress of this experiment to random simulation. It shows that test generation from single and double projection methods reached full coverage in 367 and 108 simulations respectively (after the initial 500 pseudo-randomly generated tests). In total, test generation from single and double projection methods used 867 and 608 simulations to reach full coverage, compared to 3914 simulations based on pseudo-random test generation alone. In this case study, the ILP learning started from the 57 successful tests collected in the first 500 simulations (based on pseudo-randomly generated test). This was sufficient to reach full coverage within a maximum of another 400 tests to simulate.

To open this interesting application up for the ILP community the 500 randomly generated tests used in the experiment and the resulting coverage have been made available on http://www.cs.bris.ac.uk/~eder/ILP_CDG/. This site also contains further information on the encoding of these tests and the Progol setup including background knowledge and mode declarations.

To repeat the entire experiment the complete feedback loop is needed. It includes the DUV as well as the test generator, the simulator and the coverage analysis component. Except for the DUV, which we obtained using references in [11], these are commercial products which require licenses which some of the EDA vendors offer via their higher education programmes. More information on the setup of the feedback loop used here can be obtained by contacting the authors.

5   Conclusions

This paper shows how ILP can be applied in the context of functional coverage closure as part of the CDG engine in a standard CDG feedback loop. The strength and promise of ILP-based CDG have been demonstrated in a two part experiment. In the first part rules to be used as test generation directives have been induced from existing tests and coverage. Test generation from these rules achieved a higher hit rate on their target coverage tasks than was possible with random test generation. The second part of the experiment presents a coverage closure methodology, whereby learning is applied to selected projections of a coverage hole and learning output is then combined to obtain a directive that targets this coverage hole.

Clearly, the example case study is small and a larger industry-based trial will be undertaken shortly on a realistic-sized processor. However, the results obtained provide an interesting and encouraging starting point for further work to establish ILP-based CDG alongside existing learning-based techniques.

Various aspects of the ILP-based CDG methodology would benefit from further research. With a focus on learning, one research direction is to explore the use of clustering methods that are more sophisticated than purely syntactic projection for ILP-based learning. It is anticipated that ILP techniques can be applied to identify semantically meaningful coverage clusters. The development of a kernel-based method to define a meaningful distance metric in this context is one of our next research goals. Another research task is to establish a user-friendly background acquisition methodology for ILP-based CDG. This is a key requirement for acceptance of this methodology in practice. We also intend to experiment with ILP systems that use a more descriptive induction approach compared to Progol, which in practice is mostly used for classification tasks.

In summary, this paper pioneers a methodology that makes CDG an exciting new application area for ILP. Although there is more work to be done before ILP-based CDG is mature enough to be integrated into practical verification environments, it is clear that ILP-based CDG has important advantages compared to other learning based CDG techniques. First, it seamlessly integrates into an existing verification flow without the need for encodings or models that are outside the expertise of a professional verification engineer; the learning input can be sourced from existing tests and coverage data directly via automatic translation procedures. Second, due to the declarative representation of data, ILP-based CDG requires intuitive input from the verification engineer at setup (for the background knowledge) and no non-verification expertise is needed. Application-specific libraries to cover the background knowledge (and the respective mode declarations if Progol is used) can in principle be provided to reduce the engineering input even further. Third, ILP-based CDG is fully automatic and can target user-defined functional coverage models. In addition, the transparency of the resulting directive rules, which are declarative and hence intuitively human readable, gives verification engineers an insight into the knowledge gained. This is one of the key strengths of ILP compared to other learning methods and gives ILP-based CDG a strong competitive edge.

References

1. International Technology Roadmap for Semiconductors, Design Chapter, 2005 Edition. Available at http://public.itrs.net/
2. Adir, A., Almog, E., Fournier, L., Marcus, E., Rimon, M., Vinov, M., Ziv, A.: Genesys-Pro: Innovations in test program generation for functional processor verification. IEEE Design & Test of Computers 21(2), 84–93 (2004)
3. Bergeron, J.: Writing Testbenches: Functional Verification of HDL Models, 2nd edn. Kluwer Academic Publishers, Dordrecht (2003)
4. Bose, M., Shin, J., Rudnick, E.M., Dukes, T., Abadir, M.: A genetic approach to automatic bias generation for biased random instruction generation. In: CEC2001: Congress on Evolutionary Computing, pp. 442–448 (May 2001)

5. Braun, M., Fine, S., Ziv, A.: Enhancing the Efficiency of Bayesian Network Based Coverage Directed Test Generation. In: IEEE International High-Level Validation and Test Workshop (HLDVT), IEEE Computer Society Press, Los Alamitos (2004)
6. Corno, F., Cumani, G., Reorda, M.S., Squillero, G.: Evolutionary test program induction for microprocessor design verification. In: ATS2002: IEEE Asian Test Symposium, pp. 368–373. Guam (USA) (November 2002)
7. Corno, F., Sanchez, E., Reorda, M.S., Squillero, G.: Automatic Test Program Generation: A Case Study. IEEE Design & Test of Computers 21(2), 102–109 (2004)
8. Fine, S., Levinger, M., Ziv, A.: Apparatus and method for coverage directed test. Patent Number: US2004249618, IBM (US) (December 09, 2004)
9. Fine, S., Ziv, A.: Coverage directed test generation for functional verification using Bayesian networks. In: DAC2003: 40th Design Automation Conference, pp. 286–291. California (USA) (June 2003)
10. Finn, P., Muggleton, S., Page, D., Srinivasan, A.: Pharmacophore Discovery using the Inductive Logic Programming System Progol. Machine Learning 30, 241–273 (1998)
11. Horch, J.: Entwurf eines RISC-Prozessors in der Hardwarebeschreibungssprache VHDL. Technical report, Technische Universitaet Darmstadt Institut fuer Datentechnik (1997)
12. King, R.D., Whelan, K.E., Jones, F.M., Reiser, P.G.K., Bryant, C.H., Muggleton, S.H., Kell, D.B., Oliver, S.G.: Functional genomic hypothesis generation and experimentation by a robot scientist. Nature (letters to nature) 427, 247–251 (2004)
13. Lachish, O., Marcus, E., Ur, S., Ziv, A.: Hole analysis for functional coverage data. In: DAC2002: 39th Design Automation Conference, New Orleans, Louisiana, USA (June 2002)
14. Lavrac, N., Dzeroski, S.: Inductive Logic Programming. Techniques and Applications. Ellis Horwood, New York (1994)
15. Lloyd, J.W.: Foundations of Logic Programming, 2nd edn. Springer, Heidelberg (1987)
16. Michie, D., Muggleton, S., Page, D., Srinivasan, A.: To the international computing community: A new East-West challenge. Technical report, Oxford University Computing laboratory, Oxford, UK (1994)
17. Muggleton, S.: Inverse Entailment and Progol. New Generation Computing 13(3-4), 245–286 (1995)
18. Nativ, G., Mittermaier, S., Ur, S., Ziv, A.: Cost evaluation of coverage directed test generation for the IBM mainframe. In: ITC2001: International Test Conference, pp. 793–802 (October 2001)
19. Page, D., Srinivasan, A.: ILP: A Short Look Back and a Longer Look Forward. Journal of Machine Learning Research 4, 415–430 (2003)
20. Seger, C.-J.H.: An introduction to formal verification. Technical Report 92-13, UBC, Department of Computer Science, Vancouver, BC, Canada (June 1992)
21. Smith, J., Bartley, M., Fogarty, T.: Microprocessor design verification by two-phase evolution of variable length tests. In: Proceedings of the 1997 IEEE International Conference on Evolutionary Computing, pp. 453–458. IEEE Computer Society Press, Los Alamitos (1997)
22. Ur, S., Ziv, A.: Off-the-shelf vs. custom-made coverage models, which is the one for you. In: Proceedings of the 7th International Conference on Software Testing, Analysis and Review (STAR) (May 1998)
23. Wagner, I., Bertacco, V., Austin, T.: StressTest: An automatic approach to test generation via activity monitors. In: DAC2005: 42nd Design Automation Conference, pp. 783–788, Anaheim, California (USA) (June 2005)
24. Yu, X., Fin, A., Fummi, F., Rudnick, E.M.: A Genetic Testing Framework for Digital Integrated Circuits. In: Proceedings of the International Conference on Tools with Artificial Intelligence (ICTAI), p. 521. IEEE Computer Society Press, Los Alamitos (2002)

Minimal Distance-Based Generalisation Operators for First-Order Objects*

Vicent Estruch, César Ferri, Jose Hernández-Orallo,
and María José Ramírez-Quintana

DSIC, Univ. Politècnica de València , Camí de Vera s/n, 46020 València, Spain
{vestruch,cferri,jorallo,mramirez}@dsic.upv.es

Abstract. Distance-based methods have been a successful family of machine learning techniques since the inception of the discipline. Basically, the classification or clustering of a new individual is determined by the distance to one or more prototypes. From a comprehensibility point of view, this is not especially problematic in propositional learning where prototypes can be regarded as a good generalisation (pattern) of a group of elements. However, for scenarios with structured data, this is no longer the case. In recent work, we developed a framework to determine whether a pattern computed by a generalisation operator is consistent w.r.t. a distance. In this way, we can determine which patterns can provide a good representation of a group of individuals belonging to a metric space. In this work, we apply this framework to analyse and define minimal distance-based generalisation operators (*mg* operators) for first-order data. We show that Plotkin's *lgg* is a *mg* operator for atoms under the distance introduced by J. Ramon, M. Bruynooghe and W. Van Laer. We also show that this is not the case for clauses with the distance introduced by J. Ramon and M. Bruynooghe. Consequently, we introduce a new *mg* operator for clauses, which could be used as a base to adapt existing bottom-up methods in ILP.

1 Introduction

Learning from complex data is one of the main challenges in machine learning (e.g. distance-based and kernel-based methods for structured data [4]). Nevertheless, learning from complex data while preserving comprehensibility is even more challenging and has mainly been addressed in the area of ILP [7]. Despite the fact that distance-based methods are quite intuitive and have successfully been tested in several domains, a model that explains why a new example belongs to one class or another does not exist. This is due to the fact that the information about the matches between two objects (e.g. two molecules) is lost when these matches are encoded by a number (their distance). Unfortunately,

---

* This work has been partially supported by the EU (FEDER) and the Spanish MEC under grant TIN 2004-7943-C04-02, ICT for EU-India Cross-Cultural Dissemination Project under grant ALA/95/23/2003/077-054, Generalitat Valenciana under grant GV06/301 and UPV under grant TAMAT.

S. Muggleton, R. Otero, and A. Tamaddoni-Nezhad (Eds.): ILP 2006, LNAI 4455, pp. 169–183, 2007.

this lack of explanatory patterns is incompatible for many application contexts. For example, in molecule classification it would be very interesting to describe a cluster of molecules by saying what chemical structures these molecules have in common instead of saying that they are close to one given prototype. We addressed the possibility of descriptions of this kind for distance-based algorithms in [2], where the concept of distance-based binary generalisation operator was introduced. Basically, the term 'distance-based' means that the operator computes patterns that are "consistent" with the distance employed. For instance, let (Σ^*, d) be the word space defined over the alphabet $\Sigma = \{a, b, c\}$, and let d be the edit distance. Given the words $w_1 = cabab$ and $w_2 = ababc$ a distance-based generalisation operator could compute $*abab*$, that is, all the words having the subsequence $abab$. This pattern somehow shows why $d(w_1, w_2) = 2$ because the subsequence $abab$ has been taken into account in the best match to obtain the distance. However, this is not the case for another operator computing $*c*$ (all the words having the symbol c) since the common sequence c is not considered to compute the distance.

Unfortunately, to use these generalisation operators in a real context, we need to be able to generalise more than two elements. In [1], we introduced this idea for n-ary operators and we also studied the idea of minimality. Minimality is important to prevent underfitting in the search of patterns that are consistent with the underlying distance. For instance, the pattern $*ab*$ obtained by generalising the words w_1 and w_2 looks excessively general w.r.t. another "consistent" pattern such as $*abab*$. Although the idea of generality has been studied in depth when data is represented by means of first-order logic [11], the same does not happen for other kinds of data, and especially when data is in a metric space. Therefore, in [1] we proposed a general way to define minimal distance-based generalisation operators (mg operators). We have applied this framework to several data sorts: sets, lists, graphs,... (see [3,1]).

In this paper, we focus on first-order objects (atoms and Horn clauses), which are embedded in a metric space. We show that Plotkin's lgg [11] is a mg operator for atoms using the metric defined in [13]. This means that the mg patterns computed by lgg can be used as a consistent explanation for data which has been clustered employing this distance. Then, we try to extend this result to Horn clauses (more precisely, sets of literals), and we show that the direct use of the lgg for clauses does not yield a distance-based generalisation operator using the metric defined in [12]. Consequently, we introduce a new mg for clauses. This sets out a scenario where some (but not all) generalisation operators and some (but not all) metric spaces used in ILP work well together. This suggests the applicability of other generalisation operators in ILP (such as the one introduced in this paper).

The paper is organised as follows. Section 2 introduces the framework for distance-based generalisation operators and the notion of mg. Section 3 analyses Plotkin's lgg as a mg for atoms. Section 4 extends the result to sets of literals (i.e. clauses), through the definition of a new mg which cannot be the lgg for clauses, since the latter is not distance-based. Finally, the last section presents our conclusions, possibilities for applications, some open problems, and future work.

2   Distance-Based Generalisation Framework

We present the main notions related to our framework for defining a concept of generalisation based on distances. For more details see [1].

Our approach aims to define generalisation operators for data embedded in a metric space (X, d). These operators are denoted as $\Delta(E)$, where E is a finite set of elements ($|E| \geq 2$) of X to be generalised. A generalisation computed by $\Delta(E)$ will be expressed by a pattern p belonging to a pattern language $\mathcal{L}$. In fact, every pattern p represents a set of elements of X and is denoted by $Set(p)$. Thus, we can say that an element $x \in X$ is covered by a pattern p, if $x \in Set(p)$. In the same way, p is a generalisation of E iff $E \subset Set(p)$. For instance, given the strings abb and abc, and the regular pattern $ab*$, then $Set(ab*) = \{ab, abc, aba, abb, abaa, ...\}$, and we say that $ab*$ covers the elements $abb \in Set(ab*)$ and $abc \in Set(ab*)$.

The following definition establishes the relationship between a generalisation operator defined in a metric space and the underlying distance.

Definition 1. *(Distance-based generalisation operator) Let (X, d) be a metric space and let $\mathcal{L}$ be a pattern language. We say that $\Delta : 2^X \to \mathcal{L}$ is a distance-based generalisation operator, if for every finite set $E \subset X$, $p \in \mathcal{L}$, $\Delta(E) = p$, there exists a nerve $N(E)$[1] such that, for every pair of elements x, y in E which are directly linked in $N(E)$, $Set(\Delta(E))$ includes all the elements z such that $d(x, z) + d(z, y) = d(x, y)$.*

Given a metric space (X, d), we say that, for every $x, y, z \in X$, z is between x and y if $d(x, y) = d(x, z) + d(z, y)$.

Another issue related to the generalisation operator is to determine when it performs the least general generalisation (*lgg*, in short). This is an important issue if we want the generalisations to "fit" a group of elements as closely as possible. Although the *lgg* is a widely studied concept in the field of ILP [8], it has not been studied when data is not described by means of atoms. Thus, the following constructions are an alternative and a more general notion of minimal (least general) generalisation for different sorts of data, when data is in a metric space.

First, we establish a criterion to determine which pattern is less general, given two patterns computed by two distance-based generalisation operators $\Delta(E)$ and $\Delta'(E)$, respectively. The least general generalisation operator Δ might not be unique, so we call it minimal. Then, the minimal distance-based generalisation operator Δ (*mg* operator, in short) is the one where for every set E and for every distance-based operator Δ', the pattern $\Delta(E)$ is less general than $\Delta'(E)$.

---

[1] Given a metric space (X, d) and a set of undirected connected graphs S_G, a nerve function $N : 2^X \to S_G$ maps every finite set $E \subset X$ into a graph $G \in S_G$, such that each element e in E is unequivocally represented by a vertex in G and vice versa.

In order to formalise our proposal, we could use the inclusion operation between sets ($\subset$) as a "mechanism" to compare how general two generalisations are. In other words, a generalisation $\Delta(E)$ is less general than a generalisation $\Delta'(E)$, if $Set(\Delta(E)) \subset Set(\Delta'(E))$. However, this leads to several problems (see [1] for details):

1. Most generalisations are not comparable, since neither $Set(\Delta(E)) \subset Set(\Delta'(E))$ nor vice versa.
2. The inclusion operator between sets ($\subset$) ignores the underlying distance.
3. The minimal generalisation may not exist for some pattern languages.

Therefore, these drawbacks lead us to introduce a more abstract generality criterion. It is more interesting to find some kind of 'function' that assigns a generality (cost or optimality) value to every pattern, making every pair of patterns comparable. For this purpose, we introduce a special function, called the cost function.

Definition 2. (cost function) *Let (X, d) and $\mathcal{L}$ be a metric space and a pattern language, respectively. We say that the mapping $k : 2^X \times \mathcal{L} \to \mathcal{R}$ is a cost function, if for every pattern $p \in \mathcal{L}$ and $E \subset X$, such that $E \subset Set(p) \subset X$ and $Set(p) \neq X$, then $k(E, p) < \infty$.*

Logically, this definition gives almost complete freedom for how to choose k. For the metric spaces considered in this paper, if we are looking for minimal patterns, the idea is that the cost function must depend on the fit (i.e. minimality). For this reason, we define the cost function as $k(E, p) = c(E|p)$, where $c(E|p)$ measures how well the pattern p fits the data E. However, for other metric spaces (sets, graphs, lists, . . .), more complex cost functions can be defined by also considering how complicated the pattern is [1], following the MDL/MML principle.

Definition 3. (inclusion-preserving cost function) *Let (X, d) and $\mathcal{L}$ be a metric space and a pattern language, respectively. We say that the cost function $c(E|p)$ is inclusion-preserving if for every $E \subset X$ and pair of patterns p and p' such that $Set(p) \subset Set(p')$ then $c(E|p) \leq c(E|p')$.*

One interesting point in our approach is that $c(E|p)$ is expressed in terms of the distance employed. One possible way of defining some instances for $c(E|p)$ is by using the well-known concept of border of a set[2]. Intuitively, if a pattern p_1 fits E better than a pattern p_2, $\partial Set(p_1)$ will somehow be closer to E than $\partial Set(p_2)$.

As the border of a set exists in every metric space, several definitions of $c(E|p)$ can be employed for different sorts of data, as we show in Table 1. It is easy to show that all of them are inclusion-preserving.

Now, we can introduce the definition of mg operator.

---

[2] We will say that an element e belonging to set $A \subseteq X$ is a border point, if for every $\epsilon > 0$, $B(e, \epsilon)$ (where $B(e, r)$ is the closed ball with centre on e and radius r) is not totally included in A. In the standard notation, the border of a set A will be denoted by ∂A.

Table 1. Some definitions of the function $c(E|p)$

Sort of data	$\mathcal{L}$	$c(E|p)$
Any	Any	$\sum_{\forall e \in E} inf_{r \in R} B(e, r_e) \not\subset Set(p)$
Any	Any	$\sum_{\forall e \in E} sup_{r \in R} B(e, r_e)$
Any	Any	$\sum_{\forall e \in E} min_{e' \in \partial Set(p)} d(e, e')$
Any	$Set(p)$ represents a bound set	$\sum_{\forall e \in E} (min_{e' \in \partial Set(p)} d(e, e') + max_{e'' \in \partial Set(p)} d(e, e''))$

Definition 4 (Minimal distance-based generalisation operator). *Let (X, d) be a metric space, and let Δ be a distance-based generalisation operator defined in X using the pattern language $\mathcal{L}$. Given a cost function $k(\cdot, \cdot)$, we say that Δ is a mg operator for $k(\cdot, \cdot)$ in $\mathcal{L}$, if for every distance-based generalisation operator Δ', then $k(E, \Delta(E)) \leq k(E, \Delta'(E))$, for every finite set $E \subset X$.*

In general, deriving the *mg* operator is complicated because of the high variety of nerve functions $N(\cdot)$ that can be defined. In some problems, it does not make sense to explore all the nerve functions (e.g. in clustering), and we might be interested in computing *mg* operators relative to one specific nerve function, namely:

$$k(E, \Delta_{N(E)}(E)) \leq k(E, \Delta'_{N(E)}(E)), \text{for every finite set } E \subset X.$$

Next, we analyse and/or derive *mg* operators for the specific case of first-order logic data (atoms and clauses) embedded in a metric space.

3   Minimal Distance-Based Generalisations for Atoms

The goal of this section is to compute *mg* operators for atoms embedded in a particular metric space. To do this, a distance function, a pattern language and a cost function are defined. In what follows, $\mathcal{L}$, denotes a first-order language defined over the signature $\langle \mathcal{C}, \mathcal{F}, \Pi, \mathcal{X} \rangle$, where $\mathcal{C}$ is a set of constants, $\mathcal{F}$ (and respectively Π) is a family that is indexed on N (non negative integers) with $\mathcal{F}_n$ (Π_n) being a set of n−adic function (predicate) symbols and $\mathcal{X}$ is a (infinite) denumerable set of variable symbols. In the case of no ambiguity, both predicate and function symbols are referred to as symbols, and variable symbols are referred to as variables. f/n (and respectively p/n) denotes a function symbol $f \in \mathcal{F}_n$ (and respectively $p \in \Pi_n$). Finally, the reader may refer to [5,6] for any concept about logic programming and inductive logic programming which is not explicitly defined.

3.1   The Metric Space

The distance function d we are going to employ is defined in [13]. Basically, this distance returns an ordered pair of integer values (i, j). This pair expresses how different two atoms are in terms of function symbols and variable symbols, respectively. An auxiliary function, the so-called $size(e) = (F, V)$, is required to compute d. This function encodes the structure of one atom e. That is, F is a function that counts the number of function symbols occurring in e, and V returns the sum of the squared number of occurrences of each variable in e. Finally, given atoms e_1 and e_2, $d(e_1, e_2) = [size(e_1) - size(lgg(e_1, e_2))] + [size(e_2) - size(lgg(e_1, e_2))]$.

For instance, if $e_1 = q(a, f(a))$ and $e_2 = q(b, f(X))$ and knowing that $lgg(e_1, e_2) = q(Y, f(Z))$, $size(e_1) = (3, 0)$, $size(e_2) = (2, 1)$, $size(lgg(e_1, e_2)) = (1, 2)$, the distance between e_1 and e_2 is given by the expression: $d(e_1, e_2) = [(3, 0) - (1, 2)] + [(2, 1) - (1, 2)] = (2, -2) + (1, -1) = (3, -3)$.

For non-unifiable atoms, the distance is defined by means of introducing an artificial second-order symbol $\top$, which is considered the most general [3] element, such that $size(\top) = (0, 1)$. Note that a total order relation (lexicographic order), defined over the set of ordered pairs, is needed to express how far two atoms are from each other. Given two ordered pairs $A = (F_1, V_1)$ and $B = (F_2, V_2)$, $A < B$ iff $F_1 < F_2$ or $F_1 = F_2$ and $V_1 < V_2$. As the set of tuples are ordered, it permits us to handle these objects as if they were real numbers. For this reason, all the definitions of our framework can be automatically extended for this special case.

In what follows, (X_a, d_a) denotes the metric space where X_a is the Herbrand Base with variables induced by the signature, and d_a denotes the distance described above.

3.2   The Pattern Language and the Cost Function

The pattern language is the Herbrand base with variables induced by the signature, that is, $\mathcal{L}$ coincides with X_a. For example, let $\mathcal{C} = \{a, b\}$ be a set of constants, $\mathcal{F} = \{f/1\}$ a set of function symbols, $\mathcal{X} = \{X_1, X_2, \ldots\}$ a denumerable set of variables and $\Pi = \{p/1, q/1\}$ a set of predicate symbols. Then, $\mathcal{L}_1 = \{p(a, X_1), p(X_1, a), p(X_1, X_2), p(f(a), b), \ldots q(a, X_1), q(X_1, a), \ldots\}$. Given a pattern p, $Set(p)$ denotes all the atoms in X_a which are instances of p. For example, $p(a) \in Set(p(X))$.

Regarding the cost function, $c(E|p)$ is the first function in Table 1. Clearly, it is a cost function for (X_a, d_a) and $\mathcal{L}$ since, for a finite set of elements $E \subset X_a$ and a pattern p covering E, $c(E|p) = \infty$ iff $Set(p) = X_a$.

3.3   Defining a *mg* Operator

We proved in [2] that the *lgg* for two atoms is a binary distance-based generalisation operator for (X_a, d_a). Taking this previous result into account, we can demonstrate that, where E is a finite set of two or more atoms, $lgg(E)$ is the *mg* for this metric space and this cost function.

---

[3] By *general* we mean the well-known concept from logic programming.

Proposition 1. *Given the metric space* (X_a, d_a). *If* $\mathcal{L}$ *is the Herbrand base with variables induced by the signature and* $c(E|p) = \sum_{\forall e \in E} r_e$ *(being* $r_e = \inf_{r \in \mathcal{R}} B(e, r) \not\subset Set(p))$, *then* $\Delta(E) = lgg(E)$ *is a mg operator for* d_a, $\mathcal{L}$ *and* $c(E|p)$.

Proof. First, let us show that $lgg(E)$ performs minimal patterns according to the cost function. For every generalisation p of E, $p \in \mathcal{L}$, such that $E \subset Set(p)$, by definition of lgg, $Set(lgg(E)) \subset Set(p)$, and by Definition 3, $c(E|lgg(E)) \le c(E|p)$.

Secondly, note that $lgg(E)$ is distance-based. Clearly, for every two elements $e_i, e_j \in E$, $Set(lgg(e_i, e_j)) \subset Set(lgg(E))$. According to Proposition 6 in [2], $lgg(e_i, e_j)$ is distance-based in (X_a, d_a) and so $Set(E)$ contains all the elements between e_i and e_j, for every e_i and e_j. Then, simply defining, for instance, $N(E)$ as a complete graph, $lgg(E)$ is distance-based.

This result does not necessarily hold when the cost function or even the pattern language is changed. In [1], we explore the combination of different cost functions and pattern languages in further detail.

4   Minimal Distance-Based Generalisations for Clauses

From a practical point of view, finite sets of literals (interpreted as clauses) allow us to express real-world objects more accurately than single literals do. A set of literals can represent not only the different parts of an object but also the relationships among them. A clause interprets these literals as a disjunction, which is usually expressed as a logic implication with a disjunction of all the positive literals in the consequent (head) and a conjunction of all the negative literals in the antecedent (body). For instance,

$$C = \{class(X, c_1), \neg molec(X), \neg atom(X, h)\}$$

can be interpreted and represented as: $class(X, c1) : -molec(X) \wedge atom(X, h)$[4].

In order to determine mg operators for clauses, we need to establish a distance function, a pattern language, and a cost function for this sort of data.

4.1   The Metric Space

The distance we are going to use is defined in [12]. This distance is based on minimal matchings[5] over sets and requires the elements of the sets to be embedded in a metric space as well. Given two sets A and B and the elements $a \in A$ and $b \in B$, we say that the ordered pair (a, b) belongs to the matching $\alpha_{A,B}$ between A and B (a subset of $A \times B$), if $\alpha_{A,B}(a) = b$. By $D(\alpha_{A,B})$, we denote the domain of the matching, that is, $D(\alpha_{A,B}) = \{a \in A : \exists (a, b) \in \alpha_{A,B}\}$.

---

[4] As in Prolog notation, the symbol $: -$ denotes the logic implication symbol $\leftarrow$.

[5] A matching from set A to set B is an injective mapping which is not necessarily defined over all the elements in A.

By $\alpha_{A,B}(A) = \{b \in B | (a, b) \in \alpha_{A,B} \wedge a \in A\}$, we denote the codomain of the matching.

Thus, given two sets A and B and a matching $\alpha_{A,B}$, a similarity measure $d(\alpha_{A,B}, A, B)$ can be defined by summing the distances between the elements from the ordered pairs belonging to $\alpha_{A,B}$ and adding a penalty $M/2$ for each element in A and B that is not included in the matching. More formally,

$$d(\alpha_{A,B}, A, B) = \sum_{\forall (a_i, b_j) \in \alpha_{A,B}} d(a_i, b_j) + \frac{M}{2}(|B - \alpha_{A,B}(A)| + |A - D(\alpha_{A,B})|) \quad (1)$$

Finally, the distance between A and B is given by the optimal (minimal) matching among all the possible ones:

$$d_m(A, B) = min_{\forall \alpha_{A,B}} d(\alpha_{A,B}, A, B) \quad (2)$$

Unless we say otherwise, $(2^X, d_m)$ denotes the metric space of sets, and (X, d) denotes the metric space of the elements of the sets. In our case, the metric space (X, d) to be considered, which is denoted as (X_l, d_l), is obtained by extending the space X_a and the distance d_a (defined for atoms in the previous section) to both positive and negative atoms, i.e. literals. This extension is trivial, since $p(\ldots)$ and $\neg p(\ldots)$ are considered incompatible literals. Hence it is like treating them as being built by different predicates[6]. According to [12], the constant M must be greater or equal to the maximal distance between two elements in X in order to $d_m(\cdot, \cdot)$ satisfies all the axioms of a metric. This restriction forces us to bound (restrict) the space X. Then, the restriction over X_l will consist of setting a threshold for the number of symbols in an atom, namely $R/2$. Only atoms with less than $R/2$ symbols will be permitted. These are called bounded literals. Thus, let $\bar{X}_l$ and $M = (R, R)$ be the bounded space and the penalty, respectively.

Example 1. Given the sets $A = \{a_1 \equiv p(g(a), e), a_2 \equiv p(f(a), f(b)), a_3 \equiv p(a, a)\}$ and $B = \{b_1 \equiv p(f(b), f(a)), b_2 \equiv p(f(a), e))\}$ and according to the distances among all the atoms, the optimal matching $\alpha_{A,B}$ is $\{(a_1, b_2), (a_2, b_1)\}$. Then, the distance between the sets is given by $d_m(A, B) = d(a_1, b_2) + d(a_2, b_1) + \frac{1}{2}(R, R) = (8, -6) + (\frac{R}{2}, \frac{R}{2})$.

The above restriction is finally neither a real nor theoretical problem. A representation of a real-life object always requires a finite number of symbols and all the results concerning (X_l, d_l) hold for $(\bar{X}_l, d_l)$, as the following Proposition 2 shows.

Proposition 2. *Proposition 1 (i.e. lgg for bounded literals is a mg) holds for the metric space $(\bar{X}_l, d_l)$, where $\bar{X}_l = \{x \in X_l : $ number of non-variable symbols in $x \leq k\}$ with k being a constant.*

Proof. Trivially, for every $e_i, e_j \in E \subset \bar{X}_1$, if e_k is an element between e_i and e_j in $\bar{X}_l$, it is also between them in the space X_l since the distance function is the

---

[6] The *lgg* of two incompatible literals is undefined [5].

same; thus, $e_k \in Set(lgg(E))$ and $lgg(E)$ is distance-based in $\bar{X}_l$. Also, for every generalisation p of E, such that $E \subset Set(p)$ we have that $Set(lgg(E)) \subset Set(p)$ by definition of lgg and $c(E|lgg(E)) \leq c(E|p)$ by Definition 3. Thus, lgg for literals is a mg operator.

Therefore, the metric space for clauses is $(2^{\bar{X}_l}, d_m)$.

4.2 The Pattern Language and the Cost Function

Thus, we define $\mathcal{L}$ as the set of all the logic programs we can define given a signature. Some examples of patterns could be,

$$p_1 \equiv class(X, c_1) : -molec(X), atom(X, Y, h)$$
$$class(X, c_1) : -molec(X), atom(X, Y, o)$$
$$p_2 \equiv class(X, c_2) : -molec(Y), atom(Y, Z, c)$$

The pattern p_1 says that a molecule belongs to the class/cluster c_1 if it has an atom of hydrogen or oxygen. Of course, a pattern can also be viewed as a set of clauses. For example, $p_1 = \{C_{11} \equiv \{class(X, c_1), \neg molec(X), \neg atom(X,, h)\}$, $C_{12} \equiv \{class(X, c_1), \neg molec(X), \neg atom(X,, o)\}\}$ and $p_2 = \{C_{21} \equiv \{class(X, c_2), \neg molec(Y), \neg atom(Y,, c))\}\}$. From this point of view, patterns can be combined by means of the union operator ($\cup$). Thus, the pattern $p_3 = p_1 \cup p_2$ is $p_3 = \{C_{11}, C_{12}, C_{21}\}$. Moreover, each clause C in p is a pattern as well, which is denoted as $\{C\}$.

Finally, given a pattern $p \in \mathcal{L}$, $Set(p)$ represents all those clauses in the metric space $2^{\bar{X}_l}$ which are θ-subsumed by p. Thus, the clause $\{class(m_1, c_1)$, $\neg molec(m_1), \neg atom(m_1, h)\}$ belongs to $Set(p_1)$.

As for the cost function, $c(E|p)$ is the first function in Table 1. Clearly, it is a cost function for $(2^{\bar{X}_l}, d_m)$ and $\mathcal{L}$ since for a finite set of elements E and a pattern p covering E, $c(E|p) = \infty$ iff $Set(p) = 2^{\bar{X}_l}$.

4.3 Defining mg Operators

Unlike (X_a, d_a), let us first see that $\Delta(E) = lgg(E)$ (where lgg is the *least general generalisation* for clauses [11]) is not a mg operator in $(2^{\bar{X}_l}, d_m)$. Although it can easily be shown that $lgg(E)$ is a minimal pattern in our framework, $lgg(E)$ is not distance-based for $d_m(\cdot, \cdot)$. That is, given two clauses A and B there exists a clause C such that $d(A, C) + d(C, B) = d(A, B)$ and C is not covered by $lgg(A, B)$ (see Example 2).

Example 2. Given the sets $A = \{\neg p(g(a), e), \neg p(f(a), f(b))\}$, $B = \{\neg p(f(b), f(a)), \neg p(f(a), e)\}$ and $C = \{\neg p(f(b), f(b)), \neg p(g(a), e)\}$. The optimal mappings from A to C and from C to B, respectively, are depicted below.

We can easily see that $d_m(A, B) = (8, -8) = d_m(A, C) + d_m(C, B)$. However,

$$lgg(A, B) = \{\neg p(f(X), f(Y)), \neg p(Z, e), \neg p(f(a), T), \neg p(U, V)\} \equiv$$
$$: -p(f(X), f(Y)), p(Z, e), p(f(a), T), p(U, V)$$

but $C \equiv : -p(f(b), f(b)), p(g(a), e)$ is not θ-subsumed by $lgg(A, B)$.

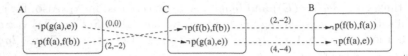

Fig. 1. The arrows and the labels indicate the optimal mappings between the different pairs of sets and the distance between the matched elements, respectively

Unfortunately, defining mg operators in this space is not as intuitive as in the previous section. We tackle the problem in a different way. First, we focus on determining binary mg operators. Then we study if we can obtain n-ary mg operators by combining these binary mg operators.

Proposition 3. *Let A, B and C be three finite sets of elements. If the equality $d_m(A, B) = d_m(A, C) + d_m(C, B)$ holds, then there exists an optimal mapping $\alpha'_{A,B}$ such that for every pair of elements (a_i, b_j) in $\alpha'_{A,B}$ there exists an element $c_k \in C$ that satisfies $d_l(a_i, b_j) = d_l(a_i, c_k) + d_l(c_k, b_j)$.*

Proof. Let $\alpha_{A,C}$, $\alpha_{C,B}$ be the optimal matchings used for the computation of $d_m(A, C)$ and $d_m(C, B)$, respectively. We can write,

$$d_m(A, C) = \sum_{\forall (a_i, c_j) \in \alpha_{A,C}} d_l(a_i, c_j) + \frac{M}{2} \cdot k_{\alpha_{A,C}}$$
$$d_m(C, B) = \sum_{\forall (c_i, b_j) \in \alpha_{C,B}} d_l(c_i, b_j) + \frac{M}{2} \cdot k_{\alpha_{C,B}}$$

where $k_{\alpha_{A,C}}$ (respectively, $k_{\alpha_{C,B}}$) denotes the number of elements of A and C (respectively, C and B) which do not belong to $\alpha_{A,C}$ (respectively, $\alpha_{C,B}$).

Next, we define the matching $\alpha'_{A,B}$ as the composition of the mappings $\alpha_{A,C}$ and $\alpha_{C,B}$. That is, $\alpha'_{A,B}(A) = \alpha_{C,B}(\alpha_{A,C}(A))$. Keeping $\alpha'_{A,B}$ in mind, the sum $d_m(A, C) + d_m(C, B)$ can be written as,

$$
\begin{aligned}
d_m(A, C) + d_m(C, B) = &\sum_{\forall (a_i, b_j) \in \alpha'_{A,B}} (d_l(a_i, \alpha_{A,C}(a_i)) + d_l(\alpha_{A,C}(a_i), b_j)) \\
&+ \sum_{\forall a_i \in D(\alpha_{A,C}) - D(\alpha'_{A,B})} d_l(a_i, \alpha_{A,C}(a_i)) \\
&+ \sum_{\forall c_i \in D(\alpha_{C,B}) - \alpha_{A,C}(A)} d_l(c_i, \alpha_{C,B}(c_i)) \\
&+ \frac{M}{2} \cdot k_{\alpha_{A,C}} + \frac{M}{2} \cdot k_{\alpha_{C,B}}
\end{aligned}
\tag{3}
$$

The first term on the right-hand side of Equation (3) considers all the ordered pairs belonging to the matchings that share an element $c_i \in C$. The second and third terms concern those ordered pairs in $\alpha_{A,C}$ and $\alpha_{C,B}$ (respectively), which were not taken into account by the first term. Finally, the two last terms come from those unmatched elements.

Next, the chain of inequalities shown in Equation (4) can be derived as follows. First, we apply the triangle inequality over the first term on the right-hand side of Expression (3). Second, we remove the second and the third terms. Third, we apply $k_{\alpha_{A,C}} + k_{\alpha_{C,B}} \geq k_{\alpha'_{A,B}}$. And, finally, the last inequality is a direct consequence of the $d_m(\cdot, \cdot)$ definition (see Equation (2)).

$$d_m(A, C) + d_m(C, B) \geq \sum_{\forall(a_i, b_j) \in \alpha'_{A,B}} d_l(a_i, b_j)$$
$$+ \sum_{\forall a_i \in D(\alpha_{A,C}) - D(\alpha'_{A,B})} d_l(a_i, \alpha_{A,C}(a_i))$$
$$+ \sum_{\forall c_i \in D(\alpha_{C,B}) - \alpha_{A,C}(A)} d_l(c_i, \alpha_{C,B}(c_i))$$
$$+ \tfrac{M}{2} \cdot k_{\alpha_{A,C}} + \tfrac{M}{2} \cdot k_{\alpha_{C,B}}$$
$$\geq \sum_{\forall(a_i, b_j) \in \alpha'_{A,B}} d_l(a_i, b_j)$$
$$+ \tfrac{M}{2} \cdot (k_{\alpha_{A,C}} + k_{\alpha_{C,B}})$$
$$\geq \sum_{\forall(a_i, b_j) \in \alpha'_{A,B}} d_l(a_i, b_j) + \tfrac{M}{2} \cdot (k_{\alpha'_{A,B}}) = d(\alpha'_{A,B}, A, B)$$
$$\geq d_m(A, B)$$

$$(4)$$

The equality $d(A, C) + d(C, B) = d(A, B)$ holds only if all the inequalities ($\geq$) on the right-hand-side of Equation (4) becomes an equality. Among all these transformations, only the first and the last one are necessary to prove the proposition. The first inequality turns into an equality if the element $c_k = \alpha_{A,C}(a_i)$ in the first term in the right-hand-side of (3) satisfies $d(a_i, b_j) = d(a_i, c_k) + d(c_k, b_j)$, for every pair (a_i, b_j) in $\alpha'_{A,B}$. The proposition is automatically proved if $\alpha'_{A,B}$ is an optimal matching, and if this occurs then the last inequality is transformed into an equality.

The fact that the $lgg(\cdot)$ for atoms is distance-based suggests a strategy to define distance-based binary generalisation operators: given two clauses A and B in $2^{\bar{X}_l}$, we could initially define $\Delta(A, B) = \{\{lgg(a_i, b_j) : (a_i, b_j) \in \alpha_{A,B}\}\}$ where $\alpha_{A,B}$ is an optimal mapping. A distance-based operator must compute a pattern covering the elements C between A and B. However, if C is between A and B, then C contains atoms c_k which are also between a_i and b_j, for every (a_i, b_j) in an optimal $\alpha_{A,B}$. Since the lgg for atoms is distance-based for the distance d_l, if c_k is between the atoms a_i and b_j, then $c_k \in Set(lgg(a_i, b_j))$. At first glance, this definition of Δ seems to be distance-based. However, two drawbacks must be analysed.

1. Variables occurring in the different $lgg(a_i, b_j)$ must be independent (i.e. never repeated). Otherwise, the corresponding pattern might not be distance-based (for further details see [1]). We deal with this crucial issue at the end of this section.
2. More than one optimal matching can be given for $d_m(A, B)$. Of course, if the matchings lead to different patterns p_1 and p_2 such as $Set(p_1) \neq Set(p_2)$, there will be elements between A and B which do not belong to $Set(p_1)$ or to $Set(p_2)$. Hence, all the optimal matchings must be taken into account. Of course, this has a negative effect on the efficiency of computing distance-based operators.

Taking both observations above into account, Propositions 4 and 5 characterise the family of all the distance-based binary generalisation operators. They show that a binary generalisation operator $\Delta(A, B)$ is distance-based if $Set(\Delta^*(A, B)) \subset Set(\Delta(A, B))$, where $\Delta^*(A, B)$ represents the union of all patterns p_i obtained by taking all the optimal matchings between A and B into account.

Proposition 4. *Given two clauses A and B in $(2^{\bar{X}_l}, d_l)$ and the pattern language $\mathcal{L}$ consisting of all logic programs defined over a signature. The binary generalisation operator $\Delta^*(A, B) = p$ defined as*

$$p = \bigcup_{\forall\ optimal\ \alpha_{A,B}} \{lgg(a_i, b_j) : \forall (a_i, b_j) \in \alpha_{A,B}\},$$

is distance-based, where the repeated variables occurring in different $lgg(a_i, b_j)$ are independent.

Proof. From Proposition 3, if a set D is between A and B (i.e. $d_m(A, B) = d_m(A, D) + d_m(D, B)$) then there exists an optimal mapping $\alpha_{A,B}$ such that for every $(a_i, b_j) \in \alpha_{A,B}$ there exists $d_k \in D$ with d_k being between a_i and b_j. As the lgg for literals is distance-based, necessarily $d_k \in Set(lgg(a_i, b_j))$ and $D \in Set(\{lgg(a_i, b_j) : \forall (a_i, b_j) \in \alpha_{A,B}\})$. Since all the optimal mappings are taken into consideration, for every set D between A and B, $D \in Set(p)$, and therefore, $\Delta^*(A, B)$ is distance-based.

Proposition 5. *Given the metric space $(2^{\bar{X}_l}, d_m)$ and the pattern language $\mathcal{L}$ consisting of all the logic programs defined over a signature. A mapping $\Delta : 2^{\bar{X}_l} \times 2^{\bar{X}_l} \to \mathcal{L}$ is distance-based iff for every pair of clauses A and B, $Set(\Delta^*(A, B)) \subset Set(\Delta(A, B))$, with Δ^* being the distance-based operator defined in Proposition 4.*

Proof. ($\to$) If $\Delta(A, B)$ is distance-based, then it means that for every D between A and B, $D \subset Set(\Delta(A, B))$. Then, for every optimal mapping $\alpha_{A,B}$, we define $D_{\alpha_{A,B}}$ as

$$D_{\alpha_{A,B}} = \{lgg(a_i, b_j) : \forall (a_i, b_j) \in \alpha_{A,B}\}$$

which is clearly between A and B. Then, for every optimal mapping $\alpha_{A,B}$, $D_{\alpha_{A,B}} \in Set(\Delta(A, B))$, and therefore $\Delta^*(A, B) \in Set(\Delta(A, B))$ and by definition of $Set(\cdot)$, $Set(\Delta^*(A, B)) \subset Set(\Delta(A, B))$.

($\leftarrow$) Thus, $Set(\Delta^*(A, B))$ is a subset of $Set(\Delta(A, B))$. Since $\Delta^*(A, B)$ is distance-based, automatically $\Delta(A, B)$ is distance-based.

Now, we must determine the mg binary operator. It is direct from Proposition 5 and Definition 3, since, for every distance-based operator $\Delta(A, B)$ and for every pair of elements A and B, we know that $Set(\Delta^*(A, B)) \subset Set(\Delta(A, B))$ and therefore, $c(\{A, B\}|\Delta^*(A, B)) \leq c(\{A, B\}|\Delta(A, B))$. Then, $\Delta^*(A, B)$ is the mg.

Given that the patterns p_i can be combined by means of the union operator, a distance-based operator can be defined for more than two elements by defining a distance-based binary operator, namely Δ', and fixing a nerve-function $N(\cdot)$. Given the set $E = \{e_1, \ldots, e_n\}$, $\Delta_{N(E)}(E) = \bigcup_{\forall (e_i, e_j) \in N(E)} \Delta'(e_i, e_j)$.

The distance-based operator which is minimal can be determined by exploring all the possible nerves $N(E)$ for a set of elements E. On the other hand, we may only be interested in computing the mg relative to a specific nerve function. Then, Proposition 6 states that if $\Delta' = \Delta^*$ in the expression above, then $\Delta_{N(E)}(E)$ is a mg that is related to a nerve function $N(E)$.

Proposition 6. *Let $\Delta^*(A, B)$ be the binary generalisation operator introduced in Proposition 4 and let $c(E|p) = \sum_{\forall e \in E} r_e$ (with $r_e = inf_{r \in \mathcal{R}} B(e, r) \not\subseteq Set(p)$) be the cost function. Then*

$$\Delta_{N(E)}(E) = \bigcup_{\forall (e_i, e_j) \in N(E)} \Delta^*(e_i, e_j)$$

is a mg operator that is related to the nerve function $N(E)$.

Proof. We will proceed by contradiction. Let us suppose that $\Delta_{N(E)}$ is not *mg*. Then there exists a distance-based $\Delta'_{N(E)}$ such that $c(E|\Delta'_{N(E)}) < c(E|\Delta_{N(E)})$. We define a binary distance-based operator Δ'' restricted to all the pairs $(e_i, e_j) \in N(E)$, such that $\Delta''(e_i, e_j) = \Delta'_{N(E)}(E) = p$. But according to Proposition 5,

$$Set(\Delta^*_{N(E)}(e_i, e_j)) \subseteq Set(\Delta''(e_i, e_j)) = Set(\Delta'_{N(E)}(E))$$

As occurs for every $(e_i, e_j) \in N(E)$, $Set(\Delta_{N(E)}(E)) \subset Set(\Delta'_{N(E)}(E))$, and, consequently, $\Delta'_{N(E)}$ cannot be *mg*. $\qed$

Before concluding, note that a pattern computed by a *mg* cannot contain repeated variables in the different $lgg(a_i, b_j)$ from the same clause. On the one hand, this makes sense since the metric does not capture the semantic of repeated variables occurring in different atoms. Hence, for the sets $A = \{p(a), q(a)\}$, $B = \{p(b), q(b)\}$, and $C = \{p(c), q(d)\}$, $d_l(A, B) = d_l(A, C)$ when, intuitively, B should be more similar to A. This is a strong constraint to express some real-world properties. However, this concerns only the *mg* operator. It does not mean that distance-based operators cannot contain repeated variables in different atoms in general. For instance, Proposition 5 suggests that we could adapt a bottom-up ILP inference algorithm to take the pattern (clauses) computed by the *mg* as input. The output of the algorithm is a more general pattern than the input pattern. It is also distance-based and contains repeated variables among different atoms. Furthermore, this fact indicates that some adaptations of the ILP algorithms can be viewed as distance-based operators.

5   Conclusions and Future Work

This work develops the notion of *mg* operator for every sort of data that is embedded in a metric space. Here we include a definition of the framework, following the main ideas explained in [1] in order to address the minimal generalisation operators for some first-order objects.

We have shown that Plotkin's *lgg* can be seen as a particular case of this setting because the classical *lgg* for atoms is a *mg* operator w.r.t. the metric space defined in [13] and a specific (but simple) cost function. We showed this result in [2], but only as a binary operator and without the notion of minimality. The notion of cost function, which is exclusively defined in terms of distances, completes the connection between the concepts of distance, pattern and generalisation that we established in previous works. Furthermore, in this work, we have suggested that different mg operators for atoms can be obtained by changing the cost function, which can be an alternative to lgg for redesigning existing ILP methods or for deriving new ones. As for clauses, Plotkin's lgg has been shown not to be a mg operator for the particular metric space derived from the distance introduced by [12]. Due to the complexity of this metric space, a new mg operator relative to one specific nerve function has been introduced. Other distances, cost functions and pattern languages have also been studied (see [1]). For instance, Plotkin's lgg for atoms is not distance-based w.r.t. the distance introduced in [9]. This is an example that some distances are more appropriate than others in a logic context.

The applicability of the framework and the new lines of research are numerous. First, we think that the new mg operators (and the new understanding of the lgg as a distance-based operator) can be useful to redefine, reunderstand, and cross different methods and ideas within ILP. For instance, some bottom-up ILP methods (some of which have almost been forgotten since the early nineties) can be adapted to work with newly derived mg operators, as we outlined at the end of the section above. Furthermore, the adapted ILP methods would be distance-based operators. For instance, some size measures for atoms and clauses (see Section 14.9 in [10]) could be used for the cost function in a similar way as they were used in the context of refinement. Second, distance-based mg would be a good link to extend ILP techniques outside ILP, since we have defined them many other data types: lists, trees, graphs, sets (see [1] [3]). Specifically, bottom-up ILP methods could by adapted to other kinds of complex objects (not necessarily first-order). For instance, we are currently investigating the possibility of applying ILP bottom-up methods of this kind to lists or graphs. Third, we think that provided that we have an adequate mg operator (as some of the ones studied or derived in this work), we could easily adapt traditional distance-based techniques to ILP such as clustering techniques (k-means, minimum-spanning tree, etc.) or classification techniques (k-nn) in a more sophisticated way than has been done to date. In other words, we can turn these techniques from instance-based techniques to model-based techniques.

One of the specific issues that must be addressed for any new mg is, logically, its efficiency. In some cases, if the mg is distance-based, but computationally expensive to find, we might need to find heuristics or approximations. Some of these approximations (as we mentioned in the specific case of the mg in Section 4) consist of making one optimal matching instead of all the possible optimal matchings between two elements. We have explored this possibility for lists (see [1]) by introducing the notion of pseudo distance-based operator. However, it is important to highlight that, in our framework, the mg operators are based on a cost function. This is more flexible than when the mg operator is solely based on the notion of generalisation or inclusion. If all the distances are pre-computed between elements, the computation of the mg can be speeded up.

We are currently adapting classical (and, for the moment, simple) machine learning techniques to our framework, such as a nearest-neighbour classifier based on mg for several data sorts or a distance-based decision tree.

Acknowledgement

We thank the anonymous reviewers for their valuable and insightful comments.

References

1. Estruch, V.: A distance-based generalisation framework for model-based learning from structured data. PhD thesis, Technical University of Valencia (2007) http://www.dsic.upv.es/~flip/#Papers
2. Estruch, V., Ferri, C., Hernández-Orallo, J., Ramírez-Quintana, M.J.: Distance-based generalisation. In: Kramer, S., Pfahringer, B. (eds.) ILP 2005. LNCS (LNAI), vol. 3625, pp. 87–102. Springer, Heidelberg (2005)
3. Estruch, V., Ferri, C., Hernández-Orallo, J., Ramírez-Quintana, M.J.: Distance-based generalisation for graphs. In: Proc. of the WS of Mining and Learning with Graphs, MLG06 (2006)
4. Gaertner, T., Lloyd, J.W., Flach, P.A.: Kernels and distances for structured data. Machine Learning 57(3), 205–232 (2004)
5. Lavrac, N., Dzeroski, S.: Inductive Logic Programming: Techniques and Applications. Ellis Horwood, New York (1994)
6. Lloyd, J.W.: Foundations of logic programming (2nd extended edn.). Springer, New York (1987)
7. Muggleton, S.: Inductive Logic Programming. New Generation Computing 8(4), 295–318 (1991)
8. Muggleton, S.H.: Inductive logic programming: Issues, results, and the challenge of learning language in logic. Artificial Intelligence 114(1–2), 283–296 (1999)
9. Nienhuys-Cheng, S-H.: Distance between Herbrand interpretations: A measure for approximations to a target concept. In: Džeroski, S., Lavrač, N. (eds.) Inductive Logic Programming. LNCS, vol. 1297, pp. 213–226. Springer, Heidelberg (1997)
10. Nienhuys-Cheng, S-H., de Wolf, R.: Foundations of Inductive Logic Programming. In: Džeroski, S., Lavrač, N. (eds.) Inductive Logic Programming. LNCS, vol. 1297, Springer, Heidelberg (1997)
11. Plotkin, G.: A note on inductive generalization. Machine Intelligence 5, 153–163 (1970)
12. Ramon, J., Bruynooghe, M.: A framework for defining distances between first-order logic objects. In: Page, D.L. (ed.) Inductive Logic Programming. LNCS, vol. 1446, pp. 271–280. Springer, Heidelberg (1998)
13. Ramon, J., Bruynooghe, M., Van Laer, W.: Distance measures between atoms. In: CompulogNet Area Meeting on Computational Logic and Machine Learning, pp. 35–41. University of Manchester, UK (1998)

Efficient and Scalable Induction of Logic Programs Using a Deductive Database System

Michel Ferreira, Nuno A. Fonseca, Ricardo Rocha, and Tiago Soares

DCC-FC & LIACC
University of Porto, Portugal
{michel,nf,ricroc,tiagosoares}@ncc.up.pt

Abstract. A consequence of ILP systems being implemented in Prolog or using Prolog libraries is that, usually, these systems use a Prolog internal database to store and manipulate data. However, in real-world problems, the original data is rarely in Prolog format. In fact, the data is often kept in Relational Database Management Systems (RDBMS) and then converted to a format acceptable by the ILP system. Therefore, a more interesting approach is to link the ILP system to the RDBMS and manipulate the data without converting it. This scheme has the advantage of being more scalable since the whole data does not need to be loaded into memory by the ILP system. In this paper we study several approaches of coupling ILP systems with RDBMS systems and evaluate their impact on performance. We propose to use a Deductive Database (DDB) system to transparently translate the hypotheses to relational algebra expressions. The empirical evaluation performed shows that the execution time of ILP algorithms can be effectively reduced using a DDB and that the size of the problems can be increased due to a non-memory storage of the data.

Keywords: Implementation, Performance, Deductive Databases.

1 Introduction

The amount of data collected and stored in databases is growing considerably in almost all areas of human activity. A paramount example is the explosion of bio-tech data that, as a result of automation in biochemistry, doubles its size every three to six months [1,2]. Most of this data is structured and stored in relational databases and, in more complex applications, can involve several relations, thus being spread over multiple tables. However, many important data mining techniques look for patterns in a single relation (or table) where each tuple (or row) is one object of interest. Great care and effort has to be made in order to store as much relevant data as possible into a single table so that propositional data mining algorithms can be applied. Notwithstanding this preparation step, propositionalizing data from multiple tables into a single one may lead to redundancy, loss of information [3] or to tables of prohibitive size [4].

On the other hand, Inductive Logic Programing (ILP) systems are able to learn patterns from relational data. However, ILP systems usually store and

S. Muggleton, R. Otero, and A. Tamaddoni-Nezhad (Eds.): ILP 2006, LNAI 4455, pp. 184–198, 2007.

manipulate data in Prolog databases as a result of being implemented in Prolog [5,6,7] or using Prolog libraries [8]. The approach often followed by ILP practitioners is to convert the data in the relational database to a format acceptable by the ILP system. A consequence of learning from Prolog databases is that the data is loaded into main memory, thus limiting ILP ability to process larger datasets. Although ILP systems load the data into main memory, they are known as being computationally expensive. To find a model, ILP systems repeatedly examine sets of candidate clauses, which in turn involves evaluating each clause on all data to determine its *quality*. On complex or sizable applications, evaluating individual clauses may take considerable time, and thus, to compute a model, an ILP system can take several hours or even days. Efficiency and scalability are thus two of the major challenges that current ILP systems must overcome.

In this work we show how an ILP system can be transparently coupled with a Relational Database Management System (RDBMS) by using a Deductive Database (DDB) system, and how this coupled environment provides an excellent framework for the efficient and scalable induction of logic programs. In particular, we will use April [9] as the ILP system and MYDDAS [10] as the DDB system. By using a DDB system, the ILP system is able to process larger databases, since the memory issues disappear, and can transparently exploit advanced features of relational databases, such as powerful indexing schemes, query optimization, efficient aggregation and joining algorithms. In particular, we describe *mode based indexing*, an optimization that many ILP systems may easily perform.

The idea of coupling ILP with relational databases is not new [11,12,13,14], but very little has been reported about the impact on performance of learning from a relational database. In fact, there is a general idea that ILP systems become slower when coupled to a RDBMS. To clarify this, we investigate the effectiveness of several high-level strategies of coupling an ILP system with a DDB. We wish to evaluate the potential performance gains that result from learning from a relational database as opposed to the more traditional approach of learning from Prolog databases. In the experiments we used four artificially generated problems [15] that allowed us to perform the evaluations while considering different data-set sizes and hypotheses complexity (number of joins in a hypothesis).

The remainder of the paper is organized as follows. First, we revise the background concepts of relational algebra operations in Prolog and introduce the problem of coverage computation in ILP. Then, we describe our approaches to couple ILP with DDB and discuss some implementation details. Next, we present the results of an empirical evaluation on the performance of the proposed approaches. We end by discussing related work and by outlining some conclusions.

2   Preliminaries

In this section we revise relevant concepts of relational algebra and the encoding of its operations in Prolog syntax. We also introduce the problem of coverage computation in the context of ILP systems.

2.1   Prolog and Relational Algebra

If we abstract the notion of order on the clauses of a Prolog predicate and restrict these clauses to ground facts with atomic arguments, then this predicate is equivalent to a database relation. Database relations are queried by RDBMS using relational algebra. In [16], Codd defined five primitive operations of relational algebra: *selection, projection, cartesian product, set union* and *set difference*. We can define Prolog predicates which are equivalent to these relational algebra operations. Assuming that $\mathcal{Q}$ and $\mathcal{R}$ are database relations with an arbitrary number of attributes, and that q and r are their associated Prolog predicates, Table 1 defines a new relation $\mathcal{P}$ and a new Prolog predicate p, based on the five primitive relational algebra operations and their equivalent encoding in Prolog syntax.

Table 1. Relational algebra operations in Prolog

Selection	$\mathcal{P} \leftarrow \sigma_{\$i=val}(\mathcal{Q})$ $p(X_1, ..., X_{i-1}, val, X_{i+1}, ..., X_n) :- q(X_1, ..., X_{i-1}, val, X_{i+1}, ..., X_n).$
Projection	$\mathcal{P} \leftarrow \pi_{\$i}(\mathcal{Q})$ $p(X_i) :- q(X_1, ..., X_i, ..., X_n).$
Cartesian Product	$\mathcal{P} \leftarrow \mathcal{Q} \times \mathcal{R}$ $p(X_1, ..., X_n, Y_1, ..., Y_m) :- q(X_1, ..., X_n), r(Y_1, ..., Y_m).$
Set Union	$\mathcal{P} \leftarrow \mathcal{Q} \cup \mathcal{R}$ $p(X_1, ..., X_n) :- q(X_1, ..., X_n).$ $p(X_1, ..., X_n) :- r(X_1, ..., X_n).$
Set Difference	$\mathcal{P} \leftarrow \mathcal{Q} - \mathcal{R}$ $p(X_1, ..., X_n) :- q(X_1, ..., X_n), not\ r(X_1, ..., X_n).$

An important difference between Prolog and relational algebra is that the Prolog's inference engine operates *tuple-at-a-time*, while the database manager operates *set-at-a-time*. To get the Prolog system to compute the equivalent of the relational algebra operations of Table 1, we need to use the $findall/3$ built-in: $findall(p(X_1, ..., X_n), p(X_1, ..., X_n), L)$, which will force backtracking to occur on goal $p(X_1, ..., X_n)$, the second argument, collecting all solutions as $p(X_1, ..., X_n)$ terms, the first argument, in list L.

Codd's relational algebra has been extended to include higher-order operations, such as aggregate functions that compute values over sets of attributes. Virtually every database system supports the following aggregate functions over relations: $sum()$, $avg()$, $count()$, $min()$ and $max()$, which compute the sum, the average, the number, the minimum and the maximum of given attributes. In relational algebra, aggregation operations are represented by $_{group}\mathcal{F}_{fun}(\mathcal{Q})$, where $\mathcal{F}$ is the aggregation operator, *group* is an optional list of attributes of relation $\mathcal{Q}$ to be grouped and *fun* is the list of aggregation functions. For example, a relational algebra expression returning a relation with a single tuple representing the number of values for the ith attribute of a relation $\mathcal{Q}$ would be: $\mathcal{P} \leftarrow \mathcal{F}_{count\ \$i}(\mathcal{Q})$.

Because of its tuple-at-a-time nature, Prolog is particularly inefficient for higher-order computations. Coupled DDB systems thus try to transfer these computations to the database manager. In the context of DDB the logic syntax to encode the aggregation operations of relational algebra is as follows:

$$p(X_i, ..., X_j, Y_1, ..., Y_m) :- Y_1 \text{ is } X_i \wedge ... \wedge X_j \wedge fun_1(X_k, q(X_1, ..., X_k, ..., X_n)),$$

$$...,$$

$$Y_m \text{ is } X_i \wedge ... \wedge X_j \wedge fun_m(X_l, q(X_1, ..., X_l, ..., X_n)).$$

where the $X_i, ..., X_j$ are the grouping attributes and the $Y_1, ..., Y_m$ are the aggregate values associated to the $fun_1, ..., fun_m$ aggregation functions. The above example of $\mathcal{P} \leftarrow \mathcal{F}_{count \ \$i}(\mathcal{Q})$ would be written in Prolog as:

$$p(Y_1) :- Y_1 \text{ is } count(X_i, q(X_1, ..., X_i, ..., X_n)).$$

Common database queries typically combine several primitive relational algebra operations. For instance, a *natural join* such as $\mathcal{P} \leftarrow \mathcal{Q} \bowtie_{\$i=\$j} \mathcal{R}$ is implemented by a composition of cartesian product, selection and projection operations: $\mathcal{P} \leftarrow \pi_{X_1,...,X_n,Y_1,...,Y_{j-1},Y_{j+1},...,Y_m}(\sigma_{\$i=\$(n+j)}(\mathcal{Q} \times \mathcal{R}))$.

An equivalent composition results in the following Prolog clause to implement the same natural join:

$$p(X_1, ..., X_i, ..., X_n, Y_1, ..., Y_{j-1}, Y_{j+1}, ..., Y_m) :- q(X_1, ..., X_i, ..., X_n),$$

$$r(Y_1, ..., Y_{j-1}, X_i, Y_{j+1}, ..., Y_m).$$

Every composition of relational algebra can be expressed in Prolog, while the reverse is not true. The subset of Prolog, extended with the $findall/3$ predicate, equivalent to relational algebra is referred as Datalog [17]. Prolog predicates which involve either direct or indirect recursion cannot be expressed in relational algebra. Relational tuples also cannot represent Prolog facts containing unbound or compound arguments.

2.2   Coverage Computation in ILP

The normal problem that an ILP system must solve is to find a consistent and complete *theory*, from a set of examples and prior knowledge, the *background knowledge*, that explains all given positive examples, while being consistent with the given negative examples [18]. In general, the background knowledge and the set of examples can be arbitrary logic programs.

To derive a theory with the desired properties, many ILP systems follow some kind of *generate-and-test* approach to traverse the *hypotheses space* [8]. A general ILP system spends most of its time evaluating hypotheses, either because the number of examples is large or because testing each example is computationally hard. For each of these hypotheses the ILP algorithm computes its *coverage*, that is, the number of positive and negatives examples that can be deduced from it. If a clause covers all of the positive examples and none of the negative examples, then the ILP system stops. Otherwise, an alternative stop criteria should be used, such as the number of hypotheses evaluated, or the number of positive examples covered, or time. A simplified algorithm for the coverage computation of a clause is presented next in Fig. 1.

```
compute_coverage(Clause,ScorePos,ScoreNeg) :-
    assert(Clause,Ref),
    reset_counter(pos,0), reset_counter(neg,0),
    (
        select_positive_example(Goal), once(Goal),
        incr_counter(pos), fail
    ;
        true
    ),
    (
        select_negative_example(Goal), once(Goal),
        incr_counter(neg), fail
    ;
        true
    ),
    counter(pos,ScorePos), counter(neg,ScoreNeg),
    erase(Ref).
```

Fig. 1. Coverage computation

The *compute_coverage*/3 predicate starts by asserting the clause being evaluated[1] and by resetting a counter *pos*. Next, the *select_positive_example*/1 predicate binds variable *Goal* to the first positive example, which is then called using the *once*/1 primitive. The *once*/1 primitive is used to avoid backtracking on alternative ways to derive the current goal. If the positive example succeeds, counter *pos* is incremented and we force failure. Failure, whether forced or unforced, will backtrack to alternative positive examples, traversing all of them and counting those that succeed. The process is repeated for negative examples and finally the asserted clause is retracted.

3   Coupling Approaches

In this section we describe several approaches to divide the coverage computation work between the logic system and the relational database system. We will describe the coupling approaches starting with the base coverage computation, and then incrementally transferring computational work from the logic system to the database system.

3.1   Selection Approach

On a typical coupled DDB system, the tuples defined extensionally in database relations are transparently mapped to Prolog predicates by using a directive such as:

$$: - \; db\_import(rel\_name, pred\_name, conn).$$

---

[1] Here we consider the general case where the clauses being evaluated can be recursive.

This directive is meant to associate a predicate *pred_name* with a database relation *rel_name* that is accessible through a connection with the database system named *conn*. What this directive does is implementing the communication layer between the Prolog engine and the database system, which involves the translation of queries written in Prolog syntax to their equivalent relational algebra expressions, as explained in subsection 2.1. Typical interfaces with relational database systems do not include support for relational algebra expressions in their textual form, requiring their further translation to SQL, the *lingua franca* of database systems.

Based on the above directive and assuming that *rel_name* is a two field relation, the query goal *pred_name(val, A)* will be translated to the following relational algebra expression: $\sigma_{\$1=val}(rel\_name)$, which is in turn translated to the SQL expression:

SELECT val, A.attr2 FROM rel_name A WHERE A.attr1 = val;

where *attr1* and *atrr2* are the attributes names of relation *rel_name*. This expression is then sent to the database system and the obtained result set is navigated *tuple-at-a-time* using backtracking. Note that the database system executes the *selection operation*, returning only the tuples that unify with the logic goal, thus freeing the logic system from the unification operation. This selection approach requires just the declaration of the background knowledge and the positive and negative examples predicates through *db_import*/3 directives. Coverage computation is done exactly as in Fig. 1.

3.2 Join Approach

A fundamental improvement to the selection approach is to transfer the computation of the join of the several database goals in the body of a clause to the database system. Prolog efficiency is compromised by the strict execution mechanism of SLD-resolution, while the query optimiser of database systems is able to use goal-reordering and extended indexing schemes to improve the efficiency of join computation.

In order to transfer the join computation to the database system, the interface of the DDB system must group together conjunctions of extensional goals and Prolog built-ins that can be expressed in relational algebra. This can be done automatically during compilation using a simple program analysis, or can be done explicitly by the user. Currently, MYDDAS follows the later approach, through a *db_view*/3 directive:

$: - db\_view(view(A_i, ..., A_j), (db\_goal_1(A_1, ..., A_n), ..., db\_goal_m(A_k, ..., A_l)), conn).$

where the first argument specifies the attributes to be fetched from the database, the second argument specifies the selection restrictions and join conditions, and the third argument identifies the connection with the database system.

The *compute_coverage*/3 predicate still works as before, but instead of asserting the given clause, it now creates a view for the goals in the body of the clause and then replaces the clause's body with the created view. For example, considering the clause '$h(A) : - p1(A, B), p2(B)$.', where $p1/2$ and $p2/1$ represent the database relations $r1$ and $r2$, the *compute_coverage*/3 predicate now creates the view:

$$db\_view(view(A), (p1(A, B), p2(B)), conn)$$

and asserts the clause '$h(A) : - view(A)$.'. The relational algebra expression generated for the view when evaluating a given example, $e1$ for instance, is:

$$\pi_{\$1}((\sigma_{\$1=e1}(r1)) \bowtie_{\$2=\$1} r2)$$

3.3 Reduced-Join Approach

Some very important issues in the coverage algorithm of Fig. 1 arise for the *once*/1 primitive: (i) the coupling interface must support deallocation of queries result sets when the *once*/1 primitive prunes the search space [19]; (ii) instead of unnecessarily computing all the alternative solutions, the database system only needs to compute the first tuple of the join.

In order to reduce the scope of the join computed by the database system, we should push the *once*/1 primitive to the database view. The asserted clause should include an *once*/1 predicate on the view definition and the DDB interface should be able to translate it to a relational algebra expression that can be efficiently executed by the database system. We introduce an extension to the relational algebra selection operation, $\sigma_{(conditions, rows)}(R)$, where the *rows* argument defines a limit to the number of tuples that the selection operation should return. In particular, if this selection operation is composed with a join operation, the query optimizer can prune the join computation as soon as the required number of tuples is reached. With this approach, the *compute_coverage*/3 predicate can be used as before and we can drop the *once*/1 call from its code. For our previous example, the view is now:

$$db\_view(view(A), once(p1(A, B), p2(B)), conn)$$

and the relational algebra operation generated when evaluating example $e1$ is:

$$\pi_{\$1}((\sigma_{(\$1=e1, 1)}(r1)) \bowtie_{\$2=\$1} r2)$$

Based on this relational algebra expression, the MYDDAS interface is able to send the following SQL query to the database system:

SELECT A.attr1 FROM r1 A, r2 B

WHERE A.attr1 = e1 AND A.attr2 = B.attr1 LIMIT 1;

3.4 Aggregation Approach

A final transfer of computation work from the logic system to the database system can be done for the aggregation operation which counts the number of examples covered by a clause. The *compute_coverage*/3 predicate uses extra-logical global variables to perform this counting operation, as it would be too inefficient otherwise.

To transfer the aggregation work to the database system we need to restrict the theories we are inducing to non-recursive theories, where the head of the clause can not appear as a goal in the body. With this restriction, we can drop the assertion of the clause to the program code, include the positive or negative examples relation as a goal co-joined with the goals in the body of the current clause, and include a *count/2* predicate on the view definition for the attributes holding the positive or negative examples. Again, the join should only test for the existence of one tuple in the body goals for each of the examples, using the *once/1* primitive on the view definition. For our example, the view would be:

$$db\_view(view(C), C \text{ } is \text{ } count(A, (h(A), once(p1(A,B), p2(B)))), conn)$$

The composition of these relational operations results in the following relational algebra expression:

$$\mathcal{F}_{count \text{ } \$1}(r0 \bowtie_{\$1=\$1} (\sigma_{(\epsilon,1)}(r1) \bowtie_{\$2=\$1} r2))$$

where $r0$ is the database relation associated with $h/1$ and ϵ represents the empty condition. We have extended the MYDDAS interface in order to generate an efficient translation to SQL for such expressions. The above view generates the following SQL expression:

$$SELECT \text{ } COUNT(A.attr1) \text{ } FROM \text{ } r0 \text{ } A$$
$$WHERE \text{ } EXISTS \text{ } (SELECT \text{ } * \text{ } FROM \text{ } r1 \text{ } B, \text{ } r2 \text{ } C$$
$$WHERE \text{ } A.attr1 = B.attr1 \text{ } AND \text{ } B.attr2 = C.attr1 \text{ } LIMIT \text{ } 1);$$

Although the '*LIMIT* 1' keyword may seem redundant for an existential sub-query, our experiments showed that MySQL performance is greatly improved if we include it on the sub-query. On the other hand, the '*LIMIT* 1' suffix has no impact on performance when using an Oracle RDBMS, as we shall see. This observation shows that MySQL query optimizer is failing somewhere on its task.

The four coupling approaches, *Selection*, *Join*, *Reduced-Join* and *Aggregation*, are gradually transferring computation from the logic system to the database system. In a future approach we plan to further transfer computation work to the database system, implementing a many-at-once optimization, as illustrated by the query packs technique [20]. Not only do some database systems perform caching of queries, but we can also extend the Prolog-to-relational-algebra translation in order to be able to send *packs* of logic queries to the database system and have their coverage computed by the database system, at once, using relational grouping operators optimized for redundancy elimination.

4   Implementation

The coupling approaches described above were implemented in the April ILP system [9] coupled with the DDB system MYDDAS. Both April and MYDDAS systems run on top of the Yap Prolog engine.

Being able to abstract the Prolog to SQL translation, task performed by MY-DDAS, we concentrated in implementing the various coupling approaches, with different distributions of work between the logic system and the database system, and considered some optimizations such as mode-based indexing, presented in the next subsection. The integration of both systems required minor changes to April's code and, in particular, to its clause evaluation component.

The impact for the ILP practitioner of using a DDB as opposed to using the Prolog database is kept to a minimum. The user first indicates, through a configuration option, which coupling approach wants to use, and then only needs to provide information regarding the database where the data resides (name, user, password, and host) and, if using the aggregation approach, the names of the tables of the positive and, if available, negative examples. When the examples are stored in tables, the ILP system automatically creates new tables for each class of examples with extra attributes that are used to keep temporary information generated during execution.

4.1   Mode-Based Indexing

ILP systems often use some kind of input/output mode declarations to supply information concerning the arguments of each predicate that may appear in the hypotheses [21,22]. These declarations specify if an argument of a predicate is intended to be a constant, an input or an output argument. Although the mode declarations are usually provided by the user, they can be also automatically extracted from the background knowledge [23].

There are two major advantages in the use of mode declarations. First, the ILP system can guarantee termination by ensuring that the hypotheses it generates are accordingly to the mode. Second, ILP systems can use the mode information to automatically create indexes in the database in order to optimize query execution. We proceed as follows. For each mode declaration (that affects some table) we create two indexes. The first index is created on the attributes indicated as constants or input arguments. The rationale is that all hypotheses (queries) generated will be mode conform and, thus, the join and projection operations in the queries will always be performed over the constant and/or the input attributes. The second index is created on all the attributes of the corresponding table (predicate). In the following section, we show that this automatic index creation, when used with the aggregation approach, reduces the execution speed significantly.

5   Performance Evaluation

We have performed a set of experiments in order to evaluate our work. The goals of the experiments were two-fold:

- Empirically compare the four coupling approaches.
- Assess if our proposal of coupling ILP with a DDB can improve the efficiency and scalability of ILP systems.

5.1   Materials and Methodology

We have used four artificially generated problems [15]. Table 2 characterizes the problems in terms of number of examples, number of relations in the background knowledge, and number of tuples. All experiments were performed using MY-DDAS 0.9, coupling Yap 5.1.0 with MySQL Server 4.1.5-gamma, on a AMD Athlon 64 Processor 2800+ with 512 Kbytes cache and 1 Gbyte of RAM. Yap performs indexing in run-time on all arguments.

Table 2. Problems characterization

Problem	# Examples	# Relations	# Tuples
$p.m8.l27$	200	8	321,576
$p.m11.l15$	200	11	440,000
$p.m15.l29$	200	15	603,000
$p.m21.l18$	200	21	844,200

A set of 688 clauses was generated for each artificial problem. The clauses were randomly generated and equally distributed by length, ranging from 1 to the number of relations available in the data-set. We used the April ILP system to randomly generate the sets of clauses.

Since the weight of coverage computation on the total execution time of an ILP system varies accordingly to the system or algorithm used, we have chosen to implement the approaches for coverage computation through simple Prolog programs[2]. This allows us to perform a comparison independent of the ILP system and to correctly measure the time spent in coverage computation. Using April's execution time as the measure does not allow us to do a precise performance evaluation since the gains would vary, depending on the search algorithm used and on the optimizations that April can perform during run-time.

5.2   Comparing the Coupling Approaches

Table 3 shows the best execution time of 5 runs, in seconds, for each problem. For the basic ILP approach, the clauses were evaluated using Yap with indexing on the first argument (IFA) and using Yap with indexing on all arguments (IAA). For the coupling approaches, the clauses were evaluated using mode-based indexing (MBI) as described in subsection 4.1. For comparison purposes, we also show the execution time for the *Aggregation* approach without mode-based indexing. Without mode-based indexing the relational tables still include indexing, but only based on the primary indexes associated to the primary keys.

A first observation should be made regarding the impact in the execution time when using full indexing in Prolog (*Basic ILP + IAA*) as opposed to use indexing solely in the first argument (*Basic ILP + IFA*). We will use the times taken by the *Basic ILP + IAA* as the base times, although full indexing is available in only a few Prolog engines.

---

[2] Available from http://www.ncc.up.pt/MYDDAS/ilpddb.html

Table 3. Performance for the different approaches (execution time in seconds)

Approach	Problem			
	p.m8.l27	p.m11.l15	p.m15.l29	p.m21.l18
Basic ILP + IFA	149	409	>1 day	>1 day
Basic ILP + IAA	15	50	33,972	>1 day
Selection + MBI	35,583	>1 day	>1 day	>1 day
Join + MBI	n.a	n.a	n.a	n.a
Reduced-Join + MBI	99	628	2,975	33,229
Aggregation	>1 day	>1 day	>1 day	>1 day
Aggregation + MBI	5	14	251	734

The core time of communication between the ILP system and the database system dilutes as we increase the computation work of the database system. For problems involving relations with thousands of tuples the *Selection + MBI* approach is unrealistic. This approach does not transfer any computation work to the database system, other than selecting tuples from individual relations. Furthermore, the number of queries generated is a factor of the number of tuples in each relation, which explains execution times of days or weeks for problems larger than *p.m8.l27*.

For the *Join + MBI* approach, as expected, we could not obtain the execution times for any problem, due to insufficient memory to compute the joins involved. Note that this approach does not implement the *once*/1 optimization, therefore the entire join is computed instead of just the first tuple. MySQL ran out of memory when trying to compute a join of several relations, each with thousands of tuples.

For the *Reduced-Join + MBI* approach the scope of the join is now reduced to compute just the first tuple. For problem *p.m11.l15* the slow-down factor compared to the *Basic ILP + IAA* approach is explained by the number of queries that are sent to the database system, one for every positive and negative example. This means that a total of 200 queries (the number of positive and negative examples) are sent to the database system for each of the 688 clauses. As the size of the joins grows larger, as with *p.m15.l29*, the time spent in communication of the queries becomes irrelevant compared to the time taken for computing the joins. This and the huge amount of backtracking performed by the *Basic ILP + IAA* approach for the two largest artificial problems, as the *Basic ILP + IAA* approach runs on a *tuple-at-a-time* form against the *set-at-a-time* database approaches, explains the speedup obtained with this approach.

On the *Aggregation* approach only two queries per clause are sent to the database system, one to compute positive coverage and one to compute negative coverage. Since all the coverage computation work is transferred to the database system, the core time of sending and storing the result set for the two queries is insignificant. However, the results are disappointing due to the lack of useful indexes on the tables.

The results obtained with the *Aggregation + MBI* approach are very good. The performance gains over the *Basic ILP + IAA* approach are clear: a 2.8

speedup for $p.m8.l27$, and a 3.4 speedup for $p.m11.l15$, and a 135 speedup for $p.m15.l29$. These results show a clear tendency for higher speedups as the size of the problems grow.

In conclusion, the *Aggregation + MBI* approach clearly outperforms the other approaches. It significantly reduces the execution time and may allow ILP systems to handle larger problems, thanks to the non-memory storage of data-sets, thus contributing to improving the scalability of ILP systems.

5.3 Impact of Query Transformations

The results presented in the previous section showed that *Aggregation + MBI* approach has the best results, even when compared to the times obtained to the *Basic ILP + IAA* approach. Although Prolog's indexing on all arguments is an improvement to indexing on the first argument (often provided by Prolog engines), that is not the only technique that may be used to improve query execution in Prolog.

Several techniques have been proposed to this effect, namely perform transformations in the query so that it can be executed more efficiently [24,20], compute an approximate evaluation [25,26] as opposed to an exact evaluation, store and reused the computations [27,28], or by exploiting parallelism [29]. Determining which technique or combinations of techniques produces the best results is out of scope of this paper. Instead, we selected one ILP technique similar to the query optimization performed by RDBMS and that has been shown to yield good results - the query transformations (QT) proposed in [24]. The results obtained with query transformations are presented in Table 4 and compared with two other approaches and with the times taken in an Oracle RDBMS.

Table 4. Comparing with query transformations (execution time in seconds)

Approach	Problem			
	p.m8.l27	p.m11.l15	p.m15.l29	p.m21.l18
Basic ILP + IAA	15	50	33,972	>1 day
Basic ILP + IAA + QT	1	4	16	39
Aggregation + MBI (MySQL)	5	14	251	734
Aggregation + MBI (Oracle)	6	9	101	164

It is obvious that the results presented are dependent of the RDBMS used. In our experiments we used MySQL which is known to be a fast database. However, our experiments suggest that the optimizer is not efficient. The results obtained for the *Aggregation + MBI* approach in the Oracle RDBMS show that it outperforms the MySQL RDBMS by almost a factor of 5 for the largest problem. This speedup also shows a clear trend to increase as the size of the data-sets grows. The Oracle optimizer also proves to be more intelligent when computing the existential sub-query on the *Aggregation* approach. When using the Oracle system, the '$LIMIT$ 1' keyword is actually redundant in terms of performance.

The impact of query transformations is impressive when compared to the basic ILP approach. Compared to our *Aggregation + MBI* approach in Oracle it is still 4 times faster for $p.m21.l18$. However, it requires the full data-set to be loaded to memory, which might not be possible for larger problems. Another interesting possibility we are exploring is the translation to relational algebra of the Prolog goals *after* applying the queries transformations optimization. Our preliminary results showed that this can in fact improve the performance on the database side. At this time, the MYDDAS interface translating Prolog to relational algebra expressions does not support the usage of the cut ($!$) predicate. The query transformations uses this extra-logical predicate to optimize queries. In Prolog, the cut operator is used to prune the search tree, but on the relational algebra the semantics of the $!/0$ predicate gives the notion of an existential sub-query. Preliminaries results of translating the cut to existential sub-queries for the goals generated by the queries transformation optimization indicate that it may have a positive impact on performance.

6   Related Work

Several previous implementations have already coupled ILP systems with relational databases, some mapping logical predicates into database relations, others translating logical clauses into SQL statements [11,12,13,14], and others using both [30]. The level of transparency (for the user) in these implementations is quite variable, ranging from no transparency (the user manually defines the views for each literal that may appear in a clause) [30] to completely transparent [14].

The idea of coupling ILP with DDB is also not new - the ILP system Warmr has been coupled with a DDB system to mine association rules [31]. The difference to our work is twofold. First, Warmr loads the data into main memory from a relational database, while in our proposal the data remains in the database. Secondly, we have performed an empirical performance study of several coupling approaches and proposed to exploit mode based indexing.

7   Concluding Remarks

In this work we have studied several approaches to couple ILP systems with RDBMS by using a DDB system. The strategy of using a DDB system brings to ILP systems the technology of relational database systems, which are very efficient in dealing with large amounts of data. We argue that this strategy is easier to implement and maintain than the approach that tries to incorporate database technology directly in the logic programming system. And, much more important, it allows a substantial increase of the size of the problems that can be solved using ILP since the data does not need to be loaded to memory by the ILP system.

The results of evaluating the several approaches to couple ILP with RDBMS show that the *Aggregation + MBI* approach: i) outperforms the other coupling approaches and significantly reduces the execution time when compared to the use of a Prolog engine (even with indexing on all arguments) and ii) may allow

ILP systems to handle larger problems, thanks to the non-memory storage of data-sets, thus contributing to improving the scalability of ILP systems.

The results also indicate that further research should be done in order to make learning from RDBMS competitive, in terms of execution time, with a fast Prolog engine (using indexing on all predicate's arguments and performing query transformations). For instance, a possible line of research could be the adaptation of techniques already developed in the ILP context (see e.g., [20,24]) to be used while learning from RDBMS. As further work we also plan to be able to implement the transformations from Prolog to SQL described in this paper as a compilation step, based on program analysis, which takes into account factors such as the size of data, database indexing information and complexity of queries. This information should guide an automatic translation of parts of a Prolog program to database accesses, using SQL as a compiler target language and a database system as an abstract machine.

Acknowledgements. This work has been partially supported by MYDDAS (POSC/EIA/59154/2004) and by funds granted to LIACC through the Programa de Financiamento Plurianual, Fundação para a Ciência e Tecnologia and Programa POSC. Tiago Soares is funded by FCT PhD grant SFRH/BD/23906/2005.

References

1. Berman, H.M., Westbrook, J., Feng, Z., Gilliland, G., Bhat, T.N., Weissig, H., Shindyalov, I.N., Bourne, P.E.: The Protein Data Bank. Nucleic Acids Research , 235–242 (2000)
2. Benson, D., Karsch-Mizrachi, I., Lipman, D., Ostell, J., Wheeler, D.: GenBank. Nucleic Acids Research 33, 235–242 (2005)
3. Wrobel, S.: Inductive Logic Programming for Knowledge Discovery in Databases. In: Relational Data Mining, pp. 74–101. Springer, Heidelberg (2001)
4. Raedt, L.D.: Attribute Value Learning versus Inductive Logic Programming: The Missing Links. In: Page, D.L. (ed.) Inductive Logic Programming. LNCS, vol. 1446, pp. 1–8. Springer, Heidelberg (1998)
5. Raedt, L.D., Laer, W.V.: Inductive Constraint Logic. In: International Conference on Algorithmic Learning Theory, pp. 80–94. Springer, Heidelberg (1995)
6. Raedt, L.D., Dehaspe, L.: Clausal Discovery. Machine Learning 26, 99–146 (1997)
7. Srinivasan, A.: The Aleph Manual (2003) Available from
   http://web.comlab.ox.ac.uk/oucl/research/areas/machlearn/Aleph
8. Muggleton, S., Firth, J.: Relational Rule Induction with CProgol4.4: A Tutorial Introduction. In: Relational Data Mining, pp. 160–188. Springer, Heidelberg (2001)
9. Fonseca, N.A., Silva, F., Camacho, R.: April - An Inductive Logic Programming System. In: Fisher, M., van der Hoek, W., Konev, B., Lisitsa, A. (eds.) JELIA 2006. LNCS (LNAI), vol. 4160, pp. 481–484. Springer, Heidelberg (2006)
10. Soares, T., Ferreira, M., Rocha, R.: The MYDDAS Programmer's Manual. Technical Report DCC-2005-10, Department of Computer Science, University of Porto (2005)
11. Shen, W.-M., Leng, B.: Metapattern Generation for Integrated Data Mining. In: Knowledge Discovery and Data Mining, pp. 152–157 (1996)
12. Brockhausen, P., Morik, K.: Direct Access of an ILP Algorithm to a Database Management System. In: MLnet Familiarization Workshop on Data Mining with Inductive Logic Programing, pp. 95–100 (1996)

13. Morik, K.: Knowledge Discovery in Databases - an Inductive Logic Programming Approach. In: Foundations of Computer Science: Potential - Theory - Cognition, pp. 429–436. Springer, Heidelberg (1997)
14. Bockhorst, J., Ong, I.M.: FOIL-D: Efficiently Scaling FOIL for Multi-Relational Data Mining of Large Datasets. In: Camacho, R., King, R., Srinivasan, A. (eds.) ILP 2004. LNCS (LNAI), vol. 3194, pp. 63–79. Springer, Heidelberg (2004)
15. Botta, M., Giordana, A., Saitta, L., Sebag, M.: Relational Learning as Search in a Critical Region. Journal of Machine Learning Research 4, 431–463 (2003)
16. Codd, E.F.: A relational model for large shared data banks. Communications of the ACM 13(6), 377–387 (1970)
17. Ullman, J.D.: Principles of Database and Knowledge-Base Systems. Computer Science Press (1989)
18. Muggleton, S., Raedt, L.D.: Inductive Logic Programming: Theory and Methods. Journal of Logic Programming 19/20, 629–679 (1994)
19. Soares, T., Rocha, R., Ferreira, M.: Generic Cut Actions for External Prolog Predicates. In: Van Hentenryck, P. (ed.) PADL 2006. LNCS, vol. 3819, pp. 16–30. Springer, Heidelberg (2005)
20. Blockeel, H., Dehaspe, L., Demoen, B., Janssens, G., Ramon, J., Vandecasteele, H.: Improving the Efficiency of Inductive Logic Programming Through the Use of Query Packs. Journal of Machine Learning Research 16, 135–166 (2002)
21. Muggleton, S.: Inverse Entailment and Progol. New Generation Computing, Special Issue on Inductive Logic Programming 13, 245–286 (1995)
22. Blockeel, H., Raedt, L.D.: Top-Down Induction of First-Order Logical Decision Trees. Artificial Intelligence 101, 285–297 (1998)
23. McCreath, E., Sharma, A.: Extraction of meta-knowledge to restrict the hypothesis space for ILP systems. In: Australian Joint Conference on Artificial Intelligence, pp. 75–82. World Scientific, Singapore (1995)
24. Santos Costa, V., Srinivasan, A., Camacho, R., Blockeel, H., Demoen, B., Janssens, G., Struyf, J., Vandecasteele, H., Laer, W.V.: Query Transformations for Improving the Efficiency of ILP Systems. Journal of Machine Learning Research 4, 465–491 (2002)
25. Srinivasan, A.: A study of two sampling methods for analysing large datasets with ILP. Data Mining and Knowledge Discovery 3(1), 95–123 (1999)
26. DiMaio, F., Shavlik, J.W.: Learning an Approximation to Inductive Logic Programming Clause Evaluation. In: Camacho, R., King, R., Srinivasan, A. (eds.) ILP 2004. LNCS (LNAI), vol. 3194, pp. 80–97. Springer, Heidelberg (2004)
27. Berardi, M., Varlaro, A., Malerba, D.: On the Effect of Caching in Recursive Theory Learning. In: Camacho, R., King, R., Srinivasan, A. (eds.) ILP 2004. LNCS (LNAI), vol. 3194, pp. 44–62. Springer, Heidelberg (2004)
28. Rocha, R., Fonseca, N.A., Santos Costa, V.: On Applying Tabling to Inductive Logic Programming. In: Gama, J., Camacho, R., Brazdil, P.B., Jorge, A.M., Torgo, L. (eds.) ECML 2005. LNCS (LNAI), vol. 3720, pp. 707–714. Springer, Heidelberg (2005)
29. Fonseca, N.A., Silva, F., Camacho, R.: Strategies to Parallelize ILP Systems. In: Kramer, S., Pfahringer, B. (eds.) ILP 2005. LNCS (LNAI), vol. 3625, pp. 136–153. Springer, Heidelberg (2005)
30. Weber, I.: Discovery of First-Order Regularities in a Relational Database Using Offline Candidate Determination. In: Džeroski, S., Lavrač, N. (eds.) Inductive Logic Programming. LNCS, vol. 1297, pp. 288–295. Springer, Heidelberg (1997)
31. Dehaspe, L., Toironen, H.: Discovery of Relational Association Rules. In: Relational Data Mining, pp. 189–208. Springer, Heidelberg (2000)

Inductive Mercury Programming

Barnaby Fisher and James Cussens

Dept of Computer Science, University of York, Heslington, York, YO10 5DD, UK
{barney,jc}@cs.york.ac.uk

Abstract. We investigate using the Mercury language to implement and design ILP algorithms, presenting our own ILP system IMP. Mercury provides faster execution than Prolog. Since Mercury is a purely declarative language, run-time assertion of induced clauses is prohibited. Instead IMP uses a problem-specific interpreter of ground representations of induced clauses. The interpreter is used both for cover testing and bottom clause generation. The Mercury source for this interpreter is generated automatically from the user's background knowledge using Moose, a Mercury parser generator. Our results include some encouraging results on IMP's cover testing speed, but overall IMP is still generally a little slower than ALEPH.

1 Introduction

In this paper we report on our research into using the Mercury language [1] to implement and design ILP algorithms. Mercury is a logical/functional programming language that provides considerably faster execution than Prolog: this was our initial motivation for examining it, however our research has uncovered additional features which may turn out to be useful for ILP.

To focus our research we set out to produce an ILP system, implemented in Mercury, which was, to a large extent, a 'clone' of the well-known ALEPH system. Our work has produced a working ILP system IMP. However, the aim of this paper is not simply to provide a progress report on our system, but to analyse general issues arising from the move from a Prolog-based system to a Mercury-based one. With this in mind, we describe not only our actually-existing system but also point to future developments which follow naturally from the move to Mercury.

The paper is organised as follows. In Section 2 we introduce the Mercury language. Section 3 describes our long-term plans for IMP, whereas Section 4 explains the currently implemented system. Section 5 describes IMP from the user's perspective. Section 6 provides benchmarking results on three ILP problems. The paper concludes, as is customary, with conclusions and suggestions for future work (Section 7).

S. Muggleton, R. Otero, and A. Tamaddoni-Nezhad (Eds.): ILP 2006, LNAI 4455, pp. 199–213, 2007.

2   The Mercury Language

The Mercury language has been developed at the University of Melbourne.[1] The motivation for the development of the language, as given by its developers, is as follows.

> Mercury is a new logic/functional programming language, which combines the clarity and expressiveness of declarative programming with advanced static analysis and error detection features. Its highly optimized execution algorithm delivers efficiency far in excess of existing logic programming systems, and close to conventional programming systems. Mercury addresses the problems of large-scale program development, allowing modularity, separate compilation, and numerous optimization/time trade-offs. (http://www.cs.mu.oz.au/research/mercury/)

Roughly speaking, one can view Mercury as Prolog together with declarations specifying the modes and types of predicates. These declarations provide two central advantages: they permit compile-time checks and they provide information which the compiler can use for optimisation. Using the information in declarations, the Mercury compiler translates Mercury source to low-level C source which can then be compiled to native code. Another feature of Mercury is that it is a declarative language in fact as well as theory:

> To ensure that programmers can actually enjoy the benefits claimed for logic programs, Mercury has no non-logical constructs that could destroy the declarative semantics that gives logic programs their power. [1]

This means that the cut operator and failure driven loops do not exist in Mercury programs. Significantly for ILP, assertion (and retraction) of clauses at run-time is also viewed as non-logical and is thus forbidden.

For a Prolog programmer with experience in writing pure Prolog, actually writing a Mercury program is quite easy. A Prolog program with predicate declarations, no non-logical constructs and a special main/2 predicate will be a Mercury program. Fig 1 shows the predicate declaration for the well known append/3 predicate, which is here written as list.append since it is implemented in Mercury's list library module. The Mercury predicate definition of append is identical to Prolog's and is not shown.

```
:- pred list.append(list(T), list(T), list(T)).
:- mode list.append(in, in, out) is det.     %(1)
:- mode list.append(in, in, in) is semidet. %(2)    % implied
:- mode list.append(in, out, in) is semidet.%(3)
:- mode list.append(out, out, in) is multi. %(4)
```

Fig. 1. Predicate declaration for append/3

---

[1] http://www.cs.mu.oz.au/research/mercury/

In Fig 1 the first line declares the *types* of the arguments for **append**. All three arguments are lists whose elements are all of some type **T**. Since **T** is a variable, **append** is *polymorphic*. The rest of the declaration connects modes to determinisms: **in** in a mode declaration represents a (fully) instantiated argument (an input), **out** represents a variable (an output). So (1) if two lists are given to append then the predicate will succeed and moreover there is exactly one output, this mode is thus *deterministic* (**det**). If (2,3) the first and third arguments are instantiated then **append** may fail, but backtracking will never produce alternative outputs, these modes are thus *semi-deterministic* (**semidet**). Finally (4), if only the third argument is instantiated, then **append** will succeed one or more times. It is thus *multisolution* (**multi**). A fourth mode (which **append** does not use) is *nondeterministic* (**nondet**) where the predicate may fail and there may be several outputs for a given input.

As noted in the *Prolog to Mercury Transition Guide*: "Mercury is a purely declarative language. Therefore it cannot use Prolog's mechanism for doing input and output with side-effects." [2]. Instead, Mercury's **io.print** predicate (provided in the **io** library) has the following declaration:

```
:- pred io.print(T::in, io::di, io::uo) is det.
```

so that the literal **io.print('Hi',s1,s2)** is true if **s1** is the state-of-the-world before printing **'Hi'** to standard output and **s2** is the state-of-the-world afterwards. "di [stands] for 'destructive input' and uo for 'unique output'. The first means that the input variable must be the last reference to the original state of the world, and that the output variable will be the only reference to the state of the world produced by this predicate" [2]. The **main/2** predicate also uses the same idea: it defines the relationship between the states-of-the-world before and after execution of the entire program.

Mercury allows the creation and calling of higher-order terms: terms which represent calls to (particular modes of) predicates. Such terms are typically passed to higher-order predicates/functions such as **solutions/2** (in the **solutions** library module) which is Mercury's version of **findall**. Here is its declaration:

```
:- pred solutions(pred(T), list(T)).
:- mode solutions(pred(out) is nondet, out) is det.
```

As the **pred** declaration states, it expects a higher-order term as its first argument. The **mode** declaration states this higher-order term should represent a monadic predicate with a single output with **nondet** mode. The output of **solutions** is the list of outputs produced by repeatedly calling this predicate. Since Mercury is purely declarative **solutions** cannot be defined entirely by Mercury code: calls to **solutions** ultimately call C functions accessed through Mercury's foreign language interface. The ability to define Mercury predicates by C functions makes it possible to define *impure* Mercury predicates. Such predicates are rigidly separated from normal ('pure') predicates to ensure the declarative semantics of the pure code are not lost.

Mercury has good support for modular design. Each Mercury source file is a module containing an *interface* section and an *implementation* section. The *interface* section consists entirely of type and predicate declarations for those types and predicates the module wishes to make visible to other modules. The *implementation* section provides the actual predicate definitions as well as the declarations for those types and predicates which the module does not wish to make visible.

3   Declarative ILP

The ILP problem addressed by IMP is essentially the same as that addressed by many other existing ILP algorithms: the user presents examples and background knowledge and the system searches for a logic program that explains the examples using the background knowledge. In addition, the user can provide various constraints on induced clauses as well as indicating what counts as a good 'explanation' of the data.

A central goal of our research is to evaluate the usefulness of 'declarative ILP' where the inductive process (not just its end result) has a declarative semantics. To this end in this section we provide a view of the ILP problem, which although only partially implemented in IMP, is the one that informs our long-term plans for the system.

3.1   Logic Programs as Data Generators

We view ILP from both a logical and statistical perspective simultaneously. From the statistical perspective the observed data is viewed as having been *generated* by some unknown probability distribution, where the distribution is defined by a Mercury program (i.e. a moded logic program). Examples are always labelled ground examples of the form:

```
p(a1,a2,a3,..ai,b1,b2,...bj)-yes
p(a'1,a'2,a'3,..a'i,b1',b'2,...b'j)-no
q(c1,c2,c3,..ck,d1,d2,...dm)-no
```

We assume further that each predicate mentioned in the examples has only one mode, that this mode is known and that the types of the arguments are known. Suppose that the example predicate $p/(i+j)$ has the following declaration

```
:- pred p(t1::in,t2::in,..ti::in,
          t'1::out,t'2::out,...t'j::out) is some_mode.
```

where the t_i, t'_j are types and `some_mode` is one of `det`, `semidet`, `multi` or `nondet`. Note that either or both of i (number of inputs) and j (number of outputs) may be zero.

All negative examples are assumed to have been generated by (1) the user posing entirely ground queries to the unknown program and (2) the unknown program responding with a `no`. Note though that the ground query:

`p(a1,a2,a3,..ai,b1,b2,...bj)`

where the `bi` are outputs, is just an abbreviation to the following conjunctive query:

`p(a1,a2,a3,..ai,X1,X2,...Xj), X1=b1, X2=b3, ..., Xj=bj`

All positive examples of a predicate with a mode of either `multi` or `nondet` are also assumed to have been generated by ground queries. However, positive examples of mode `det` or `semidet` are assumed to be the results of queries where only the inputs are ground; the observed outputs having been generated by the program. Note that each such positive example entails a set of negative examples: any other example with the same inputs but different outputs of the right type. For all positive examples, the unknown program has responded with a `yes`.

Our logical perspective on ILP is the standard one: the unknown program logically entails the positive examples, but not the negative ones. It is not difficult to see that the statistical and logical perspective are consistent: the statistical view just uses mode and determinism information to establish *how* the logical relationship between example and unknown program is established.

Since formulae (e.g. examples) either do or do not follow from a Mercury program the probability distribution defined by the program is of a very restrictive form: a conditional distribution (conditional on queries) with probabilities only of one or zero. To represent more general distributions while maintaining the assumption that the data is generated from a (pure) Mercury program, we can view examples as having a hidden extra input argument which, without loss of generality, we assume to be a `float` sampled from the uniform distribution over $[0, 1]$. Thus observed contradictory examples such as

`p(a1,a2,a3,..ai,b1,b2,...bj)-yes`
`p(a1,a2,a3,..ai,b1,b2,...bj)-no`

can be viewed as a partial representation of unobserved complete data such as

`p1(0.2754,a1,a2,a3,..ai,b1,b2,...bj)-yes`
`p1(0.5672,a1,a2,a3,..ai,b1,b2,...bj)-no`

Although the conditional distribution defined by the complete data is 'zero-one', the distribution defined by marginalising away the hidden argument need not be. With this approach the unknown Mercury program is both a declarative and procedural representation of a probability distribution, where the procedural representation defines a sampler. The hidden argument in each example can be viewed as a random seed used to generate a single instance from the sampler. (As explained in Section 4.1 only a crude approximation to this approach is currently implemented.)

3.2 Background Knowledge

Let M represent the unknown true Mercury program. We allow for the possibility that some of the clauses making up M are already known: the *background knowledge* B. So $M = H \cup B$ where H is the set of induced clauses. This entirely standard use of background knowledge is already implemented in the current version of IMP. If the user supplies non-empty background knowledge then they are required to supply consistent type and predicate declarations for this background knowledge.

3.3   Defining the Hypothesis Space

The user must state which predicates are permitted to appear in the head and body of induced clauses. All such predicates must have normal Mercury predicate declarations, specifying types, mode(s) and determinism(s). By default all well-moded clauses constructed from such predicates are considered to be candidate induced clauses, however the user can choose to effect arbitrary syntactic constraints on permissible candidates. All this is implemented in the current version of IMP, but to write constraints requires a knowledge of how IMP represents clauses, which is hardly user-friendly! The hypothesis space is the set of all logic programs defined using permitted candidate clauses.

3.4   Evaluating Induced Theories

For both complete and incomplete data, the measure of fit to data is the *likelihood* $P(E|M)$. For complete data, this number will be either zero (M contradicts the examples) or one (M does not contradict the examples). In the case of incomplete data (where there is a hidden random seed) the likelihood for a single example is given by marginalising over possible values of the unobserved random seed. In other words, given the query associated with the example, we compute the probability that a random seed drawn from $\mathcal{U}[0,1]$ would have produced the observed example: this is the likelihood. The likelihood for the entire data set is just the product of these likelihoods: conditional on queries the data is independent and identically distributed.

The likelihood $P(E|M)$ is the key function connecting model to data, however it is $P(M|E)$, the probability that a candidate model M is the true model given the data E, that is needed to score candidate models. To see this, suppose we are dealing with complete data ('noise-free' learning). Consider the model M composed of the background knowledge B and the set of positive examples as ground unit clauses. This model will have the highest possible likelihood, but would only be an acceptable model if, unusually, we had reason to believe that the observed positive examples constituted the set of all possible positive examples. We almost always have good *a priori* reasons to believe precisely the opposite and this prior knowledge needs to be made available to the system. Since $P(M|E) \propto P(M)P(E|M)$, the overall score for a candidate model is a combination of $P(M)$, the prior probability of a model and $P(E|M)$, its likelihood. As previously mentioned, IMP's current handling of probabilities remains primitive. Direct consideration of likelihoods and posterior probabilities, as described in this section, is not yet implemented: instead there is an approximation to this Bayesian approach as described in Section 4.1.

4   System Design

The key features of the IMP system are:

1. It uses a 'one-clause-at-a-time' top-down search, bounded below by a bottom clause;
2. Induced clauses are represented by ground terms;
3. Problem-specific Mercury source is generated prior to compilation; and
4. A new executable is produced for each ILP search.

The next four sections describe these features in the given order.

4.1   Search Strategy

IMP's basic search strategy is entirely conventional, and is similar to that found in PROGOL[3] and ALEPH[4]. An as yet uncovered positive example is selected, a 'bottom clause' is generated from it using saturation [5] as guided by the modes of predicates. This mode-guided generation of the bottom clause is essentially the same as PROGOL's [3]. Bottom clause construction is a similar task to that of finding all solutions to a goal, and as with Mercury's builtin solutions/2 predicate (see Section 2) we have found it necessary to use *impure* Mercury code to construct a bottom clause efficiently. Fig 2 shows a fragment of the code used: note that impure and semi-pure predicates are explicitly flagged as such and that we have made a promise_pure declaration which is a promise that the rest of the code can treat construct_bottom_body *as if* it were pure.

```
:- pragma promise_pure(construct_bottom_body/3).

construct_bottom_body(Body,Subs0,Subs) :-
        impure nb_reference.new_nb_reference(Subs0,SubsRef),
        get_body(SubsRef,[],Body),
        semipure nb_reference.value(SubsRef,Subs).
```

Fig. 2. Fragment of impure code for bottom clause construction which we promise can be treated *as if* it were pure

Once generated, the bottom clause is used to constrain a top-down uninformed breadth-first search of clauses; the 'best' clause is found, added to the theory, and a record of which examples it covers is made. The search continues until all positives are covered. We have also implemented a variant where no bottom clause is used, allowing pure top-down search.

So the Bayesian approach described in Section 3.4 is not yet implemented in IMP. Instead we have a crude approximation to it: the user defines *clause evaluation functions*. We have used two clause evaluation functions: accuracy and coverage. If P and N are the numbers of positive and negative examples covered by a clause, the clause's coverage score is $P - N$ and its accuracy is

$P/(P + N)$. The user can also limit the length of induced clauses, the length of bottom clauses and the number of negative examples a clause can cover.

Very recently, we have implemented a number of optimisations to the search mostly using ideas from ALEPH. Firstly, the search is branch-and-bound: when IMP can detect that no refinement of a given clause can possibly out-score the best clause found so far then the search is (admissibly) pruned at that point. Secondly, when a clause has more than one parent clause, then only examples in the intersection of the parents' coversets are considered as possible members of the coverset of the clause. Thirdly, each generated clause has an id which is the ordered list of the literals in the bottom clause it uses: this allows us to prune away clauses which differ from already considered clauses only in the ordering of body literals. Lastly, when considering maximally long clauses, we check coverage on negatives first: this allow early termination of cover testing if and when too many negatives are found to be covered.

So, at present, only a few ILP optimisations exist in IMP. We see no reason to prevent the eventual incorporation into IMP of more advanced optimisations such as query packs, caching and tabulation. (Mercury has built-in support for the tabulation.)

4.2   Ground Representations of Induced Clauses

In Prolog ILP systems induced clauses (including bottom clauses) are internally constructed as terms which are subsequently asserted, thus building up the induced theory. In Mercury clauses can neither be asserted nor retracted at runtime. It follows that induced clauses must remain as terms. Moreover, they will be ground terms since the current implementation of Mercury does not permit partially instantiated terms.

The IMP ground representation of clauses has two parts: a representation of the clause with no variables instantiated plus a mapping from (ground representations of) variables to ground terms which represents the instantiation state of the clause. If the clause to be represented has only variables this mapping is empty, if ground each variable is mapped to a term. Given a ground representation of a clause the issue is how to reproduce the behaviour of the program that would exist if the clause so represented *were* asserted. We have used different approaches in IMP 0.1 and IMP 0.2.

Using Higher-Order Terms. In IMP 0.1, each candidate clause is represented by a pair: its ground representation together with its representation as a higher-order term:

```
:- type clause ---> c(ground_clause,ho_clause).
```

To see whether a given clause Clause covers an example with input terms Values the following predicate is used:

```
covers_example(Clause,Values) :-
  Clause=c(GC,HOClause),
  ....
  HOClause(ValuesIn,ValuesOut), .... % cover test here
```

The ground representation is used for 'bookkeeping' and the higher-order representation (HOClause) is what actually gets called to check coverage.

The key to this approach is to ensure that the ground and higher-order terms represent the same clause. With this in mind, the refinement operator for IMP0.1 works as follows. Given a parent clause c(gc0,ho0) IMP's ground refinement operator uses gc0 to generate a set of children ground representations: gc1, gc2, .., gcn by adding a single (ground representation of a) literal. New higher-order terms can then be constructed from ho0 and these literals.

Interpreting Ground Representation of Clauses. Although encoding induced clauses as higher-order terms which are then called on examples is quite a natural approach it has a number of drawbacks. Firstly, we have found it impossible to encode recursive clauses using this approach; secondly, higher-order terms have a different instantiation state from normal ground terms which makes them harder to manipulate and store during the search process and thirdly, we suspected that higher-order terms, being created at runtime, were not the most efficient approach.

In IMP0.2 a different, simpler approach is taken: an interpreter is used to decode 'calls' to the ground representation of clauses. Fig 3 show the type declarations for clauses represented as ground terms and an examples of such a term (the third argument subs is not actually used in our current implementation).

```
:- type clause ---> c(head :: literal, body :: literals,
                      subs :: substitution_map ).

:- type literal ---> l(pred_id,arguments).
:- type literals == list(literal).

:- type argument ---> a(arg_mode,arg_id,type_id).
:- type arguments == list(argument).

% eastbound(H0) :- has_car(H0,B2), load(B2,hexagon,1)
% is represented as:
c(l(bg_lit(12), [a(in, head_arg(0), train)]),
 [l(bg_lit(11), [a(in, head_arg(0), train), a(out, body_arg(2), car)]),
  l(bg_lit(9),  [a(in, body_arg(2), car), a(constant, constant_arg(4),shape),
                 a(constant,constant_arg(2), int)])],
array([]))
```

Fig. 3. Ground representation of clauses: type declaration and an example

Fragments of the interpreter are given in Fig 4: it is similar to a Prolog-implemented Prolog interpreter except that substitution maps, not partial instantiations, are used to keep track of the instantiation state of variables.

Since the induced theory Theory is threaded through the interpreter, induced recursive clauses can be properly interpreted. To avoid possible non-termination due to induced recursive clauses the interpreter implements a depth-bounded call (the depth is supplied by the user). This is similar to ALEPH and PROGOL. Calls to background predicates are not depth-bounded: IMP puts the responsibility on the user to ensure that background predicates terminate. Fig 4 includes the problem-specific predicate 'wrapper' predicate bk_implies/3: the example used is a fragment of the 'trains' example. This predicate is used (in different modes) both for cover testing and for constructing the bottom clause.

The ground representation of literals, clauses and theories is also ultimately problem-specific since these types are defined in terms of problem-specific types examples of which (for the trains) are given in Fig 5.

4.3   Generating Problem-Specific Mercury Source

For both IMP0.1 and IMP0.2 there must be wrappers connecting ground representations of predicates to actual predicates. Requiring the user to actually write these would be a tedious and error-prone burden. Instead IMP automatically generates correct problem-specific wrapper predicates prior to compilation. IMP uses Moose, a parser generator for Mercury that "does the same sort of thing for Mercury that Yacc and Bison do for C." (Moose README file). Moose is distributed in the 'extras' part of the current Mercury distribution.

5   Using IMP

The basic philosophy behind IMP's operation is that what is known at compile time should be compiled. An exception to this is that the examples are read in at run time: compiling a large number of examples (represented as ground facts) proved to be unacceptably slow. An advantage of inputting examples at runtime is that different subsets of the data can be used without recompiling IMP.

When IMP is installed there is a one-time compilation of the system modules to object code. Thereafter, for a given ILP problem there is the following sequence of events (the execution of which is organised by Makefile dependencies).

1. The user writes only two Mercury modules. The first, called background.m, is just the background knowledge. Predicates which may appear in induced clauses are declared in the interface section, others are hidden in the implementation section. The user also provides a problem-specific options.m file defining parameters such as how much noise is permitted, the depth-bound, etc. This is most easily done by editing a copy of the system's options.m file which contains default values.

```
%FRAGMENT FROM SYSTEM MODULE interpreter.m

:- pred implies_example_aux(theory,example,sub,sub,sub).
:- mode implies_example_aux(in,in(example),sub_di,sub_uo,sub_ui) is cc_nondet.

implies_example_aux(Theory,Example,!BodySubs,ConstantSubs) :-
  example.example(ExampleAtom,ExampleSubs,_,Example),
  ( theory.clause_member(Clause,Theory),
    clause.clause(Head,Body,_,Clause),
    literal.same_literal_type(ExampleAtom,Head),
    arg_sub.make_start_clause_subs(ExampleSubs,!.BodySubs,ConstantSubs,ExampleBodySubs),
    implies_conj(1,_,Theory,Body,ExampleBodySubs,ExampleBodySubOut),
    arg_sub.get_body_subs(ExampleBodySubOut,!:BodySubs)
  ;
    bk_implies(ExampleAtom,ExampleSubs,_ExampleSubsOut)
  ).

%FRAGMENT FROM PROBLEM-SPECFIC MODULE bk_implies.m

:- pred bk_implies(literal,substitution_map,substitution_map).
:- mode bk_implies(in,in,out) is nondet.  % cover testing
:- mode bk_implies(out,in,out) is nondet. % bottom clause construction

bk_implies(Literal,Subs0,SubsOut) :-
  literal(Id,Args,Literal),
  (
    Id=bg_lit(14),   % 'closed' literal
    Args=[Arg1],
    clause.argument(in,A1,car,Arg1),
    substitution_map.subs_lookup(Subs0,A1,V1),
    value(car(B1),V1),
    SubsOut=Subs0,
    closed(B1)       % call to background predicate HERE
  ;
    Id=bg_lit(11),  % 'has_car' literal
    Args=[Arg1,Arg2],
    clause.argument(in,A1,train,Arg1),
    clause.argument(out,A2,car,Arg2),
    substitution_map.subs_lookup(Subs0,A1,V1),
    substitution_map.insert_and_check(Subs0,A2,V2,Subs1),
    value(train(B1),V1),
    value(car(B2),V2),
    SubsOut=Subs1,
    has_car(B1,B2) % call to background predicate HERE
    ....
  ).
```

Fig. 4. IMP0.2 interpreter showing code from a system module and from an automatically-generated problem specific module for Michalski's trains

```
:- type type_id ---> car; train; shape; int.
:- type pred_name ---> closed; double; eastbound; has_car; jagged;
                       load; long; open_car; shape; short; wheels.
:- type problem_value ---> car(car); train(train); shape(shape); int(int).
```

Fig. 5. Automatically generated problem specific types for Michalski's trains. The types car, train and shape needed for the definition problem_value are defined by the user in the background file.

2. The problem-specific background.m is compiled by the Mercury compiler. As well as generating C and object code, a number of other files are created including a module interface file background.int containing all public type and predicate declarations.
3. The Moose pre-processor uses background.int to generate the Mercury modules background_interface.m which provides types and predicates for manipulating the ground representation of clauses, and bk_implies.m which connects this ground representation to the actual background predicates.
4. These two modules and options.m are then compiled and linked with the system object code to provide a problem-specific executable.
5. This executable is then run with the file containing the examples as a command-line argument.

6   Benchmarking Results

We have evaluated IMP on the following ILP problems:

Trains Michalski's train problem [6]
MSD Morpho-syntactic tagging for Slovene [7]
Muta Mutagenesis [8]

6.1   IMP0.1 Versus IMP0.2

For TRAINS with 40,000 examples and a single clause search of 83 clauses in both cases, IMP0.1 took 23 seconds and IMP0.2 took 10 seconds. The TRAINS data was from an example dataset that comes with ALEPH; examples were repeated to form a big enough dataset. For MSD with 2,815 examples, IMP0.1 inspected 20,058 clauses in 54 seconds whereas IMP0.2 inspected 20,024 clauses in 22 seconds. These experiments were sufficient to convince us that the 'higher-order' approach in IMP0.1 was inferior to the 'interpreter' approach of IMP0.2, and so all further benchmarking was restricted to IMP0.2.

6.2   Benchmarking Cover Testing

The performance of an ILP system depends on a number of factors a key one of which is speed of *cover testing*. Cover testing finds which examples are covered by a single clause: that is, which examples would follow if the clause were added to the background knowledge. In an attempt to compare speed of *cover testing* in IMP0.2 and ALEPH, as opposed to speed of the systems overall, we ran both IMP0.2 and ALEPH without a bottom clause on the MSD dataset. The search was thus pure top-down (breadth-first) search. This was done because it effectively disables various optimisations in ALEPH which prevent it doing full cover testing when this is not necessary. We ran the experiment with various limits on the number of clauses to inspect in a single clause search. The results in Fig 6 show that for this problem, with this artificial restriction, IMP is computing cover sets more quickly than ALEPH. Although, these results are encouraging we have not done further such comparisons, since our real interest is in comparing the performance of IMP and ALEPH in normal operation.

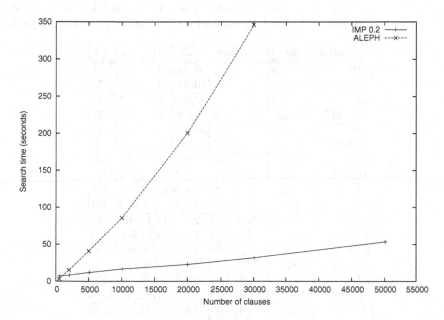

Fig. 6. Cover testing speed comparison of IMP0.2 and ALEPH using no bottom clause for MSD using 2,815 examples

6.3   Benchmarking Searches

Comparing normal operation of ALEPH and IMP showed that, despite the encouraging results of Section 6.2, ALEPH remains the faster algorithm. The results for TRAINS and MSD are shown in Table 1. In almost all cases, ALEPH is the winner although IMP is generally not far behind. In contrast for MUTA, IMP is *massively slower* than ALEPH: we had to terminate execution after waiting 20 minutes for the bottom clause to appear.

Comparing the clauses found by the two systems, for TRAINS the two systems always find the same 'best' clause. However, for the MSD domain we found that although IMP's search was a little slower than ALEPH's, it usually found a better clause. In all cases, ALEPH returns a clause covering 7 positives and 0 negatives and indeed for $|C| = 4, lim(n) = \infty$, IMP finds this same clause (see Table 1 for an explanation of the notation). However, for $|C| = 5, lim(n) = 5,000/10,000$, IMP finds a clause covering 11 positives and 0 negatives, and for $|C| = 5, lim(n) > 10,000$ IMP finds a clause covering 46 positives and 0 negatives. In all these cases IMP and ALEPH have inspected the same number of clauses: we suspect that IMP is doing a better job of avoiding duplicate clauses thus allowing it, in effect, to do a bigger search and thus find these better clauses.

Table 1. Comparing IMP and ALEPH (normal operation for a single clause search). $|C|$ is the limit on clause length, $lim(n)$ is the limit on the number of clauses, $|Ex|$ is the number of examples, t is the time taken in seconds for the search, n is the number of clauses actually generated and n/t show the number of clauses generated per second.

Algorithm	Dataset	$|C|$	$lim(n)$	$|Ex|$	t	n	n/t
IMP	TRAINS	4	∞	10,000	1	38	38
ALEPH	TRAINS	4	∞	10,000	1	73	73
IMP	TRAINS	4	∞	20,000	2	38	19
ALEPH*	TRAINS	4	∞	20,000	2	73	36
IMP	TRAINS	4	∞	30,000	3	38	13
ALEPH	TRAINS	4	∞	30,000	2	73	37
IMP	MSD	4	∞	2,815	7	4,148	593
ALEPH	MSD	4	∞	2,815	3	4,293	1431
IMP	MSD	5	5,000	2,815	12	5,000	417
ALEPH	MSD	5	5,000	2,815	13	5,000	385
IMP	MSD	5	10,000	2,815	17	10,000	588
ALEPH	MSD	5	10,000	2,815	14	10,000	714
IMP	MSD	5	20,000	2,815	21	20,000	952
ALEPH	MSD	5	20,000	2,815	18	20,000	1111
IMP	MSD	5	30,000	2,815	25	30,000	1200
ALEPH	MSD	5	30,000	2,815	21	30,000	1428
IMP	MSD	5	40,000	2,815	30	40,000	1333
ALEPH	MSD	5	40,000	2,815	24	40,000	1666

7   Conclusions and Future Work

One clear outcome of this research is a (constructive) existence proof that a PROGOL/ALEPH-style ILP algorithm can be implemented in Mercury. Beyond this, we have shown that for two example problems (TRAINS and MSD) IMP is only a little slower than ALEPH and in some cases finds better clauses. On the other hand we have terrible results for MUTA and our immediate future work is to discover whether this is a fundamental problem with IMP or due to an avoidable inefficiency in our implementation. In the mid-term, we intend to take further optimisations from ALEPH: caching is an obvious candidate.

In the longer term we hope to take fuller advantage of the modularity of Mercury. At present user-defined options are provided at compile time. We hope to extend this to the search algorithm itself so that the different components of a search (bottom clause vs. no bottom clause, breadth-first vs. A-*, etc) are made available at compile time by specifying the appropriate system object files to link to. The problem specific pre-processor could also be exploited further. One interesting possibility would be to use it to generate specialised problem-specific refinement operators. Finally, we are looking to actually implement the probabilistic approach presented in Section 3.

Acknowledgements

This work was supported by the AI Group of the Dept of Computer Science, University of York and by the *Applications of Probabilistic Inductive Logic Programming II* project funded by the European Commission. Thanks to Ashwin Srinivasan for information on ALEPH and to our three anonymous referees for helpful suggestions for improvements.

References

1. Somogyi, Z., Henderson, F., Conway, T.: The execution algorithm of Mercury: an efficient purely declarative logic programming language. Journal of Logic Programming 29(1–3), 17–64 (1996)
2. Melbourne University: The Prolog to Mercury Transition Guide. Version 0.13.0 edn. Mercury documentation (2006)
3. Muggleton, S.: Inverse entailment and Progol. New Generation Computing Journal 13, 245–286 (1995)
4. Srinivasan, A.: The Aleph Manual. Version 4 and above edn. (2004)
5. Rouveirol, C.: Flattening and saturation: Two representation changes for generalization. Machine Learning 14(2), 219–232 (1994)
6. Michalski, R., Stepp, R.: Learning from observation: conceptual clustering. In: Michalski, R., Carbonnel, J., Mitchell, T. (eds.) Machine Learning: An Artificial Intelligence Approach. Tioga, Palo Alto, CA, pp. 331–364 (1983)
7. Cussens, J., Džeroski, S., Erjavec, T.: Morphosyntactic tagging of Slovene using Progol. In: Džeroski, S., Flach, P.A. (eds.) Inductive Logic Programming. LNCS (LNAI), vol. 1634, Springer, Heidelberg (1999)
8. Srinivasan, A., Muggleton, S., Sternberg, M., King, R.: Theories for mutagenicity: a study of first-order and feature-based induction. Artificial Intelligence 85(1,2), 277–299 (1996)

An ILP Refinement Operator
for Biological Grammar Learning

Daniel C. Fredouille[1], Christopher H. Bryant[1,*],
Channa K. Jayawickreme[2], Steven Jupe[3], and Simon Topp[4]

[1] School of Computing, The Robert Gordon University, Aberdeen, UK
chb@comp.rgu.ac.uk
[2] Discovery Research Biology, GlaxoSmithKline, Durham, USA
[3] Department of Bioinformatics, GlaxoSmithKline, Stevenage, UK
[4] Department of Bioinformatics, GlaxoSmithKline, Harlow, UK

Abstract. We are interested in using Inductive Logic Programming
(ILP) to infer grammars representing sets of biological sequences. We
call these biological grammars. ILP systems are well suited to this task
in the sense that biological grammars have been represented as logic
programs using the Definite Clause Grammar or the String Variable
Grammar formalisms. However, the speed at which ILP systems can
generate biological grammars has been shown to be a bottleneck. This
paper presents a novel refinement operator implementation, specialised
to infer biological grammars with ILP techniques. This implementation
is shown to significantly speed-up inference times compared to the use
of the classical refinement operator: time gains larger than 5-fold were
observed in $\frac{4}{5}$ of the experiments, and the maximum observed gain is
over 300-fold.

1 Introduction

A significant challenge in the analysis and interpretation of biological sequence
data is the discovery of patterns common to sequences sharing a given biological
function. The use of such patterns is twofold: (1) they can be used to annotate
sequences of unknown function, providing molecular biologists with a likely function for such sequences; (2) they can help biologists to understand how functions
are realised because they represent common points between sequences of similar
functions.

Patterns in the form of grammars have been used with success to model biological sequences, we call these *biological grammars*. Many formalisms have been
used for this task, including String Variable Grammars (SVG) [Sea93], Patscan
patterns [DLO97], Prosite patterns [FPB+02], Basic Gene Grammars [LMR01]
and Probabilistic Regular or Context-Free Grammars [BCD+04, SBH+94]. However, the hand development of grammars, using for example the formalisms of
[Sea93] or of [LMR01], is difficult and requires expensive human expertise. Moreover, some patterns might be too subtle to be recognised by a human expert.

---

* Corresponding author.

S. Muggleton, R. Otero, and A. Tamaddoni-Nezhad (Eds.): ILP 2006, LNAI 4455, pp. 214–228, 2007.

Thus, given the enormous volume of data arising from genome projects, the acquisition of biological grammars from sets of biological sequences needs to be automated.

We propose to use Inductive Logic Programming (ILP) to infer biological grammars. The advantage of ILP for this purpose is twofold: first ILP infers logic programs, and logic programs have been shown to be useful for representing hand designed biological grammars (*e.g.*, [Sea93]); second, unlike most machine learning technique, ILP is able to bias inference to take expert knowledge into account. This is certainly an advantage in this application domain since, as biological sequences are not just sequences but represent molecules with physical and chemical properties, potential parts of the target grammar are often available as expert knowledge.

ILP however has an important drawback: inference speed. The usual approach to obtaining a more efficient inference process is to use language and search biases. The former allows the search space to be reduced, while the latter influences its exploration [LD94, sec. 1.3]. This approach have been used to infer grammars over proteins [MBS$^+$01], the biases being integrated into mode declarations and pruning predicates. However, despite the efforts of Muggleton et al. [MBS$^+$01], some inference processes took days to run while exploring a small fraction of the search space. Such long running times were also confirmed by Bryant & Fredouille [BF05]. This drawback has made it difficult to discover the true potential of ILP for biological grammar acquisition.

We propose to tackle this speed problem by hard-coding the languages and search biases of Muggleton et al. [MBS$^+$01] in Muggleton's refinement operator [Mug95] (Section 2). Compared to classical techniques influencing refinements with respect to background knowledge (*e.g.*, mode declarations, typing, . . . , see [Tau94] for an early review), our technique sacrifices the range of applications to the advantage of efficiency. We empirically show that this sacrifice is worthwhile since our refinement operator can lead to very significant speeds-up of biological grammar inference: gains in inference times larger than 5-fold were obtained in $\frac{4}{5}$ of the experiments, with the maximum observed gain being over 300-fold (Section 3).

Grammars and Biological Sequences. Biological sequences are defined either over an alphabet of 4 letters (DNA or RNA sequences), or over an alphabet of 20 letters (protein sequences). Each letter of such sequences represents a chemical unit which is called a nucleic acid for DNA or RNA sequences, or an amino-acid for proteins.

A *context-free grammar* can be seen as a set of rules which represents sets of sequences. For biological grammars, these sequences are biological sequences. The rules of a context-free grammar can be represented using the logic formalism known as *Definite Clause Grammar* (DCG) [PW80]. In this formalism a sequence over a finite alphabet of letters is represented as a list, each element of the list corresponding to a letter of the sequence. Figure 1 gives an example of such a grammar.

```
target(A,B)  :- gap(A,C), al(C,D), bl(D,E), gap(E,B).
gap(A,A).                       al([a|X],X).
gap(A,[_|B])  :- gap(A,B).      bl([b|X],X).
```

Each predicate in a DCG clause takes as input (first argument) a list representing the sequence to analyse, and outputs (second argument) the part of the list remaining when removing a prefix that the predicate matches. For this DCG, a call target(Seq,[]) *will succeed if and only if* Seq *contains the sublist* [a,b] *(i.e., the subsequence 'a b'). Indeed, the* gap/2 *predicate matches any sequence, and the* al/2 *(resp.* bl/2*) predicate matches sequences starting with 'a' (resp. 'b'). The main rule (*target/2*) therefore accepts all sequences starting with any sequence, followed by 'a b', followed by any sequence.*

Fig. 1. A simple grammar represented as a DCG

We denote the length of a sequence s by $|s|$. Biological sequences are of very variable length, protein sequences' lengths range from roughly 50 to many thousands of letters. Note the contrast with natural language, where sequences rarely exceed 500 letters. This implies that it is very unlikely that any grammar of reasonable size can characterise all parts of a set of biological sequences (even if these sequences share a common biological function). From this observation, the notion of gap – as introduced by Figure 1 – is very important to biological grammars: gap/2 is the predicate which can be used to cover parts of the biological sequences uncharacterised by the rest of the grammar rules. A typical biological grammar therefore includes some well characterised parts separated by gaps.

Inference of Biological Grammars with ILP. Different approaches to grammar learning with ILP have been considered, mainly [CP99, PC01, MBS+01]. These papers differ in two main points. The first application is natural language grammars [CP99, PC01] while the application in [MBS+01] is biological grammars. Second, the representation of grammars in [CP99, PC01] uses chart parsing tables, while [MBS+01] uses DCGs.

Our work takes its roots in the approach of Muggleton et al. [MBS+01] and uses the DCG formalism. To infer a rule like the target/2 rule of Figure 1, the idea of [MBS+01] is to provide: (1) examples under the form target(L,[]). where L is a list of letters representing a biological sequence; and (2) DCG predicates as background knowledge (in Figure 1 this corresponds to providing the gap/2, al/2 and bl/2 definitions). The inference process aim is to combine them into new DCG rules optimising the evaluation function.

In this framework, the ILP system has to be prevented from inferring logic rules which do not represent DCGs. A main constraint is that the user can only provide background predicates respecting the DCG semantic, *i.e.*, they must have two arguments, take a sequence s as first argument, and return in the second argument a suffix of s. We also have to ensure that the inferred rule is a DCG, leading to the following constraints:

c0) the head of the rule contains two variables;

c1) the first variable of the head must be unified with the first variable in the first literal of the body;

c2) the second variable of all body literals but the last must be unified with the first variable of the following literal;

c3) the second variable of the head must be unified with the second variable of the last body literal;

c4) all couples of variables unspecified by points (c1-c3) must not be unified[1].

Part of these constraints can be enforced using mode declarations of the following form [MBS+01]: modeh(1,target(+rl,-rl)) and modeb(n,bk_predicate(+rl, -rl)). In these declarations, rl is a predicate accepting lists of letters; target is the predicate to infer; bk_predicate is a background knowledge predicate and n is its ambiguity (*i.e.*, the maximum number of times a backtrack on this predicate can succeed). These declarations enforce c0-c1 but only partially c2-c4[2]: Muggleton et al. [MBS+01] had to use pruning predicates to enforce the remaining parts (Subsection 2.2 gives more details on this point).

2   A Refinement Operator for Biological Grammar Inference

This section is divided in two parts. Subsection 2.1 considers the notion of bottom clause and how this notion can be simplified for biological grammars. The bottom clause defines elements of the search space. Subsection 2.2 details the proposed refinement operator to explore this space.

2.1   Bottom Clause Construction

Bottom Clause for Biological Grammar Learning. The notion of bottom clause was introduced by Muggleton in [Mug95]. Such a clause, denoted by $bot_c(e)$ is constructed from a positive example e and represents the most specific logic program, defined using the background knowledge and respecting the mode declarations, that covers e. The CPROGOL algorithm [Mug95] works by taking an example e_1 and constructing its bottom clause $bot_c(e_1)$. It then searches through the sets of clauses θ-subsuming $bot_c(e_1)$ to return the best one with respect to the evaluation function. Further clauses are inferred using the same strategy iteratively, but starting from the set of yet uncovered examples (uncovered by any of the already inferred clauses); this is the principle of the *cover set* algorithm.

An example of bottom clause for biological grammar learning is given in Figure 2. In this example the background knowledge predicates are limited (for the sake of explanation) to two physical properties of the letters (representingamino-acids). The neg/2 (resp. small/2) predicate corresponds to negatively

---

[1] For example, a rule target(A,B):-foo1(A,A),foo2(A,B). is not a DCG rule but respects (c0-c3).

[2] For example, a rule target(A,B):-foo1(A,C),foo2(A,C),gap(C,B). respects the mode declarations but violates c2.

```
target(A₀,A₄) :-    gap(A₀,A₀), gap(A₀,A₁),..., gap(A₄,A₄),
                    neg(A₀,A₁), neg(A₃,A₄), small(A₀,A₁), small(A₁,A₂).
```

Fig. 2. Bottom clause for a (fake) protein sequence [d,p,i,e] using background knowledge from three predicates: the gap/2 predicate and two predicates related to physical properties of amino-acids (neg/2 and small/2).

charged (resp. small) amino-acids. They can be defined by the sets of rules: $\{neg([\alpha|X],X).:\alpha \in \{d,e\}\}$ and $\{small([\alpha|X],X).:\alpha \in \{a,c,d,g,n,p,s,t\}\}$. Then there is the gap/2 predicate which, as explained in Section 1, can be considered to be compulsory for biological grammar inference processes and allows parts of the sequences uncharacterised by the inferred grammar to be covered.

Calls to DCG predicates which succeed match a prefix of the input sequence and return the remaining suffix. Therefore, each variable of the bottom clause $bot_c(e)$ corresponds to a suffix of the sequence e. We emphasise this fact in Figure 2 by using notation A_i for the variable corresponding to the suffix of e starting at position i in e (positions are between letters of e, and 0 is the position before the first letter). Therefore, on Figure 2, the presence of a predicate foo(A_i,A_j) means that foo/2 matches the subsequence of e between positions i and j. This particularity of bottom clauses constructed over DCGs enables the use of a simplified representation: we call it the *bottom automaton*.

From Bottom Clause to Bottom Automaton. In the bottom automaton, denoted by $bot_a(e)$, positions are represented by states and transitions represent background predicates: a transition foo between states i and j meaning that predicate foo/2 matches sequence e between positions i and j. Since they violate (c4), transitions such that $i = j$ are ignored (*i.e.*, transitions corresponding to predicates of the form foo(X,X) in the bottom clause). A bottom automaton is represented in Figure 3. On this figure, unlabelled transitions are those for the gap/2 predicate. The initial (resp. final) state of this automaton corresponds to position 0 (resp. $|e|$) of e, and is represented with a short incoming (resp. outgoing) arrow.

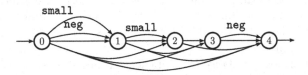

Fig. 3. The bottom automaton $bot_a(e)$ equivalent to the bottom clause $bot_c(e)$ of Figure 2

By definition, the bottom automaton and the bottom clause are two equivalent representations of the same concept. The important things to see is that all DCG θ-subsuming the bottom clause and respecting constraints (c0) to (c4)

correspond to a path from the initial state 0 to the final state $|e|$ in bot_a(e).
For example, the path: $0 \rightarrow$ gap $\rightarrow 1 \rightarrow$ small $\rightarrow 2 \rightarrow$ gap $\rightarrow 4$, which accepts
sequence gap small gap, corresponds to rule:
target(A,B):-gap(A,C),small(C,D),gap(D,B). In addition, a path not end-
ing in state $|e|$ corresponds to a rule respecting all constraints but (c3). (This
fact will be useful later on.) For example, the path: $0 \rightarrow$ neg $\rightarrow 1 \rightarrow$ small $\rightarrow 2$
corresponds to rule: target(A,_):-neg(A,B),small(B,_).

Creating the Bottom Automaton. Algorithm 1. shows how to create the
bottom automaton. A similar procedure could be used to create a bottom clause
specialised to biological grammar learning, but the formalism of the bottom
automaton turned out to be easier to use. Optimisations of this algorithms use
properties (p1) and (p2), linked to the gap/2 predicate:

p1) All states of $bot_a(e)$ can be reached from state 0 (equivalently, $bot_c(e)$ con-
tains $|e| + 1$ different variables)[3].

p2) We have $\frac{(|e|)(|e|+1)}{2}$ transitions by symbol gap in the bottom automaton
(equivalently, $\frac{(|e|+1)(|e|+2)}{2}$ gap/2 predicates in the bottom clause, this num-
ber is larger than the number of transitions in the bottom automaton to
count predicates of the form foo(X,X)).

Property (p1) allows us not to compute the set of positions of e that can be
reached by the use of the background knowledge: we know that all positions are
reached (hence the loop on line 2 of Algorithm 1.). Property (p2) means that
very large bottom clauses are considered during inference (*e.g.*, if $|e| = 200$, the
bottom clause is of minimal size 20301). We can circumvent this problem; since
it is known that gap transitions are present between each couple of states of the
automaton, it is easier not to store them (line 3, condition pred$\neq$gap): instead,
a particular treatment in the refinement operator can be used to introduce gaps
when needed. The advantage is twofold: gain in memory, since this prevents the
bottom clause size being quadratic in the sequence length; gain in execution
time, since the bottom automaton can then be constructed faster.

The size of the resulting automaton is in $O(|e| \times |BK| \times max(ma))$, where $|BK|$
is the number of background knowledge predicates and $max(ma)$ is the maximum ambiguity encountered for a predicate different from gap/2. As $max(ma)$
can be considered much smaller than the sequence length[4], the automaton size
can be considered linear in this length (compare with the $O(|e|^2)$ number of
elements in a bottom clause storing gaps). The time complexity of Algorithm 1.
is in $O(|e| \times |BK| \times (K_1 + max(ma) \times K_2))$, where K_1 is the cost of obtaining
the list S (which depends on the background predicates implementation), and
where K_2 is the cost of inserting a transition in the automaton (line 7); this cost
is, in our implementation, in $O(log(|BK|))$.

---

[3] This is because the gap/2 predicate can return all suffixes of its input sequence.
[4] In practice, only the gap predicate is so ambiguous that it can match in between all
positions of the example sequence.

Algorithm 1. Construction of the bottom automaton without the gap transitions over a sequence e.

1: Create $|e| + 1$ states, labelled 0 to $|e|$.
2: **for** i in $[0, |e|]$ **do**
3:     **for all** background knowledge predicate **pred** (**pred**$\neq$**gap**) **do**
4:         **let** ma **be** the ambiguity degree of **pred** as stated by mode declarations
5:         **let** S **be** the list of A_j obtained by backtracking up to ma times on **pred**(A_i, A_j)
6:         **for all** A_j in S **do**
7:             Add a transition between states i and j labelled by **pred**

2.2 Refinement Operator

Using the bottom automaton, we propose a refinement operator adapted to biological grammar learning. Our operator can be seen as a specialisation of the classical ILP refinement operator introduced by Muggleton [Mug95]. This is the same specialisation that Muggleton et al. [MBS+01] achieved using pruning predicates. We therefore start by describing [MBS+01] pruning, and then explain how we integrate this pruning into the refinement operator.

Removing Non DCG Rules using Pruning. Muggleton et al. [MBS+01] pruned all rules not respecting constraints (c2) or (c4). Rules with two following gaps in the body were also pruned since two following gaps are equivalent to a single gap. Rules violating (c0) and (c1) do not need to be pruned: they are not present in the space thanks to mode declarations. Finally, rules only violating (c3) were not pruned: they were refined to enable all DCG rules of the search space to be reached. The rules returned by inference processes do however respect (c3): indeed, the mode declarations allow them to be present in the search space but not to be returned by the inference process.

In practice this corresponds to refining rules of the form:

$$\texttt{target(A,\_)} \;\; \texttt{:-} \;\; \texttt{foo}_0\texttt{(A,B)}, \;\; \ldots, \;\; \texttt{foo}_m\texttt{(X,\_)}. \tag{r0}$$

into rules of the following forms:

$$\texttt{target(A,\_)} \;\; \texttt{:-} \;\; \texttt{foo}_0\texttt{(A,B)}, \;\; \ldots, \;\; \texttt{foo}_m\texttt{(X,Y)}, \;\; \texttt{foo}_{m+1}\texttt{(Y,\_)}. \tag{r1}$$
$$\texttt{target(A,Z)} \;\; \texttt{:-} \;\; \texttt{foo}_0\texttt{(A,B)}, \;\; \ldots, \;\; \texttt{foo}_m\texttt{(X,Y)}, \;\; \texttt{foo}_{m+1}\texttt{(Y,Z)}. \tag{r2}$$

Rules (r0) and (r1) violates (c3) while rule (r2) is an inferable DCG rule. Using this strategy, the search space was reduced to a tree containing all DCG rules θ-subsuming $bot_c(e)$ (*i.e.*, the operator is optimal for the DCG rules), the rules respecting (c0) to (c4) being the leaves of the tree and internal nodes being rules violating only (c3). Such a tree, corresponding to the bottom clause of Figure 2, is given in Figure 4.

The Proposed Refinement Operator. By integrating the constraints in the refinement operator, we generate only rules that are correct for the application, instead of generating rules that need to be pruned. Our refinement operator is described by Algorithm 2.

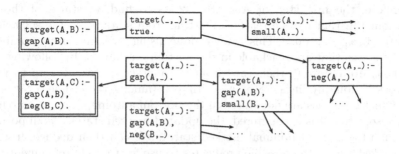

Fig. 4. First levels of the search space associated with the pruning proposed by [MBS⁺01] and the bottom clause of Figure 2. Refinements are represented by arrows. Double boxes correspond to inferable rules, while single boxes are internal nodes of the search space.

Algorithm 2. Refinement operator for grammar inference in the space defined by $bot_a(e)$.

1: let tgt(A,_):- foo$_0$(A,B),...,foo$_m$(X,_) be the rule to refine
2: Compute the set of reachable states in $bot_a(e)$ by foo$_0$,...,foo$_m$
3: $M \leftarrow \{0\}$ (The marked states, starting with the initial state)
4: **for** $v \in [0, m]$ **do**
5:     **if** foo$_v$=gap **then** $M \leftarrow \{i \in \mathbb{N} : min(M) < i \le |e|\}$
6:     **else** $M' \leftarrow \emptyset$
7:        **for** transitions $i \xrightarrow{foo_v} j$ in $bot_a(e)$ with $i \in M$ **do** $M' \leftarrow M' \cup \{j\}$
8:        $M \leftarrow M'$
9: Compute predicates that can be added at the end of the refined rule
10: **if** foo$_m$ = gap **then** $P_2 \leftarrow P_1 \leftarrow \emptyset$ **else** $P_1 \leftarrow P_2 \leftarrow \{gap\}$
11: **for** $i \in M$ **do**
12:     **for** transitions $i \xrightarrow{pred} j$ in $bot_a(e)$ **do**
13:        $P_1 \leftarrow P_1 \cup \{pred\}$
14:        **if** $j = |e|$ **then** $P_2 \leftarrow P_2 \cup \{pred\}$
15: Compute the set of possible refinements
16: $R \leftarrow \emptyset$ (The set of refinements)
17: **for** pred $\in P_1$ **do** $R \leftarrow R \cup \{tgt(A,\_):-foo_0(A,B),...,foo_m(X,Y),pred(Y,\_)\}$
18: **for** pred $\in P_2$ **do** $R \leftarrow R \cup \{tgt(A,Z):-foo_0(A,B),...,foo_m(X,Y),pred(Y,Z)\}$

Consider rule (r0), to refine it the algorithm has to add a predicate at its end, but also has to ensure that the obtained rule is in the search space defined by $bot_a(e)$. As legal predicates correspond to paths in the bottom automaton, the problem can be reduced to path searching. Refinements into rules of the (r1) form have to correspond to paths starting from state 0, but which can end in any state i of the automata. This means that the rule can cover the first i letters of e and that further refinement is needed to cover the remaining letters. For rules of the form (r2) the paths have, in addition, to end in state $|e|$: this ensures that the rule is able to cover e.

Therefore, the first step of Algorithm 2. is to find all states of the bottom automaton that can be reached, starting from state 0, by the sequence of predicates $foo_0 \ldots foo_m$. This can be done using dynamic programming to mark the states that are reachable in the bottom automaton by following transition foo_0 from state 0, then foo_1 from the marked states, ..., up to foo_m. This work is done by lines 2-8 of Algorithm 2. (among these, line 5 takes into account that gap rules are not stored in the bottom automaton: gaps match any sequence so, when it is encountered, the updated marked states are all positions larger than the current minimal marked state). We can then deduce, from the set of marked states, the possible predicates to use for the (r1) refinements: *i.e.*, all predicates present on outgoing transitions of the marked states (lines 9-14 of Algorithm 2.); and for (r2) refinements, *i.e.*, those that also enable to reach state $|e|$. Finally, we construct the set of refined rules from the original rule and these sets of predicates (lines 15-18). Algorithm 2. avoids returning redundant rules by working with sets instead of lists, and prevents rules which contain 2 consecutive gaps, which is meaningless (condition line 10).

3   Experimental Evaluation

In this section we report our empirical investigation of the time gain obtained by using our refinement operator.

3.1   Experimental Method

The experiments concern inference of grammars over protein sequences. We consider two aspects of the problem: inference of a grammar from positive and random examples as proposed by Muggleton [Mug97], and inference from positive and negative examples. The implementation of the bottom automaton algorithm and the refinement operator, as well as the public part of the datasets, can be found at `http://www.comp.rgu.ac.uk/staff/chb/research/data_sets/ilp06/refine_op`

Positive and Random Dataset. The dataset for positive only learning was provided by experiments of Muggleton et al. [MBS+01]. Among the different experiments reported in [MBS+01] we selected the one that took the longest to complete because in this case the efficiency of the grammar acquisition was a bottleneck. This experiment involved inferring on subsequences, called *middle*, of Neuropeptide Precursors Proteins (NPPs). The examples comprise 76 positive and 2 910 random *middle* sequences. The length of these sequences vary from 5 letters to 95. We denote this dataset by PosRand. This dataset is in the public domain.

Positive and Negative Dataset. The data set for discriminative learning consists of two sets of sequences representing two qualitatively distinct classes, Gi/o and Gs/q, of a protein family known as the G-protein coupled receptors (GPCRs) [PPL02]. Data allowing the classification of these proteins into the two sets is proprietary. The Gi/o and Gs/q datasets contain 43 and 94 sequences respectively. GPCRs have a characteristic 7 membrane-spanning regions and thus have regions outside the cell, within the cell membrane and inside the cell.

In this paper we present results for one of the parts inside the cell, called intra-cellular loop #2, and for this inference process, the Gs/q sequences were used as positive examples while the Gi/o sequences were used as negative examples. The lengths of these sequences vary from 12 to 46 letters. We denote this dataset by POSNEG.

Inference Processes and Parameters. All experiments have been running on a SunBlade2500 under SunOS 5.8. We used the ALEPH [Sri93] implementation of Muggleton's refinement operator [Mug95] to test our ideas, instead of the original CPROGOL implementation. This choice was made because ALEPH is much easier to modify than CPROGOL: it gives the user a large number of options including defining a user refinement operator and preventing the default bottom clause construction. We denote inference with ALEPH, using Muggleton's opera-tor [Mug95], by REF-ℵ, and inference with ALEPH, using our biological grammar dedicated bottom clause construction and refinement operator, by REF-G.

The principle of the experiments is to explore the search space up to a given depth with both systems and observe execution times, knowing that the inferred rules from both systems are the same (see Appendix A) because the explored search spaces are the same. We considered maximum exploration depths in the search space (corresponding to ALEPH parameter `clauselength`) of 4, 5 and 6 for the POSRAND dataset, and of 5 and 6 for the POSNEG dataset. Inference with `clauselength` less than 5 on POSNEG is not interesting because, for biological reasons on this dataset, rules are required to start and end with the gap predicate: the head and the two gaps already count for 3, so a value of 4 corresponds to using background knowledge rules one at a time, hence the starting value of 5.

The evaluation function used for POSRAND dataset was Muggleton's evalua-tion function for positive only learning [Mug97]. A different evaluation function was needed for the POSNEG dataset because it does not contain randoms. The Gi/o and Gs/q subsets of the POSNEG dataset contain a very different number of sequences while having the same importance to the biologists. Therefore, to avoid biasing the inference toward one class, we decided to use an evaluation function which weights the examples of each class by the inverse of the number of instances of the class available. The evaluation function used is the accuracy over the weighted examples, *i.e.*, acc $= \frac{1}{2} * (\frac{p}{P} + \frac{n}{N})$, where P (resp. N) is the size of the positive (resp. negative) training set size, and p (resp. n) is the number of positive (resp. negative) training examples covered (resp. rejected) by the rule.

After preliminary experiments, it became clear that inference times were strongly influenced by the `minacc` setting of ALEPH. This parameter is a thresh-old on the minimal precision of inferable rules with respect to the training examples[5]. We therefore considered inferences with different `minacc` values (0.1, 0.5 and 0.9) to obtain an idea of the gain in different inference situations.

---

[5] Precision is defined here as the number of accepted positives over the sum of the number of accepted positives and accepted negatives.

Table 1. Inference times (seconds) on the PosRand and PosNeg datasets. (*): Experiments where the **nodes** limit of ALEPH was exceeded. (+): Experiments stopped after running more than the indicated time.

Algo	min acc	PosRand clauselength 4	5	6	PosNeg clauselength 5	6
REF-ℵ	0.1	1 213	*17 530	*+324 000	956	* 69 329
REF-G		151	1 897	38 899	1 087	52 299
Gain		8.0	9.24	>8.3	0.9	1.3
REF-ℵ	0.5	1 311	*+334 000	*+413 280	834	* 60 827
REF-G		131	1 944	55 878	265	12 098
Gain		10.0	>171.8	>7.4	3.1	5.0
REF-ℵ	0.9	1 802	*+511 220	*+511 200	1232	* 120 030
REF-G		156	1 601	63 253	186	5 541
Gain		11.6	> 319.0	>8.1	6.6	21.7

3.2 Results of the Experiments

The running times are listed in Table 1. Very different speed-ups were obtained depending on the data, the **minacc** and the **clauselength** parameters. Speed-up factors over 5 were obtained in $\frac{4}{5}$ of the experiments, the best speed-up obtained being over 300-fold (PosRand, **minacc**= 0.9, **clauselength**= 5). It is possible that even greater speed-ups can be achieved since many experiments on PosRand using the default refinement operator had to be stopped after running more than 90h, while the corresponding experiments using the hand-made refinement finished by themselves (always in less than a day). Moreover, many REF-ℵ experiments reached the limit on the maximum number of nodes to be explored by the algorithm on at least some of the algorithm cycles (the **nodes** parameter of ALEPH was set to 500 000). Inference with REF-G never reached this limit. This implies two things: (1) the potential gains, given an unlimited value for **nodes** are larger than those shown in Table 1 (cells with the * symbol); (2) given that the search is exhaustive, the results of the REF-G experiments guarantee that the obtained clauses are the best possible up to the given **clauselength**.

The inference times of Table 1 clearly show the advantages of our refinement operator, both in the PosRand and the PosNeg experiments. In practice only one inference process was slower when using our refinement operator (Table 1, PosNeg, **minacc**= 0.1, **clauselength**= 5). This possible loss is however small compared to the potential gains observed for all other parameters. The best gains were obtained with larger values for the **minacc** setting. This is good news because maximising the precision is usually desirable.

3.3 Interpretation of Experiments

Even if the results obtained are very satisfying, being able to explain their variation can help us understand how to improve them. A potential explanation of this variation is that ALEPH is using different optimisations to speed-up the search. We discuss how two of these optimisations can explain the variation of the results of Table 1.

The gain of 0.9 observed with PosNeg, `clauselength`=5 and `minacc`=0.1 We will refer to the first of these optimisations as optimisation A. Optimisation A, which is only available to REF-ℵ, is that ALEPH knows that its default refinement operator is working by specialising rules. It can use this information to prevent, when evaluating the performance of a rule, the parsing of examples which were rejected by its father rule. This optimisation does not take place if the user provides his own refinement since ALEPH does not know if the refinement operator works by specialisation or generalisation (or both). The gain of 0.9 for PosNeg with `minacc`=0.1 and `clauselength`=5 could be the extra parsing time needed outweighing the optimisations brought by the refinement operator.

The Improvement in Gain when Augmenting `minacc`. Another optimisation of ALEPH, Optimisation B, uses the `minacc` value to prevent the parsing of some examples when the evaluated clauses are at maximum depth. This is done using the formulae $\texttt{minacc} = \frac{p}{p+n}$ (where p and n are respectively the number of positives and negatives/randoms accepted by the rule), ALEPH computes the maximum number of negatives/randoms that the rule can accept once the number of positives covered is known (*i.e.*, $\frac{(1-\texttt{minacc})p}{\texttt{minacc}}$). It then stops parsing if this number is reached and if the clause is of size `clauselength` (smaller rules have to be evaluated as they could be refined). This optimisation is available both for REF-ℵ and REF-G.

Conjecture. To summarize, thanks to optimisation B, the higher the `minacc` value, the smaller is the number of examples to parse. Now, there is an effect of optimisation B on optimisation A: when `minacc` is high, optimisation B is very efficient and optimisation A cannot reduce the number of examples to parse much more. We therefore make the following conjecture to explain the increasing gains with respect to `minacc`: when increasing `minacc`, optimisation A has less and less effect, and the gain offered by REF-G over REF-ℵ is more and more visible. This suggests that:

- the true gain of our optimisation is closer to that observed when `minacc`=0.9;
- both higher and more stable gains with respect to `minacc` could be obtained by making Optimisation A available for inference with REF-G.

4   The Quality of the Resulting Grammars

This paper has focused on the speed at which ILP systems can generate biological grammars. Elsewhere [BFW+06] we have published results concerning the quality of the resulting grammars. We have applied our refinement operator implementation to a hard protein function inference task: the prediction of the coupling preference of GPCR proteins [BFW+06]. The time needed to execute the experiments reported in [BFW+06] was approximately two months. It would have taken much longer to obtain the same results if we had used the default refinement operator (REF-ℵ). We estimate that it would have taken 10 months given that Table 1 suggests a five fold time gain for similar tasks (PosNeg, minacc=0.5).

While this does illustrate why our refinement operator implementation (REF-G) is important for hard protein function inference tasks, further work is need to establish whether, given the same amount of run-time, REF-G results in significant improvements in the quality of the resulting grammars in comparison to REF-ℵ.

5   Other Applications of the Bottom Automaton Formalism

This paper has shown how our bottom automaton formalism can be used to implement one particular refinement operator, namely the one introduced by [Mug95]. However it could be used to implement other refinement operators; the formalism itself does not place constraints on the exploration strategy.

Moreover, we believe that the strategy used to create the bottom automaton could be usefully reused for problems involving complex examples (e.g., trees, graphs,...) which involve trying to find rules matching substructures of those examples (e.g., subgraphs or subtrees). Indeed simplifications similar to those proposed in Algorithms 1 and 2 (i.e. those linked to the gap/2 predicate) could also be considered in such problems.

6   Conclusion

We have integrated the biases of biological grammar inference into a dedicated ILP refinement operator. We have shown that, by using this operator, inference running times can decrease very significantly compared to the previously used technique using pruning predicates: time gains larger than 5-fold where obtained in most experiments, and the best observed gain is over 300-fold.

Acknowledgements. This work is funded by the UK EPSRC grant GR/S68682. The authors would like to thank Ashwin Srinivasan of IBM, India for his very informative insights about the ALEPH ILP system, and for his fast updates of the system. The authors would like to acknowledge the contributions made by the Systems Research, Transgenics & Gene Cloning, and Gene Expression & Protein Biochemistry groups at GlaxoSmithKline to the proprietary GPCR classification data used in this work.

References

[BCD⁺04]   Bateman, A., Coin, L., Durbin, R., Finn, R.D., Hollich, V., Griffiths-Jones, S., Khanna, A., Marshall, M., Moxon, S., Sonnhammer, E.L.L., Studholme, D.J., Yeats, C., Eddy, S.R.: The Pfam protein families database. Nucleic Acids Research 32, 138–141 (2004)

[BF05]   Bryant, C.H., Fredouille, D.: A parser for the efficient induction of biological grammars. In: Kramer, S., Pfahringer, B. (eds.) 15th International Conference on ILP: late-breaking paper track. University of Bonn (2005), http://wwwbib.informatik.tu-muenchen.de/infberichte/2005/TUM-I0510.idx

[BFW⁺06]   Bryant, C.H., Fredouille, D., Wilson, A., Jayawickreme, C.K., Jupe, S., Topp, S.: Pertinent background knowledge for learning protein grammars. In: Fürnkranz, J., Scheffer, T., Spiliopoulou, M. (eds.) ECML 2006. LNCS (LNAI), vol. 4212, pp. 54–65. Springer, Heidelberg (2006)

[CP99]   Cussens, J., Pulman, S.: Experiments in inductive chart parsing. In: Cussens, J. (ed.) LLL'99, pp. 72–83, Bled, Slovenia (June 1999)

[DLO97]   Dsouza, M., Larsen, N., Overbeek, R.: Searching for patterns in genomic data. Trends in Genetics 13(12), 497–498 (1997)

[FPB⁺02]   Falquet, L., Pagni, M., Bucher, P., Hulo, N., Sigrist, C.J., Hofmann, K., Bairoch, A.: Protein data bank. Nucleic Acid Research 30, 235–238 (2002)

[LD94]   Lavrač, N., Džeroski, S.: Inductive Logic Programming: Techniques and Applications. Ellis Hortwood, New York (1994)

[LMR01]   Leung, S.-W., Mellish, C., Robertson, D.: Basic Gene Grammars and DNA-ChartParser for language processing of *Escherichia coli* promoter DNA sequences. Bioinformatics 17(3), 226–236 (2001)

[MBS⁺01]   Muggleton, S.H., Bryant, C.H., Srinivasan, A., Whittaker, A., Topp, S., Rawlings, C.: Are grammatical representations useful for learning from biological sequence data? – a case study. Journal of Computational Biology 5(8), 493–522 (2001)

[Mug95]   Muggleton, S.H.: Inverse entailment and Progol. New Generation Computing, Special issue on Inductive Logic Programming 13(3-4), 245–286 (1995)

[Mug97]   Muggleton, S.H.: Learning from positive data. In: Inductive Logic Programming. LNCS, vol. 1314, pp. 358–376. Springer, Heidelberg (1997)

[PC01]   Pulman, S., Cussens, J.: Grammar learning using inductive logic programming. Oxford University Working Papers in Linguistics, Philology and Phonetics 6, 31–45 (2001)

[PPL02]   Pierce, K.L., Premont, R.T., Lefkowitz, R.J.: Seven-transmembrane receptors. Nat. Rev. Mol. Cell. Biol. 3(9,6), 39–50 (2002)

[PW80]   Pereira, F., Warren, D.H.D.: Definite clause grammars for language analysis – a survey of the formalism and a comparison with augmented transition networks. Artificial Intelligence 13(3), 231–278 (1980)

[SBH⁺94]   Sakakibara, Y., Brown, M., Hughey, R., Saira Mian, I.: Stochastic context-free grammars for tRNA modeling. Nucleic Acids Research 22, 5112–5120 (1994)

[Sea93]   Searls, D.B.: String variable grammar: A logic grammar formalism for the biological language of DNA. Journal of logic Programming, 12 (1993)

[Sri93]   Srinivasan, A.: A Learning Engine for Proposing Hypotheses (Aleph) (1993), http://web.comlab.ox.ac.uk/oucl/research/areas/machlearn/Aleph

[Tau94]   Tausend, B.: Representing biases for inductive logic programming. In: Bergadano, F., De Raedt, L. (eds.) Machine Learning: ECML-94. LNCS, vol. 784, pp. 427–430. Springer, Heidelberg (1994)

A   Appendix: The Equality of Rules Inferred by REF-G and REF-ℵ

In the REF-G implementation, ALEPH is prevented from constructing the bottom clauses, therefore the inferred rules are *not* checked for consistency with the mode declarations. This means that rules violating (c3) (*i.e.*, of the form $target(A,\_)$:- $foo_0(A_0,A_1),\ldots,foo_m(A_m,\_)$) can be inferred when using REF-G but not when using REF-ℵ. For the sake of comparison between REF-G and REF-ℵ, we added in REF-G an ALEPH false/0 predicate rejecting clauses violating (c3). (Like the prune/1 predicate, the false/0 predicate can be used to prevent the inference of some rules; however, unlike rules rejected by prune/1, rules rejected by false/0 are refined.) After this modification of the REF-G code, the rules inferred by both systems were the same.

When using the REF-G operator in other frameworks, adding a false/0 predicate is not needed. Indeed, since gap/2 predicates are allowed in rules, we can systematically transform a rule violating (c3), *i.e.*, of the form: $target(A,Z)$:- $foo_0(A,B),\ldots,foo_m(X,Y)$, where Z and Y are free variables, into a rule: $target(A,Z)$:- $foo_0(A,B),\ldots,foo_m(X,Y),gap(Y,Z)$.

These two rules cover the same examples. Therefore, without adding a false/0 predicate, the algorithm explores for free, for all rules ending with a gap, one step deeper in the search space. The only drawback is that a small syntactic correction must be applied to the inferred rules.

Combining Macro-operators with Control Knowledge

Rocío García-Durán, Fernando Fernández, and Daniel Borrajo

Universidad Carlos III de Madrid
Avda de la Universidad 30, 28911-Leganés (Madrid), Spain
{rgduran,ffernand}@inf.uc3m.es, dborrajo@ia.uc3m.es

Abstract. Inductive Logic Programming (ILP) methods have proven to succesfully acquire knowledge with very different learning paradigms, such as supervised and unsupervised learning or relational reinforcement learning. However, very little has been done on applying it to General Problem Solving (GPS). One of the ILP-based approaches applied to GPS is HAMLET. This method learns control rules (heuristics) for a non linear planner, PRODIGY4.0, which is integrated into the IPSS system; control rules are used as an effective guide when building the planning search tree. Other learning approaches applied to planning generate macro-operators, building high-level blocks of actions, but increasing the branching factor of the search tree. In this paper, we focus on integrating the two different learning approaches (HAMLET and macro-operators learning), to improve a planning process. The goal is to learn control rules that decide when to use the macro-operators. This process is successfully applied in several classical planning domains.

1 Introduction

Planning is a problem solving task that consists on, given a domain theory (set of states and operators) and a problem (initial state and set of goals), obtaining a plan (set of operators and a partial order of execution among them), such that, when executed, transforms the initial state into a state where all goals are achieved. Planning is computationally hard (PSPACE) in general. To reduce the difficulty of finding a solution to a problem, many solvers employ learning techniques that improve noticeably the original behaviour of the solvers [1].

One successful technique consists of learning macro-operators, that are compositions of simpler operators. Their main advantage is the decrease of the depth in the search tree, reducing the number of nodes and the number of variables to bind; that is memory and time. However, their main drawback is the utility problem [2]. The addition of macro-operators to the domain description increases the branching factor and the processing cost per node, which can worsen search performance. One way of partially solving this problem, as was applied in [3], consists on filtering macro-operators to the most used ones. But even using this filtering, we still encounter the utility problem.

S. Muggleton, R. Otero, and A. Tamaddoni-Nezhad (Eds.): ILP 2006, LNAI 4455, pp. 229–243, 2007.

In order to alleviate this problem, we propose to learn heuristics that can guide the problem solver when deciding which operator (or macro-operator) to use in a given decision. Thus, a second learning approach obtains control rules from search episodes [4]. It is based on a relational approach that combines an analytical learning strategy (based on EBL) with an inductive strategy for incremental refinement of learned knowledge. As most relational learning systems, it learns by generalizing and specializing a set of rules. In this paper we use HAMLET to find a set of control rules that are able to decide when to use the acquired macro-operators. Using control rules, IPSS reduces the number of nodes of the search tree and, thus, the planning time.

A similar combination was used in [5], where macro-operators and chunks (structures similar to rules) are used together to improve the results of the solver. However, the selected macro-operators were not filtered before using them, potentially leading to the utility problem. Also the chunks were created only from a given macro-operator, instead of learning them when using all operators in the domain. Finally, there were no experiments reported, so we can not evaluate its performance.

In the next section, we describe the nonlinear planner used for the experiments, PRODIGY4.0, and the two learning modules: macro-operators generator and the learning system, HAMLET. The third section describes the method we use to filter the macro-operators and to generate the control rules. Section 4 shows the experiments on five domains of the International Planning Competition (IPC). Finally we introduce some conclusions and outlines future work.

2   IPSS

IPSS is an integrated tool for planning and scheduling [6], which is based on PRODIGY [7] as the planner component. The two learning modules used in this work, macro-operators learning module and HAMLET, are integrated into IPSS. In Figure 1 we can see an schema of the three components. The three subsections describe all of them.

2.1   The Problem Solver

PRODIGY4.0 is a nonlinear planner, that follows a means-end analysis and bidirectional search procedure. Its inputs are: a domain theory, that includes the operators and an object hierarchy; the problem to be solved, defined by an initial state and a set of goals; and control knowledge, described as a set of control rules, that guide the search process.

The planner has several decision points, such as: select a goal, select an operator, select a binding of the operator and decide whether to subgoal on a pending goal or apply an operator when its preconditions are true in the current state. From a learning perspective the important fact about how the planner behaves is that it consists of a search process that can be controlled by heuristics (in form of control rules) that can be learned.

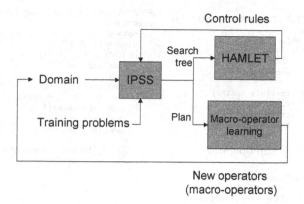

Fig. 1. Diagram of the IPSS planner, Macro-operator learning module and HAMLET

In [8], a meta-model valid for most planners that characterize all of them in terms of those search decisions is presented.

2.2   The Macro-operators Module

A macro is an operator that summarizes the execution of several simpler opera-tors. Given each solved problem, a macro-operator is created using a triangular table [9]. In Figure 2 (a) and (b) we can see two examples of simple operators in the Blocksworld domain.

The Blocksworld domain used in the second IPC consists of a set of blocks that are all of the same size, a table and a robot arm. The robot arm can *pick up* a single block from the table and *stack* it on another clear block. Also it can *unstack* a clear block and *put down* a block on the table. The table can hold an infinite number of blocks.

Figure 2 (a) shows the operator that allows the robot to pick up a block from the table, and with the Figure 2 (b) shows the operator that allows the robot to stack a block on top of another block. The macro-operator composed of these two simple operators can be seen in Figure 2 (c). All variables refered to in the examples are written within brackets.

The main drawback of macro-operators is the utility problem [2,10]: adding macro-operators can increase the branching factor and the processing cost per node, without necessarily improving search performance.

Including a partial ordering of the operators in the macro-operator or com-bining the use of macro-operators with techniques such as the relaxed graphplan computation implemented in FF, can show significant improvements in different domains [3,8].

Based on that work we also filter macro-operators using, as utility measure, the frequency of appearance of several simple operators sequentially together in a set of obtained solution plans. These total-ordered plans are generated from

```
(OPERATOR PICK-UP (params <ob1>)          (OPERATOR STACK (params <ob> <underob>)
   (preconds                                  (preconds
      ((<ob1> object))                            ((<ob> object)
      (and (clear <ob1>)                            (<underob> object))
           (on-table <ob1>)                        (and (clear <underob>)
           (arm-empty)))                                 (holding <ob>)))
   (effects ()                                (effects ()
      ((del (on-table <ob1>))                    ((del (holding <ob>))
       (del (clear <ob1>))                        (del (clear <underob>))
       (del (arm-empty))                          (add (arm-empty))
       (add (holding <ob1>)))))                   (add (clear <ob> ))
                                                  (add (on <ob> <underob>)))))
```

(a) pickup operator   (b) stack operator

```
(OPERATOR m2-2-pickup-stack
   (params <e-object> <d-object>)
   (preconds ((<d-object> object)
              (<e-object> object))
      (and
         (clear <d-object>)
         (clear <e-object>)
         (on-table <e-object>)
         (arm-empty)))
   (effects nil
      ((add (on <e-object> <d-object>))
       (del (clear <d-object>))
       (del (on-table <e-object>)))))
```

(c) pickup+stack macro-operator

Fig. 2. Example of two simple operators and the corresponding macro-operator in the Blocksworld domain

solving a set of random training problems. The six more common combinations of two and three simple operators are selected.

2.3 The HAMLET Learning Module

HAMLET is an incremental learning method based on EBL (Explanation Based Learning) and inductive refinement of control rules [4]. The main inputs of HAMLET are a domain and a set of training problems. HAMLET calls IPSS and receives as input the search tree expanded by the planner in order to decide where and what to learn. HAMLET's output is a set of control-rules that potentially guide the planner towards good quality solutions.

In Figure 3 we can see an example of a control rule in the Blocksworld domain. Each control rule has an *if*-part and a *then*-part. The *if*-part refers to conditions about the meta-states of the search process that can include conditions refering to the current state, the goal in which the planner is working on or the operator that can achieve a given goal. These conditions are represented using meta-predicates, such as *true-in-state*, *current-goal* and *some-candidate-goals* shown in Figure 3. Some meta predicates can have as arguments literals from the state, such as *clear* of *arm-empty*. Other arguments can be types or operator names.

The *then*-part describes what decision should be made and how. HAMLET has five kinds of control rules, corresponding to PRODIGY's decisions: apply an operator, decide to subgoal, select an unachieved goal, select an operator and select a binding for an operator (the target concepts). The rule in Figure 3 selects the *unstack* operator for achieving the goal of clearing an object when that object currently is under another one.

```
(control-rule INDUCED-SELECT-UNSTACK
    (if (and (current-goal (clear <object-2>))
             (true-in-state (on <object-1> <object-2>))
             (type-of-object <object-1> object)
             (type-of-object <object-2> object)))
    (then select operators unstack))
```

Fig. 3. Example of control rule in the Blocksworld domain

HAMLET has two main modules: the Bounded Explanation and the Refinement modules. The first module uses the decisions made by the planner after solving the training problems in order to generate control rules. The second module performs incremental inductive refinement of rules. First, HAMLET generalizes control rules, as soon as it finds more examples of the same target concept. In this case, it tries to apply the following main steps: (i) intersect preconditions of two rules of the same target concept; (ii) delete rules that are subsumed by others; and (iii) unify two rules that are similar except for two variables of which subtypes belong to a common type.

Also it analyses negative examples (when applying a control rule leads to a failure or a worse solution than the best one expected) to make more specific the overly-general control rules. When a negative example of a control rule is found, HAMLET redefines the rule using the following steps, until the rule does not subsume a negative example: (i) use different substitution from the ones used for intersecting two more specific rules; (ii) add one literal refering to the state to the preconditions; (iii) specialize the type of objects; and (iv) delete the most general control rule.

A more detailed definition and some examples of generalization and specialization can be found in [11]. The reader can also find there comparative results to other ILP systems, showing that HAMLET outperforms other ILP techniques such as FOIL or PROGOL, on this learning task.

3   Experimental Setup

In this work, we have used macro-operators and control rules together, with the aim of generating control rules that define when a specific macro-operator shall be used. To select the macros and rules for the experiments, two automated steps have been developed. Finally, we compare our results to the two learning techniques separately. These steps are the following:

1. The first step is to generate and select some macro-operators composed by two and three simple operators. We have bounded the number of operators that can appear in a macro-operator by an experimental analysis of the type of macro-operators that are more useful, which is also based on the work of [3]. We provide IPSS a set of random training problems to be solved. From the resulting total-ordered plans, all the different combinations of two and three operators are obtained. These operators must appear in sequence and have, at least, one object in common. The three most common sequences of each size are selected for the second step.

   In Figure 4 we can see an example of a solution plan in the Logistics domain, where all possible macros composed by two simple operators have been shown. The most common macro-operators from all solution plans will be selected for the experiments.

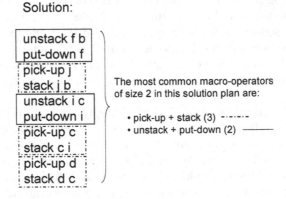

Fig. 4. Example to obtain the most common macros of size 2 from a solution plan

2. The next step consists of learning control rules when the domain is expanded with each macro-operator separately,[1] using always the same training set of random problems. We also learn control rules using the original domain (without macro-operators) for comparison.
3. Finally, the same test set is used for each resulting domain: (i) the original domain, (ii) the domain with each selected macro-operator, (iii) the original domain with its own learned control rules, and (iv) the macro-operators and the control rules together. In Figure 5 we can see the four approaches.

---

[1] Each macro-operator is pushed into the operator list in the domain definition. Since the default decision of the planner is always to select the first possible operator found in the domain for achieving each goal, this will force the planner to select the macro-operator as the first option.

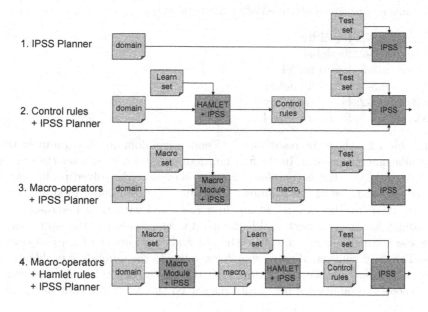

Fig. 5. Scheme of the four approaches applied for the experiments

4   Experiments

This section describes the experiments performed in some of the planning domains used in the IPC: Zeno-travel, Logistics, Miconic, Blocksworld and Satellite domains. We set the time bound to 30 seconds for solving problems both when learning and training. We now describe each domain separately.

4.1   Zeno-Travel

The objective in the Zeno-travel domain is to transport people from a city to another one by aircrafts, which need some fuel to fly. The operators are: *board* a person into an aircraft in a city; *depart* a person from an aircraft into a city; *fly* an aircraft from a city to another city; *zoom* that flies an aircraft faster (consuming more fuel) from a city to another one; and *refuel* the aircraft in a city.

We used:

- Macro-operator learning set: 25 random problems. The first one with one goal, the next 20 problems with two goals and the last four with three goals. Each one of them is described by an average of 10 literals and 2.1 goals.
- Control-rules learning set: 100 random problems, 75 with two goals and 25 with three. An average of 10 literals and 2.3 goals describe each problem.
- Test set: 170 random problems. All of them have two aircrafts, from seven up to 15 people, three cities, seven levels of fuel and from three up to 14 goals. Each test problem is composed by an average of 20.7 literals and 7.4 goals.

The macro-operators obtained after filtering were:

1. Macro m2-1: refuel fly
2. Macro m2-2: fly debark
3. Macro m2-3: board refuel
4. Macro m3-1: refuel fly debark
5. Macro m3-2: board refuel fly
6. Macro m3-3: fly board refuel

In Table 1 we show the results in the Zeno-travel domain, Z, without or with an specific macro-operator. In the first multicolumn, IPSS, we can see the number of *solved* problems, the *accumulated time* in seconds of the solved problems and the *accumulated cost* of the solutions, computed as the number of simple operators on them by the planner alone (first row) and with each macro-operator (remaining rows). The next multicolumn, HAMLET, presents the same results using the learned control rules in each case and the number of learned control rules. The third column, *Worse using rules*, refers to the number of problems not solved with rules that were solved without them. The last column, *Better using rules*, shows the number of new problems solved thanks to the control rules.

Table 1. Results of a test set with 170 random problems in the Zeno-travel domain

Domain	IPSS			HAMLET				Worse using rules	Better using rules
	Solved	Time	Cost	Solved	Time	Cost	Rules	Unsolved	Solved
Z	0	0	0	0	0	0	3	0	0
Z+m2-1	154	37.74	4439	156	50.67	4499	2	0	2
Z+m2-2	6	5.16	123	6	5.16	123	0	0	0
Z+m2-3	76	28.29	3203	76	28.29	3203	0	0	0
Z+m3-1	15	4.15	294	18	6.68	370	2	0	3
Z+m3-2	12	4.77	272	38	89.16	1387	6	5	31
Z+m3-3	82	81.62	3407	84	85.71	3327	2	0	2

As we can see in Table 1, when using IPSS alone, no problem was solved in the time bound of 30 seconds. If we apply HAMLET, although we learn three rules, no problem was solved either. This is an example where control rules are not useful. However, after modifying the domain with the respective macro-operators, results are improved. Some macro-operators are better than others, such as *m2-1*, *m2-3* and *m3-3*, reaching a percentage of solved problems of 91, 45 and 48%, respectively. In all cases using both macro-operators and control rules, results improve in terms of solved problems.

To understand why a macro-operator works better than another one, we compare in this domain the best one, *refuel+fly*, to the worst one, *fly+debark*. Let us suppose that the current goal is to fly from city1 to city2. *Refuel+fly* will be selected to achieve the goal of being at city2 and, besides, the tank of the aircraft is refueled. But this second effect does not achieve any other goal and it is always necessary to fly. That is, every time an aircraft flies, it is going to need fuel. Let us suppose now that the current goal is to refuel the tank of an aircraft. When we use *refuel+fly*, the tank of the aircraft refuels and it flies too.

The only possibility in this domain to need fuel occurs when we are going to fly, so the macro-operator is well applied in this case too.

Using the second macro-operator *fly+debark* the situation is different. In Figure 6 (a) we can see an example where the current goal is to fly from city0 to city1, maybe to pick a person up. By selecting *fly+debark*, we add the goal of having someone inside the aircraft, although we do not need anyone really in case we do not have any person inside the airplane. The second situation can be seen in Figure 6 (b), where the current goal is to debark person0 from aircraft0 in city0. The macro-operator *fly+debark* is selected to debark the person0 in city0, what forces aircraft0 to fly to another city before.

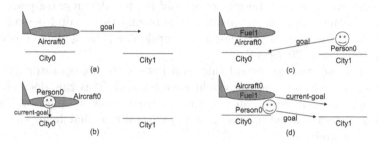

Fig. 6. Examples of problems in the Zeno-travel domain

Also to study the behaviour of the control rules learned in the third step, we show an example. If we run the planner with the original domain using the macro-operator *m3-1*, that is *refuel+fly+debark*, it can solve 15 problems, and with their two learned control rules, it can solve three problems more. One of these two rules can be seen in Figure 7.

```
(control-rule INDUCED-SELECT-FLY
    (if (and (current-goal (at <aircraft-3> <city-4>))
             (true-in-state (at <aircraft-3> <city-1>))
             (true-in-state (fuel-level <aircraft-3> <flevel-2>))
             (some-candidate-goals nil)
             (type-of-object <flevel-2> flevel)
             (type-of-object <city-1> city)
             (type-of-object <city-4> city)
             (type-of-object <aircraft-3> aircraft)))
    (then select operators fly))
```

Fig. 7. Control rule learned in the Zeno-travel domain with the macro-operator *refuel+fly+debark*

This rule says that if there is an aircraft in a city and the current goal is to have it in another city (variables city1 and city4 must be bound to different values), the planner should select the operator *fly*. That could be obvious, but it is important, given that without it the planner will always choose first to use the macro-operator *refuel+fly+debark*, because it appears in the domain description before the simple operator *fly*.

In Figure 6 (c) we can see a part of a problem, where we have an aircraft0 in a city0 and a person0 in a city1. The goal is to take this person to city0. Given that the planner follows a backward chaining process, the task would be to debark this person in the final city0, and the first operator that provides this is the macro *refuel+fly+debark*, flying from city1 to city0 with the person. After that the two goals to reach are: (i) to have the person0 into the aircraft0 and (ii) to have the aircraft0 in city1. To reach (i), the only operator that provides it is *board* person0 into aircraft0. The next goals to reach are: (iii) to have the person0 in the city1, that is true from the begining, and (iv) to have aircraft0 in city1, similar to goal (ii).

Now, to reach (ii) and without the second rule, *refuel+fly+debark* would be applied first, which means, besides refuel and fly, to take an extra person to be debarked. At this moment, the planner tries to find this second person only to have the aircraft in city1. This is not a good option and the planner ends without finding a solution in 30 seconds.

However, if we use the second rule seen before, the *fly* operator from city0 to city1 will be selected, and we would have finished. This rule does not select a macro-operator but selects an operator to avoid a macro-operator. This is a good induced (generalized in several steps) control rule that helps the planner to guide the search.

The control rules can work worse in other examples, such as the five cases where the macro-operator *m3-2*, *board+refuel+fly*, and their six resulting control rules are used. These cases are harder to explain because they include many goals and many objects. In Figure 6 (d) we can see a small example where the control rule has not the expected effects. We can see this control rule in Figure 8. It says that if there is an aircraft in a city and the current goal is to have the aircraft in another city, it must select the *fly* operator. In the example of Figure 6 (d), the current goal is to have airplane1 in city1, maybe to pick someone up. The control rule will be fired, although it would be better to apply the macro-operator because the final goal for person1 is to be in city1 too. Finding the right conditions to be inserted into the *if*-part of the rule is a hard problem and it is not easier for standard ILP techniques either [11].

```
(control-rule SELECT-FLY-L157-03-MAROB-61860753
  (if (and (current-goal (at <aircraft-1> <city-2>))
           (true-in-state (at <aircraft-1> <city-5>))
           (true-in-state (next <flevel-6> <flevel-12>))
           (true-in-state (fuel-level <aircraft-1> <flevel-6>))
           (some-candidate-goals nil)
           (type-of-object <aircraft-1> aircraft)
           (type-of-object <city-2> city)
           (type-of-object <city-5> city)
           (type-of-object <flevel-6> flevel)
           (type-of-object <flevel-12> flevel)))
    (then select operators fly))
```

Fig. 8. Control rule learned in the Zeno-travel domain with the macro-operator *board+refuel+fly*

Although the rules learned for *board+refuel+fly* work worse in five problems, they solve 31 new problems that were not solved without them.

4.2 Logistics

The goal in this domain is to carry packages from one place to another one. These places can be post-offices or airports that are inside cities. Each package can be carried by trucks, from one place to another one in the same city, or by airplanes, from an airport to another airport, that can be in different cities. The operators are: *load-truck*, loads a package in a truck; *load-airplane*, loads a package in an airplane; *unload-truck*; *unload-airplane*; *drive-truck*, a truck drives from a place to another one in the same city; and *fly-airplane* an airplane flies from an airport to another.

We use the version of the Logistics domain, as was first defined [12]. The main difference with the first IPC version is that the predicates for describing where packages, trucks and airplanes are have changed from the specific *at-object*, *at-truck* and *at-airplane* in our version to the generic *at* in the IPC version.

We have used a random problem generator to create different problem sets for learning and test. To learn the macro-operators and the control rules we have used the same set of 30 random problems with three cities, three objects and a maximum of three goals. Each one of them is described by an average of 20.7 literals and 1.3 goals. The test set is composed by 70 random problems. The first 30 have seven cities, 10 objects and from one to 10 goals. The next 40 problems are more complex. 10 of them are of type (3, 5, 5), other 10 are (5, 10, 10), the next 10 problems are (8, 15, 15) and the last 10 are (10, 20, 20), where (c, o, g) refers to number or cities (c), number of objects (o) and number of goals (g) respectively. An average of 47.3 literals and nine goals describe each test problem.

The complete list of learned macro-operators obtained in the second step are the following: (m2-1) drive-truck+unload-truck; (m2-2) fly-airplane+unload-airplane; (m2-3) load-truck+drive-truck; (m3-1) load-truck+drive-truck+unload-truck; (m3-2) drive-truck+load-truck+drive-truck; and (m3-3) load-airplane+fly-airplane+unload-airplane.

Table 4 shows the results of solving the test problems in the same format that in the previous Table 1. We can observe that *m2-2* and *m3-3* improve the number of solved problems with respect to using the planner alone or with control rules. In all cases, using HAMLET the number of solved problems increases. Except for the original domain without macros, where the time to solve the problem with control rules is much lower than without them. For the rest, the time increases using control rules, and also the cost. This is caused by the utility problem again.

4.3 Miconic

The version of this domain is the one used in the IPC-2000 with a change done in the domain definition reported in [13]. Also we used the 150 problems of IPC.

Table 2. Results of a test set with 70 random problems in the Logistics domain

Domain	IPSS			HAMLET				Worse using rules	Better using rules
	Solved	Time	Cost	Solved	Time	Cost	Rules	Unsolved	Solved
L	7	34.67	94	8	1.62	82	9	2	3
L+m2-1	4	0.72	25	6	0.77	40	4	0	2
L+m2-2	18	7.17	560	25	9.73	565	8	1	8
L+m2-3	3	0.17	14	3	0.17	14	6	0	0
L+m3-1	4	0.92	19	6	1.48	36	4	0	2
L+m3-2	6	22.5	64	6	22.5	64	9	0	0
L+m3-3	11	20.9	279	46	50.96	1690	9	0	35

In this domain there are two types of objects: passengers and floors. The goal is to bring people using an elevator to different floors. The operators are: *board* a person into the elevator in a floor; *depart* a person from the elevator in a floor; move *up* the elevator from a floor to a higher floor; and move *down* the elevator from a floor to a lower floor.

A set of 15 random problems with two up to six floors was used to learn the macros. Each problem is composed by an average of 12.3 literals and two goals. The 10 most simple problems of the 150 problems of the competition have been used to learn the control rules in HAMLET, which are problems with two and four floors and have an average of 7.5 literals and 1.5 goals. The rest 140 problems of the competition have been used to test and are problems with from six up to 60 floors. An average of 692.5 literals and 16.5 goals describe each test problem.

The learned macro-operators in the second step are: (m2-1) up+board; (m2-2) board+down; (m2-3) down+depart; (m3-1) board+down+depart; (m3-2) up+board+down; and (m3-3) board+up+depart.

Table 3 shows the results of solving the test problems in the same previous format. We can find two macro-operators with a very bad behaviour, *m2-2* and *m3-2*, also using their learned control rules. In this domain, we can find two other cases, such as *m2-1* and *m2-3*, in which, using control rules, the total number of solved problems decreases, by one and two problems respectively. We can observe the macro-opeator *m3-1* that, using control rules, the number of solved problems increases in four and the time to solve them decreases in more than seven seconds.

Table 3. Results of a test set with 140 random problems in the Miconic domain

Domain	IPSS			HAMLET				Worse using rules	Better using rules
	Solved	Time	Cost	Solved	Time	Cost	Rules	Unsolved	Solved
M	4	6.17	117	14	7.07	566	2	0	10
M+m2-1	22	42.2	1330	21	34.62	1172	4	8	7
M+m2-2	1	0.06	7	2	0.43	15	3	0	1
M+m2-3	16	8.53	449	14	16.25	342	3	2	0
M+m3-1	6	25.99	92	10	18.44	162	3	0	4
M+m3-2	2	0.14	16	5	0.44	45	3	0	3
M+m3-3	21	7.04	594	23	12.45	731	3	0	2

4.4 Blocksworld

We have used a random problem generator to create the set of problems. The problem set to learn macro-operators is composed of 30 problems, 10 of them are (5, 2), other 10 are (5, 3) and the last 10 are (10, 4), where (b, g) refers to number of blocks (b) and number of goals (g) respectively. Each problem is composed by an average of 10.5 literals and 3.2 goals. The problem set to learn control rules is similar to the one used for learning macro-operators. The test set is composed of 160 problems. There are eight subsets of 20 problems: (5, 1), (5, 2), (10, 3), (10, 5), (15, 10), (25, 15), (30, 20) and (55, 50). An average of 26.9 literals and 13.3 goals describe each test problem.

The macro-operators obtained in the Blocksworld domain are the following: (m2-1) unstack+putdown; (m2-2) pickup+stack; (m2-3) unstack+stack; (m3-1) unstack+putdown+unstack; (m3-2) unstack+putdown+pickup; and (m3-3) putdown+pickup+stack.

The results of solving the test problems can be seen in Table 4. In the Blocksworld domain, there is only one macro-operator, *m2-1*, that improves the results of the planner alone. However, the number of solved problems after applying the control rules is lower than without them. In the rest of the cases, although the results do not improve the one of using the planner alone or with their control rules, the number of solved problems does increase when HAMLET is used. The time using control-rules decreases in the last case, from 87 to 20 seconds, although it solves five problems more. There are four problems solved without rules too, that needed around 15 seconds to be solved for each one.

Table 4. Results of a test set with 160 random problems in the Blocksworld domain

Domain	IPSS			HAMLET				Worse using rules	Better using rules
	Solved	Time	Cost	Solved	Time	Cost	Rules	Unsolved	Solved
B	69	124.21	472	73	115.55	573	5	5	9
B+m2-1	119	78.36	1899	112	122.31	1462	8	10	3
B+m2-2	65	172.55	393	68	181.28	454	6	6	9
B+m2-3	45	21.02	234	47	62.38	265	3	1	3
B+m3-1	53	34.29	340	53	34.29	340	0	0	0
B+m3-2	28	22.04	122	36	75.36	182	9	0	8
B+m3-3	30	87.68	131	35	20.02	135	7	4	9

4.5 Satellite

The Satellite domain involves a collection of observation tasks between multiple satellites, each equipped with different instruments. Satellites can point to different directions (*turn-to*), supply power to one selected instrument (*switch-on* and *switch-off*), *calibrate* it to one target and *take-image* of a target. This domain is the one used in the IPC-2002. We also use the IPC problems as test set.

To learn macros we have used 30 random problems, with one satellite, two instruments and with from one up to three goals. Each one of them is described by an average of 10 literals and 1.8 goals. To learn control rules only six problems have been used with from one up to three satellites, from two up to nine instruments, and from three up to eight goals. The average of literals and goals for each problem are 21.2 and 5.3 respectively. The test set is composed of 36 problems with from four up to 10 satellites, and from nine up to 123 goals, with an average of 77.4 literals and 52.4 goals to describe each test problem.

The macro-operators obtained in the Satellite domain are: (m2-1) turn-to+ take-image; (m2-2) switch-on+turn-to; (m2-3) turn-to+calibrate; (m3-1) switch-on+turn-to+calibrate; (m3-2) calibrate+turn-to+take-image; and (m3-3) turn-to+calibrate+turn-to.

The results of solving the test problems can be seen in Table 5. In this domain no macro-operator alone or combination of macro-operator and control rules improves the results obtained with the planner alone, which solves 100% of the problems. The only good behaviour is using the macro *m2-1* when control rules are used.

Table 5. Results of a test set with 36 random problems in the Satellite domain

Domain	IPSS			HAMLET				Worse using rules	Better using rules
	Solved	Time	Cost	Solved	Time	Cost	Rules	Unsolved	Solved
S	36	110.75	4453	36	110.75	4453	0	0	0
S+m2-1	0	0	0	22	106.54	1766	1	0	22
S+m2-2	0	0	0	0	0	0	0	0	0
S+m2-3	24	103.16	2707	23	71.98	2384	1	1	0
S+m3-1	27	117.54	4453	21	71.07	2101	3	6	0
S+m3-2	8	38.86	1303	8	17.74	533	3	5	5
S+m3-3	23	129.77	319	23	129.77	319	0	0	0

5   Conclusions and Future Work

In this paper, we propose to learn control rules using an ILP-based approach after learning macro-operators. These control rules have been obtained by the relational learning system HAMLET, which finds a set of rules that are able to decide when to use the acquired macro-operators. The experiments have been made in several classical domains in planning.

In this paper, we have shown that the combination of macro-operators and control rules obtained from a relational learning technique can improve the results of the IPSS planner alone. We have also shown that the different learned macro-operators do not always outperform the results of the base planner. However, in most cases, when learned control rules are applied over a good resulting macro-operator, the results improve over using the macro-operator alone.

Also, there are many domains in which this integration must be tested and we have to increase even more the number of simple operators that compose the used macro-operators.

Acknowledgements

This work has been partially supported by the Spanish MEC project TIN2005-08945-C06-05 and regional CAM-UC3M project UC3M-INF-05-016.

References

1. Zimmerman, T., Kambhampati, S.: Learning-assisted automated planning: Looking back, taking stock, going forward. AI Magazine 24(2), 73–96 (2003)
2. Minton, S.: Learning Effective Search Control Knowledge: An Explanation-Based Approach. Kluwer Academic Publishers, Dordrecht (1988)
3. Botea, A., Enzenberger, M., Mueller, M., Schaeffer, J.: Macro-ff: Improving ai planning with automatically learned macro-operators. Journal of Artificial Intelligence Research 24, 581–621 (2005)
4. Borrajo, D., Veloso, M.: Lazy incremental learning of control knowledge for efficiently obtaining quality plans. AI Review Journal 11(1-5), 371–405 (1997)
5. McCluskey, T.: Combining weak learning heuristics in general problems solvers. In: Proceedings of the 10th International Joint Conference on Artificial Intelligence, pp. 331–333 (1987)
6. Rodríguez-Moreno, M.D., Oddi, A., Borrajo, D., Cesta, A.: A hybrid approach for integrating planning and scheduling: IPSS. IEEE Transactions on Knowledge and Data Engineering (in press)
7. Veloso, M., Carbonell, J., Pérez, A., Borrajo, D., Fink, E., Blythe, J.: Integrating planning and learning: The prodigy architecture. Journal of Experimental and Theoretical AI 7, 81–120 (1995)
8. Fernández, S., Aler, R., Borrajo, D.: Transfering learned control-knowledge between planners. In: Proceedings of the 20th International Joint Conference on Artificial Intelligence (2007)
9. Fikes, R., Hart, P., Nilsson, N.: Learning and executing generalized robot plans. Artificial Intelligence 3, 251–288 (1972)
10. McCluskey, T.L., Porteous, J.M.: Engineering and compiling planning domain models to promote validity and efficiency. Artificial Intelligence 95(1), 1–65 (1997)
11. Borrajo, D., Camacho, D., Silva, A.: Multistrategy relational learning of heuristics for problem solving. In: Proceedings of Expert Systems 99, The 19th SGES International Conference on Knowledge Based Systems and Applied Artificial Intelligence, Cambridge, England, pp. 57–71. Springer, Heidelberg (1999)
12. Veloso, M.: Planning and Learning by Analogical Reasoning. In: Veloso, M.M. (ed.) Planning and Learning by Analogical Reasoning. LNCS, vol. 886, Springer, Heidelberg (1994)
13. García-Durán, R.: Integrating macro-operators and control-rules learning. Doctoral Consortium. In: International Conference on Planning and Scheduling, pp. 34–37 (2006)

Frequent Hypergraph Mining[*]

Tamás Horváth[1], Björn Bringmann[2], and Luc De Raedt[2]

[1] Fraunhofer IAIS, Sankt Augustin, Germany
tamas.horvath@iais.fraunhofer.de
[2] Dept. of Computer Science, Katholieke Universiteit Leuven, Belgium
{bjoern.bringmann,luc.deraedt}@cs.kuleuven.be

Abstract. The class of frequent hypergraph mining problems is introduced which includes the frequent graph mining problem class and contains also the frequent itemset mining problem. We study the computational properties of different problems belonging to this class. In particular, besides negative results, we present practically relevant problems that can be solved in incremental-polynomial time. Some of our practical algorithms are obtained by reductions to frequent graph mining and itemset mining problems. Our experimental results in the domain of citation analysis show the potential of the framework on problems that have no natural representation as an ordinary graph.

1 Introduction

The field of data mining has studied increasingly expressive representations in the past few years. Whereas the original formulation of frequent pattern mining still employed itemsets [1], researchers have soon studied more expressive representations such as sequences and episodes (e.g., [16]), trees (e.g., [4,21]), and more recently, graph mining has become an important focus of research (e.g., [13,18,19]). These developments have been motivated and accompanied by new and challenging application areas. Indeed, itemsets apply to basket-analysis, sequences and episodes to alarm monitoring, trees to document mining, and graph mining to applications in computational chemistry.

In this paper, we introduce the next natural step in this evolution: the mining of *labeled hypergraphs*. In a similar way that tree mining generalizes sequence mining, and graph mining generalizes tree mining, hypergraph mining is a natural generalization of frequent pattern mining in *undirected* graphs. The presented framework is especially applicable to problem domains which do not have a natural representation as ordinary graphs. One such application is used in the experimental section of this paper. It is concerned with citation analysis, more specifically, with analyzing bibliographies of a set of papers. The bibliography of a paper can be viewed as a hypergraph, in which each author corresponds to a vertex and each paper to the hyperedge containing all authors of the paper.

---

[*] An early version of this paper appeared in T. Gärtner, G.C. Garriga, and T. Meinl (Eds.), *Proc. of the International Workshop on Mining and Learning with Graphs*, pages 25–36, ECML/PKDD'06 workshop proceedings, Berlin, Germany, 2006.

S. Muggleton, R. Otero, and A. Tamaddoni-Nezhad (Eds.): ILP 2006, LNAI 4455, pp. 244–259, 2007.

By mining for frequent subhypergraphs in the bibliographies of a set of papers (e.g. past KDD conference papers), one should be able to discover common citation patterns in a particular domain (such as SIGKDD). These patterns might then be employed in a recommender system that assists scientists while making bibliographies. A similar approach in a basket-analysis context allows one to represent the transactions over a specific period of time of *one family* as a hypergraph, where the products correspond to the vertices and the transactions to the hyperedges. Mining such data could provide insight into the overall purchasing behavior of families.

The main contribution of this paper is the introduction of a general framework of mining frequent hypergraphs. The framework can be specialized in a number of different ways, according to the notion of the generalization relation employed as well as the class of hypergraphs considered. We consider different problems where the generalization relation is defined by *subhypergraph isomorphism*, study their computational properties, and present positive and negative results. More specifically, we show that there is no output-polynomial time algorithm for mining frequent connected subhypergraphs, and even in the case of strong *structural* assumptions on the hyperedges, this problem cannot be solved efficiently by the usual level-wise frequent pattern mining approach (see, e.g., [15]). On the other hand, by restricting the functions labeling the vertices, we achieve positive results. Some of the results are obtained by employing reductions from frequent hypergraph mining problems to ordinary graph mining and itemset mining problems. We also present experiments in the above sketched citation analysis domain which indicate that these reductions can effectively be applied in practice. Essentially, we gathered the bibliographies of 5 SIGKDD, 30 SIGMOD, and 30 SIGGRAPH conferences and searched for frequent hypergraphs in each conference.

The rest of the paper is organized as follows: in Section 2, we introduce the necessary notions concerning hypergraphs and in Section 3, we define the problem class of frequent hypergraph mining. In Section 4, we study the frequent subhypergraph mining problem. In Section 5, we present some experiments using the citation analysis problem, and finally, in Section 6, we conclude and list some problems for future work. Due to space limitations, some of the proofs are only sketched in this version.

2   Notions and Notations

We recall some basic notions and notations related to graphs and hypergraphs (see, e.g., [2,6]). For a set S and non-negative integer k, $[S]^k$ denotes the family of all k-subsets of S, i.e., $[S]^k = \{S' \subseteq S : |S'| = k\}$.

Graphs and Hypergraphs. An *(undirected) graph* G consists of a finite set V of *vertices* and a family $\mathcal{E} \subseteq [V]^2$ of *edges*. G is *bipartite* if G has a vertex 2-coloring, i.e., if V admits a partition into V_1 and V_2 such that $E \notin [V_1]^2 \cup [V_2]^2$ for every $E \in \mathcal{E}$. A *hypergraph* H is a pair $(V, \mathcal{E})$, where V is a finite set and $\mathcal{E}$ is a family of nonempty subsets of V such that $\bigcup_{E \in \mathcal{E}} E = V$. The elements of V and

$\mathcal{E}$ are called *vertices* and *edges* (or *hyperedges*), respectively. H is *r-uniform* for some integer $r > 0$ if $\mathcal{E} \subseteq [V]^r$. The *rank* of H, denoted $r(H)$, is the cardinality of its largest hyperedge, i.e., $r(H) = \max_{E \in \mathcal{E}} |E|$, and the *size* of H, denoted $\mathrm{size}(H)$, is the number of hyperedges of H, i.e., $\mathrm{size}(H) = |\mathcal{E}|$.

By definition, a hyperedge may contain one or more vertices. Note that ordinary undirected graphs without isolated vertices form a special case of hypergraphs, i.e., the class of 2-uniform hypergraphs. We note that every hypergraph $H = (V, \mathcal{E})$ can be represented by a *bipartite incidence* graph $B(H) = (V \cup \mathcal{E}, \mathcal{E}')$, where $\mathcal{E}' = \{\{v, E\} : v \in V, E \in \mathcal{E}, \text{ and } v \in E\}$.

Labeled Hypergraphs. A *labeled hypergraph* is a triple $H = (V, \mathcal{E}, \lambda)$, where $(V, \mathcal{E})$ is a hypergraph, and $\lambda : V \to \mathbb{N}$ is a *labeling function*[1]. Unless otherwise stated, by hypergraphs (resp. graphs) we always mean labeled hypergraphs (resp. labeled graphs), and denote the set of vertices, the set of edges, and the labeling function of a hypergraph (resp. graph) H by V_H, $\mathcal{E}_H$, and λ_H, respectively. The set of all hypergraphs is denoted by $\mathcal{H}$ and $\mathcal{H}_r$ denotes the set of all r-uniform hypergraphs. For a hypergraph $H \in \mathcal{H}$ and subset $V' \subseteq V_H$, we denote the *multiset*[2] $\{\lambda_H(v) : v \in V'\}$ by $\lambda^H(V')$. A *path* connecting the vertices $u, v \in V_H$ is a sequence $E_1, \ldots, E_k$ of edges of H such that $u \in E_1$, $v \in E_k$, and $E_i \cap E_{i+1} \neq \emptyset$ for every $i = 1, \ldots, k - 1$. A hypergraph is *connected* if there is a path between any pair of its vertices. The set of connected hypergraphs is denoted by $\mathcal{H}^c$. Clearly, $\mathcal{H}^c \subset \mathcal{H}$.

Injective Hypergraphs. Depending on the labeling functions, in this paper we will consider two special classes of hypergraphs. A hypergraph $H \in \mathcal{H}$ is *node injective* if λ_H is injective, and it is *edge injective* whenever $\lambda^H(E) = \lambda^H(E')$ if and only if $E = E'$ for every $E, E' \in \mathcal{E}_H$. The sets of node and edge injective hypergraphs will be denoted by $\mathcal{H}^{ni}$ and $\mathcal{H}^{ei}$, respectively. Clearly, $\mathcal{H}^{ni} \subseteq \mathcal{H}^{ei} \subseteq \mathcal{H}$.

Hypergraph Isomorphism. Let $H_1, H_2 \in \mathcal{H}$ be hypergraphs. H_1 and H_2 are called *isomorphic*, denoted $H_1 \simeq H_2$, if there is a bijection $\varphi : V_{H_1} \to V_{H_2}$ such that

- φ preserves the labels, i.e., $\lambda_{H_1}(v) = \lambda_{H_2}(\varphi(v))$ for every $v \in V_{H_1}$, and
- φ preserves the hyperedges in both directions, i.e., for every $E \subseteq V_{H_1}$ it holds that $E \in \mathcal{E}_{H_1}$ if and only if $\{\varphi(v) : v \in E\} \in \mathcal{E}_{H_2}$.

Throughout this paper, two hypergraphs H_1 and H_2 are considered to be the same if $H_1 \simeq H_2$.

---

[1] We will only consider labeling functions defined on the vertex set because any hypergraph $H = (V, \mathcal{E}, \lambda)$ with $\lambda : V \cup \mathcal{E} \to \mathbb{N}$ satisfying $\lambda(v) \neq \lambda(E)$ for every $v \in V$ and $E \in \mathcal{E}$ can be transformed into a hypergraph $H' = (V', \mathcal{E}', \lambda')$ with $V' = V \cup \{v_E : E \in \mathcal{E}\}$, $\mathcal{E}' = \{E \cup \{v_E\} : E \in \mathcal{E}\}$, and with $\lambda' : V' \to \mathbb{N}$ mapping every new vertex $v_E \in V' \setminus V$ to $\lambda(E)$ and every $v \in V$ to $\lambda(v)$.

[2] A *multiset* M is a pair (S, f), where S is a set and f defines the multiplicity of the elements of S in M, i.e., f is a function mapping S to the cardinal numbers greater than 0.

Subhypergraphs. A *subhypergraph* of a hypergraph $H \in \mathcal{H}$ is a hypergraph $H' \in \mathcal{H}$ satisfying $V_{H'} \subseteq V_H$, $\mathcal{E}_{H'} \subseteq \mathcal{E}_H$, and $\lambda_{H'}(v) = \lambda_H(v)$ for every $v \in V_{H'}$.

3 Frequent Hypergraph Mining

Many problems in data mining can be viewed as a special case of the problem of enumerating the elements of a *quasiordered* set[3], which satisfy some monotone property (see, e.g., [3,12]). In this section, we define a new class of subproblems of this enumeration problem, the class of *frequent hypergraph mining problems*. In the next section, we then discuss the computational aspects of some problems belonging to this class. We start with the definition of a more general problem class.

The Frequent Pattern Mining Problem Class ($\mathcal{C}_{\text{FPM}}$): Each problem belonging to this class is given by a *fixed* triple $(\mathcal{L}_D, \mathcal{L}_P, \preccurlyeq)$, where $\mathcal{L}_D$ is a *transaction language*, $\mathcal{L}_P$ is a *pattern language*, and $\preccurlyeq$, called the *generalization relation*, is a quasiorder on $\mathcal{L}_D \cup \mathcal{L}_P$. For such a triple, the $(\mathcal{L}_D, \mathcal{L}_P, \preccurlyeq)$-FREQUENT-PATTERN-MINING problem is defined as follows: Given a finite set $\mathcal{D} \subseteq \mathcal{L}_D$ of *transactions* and an integer $t > 0$, called *frequency threshold*, compute the set $\mathcal{F}_{(\mathcal{L}_D, \mathcal{L}_P, \preccurlyeq)}(\mathcal{D}, t)$ of *frequent patterns* defined by

$$\mathcal{F}_{(\mathcal{L}_D, \mathcal{L}_P, \preccurlyeq)}(\mathcal{D}, t) = \{\varphi \in \mathcal{L}_P : |\{\tau \in \mathcal{D} : \varphi \preccurlyeq \tau\}| \geq t\} \ .$$

The transitivity of $\preccurlyeq$ implies that frequency is a monotone property, i.e., for every $\varphi, \theta \in \mathcal{L}_P$ it holds that $\theta \in \mathcal{F}_{(\mathcal{L}_D, \mathcal{L}_P, \preccurlyeq)}(\mathcal{D}, t)$ whenever $\varphi \in \mathcal{F}_{(\mathcal{L}_D, \mathcal{L}_P, \preccurlyeq)}(\mathcal{D}, t)$ and $\theta \preccurlyeq \varphi$.

We now define two subclasses of $\mathcal{C}_{\text{FPM}}$ by restricting the transaction and pattern languages to hypergraphs ($\mathcal{C}_{\text{FHM}}$) and graphs ($\mathcal{C}_{\text{FGM}}$).

The Frequent Hypergraph Mining Problem Class ($\mathcal{C}_{\text{FHM}}$): It consists of the set of $(\mathcal{L}_D, \mathcal{L}_P, \preccurlyeq)$-FREQUENT-PATTERN-MINING problems, where $\mathcal{L}_D, \mathcal{L}_P \subseteq \mathcal{H}$ (i.e., $\mathcal{L}_D$ and $\mathcal{L}_P$ are sets of labeled hypergraphs).

The Frequent Graph Mining Problem Class ($\mathcal{C}_{\text{FGM}}$): It is the set of $(\mathcal{L}_D, \mathcal{L}_P, \preccurlyeq)$-FREQUENT-PATTERN-MINING problems, where $\mathcal{L}_D, \mathcal{L}_P \subseteq \mathcal{H}_2$ (i.e., $\mathcal{L}_D$ and $\mathcal{L}_P$ are sets of labeled graphs).

Clearly, $\mathcal{C}_{\text{FGM}} \subsetneqq \mathcal{C}_{\text{FHM}} \subsetneqq \mathcal{C}_{\text{FPM}}$. It also holds that the *frequent itemset mining problem* [1] belongs to $\mathcal{C}_{\text{FPM}}$; for this problem we have $\mathcal{L}_D = \mathcal{L}_P = \{X \subset \mathbb{N} : |X| < \infty\}$ and $\preccurlyeq$ is the subset relation. In fact, the frequent itemset mining problem is contained by $\mathcal{C}_{\text{FHM}}$. Indeed, this problem can be considered as the $(\mathcal{H}_1^{\text{ni}}, \mathcal{H}_1^{\text{ni}}, \preccurlyeq)$-FREQUENT-HYPERGRAPH-MINING problem, where $\preccurlyeq$ is the subhypergraph relation and the transaction and pattern languages are the set of 1-uniform node injective hypergraphs.

---

[3] A binary relation is a *quasiorder* (or *preorder*), if it is reflexive and transitive.

The *parameter* of a $(\mathcal{L}_D, \mathcal{L}_P, \preccurlyeq)$-FREQUENT-HYPERGRAPH-MINING problem formulated above is the *size* of $\mathcal{D}$ defined by

$$\mathrm{size}(\mathcal{D}) = \max \left\{ \sum_{H \in \mathcal{D}} \mathrm{size}(H), \max_{H \in \mathcal{D}} r(H) \right\} .$$

Note that the size of the output, i.e. the set to be enumerated, can be exponential in the size of the input. Because in such cases, it is impossible to compute them in time polynomial only in the size of the input, we investigate whether the enumeration problems can be solved in *incremental polynomial time* or at least in *output-polynomial time* (or *polynomial total time*) (see, e.g., [9,14]). In the first, more restrictive case, the algorithm is required to list the first N elements of the output in time polynomial in the *combined size* of the input and the set of these N elements for every integer $N > 0$. In the second, more liberal case, the algorithm has to solve the problem in time polynomial in the combined size of the input and the *entire* set to be enumerated. Note that the class of output-polynomial time algorithms entails the class of incremental polynomial time algorithms.

To sketch the relation among frequent pattern mining problems, we need the notion of *polynomial reduction*. More precisely, we say that the frequent pattern mining problem $P_1 = (\mathcal{L}_{D,1}, \mathcal{L}_{P,1}, \preccurlyeq_1)$ is *polynomially reducible* to the frequent pattern mining problem $P_2 = (\mathcal{L}_{D,2}, \mathcal{L}_{P,2}, \preccurlyeq_2)$ if there exist functions

$$g : 2^{\mathcal{L}_{D,1}} \times \mathbb{N} \to 2^{\mathcal{L}_{D,2}} \times \mathbb{N} \quad \text{and} \quad f : \mathcal{L}_{P,2} \to \mathcal{L}_{P,1}$$

satisfying the following properties:

(i) $|\mathcal{F}_{(\mathcal{L}_{D,1}, \mathcal{L}_{P,1}, \preccurlyeq_1)}(I)| = |\mathcal{F}_{(\mathcal{L}_{D,2}, \mathcal{L}_{P,2}, \preccurlyeq_2)}(g(I))|$ for every $I \in 2^{\mathcal{L}_{D,1}} \times \mathbb{N}$,

(ii) f is injective, and

(iii) g and f can be computed in polynomial time.

That is, a pattern $\varphi \in \mathcal{L}_{P,1}$ is frequent for I if and only if it is the image (under f) of a pattern $\varphi' \in \mathcal{L}_{P,2}$ which is frequent for $g(I)$. Thus, if P_1 is polynomial-time reducible to P_2 then any enumeration algorithm solving P_2 in incremental polynomial (resp. output-polynomial) time can be used to solve P_1 in incremental polynomial (resp. output-polynomial) time.

Clearly, several frequent hypergraph mining problems, even frequent graph mining problems, cannot be solved in output-polynomial time (unless P = NP). In Proposition 1 below we present a simple example of such a hard problem.

Proposition 1. *Let $\mathcal{L}_D \subseteq \mathcal{H}_2$ and let $\mathcal{L}_P \subseteq \mathcal{H}_2$ be the set of complete graphs such that every vertex of every graph in $\mathcal{L}_D \cup \mathcal{L}_P$ is labeled by the same symbol, say 1, and let $\preccurlyeq$ be the homomorphism $\preccurlyeq_h$ between labeled graphs[4]. Then, unless $P = NP$, the $(\mathcal{L}_D, \mathcal{L}_P, \preccurlyeq_h)$-FREQUENT-GRAPH-MINING problem cannot be solved in output polynomial time.*

---

[4] A *homomorphism* from a hypergraph $H_1 \in \mathcal{H}$ to a hypergraph $H_2 \in \mathcal{H}$, denoted $H_1 \preccurlyeq_h H_2$, is a function $\varphi : V_{H_1} \to V_{H_2}$ preserving the labels and edges.

Proof. Let $G = (V, \mathcal{E})$ be an unlabeled graph and let G' be the labeled graph obtained from G by assigning 1 to each vertex of G. Then, for $\mathcal{D} = \{G'\}$ and $t = 1$, we have that G has a clique of size k if and only if there is a pattern $C \in \mathcal{F}_{(\mathcal{L}_D, \mathcal{L}_P, \preccurlyeq_h)}(\mathcal{D}, t)$ with k vertices. Since $|\mathcal{F}_{(\mathcal{L}_D, \mathcal{L}_P, \preccurlyeq_h)}(\mathcal{D}, t)| \leq |V|$, the size of the output is bounded by a polynomial of the input parameters. But this implies that the $(\mathcal{L}_D, \mathcal{L}_P, \preccurlyeq_h)$-FREQUENT-GRAPH-MINING problem cannot be computed in output polynomial time (unless P = NP), as otherwise the maximum clique problem[5] could be decided in polynomial time by computing first $\mathcal{F}_{(\mathcal{L}_D, \mathcal{L}_P, \preccurlyeq_h)}(\mathcal{D}, t)$ and then the pattern of maximum size from $\mathcal{F}_{(\mathcal{L}_D, \mathcal{L}_P, \preccurlyeq_h)}(\mathcal{D}, t)$. $\qquad\square$

4   Frequent Subhypergraph Mining

By Proposition 1, the class $\mathcal{C}_{\text{FGM}}$, and thus the more general class $\mathcal{C}_{\text{FHM}}$ as well, contains problems that cannot be solved in output polynomial time (unless P = NP). This negative result raises the challenge of identifying practically relevant and tractable problems belonging to $\mathcal{C}_{\text{FHM}}$. In this section, we take a first step towards this direction by considering the problem of frequent hypergraph mining w.r.t. *subhypergraph isomorphism*. This problem, called *frequent subhypergraph mining*, is a natural problem of the frequent hypergraph mining problem class $\mathcal{C}_{\text{FHM}}$ and can be applied to many practical problems. In Section 5, we will employ this setting to tackle the citation analysis problem sketched in the introduction.

We start with the definition of the generalization relation used in this section. Let $H_1, H_2 \in \mathcal{H}$. H_1 can be embedded into H_2 by *subhypergraph isomorphism*, denoted by $H_1 \preccurlyeq_i H_2$, if H_2 has a subhypergraph isomorphic to H_1. Note that $\preccurlyeq_i$ generalizes the notion of subgraph isomorphism between ordinary labeled graphs to hypergraphs. Since $\preccurlyeq_i$ is a partial order on $\mathcal{H}$, it is a generalization relation on every subset of $\mathcal{H}$. Using $\preccurlyeq_i$, in this section we consider the

$$(\mathcal{H}, \mathcal{H}^c, \preccurlyeq_i)\text{-FREQUENT-HYPERGRAPH-MINING}$$

problem of $\mathcal{C}_{\text{FHM}}$ and will refer to this problem as the *frequent subhypergraph mining problem*.

Although the pattern language in the frequent subhypergraph mining problem is restricted to *connected* hypergraphs, any enumeration algorithm for this problem can in fact be used to enumerate frequent, not necessarily connected, subhypergraphs as well. Indeed, for a set $\mathcal{D} \subseteq \mathcal{H}$ of hypergraphs, one can consider the set of connected hypergraphs obtained from $\mathcal{D}$ by the following transformation: Let $\ell \in \mathbb{N}$ be a label not used in any of the hypergraphs in $\mathcal{D}$. For every $H \in \mathcal{D}$, introduce a new vertex v, label it by ℓ, and add v to each edge of H. Clearly, any subhypergraph of the obtained hypergraph is connected and uniquely represents a (not necessarily connected) subhypergraph of H.

---

[5] *Given an unlabeled graph $G = (V, \mathcal{E})$, find a clique of maximum size in G. This problem is NP-complete [11]. A clique of G is a subset $V' \subseteq V$ such that each pair of vertices in V' are joined by and edge in $\mathcal{E}$.*

4.1 Negative Results

In this section we show that the frequent subhypergraph mining problem cannot be solved in output-polynomial time. This follows directly from Theorem 2 below which states that even for ordinary graphs (i.e., 2-uniform hypergraphs), the frequent subhypergraph mining problem is intractable in output-polynomial time. Since this is one of the most frequently considered frequent graph mining problems, this negative result may be of interest in itself.

Theorem 2. *If $P \neq NP$, there is no output-polynomial time algorithm solving the frequent subhypergraph mining problem even in the case of 2-uniform hypergraphs (i.e., ordinary graphs).*

Proof. We show that if such an algorithm would exist then the NP-complete Hamiltonian path problem could be decided in polynomial time. Let $G = (V, \mathcal{E})$ be an ordinary undirected graph with n vertices. Let $H_G, H \in \mathcal{H}_2$ be labeled graphs such that

- $V_{H_G} = V$, $\mathcal{E}_{H_G} = \mathcal{E}$,
- $|V_H| = n$, and $\mathcal{E}_H$ consists of $n - 1$ (hyper)edges that form a simple path (i.e., each vertex of H occurs exactly once in the path), and
- each vertex in H_G and H has the same label.

H will be used to make sure the size of the output is small. One can easily check that G has a Hamiltonian path if and only if there is a path of length $n - 1$ in $F = \mathcal{F}_{(\mathcal{H}, \mathcal{H}^c, \preccurlyeq_i)}(\{H_G, H\}, 2)$. Since $|F| \leq n$, this can be decided in time polynomial in n if F can be enumerated in output-polynomial time. □

As another restriction, we consider the frequent subhypergraph mining problem restricted to acyclic hypergraphs [10] because several NP-hard problems on hypergraphs become polynomial for acyclic hypergraphs. A hypergraph $H \in \mathcal{H}$ is α-*acyclic* if one can remove all of its vertices and edges by deleting repeatedly either an edge that is empty or is contained by another edge, or a vertex contained by at most one edge [20]. Note that α-acyclicity is not a hereditary property, that is, α-acyclic hypergraphs may have subhypergraphs that are not α-acyclic. Consider for example the hypergraph $H \in \mathcal{H}$ such that $\mathcal{E}_H = \{\{a, b\}, \{b, c\}, \{a, c\}, \{a, b, c\}\}$. While H is α-acyclic, its subhypergraph obtained by removing the edge $\{a, b, c\}$ is not α-acyclic. To overcome this anomaly, the following proper subclass of α-acyclic hypergraphs is introduced in [10]: An α-acyclic hypergraph is β-*acyclic*, if each of its subhypergraphs is also α-acyclic. Note that forests are 2-uniform β-acyclic hypergraphs.

Let $\mathcal{B}_3$ denote the set of 3-uniform β-acyclic hypergraphs. For connected subhypergraphs of 3-uniform β-acyclic hypergraphs, the following negative result holds:

Proposition 3. *Given a finite set $\mathcal{D} \subseteq \mathcal{B}_3$ and integer $t > 0$, deciding whether $H \in \mathcal{F}_{(\mathcal{B}_3, \mathcal{H}^c, \preccurlyeq_i)}(\mathcal{D}, t)$ is NP-hard.*

Proof (sketch). We use a polynomial reduction from the *subforest isomorphism* problem[6]. Let F be a forest and T be a tree and consider the hypergraph F' (resp. T') obtained from F (resp. T) by introducing a new vertex labeled by a symbol $\ell \in \mathbb{N}$ used neither in F nor in T, and by adding the new vertex to each edge of F (resp. T). Clearly, $F', T' \in \mathcal{B}_3$ and there is a subgraph isomorphism from F to T if and only if $F' \preccurlyeq_i T'$, from which the statement follows.   □

Proposition 3 above indicates that for the frequent subhypergraph mining problem, the usual frequent pattern mining approaches (such as the level-wise one) will not work in incremental polynomial time (unless $P = NP$) because they repeatedly test whether candidate patterns satisfy the frequency threshold (see, e.g., [12,15]).

4.2 A Naïve Algorithm

Despite the negative worst-case result stated in the previous section, in this section we present a naïve algorithm for the frequent subhypergraph mining problem. The algorithm is based on a reduction to mining frequent subgraphs from labeled bipartite graphs.[7]

More precisely, for an instance $(\mathcal{D}, t)$ of the frequent subhypergraph mining problem, let $n \in \mathbb{N}$ be an upper bound on the labels occurring in the hypergraphs of $\mathcal{D}$ and let μ be an injection assigning an integer greater than n to every finite multiset of $\mathbb{N}$. For a hypergraph $H \in \mathcal{D}$, let $LB(H) \in \mathcal{H}_2$ be the (labeled) *bipartite* graph such that

(i) $(V_{LB(H)}, \mathcal{E}_{LB(H)})$ is the *unlabeled* bipartite incidence graph of the unlabeled hypergraph $(V_H, \mathcal{E}_H)$, and
(ii) for every $v \in V_{LB(H)} = V_H \cup \mathcal{E}_H$,

$$\lambda_{LB(H)}(v) = \begin{cases} \lambda_H(v) & \text{if } v \in V_H \\ \mu(\lambda^H(v)) & \text{otherwise (i.e., } v \in \mathcal{E}_H) \end{cases} .$$

Clearly, a subgraph G of $LB(H)$ represents a subhypergraph of H if and only if each vertex of G corresponding to a hyperedge $E \in \mathcal{E}_H$ is connected with exactly $|E|$ vertices in G. Using the above transformation and considerations, the set $\mathcal{F}_{(\mathcal{H}, \mathcal{H}^c, \preccurlyeq_i)}(\mathcal{D}, t)$ of t-frequent subhypergraphs for the instance $(\mathcal{D}, t)$ can be computed by Algorithm 1.

Although by Theorem 2, Algorithm 1 does not work in output-polynomial time in the worst case, using a state-of-the-art frequent graph mining algorithm it proved to be effective in time on the citation analysis domain (see Section 5).

---

[6] Given a forest F and a tree T, decide whether T has a subgraph isomorphic to F. This problem is known to be NP-complete [11].
[7] Another naïve approach could be the following algorithm: Select a hyperedge E of a frequent pattern, attach a hyperedge E' to E, and compute the support count of the obtained pattern. Beside the intractability of deciding subhypergraph isomorphism, the number of possible attachments of E' to E can be exponential in their cardinality.

Algorithm 1. FREQUENT SUBHYPERGRAPH MINING

Require: an instance $(\mathcal{D}, t) \in 2^{\mathcal{H}} \times \mathbb{N}$
Ensure: $\mathcal{F}_{(\mathcal{H}, \mathcal{H}^c, \preccurlyeq_i)}(\mathcal{D}, t)$

1: $\mathcal{F} := \emptyset$
2: $\mathcal{B}_{\mathcal{D}} := \{LB(H) : H \in \mathcal{D}\}$
3: Compute a next t-frequent connected bipartite subgraph B of the set $\mathcal{B}_{\mathcal{D}}$ if it exists;
   otherwise **return** $\mathcal{F}$
4: **if** B corresponds to some hypergraph H_B **then**
      $\mathcal{F} := \mathcal{F} \cup \{H_B\}$
5: **goto** 3

4.3 Tractable Cases

In this section we present positive results for two special cases of the frequent subhypergraph mining problem obtained by making assumptions on the *labeling functions* of the transaction hypergraphs. We first consider the problem for *node injective* hypergraphs, i.e., where the labeling functions are injective. We show that for this case, the frequent subhypergraph mining problem is polynomially reducible to the frequent itemset mining problem and hence, it can be solved in incremental-polynomial time [1]. We then generalize this positive result to edge injective hypergraphs, i.e., to hypergraphs not containing two different hyper-edges that are mapped to the same multiset by the labeling function. Although node injective hypergraphs are a special case of edge injective hypergraphs, we discuss the two cases separately because node injective hypergraphs can be used to model many practical problems and they permit a simplified algorithmic approach.

Node Injective Hypergraphs. As mentioned above, many practical data mining problems can be modeled by node injective hypergraphs, i.e., by hypergraphs from $\mathcal{H}^{ni}$. Such applications include problem domains consisting of a finite set of objects (vertices) with a unique identifier. For node injective hypergraphs, we consider the $(\mathcal{H}^{ni}, \mathcal{H}^{ni}, \preccurlyeq_i)$-FREQUENT-HYPERGRAPH-MINING problem which is a special case of the frequent subhypergraph mining problem.

As an example of a practical application of this problem, we consider the *citation analysis* task mentioned in the introduction (see also Section 5): *Given a set $\mathcal{D}$ of articles and a frequency threshold $t > 0$, compute each family $\mathcal{F}$ of groups of authors satisfying the following property: there exists a subset $\mathcal{D}' \subseteq \mathcal{D}$ of articles of cardinality at least t such that for every group $F \in \mathcal{F}$ of authors and for every article $D \in \mathcal{D}'$ it holds that D cites some article written by (exactly) the authors belonging to F*. In this enumeration problem, we can assign a unique non-negative integer to each author, whose papers are cited by at least one article in $\mathcal{D}$.

We can use the *node injective hypergraph representation* of a paper's bibliography defined as follows. For each author cited in the bibliography, introduce a vertex and label it by the integer assigned to the author. Furthermore, for each

1. R. Agrawal, R. Srikant. *Publication 1.*
2. H. Mannila, H. Toivonen. *Publication 2.*
3. J. Quinlan. *Publication 3.*
4. H. Toivonen, R. Srikant, R. Agrawal. *Publication 4.*

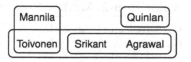

Fig. 1. An example reference-list and the according hypergraph

cited work add a hyperedge E to the set of hyperedges, where E consists of the vertices representing the cited work's authors. Clearly, the hypergraph obtained in this way is always node injective, similar to the example in Figure 1.[8] Our database $\mathcal{D}$ is a set of such node injective hypergraphs.

Theorem 4 below states that for node injective hypergraphs, the frequent subhypergraph mining problem is polynomially reducible to the frequent itemset mining problem. We recall that the frequent itemset mining problem can be considered as a problem belonging to the class $\mathcal{C}_{\text{FHM}}$ (see Section 3). Notice that in the theorem below, subhypergraphs may be non-connected. The theorem is based on the fact that for every node injective hypergraphs $H_1, H_2 \in \mathcal{H}^{\text{ni}}$, $H_1 \preccurlyeq_i H_2$ if and only if for every $E_1 \in \mathcal{E}_{H_1}$, there is a hyperedge $E_2 \in \mathcal{E}_{H_2}$ such that $\lambda^{H_1}(E_1) = \lambda^{H_2}(E_2)$, i.e.,

$$H_1 \preccurlyeq_i H_2 \iff \{\lambda^{H_1}(E) : E \in \mathcal{E}_{H_1}\} \subseteq \{\lambda^{H_2}(E) : E \in \mathcal{E}_{H_2}\} \ .$$

Note that the above equivalence implies that $\preccurlyeq_i$ can be decided efficiently for node injective hypergraphs.

Theorem 4. *The frequent subhypergraph mining problem for node injective hypergraphs is polynomially reducible to the frequent itemset mining problem.*

Proof (sketch). The proof follows by considering the set of vertex labels of a hyperedge as an item for every hyperedge occurring in the transaction hypergraphs.   □

Combining the above theorem with the results of [1], we have the following result on listing frequent subhypergraphs for node injective hypergraphs.

Corollary 5. *The frequent subhypergraph mining problem for node injective hypergraphs can be solved in incremental polynomial time.*

Edge Injective Hypergraphs. In Theorem 6 below we generalize the previous positive result to *edge injective hypergraphs.* Since edge injective hypergraphs may contain different vertices with the same label, they are not determined by a family of multisets of vertex labels (in contrast to the previous case). Hence, a polynomial reduction to frequent itemset mining is not applicable to this case.

---

[8] To facilitate better comprehensibility the artificial node connecting all hyperedges is omitted in this example.

Algorithm 2. MINING EDGE INJECTIVE HYPERGRAPHS

Require: an instance $(\mathcal{D}, t) \in 2^{\mathcal{H}^{ei}} \times \mathbb{N}$
Ensure: $\mathcal{F}_{(\mathcal{H}^{ei}, \mathcal{H}^{ei}, \preccurlyeq_i)}(\mathcal{D}, t)$

1: $X := \bigcup_{H \in \mathcal{D}} \{\lambda^H(E) : E \in \mathcal{E}_H\}$
2: $F := \emptyset$
3: $k := 0$
4: **while** $k = 0 \vee L_k \neq \emptyset$ **do**
5:     $k := k + 1$
6:     $C_k := \begin{cases} X & \text{if } k = 1 \\ \{Y_1 \cup Y_2 \in [X]^k : Y_1, Y_2 \in L_{k-1}\} & \text{otherwise} \end{cases}$
7:     $L_k := \emptyset$
8:     **forall** $X' \in C_k$ **do**
9:         $Q := \emptyset$
10:         **forall** $H \in \mathcal{D}$ **do**
11:             **if** H has a subhypergraph H' s.t. $X' = \{\lambda^{H'}(E) : E \in \mathcal{E}_{H'}\}$ **then**
12:                 **if** $\exists (H'', f) \in Q$ s.t. $H'' \simeq H'$ **then**
13:                     change (H'', f) in Q to $(H'', f+1)$
14:                 **else** $Q := Q \cup \{(H', 1)\}$
15:             **endfor**
16:             flag := TRUE
17:             **forall** $(H, f) \in Q$ s.t. $f \geq t$ **do**
18:                 $F := F \cup \{H\}$
19:                 **if** flag **then**
20:                     $L_k := L_k \cup \{X'\}$
21:                     flag := FALSE
22:                 **endif**
23:             **endfor**
24:     **endfor**
25: **endwhile**
26: **return** F

Theorem 6. *The frequent subhypergraph mining problem for edge injective hypergraphs can be solved in incremental polynomial time.*

Proof (sketch). Due to space limitations, we only sketch the proof. Without proof we first note that subhypergraph isomorphism between edge injective hypergraphs can be decided in polynomial time. To compute the set of frequent hypergraphs, we use a level-wise algorithm given in Algorithm 2.

In line 1 of the algorithm, X is initialized as the set of multisets corresponding to the edges in the transaction hypergraphs. In C_k (line 6), we compute a family of candidate sets of multisets; the elements of C_k consist of k multisets corresponding to the vertex labels of k hyperedges. For every X' in C_k (see the loop starting at line 8), we check for every $H \in \mathcal{D}$ whether H has a subhypergraph H' such that the set of multisets defined by the vertex labels of the edges of H' is equal to X'. Since edges are injectively labeled, H' must contain exactly k hyperedges. If H has such a subhypergraph H' then we check whether we have already found another hypergraph in the database which has a subhypergraph isomorphic to H'. If so, we increment the counter of this subhypergraph (line 13); otherwise we add H' with frequency 1 to the set Q (line 14). In the loop (17–23) we update the set of frequent hypergraphs and L_k. One can show that this algorithm works in incremental polynomial time.   □

5   Experimental Evaluation

In this section, we empirically evaluate (i) the naïve algorithm (see Sect. 4.2) and (ii) the method based on the reduction of the node injective case to frequent itemset mining (see Sect. 4.3) on the citation analysis problem discussed earlier.

5.1   Bibliographic Datasets

Three different bibliographic data sets were constructed from the ACM Digital library[9]: KDD, SIGMOD, and SIGGRAPH. They correspond to the set of all reference lists of papers found in the proceedings of the respective conferences. The characteristics of the data-sets are listed in Table 1.

Table 1. Datasets used. We list the total number of papers in the proceedings and the number of authors occurring in the reference lists of the corresponding papers.

dataset	years	papers	authors
KDD	99-04	499	6966
SIGMOD	74-04	1404	11984
SIGGRAPH	74-04	1519	13192

A simple parser was used to extract the authors and cited papers occurring in the reference lists. Each paper was then represented as a hypergraph, as already discussed above. The resulting hypergraphs are *node injective* and disconnected in almost all cases. Most existing graph miners only consider *connected* graphs. Hence, we added one special hyperedge to each paper, which connects all authors cited in that paper such that the naïve algorithm could be employed.

All experiments were run on a workstation, running Suse Linux 9.2, 3.2 GHz, 2GB of RAM. As graph miner for the naïve algorithm, we employed Siegfried Nijssen's implementation of GASTON [18] and as item-set miner for the reduction method, Bart Goethals' implementation of Apriori[10]. Since we did not employ a specialized hypergraph or graph miner, the data had to be pre- and postprocessed. The pre- and post-processing steps run in time linear in the number of hypergraphs.

---

[9] *http://www.acm.org/*

[10] *http://www.cs.helsinki.fi/u/goethals/software/*

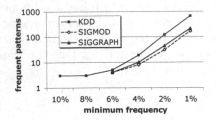
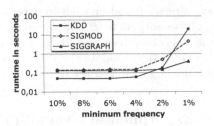

Fig. 2. Frequent patterns in the *node* injective setting

Fig. 3. Runtimes for the naïve approach in the *node* injective setting

5.2 Experimental Results

As mentioned above, we performed experiments employing reductions to frequent bipartite graph mining and to frequent item-set mining. The empirical results are given in Figures 2 and 3.

The runtime of the method based on the reduction to frequent item-set mining was always below 0.01 seconds. Different from that, the naïve approach based on the reduction to frequent bipartite graph mining shows much higher runtimes. In detail, the 1% settings required 20.36, 4.55, and 0.4 seconds for KDD, SIGMOD, and SIGGRAPH respectively. The higher runtimes for the naïve approach are essentially due to the problem that only a fraction of the frequent bipartite graphs are in fact subhypergraphs (see line 4 of Algorithm 1). As usual for frequent pattern mining techniques, the runtime and size of the frequent pattern space increase exponentially with a decreasing level of minimum support (see Figures 2 and 3). One of the frequent subhypergraphs in the KDD dataset was $\{\{Agrawal, Srikant\}, \{Agrawal, Swami, Imielinski\}\}$, while in the SIGGRAPH dataset the hypergraph $\{\{Sproull, Newmann\}\}$ was very frequent. The experimental results reveal that the reduction approach can be successfully employed in practice. As expected due to the theoretical results, the reduction to item-set mining for injective subhypergraphs is much less computationally expensive. All experiments w.r.t. node injective subhypergraphs were finished in less than a fraction of a second, which – in our opinion – indicates that it is not worth-while to implement a special purpose data mining system for this task.

6   Conclusion and Further Research

In this paper the problem class $\mathcal{C}_{FHM}$ of frequent hypergraph mining was introduced. It forms a natural extension of traditional frequent itemset and graph mining. Several problems of $\mathcal{C}_{FHM}$ were studied and positive and negative complexity results were obtained.

In our first step of studying some problems of $\mathcal{C}_{FHM}$ we deliberately did not develop and implement a special hypergraph mining algorithm, because there are many problems of $\mathcal{C}_{\text{FHM}}$ that are interesting (which implies the need for implementing many variants and optimizations). Instead, some of our theoretical and practical results have been obtained by reductions to frequent graph mining and itemset mining problems. The experiments clearly indicate that – at least for the citation analysis problems studied – these reductions can be quite effective in practice. In addition, these experiments provide evidence that frequent hypergraph mining is indeed a useful generalization of frequent itemset and graph mining and is likely to yield many interesting applications.

Finally we list some open questions.

(i) One of the challenges is to identify further problems of $\mathcal{C}_{\text{FHM}}$ that are enumerable in incremental or at least in output-polynomial time.

(ii) Besides subhypergraph isomorphism, it would be interesting to investigate frequent hypergraph mining problems, where the generalization relation is defined by (constrained) *homomorphisms*.

(iii) Since many problems of $\mathcal{C}_{\text{FHM}}$ can be reduced to frequent graph mining in bipartite graphs, it would be interesting to develop frequent graph mining algorithms specific to bipartite graphs.

(iv) The work on frequent hypergraph mining can be related to multi-relational data mining [7], where each instance consists of multiple tuples over multiple tables in a relational database. Multi-relational data mining techniques have been applied to graph mining problems. Hence, the question arises if they are also applicable to hypergraph mining, and vice versa.

(v) In a similar way that frequent hypergraph mining generalizes frequent graph mining in *undirected* graphs, frequent pattern mining in *relational structures* (see, e.g., [8]) can be considered as a generalization of frequent graph mining in *directed* graphs. Similarly to the problem class $\mathcal{C}_{\text{FHM}}$, the *Frequent Relational Structure Mining Problem Class* ($\mathcal{C}_{\text{FRSM}}$) can be defined as the set of $(\mathcal{L}_D, \mathcal{L}_P, \preccurlyeq)$-FREQUENT-PATTERN-MINING problems, where $\mathcal{L}_D$ and $\mathcal{L}_P$ are classes of relational τ-structures over some vocabulary τ. Thus, the $(\mathcal{L}_D, \mathcal{L}_P, \preccurlyeq)$-FREQUENT-RELATIONAL-STRUCTURE-MINING problem can be defined as follows: *Given* a finite set $\mathcal{D} \subseteq \mathcal{L}_D$ of relational τ-structures and an integer $t > 0$, *compute* the set of relational τ-structures from $\mathcal{L}_P$ that generalize at least t structures of $\mathcal{D}$ with respect to $\preccurlyeq$. To the best of our knowledge, there are only a few results towards this direction. In particular, related problems have been considered only for the generalization relations *relational homomorphism* [5] and *relational substructure isomorphism* [17]. The challenge is to identify tractable problems of $\mathcal{C}_{\text{FRSM}}$.

Acknowledgments

The authors thank Mario Boley, Thomas Gärtner, Stefan Wrobel, and the anonymous reviewers for useful comments. Tamás Horváth was partially supported by the DFG project (WR 40/2-2) *Hybride Methoden und Systemarchitekturen für heterogene Informationsräume*. Björn Bringmann and Luc De Raedt were partially supported by the IQ project (EU grant IST-FET FP6-516169).

References

1. Agrawal, R., Mannila, H., Srikant, R., Toivonen, H., Verkamo, A.I.: Fast discovery of association rules. In: Advances in Knowledge Discovery and Data Mining, pp. 307–328. AAAI/MIT Press (1996)
2. Berge, C.: Hypergraphs. North Holland Mathematical Library, vol. 445. Elsevier, Amsterdam (1989)
3. Boros, E., Elbassioni, K., Gurvich, V., Khachiyan, L., Makino, K.: Dual bounded hypergraphs: A survey. In: Proc. of the 2nd SIAM Conference on Data Mining, pp. 87–98 (2002)
4. Chi, Y., Nijssen, S., Muntz, R.R., Kok, J.N.: Frequent subtree mining–an overview. Fundamenta Informaticae 66, 161–198 (2005)
5. Dehaspe, L., Toivonen, H.: Discovery of frequent DATALOG patterns. Data Mining and Knowledge Discovery 3, 7–36 (1999)
6. Diestel, R.: Graph theory, 3rd edn. Springer, Heidelberg (2005)
7. Džeroski, S., Lavrač, N. (eds.): Relational Data Mining. Springer, New York (2002)
8. Ebbinghaus, H.-D., Flum, J.: Finite Model Theory, 2nd edn. Springer, Heidelberg (1999)
9. Eiter, T., Gottlob, G.: Identifying the minimal transversals of a hypergraph and related problems. SIAM Journal on Computing 24(6), 1278–1304 (1995)
10. Fagin, R.: Degrees of acyclicity for hypergraphs and relational database schemes. Journal of the ACM 30(3), 514–550 (1983)
11. Garey, M.R., Johnson, D.S.: Computers and Intractability: A Guide to NP-Completeness. Freeman, San Francisco, CA (1979)
12. Gunopulos, D., Khardon, R., Mannila, H., Saluja, S., Toivonen, H., Sharm, R.S.: Discovering all most specific sentences. ACM Transactions on Database Systems 28(2), 140–174 (2003)
13. Horváth, T., Ramon, J., Wrobel, S.: Frequent subgraph mining in outerplanar graphs. In: Proc. of the 12th ACM SIGKDD International Conference on Knowledge discovery and Data Mining, pp. 197–206. ACM Press, New York (2006)
14. Johnson, D.S., Yannakakis, M., Papadimitriou, C.H.: On generating all maximal independent sets. Information Processing Letters 27(3), 119–123 (1988)
15. Mannila, H., Toivonen, H.: Levelwise search and borders of theories in knowledge discovery. Data Mining and Knowledge Discovery 1(3), 241–258 (1997)
16. Mannila, H., Toivonen, H., Verkamo, A.I.: Discovery of frequent episodes in event sequences. Data Mining and Knowledge Discovery 1(3), 259–289 (1997)
17. Nijssen, S., Kok, J.N.: Efficient frequent query discovery in FARMER. In: Proc. of the 17th International Joint Conference on Artificial Intelligence, pp. 891–896. Morgan Kaufmann, San Francisco (2001)
18. Nijssen, S., Kok, J.N.: A quickstart in frequent structure mining can make a difference. In: Proceedings of the 10th ACM SIGKDD International Conference on Knowledge Discovery and Data Mining, pp. 647–652. ACM Press, New York (2004)
19. Yan, X., Han, J.: gSpan: Graph-based substructure pattern mining. In: Proceedings of the 2002 IEEE International Conference on Data Mining, pp. 721–724. IEEE Computer Society Press, Los Alamitos (2002)

20. Yu, C.T., Ozsoyoglu, M.Z.: An algorithm for tree-query membership of a distributed query. In: Proceedings of Computer Software and Applications Conference, pp. 306–312. IEEE Computer Society Press, Los Alamitos (1979)
21. Zaki, M.J.: Efficiently mining frequent trees in a forest. In: Proceedings of the 8th ACM SIGKDD International Conference, pp. 71–80. ACM Press, New York (2002)

Induction of Fuzzy and Annotated Logic Programs

Tomáš Horváth[1] and Peter Vojtáš[2]

[1] ICS, Faculty of Science, Pavol Jozef Šafárik University, Košice, Slovakia
Tomas.Horvath@upjs.sk
[2] ICS, Czech Academy of Sciences, Prague, Czech Republic
Peter.Vojtas@mff.cuni.cz

Abstract. The new direction of the research in the field of data mining is the development of methods to handle imperfection (uncertainty, vagueness, imprecision, ...). The main interest in this research is focused on probability models. Besides these there is an extensive study of the phenomena of imperfection in fuzzy logic. In this paper we concentrate especially on fuzzy logic programs (FLP) and Generalized Annotated Programs (GAP). The lack of the present research in the field of fuzzy inductive logic programming (FILP) is that every approach has its own formulation of the proof-theoretic part (often dealing with linguistic hedges) and lack sound and compete formulation of semantics. Our aim in this paper is to propose a formal model of FILP and induction of GAP programs (IGAP) based on sound and complete model of FLP (without linguistic hedges) and its equivalence with GAP. We focus on learning from entailment setting in this paper. We describe our approach to IGAP and show its consistency and equivalence to FILP. Our inductive method is used for detection of user preferences in a web search application. Finally, we compare our approach to several fuzzy ILP approaches.

1 Introduction

In a standard logical framework, we are restricted to represent only facts that are true absolutely. Thus, this framework is unable to represent and reason with imperfect - uncertain, vague, noisy, ranked/preferenced - information. This is a significant gap in the expressive power of the framework, and a major barrier to its use in many real-world applications. We use imperfection in the generic sense of uncertainty. Imperfection is unavoidable in the real world: our information (and particularly our classification) is often inaccurate and always incomplete, and only a few of the "rules" that we use for reasoning are true in all (or even most) of the possible cases.

Furthermore, it is hard to represent the notions of a natural language just with two values (true, false). If we consider the concept "cheap", in a standard two-valued logic we can say that it holds (an object is cheap) or not (an object is not cheap). But in two valued logic we cannot express easily that one item is cheaper than another. So, it is convenient to use several degrees of truth to the facts, in order to represent the "more" or "less" cheap. For these purpose we can use the multi-valued logical framework, in which a truth value is assigned to facts, information expressing their accuracy, trustworthiness, preference, especially different user preferences, etc.

S. Muggleton, R. Otero, and A. Tamaddoni-Nezhad (Eds.): ILP 2006, LNAI 4455, pp. 260–274, 2007.

This limitation, which is critical in many domains (e.g., medical diagnosis), has led over the last decade to the resurgence of probabilistic reasoning in data mining. Probability theory models uncertainty by assigning a probability to each of the states of the world that an agent considers possible (see [7]). Besides probabilistic models there is an extensive study of these phenomena in many valued logic.

To capture different independencies between predicates, in many valued logical framework we have several many valued connectives, which from each one are convenient for another, specific case. Notice, the standard logical framework deals only with "strict" but "uncomplicated" two-valued connectives (&, ∨, →) for each case.

In this paper we concentrate on multi valued logical framework, especially on fuzzy logic programming (FLP) and generalized annotated logic programming (GAP). There are no research – as we know – on induction of GAP programs (IGAP), and just a few studies on fuzzy inductive logic programming (FILP). The lack of the present research on FILP is that every approach has its own formulation of the deductive part. These differs each other and are considered mainly from the proof-theoretic view. The model-theoretic part of these approaches lacks correct and sound formulation.

In [12] we proposed an approach to induction of FLP via inducing Generalized Annotated Programs (GAP) [14]. The formal model of FILP was not introduced in the mentioned paper (or any paper before), as well as the consistency of our approach was never proved before. The main contributions of this paper are to give a correct and sound formal model of FILP and IGAP for learning from entailment setting, to show the correctness of our approach and to determine the main challenges and problems in the process of induction in fuzzy logic framework.

This paper is structured as follows: In the next chapter we introduce our formal model of FLP from the proof-theoretic and model-theoretic view. We follow closely Lloyd's presentation and even notation [16]. We show the correctness and completeness of this model, too. Based on this model, we propose our model of FILP in the following chapter and show that our model of FILP is a generalization of crisp ILP. In the next two chapters we describe the formal model of GAP and IGAP. We show in the latter chapter that our IGAP task is equivalent to FILP task. In this chapter we further describe our IGAP approach (with an illustrative toy example) and show its consistency. In the chapter 6 we discuss the role of our approach in the Slovak project NAZOU [19]. Finally, we discuss some recent work and future directions.

2 Fuzzy Logic Programming

In order to describe different interrelations between properties, our language has finitely many conjunctions $\&_1, ..., \&_k$, disjunctions $\vee_1, ..., \vee_l$ and their truth functions conjunctors $\&_1^{\bullet}, ..., \&_k^{\bullet}$, disjunctions $\vee_1^{\bullet}, ..., \vee_l^{\bullet}$ (coupled with conjunctors via de Morgan laws with respect to the negation 1-x). In order to describe the increasing fulfillment of requirements we have aggregation operators of different arity $@_1, ...,$ $@_m$ in our language. Their truth functions $@_1^{\bullet}, ..., @_m^{\bullet}$ are order preserving. Usually we assume that $@^{\bullet}(0,...,0)=0$ and $@^{\bullet}(1,...,1)=1$ hold, but sometimes we relax these. We assume all truth functions of conjunctions, disjunctions and aggregations are left continuous (in the sense of functions of real numbers). Implications $\rightarrow_1, ..., \rightarrow_n$ have truth functions implicators $\rightarrow_1^{\bullet}, ..., \rightarrow_n^{\bullet}$.

Example 1. Let x the truth value of an event X and y the truth value of an event Y. The common connectives are the *Lukasiewicz* connectives

$$\&_L{}^{\bullet}(x,y) = max(0, x+y-1)$$
$$\vee_L{}^{\bullet}(x,y) = min(1, x+y)$$
$$\rightarrow_L{}^{\bullet}(x,y) = min(1, 1-x+y)$$

(in case if X and Y are disjunctive)
the *Goedel* connectives

$$\&_G{}^{\bullet}(x,y) = min(x,y)$$
$$\vee_G{}^{\bullet}(x,y) = max(x,y)$$
$$\rightarrow_G{}^{\bullet}(x,y) = y \text{ if } x > y, \text{ else } 1$$

(in case if X and Y are inclusive) and
the *product* connectives

$$\&_P{}^{\bullet}(x,y) = x.y$$
$$\vee_P{}^{\bullet}(x,y) = x+y-xy$$
$$\rightarrow_P{}^{\bullet}(x,y) = min(1, y/x)$$

(in case if X and Y are independent).

In our computational model, we have conjunctors $C_1,...,C_n$ which are residual to implicators $I_1, ..., I_n$. Assume, our conjunctors and implicators fulfill property (a) from (1) (in what follows, b, h, r are universally quantified and range through [0,1]).

$$(a)(C,I) \ r \leq I(b,h) \text{ iff } C(b,r) \leq h$$
$$\phi 2(C,I) \ C(b,I(b,h)) \leq h \qquad\qquad (1)$$
$$\phi 3(C,I) \ r \leq I(b, C(b,r))$$

The following observations hold:

- (a)(C,I) iff (ϕ2(C,I) and ϕ3(C,I))
- if (a)(C,I) then $I(b,h) = sup\{r: C(b,r) \leq h\}$ and $C(b,r) = inf\{h: I(b,h) \geq r\}$.
- given C, then there is an I such that (a)(C,I) iff C is left continuous in r.
- given I, then there is a C such that (a)(C,I) iff I is right continuous in h.

Any formula built from atoms using conjunctions, disjunctions and aggregations is called a *body*. Every composition of conjunctors, disjunctors and aggregation operators is again an aggregation operator. Hence, without a loss of generality, we can assume that each body is of the form $B=@(B_1,... ,B_n)$.

A *rule* of FLP is a graded implication

$$(H \leftarrow (B_1,...,B_n).r),$$

where H is an atom called *head*, $@(B_1,...,B_n)$ is a body and $r \in Q \cap [0,1]$ is a rational number. (H ← $@((B_1,...,B_n))$ is the logical and r is the quantitative part of the rule).

A *fact* is a graded atom *(B.b)*.

A finite set P of positively graded FLP rules and facts is said to be a *fuzzy logic program* if there are no two rules (facts) with the same logical parts and different quantitative parts. It can be represented as a partial mapping *P: Formulas→(0,1]* with the *domain* of P *dom(P)* consisting only of atoms and logical parts of FLP rules of the form H←$@(B_1,...,B_n)$. The quantitative part of the rule is $r=P(H \leftarrow @((B_1,...,B_n)))$.

Example 2. An example of a fuzzy logic program

p(a,b).3/4   p(b,c).1/4   p(a,d).2/3   p(d,c).1/3

(p(X,Z) $\leftarrow_G$ p(X,Y) $\&_P$ p(Y,Z)).1/4

Let $\mathfrak{B}_L$ be the Herbrand base. A mapping f: $\mathfrak{B}_L \rightarrow[0,1]$ is said to be a *fuzzy Herbrand interpretation*. Our fuzzy logic is truth functional i.e. f can be extended to f all formulas along the complexity of formula using the truth function of connectives. A graded formula (φ.x) is *true in an interpretation* f (f $\models_{FLP}$ φ.x) if f(φ)$\geq$x. For a rule ($\leftarrow$·, @· are truth functions of $\leftarrow$, @) it means (2):

$$\mathit{f}(H\leftarrow@((B_1,...,B_n)))=\leftarrow\cdot(f(H),@\cdot(f(B_1),...,f(B_n))) \geq r \qquad (2)$$

A pair *(x; θ)* consisting of a real number 0<x≤1 and a substitution θ is a *correct answer* for a program P and a query "?-A" if for arbitrary interpretation f, which is a model of P, we have $\mathit{f}(\forall(A\theta))\geq x$.

We base our procedural semantics on the backward usage of *fuzzy modus ponens* (3) – no refutation nor resolution is applied here (we know by the residuality of C_i that this is a sound rule[21]).

$$\{(B. b), (H \leftarrow_I B. r)\} \models_{FLP} (H. C_i(b,r)) \qquad (3)$$

In the computation we deal with four types of inference rules:

Rule 1: from $((XA_mY);\upsilon)$ infer $((X\mathcal{C}(B,r)Y)\theta;\upsilon°\theta)$ if
- A_m is an atom (called the selected atom)
- θ is an mgu of A_m and H,
- P(H$\leftarrow$B)=r and B is a (nonempty) body.

$\mathcal{C}$ means a residual conjunction (see fuzzy modus ponens).

Rule 2: From (XA_mY) infer $(X0Y)$ if in an aggregation an argument is missing.

Rule 3: From $((XA_mY);\upsilon)$ infer $((XrY)\theta;\upsilon°\theta)$ if
- A_m is an atom (called the selected atom)
- θ is an mgu of A_m and A,
- P(A)=r (i.e. A is a fact).

Rule 4: If the word does not contain any predicate symbols rewrite all connectives (&'s, $\vee$'s and @'s) to $\&^\bullet$, $\vee^\bullet$ and $@^\bullet$. As this word contains only some additional $\mathcal{C}$'s and real numbers, evaluate it (of course the substitution remains untouched).

A pair *(r; θ)* consisting of a (rational) number r and a substitution θ is said to be a *computed answer* for a program P and a goal "?-A" if there is a sequence G_0, ..., G_n such that
- every G_i is a pair consisting of a word and a substitution,
- G_0=(A,id)
- every G_{i+1} is inferred from G_i by one of the inference rules (we do not forget the usual Prolog renaming of variables along derivation),
- G_n=(r,θ') and θ=θ' restricted to variables of A.

$$T_P(f)(A) = \max\{\sup\{C_i(f(B),r): (A\leftarrow_i B. r) \text{ is a ground instance of a rule in the program P}\}, \sup\{b: (A. b) \text{ is a ground instance of a fact in the program P}\}\}. \qquad (4)$$

We know that T_P *operator* (4) is continuous [21] and it's fixpoint is the minimal fuzzy model of the fuzzy logic program P.

Example 3. We find the minimal model of program from the example 2:

$T_P^0(0) = \varnothing$
$T_P^1(0) = T_P(T_P(0)) = \{p(a,b).3/4, p(b,c).1/4, p(a,d).2/3, p(d,c).1/3 \}$
$T_P^2(0) = T_P(T_P(T_P(0))) = \{p(a,b).3/4, p(b,c).1/4, p(a,d).2/3, p(d,c).1/3, p(a,c).2/9 \}$
$T_P^3(0) = T_P^2(0)$, so $T_P^2(0)$ is the minimal model of P

The truth value of the fact p(a,c) in the minimal model is computed as follows:

$T_P(0)(p(a,c)) = \max\{\sup\{\&_G(T_P^1(p(a,b)\&_Pp(b,c)),1/4), \&_G(T_P^1(p(a,d)\&_Pp(d,c)),1/4)\},0\}$
$=\max\{\sup\{\&_G(\&_P(3/4,1/4),1/4),\&_G(\&_P(2/3,1/3),1/4) \},0\}=$
$=\max\{\sup\{\&_G(3/4.1/4,1/4),\&_G(\&_P(2/3.1/3,1/4)\},0\}=$
$=\max\{\sup\{\min\{3/16,1/4\},\min\{2/9,1/4 \}\},0\}=\max\{\sup\{3/16,2/9\},0\}=2/9.$

From this computation we can see the inference rules and the many valued modus ponens. We show an example of a computation:

?-p(a,c).	// substitution {X/a, Y/b, Z/c}
?-$\&_G((p(a,b)\&_Pp(b,c)),1/4)$.	// $\&_G$ is residual to $\to_G$
?-$\&_G(\&_P(3/4,1/4),1/4)$.	// =min{3/4.1/4, 1/4}=3/16
?-3/16.	// the answer is 3/16
?-$\&_G((p(a,d)\&_Pp(d,c)),1/4)$.	// substitution {X/a, Y/d, Z/c}
?-$\&_G(\&_P(2/3,1/3),1/4)$.	// $\&_G$ is residual to $\to_G$
?-2/9.	// the answer is 2/9

Notice, that in classical logic programming (if we do not consider truth values, resp. every truth value is 1.0 in example 2) the answer to goal "?-p(a,c)." would be "yes".

Theorem 1 (soundness of our formal model of FLP [21]). Every computed answer for a definite fuzzy logic program P and a goal "?-A" is a correct answer.

Theorem 2 ((approximate) completeness of our formal model of FLP [21]). For every correct answer $(x;\theta)$ for a definite fuzzy logic program P and a query "?-A" and for every $\varepsilon > 0$ there is a computed answer $(r;\upsilon)$ for P and "?-A" such that $x-\varepsilon<r$ and $\theta=\upsilon\gamma$ (for some γ).

3 Fuzzy Inductive Logic Programming

The most important requirement to FILP is that its formal model must be a generalization of the classical ones (as every many valued logic is a generalization of the classical one).

Briefly, the task of ILP is to find a correct hypothesis from the sets of positive and negative examples under the presence of background knowledge. We distinguish three settings in Inductive Logic Programming (ILP), namely *learning from entailment* [6], *learning from interpretations* [2], and *learning from proofs* [5]. As we stated in the introductory part, we concentrate on learning from entailment setting in this paper:

Definition 1 (the learning from entailment setting of the ILP task). When *learning from entailment*, given is a set of examples $E = P \cup N$, consisting of positive P and negative N examples. Given is the background knowledge B. The task is to find a hypothesis H, such that the following conditions hold:

$(\forall e \in P)\ H \wedge B \models e$ *(crisp-completeness of H)*

$(\forall e \in N)\ H \wedge B \not\models e$ *(crisp-consistency of H)*

E consists of facts, B is a definite program, H consists of definite program clauses. The conditions of completeness and consistency mean that we want all positive examples to belong to the minimal model of $H \wedge B$ and none of the negative examples belong to the minimal model of $H \wedge B$.

In previous chapter we introduced the concepts necessary to formulate the FILP task (i.e. fuzzy Herbrand interpretation, fuzzy definite clause, fuzzy model, ...). These allows us to define the FILP task taking into account that it have to be a generalization of the classical ILP task.

We face a problem. A straightforward rewriting of classical ILP definition does not make sense because we have no clear positive and negative examples. From the semantics of truth values (see previous chapter) it is clear, that $e:\alpha \in E$ holds in all degrees $\alpha' \leq \alpha$ and does not holds in all degrees $\alpha'' > \alpha$. Thus the conditions of completeness and consistency will be different from the classical ones.

Definition 2 (the learning from entailment setting of the FILP task). When learning from fuzzy entailment, given is a set of fuzzy examples E. Given is the fuzzy background knowledge B. The task is to find a fuzzy hypothesis H, such that the following conditions hold:

$(\forall e.\alpha \in E)\ H \wedge B \models_{FLP} e.\alpha$ *(fuzzy-completeness of H)*

$(\forall e.\alpha \in E)\ (\forall \beta > \alpha)\ H \wedge B \not\models_{FLP} e.\beta$ *(fuzzy-consistency of H)*

E consists of fuzzy facts, B is a fuzzy definite program and H consists of fuzzy definite clauses. Nevertheless, these definitions seems to be very similar but they are still very different. First, the fuzzy meaning of a model, entailment, fact, definite program and definite clause differ from the classical meaning of these concepts. Second, in the FILP task we do not have only positive and negative examples. Indeed we have examples with truth values belonging to the interval [0,1]. However, the FILP task differs more from the classical ones it still remains it's generalization.

Observation 1. Our formal model of the FILP task (definition 2) is a generalization of the classical, crisp ILP task (definition 1).

Proof. Reduce the fuzzy truth value interval ftv=[0,1] (or ftv=[0,1]∩Q) to crisp truth value interval ctv={0,1}. As can be seen from our formal model of FLP (in the previous chapter), in this case fuzzy facts becomes crisp. In case of ctv the "fuzzy" examples e.0 and e.1 correspond to crisp negative and positive examples, respectively.

Similarly, for ctv the truth values of fuzzy conjunctions will correspond to truth values of crisp conjunctions (because the fuzzy conjunctions are the generalizations of the classical ones). Thus the fuzzy definite clauses and fuzzy definite programs will be equivalent to crisp definite clauses and crisp definite programs, respectively.

Now, we prove for ctv, that if the "fuzzy" hypothesis (respectively, its reduced crisp form) is fuzzy-complete, it is crisp-complete, too. The fuzzy-completeness condition $(\forall e.\alpha \in E)$ $H \wedge B \models_{FLP} e.\alpha$ holds, if $(H \wedge B)(e) \geq \alpha$ for every $e.\alpha \in E$. If $\alpha=1$ then $(H \wedge B)(e) \geq \alpha=1$. Thus $(H \wedge B)(e) \geq 1$ and since every truth value can be 0 or 1, $(H \wedge B)(e)=1$ what means that all "positive" examples $(e.\alpha=e.1)$ are entailed by $H \wedge B$.

Similarly, for ctv, if the "fuzzy" hypothesis (its reduced crisp form) is fuzzy-consistent, it is crisp-consistent, too. The fuzzy-consistency condition $(\forall e.\alpha \in E)$ $(\forall \beta > \alpha)$ $H \wedge B \not\models_{FLP} e.\beta$ holds, if $(H \wedge B)(e) < \beta$ for every $e.\alpha \in E$ and $\beta > \alpha$. If $\alpha=0$ then $\beta=1$. Thus $(H \wedge B)(e) < \beta=1$, so $(H \wedge B)(e) < 1$. Since every truth value can be 0 or 1, $(H \wedge B)(e)=0$ what means, that e does not belong to minimal model of $H \wedge B$. It means, that none of the "negative" examples $(e.\alpha=e.0)$ are entailed by $H \wedge B$.   □

As we see from the example 3, the deductive part of FLP is computationally not difficult. That is mainly, because we know all truth functions of connectives and aggregations. In the inductive part it is the opposite. In the beginning of induction we have just the known connectives or aggregations. But these need not to fit the data we are learning from. There can be (infinitely) many unknown types of connectives and aggregations (and thus hypotheses) our data correspond to.

There can be several approaches to solve the FILP task. For example, we can use just the known connectives, aggregations, and try to find some hypotheses. Another approach can be the genetic algorithms, where we can find some previously unknown connectives, aggregations in rules. We can construct several approaches by this way. All these approaches need to implement an own deductive part, because the inference is different from the classical Prolog inference (even though the fuzzy inference rules are the generalization of the Prolog inference rules).

There is an interesting approach to FILP task, namely to induce Generalized Annotated Programs (GAP) [14]. The advantage of this approach is that GAP deals with crisp connectives and they are "equivalent" to FLP [15], i.e. GAP can be transformed to FLP and FLP can be transformed to GAP. Notice that GAP differs from Logic Programs with Annotated Disjunctions [3], known in the ILP community.

Since our approach to FILP task is based on induction of GAP, we introduce GAP in the next chapter. So far we do not know about any inductive GAP system (also personally confirmed by V.S. Subrahmanian [14]).

4   Generalized Annotated Programs

In [14] the generalized annotated logic programs (GAP) that unify and generalize various results and treatments of multivalued logic programming are introduced.

In multivalued logic, the set of truth values represents our set of preferences, the degree of trustworthiness of data, or the relevancy of information. The whole theory of GAP is developed in a general setting for truth value set being lattices. We restrict here ourselves to finite subsets of the unit interval of real numbers [0,1].

The language of annotated programs consists of qualitative and quantitative parts. The qualitative part is the usual language of predicate logic (with variables, constants, predicates and function symbols). The quantitative part of the language in our approach is typed (sorted) and for each logical predicate p there is a (possibly different) truth values set T_P with ordering $\leq_P$. The quantitative part of the language consists of annotation terms. These are composed from annotation variables, annotation constants and a set of basic annotation functions of different arity. Every basic annotation term (considered as a symbol of our alphabet) is assigned an annotation function. In [14] it is assumed that every annotation function is total continuous (hence monotonic) in the sense of lattice theory. This lattice continuity means that all annotation functions are non-decreasing and left continuous in the topology of real line. More complex annotation terms are built from these annotation functions preserving arity.

If A is an atomic formula and α is an annotation term, then A:α is an *annotated atom*. If $\alpha \in [0, 1]$ then A:α_is constant-annotated (or c-annotated). When α is an annotation variable, then A:α_is said to be variable-annotated (or v-annotated).

If A:ρ is a possibly complex annotated atom and $B_1:\mu_1$, ..., $B_k:\mu_k$ are variable-annotated atoms, then A:$\rho(\mu_1, ..., \mu_k) \leftarrow B_1:\mu_1$ & ... & $B_k:\mu_k$ is an *annotated clause*.

We stress here, that atoms in the body of a rule have only variable annotations (to avoid problems with discontinuous restricted semantics). Only facts can have constant annotations. We assume that variables occurring in the annotation of the head also appear as annotations of the body literals and different literals in the body are annotated with different variables. All object and annotation variables are assumed to be generally quantified.

Let B_L be the Herbrand base of the qualitative part of the GAP language. A mapping f: $B_L \rightarrow [0,1]$ is said to be a *Herbrand interpretation for annotated logic*.

The satisfaction is defined along the complexity of formulas as in the classical logic.

Suppose f: $B_L \rightarrow [0,1]$ is an interpretation, $\mu \in [0,1]$ and A is ground atom, then f$\models_{GAP}$ A:μ, i.e. f is a *model* of A:μ iff f(A) $\geq \mu$. The rest of satisfaction is defined similarly as in the two valued logic:

> f $\models_{GAP}$ F_1&F_2 iff f is a model of F_1 and f is a model of F_2.
> f $\models_{GAP}$ $F_1 \vee F_2$ iff f is a model of F_1 or f is a model of F_2.
> f $\models_{GAP}$ F1$\leftarrow$F2 iff f is a model of F_1 or f is not a model of F_2.

Quantification of object or annotated variables is defined as usual by substitution of ground terms (object or annotation).

Example 4. In the case of propositional logic the Herbrand base is represented by the set of propositional variables PV. Assume, we have an annotated clause

C= p:(1+2x)/4 $\leftarrow$ p:x and an interpretation f: PV $\rightarrow$ [0, 1].

Then f $\models_{GAP}$ C iff for every x from the unit interval [0, 1], f(p)$\geq$x implies f(p)$\geq$(1+2x)/4. It is fulfilled, if f(p)$\geq$1/2.

Example 5. Constantly annotated clauses are important for applications, because they can describe dependencies observed in data. Assume we have an annotated clause D= q:0.5 $\leftarrow$ p:0.5 and an interpretation f: PV $\rightarrow$ [0, 1].

Then f $\models_{GAP}$ D if either f(p)<0.5 or f(q)≥0.5. This rule with constant annotation illustrates also discontinuity of restricted semantics, because in every model f(q) ≥0.5 but no finite computation can confirm this.

In other words, we can say, that the annotated rule is true in the interpretation f

$$f \models_{GAP} A{:}\rho\,(\mu_1, ..., \mu_k) \leftarrow B_1{:}\mu_1\,\&\,...\,\&\,B_k{:}\mu_k$$
if for all assignments e of annotation variables we have   (5)
$$f(A) \geq_A \rho(e(\mu_1), ..., e(\mu_k)) \leftarrow f(B_1) \geq_{B1} e(\mu_1)\,\&\,...\,\&\,\,f(B_k) \geq_{Bk} e(\mu_k)$$

Definition 3 (FLP and GAP transformations [15]). Assume C= A:ρ ← $B_1{:}\mu_1$ &...
...& $B_k{:}\mu_k$ is an annotated clause. Then flp(C) is the fuzzy rule A← ρ($B_1,...,B_k$).1, here ρ is understood as an n-ary aggregator operator.

Assume D = A←$_i$ @($B_1,...,B_n$).r is a fuzzy logic program rule. Then gap(D) is the annotated clause A:C_i(@($x_1,...,x_n$),r) ← $B_1{:}x_1,...,B_n{:}x_n$.

The definition 3 enable to us to transform FLP programs to GAP programs and vice versa. Note, that this transformation is on the syntactical level. The next theorem 3 claims the equivalence of FLP and GAP on the syntactical level.

Theorem 3 (FLP and GAP equivalence [15]). ssume C is an annotated clause, D is a fuzzy logic program rule and F is a fuzzy Herbrand interpretation. Then

f is a model of C iff f is a model of flp(C),
f is a model of D iff f is a model of gap(C).

5   Inductive Generalized Annotated Programming

Because of definition 3 and theorem 3 we can construct an alternative approach to our FILP task. By this idea we transform the FILP task to Inductive Generalized Annotated Programming (IGAP) task. We find an IGAP hypothesis (GAP program) what we again transform to FILP hypothesis (FLP program).

Definition 4 (the learning from entailment setting of the IGAP task). When learning from GAP entailment, given is a set of GAP examples E. Given is the GAP background knowledge B. The task is to find a GAP hypothesis H, such that the following conditions hold:

$(\forall e.\alpha \in E)$ H∧B $\models_{GAP}$ e.α *(gap-completeness of H)*
$(\forall e.\alpha \in E)\,(\forall \beta > \alpha)$ H∧B $\not\models_{GAP}$ e.β *(gap-consistency of H)*

Observation 2. The FILP task can be transformed to IGAP task and the IGAP task can be transformed to FILP task.

Proof: Arising from equivalence of FLP and GAP (definition 3 and theorem 3).   □

In [12] we have introduced our approach to IGAP task, although the above formal model (definition 4) was not determined yet.

Our approach to IGAP is based on multiple use of a classical ILP system with monotonicity axioms in the background knowledge (illustrated in algorithm 1).

Algorithm 1. Our IGAP approach

Input: Annotated E, Annotated B.
Output: Annotated H.
1. Initialize the two-valued hypothesis $H^* = \emptyset$.
2. Find out every n classes of truth values which are present in E ($TV_1 < \ldots < TV_n$).
3. Find out every $m_1, \ldots, m_k$ classes of truth values which are present in B for every predicate $p_1, \ldots, p_k$ ($TVp_{1,1} < \ldots < TVp_{1,m1}, \ldots, TVp_{k,1} < \ldots < TVp_{k,mk}$).
4. Transform the annotated background knowledge B to a two-valued background knowledge B^* by an extra attribute TV ($p_i(x_1, \ldots, x_{is}):TVp_{i,j} \Rightarrow p_i(x_1, \ldots, x_{is}, TVp_{i,j})$).
5. Add monotonicity axioms to B^* for every annotated predicate p_i, $i \in \{1, \ldots, k\}$
   ($p_i(x_1, \ldots, x_{is}, X) \leftarrow le(X, Y), p_i(x_1, \ldots, x_{is}, Y).,$
   $le(TVp_{i,1}, TVp_{i,2})., \ldots, le(TVp_{i,mi-1}, TVp_{i,mi}).$)
6. For all TV_i, where $1 < i \leq n$ do the following:
   a. split the example set E to negative $E- = \{e:\alpha \in E | \alpha < TV_i\}$ and positive $E+ = \{e:\alpha \in E | \alpha \geq TV_i\}$ parts.
   b. With the ILP system ALEPH compute the hypothesis H_i^* for the two-valued background knowledge B, positive E+, and negative E- examples.
   c. Add the hypothesis H_i^* to H^*.
7. Transform two-valued hypothesis H^* to annotated hypothesis H by transforming the extra attributes TV in literals back ($p_i(x_1, \ldots, x_{is}, TVp_{i,j}) \Rightarrow p_i(x_1, \ldots, x_{is}):TVp_{i,j}$).

Informally, we search every present truth values of examples and background knowledge predicates. Then we transform predicates in B to crisp form, thus achieving crisp background knowledge B^*. Then we extend B^* with the "monotonicity axioms" which states that if the predicate holds with truth Y it also holds in truth X less or equal to Y. Predicates "le" states the relation less or equal. This correspond to natural meaning of truth values to B^*. Then we split the example set to positive and negative parts according to truth values present in E as follows: learning rules that guarantee our annotation function has value at least α, every example higher or equal than α belongs to positive example set, the others create the negative example set (note that when learning witness for α in B* all truth values take part). Thus, the hypothesis for the grade α holds in grade "at least" α, what agree with the natural meaning of truth in GAP.

Example 6. The background knowledge consist of crisp facts of "hotel(hotel_name, location, price)", "conference(name, location)" and annotated facts of "cheap(price)", "near(location1, location2)":

hotel(africa,centre,20).   hotel(america,east,50).   hotel(antarctica,west,80).
hotel(australia,east,110).   hotel(asia,west,50).   hotel(europe,centre,80).
conference(icml,centre).   conference(ecml,east).   conference(ilp,west).
cheap(20):1.0   cheap(50):0.7   cheap(80):0.4   cheap(110):0.1
near(centre,centre):1.0   near(east,centre):0.7   near(west,centre):0.4
near(centre,east):0.7   near(east,east):1.0   near(west,east):0.1
near(centre,west):0.4   near(east,west):0.1   near(west,west):1.0

The example set consist of annotated facts of "good(hotel,conference_for)":

good (africa,icml):1.0   good(america,icml):1.0   good(antarctica,icml):0.4
good(australia,icml):0.1   good(asia,icml):0.7   good(europe,icml):0.4
good(africa,ecml):1.0   good(america,ecml):1.0   good(antarctica,ecml):0.1
good(australia,ecml):0.1   good(asia,ecml):0.1   good(europe,ecml):0.4
good(africa,ilp):0.7   good(america,ilp):0.1   good(antarctica,ilp):0.4
good(australia,ilp):0.1   good(asia,ilp):1.0   good(europe,ilp):0.4

The annotated hypothesis (result of our approach) is the following:

good(A,B):1.0 :- hotel(A,C,D), cheap(D):0.7, conference(B,C).
good(A,B):1.0 :- hotel(A,C,D), cheap(D):0.7, conference(B,E), near(E,C):0.7.
good(A,B):0.7 :- hotel(A,C,D), cheap(D):0.7, conference(B,E), near(E,C):0.4.
good(A,B):0.4 :- hotel(A,C,D), cheap(D):0.4, conference(B,E), near(E,C):0.4.

All these rules cover all positive examples (in relevant truth). The meaning of these rules (for example for the third rule) is "if a hotel is cheap with truth (at least) 0.7 and near to conference location with truth (at least) 0.4 then this hotel is good for the conference with truth (at least) 0.7".

Our illustrative example 6 is very simple but convenient for demonstration. As we see, we deal with mixed (crisp and annotated) predicates. However, in case of our example the completeness and consistency conditions are fulfilled. In general, it often happens that the completeness condition do not hold. But the consistency condition is always fulfilled (proved in theorem 4).

Theorem 4. Given annotated B and annotated E. Our algorithm 1 finds a gap-consistent annotated hypothesis H.

Proof: The gap-consistency condition requires that for every e:α∈E the following holds $(\forall \beta > \alpha)$ H∧B $\not\models$ $_{GAP}$ e:β, so the minimal model $M_{H∧B}$ of H∧B can not assign a truth value β (higher than α) to example e:α. By contradiction, assume that our algorithm assigns a truth value β higher than α to an example e:α. From the construction of positive and negative example sets in our algorithm, and from the consistency of ALEPH (the hypothesis can not cover negative examples) it is clear that an example e:α can be covered only with a hypothesis of the truth value δ≤α. So, it is not possible that minimal model $M_{H∧B}$ assigns truth value β to the example e:α. It is a contradiction.   □

Notice, that it can happen, that we do not cover an example e:α right in the grade α, but in grade δ<α. So, that means, that our algorithm can find hypotheses that are not complete.

Observation 3. Given fuzzy B and fuzzy E. Let us transform the fuzzy E and fuzzy B to annotated E_A and annotated B_A, compute with our algorithm 1 an annotated hypothesis H_A and transform this H_A to fuzzy H. Then this fuzzy H is fuzzy-consistent.
Proof: Arising from observation 2.   □

Observation 4. Given an annotated B and annotated E. Our algorithm 1 finds an annotated H such that

$$E \models_{GAP} H∧B$$

Proof: This relation means, that E assigns a truth value higher than H∧B to an example e:α (E(e)≥H∧B(e)). From our algorithm and the theorem 4 it is clear, that an example e:α is covered with a hypothesis of the truth value δ≤α.   □

Our approach (algorithm 1) is implemented in the Slovak project "NAZOU – Tools for acquisition, organization and maintenance of knowledge in an environment of heterogeneous information resources" [19]. Our method in this project is used to learn the user's preferences [9]. To explain the idea imagine a situation from example 6. Say, that the user wants to find a hotel in a selected city with a few hundreds of hotels. We want to serve to the user the preferable hotels first. We do it as follows: The objects are given to the user without any knowledge about him/her preferences. He/she evaluates a couple of hotels in several classes – e.g. poor (0.1), good (0.7) and excellent (1.0) – and restarts the search. Then – by our approach – the user's classification is learned and the hotels are given to him/her according to his/her preferences. The process is repeated until the convenient hotels are founded.

Our approach was successfully applied to measuring impact of information systems on business competitiveness [10] and to classify cars according to their fuel consumption for the well known auto-mpg database from the UCI repository [11]. In all of these applications, our approach was used for ordinal (monotone) classification. Since, our aim in this paper is to give a formal model for FILP (and not to introduce our approach), we omit the descriptions of these experiments. We introduced the formal model of IGAP because it seems to be an interesting approach to FILP.

6 Fuzzy Data vs. Crisp Data

As mentioned before, our approach is used to learn user preferences [9] in the NAZOU project [19]. If we talk about user's preferences, an interesting phenomenon arises: *The crisp data becomes fuzzy in the moment, if the user evaluates them.* Let's explain it on example:

Example 7. Imagine, we have one hotel which costs 70$/night and is located 2km far from the conference location. For a student this hotel is "cheap" with truth value 0.1 and "near" with truth value 0.8. For a professor, the situation is a little bit different, this hotel is "cheap" and "near" with truth values 0.4. Finally, a manager of an international company evaluates this hotel as "cheap" with truth value 0.9 and "near" with truth value 0.1.

We see (example 7) that every crisp attribute can be evaluated variously according to the user. This is an advantage of the fuzzy framework, that we can easily represent every type of "ordering of the domains of attributes". This evaluations (orderings of attribute domains) we can easily represent by *fuzzy membership functions* (figure 1).

Note, that in our approach we can easily encode all types of orderings, in case of continuous and discrete attribute domains, too (in case of continuous attributes, we discretize the attribute domain to intervals and we encode the ordering of these intervals).

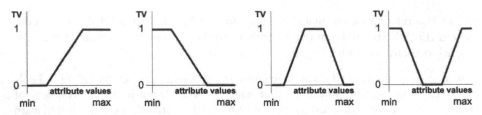

Fig. 1. The four main types of fuzzy membership functions. The higher values the better, the lowest values the better, the middle values the better and the marginal values the better (from left to right).

In the project NAZOU [19] we implemented to our algorithm a module which checks the ordering of the attribute domain. It is achieved by adjusted statistical regression or by the algorithm QUIN [4] for learning qualitative models. Moreover, there is implemented a module, which allows to user to specify his/her orderings.

7 Recent Work

To create a more suitable set of rules using ILP in [1] an algorithm called FS FOIL was developed, that extends the original FOIL algorithm, modified to be able to handle first order fuzzy predicates where cover compares confidence and support of fuzzy predicates. A version of FOIL that handles membership degree has already been developed in [20] but the rules induced still keep a classical meaning. In [17] a system enriching relational learning with several types of fuzzy rules - flexible, gradual and certainty - was introduced. In this approach a fuzzy rule is associated by crisp rules where the truth of a head is the same or complementary of the truth of a body (on an α-cut). These types of rules are considered in [18], too, where hypotheses are computed by a fixed T-norm and are more flexible as in [17]. All these approaches are using vague linguistic hedges and are implemented in FOIL. All these approaches are using vague linguistic hedges and are implemented in FOIL. These approaches have some disadvantages: [20] uses only Lukasiewicz logic, [18] and [20] deals with fixed types of fuzzy rules, moreover in [18] the truth values of the head of a rule and the body have the same truth value (or they are complements α and 1-α) while in [20] a fixed t-norm (aggregation) is used in learning.

As we mentioned before we do not know about any inductive GAP system.

Our FILP task does not consider probability distributions as in probabilistic models [5]. Embedding of FILP to Bayesian Logic Programs (BLP) is studied in [22]. In [23] the transformations of GAP to several frameworks are introduced (shown on figure 2). In each of these models of logic programs we have sound and complete continuous semantics with production operator and minimal Herbrand model. Moreover all models have the syntactic and computational part same as in classical Logic Programs [16]. Models differ in quantitative (many valued, probabilistic) part.

Finally, note that GAP (and thus FLP) differs from Logic Programs with Annotated Disjunctions (LPAD) [3]. An LPAD rule is a first order logic clause where the head literals are annotated with probabilities $((h_1:\alpha_1), (h_2:\alpha_2), ..., (h_n:\alpha_n) \leftarrow b_1, b_2, ..., b_m)$, where h_i and b_i are crisp literals and $\alpha_i \in [0,1]$. As we see, this rule have no annotated literals in body. Moreover in GAP rules α means the truth of a literal while in LPAD rule α means the probability of a literal being true (what is the difference between the fuzzy and probabilistic frameworks).

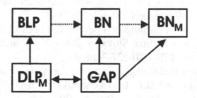

Fig. 2. The transformations of GAP to models of Bayesian Logic Programs (BLP [13]), Bayesian Nets (BN [8]), Definite Logic Programs with monotonicity axioms (DLP$_M$) and a special monotonised version of BN (BN$_M$)

8 Conclusions

The main contribution of paper was to give a correct and sound formal model of FILP and IGAP. For this purpose we described our complete and sound FLP model, our formal model of FILP is based on. We showed that FILP is a generalization of ILP. We introduced the framework of GAP (equivalent to FLP). This enables us to introduce the formal model of IGAP. We showed that the IGAP is equivalent to FILP. We described our approach to IGAP and show that it is gap-consistent and thus, fuzzy-consistent. We mentioned about fuzzy membership functions and stated that these functions are user specific and thus we can not compute with fixed fuzzy membership functions. We described an application of our approach for induction of user preferences in a web search application. Finally we described recent works in fuzzy ILP and compared GAP with other probabilistic approaches.

Acknowledgement. *Supported by Czech project 1ET 100300517 and Slovak projects VEGA 1/3129/06 and NAZOU.*

References

[1] Bodenhofer, U., Drobics, M., Klement, E-P.: FS-FOIL: An Inductive learning method for extracting interpretable fuzzy descriptions. Int.J. Approximate Reasoning 32, 131–152 (2003)
[2] Blockeel, H., Raedt, L.D., Jacobs, N.: Scaling up inductive logic programming by learning from interpretations. Data Mining and Knowledge Discovery 3(1), 59–93 (1999)
[3] Blockeel, H: Two Novel Methods for Learning Logic Prorams with Annotated Disjunctions. In: Proceedings of short papers on ILP '06, Santiago De Compostela, Spain, UDC Press Service, pp. 31–33 (2006) ISBN:84-9749-206-4
[4] Bratko, I., Šuc, D.: Learning qualitative models. AI Magazine 24, 107–119 (2003)
[5] De Raedt, L., Kersting, K.: Probabilistic Inductive Logic Programming. In: Ben-David, S., Case, J., Maruoka, A. (eds.) ALT 2004. LNCS (LNAI), vol. 3244, pp. 19–36. Springer, Heidelberg (2004)

[6] Džeroski, S., Lavrač, N.: An introduction to inductive logic programming. In: Džeroski, S., Lavrač, N. (eds.) Relational data mining, pp. 48–73. Springer, Heidelberg (2001)

[7] Getoor, L., et al.: Learning probabilistic relational models. In: Džeroski, S., Lavrač, N. (eds.) Relational data mining, pp. 307–335. Springer, Heidelberg (2001)

[8] Heckerman, D.: A Tutorial on Learning with Bayesian Networks. Technical Report MSR-TR-95-06, Microsoft Research (March 1995)

[9] Horváth, T.: Unsupervised Learning of User Preferences by Ordinal Classification. In: Workshop NAZOU, Bystra Dolina, Slovakia, 2006: Vydavatelstvo STU. Bratislava, Slovakia, pp. 125–134 (2006) ISBN 80-227-2468-8

[10] Horváth, T., Sudzina, F.: Measuring impact of information systems on business competitiveness using regression and ILP. In: Ekonomika firiem, Michalovce, Slovakia, 2004: PHF EU Bratislava, Košice, Slovakia, 2004, pp. 296–300 (2004) ISBN 80-225-1879-4

[11] Horváth, T., Vojtáš, P.: GAP - Rule Discovery for Graded Classifciation. In: Fuernkranz, J. (eds.) Workshop of Advances in Inductive Rule Learning (W8) of ECML/PKDD '04, Pisa, Italy, 2004: TU Darmstadt, Darmstadt, Germany, 2004, pp. 46–63 (2004)

[12] Horváth, T., Vojtáš, P.: Fuzzy induction via generalized annotated programs. In: FDD '04, Dortmund, Germany, 2004, pp. 419–433. Springer, Heidelberg (2005)

[13] Kersting, K., De Raedt, L.: Bayesian Logic Programs, Technical Report 151, University of Freiburg, 52 pages

[14] Kifer, M., Subrahmanian, V.S.: Theory of generalized annotated logic programming and its applications. J. Logic Programming 12, 335–367 (1992)

[15] Krajči, S., Lencses, R., Vojtáš, P.: A comparison of fuzzy and annotated logic programming. Fuzzy Sets and Systems 144, 173–192 (2004)

[16] Lloyd, J.W.: Foundations of Logic Programming. Springer, Heidelberg (1987)

[17] Prade, H., Richard, G., Serrurier, M.: Enriching relational Learning with fuzzy predicates. In: Lavrač, N., Gamberger, D., Todorovski, L., Blockeel, H. (eds.) PKDD 2003. LNCS (LNAI), vol. 2838, pp. 399–410. Springer, Heidelberg (2003)

[18] Prade, H., Richard, G., Dubois, D., Sudkamp, T., Serrurier, M.: Learning first order fuzzy rules with their implication operator. In. Proc. of IPMU (2004)

[19] Project NAZOU: http://nazou.fiit.stuba.sk/

[20] Shibata, D., et al.: An induction algorithm based on fuzzy logic programming. In: Zhong, N., Zhou, L. (eds.) Methodologies for Knowledge Discovery and Data Mining. LNCS (LNAI), vol. 1574, pp. 268–273. Springer, Heidelberg (1999)

[21] Vojtáš, P.: Fuzzy logic programming. Fuzzy Sets and Systems 124(3), 361–370 (2004)

[22] Vojtáš, P., Vomlelová, M.: Transformation of deductive and inductive tasks between models of logic programming with imperfect information. In: Proceedings of IPMU, Editrice Universita La Sapienza, Roma, pp. 839–846 (2004)

[23] Vojtáš, P., Vomlelová, M.: On models of comparison of multiple monotone classifications. In: Proc. IPMU'2006, Paris, France, Éditions EDK, Paris, pp. 1236–1243

Boosting Descriptive ILP for Predictive Learning in Bioinformatics

Ning Jiang and Simon Colton

Department of Computing, Imperial College, London
{nj2,sgc}@doc.ic.ac.uk

Abstract. Boosting is an established propositional learning method to promote the predictive accuracy of weak learning algorithms, and has achieved much empirical success. However, there have been relatively few efforts to apply boosting to Inductive Logic Programming (ILP) approaches. We investigate the use of boosting descriptive ILP systems, by proposing a novel algorithm for generating classification rules which searches using a hybrid language bias/production rule approach, and a new method for converting first-order classification rules to binary classifiers, which increases the predictive accuracy of the boosted classifiers. We demonstrate that our boosted approach is competitive with normal ILP systems in experiments with bioinformatics datasets.

1 Introduction

Inductive Logic Programming (ILP) has been very successful in application to relational predictive tasks. Sophisticated predictive ILP systems, such as Progol [1] and FOIL [2], can achieve high predictive accuracy, while the learning results remain understandable. To achieve higher predictive accuracy, there have been attempts to combine ILP with propositional learning algorithms, such as Support Vector Machines [3]. While the predictive accuracy of such systems can be better than ILP systems, the learning results can be less understandable due to the complex representations employed.

Boosting [4] is an established method to increase the predictive accuracy of other learning algorithms, which are known as base learners. The result of boosting is a weighted sum of the predictions of the classifiers received from the base learner, and therefore can be easily understood. Although boosting has many advantageous characteristics, there have been relatively few efforts to apply it to ILP systems. Some studies include [5], which applied AdaBoost [4] to the FFOIL ILP system, and [6], in which MOLFEA, a domain-specific ILP system, was used as the base learner for AdaBoost. While these studies showed that the predictive accuracy of ILP can often be increased by boosting, there is still much room for improvement. In particular, the run-time performance of ILP systems becomes an issue because AdaBoost has to invoke them many times to produce base classifiers. This prevents boosting from running more iterations to achieve higher predictive accuracy. Also, base classifiers generated by these ILP systems tend to be fairly accurate, which causes boosting to converge quickly, hence it

S. Muggleton, R. Otero, and A. Tamaddoni-Nezhad (Eds.): ILP 2006, LNAI 4455, pp. 275–289, 2007.

is liable to overfitting, particularly on noisy datasets. Moreover, boosting needs to apply a weighting over training examples when the base learner is invoked, and it expects that the base learner can minimise the weighted training error instead of the normal one. As ILP systems are usually not able to handle weighted examples, resampling is adopted, in which low weighted examples may be lost.

To attempt to overcome these weaknesses, we have investigated the use of boosting with descriptive ILP systems, which generate first-order classification rules from training data in a class-blind manner. In order to control the generation of classification rules, we have introduced a novel descriptive ILP system that employs a declarative language bias which in turn enables a new method to convert classification rules to binary classifiers. We present the results of this approach for four bioinformatics datasets, and show that our method is competitive with state of the art ILP systems.

This paper is structured as follows. Section 2 gives a brief introduction to descriptive ILP and boosting algorithms. An overview of our boosted descriptive ILP approach is given at the beginning of section 3, followed by the details of the language bias, rule conversion and boosting steps. The benefits of combining boosting with ILP is also explained. Our experiments with bioinformatics datasets are described in section 4, and we describe some directions for further work in section 5.

2   Background

2.1   Boosting

Boosting is a machine learning algorithm that attempts to increase the predictive accuracy of a weak learning algorithm (known as a base learner) by aggregating multiple classifiers from it (known as base classifiers). Early studies of boosting were motivated by Kearns and Valiant's research on the PAC learning model [7]. The most widely used boosting algorithm, AdaBoost, was introduced by Freund and Schapire [4]. AdaBoost is simple to implement, and has many favourable characteristics. In particular, while the learning algorithm is understood as a stepwise optimisation [8] in training accuracy, its generalisation error is efficiently bounded by margins independent of the number of base classifiers [9,10]. The effectiveness of AdaBoost at minimising margins was observed in early experiments: the generalisation error often keeps dropping even after the training error reaches zero. However, it was later found that AdaBoost does overfit sometimes, especially when the data is noisy [11]. A strong connection between AdaBoost and logistic regression was also discovered [12], which showed that both algorithms essentially solve the same constrained optimisation problems.

The AdaBoost algorithm tries to construct an accurate combining classifier via a weighted majority vote of base classifiers. The base classifiers are obtained by repeatedly calling the base learner, which is supplied with a weighting that affects the evaluation of training errors of the base learner. Each time it is called, the base learner is applied to the training examples and returns the classifier which minimises the weighted training error. AdaBoost then chooses a weight for the received base classifier according to the weighted training error and updates the weighting of training examples such that the total weight of correctly classified examples are the same as that of misclassified examples. This process is repeated until AdaBoost has received a specified number of base classifiers – a typical setting of 200 to 300 base classifiers is widely used. The final classifier is the weighted sum of all of the received base classifiers.

2.2 Descriptive ILP

In contrast to predictive learning, which learns a target concept from labelled examples, a descriptive learning system requires no class labels when performing non-predictive learning tasks such as association rule learning and frequent pattern discovery. Descriptive ILP systems often perform learning from interpretations [13], assuming each training example is an independent set of ground facts and using coverage tests to validate candidate rules or patterns. Such patterns are referred to as *classification rules* in this paper, as each rule specifies a binary classification of objects according to the truth-value. Without any limitation, descriptive ILP systems search over an excessively large rule space, and this may require an impractically long time to finish. To avoid this problem, searching is often limited to a specific type of rule specified by an explicit declarative *language bias*. Well known descriptive ILP systems include $\mathcal{C}$LAUDIEN [14] and HR [15].

$\mathcal{C}$LAUDIEN performs characterising induction on positive examples to produce classification rules which characterise training examples. To restrict the language to search over, $\mathcal{C}$LAUDIEN employs the $\mathcal{D}$LAB language bias. $\mathcal{D}$LAB defines the syntax of association rules by using a grammar that has the expressive power of a regular expression, but with a more convenient notation.

We refer to this type of language bias as a *syntactical language bias*. In contrast, other ILP systems use a *constructive language bias*, which operates by repeatedly applying production rules to existing classification rules to construct new ones. Note that in a syntactical language bias, production rules are used differently, namely to develop an intermediate rule into either another intermediate rule or a classification rule (as is the case in a context-free grammar). An important difference between the two types of language biases is that constructive language biases typically allow for recursive language definitions, producing infinite language spaces and usually requiring classification rules to meet other constraints, such as the maximum number of literals in a rule. In contrast, syntactical language biases generally do not take recursive definitions, and produce a finite search space.

HR is a descriptive ILP system that performs automated theory formation via a constructive language bias [15]. Starting from a set of initial classification rules provided as background knowledge, HR repeatedly applies a set of production rules to develop an existing rule or combine two existing rules. For instance, the *compose* rule makes conjunctions of two existing classification rules, while the *split* rule instantiates some variables in an existing classification rule. HR employs a weighted sum – with weights provided by the user – of measures of interestingness to guide the search for classification rules.

3 Boosting Descriptive ILP

Our boosted descriptive ILP approach is composed of three steps:

Rule generation. In this step, a new descriptive ILP system, *WeakILP*, is used to produce a set of first order classification rules, which are specified in a syntactical language bias. The rules may have to meet certain criteria with respect to training examples and background knowledge.

Rule conversion. In this step, the received classification rules are converted into binary classifiers, from which boosting chooses base classifiers. Different rule conversion methods may be used, as discussed in section 3.2.

Boosting. In this step, we use an adaptation of AdaBoost to choose some classifiers to aggregate into the boosted classifier. Instead of specifying the number of base classifiers in advance, we employ cross validation sets to determine when to stop adding base classifiers.

Compared to existing boosted ILP approaches, our descriptive ILP based approach has certain advantages. Firstly, the new framework separates the ILP and boosting steps, which avoids the necessity of resampling weighted examples. Hence, the boosting step can handle weightings of examples more accurately. Secondly, the learning process is more efficient, because descriptive ILP is invoked only once. This enables boosting to run as many rounds as necessary without significant increase in computational time. In previous boosted ILP experiments, such as [5], the number of base classifiers was set to between 10 and 20, whereas the typical setting in our experiments is between 50 and 200 base classifiers. In general, this means that a higher predictive accuracy can be achieved. Thirdly, although some predictive ILP systems may produce multiple classification rules at once, descriptive ILP can make better use of boosting. Boosting's performance is conditional on the ability of the base learner to return a proper[1] base classifier for arbitrarily weighted training examples. As descriptive ILP does not have a target concept to learn, classification rules from it describe a wide variety of classifications of training examples. Hence, rules from a descriptive ILP system are much more likely to fit different weightings than those from predictive ILP, which enables boosting to perform properly.

3.1 Rule Generation

Our approach employs descriptive ILP to exhaustively generate classification rules, regardless of accuracy. In contrast to predictive ILP which produces only a few of the most accurate rules, the number of rules generated in this step may

---

[1] The weighted training error of a proper base classifier must be less than 50% for binary learning tasks.

be quite large. Hence, to improve efficiency, it is essential to have an expressive language bias to specify a language where no rule is irrelevant to the learning target.

As an example, a typical learning task in bioinformatics is to predict a certain biological characteristic of a molecule given its structural information, usually atoms in the molecule and bonds between atoms. For simplicity, we assume the predicates are of the form: $atom(X, A, E)$ and $bond(X, A, B)$, where X is the unique identifier of a molecule, A and B are atoms, and E represents the element type of atom A. Continuing with the example, suppose that domain experts believe that the biological characteristic is determined by linear (i.e., non-cyclic) connected substructures of the molecule. In this case, we need a language which specifies a sequence of atoms of any type and any length.

This is not straightforward to specify with existing syntactical language biases, as the maximum number of variables in the rule is indefinite due to the indefinite length of the sequence. Hence, because existing syntactical language biases do not allow recursive production rules, to cover all rules in this language, we have to use a more powerful language specification. However, existing constructive language biases also have difficulty to restrict rules to non-cyclic sequences of atoms, and often an excessive number of irrelevant rules are produced. Our solution has been to develop a new light-weight descriptive ILP system, called WeakILP, which uses a syntactical language bias of more expressive power. WeakILP allows recursive production rules and can employ a novel rule conversion approach.

Language bias
A classification rule in WeakILP has the following form:

$$rule(X, \{X_1, X_2, \ldots\}) : Body$$

where X represents the object to classify (i.e., a training or test set example), $\{X_1, X_2, \ldots\}$ is a set of *key variables* which occur in the *Body*, which is a well-formed formula in first-order logic[2], though it is often a conjunction of literals. For example, below is a rule specifying a non-cyclic sub-molecule structure:

$$rule(X, \{A, B, C\}) : atom(X, A, o) \wedge bond(X, A, B) \wedge bond(X, B, C) \wedge atom(X, C, n)$$

where X is the molecule to classify and A, B and C are strictly different atoms.

The set of key variables is referred to as a *key set*, which is used to highlight interesting properties or structures of the rule. In the above example, the variables A, B and C can help identify each unique occurrence of the substructure. To specify key sets for classification rules and allow recursive definitions in the language, WeakILP adopts a new syntactical language bias. The language bias defines the grammar of classification rules by using production rules.

---

[2] Note that *Body* is not theoretically restricted to first-order logic, as the language bias is simply a set of grammatical definitions. Any logic can be accepted if the produced rules can be interpreted by the runtime system. Our current implementation is based on Prolog, hence rules are restricted to Prolog queries. In the experiments presented here, all classification rules are a conjunction of literals.

A grammar is composed of several production rules: $A_1 \to B_1, \ldots, A_k \to B_k$, where each A_i is a positive literal or a function symbol, to be replaced by one of the formulae on the right-hand side, and B_i is a well-formed formula. Each A_i is a *nonterminal symbol*, as defined below.

Definition 1 (Terminal and Nonterminal symbols). *A nonterminal symbol is any positive literal which occurs on the left-hand side of a production rule, and may or may not be ground. The nonterminal symbol is in fact a placeholder, which is absent from the produced classification rules. On the other hand, literals which must occur in the produced classification rules are called terminal symbols.*

Note that, to avoid confusion, any nonterminal symbol must not be used as a terminal symbol.

A replacing formula, B_i, can be any well-formed logic formula, which may include nonterminal symbols to allow recursive definitions of rules. In particular, to allow the specification of the key set, some variables may be enclosed by the function symbol $key/1$. In the generated classification rules (which include no nonterminal symbol), if a variable occurs in a $key/1$ functor, it will be put into the key set, and the functor itself will be ignored.

The following is an example of the syntactical grammar which defines a sequence of atoms of arbitrary length for the above bioinformatics problem.

$$rule(X) \to sequence(X, key(A) \wedge key(B))$$
$$sequence(X, A, B) \to bond(X, A, B)$$
$$sequence(X, A, B) \to bond(X, A, key(C)) \wedge sequence(X, key(C), B)$$

The above grammar produces classification rules, of which the key set comprises all atoms in a sequence of atoms. For instance, the grammar can produce the rule $bond(key(A), key(C)), bond(key(C), key(B))$, which is interpreted as this classification rule, which defines a sequence of three connected atoms: $rule(X, \{A, B, C\}) : bond(X, A, C) \wedge bond(X, C, B)$. Note that the $key/1$ functor enclosing variables A, B and C has been removed, and these variables have been put into the key set (the importance of which becomes clearer when this classification rule is interpreted as a binary classifier, as described below).

When a production rule is chosen to apply to a formula which contains nonterminal symbols, one of the nonterminals is replaced by the formula defined in the production rule. The replacing continues until there are no nonterminal symbols left. More formally, the application of a production rule to a formula including nonterminals is defined as follows:

Definition 2 (Application of production rules). *Given a well-formed formula $F(A')$, where A' is an occurrence of some nonterminal symbol in $F(A')$, a production rule $A \to B$ can be applied to A' if and only if there is a unification of A' and A. Suppose θ is the most general unifier of A' and A. Application of the production rule to A' of $F(A')$ produces a well-formed formula $F(B)\theta$.*

The generation of classification rules starts from a rule including only one nonterminal symbol, known as the start symbol: $rule(X)$. The language defined by a grammar is the set of all classification rules that contain no nonterminal symbols and can be derived from the start symbol by applying production rules. Note that, when there are recursive production rules in a grammar, the set of rules defined by the grammar may be infinite. Therefore, it is often necessary to specify a maximum length of classification rules or the maximum steps to derive a classification. Some classification rules defined by the above grammar include:

$$rule(X, \{A, B\}) : bond(X, A, B)$$

$$rule(X, \{A, C, B\}) : bond(X, A, C) \wedge bond(X, C, B)$$

$$rule(X, \{A, C, D, B\}) : bond(X, A, C) \wedge bond(X, C, D) \wedge bond(X, D, B)$$

Importantly, the key set can be used for counting purposes. For instance, in the above example, suppose we require variables to be instantiated into strictly different constants. In this case, we can count different ground instantiations of rules for a molecule, which gives information about the occurrences of a specific substructure. This information is then used to obtain more sophisticated base classifiers, as described in section 3.2.

The following grammar extends the above example grammar with $atom/3$ predicates to restrict the element type of atoms. For the purposes of the example, we specify that the first and last atoms in a sequence must be assigned a specific element, with other atoms being optional.

$$rule(X) \rightarrow atomtype(X, A) \wedge sequence(X, key(A), key(B)) \wedge atomtype(X, B)$$

$$sequence(X, A, B) \rightarrow bond(X, A, B)$$

$$sequence(X, A, B) \rightarrow bond(X, A, key(C)) \wedge optional(X, C) \wedge sequence(X, key(C), B)$$

$$optional(X, A) \rightarrow atom(X, A, \_)$$

$$optional(X, A) \rightarrow atomtype(X, A)$$

$$atomtype(X, A) \rightarrow atom(X, A, o)$$

$$atomtype(X, A) \rightarrow atom(X, A, n)$$

$$atomtype(X, A) \rightarrow atom(X, A, c)$$

$$atomtype(X, A) \rightarrow atom(X, A, h)$$

Continuing the example, we add production rules to the above grammar, so that the generated classification rules will include combinations of genotoxicity properties of a molecule, such as $salmonella/1$, $cytogen/1$, and $drosophila/1$.

$$rule(X) \rightarrow properties(X, 2) \wedge atom(X, A)$$

$$\wedge sequence(X, key(A), key(B)) \wedge atom(X, B)$$

$$property(X, Last, New) \rightarrow salmonella(X)$$

$$properties(X, N) \rightarrow salmonella(X) \wedge properties1(X, M)$$

$$properties(X, N) \rightarrow properties1(X, N)$$

$$properties1(X, N) \rightarrow cytogen(X) \wedge properties2(X, M)$$

$$properties1(X, N) \rightarrow properties2(X, N)$$

$$properties2(X, N) \rightarrow drosophila(X, N)$$

Pruning

Given a grammar as above, WeakILP exhaustively produces all classification rules in the language, except those which are true for fewer examples than requested by a user-specified minimum coverage. Such pruning is mainly to improve computational efficiency. In the case that a classification rule covers no training examples, it cannot contribute to classification, because its training accuracy could not be higher than the default classifier regardless of weighting over training examples. As a consequence, boosting does not choose a base classifier derived from a classification rule of zero coverage. Moreover, those rules that cover very few training examples may be too specific to these examples, and might not affect the training result significantly. Pruning those examples can dramatically reduce the number of classifiers that boosting has to evaluate.

3.2   Rule Conversion

For predictive learning tasks, we convert first-order classification rules from descriptive ILP into binary classifiers according to their evaluation for each training example, as described below. These classifiers are then used as candidate base classifiers for boosting. We have experimented with the conventional method for performing this conversion which uses truth values. We have also experimented with a novel method which finds coefficients of instantiations, as described below.

Truth-based Conversion Method

An intuitive means for converting a classification rule into a classifier is based on its truth-value for each example, which is the method adopted in previous attempts to combine ILP with propositional learning systems [6,5]. In this case, supposing that $R(X, K)$ is a classification rule, then the corresponding classifier is defined as:

$$f(x_i) = \begin{cases} +1 & \text{if } R(x_i, K) \text{ is true} \\ -1 & \text{otherwise} \end{cases}$$

where $R(x_i, K)$ is the instantiation of $R(X, K)$ gained by replacing X with a specific example x_i.

Instantiation-based Conversion Method

We also propose a different rule conversion method based on the number of ground instantiations of the classification rule. Given a classification rule $R(X, K)$, the corresponding binary classifiers are defined as:

$$f(x_i, \beta) = \begin{cases} +1 & \text{if } \big| \{K\theta \,|\, R(x_i, K)\theta \text{ is ground and true}\} \big| \geq \beta \\ -1 & \text{otherwise} \end{cases}$$

where β is a non-negative integer and θ is a ground substitution that maps variables into ground terms.

As $R(x_i, K)\theta$ is ground, the substituted key set $K\theta$ is also ground. The set $\{K\theta \,|\, R(x_i, K)\theta \text{ is ground and true}\}$ is therefore the set of all ground instantiations of the key variables that make the classification rule $R(X, K)$ true for the example x_i. The cardinality of the instantiation set counts the different key sets that make the classification rule true for the example, which can be understood as the degree to which a rule holds for an example. Note that only instantiations of the key set to strictly different ground instances are counted, and permutations of an instantiation which has been counted already are similarly not counted.

To illustrate this novel rule conversion method, we consider the above bioinformatics problem. Each rule defined in the language represents a non-cyclic sequence of atoms. The key set is composed of the *atom* variables, therefore the cardinality of the instantiation set describes the number of distinct occurrences of the sequence in a molecule. Illustrated below are 6 instantiations of this classification rule: $rule(X, \{A, B, C\}) : bond(X, A, B), bond(X, B, C)$, for a particular example x_i.

$$rule(x_i, \{a, b, c\}) : bond(x_i, a, b), bond(X, b, c) \tag{1}$$

$$rule(x_i, \{c, b, a\}) : bond(x_i, c, b), bond(X, b, a) \tag{2}$$

$$rule(x_i, \{a, b\}) : bond(x_i, a, b), bond(X, b, a) \tag{3}$$

$$rule(x_i, \{b, a\}) : bond(x_i, b, a), bond(X, a, b) \tag{4}$$

$$rule(x_i, \{b, c\}) : bond(x_i, b, c), bond(X, c, b) \tag{5}$$

$$rule(x_i, \{c, b\}) : bond(x_i, c, b), bond(X, b, c) \tag{6}$$

We note that only instantiation (1) will be counted. This is because the key set in (2) is a permutation of that in (1), and instantiations (3), (4), (5) and (6) have instantiated two variables to the same ground term, hence are not counted. Therefore, for this classification rule, the instantiation coefficient used in the second rule conversion method described above will be 1. Note that the requirement to instantiate to strictly different terms is referred to in $\mathcal{C}$LAUDIEN as injectivity. Note also that the first conversion method is clearly a special case of the second method, namely when β is set to 1, and, when β is set to 0, $f(x_i, \beta)$ is a naive classifier that gives the same positive prediction for any example.

Further Pruning
When the instantiation-based conversion is adopted, each classification rule corresponds to multiple binary classifiers with different choices of the parameter β. To improve efficiency, we prune certain classifiers. In many descriptive ILP systems, a prover is used to determine whether two rules are logically equivalent. Logically equivalent rules can be safely pruned, as they always give the same prediction with respect to the background theory. In WeakILP, we choose to prune any classifier which gives the same predictions for training examples as another, i.e., predictively equivalent classifiers. Note that such pruning does not affect the learning process of boosting, as the boosting algorithm cannot distinguish those classifiers, and might randomly (depending on the implementation) choose one of them as a base classifier when appropriate. As all logically equivalent classifiers must also be predictively equivalent, this approach is more efficient in reducing redundant classifiers than using a logic prover.

However, because the converse statement is not true, i.e., predictively equivalent classifiers are not necessarily logically equivalent, predictively equivalent classifiers (for training examples) might give different predictions for test examples. It has been suggested in [16] that a syntactically less complex classifier tends to have better generalization performance than a more specific one. Hence, we choose to prune the more complex classifiers, i.e., in WeakILP, given a set of predictively equivalent classifiers, we take the shortest one in terms of the number of literals in the classification rule.

3.3 Boosting

Once binary classifiers are produced, the AdaBoost algorithm will be applied to construct a combining classifier from them. The boosting algorithm is presented in Figure 1, in which boosting does not invoke a separate base learner to obtain base classifiers, but, instead, evaluates received binary classifiers against weighted examples directly and chooses the one of the highest weighted accuracy.

Given $(x_1, y_1), \ldots, (x_m, y_m)$ where $x_i \in X, y_i \in Y = \{+1, -1\}$
Initialise $d_1(x_i) = 1/m$ for each example x_i
Generate candidate base classifiers Γ from descriptive ILP
For $t = 1, \ldots, T$:
  − select $h_t(x) \in \Gamma$ to minimise $\epsilon_t = \sum_i h_t(x_i) y_i d_t(x_i)$
  − let $\alpha_t = \frac{1}{2} \ln \frac{1-\epsilon_t}{\epsilon_t}$
  − update $d_{t+1}(x_i) = d_t(x_i) \exp(-\alpha_t y_i h_t(x_i))$
Output the final classifier: $\text{H}(x) = \text{sign}\left(\sum_t \alpha_t h_t(x)\right)$

Fig. 1. The boosting descriptive ILP algorithm, where T is the specified number of base classifiers to combine in the boosted classifier

In experiments with boosting, the learning results are often presented on a stepwise basis, i.e., results after every step are listed. This is particularly useful to demonstrate the efficiency of boosting for improving the accuracy of the base learner. However, it is more appropriate to evaluate the generalisation performance of the learning algorithm as a whole. This is because, in practical applications, we have to choose a combining classifier produced at a particular step. Hence, we need to estimate AdaBoost's parameter, i.e., determine when to stop adding base classifiers to the boosted classifier.

For our experiments, when n-fold cross validation is used for an experiment, we use $(n - 1)$-fold cross validation to evaluate the parameter on the training set. This strategy roughly maintains the size of the validation sets employed comparable to that of the test set. Hence, after each base classifier is added to the boosted classifier, we use 9-fold cross validation over the training set to determine the performance of the boosted classifier. Our system then backtracks to the boosted classifier which performed best, and outputs this as the final result. We have found that this improves performance over the usage of a single validation set. In the case of separate training and test sets, 10-fold cross validation is typically used.

4 Experiments with Bioinformatics Datasets

We performed experiments with four bioinformatics datasets: mutagenicity [17], DSSTox [3], carcinogenicity [18], and KDD Cup 2001 [19]. For each dataset, we evaluated our method using four different settings: WeakILP with and without boosting and using both of the rule conversion methods. When WeakILP was used without boosting, we chose the most accurate classifier in terms of predictive accuracy on training examples. We performed cross validation for all datasets except the KDD Cup dataset (which has a independent test set) to estimate the generalisation performance. In the KDD Cup dataset, for pruning purposes, the minimum coverage of classification rules was set to 15 to reduce the number of classifiers produced. In all the other experiments, we used a minimum coverage of one.

- **Mutagenicity.** The mutagenicity problem, reported in [17], is one of the most widely used datasets in ILP. The task regards learning a theory of mutagenesis from a set of 188 nitroaromatic molecules, of which 125 are mutagenic (active) and 63 are non-mutagenic (non-active). The background knowledge includes atoms which occur in a molecule, bonds between the atoms, certain chemical features, structural attributes, and predefined function groups in the molecule. The language bias used for this experiment is presented in table 1. The maximum length of classification rules was set to be 4. We performed 10-fold cross validation to estimate the generalisation performance on this dataset. Table 2 gives a partial example of an output combining classifier, which achieves a predictive accuracy of 89.47% (on both training and test examples) when six base classifiers are chosen.

- **DSSTox.** DSSTox is the predictive toxicity dataset used in [3], which consists of 576 molecules. The language bias and other settings were the same as in the mutagenicity experiment, except that 5-fold cross validation was used, to be consistent with the previous study [3].

- **Carcinogenicity.** The carcinogenicity dataset includes 337 chemicals, which is composed of both training and test datasets used from a previous predictive toxicology competition. The task is to predict the cancerous activity of the chemicals. Similar settings were used in this experiment as with the mutagenicity dataset, except that the language bias allowed arbitrary combinations of genotoxicity properties and structural indicators [18].

- **KDD Cup 2001.** This competition [19] was composed of three tasks, of which we consider only the second task, the prediction of *functions* of genes. The dataset consists of 862 genes as training examples and 381 genes as test examples. Each gene can belong to any combination of 14 classes, so we can break down the leaning task into 14 binary classification sub-tasks. We used a language bias similar to that used in [20], except that no negation was allowed.

Table 2 shows a typical training result from our boosted WeakILP experiments. We found most weightings concentrate on the first few base classifiers and if we reduce the boosted classifier to ten base classifiers, in most cases, the

Table 1. Language bias for the mutagenicity dataset. Production rules with the same left-hand side nonterminal symbol are grouped together for ease of reading.

$$bound\_type(X, A, B) \rightarrow bond(X, key(A), key(B), 1) \quad \text{or}$$
$$bond(X, key(A), key(B), 2) \quad \text{or}$$
$$\ldots$$
$$atom\_type(X, B) \rightarrow atom(X, B, h) \quad \text{or}$$
$$atom(X, B, c) \quad \text{or}$$
$$\ldots$$
$$connection(X, A, B) \rightarrow bond\_type(X, A, B) \quad \text{or}$$
$$bond\_type(X, A, B) \wedge atom\_type(X, B)$$
$$sequence(X, A, B) \rightarrow connection(X, A, B) \quad \text{or}$$
$$connection(X, A, C) \wedge sequence(X, C, B)$$
$$structure(X, A, B) \rightarrow arc(X, A, B) \quad \text{or}$$
$$arc(X, A, B) \wedge structure(X, A, B) \quad \text{or}$$
$$arc(X, A, C) \wedge arc(X, C, B) \wedge structure(X, C, D)$$
$$rule(X) \rightarrow structure(X, A, B) \quad \text{or}$$
$$atom\_type(X, A) \wedge structure(X, A, B)$$

Table 2. The first six base classifiers of a boosted classifier for the mutagenicity dataset. *Acc.* represents the test accuracy of the corresponding combining classifier. *Wt.* is the weight assigned to the corresponding base classifier. *Pred.* is the prediction of the base classifier, which may be either active (+), or non-active (-). We only give the body of the classification rule, as all variables except X are key variables. The classifier is read as: *the molecule is* Pred. *if the number of ground instantiations is equal to or greater than the threshold, β.*

Acc.	Wt.	Pred.	β	Body of the classification rule
73.68%	0.82	+	16	$bond(X, A, C, 1) \wedge bond(X, C, B, 7)$.
73.68%	0.45	+	6	$bond(X, A, C, 2) \wedge bond(X, C, D, 1) \wedge bond(X, D, E, 7)$ $\wedge bond(X, E, B, 7)$.
73.68%	0.37	+	28	$bond(X, A, B, 7)$.
73.68%	0.43	−	2	$bond(X, A, C, 1) \wedge atom(X, C, o) \wedge bond(X, C, B, 1)$ $\wedge atom(X, B, c)$.
78.94%	0.38	+	8	$bond(X, A, C, 1) \wedge bond(X, C, B, 1) \wedge bond(X, C, D, 1)$ $\wedge atom(X, D, c)$.
89.47%	0.28	−	16	$bond(X, A, C, 1) \wedge bond(X, C, D, 7) \wedge bond(X, D, B, 1)$ $\wedge atom(X, B, h)$.

result is still fairly accurate but much simpler. Hence, the training result can be made more understandable at a minor cost to predictive accuracy. Table 3 lists the predictive accuracies of WeakILP and boosted WeakILP using both rule conversion methods. The result shows that with only one exception, boosting is able to improve the generalization performance of WeakILP, and the improvement is

Table 3. Test accuracy or estimated generalization accuracy of WeakILP and boosted WeakILP for the four datasets, using truth-value and instantiation based rule conversion methods

Rule conversion	Truth-value based		Instantiation based	
Boosting	WeakILP	boosted	WeakILP	boosted
Mutagenicity	66.5%	76.6%	80.9%	90.5%
DSSTox	63.0%	66.1%	68.4%	75.6%
Carcinogenicity	58.4%	57.5%	58.7%	61.1%
KDD Cup 2001	90.5%	91.8%	90.5%	91.8%

Table 4. The comparison of our boosted WeakILP approaches with other state of the art systems. The results for the mutagenicity dataset are mostly taken from [21] and the results for DSSTox are from [3]. RELAGGS was the winner of KDD Cup 2001 task 2 [19] and ICL results are collected from [20]. Aleph results are based on [22]. It is worth noting that many experiments were done in different settings, including different background knowledge and performance estimation. † This result has large variations between 60% and 64% in different bagging steps. ‡ The STILL experiment did not perform 10-fold cross validation, but held 10% examples back as test examples. †† All other methods except boosted WeakILP had access to background knowledge which is not currently available in the public domain.

Category	Method	Mutagenesis	Carcinogenesis	DSSTox ††	KDD Cup 2001
ILP	Progol	88.0%		55.0%	
	FOIL	86.7%			
	STILL	93.6%‡			
	ICL	88.3%			92.2%
	Aleph	88.8%	57.9%		
Kernel based	SVILP			73.0%	
	CHEM			58.0%	
	MIK	93.0%		60.0%	
	PLS			71.0%	
Bagging/ Boosting Based	RS	95.8%			
	Bagging Aleph		64.0%†		
	Boosted FFOIL	88.3%			
	Boosted WeakILP	90.5%	61.1%	59.3%	91.8%
Others	RELAGGS	88.0%			93.0%

more than 10% in two out of four datasets. We also observed that the new instantiation-based rule conversion method resulted in better test accuracy with no exceptions, and when used together with the boosted WeakILP approach, it always produces better predictive accuracy than with other settings. We compare our results (using boosted WeakILP with the instantiation based rule conversion) with other methods in Table 4. The predictive accuracy we achieve is in line with the top ranking approaches for all experiments except DSSTox. Note that all the other methods had access to certain more sophisticated background information for the DSSTox dataset, which was not available to us. Our experiments involved minimum use of background knowledge, and we hope to improve our results by using more background knowledge.

5   Conclusions and Further Work

We have explored the use of boosted descriptive ILP for predictive learning tasks, and presented some experimental results for bioinformatics datasets. The main contributions of our study include the following:

- We distinguish two types of language biases, namely constructive and syntactical, and we highlight the limitation of existing language biases.
- To take advantage of both types of language biases, we suggest a new declarative language bias, used in our WeakILP system. The new language bias adopts a context-free style grammar to define languages, which is more expressive than $\mathcal{D}$LAB in that it allows recursive definitions of the language.
- We have proposed a new propositionalization technique, which counts the ground instantiations of a logic rule to indicate the degree that the classification rule supports its prediction. This approach has been shown to be effective in some learning tasks, in which both training and test accuracies have been improved significantly.
- We have shown that the boosted WeakILP approach performs well with four bioinformatics datasets, and it outperforms many widely used ILP systems. Hence, there is some evidence that the boosted WeakILP approach is competitive with state of the art ILP systems in terms of predictive accuracy. This is encouraging, especially given that the learning results are understandable compared to other propositionalization based methods.

In further work, we plan to perform further experiments to investigate both runtime and predictive performance of the proposed approach in non-bioinformatics domains. Also, further theoretical and experimental studies are necessary to compare the performance of boosting with other machine learning methods including SVM and logistic regression. Moreover, we aim to find a theoretical explanation to answer questions about when our approach is suitable and when it is not.

Acknowledgments

The authors thank Stephen Muggleton for making the DSSTox dataset available and the three reviewers, whose comments and references provided important information to improve the quality of this paper.

References

1. Muggleton, S.: Inverse entailment and Progol. New Generation Computing, Special issue on Inductive Logic Programming 13(3-4), 245–286 (1995)
2. Quinlan, J., Cameron-Jones, R.: FOIL: A midterm report. In: Brazdil, P.B. (ed.) Machine Learning: ECML-93. LNCS, vol. 667, pp. 3–20. Springer, Heidelberg (1993)

3. Muggleton, S., Lodhi, H., Amini, A., Sternberg, M.: Support vector inductive logic programming. In: Holmes, D., Jain, L.C. (eds.) Innovations in Machine Learning: Theory and Applications, Springer, Heidelberg (2006)
4. Schapire, R.: The boosting approach to machine learning: An overview. In: MSRI Workshop on Nonlinear Estimation and Classification (2001)
5. Quinlan, J.: Boosting first-order learning. In: Arikawa, S., Sharma, A.K. (eds.) ALT 1996. LNCS, vol. 1160, pp. 143–155. Springer, Heidelberg (1996)
6. Kramer, S.: Demand-driven construction of structural features in ILP. In: Rouveirol, C., Sebag, M. (eds.) ILP 2001. LNCS (LNAI), vol. 2157, pp. 132–141. Springer, Heidelberg (2001)
7. Valiant, L.: A theory of the learnable. Communications of the ACM 27(11), 1134–1142 (1984)
8. Friedman, J., Hastie, T., Tibshirani, R.: Additive logistic regression: a statistical view of boosting. Technical report, Dept. of Statistics, Stanford University (1998)
9. Meir, R., Rätsch, G.: An introduction to boosting and leveraging. In: Mendelson, S., Smola, A.J. (eds.) Advanced Lectures on Machine Learning. LNCS (LNAI), vol. 2600, pp. 118–183. Springer, Heidelberg (2003)
10. Schapire, R., Freund, Y., Bartlett, P., Lee, W.: Boosting the margin: a new explanation for the effectiveness of voting methods. In: 14th International Conference on Machine Learning, pp. 322–330 (1997)
11. Jin, R., Liu, Y., Si, L., Carbonell, J., Hauptmann, A.: A new boosting algorithm using input-dependent regularizer. In: 20th International Conference on Machine Learning (2003)
12. Lebanon, G., Lafferty, J.: Boosting and maximum likelihood for exponential models. Advances in Neural Information Processing Systems 15 (2001)
13. Raedt, L., Džeroski, S.: First-order jk-clausal theories are pac-learnable. Artif. Intell. 70(1-2), 375–392 (1994)
14. Deraedt, L., Dehaspe, L.: Clausal discovery. Machine Learning 26, 99–146 (1997)
15. Colton, S., Muggleton, S.: Mathematical applications of inductive logic programming. Machine Learning 64(1-3), 25–64 (2006)
16. Muggleton, S.: Learning from positive data. In: Inductive Logic Programming. LNCS, vol. 1314, pp. 358–376. Springer, Heidelberg (1997)
17. Srinivasan, A., Muggleton, S., Sternberg, M., King, R.: Theories for mutagenicity: A study in first-order and feature-based induction. Artificial Intelligence 85(1-2), 277–299 (1996)
18. Srinivasan, A., King, R., Muggleton, S., Sternberg, M.: Carcinogenesis predictions using ILP. In: Džeroski, S., Lavrač, N. (eds.) Inductive Logic Programming. LNCS, vol. 1297, pp. 273–287. Springer, Heidelberg (1997)
19. Cheng, J., Hatzis, C., Hayashi, H., Krogel, M., Morishita, S., Page, D., Sese, J.: KDD cup 2001 report. SIGKDD Explorations 3(2), 47–64 (2002)
20. Laer, W.: From Propositional to First Order Logic in Machine Learning and Data Mining - Induction of first order rules with ICL. PhD thesis, Department of Computer Science, Katholieke Universiteit Leuven (2002)
21. Lodhi, H., Muggleton, S.: Is mutagenesis still challenging? In: 15th International Conference on Inductive Logic Programming, pp. 35–40 (2005)
22. Zelezny, F., Srinivasan, A., Page, D.: Lattice-search runtime distributions may be heavy-tailed. In: Matwin, S., Sammut, C. (eds.) ILP 2002. LNCS (LNAI), vol. 2583, Springer, Heidelberg (2003)

Relational Sequence Alignments and Logos

Andreas Karwath and Kristian Kersting

University of Freiburg, Institute for Computer Science, Machine Learning Lab
Georges-Koehler-Allee, Building 079, 79110 Freiburg, Germany
{karwath,kersting}@informatik.uni-freiburg.de

Abstract. The need to measure sequence similarity arises in many applicitation domains and often coincides with sequence alignment: the more similar two sequences are, the better they can be aligned. Aligning sequences not only shows how similar sequences are, it also shows where there are differences and correspondences between the sequences.

Traditionally, the alignment has been considered for sequences of flat symbols only. Many real world sequences such as natural language sentences and protein secondary structures, however, exhibit rich internal structures. This is akin to the problem of dealing with structured examples studied in the field of inductive logic programming (ILP). In this paper, we introduce REAL, which is a powerful, yet simple approach to align sequence of structured symbols using well-established ILP distance measures within traditional alignment methods. Although straight-forward, experiments on protein data and Medline abstracts show that this approach works well in practice, that the resulting alignments can indeed provide more information than flat ones, and that they are meaningful to experts when represented graphically.

1 Introduction

Sequential data are ubiquitous and are of interest to many communities. Such data can be found in virtually all application areas of machine learning including computational biology, user modeling, speech recognition, empirical natural language processing, activity recognition, information extractions, etc. Therefore, it is not surprising that sequential data has been the subject of active research for decades. One of the many tasks investigated is that of *sequence alignment*. Informally speaking, a sequence alignment is a way of arranging sequences to emphasize their regions of similarity. Sequence alignments are employed in a variety of domains: in bioinformatics they are for instance used to identify similar DNA sequence, to produce phylogenetic trees, and to develop homology models of protein structures; in empirical language processing, they are for instance used for automatically summarizing, paraphrasing, and translating texts.

Most of the alignment approaches assume sequences of flat symbols. Many sequences occurring in real-world problems such as in computational biology, planning, and user modeling, natural language processing, however, exhibit internal structure. The elements of such sequences can be seen as atoms in a relational logic.

S. Muggleton, R. Otero, and A. Tamaddoni-Nezhad (Eds.): ILP 2006, LNAI 4455, pp. 290–304, 2007.

Example 1. Consider the following sentence adapted from [1]: *'A purple latex balloon blew himself up in a southern city Wednesday, bursting two other balloons and deforming 27'.* The sentences actually provides much more complex data than shown. Applying Brill's rule-based part of speech tagger, cf. [2], which is one of the most widely used tools for assigning parts of speech to words, yields the following sequence of structured objects:

dt(a), jj(purple), nn(latex), nn(balloon), vbd(blew), prp(himself), in(up),

in(in), dt(a), jj(southern), nn(city), nnp(wednesday), comma, vbg(bursting),

cd(two), jj(other), nns(balloons), cc(and), vbg(deforming), cd(27)

The application of traditional alignment algorithms to such sequences requires one to either ignore the structure of the atoms, which results in a loss of information, or to take all possible combinations of arguments into account, which leads to a combinatorial explosion in the number of parameters. In other words, relational sequence alignment is a significant problem.

Surprisingly few works have investigated sequences of complex objects so far. Ketterlin [14] considered the clustering of sequences of complex objects but did not employ logical concepts. Likewise, Jiang *et al.* [11] and Weskamp *et al.* [27] proposed alignment algorithms for trees respectively graphs. Lee and De Raedt [15] and Jacobs [10] introduced ILP frameworks for reasoning and learning with relational sequences. Recently, Tobudic and Widmer [26] used relational instance-based learning for mining music data, where sequential, relational information is employed. To the best of our knowledge, however, none of these works investigate the alignment of relational sequences.

Indeed within bioinformatics most advances of sequence alignment for biological sequence analysis (see [6] for a good overview) have been made by incorporating additional sources of information such as sequence profiles or secondary structure predictions. As these works demonstrate, incorporating additional information can often yield considerable benefits to alignment quality. These methods, however, do not employ relational sequences, are domain-dependent and do not easily generalize across different domains. Therefore, Do *et al.* [5], McCallum *el al.* [17], Parker *et al.* [21] and Sato and Sakakibara [24] proposed more advanced probabilistic methods such as conditional random fields (CRFs) to discriminatively learn edit distances for propositional strings and trees [24]. CRFs allow to use arbitrary even relational features [8] to define the potential functions involved. This, however, leaves one with the difficult task of choosing the right representation or with the difficult task of automatically selecting the features form data, see e.g. [8]. This might explain why CRFs have so far not been used for aligning relational sequences.

In this context, we present REAL: a general, domain-independent approach to relational sequence alignments and logos. The contributions of REAL are three-fold. First of all, REAL is a simple, yet powerful approach to align relational sequences. In particular, we propose to use well-established ILP distance measures within traditional alignment methods. Second, it defines the information content of relational sequence alignments. This is an important question as it allows to evaluate alignments of and to find common motifs in relational sequences. Moreover, it can be graphically represented by so-called *relational sequence logos*, which are the third contribution of REAL. Although straightforward, experiments on real world data show that REAL works well in practice, that the resulting alignments can indeed provide more information than flat ones, and that the logos generated are meaningful to experts.

We proceed as follows. After discussing related work, we review basic alignment algorithms in Section 2. Then, we discuss relational sequences and relational distance measures in Section 3. Afterwards, in Section 3.1, we define the information content of relational sequence alignments. Based on this, we introduce relational sequences logos in Section 4. Before concluding, we empirically evaluate REAL on real-world data sets.

2 Sequence Alignment Algorithms

Alignment plays a major role in analyzing biological sequences. Consider e.g. the protein fold recognition problem, which is concerned with how proteins fold in nature, i.e., their three-dimensional structures. This is an important problem as the biological functions of proteins depend on the way they fold. Given a sequence of an unknown protein (query sequence) all approaches work in principle in a similar fashion: they scan an existing database of amino acids sequences (from more or less known proteins) and extract the most similar ones with regard to the query sequence. The result is usually a list, ordered by some score, with the best hits at the top of this list. The common approach for biologists, is to investigate these top scoring alignments or hits to conclude about the function, shape, or other features of query sequence.

One of the earliest alignment algorithm is that for global alignment by Needleman and Wunsch in 1970 [19]. The algorithm is based on dynamic programming, and finds the alignment of two sequences with the maximal overall similarity w.r.t. a given pairwise similarity model. In the biological domain, this similarity model is typically represented by pair-wise similarity or dissimilarity scores of pairs of amino acids. These scores are commonly specified by using a so-called similarity matrix, like the PAM [4] or BLOSUM [9] families of substitution matrices. The scores, or costs, associated with a match or mismatch between two amino acids, reflect to some extent the probability that this change in amino acids might have occurred over time of evolution.

More precisely, the Needleman-Wunsch algorithm proceeds as follows: initially, for two sequences of length m and n, a matrix with $m + 1$ columns and $n + 1$ rows is created. The matrix then is filled with the maximum score as follows:

$$M_{i,j} = \max \begin{cases} M_{i-1,j-1} + S_{i,j} & : \text{a match or mismatch} \\ M_{i,j-1} + w & : \text{a gap in the first sequence} \\ M_{i-1,j} + w & : \text{gap in the second sequence} \end{cases} \quad (1)$$

where $S_{i,j}$ is pairwise similarity of amino acids and w reflects a linear gap (insert step) penalty. The overall score of the alignment can be found in cell $M_{m,n}$.

To calculate the best *local* alignment of two sequences, one often employs the Smith-Waterman local alignment algorithm [25]. The main difference in this algorithm when compared to the Needleman-Wunsch algorithm, is that all negative scores are set to 0. When visualizing the resulting alignment matrix, strands of non negative numbers correspond to a good local alignment. For both algorithms versions using affine gaps costs exist, i.e. one employs different kind of gap costs for opening a gap or for extending one. To discourage the splitting of connected regions due the enforcement of a gap in the middle of the alignment, commonly extra gaps are allowed to be inserted at the end and at the beginning at either no additional costs or relatively low costs (padding costs).

In general, the alignments resulting from an global or local alignment, show then the more *conserved* regions between two sequences. To enhance the detection of these conserved regions, commonly multiple sequence alignments are constructed. Given a number of sequences belonging to the same class, i.e. in biological terms believed to belong to the same family, fold, or are otherwise somehow related, alignments are constructed aligning all sequences in one single alignment, a so-called profile. A common approach for the construction of a multiple alignment is a three step approach: First, all pairwise alignments are constructed. Second, using this information as starting point a phylogenetic tree is created as *guiding tree*. Third, using this tree, sequences are joined consecutively into one single alignment according to their similarity. This approach is known as the neighbour joining approach [23].

Example 2. Reconsider our natural language example from the beginning. Table 1 shows the global alignment of all five example sentences used by Barzilay and Lee [1] (adapted appropriately). As similarity measure we used the identity function, i.e., for instance $S(\texttt{balloon}, \texttt{balloon}) = 1$ but $S(\texttt{wednesday}, \texttt{sunday}) = 0$. The underlined sub-structures show the conserved regions computed by a propositional, global sequence alignment with arbitrarily chosen gap costs: gap opening cost 1.5, gap extention cost 0.5, and padding cost 0.25.

A good overview of alignment algorithms, including construction of multiple alignments and the generation of phylogenetic trees, can be found in [6].

3   Alignment of Sequences of Relational Objects

The alignment algorithms discussed in the previous section assume a given similarity measure $S_{i,j}$. Typically, this similarity measure is flat because the considered sequences consist of flat symbols. For instance the similarity measure used in Example 2 was simply the identity function. Many sequences occurring in real-world problems such as in computational biology, planning, user modeling, and natural language processing, however, exhibit internal structure. The elements of such sequences can elegantly be represented as objects in a relational logic (see e.g. [16] for an introduction to logic).

Table 1. Five sentences adapted from the example given by Barzilay and Lee [1]. Underlined words show the conserved regions (exact matches across all sequences) computed by a propositional sequence alignment using gap opening cost 1.5, gap extention cost 0.5, and padding cost 0.25. The bold parts denote the conserved regions of the corresponding relational sequence alignment using the same gap costs. The italic words show *lgg* conserved regions, i.e., the lgg of all atoms at a position exists.

1. **A** purple **latex balloon blew himself up in** *a* southern city *Wednesday,* **bursting** two other balloons and deforming 27.

2. **A latex balloon blew himself up in** *the* area of Freiburg, on *Sunday,* **bursting** itself and disfiguring seven balloons.

3. **A latex balloon blew himself up in** *the* coastal resort of *Cuxhaven,* **bursting** three other balloons and deforming dozens more.

4. **A** purple **latex balloon blew himself up in** *a* garden cafe on *Saturday,* **bursting** 10 balloons and deforming 54.

5. **A latex balloon blew himself up in** *the* centre of Berlin on *Sunday,* **bursting** three balloons as well as itself and disfiguring 40.

Example 3. Recall the extended version of the *balloon* sentence in Example 1 dt(a), jj(purple), nn(latex), nn(balloon), vbd(blew), ... representing determiners dt(*Word*), nouns nn(*Word*) etc. The secondary structure of the Ribosomal protein L4 can be represented as st(null, short), he(h(right, alpha), *long*), st(plus, short), ... representing helices and strands of certain types, orientations, and lengths, he(*HelixType,Length*) respectively st(*Orientation, Length*).

The symbols dt, nn, ..., st, null, short, he, h, ... have an associated *arity*, i.e., number of arguments such as st/2, he/2, and h/2 having arity 2, dt/1 and nn/1 having arity 1, and plus/0, 1/0, having arity 0. A *structured term* is a placeholder or a symbol followed by its arguments in brackets such as nn(balloon), medium, h(right, X), and he(h(right, X), medium). A *ground term* is one that does not contain any variables such as nn(balloon), st(null, short), he(h(right, alpha), long), ...

Relational sequence alignment simply denotes the alignment of sequences of such structured terms. More formally, the relational alignment problem can be defined as follows.

Definition 1 (Relational Sequence Alignment Problem). *Let* $\mathbf{x} = \langle \mathbf{x}_i \rangle_{i=1}^n$, $n > 0$, *and* $\mathbf{y} = \langle \mathbf{y}_i \rangle_{i=1}^m$, $m > 0$, *be two sequences of logical objects and let* $S_{i,j}$ *be a similarity measure indicating the score of aligning object* $\mathbf{x}_i$ *with object* $\mathbf{y}_j$. *Then, the global alignment problem seeks to find the match with highest score of both sequences in their entirety. The local alignment problem seeks to find the subsequence match with highest score.*

One attractive way to solve this problem is to use a standard alignment algorithm but to replace the flat similarity measure $S_{i,j}$ in Eq. (1) by a structured one.

In this paper, we propose to use one of the many distance measures developed within Inductive Logic Programming [18]. As an example, consider one of the most basic measures proposed by Nienhuys-Cheng [20] [1]. It treats ground structured terms as hierarchies, where the top structure is most important and the deeper, nested sub-structures are less important. Let S denote the set of all symbols, then Nienhuys-Cheng distance d is inductively defined as follows:

$$\forall c/0 \in S : \qquad\qquad d(c,c) = 0$$
$$\forall p/n, q/m \in S : p/n \neq q/m : d(p(t_1,\ldots,t_n), q(s_1,\ldots,s_m)) = 1$$
$$\forall p/n \in S : \qquad\qquad d(p(t_1,\ldots,t_n), p(s_1,\ldots,s_n)) = \frac{1}{2n}\sum_{i=1}^{n} d(t_i, s_i)$$

For different symbols the distance is one; however, when the symbols are the same, the distance linearly decreases with the number of arguments that have different values, and is at most 0.5. The intuition is that longer tuples are more error-prone and that multiple errors in the same tuple are less likely.

Example 4. At this point the reader may verify that

$$d(\texttt{nnp}(\texttt{wednesday}), \texttt{nnp}(\texttt{wednesday})) = 1/(2 \cdot 0) \cdot (1) = 0.0$$
$$d(\texttt{nnp}(\texttt{wednesday}), \texttt{nnp}(\texttt{sunday})) = 1/(2 \cdot 1) \cdot (0) = 0.5$$
$$d(\texttt{dt}(\texttt{a}), \texttt{dt}(\texttt{the})) = 1.0$$

so that it smooths the dichotomic identity function of the propositional case.

To solve the corresponding relational alignment problem, we simply set $S_{i,j} = 1 - d(x_i, y_i)$ in Equation (1).

Example 5. Continuing with our *Balloon* example but now employing the relational representation based on Brill's rule-based part of speech tagger, cf. [2], the bold parts in Table 1 show the conserved regions of the corresponding relational sequence alignment. We used the same gap costs as before but replaced the identity function by the Nienhuys-Cheng measure.. As one can see, the consensus regions of the propositional sequence alignment are proper sub-regions of the relational one.

3.1 Information Content

Now that we have introduced relational sequence alignments, we will investigate how informative they are. To this aim, we will introduce the concept of *information content* of relational sequence alignments. The information content is a significant concept as it allows to evaluate alignments of and to find common motifs in relational sequences. Moreover, it allows (see next Section) one to represented alignments graphically by so-called *relational sequence logos*.

---

[1] For sequences of more complex logical objects such as interpretations and queries, a different, appropriate similarity function has to be chosen. We refer to Jan Ramon's PhD Thesis [22] for a nice review of them.

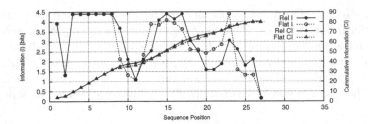

Fig. 1. Information content (IC) for the *balloon* example. The graph shows both the IC at each position (circle) and the cumulative IC (triangle) for the relational representation (solid, filled) and for the flat representation (dotted, unfilled).

Following Gorodkin *et al.* [7], the information content I_i of position i of a relational sequence alignment is

$$I_i = \sum_{k \in G} I_{ik} = \sum_{k \in G} q_{ik} \log_2 \left(\frac{q_{ik}}{p_k} \right),$$

where G is the Herbrand base over the language of the aligned sequences including gaps (denoted as '$-$') and q_{ik} is the fraction of ground atoms k at position i. When k is not a gap, we interpret p_k as the *a priori* distribution of the ground atom. Following Gorodkin *et al.*, we set $p_- = 1.0$, since then $q_{i-} \log_2(q_{i-}/p_-)$ is zero for q_{i-} equal to zero or one. For the work reported here, we set $p_k = 1/(|G|-1)$ when $k \neq -$. The intuition is as follows:

> *if I_{ik} is negative, we observe fewer copies of ground atom k at position i than expected, and vice versa if I_{ik} is positive, we observe more of it.*

Example 6. Figure 1 shows the (cumulative) information content for our running *balloon* example. As prior we use the empirical frequencies over all five sentences. As one can see, both the relational and the flat representation agree on the information content for '*A [...] latex balloon blew himself up in [...]*'. They, however, disagree on the rest. Actually, the relational representation puts more information into the positions 14–18 whereas the flat representation put more information into the positions 19–23.

The total information content becomes $I = \sum_i I_i$ and can be used to evaluate relational sequence alignments.

Example 7. In the *balloon* example, the relational representation provides more information than the flat one, 80.7 vs. 79.8.

So far, we have defined the information content at the most informative level, namely the level of ground atoms. Relational sequences exhibit a rich internal structure and, due to that, multiple abstraction levels can be explored: variables allow to make abstraction of specific symbols. To compute the information content at a higher abstraction levels, i.e., of an atom a replacing all covered ground atoms k at position i, we view q_{ia} (resp. p_a) as the sum of q_{ik} (resp. p_k) of the ground atoms k covered by a.

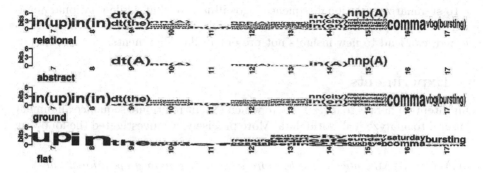

Fig. 2. Sequence logos (positions 7 – 17) for the *balloon* example (from bottom to top: flat , ground, abstract, and relational)

4   Relational Sequence Logos

Reconsider the alignment in Table 1. It consists of several lines of textual information. This makes it difficult – if not impossible – to read off information such as the general consensus of the sequences, the order of predominance of the symbols at every position, their relative frequencies, the amount of information present at every position, and significant locations within the sequences. In contrast, the corresponding sequence logo as shown in Figure 2 concentrates all of this into a single graphical representation. In other words, *'a logo says more than a thousand lines alignment'*.

Each position i in a *relational sequence logo* is represented by a stack consisting of the atoms at position i in the corresponding alignment. The height of the stack at position i indicates the information content I_i available. The height h_{ik} of each atom k at position i is proportional to its frequency relative to the expected frequency, i.e.,

$$h_{ik} = \alpha_i \cdot \left(\frac{q_{ik}}{p_k} \right) \cdot I_i \,,$$

where α_i is a normalization constant. The atoms are sorted according to their heights. If I_{ik} is negative, the atom is shown upside-down.

Sequence logos at lower abstraction levels can become quite complex. Relational abstraction can be used to straighten them up. Reconsider Fig. 2. It also shows the logo at the highest abstraction level, where we considered as symbols the *least general generalization* of all ground atoms over the same predicate at each position in the alignment only. Because the prior probabilities change dramatically, the *abstract logo* looks totally different from the ground one. It actually highlights the determiner at position 9 and the propositional phrase at positions 14 and 15. Both views provide relevant information. *Relational logos* now combine both by putting at each position the individual stack items together and sort them in ascending order of heights.

To summarize, relational sequence logos illustrate that while relational alignments can be quite complex, they exhibit rich internal structures which, if exploited, can lead to new insights not present in flat alignments.

5   Experiments

Our intention here is to investigate to which extent relational sequence alignment is useful to analyze real-world data. More precisely, we investigated the following questions:

(Q1) *Can* REAL*'s alignments be more informative than propositional ones?*
(Q2) *If so, can there be a gain in applications over propositional alignments?*
(Q3) *Can* REAL *easily be applied across different domains?*
(Q4) *Is* REAL *competitive with advanced ILP approaches?*

To this aim, we implemented REAL in Python and Prolog and conducted a number of experiments on real-world data sets. In the following we will present their results.

5.1   (Q1) Alignment of Protein Sequences

To answer **(Q1)**, we considered as real-world data set the five most populated folds in the SCOP class *Alpha and beta proteins (a/b)*, i.e., folds c.1, *TIM beta/alpha-barrel*, c.2, *NAD(P)-binding Rossmann-fold domains*, c.23, *Flavodoxin-like*, c.37, *P-loop containing nucleotide triphosphate hydrolases*, and c.55. *Ribonuclease H-like motif*. The examples are sequences of secondary structure elements of proteins which are similar in their three dimensional shape, but in general do not share a common ancestor (i.e. are not homologous). In total there are 2086 sequence distributed over the folds as follows: (c.1: 721), (c.2: 360), (c.23, 274), (c.37, 441), (c.55,290). The data set was generated using the ASTRAL database for the SCOP version 1.63[2].

We actually considered the subset of proteins which do not share more than 40 per cent amino acid sequence identity (*cut 40*). Overall, there are 522 example sequences (c.1: 182, c.2: 100, c.23: 66, c.37: 121, c.55: 53). We aligned sequences from one fold into a multiple alignment. Here we used the global alignment algorithm Needleman-Wunsch with affine gap penalties. The question of finding the appropriate gap costs in computational Biology is commonly answered by a trial and error approach. Here, we have solely concentrated on global alignments with affine gap costs using low padding costs. We have arbitrarily chosen the following gap costs: opening 1.5, extentsion 0.5, and padding 0.25.

Overall, REAL yield a larger information content than the propositional approach (treating each ground atom as a different symbol). More precisely, the information contents for all folds were (relational/flat): c.1 (6.14/5.01), c.2 (7.66/7.54), c.23 (6.65/5.34), c.37 ($-0.12/-0.62$), c.55 (1.05/-0.24). Making gaps less expensive even increased the difference in information content. This affirmatively answers question **Q1**.

---

[2] http://astral.berkeley.edu/scopseq-1.63.html

Fold: SH3 (1 002 032)

SCOP: barrel, partly opened; np 1/4 4; Sp 1/4 8; meander; the last **strand** is **interrupted by** a turn of 310 **helix**

Fold: Barrel-sandwich hybrid (1 002 079)

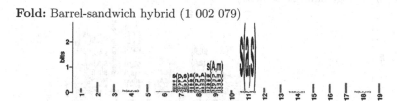

SCOP: sandwich of half-barrel-shaped b-**sheets**

Fig. 3. Comparison of REAL's logos to SCOP descriptions for several folds. The logos are compared to the expert-like descriptions of those folds taken from the SCOP database (caption). **Bold** words denote matches.

5.2 (Q2, Q3) Information Extraction

5.3 (Q4) Protein Fold Classification and Description

In general, however, more informative alignments can also come at an expense: even apparent unrelated sequences get higher similarity scores. For instance, in our protein sequence data set, we found sequences from different folds, where the relational alignment score is 4.75 times higher than the flat one. This can be a drawback in discriminative machine learning tasks. To validate this, we performed a 10-fold cross-validated nearest neighbour classification ($k=7$) on the cut 40 protein data set. This yielded 74.33% for the flat and 68.01% for the relational representation. On the full protein data sets, the predicative accuracies increase to 93.86% respectively 90.17%. The reason for the increase are obviously in the missing of close homologues in the cut 40 subset. Although, the experimental results favour the flat representation, the performances themselves are very good. They are comparable to more sophisticated statistical relational learning results on similar data: LoHHMs 74.0% [12], Fisher kernels 84% [13], CRFs 92.96% [8]. This tends to affirmatively answer **Q4**.

To further investigate **(Q4)** empirically, we investigated to which extend REAL's logos can be used to describe structural principles underlying SCOP folds. Understanding how proteins fold in nature, i.e., their three-dimensional shapre and structure is an important research question because the biological functions of proteins depend on the way they fold. We considered the SCOP protein data set used by Cotes *et al.* [3]. We computed the logos for those protein

Fold: Long a-hairpin (1 001 002)

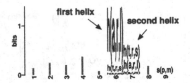

SCOP:**two helices**; antiparallel hairpin, left-handed twist

Fold: Immunoglobulin (1 002 001)

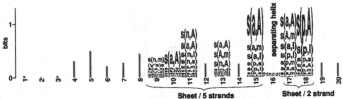

SCOP: sandwich; **seven strands** in **two sheets**; greek-key; some members of the fold have additional strands

Fig. 4. Comparison of REAL's logos to SCOP descriptions for several folds. The logos are compared to the expert-like descriptions of those folds taken from the SCOP database (caption). **Bold** words denote matches.

folds for which Cotes *et al.* [3] provide the ILP rules computed using PROGOL. The logos together with a comparison to SCOP's expert-like descriptions of the folds are shown in Figures 3–6.

The relational logos match surprisingly well the fold descriptions[3]: only the parts of the SCOP descriptions, which can not be expressed using our simple

Fold: Prealbumin-like (1 002 003)

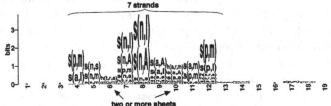

SCOP: sandwich; **seven strands** in **two sheets**, greek-key; variations: some members have additional one or two strands to common fold

Fig. 5. Comparison of REAL's logo to SCOP description for the Prealbumin-like fold. The logo is compared to the expert-like descriptions of this folds taken from the SCOP database (caption). **Bold** words denote matches.

---

[3] Using the flat representation, we were not able to discover the SCOP descriptions.

Fold: TIM barrel (1 003 001)

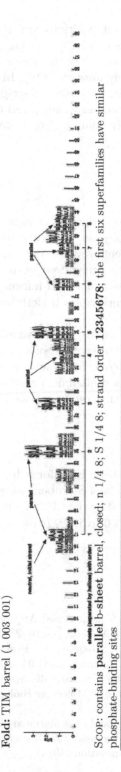

SCOP: contains **parallel b-sheet** barrel, closed; n 1/4 8; S 1/4 8; strand order **12345678**; the first six superfamilies have similar phosphate-binding sites

Fold: Rossmann-like (1 003 002)

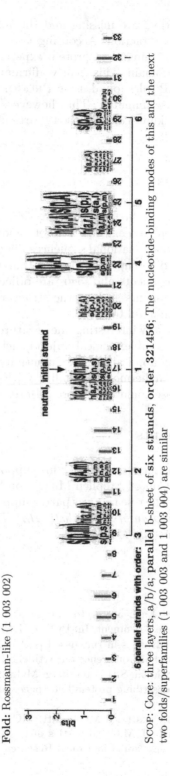

SCOP: Core: three layers, a/b/a; **parallel** b-sheet of **six strands**, **order 321456;** The nucleotide-binding modes of this and the next two folds/superfamilies (1 003 003 and 1 003 004) are similar

Fig. 6. Comparison of REAL's logos to SCOP descriptions for the TIM barrel and the Rossmann-like folds. The logos are compared to the expert-like descriptions of those folds taken from the SCOP database (caption). **Bold** words denote matches.

protein representation, are missing and the relevant positions are highlighted due to relational abstraction. According to Cotes *et al.* [3], the logos can be considered to be meaningful to protein experts and, hence, a success in terms of the application domain. This clearly affirmatively answers **(Q4)**. In contrast to Cotes *et al.*'s ILP rules found using PROGOL, our discovered descriptions are less detailed and discriminative. This, however, is not surprising given the small amount of domain knowledge we used (particularly compared to Cotes *et al.*'s PROGOL approach).

6   Conclusions

We presented REAL, the first – to the best of our knowledge – alignment approach for relational sequences, i.e., sequences of logical objects. The experimental results clearly show that relational sequences alignments reveal useful information in practice across different domains and that they can indeed be more informative. REAL's alignments and logos are objective and reveal information not present in flat alignments such as the structural principles underlying protein folds in a way meaningful to experts.

REAL suggests a very interesting line of future research, namely to address the alignment of more complex logical objects such as interpretations, i.e., graphs. This has interesting applications e.g. in activity recognition, music mining, and plan recognition. Furthermore, extending CRF-based alignment methods [21,8] to the relational case could be explored. Here, REAL should serve as a baseline.

Acknowledgments

The authors thank Luc De Raedt for his support, Ross King for helpful discussions, and Adrian Cootes, Stephen Muggleton, Michael Sternberg for providing their protein data. The research was partly supported by the EU IST programme: FP6-508861, *Application of Probabilistic ILP II*; FP6-516169, *Inductive Queries for Mining Patterns and Models*.

References

1. Barzilay, R., Lee, L.: Learning to Paraphrase: An Unsupervised Approach Using Multiple-Sequence Alignment. In: Proc. of HLT-NAACL-03, pp. 16–23 (2003)
2. Brill, E.: Some advances in rule-based part of speech tagging. In: Proceedings of the Twelfth National Conference on Artificial Intelligence (AAAI-94) (1994)
3. Cootes, A., Muggleton, S.H., Sternberg, M.J.E.: The automatic discovery of structural principles describing protein fold space. Journal of Molecular Biology 330(4), 839–850 (2003)
4. Dayhoff, M.O., Schwartz, R.M., Orcutt, B.C.: A model of evolutionary change in proteins. In: Dayhoff, M.O (ed.) Atlas of Protein Sequence and Structure, vol. 5, ch. 22, pp. 345–352. Nat. Biomedical Research Foundation (1978)

5. Do, C.B., Gross, S.S., Batzoglou, S.: CONTRAlign: Discriminative Training for Protein Sequence Alignment. In: Apostolico, A., Guerra, C., Istrail, S., Pevzner, P., Waterman, M. (eds.) RECOMB 2006. LNCS (LNBI), vol. 3909, pp. 60–74. Springer, Heidelberg (2006)

6. Durbin, R., Eddy, S., Krogh, A., Mitchinson, G.: Biological Sequence Analysis. Cambridge University Press, Cambridge (1998)

7. Gorodkin, J., Heyer, L.J., Brunak, S., Stormo, G.D.: Displaying the information contents of structural RNA alignments: the structure logos. CABIOS 13(6), 583–586 (1997)

8. Gutmann, B., Kersting, K.: TildeCRF: Conditional Random Fields for Logical Sequence. In: Fürnkranz, J., Scheffer, T., Spiliopoulou, M. (eds.) ECML 2006. LNCS (LNAI), vol. 4212, pp. 174–185. Springer, Heidelberg (2006)

9. Henikoff, S., Henikoff, J.G.: Amino acid substitution matrices from protein blocks. Proc. Natl Acad. Sci. 89, 10915–10919 (1992)

10. Jacobs, N.: Relational Sequence Learning and User Modelling. PhD thesis, Computer Science Department, Katholieke Universiteit Leuven, Belgium (2004)

11. Jiang, T., Wang, L., Zhang, K.: Alignment of trees: an alternative to tree edit. Theoretical Computer Science 143(1) (1995)

12. Kersting, K., De Raedt, L., Raiko, T.: Logial Hidden Markov Models. Journal of Artificial Intelligence Research (JAIR) 25, 425–456 (2006)

13. Kersting, K., Gärtner, T.: Fisher Kernels for Logical Sequences. In: Boulicaut, J.-F., Esposito, F., Giannotti, F., Pedreschi, D. (eds.) ECML 2004. LNCS (LNAI), vol. 3201, pp. 205–216. Springer, Heidelberg (2004)

14. Ketterlin, A.: Clustering Sequences of Complex Objects. In: Proc. of the 3rd Int. Conf. on Knowledge Discovery and Data Mining (KDD-97), pp. 215–218 (1997)

15. Lee, S.D., De Raedt, L.: Constraint Based Mining of First Order Sequences in SeqLog. In: Meo, R., Lanzi, P.L., Klemettinen, M. (eds.) Database Support for Data Mining Applications. LNCS (LNAI), vol. 2682, pp. 154–173. Springer, Heidelberg (2004)

16. Lloyd, J.W.: Foundations of Logic Programming, 2nd edn. Springer, Heidelberg (1989)

17. McCallum, A., Bellare, K., Pereira, F.: A Conditional Random Field for Discriminatively-trained Finite-state String Edit Distance. In: Bacchus, F., Jaakkola, T. (eds.) Proceedings of the Twenty-Firstst Conference on Uncertainty in Artificial Intelligence (UAI-05), Edinburgh, Scotland, July 26–29, 2005 (2005)

18. Muggleton, S.H, De Raedt, L.: Inductive Logic Programming: Theory and Methods. Journal of Logic Programming 19(20), 629–679 (1994)

19. Needleman, S., Wunsch, C.: A general method applicable to the search for similarities in the amino acid sequence of two proteins. J. Mol. Biol. 48(3), 443–453 (1970)

20. Nienhuys-Cheng, S.-H.: Distance between Herbrand interpretations: A measure for approximations to a target concept. In: Proc. of the 8. International Conference on Inductive Logic Programming (ILP-97), pp. 250–260 (1997)

21. Parker, C., Fern, A., Tadepalli, P.: Gradient Boosting for Sequence Alignment. In: Gil, Y., Mooney, R.J. (eds.) Proceedings of National Conference on Artificial Intelligence (AAAI-06), Boston, Massachusetts, USA, July 16-20, 2006, AAAI Press, Stanford (2006)

22. Ramon, J.: Clustering and instance based learning in first order logic. PhD thesis, Department of Computer Science, K.U. Leuven, Leuven, Belgium (October 2002)

23. Saitou, N., Nei, M.: The neighbor-joining method: a new method for reconstructing phylogenetic trees. Mol. Evol. Biol. 4(4), 406–425 (1987)

24. Sato, K., Sakakribara, Y.: RNA secondary structural alignment with conditional random field. Bioinformatics 25(Suppl. 2), ii237–ii242 (2005)
25. Smith, T.F., Waterman, M.S.: Identification of common molecular subsequences. Journal of Molecular Biology 147, 195–197 (1981)
26. Tobudic, A., Widmer, G.: Relational IBL in Classical Music. Machine Learning 2006 (To be published)
27. Weskamp, N.: Graph Alignments: A New Concept to Detect Conserved Regions in Protein Active Sites. In: Giegerich, R., Stoye, J. (eds.) Proceedings German Conference on Bioinformatics, pp. 131–140 (2004)

On the Missing Link Between Frequent Pattern Discovery and Concept Formation

Francesca A. Lisi and Floriana Esposito

Dipartimento di Informatica, Università degli Studi di Bari,
Via Orabona 4, 70125 Bari, Italy
{lisi, esposito}@di.uniba.it

Abstract. Concept Formation is a unsupervised learning task usually decomposed into the two subtasks of clustering and characterization. This paper presents a novel approach to Concept Formation in First Order Logic (FOL) which adopts a pattern-based approach to clustering and a bias-based approach to characterization. The resulting method extends therefore the levelwise search method for Frequent Pattern Discovery. The FOL fragment chosen is $\mathcal{AL}$-log, a hybrid language that merges the description logic $\mathcal{ALC}$ and the clausal logic DATALOG and turns out to be suitable for applications in the context of Ontology Refinement. Indeed the method returns a taxonomy rooted into the concept that occurs in an existing taxonomic ontology and needs to be refined in the light of new knowledge coming from an external data source. Experimental results have been obtained on an $\mathcal{ALC}$ ontology enriched with DATALOG data extracted from the on-line CIA World Fact Book.

1 Introduction

Concept Formation is about the incremental and unsupervised acquisition of conceptual knowledge. In their review of human concepts and concept formation, Medin and Smith [21] summarized three views: the classical, probabilistic and exemplar views. The *classical* view holds that all instances of a concept share common properties that are necessary and sufficient conditions for defining the concept. The *probabilistic* view argues that concepts are represented in terms of properties that are only characteristic or probable of class members. Membership in a category can thus be graded rather than all-or-one. The *exemplar* view claims that categories may be represented by their individual exemplars, and that assignment of a new instance to a category is determined by whether the instance is sufficiently similar to one or more of the category's known exemplar. One of the functions a concept serves is simple categorization [24]: the means by which people decide whether or not something belongs to a simple class. The defining properties in the classic view of concepts are most effective in performing simple categorization. However, to obtain the defining properties directly has been proved to be very difficult [21]. As a subject of interest in AI, Concept Formation indicates a task of Machine Learning that refers to the acquisition of conceptual hierarchies in which each concept has a flexible,

S. Muggleton, R. Otero, and A. Tamaddoni-Nezhad (Eds.): ILP 2006, LNAI 4455, pp. 305–319, 2007.

non-logical definition and in which learning occurs incrementally and without supervision [11]. More precisely, it is to take a large number of unlabeled training instances; to find clusterings that group those instances in categories; to find an intensional definition for each category that summarized its instances; and to find a hierarchical organization for those categories [6]. Note that Machine Learning researchers focus on the probabilistic and exemplar concepts. Concept Formation stems from *Conceptual Clustering* [22]. The two differ substantially in the methods: The latter usually applies bottom-up batch algorithms whereas the former prefers top-down incremental ones. Yet the methods are similar in the scope of induction, i.e. *prediction*, as opposite to (Statistical) Clustering [10] whose goal is to describe a data set.

Close to (Statistical) Clustering as it aims to *description*, **Frequent Pattern Discovery** is about the discovery of regularities in a data set [20]. A frequent pattern is an intensional description, expressed in a language $\mathcal{L}$, of a subset of a given data set $\mathbf{r}$ whose cardinality exceeds a user-defined threshold (*minimum support*). Note that patterns can refer to multiple levels of description granularity (*multi-grained patterns*) [9]. Here $\mathbf{r}$ typically encompasses a taxonomy $\mathcal{T}$. More precisely, the problem of *frequent pattern discovery at l levels of description granularity*, $1 \leq l \leq maxG$, is to find the set $\mathcal{F}$ of all the frequent patterns expressible in a multi-grained language $\mathcal{L} = \{\mathcal{L}^l\}_{1 \leq l \leq maxG}$ and evaluated against $\mathbf{r}$ w.r.t. a set $\{minsup^l\}_{1 \leq l \leq maxG}$ of minimum support thresholds by means of the evaluation function *supp*. In this case, $P \in \mathcal{L}^l$ with support s is frequent in $\mathbf{r}$ if (i) $s \geq minsup^l$ and (ii) all ancestors of P w.r.t. $\mathcal{T}$ are frequent in $\mathbf{r}$. The blueprint of most algorithms for frequent pattern discovery is the *levelwise search* method [20] which searches the space $(\mathcal{L}, \succeq)$ of patterns organized according to a generality order $\succeq$ in a breadth-first manner, starting from the most general pattern in $\mathcal{L}$ and alternating candidate generation and candidate evaluation phases. The underlying assumption is that $\succeq$ is a quasi-order monotonic w.r.t. *supp*. Note that the method proposed in [20] is also at the basis of algorithms for the variant of the task defined in [9].

In this paper we identify that missing link between Frequent Pattern Discovery and Concept Formation which allows us to formulate a solution approach for Concept Formation that exploits the results obtained for Frequent Pattern Discovery. The application context for our study is *Ontology Learning* [18] for the case of taxonomic ontologies [7]. In particular, we consider the Concept Formation problem of finding subconcepts of a known concept C_{ref}, called *reference concept*, belonging to an existing taxonomic ontology Σ in the light of new knowledge coming from a relational data source Π. We call this problem **Concept Refinement**. Also we assume that a *concept* C consists of two parts: an *intension* $int(C)$ and an *extension* $ext(C)$. The former is an expression belonging to a logical language $\mathcal{L}$ whereas the latter is a set of objects that satisfy the former. Then, the goal of Concept Refinement is to find a taxonomy $\mathcal{G}$ of concepts C_i such that (i) $int(C_i) \in \mathcal{L}$ and (ii) $ext(C_i) \subset ext(C_{ref})$. Note that C_{ref} is among both the concepts defined in Σ and the symbols of $\mathcal{L}$. Furthermore $ext(C_i)$ relies on a notion of satisfiability of $int(C_i)$ w.r.t. $\mathcal{B} = \Sigma \cup \Pi$. The taxonomy

Table 1. Syntax and semantics of $\mathcal{ALC}$

bottom (resp. top) concept	$\bot$ (resp. $\top$)	$\emptyset$ (resp. $\Delta^{\mathcal{I}}$)
atomic concept	A	$A^{\mathcal{I}} \subseteq \Delta^{\mathcal{I}}$
role	R	$R^{\mathcal{I}} \subseteq \Delta^{\mathcal{I}} \times \Delta^{\mathcal{I}}$
individual	a	$a^{\mathcal{I}} \in \Delta^{\mathcal{I}}$
concept negation	$\neg C$	$\Delta^{\mathcal{I}} \setminus C^{\mathcal{I}}$
concept conjunction	$C \sqcap D$	$C^{\mathcal{I}} \cap D^{\mathcal{I}}$
concept disjunction	$C \sqcup D$	$C^{\mathcal{I}} \cup D^{\mathcal{I}}$
value restriction	$\forall R.C$	$\{x \in \Delta^{\mathcal{I}} \mid \forall y\ (x,y) \in R^{\mathcal{I}} \rightarrow y \in C^{\mathcal{I}}\}$
existential restriction	$\exists R.C$	$\{x \in \Delta^{\mathcal{I}} \mid \exists y\ (x,y) \in R^{\mathcal{I}} \wedge y \in C^{\mathcal{I}}\}$
equivalence axiom	$C \equiv D$	$C^{\mathcal{I}} = D^{\mathcal{I}}$
subsumption axiom	$C \sqsubseteq D$	$C^{\mathcal{I}} \subseteq D^{\mathcal{I}}$
concept assertion	$a : C$	$a^{\mathcal{I}} \in C^{\mathcal{I}}$
role assertion	$\langle a, b \rangle : R$	$(a^{\mathcal{I}}, b^{\mathcal{I}}) \in R^{\mathcal{I}}$

$\mathcal{G}$ is structured according to the *subset relation* between concept extensions. A Knowledge Representation and Reasoning (KR&R) framework suitable for our purposes is the one offered by the *hybrid* KR&R system $\mathcal{AL}$-log [3] because it provides a unified framework for dealing with both the taxonomic ontology and the relational data source. Therefore, as a solution approach to the Concept Refinement problem, we propose to extend our previous work on Frequent Pattern Discovery [15] because it adapts [20,9] to the KR&R framework of $\mathcal{AL}$-log. A preliminary study of the problem is reported in [12,14].

The paper is structured as follows. Section 2 clarifies how concepts are defined with $\mathcal{AL}$-log in our approach to the Concept Formation problem in hand. Section 3 illustrates our approach to the problem. Section 4 discusses experimental results obtained on a taxonomic ontology. Section 5 concludes with final remarks and directions of future work.

2   Representing Concepts

The KR&R framework for conceptual knowledge is the one offered by $\mathcal{AL}$-log [3] which allows for the specification of both structural and relational data: the former is based on the description logic $\mathcal{ALC}$ [25], the latter on DATALOG [2]. The integration of the two forms of representation is provided by the so-called constrained DATALOG clause, i.e. a DATALOG clause with variables possibly constrained by concepts expressed in $\mathcal{ALC}$.

Input concepts are the concepts occurring in the taxonomic ontology Σ considered as input to the problem and represented with $\mathcal{ALC}$. In $\mathcal{ALC}$ knowledge is in terms of classes (*concepts*), binary relations between classes (*roles*), and instances (*individuals*). Complex concepts can be defined from atomic concepts and roles by means of constructors (see Table 1). Also Σ can state both is-a relations between concepts (*axioms*) and instance-of relations between individuals (resp. couples of individuals) and concepts (resp. roles) (*assertions*). Concepts and axioms form the so-called TBox $\mathcal{T}$ of Σ whereas individuals and assertions form the so-called ABox $\mathcal{A}$ of Σ. An *interpretation* $\mathcal{I} = (\Delta^{\mathcal{I}}, \cdot^{\mathcal{I}})$ for Σ consists of a domain $\Delta^{\mathcal{I}}$ and a mapping function $\cdot^{\mathcal{I}}$. In particular, individuals are mapped to elements of $\Delta^{\mathcal{I}}$ such that $a^{\mathcal{I}} \neq b^{\mathcal{I}}$ if $a \neq b$ (*unique names* assumption). If $\mathcal{O} \subseteq \Delta^{\mathcal{I}}$ and $\forall a \in \mathcal{O} : a^{\mathcal{I}} = a$, $\mathcal{I}$ is called $\mathcal{O}$-*interpretation*. The main reasoning task for Σ is the *consistency check*. This test is performed with a *tableau calculus* that starts with the tableau branch $S = \mathcal{T} \cup \mathcal{A}$ and adds assertions to S by means of *propagation rules* until either a contradiction is generated or an interpretation satisfying S can be easily obtained from it.

Example 1. Throughout this paper, we will refer to $\mathcal{ALC}$ ontology Σ_{CIA} concerning countries, ethnic groups, languages, and religions of the world, and built according to Wikipedia[1] taxonomies. For instance, the expression

`MiddleEastCountry ≡ AsianCountry ⊓ ∃Hosts.MiddleEasternEthnicGroup.`

is an equivance axiom that defines the concept `MiddleEastCountry` as an Asian country which hosts at least one Middle Eastern ethnic group.

Output concepts are the concepts automatically formed out of the input ones. The language $\mathcal{L}$ contains expressions, called $\mathcal{O}$-*queries*, relating individuals of C_{ref} to individuals of other concepts (*task-relevant concepts*). These concepts also must occur in Σ. An $\mathcal{O}$-*query* is a constrained DATALOG clause of the form

$$Q = q(X) \leftarrow \alpha_1, \dots, \alpha_m \& X : C_{ref}, \gamma_2, \dots, \gamma_n,$$

where X is the *distinguished variable* and the remaining variables occurring in the body of Q are the *existential variables*. Note that α_j, $1 \leq j \leq m$, is a DATALOG literal whereas γ_k, $1 \leq k \leq n$, is an assertion that constrains a variable already appearing in any of the α_j's to vary in the range of individuals of a concept defined in Σ. Also $\mathcal{O}$-queries are compliant with the properties of *linkedness* and *connectedness* [23] and the bias of *Object Identity* (OI)[2] [26]. The $\mathcal{O}$-query

$$Q_t = q(X) \leftarrow \& X : C_{ref}$$

is called *trivial* for $\mathcal{L}$ because it only contains the constraint for X. Furthermore the language $\mathcal{L}$ is *multi-grained*, i.e. it contains expressions at multiple levels of description granularity. Indeed it is implicitly defined by a *declarative bias specification* which consists of a finite alphabet $\mathcal{A}$ of DATALOG predicate names and finite alphabets Γ^l (one for each level l of description granularity) of $\mathcal{ALC}$ concept names. Note that α_i's are taken from $\mathcal{A}$ and γ_j's are taken from Γ^l. We impose $\mathcal{L}$ to be finite by specifying some bounds, mainly $maxD$ for the maximum depth of search and $maxG$ for the maximum level of granularity.

---

[1] http://www.wikipedia.org/

[2] The OI bias can be considered as an extension of the unique names assumption from the semantics of $\mathcal{ALC}$ to the syntax of $\mathcal{AL}$-log. It boils down to the use of substitutions whose bindings avoid the identification of terms.

Example 2. We want to refine the concept `MiddleEastCountry` belonging to Σ_{CIA} in the light of the new knowledge coming from the external data source Π_{CIA} consisting of DATALOG facts[3] extracted from the on-line 1996 CIA World Fact Book[4]. More precisely we want to describe Middle East countries (individuals of the reference concept) with respect to the religions believed and the languages spoken (individuals of the task-relevant concepts) at three levels of granularity ($maxG = 3$). To this aim we define $\mathcal{L}_{\text{CIA}}$ as the set of $\mathcal{O}$-queries with $C_{ref} = $ `MiddleEastCountry` that can be generated from the alphabet

$\mathcal{A}= \{\texttt{believes/2, speaks/2}\}$

of DATALOG binary predicate names, and the alphabets

$\Gamma^1 = \{\texttt{Language, Religion}\}$
$\Gamma^2 = \{\texttt{IndoEuropeanLanguage}, \dots, \texttt{MonotheisticReligion}, \dots\}$
$\Gamma^3 = \{\texttt{IndoIranianLanguage}, \dots, \texttt{MuslimReligion}, \dots\}$

of $\mathcal{ALC}$ concept names for $1 \leq l \leq 3$, up to $maxD = 5$. Note that the names in $\mathcal{A}$ are taken from Π_{CIA} whereas the names in Γ^l's are taken from Σ_{CIA}. Examples of $\mathcal{O}$-queries in $\mathcal{L}_{\text{CIA}}$ are:

$Q_t = \texttt{q(X)} \leftarrow \& \texttt{ X:MiddleEastCountry}$
$Q_1 = \texttt{q(X)} \leftarrow \texttt{speaks(X,Y)} \& \texttt{ X:MiddleEastCountry, Y:Language}$
$Q_2 = \texttt{q(X)} \leftarrow \texttt{speaks(X,Y)} \& \texttt{ X:MiddleEastCountry, Y:IndoEuropeanLanguage}$
$Q_3 = \texttt{q(X)} \leftarrow \texttt{believes(X,Y)} \& \texttt{ X:MiddleEastCountry, Y:MuslimReligion}$

where Q_t is the trivial $\mathcal{O}$-query for $\mathcal{L}_{\text{CIA}}$, $Q_1 \in \mathcal{L}^1_{\text{CIA}}$, $Q_2 \in \mathcal{L}^2_{\text{CIA}}$, and $Q_3 \in \mathcal{L}^3_{\text{CIA}}$.

Thus, an output concept $\mathcal{C}$ has an $\mathcal{O}$-query Q as intension and the set *answerset* $(Q, \mathcal{B})$ of correct answers to Q w.r.t. $\mathcal{B}$ as extension. Note that *answerset*$(Q, \mathcal{B})$ contains the substitutions θ_i's for the distinguished variable of Q such that there exists a correct answer to $body(Q)\theta_i$ w.r.t. $\mathcal{B}$. In other words, the extension is the set of individuals of C_{ref} satisfying the intension.

Example 3. The concept having Q_1 as intension has extension *answerset* $(Q_1, \mathcal{B}_{\text{CIA}}) = \{\texttt{'ARM', 'IR', 'SA', 'UAE'}\}$. In particular, the substitution $\theta = \{\texttt{X/'ARM'}\}$ is a correct answer to Q_1 w.r.t. $\mathcal{B}_{\text{CIA}}$ because there exists a correct answer $\sigma=\{\texttt{Y/ 'Armenian'}\}$ to $body(Q_1)\theta$ w.r.t. $\mathcal{B}_{\text{CIA}}$. Note that $\mathcal{B}_{\text{CIA}}=\Sigma_{\text{CIA}} \cup \Pi_{\text{CIA}}$.

Output concepts are organized into a taxonomy $\mathcal{G}$ rooted in C_{ref} and structured as a Directed Acyclic Graph (DAG) according to the *subset relation* between concept extensions. Note that one such ordering is in line with the set-theoretic semantics of the subsumption relation in ontology languages (see, e.g., the semantics of $\sqsubseteq$ in $\mathcal{ALC}$).

---

[3] http://www.dbis.informatik.uni-goettingen.de/Mondial/
mondial-rel-facts.flp
[4] http://www.odci.gov/cia/publications/factbook/

3 Forming Concepts Out of Frequent Patterns

According to the commonly accepted formulation of the task [11,6], Concept Formation can be decomposed in two sub-tasks:

1. clustering
2. characterization

The former consists in using internalised heuristics to organize the observations into categories whereas the latter consists in determining a concept (that is, an intensional description) for each extensionally defined subset discovered by clustering. We propose a **pattern-based** approach for the former (see Section 3.1) and a **bias-based** approach for the latter (see Section 3.2). Prior formulations of the two approaches are reported in [12] and [14], respectively.

3.1 Pattern-Based Clustering

A frequent pattern highlights a regularity in **r**, therefore it can be considered as the clue of a data cluster. Note that clusters are concepts partially specified (called *emerging concepts*): only the extension is known. We propose to detect emerging concepts by applying the method of [15] for frequent pattern discovery at l, $1 \leq l \leq maxG$, levels of description granularity and k, $1 \leq k \leq maxD$, levels of search depth. It adapts [20,9] to the KR&R framework of $\mathcal{AL}$-log as follows. For $\mathcal{L}$ being a multi-grained language of $\mathcal{O}$-queries, we need to define first *supp*, then $\succeq$. The *support* of an $\mathcal{O}$-query $Q \in \mathcal{L}$ w.r.t. an $\mathcal{AL}$-log knowledge base $\mathcal{B}$ is defined as

$$supp(Q, \mathcal{B}) = \mid answerset(Q, \mathcal{B}) \mid / \mid answerset(Q_t, \mathcal{B}) \mid$$

and supplies the percentage of individuals of C_{ref} that satisfy Q.

Example 4. The value $supp(Q_1, \mathcal{B}_{\text{CIA}}) = 26.6\%$ is obtained from $\mid answerset (Q_1, \mathcal{B}_{\text{CIA}}) \mid = 4$ and $\mid answerset(Q_t, \mathcal{B}_{\text{CIA}}) \mid = 15 = \mid$ `MiddleEastCountry` $\mid$.

Patterns are ordered according to $\mathcal{B}$-*subsumption* [15] which can be tested by resorting to constrained SLD-resolution: Given two $\mathcal{O}$-queries $H_1, H_2 \in \mathcal{L}$, $\mathcal{B}$ an $\mathcal{AL}$-log knowledge base, and σ a Skolem substitution for H_2 w.r.t. $\{H_1\} \cup \mathcal{B}$, we say that H_1 $\mathcal{B}$-subsumes H_2, denoted as $H_1 \succeq_\mathcal{B} H_2$, iff there exists a substitution θ for H_1 such that (i) $head(H_1)\theta = head(H_2)$ and (ii) $\mathcal{B} \cup body(H_2)\sigma \vdash body(H_1)\theta\sigma$ where $body(H_1)\theta\sigma$ is ground. It has been proved that $\succeq_\mathcal{B}$ is a quasi-order that fulfills the condition of monotonicity w.r.t. *supp* [15].

Example 5. It can be checked that $Q_1 \succeq_\mathcal{B} Q_2$ by choosing $\sigma = \{$X/a, Y/b$\}$ as a Skolem substitution for Q_2 w.r.t. $\mathcal{B}_{\text{CIA}} \cup \{Q_1\}$ and $\theta = \emptyset$ as a substitution for Q_1. Similarly it can be proved that $Q_2 \not\succeq_\mathcal{B} Q_1$. Furthermore, it can be easily verified that Q_3 $\mathcal{B}$-subsumes the following $\mathcal{O}$-query in $\mathcal{L}^3_{\text{CIA}}$

$Q_4 =$ `q(A)` $\leftarrow$ `believes(A,B), believes(A,C)` &
         `A:MiddleEastCountry, B:MuslimReligion`

by choosing $\sigma = \{$A/a, B/b, C/c$\}$ as a Skolem substitution for Q_4 w.r.t. $\mathcal{B}_{\text{CIA}} \cup \{Q_3\}$ and $\theta = \{$X/A, Y/B$\}$ as a substitution for Q_3. Note that $Q_4 \not\succeq_B Q_3$ under the OI bias. Indeed this bias does not admit the substitution $\{$A/X, B/Y, C/Y$\}$ for Q_4 which would make it possible to verify conditions (i) and (ii) of the $\succeq_B$ test.

3.2 Bias-Based Characterization

Since several frequent patterns can have the same set of supporting individuals, turning clusters into concepts is crucial in our approach. The choice criterion for concept intensions has been obtained by combining two orthogonal biases: a language bias and a search bias [23]. The former allows the user to define conditions on the form of $\mathcal{O}$-queries to be accepted as concept intensions. E.g., it is possible to state which is the minimum level of description granularity (parameter $minG$) and whether (all) the variables must be ontologically constrained or not. The latter allows the user to define a preference criterion based on $\mathcal{B}$-subsumption. More precisely, it is possible to state whether the *most general description (m.g.d.)* or the *most specific description (m.s.d.)* w.r.t. $\succeq_B$ has to be preferrred. Since $\succeq_B$ is not a total order, it can happen that two patterns P and Q, belonging to the same language $\mathcal{L}$, can not be compared w.r.t. $\succeq_B$. In this case, the m.g.d. (resp. m.s.d) of P and Q is the union (resp. conjunction) of P and Q.

Example 6. The patterns

q(A) ← speaks(A,B), believes(A,C) & A:MiddleEastCountry, B:ArabicLanguage

and

q(A) ← believes(A,B), speaks(A,C) & A:MiddleEastCountry, B:MuslimReligion

have the same answer set $\{$ARM, IR$\}$ but are incomparable w.r.t. $\succeq_B$. Their m.g.d. is the union of the two:

q(A) ← speaks(A,B), believes(A,C) & A:MiddleEastCountry, B:ArabicLanguage
q(A) ← believes(A,B), speaks(A,C) & A:MiddleEastCountry, B:MuslimReligion

Their m.s.d. is the conjunction of the two:

q(A) ← believes(A,B), speaks(A,C), speaks(A,D), believes(A,E) &
        A:MiddleEastCountry, B:MuslimReligion, C:ArabicLanguage

The extension of the subsequent concept will be $\{$ARM, IR$\}$.

The two biases are combined as follows. For each frequent pattern $P \in \mathcal{L}$ that fulfills the language bias specification, the procedure for building the DAG $\mathcal{G}$ from the set $\mathcal{F} = \{\mathcal{F}_k^l \mid 1 \leq l \leq maxG, 1 \leq k \leq maxD\}$ checks whether a concept $\mathcal{C}$ with $ext(\mathcal{C}) = answerset(P)$ already exists in $\mathcal{G}$. If one such concept is not retrieved, a new node $\mathcal{C}$ with $int(\mathcal{C}) = P$ and $ext(\mathcal{C}) = answerset(P)$ is added to $\mathcal{G}$. Note that the insertion of a node can imply the reorganization of the DAG to keep it compliant with the subset relation on extents. If the node already occurs in $\mathcal{G}$, its intension is updated according to the search bias specification.

4   Experimental Results

In order to test the approach presented in Section 3 we have extended the system $\mathcal{AL}$-QuIn [13] with a module for post-processing frequent patterns into concepts. The goal of the experiments is to provide an empirical evidence of the orthogonality of the two biases and of the potential of their combination as choice criterion.

In the next subsections we report the experimental results obtained for the problem introduced in Example 2 by setting the parameters for the frequent pattern discovery phase as follows: $maxD = 5$, $maxG = 3$, $minsup^1 = 20\%$, $minsup^2 = 13\%$, and $minsup^3 = 10\%$. Thus each experiment starts from the same set $\mathcal{F}$ of 53 frequent patterns out of 99 candidate patterns. Also all the experiments require the descriptions to have all the variables ontologically constrained but vary as to the user preferences for the minimum level of description granularity and the search bias. They are grouped according to the value assigned to $minG$.

4.1   Experiments with $minG = 2$

The first two experiments both require the descriptions to have all the variables ontologically constrained by concepts from the second granularity level on. When the m.g.d. criterion is adopted, the procedure of taxonomy building returns the following twelve concepts:

```
C-1111 ∈ F₁¹
```
$C\text{-}1111 \in \mathcal{F}_1^1$
```
q(A) ← A:MiddleEastCountry
{ARM, BRN, IR, IRQ, IL, JOR, KWT, RL, OM, Q, SA, SYR, TR, UAE, YE}
```

$C\text{-}5233 \in \mathcal{F}_3^2$
```
q(A) ← believes(A,B) & A:MiddleEastCountry, B:MonotheisticReligion
{ARM, BRN, IR, IRQ, IL, JOR, KWT, RL, OM, Q, SA, SYR, TR, UAE}
```

$C\text{-}2233 \in \mathcal{F}_3^2$
```
q(A) ← speaks(A,B) & A:MiddleEastCountry, B:AfroAsiaticLanguage
{IR, SA, YE}
```

$C\text{-}3233 \in \mathcal{F}_3^2$
```
q(A) ← speaks(A,B) & A:MiddleEastCountry, B:IndoEuropeanLanguage
{ARM, IR}
```

$C\text{-}8256 \in \mathcal{F}_5^2$
```
q(A) ← speaks(A,B), believes(A,C) &
       A:MiddleEastCountry, B:AfroAsiaticLanguage, C:MonotheisticReligion
{IR, SA}
```

$C\text{-}6256 \in \mathcal{F}_5^2$
```
q(A) ← believes(A,B), believes(A,C) &
       A:MiddleEastCountry, B:MonotheisticReligion, C:MonotheisticReligion
{BRN, IR, IRQ, IL, JOR, RL, SYR}
```

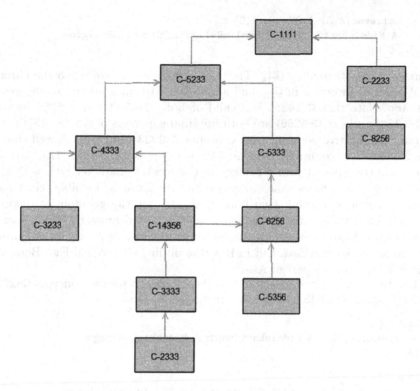

Fig. 1. Taxonomy $\mathcal{G}'_{\text{CIA}}$ for $minG = 2$

C-2333 $\in \mathcal{F}^3_3$
q(A) $\leftarrow$ believes(A,'Druze') & A:MiddleEastCountry
{IL, SYR}

C-3333 $\in \mathcal{F}^3_3$
q(A) $\leftarrow$ believes(A,B) & A:MiddleEastCountry, B:JewishReligion
{IR, IL, SYR}

C-4333 $\in \mathcal{F}^3_3$
q(A) $\leftarrow$ believes(A,B) & A:MiddleEastCountry, B:ChristianReligion
{ARM, IR, IRQ, IL, JOR, RL, SYR}

C-5333 $\in \mathcal{F}^3_3$
q(A) $\leftarrow$ believes(A,B) & A:MiddleEastCountry, B:MuslimReligion
{BRN, IR, IRQ, IL, JOR, KWT, RL, OM, Q, SA, SYR, TR, UAE}

C-14356 $\in \mathcal{F}^3_5$
q(A) $\leftarrow$ believes(A,B), believes(A,C) &
        A:MiddleEastCountry, B:ChristianReligion, C:MuslimReligion
{IR, IRQ, IL, JOR, RL, SYR}

C-5356 $\in \mathcal{F}^3_5$

```
q(A) ← believes(A,B), believes(A,C) &
        A:MiddleEastCountry, B:MuslimReligion, C:MuslimReligion
{BRN, IR, SYR}
```

organized in the taxonomy $\mathcal{G}'_{CIA}$. They are numbered according to the chronological order of insertion in $\mathcal{G}'_{CIA}$ and annotated with information of the generation step. Note that C-14356 is a child of both C-4333 and C-6256 because ext(C-4333) and ext(C-6256) are both minimal supersets of ext(C-14356).

From a qualitative point of view, concepts C-2233[5] and C-5333 well characterize Middle East countries. Armenia (ARM), as opposite to Iran (IR), does not fall in these concepts. It rather belongs to the weaker characterizations C-3233 and C-4333. This proves that our procedure performs a 'sensible' clustering. Indeed Armenia is a well-known borderline case for the geo-political concept of Middle East, though the Armenian is usually listed among Middle Eastern ethnic groups. Modern experts tend nowadays to consider it as part of Europe, therefore out of Middle East. But in 1996 the on-line CIA World Fact Book still considered Armenia as part of Asia.

When the m.s.d. criterion is adopted, the intensions for the concepts C-2233, C-3233, C-8256, C-2333 and C-3333 change as follows:

```
C-2233 ∈ 𝓕³²
q(A) ← speaks(A,B) & A:MiddleEastCountry, B:ArabicLanguage
{IR, SA, YE}
```

```
C-3233 ∈ 𝓕³²
q(A) ← speaks(A,B) & A:MiddleEastCountry, B:IndoIranianLanguage
{ARM, IR}
```

```
C-8256 ∈ 𝓕⁵²
q(A) ← speaks(A,B), believes(A,C) &
        A:MiddleEastCountry, B:ArabicLanguage, C:MuslimReligion
{IR, SA}
```

```
C-2333 ∈ 𝓕³³
q(A) ← believes(A,'Druze'), believes(A,B),
        believes(A,C), believes(A,D) &
        A:MiddleEastCountry, B:JewishReligion,
        C:ChristianReligion, D:MuslimReligion
{IL, SYR}
```

```
C-3333 ∈ 𝓕³³
q(A) ← believes(A,B), believes(A,C), believes(A,D) &
        A:MiddleEastCountry, B:JewishReligion,
        C:ChristianReligion, D:MuslimReligion
{IR, IL, SYR}
```

In particular C-2333 and C-3333 look quite overfitted to data. Yet overfitting allows us to realize that what distinguishes Israel (IL) and Syria (SYR) from

---

[5] C-2233 is less populated than expected because $\mathcal{B}_{CIA}$ does not provide facts on the languages spoken for all countries.

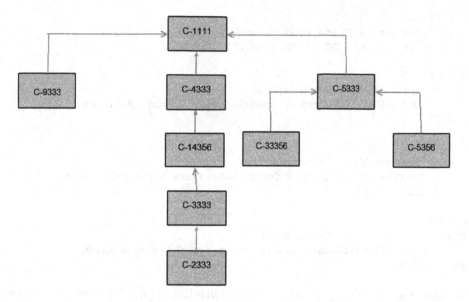

Fig. 2. Taxonomy $\mathcal{G}''_{\text{CIA}}$ for $minG = 3$

Iran is just the presence of Druze people. Note that the clusters do not change because the search bias only affects the characterization step.

4.2   Experiments with $minG = 3$

The other two experiments further restrict the conditions of the language bias specification. Here only descriptions with variables constrained by concepts of granularity from the third level on are considered. When the m.g.d. option is selected, the procedure for taxonomy building returns the following nine concepts:

C-1111 $\in \mathcal{F}_1^1$
q(A) ← A:MiddleEastCountry
{ARM, BRN, IR, IRQ, IL, JOR, KWT, RL, OM, Q, SA, SYR, TR, UAE, YE}

C-9333 $\in \mathcal{F}_3^3$
q(A) ← speaks(A,B) & A:MiddleEastCountry, B:ArabicLanguage
{IR, SA, YE}

C-2333 $\in \mathcal{F}_3^3$
q(A) ← believes(A,'Druze') & A:MiddleEastCountry
{IL, SYR}

C-3333 $\in \mathcal{F}_3^3$
q(A) ← believes(A,B) & A:MiddleEastCountry, B:JewishReligion
{IR, IL, SYR}

C-4333 $\in \mathcal{F}_3^3$
q(A) ← believes(A,B) & A:MiddleEastCountry, B:ChristianReligion
{ARM, IR, IRQ, IL, JOR, RL, SYR}

$\text{C-5333} \in \mathcal{F}_3^3$
q(A) ← believes(A,B) & A:MiddleEastCountry, B:MuslimReligion
{BRN, IR, IRQ, IL, JOR, KWT, RL, OM, Q, SA, SYR, TR, UAE}

$\text{C-33356} \in \mathcal{F}_5^3$
q(A) ← speaks(A,B), believes(A,C) &
        A:MiddleEastCountry, B:ArabicLanguage, C:MuslimReligion
{IR, SA}

$\text{C-14356} \in \mathcal{F}_5^3$
q(A) ← believes(A,B), believes(A,C) &
        A:MiddleEastCountry, B:ChristianReligion, C:MuslimReligion
{IR, IRQ, IL, JOR, RL, SYR}

$\text{C-5356} \in \mathcal{F}_5^3$
q(A) ← believes(A,B), believes(A,C) &
        A:MiddleEastCountry, B:MuslimReligion, C:MuslimReligion
{BRN, IR, SYR}

organized in a DAG $\mathcal{G}''_{CIA}$ which partially reproduces $\mathcal{G}'_{CIA}$. Note that the stricter conditions set in the language bias cause three concepts occurring in $\mathcal{G}'_{CIA}$ not to appear in $\mathcal{G}''_{CIA}$: the scarsely significant C-5233 and C-6256, and the quite interesting C-3233. Therefore the language bias can prune the space of clusters. Note that the other concepts of $\mathcal{G}'_{CIA}$ emerged at $l = 2$ do remain in $\mathcal{G}''_{CIA}$ as clusters but with a different characterization: C-9333 and C-33356 instead of C-2233 and C-8256, respectively.

When the m.s.d. condition is chosen, the intensions for the concepts C-2333 and C-3333 change analogously to $\mathcal{G}'_{CIA}$. Note that $\mathcal{G}''_{CIA}$ in both cases of m.g.d. and m.s.d. is a hierarchical taxonomy. It can be empirically observed that the possibility of producing a hierarchy increases as the conditions of the language bias become stricter.

5   Final Remarks

Summary. In this paper we have briefly described a top-down incremental method for Concept Formation within the KR&R framework of $\mathcal{AL}$-log. Note that it is not hierarchical because it returns a DAG instead of a tree structure. Hierarchical taxonomies are to be preferred for better human understanding and machine management [7]. We would like to emphasize that the biases involved in the criterion of choice are powerful enough to force the method towards the construction of a hierarchical taxonomy. Also it builds overlapping clusters. Therefore the pattern-based clustering method proposed is better defined as a clumping technique.

It is straightforward to reformulate the problem of Concept Refinement considered in this paper as a problem of *Ontology Refinement* [18]. Indeed our solution approach takes a taxonomic ontology as input and returns subconcepts of one of the concepts in the ontology, thus adapting the ontology to, e.g., a specific domain or the needs of a particular user. This is done by discovering strong associations between concepts in the input ontology.

Related work. The relation between Frequent Pattern Discovery and Concept Formation as such has never been investigated. Rather our pattern-based approach to clustering is inspired by [29]. Some contact points can be also found with [30] that defines the problem of cluster-grouping and a solution to it that integrates Subgroup Discovery, Correlated Pattern Mining and Conceptual Clustering. Note that neither [29] nor [30] deal with (fragments of) First Order Logic (FOL). Conversely, [27] combines the notions of frequent DATALOG query introduced in ILP and iceberg concept lattice borrowed from Formal Concept Analysis (FCA) [5][6]. As a result of this cross-fertilization between the two fields, *iceberg query lattices* provide a condensed representation of frequent DATALOG queries. Generally speaking, very few works on Conceptual Clustering and Concept Formation in FOL can be found in the literature. They vary as for the approaches (distance-based, probabilistic, etc.) and/or the representations (description logics, conceptual graphs, E/R models, etc.) adopted. The closest work to ours is Vrain's proposal [28] of a top-down incremental but distance-based method for Conceptual Clustering in a mixed object-logical representation. Also the idea of resorting to Frequent Pattern Discovery in Ontology Learning has been already investigated in [16]. Yet there are several differences between [16] and the present work: [16] is conceived for Ontology Extraction instead of Ontology Refinement, uses generalized association patterns (bottom-up search) instead of multi-level association patterns (top-down search), adopts propositional logic instead of FOL. Within the same application area, [19] proposes a distance-based method for clustering in RDF[7] which is not conceptual. Without doubt, there is a lack of evaluation standards in Ontology Learning. Comparative work in this field would help an ontology engineer to choose the appropriate method. One step in this direction is the framework presented in [1] but it is conceived for Ontology Extraction. Regardless of performance, each approach has its own benefits. Our approach has the advantages of dealing with expressive ontologies and being conceptual. One such approach, and in particular the possibility of forming concepts with an intensional description in the form of rule, has been considered interesting in the case of concepts defining processes, e.g. within the ontology EXPO for scientific experiments[8].

Future work. For the future we plan to extensively evaluate this approach on significantly big ontologies, hopefully on ResearchCyc[9]. The evaluation can follow several directions. It could measure the cluster validity [8], or the category

---

[6] FCA is a well-established and widely used approach for Conceptual Clustering. More recently, it has been applied to Closed Pattern Mining. Note that the notion of concept adopted in our approach is similar to the notion of formal concept at the basis of FCA.

[7] RDF is a simple ontology language for the World Wide Web.

[8] Private communication with Larisa N. Soldatova, Department of Computer Science, The University of Wales, Aberystwyth.

[9] http://research.cyc.com/

utility [4], or the similiarity with human-modeled ontologies for the problem at hand [17]. Along each of these directions there is a lot of work to be done from a methodological point of view.

References

1. Bisson, G., Nedellec, C., Cañamero, D.: Designing clustering methods for ontology building - the Mo'K workbench. In: Staab, S., Maedche, A., Nedellec, C., Wiemer-Hastings, P. (eds.) ECAI Workshop on Ontology Learning, vol. 31, CEUR Workshop Proceedings. CEUR-WS.org (2000)
2. Ceri, S., Gottlob, G., Tanca, L.: Logic Programming and Databases. Springer, Heidelberg (1990)
3. Donini, F.M., Lenzerini, M., Nardi, D., Schaerf, A.: $\mathcal{AL}$-log: Integrating Datalog and Description Logics. Journal of Intelligent Information Systems 10(3), 227–252 (1998)
4. Fisher, D.H.: Knowledge acquisition via incremental conceptual clustering. Machine Learning 2(2), 139–172 (1987)
5. Ganter, B., Stumme, G., Wille, R. (eds.): Formal Concept Analysis. LNCS (LNAI), vol. 3626. Springer, Heidelberg (2005)
6. Gennari, J.H., Langley, P., Fisher, D.: Models of incremental concept formation. Artificial Intelligence 40(1-3), 11–61 (1989)
7. Gómez-Pérez, A., Fernández-López, M., Corcho, O.: Ontological Engineering. Springer, Heidelberg (2004)
8. Halkidi, M., Batistakis, Y., Vazirgiannis, M.: On clustering validation techniques. Journal of Intelligent Information Systems 17(2-3), 107–145 (2001)
9. Han, J., Fu, Y.: Mining multiple-level association rules in large databases. IEEE Transactions on Knowledge and Data Engineering, 11(5) (1999)
10. Hartigan, J.A.: Statistical clustering. In: Smelser, N.J., Baltes, P.B. (eds.) International Encyclopedia of the Social and Behavioral Sciences, pp. 15014–15019. Oxford Press, Oxford (2001)
11. Langley, P.: Machine learning and concept formation. Machine Learning 2(2), 99–102 (1987)
12. Lisi, F.A.: A Pattern-Based Approach to Conceptual Clustering in FOL. In: Schärfe, H., Hitzler, P., Øhrstrøm, P. (eds.) ICCS 2006. LNCS (LNAI), vol. 4068, pp. 346–359. Springer, Heidelberg (2006)
13. Lisi, F.A., Esposito, F.: ILP Meets Knowledge Engineering: A Case Study. In: Kramer, S., Pfahringer, B. (eds.) ILP 2005. LNCS (LNAI), vol. 3625, pp. 209–226. Springer, Heidelberg (2005)
14. Lisi, F.A., Esposito, F.: Two Orthogonal Biases for Choosing the Intensions of Emerging Concepts in Ontology Refinement. In: Brewka, G., Coradeschi, S., Perini, A., Traverso, P. (eds.) ECAI 2006. Proceedings of the 17th European Conference on Artificial Intelligence, pp. 765–766. IOS Press, Amsterdam (2006)
15. Lisi, F.A., Malerba, D.: Inducing Multi-Level Association Rules from Multiple Relations. Machine Learning 55, 175–210 (2004)
16. Maedche, A., Staab, S.: Discovering Conceptual Relations from Text. In: Horn, W. (ed.) Proceedings of the 14th European Conference on Artificial Intelligence, pp. 321–325. IOS Press, Amsterdam (2000)
17. Maedche, A., Staab, S.: Measuring similarity between ontologies. In: Gómez-Pérez, A., Benjamins, V.R. (eds.) EKAW 2002. LNCS (LNAI), vol. 2473, pp. 251–263. Springer, Heidelberg (2002)

18. Maedche, A., Staab, S.: Ontology Learning. In: Staab, S., Studer, R. (eds.) Handbook on Ontologies, Springer, Heidelberg (2004)
19. Maedche, A., Zacharias, V.: Clustering Ontology-Based Metadata in the Semantic Web. In: Elomaa, T., Mannila, H., Toivonen, H. (eds.) PKDD 2002. LNCS (LNAI), vol. 2431, pp. 348–360. Springer, Heidelberg (2002)
20. Mannila, H., Toivonen, H.: Levelwise search and borders of theories in knowledge discovery. Data Mining and Knowledge Discovery 1(3), 241–258 (1997)
21. Medin, D., Smith, E.: Concepts and concept formation. Annual Review of Psychology 35, 113–138 (1984)
22. Michalski, R.S., Stepp, R.E.: Learning from observation: Conceptual clustering. In: Michalski, R.S., Carbonell, J.G., Mitchell, T.M. (eds.) Machine Learning: an artificial intelligence approach, Morgan Kaufmann, San Francisco (1983)
23. Nienhuys-Cheng, S.-H., de Wolf, R. (eds.): Foundations of Inductive Logic Programming. LNCS, vol. 1228. Springer, Heidelberg (1997)
24. Rey, G.: Concepts and stereotypes. Cognition 15, 237–262 (1983)
25. Schmidt-Schauss, M., Smolka, G.: Attributive concept descriptions with complements. Artificial Intelligence 48(1), 1–26 (1991)
26. Semeraro, G., Esposito, F., Malerba, D., Fanizzi, N., Ferilli, S.: A logic framework for the incremental inductive synthesis of Datalog theories. In: Fuchs, N.E. (ed.) LOPSTR 1997. LNCS, vol. 1463, pp. 300–321. Springer, Heidelberg (1998)
27. Stumme, G.: Iceberg query lattices for DATALOG. In: Wolff, K.E., Pfeiffer, H.D., Delugach, H.S. (eds.) ICCS 2004. LNCS (LNAI), vol. 3127, pp. 109–125. Springer, Heidelberg (2004)
28. Vrain, C.: Hierarchical conceptual clustering in a first order representation. In: Michalewicz, M., Raś, Z.W. (eds.) ISMIS 1996. LNCS, vol. 1079, pp. 643–652. Springer, Heidelberg (1996)
29. Xiong, H., Steinbach, M., Ruslim, A., Kumar, V.: Characterizing pattern based clustering. Technical Report TR 05-015, Dept. of Computer Science and Engineering, University of Minnesota, Minneapolis, USA (2005)
30. Zimmermann, A., De Raedt, L.: Cluster-grouping: From subgroup discovery to clustering. In: Boulicaut, J.-F., Esposito, F., Giannotti, F., Pedreschi, D. (eds.) ECML 2004. LNCS (LNAI), vol. 3201, pp. 575–577. Springer, Heidelberg (2004)

Learning Modal Theories

John W. Lloyd[1] and Kee Siong Ng[2]

[1] Computer Sciences Laboratory
Research School of Information Sciences and Engineering
The Australian National University
jwl@mail.rsise.anu.edu.au
[2] Symbolic Machine Learning and Knowledge Acquisition
National ICT Australia*
kee.siong@nicta.com.au

Abstract. This paper discusses how to learn theories that are modal, concentrating on the issue of how modal hypotheses are formed. Illustrations are given to show the usefulness of the ideas for agent applications.

1 Introduction

This paper introduces the idea of learning theories that are modal. To motivate the development, we first discuss why learning modal theories is useful, particularly in agent applications.

Consider an agent situated in some environment that can receive percepts from the environment and can apply actions to the environment. Included in a state of the agent may be information about the environment or something that is internal to the agent. The state may be updated as a result of receiving a percept. As well as some state, the agent's model includes its belief base, which can also be updated. Each action changes the current state to a new state. The agent selects an action that maximises its expected performance. An agent architecture based on the rationality principle of choosing an action that maximises expected utility is in [1] and discussion of the learning component of such agents is in [2].

We now concentrate on action selection. Agents use their belief bases to determine which action to select. It is common for the beliefs that are needed for this to have a modal nature, usually temporal or epistemic. For example, on the temporal side, it might be important that at the last time or at some time in the past, some situation held and, therefore, a certain action is now appropriate. Similarly, on the epistemic side, beliefs about the beliefs of other agents may be used to determine which action to perform. The usefulness of modal beliefs for agents is now well established, in [3] and [4], for example. Besides, introspection reveals that people use temporal and epistemic considerations when deciding what to do; essentially, we are exploiting here the fact that modal logic is a part

---

* NICTA is funded through the Australian Government's Backing Australia's Ability initiative, in part through the Australian Research Council.

S. Muggleton, R. Otero, and A. Tamaddoni-Nezhad (Eds.): ILP 2006, LNAI 4455, pp. 320–334, 2007.
© Springer-Verlag Berlin Heidelberg 2007

of mathematics which is useful for building agents that aspire to have similar capabilities.

While many beliefs can be built into agents beforehand by their designers, it is also common for beliefs to be acquired by some kind of learning process during deployment. Since beliefs can be modal, the hypothesis languages used by the learning system need to be modal. We are thus led to the conclusion that symbolic machine learning needs to be generalised beyond classical logics, such as first-order logic, to modal logics. In fact, modal higher-order logic will be employed in this paper.

This paper investigates the potential usefulness of modalities for learning applications. Its two main contributions are machinery for specifying modal hypotheses and illustrations that show the usefulness of modal hypotheses in agent applications. Given the generality of the agent paradigm and the ubiquity of agent applications, we believe that agents will be a fertile application area for symbolic machine learning techniques.

The next section contains a discussion of the logical machinery needed to construct modal hypotheses. Section 3 contains two illustrations of the ideas for agent applications. Section 4 gives some conclusions and discusses related work.

2 Modal Hypotheses

An approach to symbolic learning based on higher-order logic is presented in [5] that introduces the concept of a predicate rewrite system which is a grammar formalism for specifying search spaces of predicates that are used in hypothesis languages. Thus, to achieve the desired generalisation to learning *modal* theories, a key step is to extend predicate rewrite systems to the modal case. This is done in this section. Along the way, we introduce a modal, higher-order logic which provides a suitable setting for the development.

2.1 Modal Higher-Order Logic

We outline the most relevant aspects of the logic, focussing to begin with on the monomorphic version. We define types and terms, and give an introduction to the modalities that will be most useful in this paper. Full details of the logic, including its reasoning capabilities, can be found in [6].

Definition 1. *An* alphabet *consists of three sets:*

1. *A set $\mathfrak{T}$ of type constructors.*
2. *A set $\mathfrak{C}$ of constants.*
3. *A set $\mathfrak{V}$ of variables.*

Each type constructor in $\mathfrak{T}$ has an arity. The set $\mathfrak{T}$ always includes the type constructor Ω of arity 0. Ω is the type of the booleans. Each constant in $\mathfrak{C}$ has a signature. The set $\mathfrak{V}$ is denumerable. Variables are typically denoted by $x, y, z, \ldots$. Types are built up from the set of type constructors, using the symbols $\rightarrow$ and $\times$.

Definition 2. A type *is defined inductively as follows.*

1. *If T is a type constructor of arity k and $\alpha_1, \ldots, \alpha_k$ are types, then $T \, \alpha_1 \ldots \alpha_k$ is a type. (Thus a type constructor of arity 0 is a type.)*
2. *If α and β are types, then $\alpha \to \beta$ is a type.*
3. *If $\alpha_1, \ldots, \alpha_n$ are types, then $\alpha_1 \times \cdots \times \alpha_n$ is a type.*

The set $\mathfrak{C}$ always includes the following constants.

1. $\top$ and $\bot$, having signature Ω.
2. $=_\alpha$, having signature $\alpha \to \alpha \to \Omega$, for each type α.
3. $\neg$, having signature $\Omega \to \Omega$.
4. $\wedge, \vee, \longrightarrow, \longleftarrow$, and $\longleftrightarrow$, having signature $\Omega \to \Omega \to \Omega$.
5. Σ_α and Π_α, having signature $(\alpha \to \Omega) \to \Omega$, for each type α.

The intended meaning of $=_\alpha$ is identity (that is, $=_\alpha x \, y$ is $\top$ iff x and y are identical), the intended meaning of $\top$ is true, the intended meaning of $\bot$ is false, and the intended meanings of the connectives $\neg, \wedge, \vee, \longrightarrow, \longleftarrow$, and $\longleftrightarrow$ are as usual. The intended meanings of Σ_α and Π_α are that Σ_α maps a predicate to $\top$ iff the predicate maps at least one element to $\top$ and Π_α maps a predicate to $\top$ iff the predicate maps all elements to $\top$. The type $\{\alpha\}$ is a synonym for $\alpha \to \Omega$, used when we are intuitively thinking of a term as a set of elements rather than as a predicate.

We assume there are necessity modality operators $\Box_i$, for $i = 1, \ldots, m$.

Definition 3. A term, *together with its type, is defined inductively as follows.*

1. *A variable in $\mathfrak{V}$ of type α is a term of type α.*
2. *A constant in $\mathfrak{C}$ having signature α is a term of type α.*
3. *If t is a term of type β and x a variable of type α, then $\lambda x.t$ is a term of type $\alpha \to \beta$.*
4. *If s is a term of type $\alpha \to \beta$ and t a term of type α, then $(s \, t)$ is a term of type β.*
5. *If $t_1, \ldots, t_n$ are terms of type $\alpha_1, \ldots, \alpha_n$, respectively, then $(t_1, \ldots, t_n)$ is a term of type $\alpha_1 \times \cdots \times \alpha_n$.*
6. *If t is a term of type α and $i \in \{1, \ldots, m\}$, then $\Box_i t$ is a term of type α.*

Terms of the form $(\Sigma_\alpha \, \lambda x.t)$ are written as $\exists_\alpha x.t$ and terms of the form $(\Pi_\alpha \, \lambda x.t)$ are written as $\forall_\alpha x.t$ (in accord with the intended meaning of Σ_α and Π_α). Thus, in higher-order logic, each quantifier is obtained as a combination of an abstraction acted on by a suitable function (Σ_α or Π_α).

If α is a type, then $\mathfrak{B}_\alpha$ is the set of basic terms of type α [5]. Basic terms represent individuals. For example, $\mathfrak{B}_\Omega$ is $\{\top, \bot\}$.

The polymorphic version of the logic extends what is given above by also having available parameters which are type variables (denoted by $a, b, c, \ldots$). The definition of a type as above is then extended to polymorphic types that may contain parameters and the definition of a term as above is extended to terms that may have polymorphic types. We work in the polymorphic version of the logic in the remainder of the paper. In this case, we drop the α in $\exists_\alpha$, $\forall_\alpha$, and $=_\alpha$, since the types associated with $\exists$, $\forall$, and $=$ are now inferred from the context.

An important feature of higher-order logic is that it admits functions that can take other functions as arguments. (First-order logic does not admit these so-called higher-order functions.) This fact can be exploited in applications, through the use of predicates to represent sets and predicate rewrite systems that are used for learning, for example.

The reasoning system employed by the learner combines a theorem prover and an equational reasoning system. The theorem prover is a fairly conventional tableau theorem prover for modal higher-order logic. The equational reasoning system is, in effect, a computational system that significantly extends existing functional programming languages by adding facilities for computing with modalities. The proof component and the computational component are tightly integrated, in the sense that either can call the other. Furthermore, this synergy between the two makes possible all kinds of interesting reasoning tasks. It turns out that, for agent applications, the most common reasoning task is a computational one, that of evaluating a function call. In this case, the theorem-prover plays a subsidiary role, usually that of performing some rather straightforward modal theorem-proving tasks.

We remark that the treatment of modalities in a computation has to be carefully handled. The reason is that even such a simple concept as applying a substitution is greatly complicated in the modal setting by the fact that constants generally have different meanings in different worlds and therefore the act of applying a substitution may not result in a term with the desired meaning. A similar problem occurs when the redex chosen for a computation step is in the scope of a modality. A standard way to handle these problems is to insist that some constants be *rigid*, that is, have the same meaning in each world (in the semantics). In the modal higher-order logic setting, it is entirely natural for some constants to be rigid; for example, all constants (data constructors and functions alike) in the Haskell prelude can be declared to be rigid, except in the most sophisticated applications. For non-rigid constants, of which there are usually many in the belief bases of typical agents, great care must be taken to ensure that they are only ever used in the correct modal contexts.

Theories in the logic consist of two kinds of assumptions, global and local. The essential difference is that global assumptions are true in each world in the intended interpretation, while local assumptions only have to be true in the actual world in the intended interpretation. Each kind of assumption has a certain role to play when proving a theorem.

As is well known, modalities can have a variety of meanings, depending on the application. Some of these are indicated here; much more detail can be found in [3], [4] and [6], for example.

In multi-agent applications, one meaning for $\square_i\varphi$ is that 'agent i knows φ'. In this case, the modality $\square_i$ is written as $\boldsymbol{K}_i$. The logic $\mathbf{S5}_m$ is commonly used to capture the intended meaning of knowledge.

A weaker notion is that of belief. In this case, $\square_i\varphi$ means that 'agent i believes φ' and the modality $\square_i$ is written as B_i. The logic $\mathbf{KD45}_m$ is commonly used to capture the intended meaning of belief.

The modalities also have a variety of temporal readings. We will make use of the (past) temporal modalities ● ('last') and ■ ('always in the past'). We can also define the modality ◆ ('sometime in the past'), which is dual to ■, by $◆t \equiv \neg■\neg t$, where t is either a formula or a predicate. (The negation of a predicate is defined below.)

Modalities can be applied to terms that are not formulas. Thus terms such as $B_i 42$ and $●A$, where A is a constant, are admitted. We will find to be particularly useful terms that have the form $\square_{j_1}\cdots\square_{j_r}f$, where f is a function and $\square_{j_1}\cdots\square_{j_r}$ is a sequence of modalities.

For a particular agent in some application, the *belief base* of the agent is a theory. There are no restrictions placed on theories. Each assumption in a belief base is called a *belief*. Typically, for agent j, local assumptions in its belief base have the form $B_j\varphi$, with the intuitive meaning 'agent j believes φ'. Often φ is an equation. Other typical local assumptions have the form $B_j B_i\varphi$, meaning 'agent j believes that agent i believes φ'. Global assumptions in a belief base typically have the form φ, with no modalities at the front since the fact that they are global implicitly implies any sequence of (necessity) modalities effectively appears at the front. Thus, in general, beliefs commonly have the form $B_{j_1}\cdots B_{j_r}\varphi$, where $r \geq 0$. If there is a temporal component to beliefs, this is often manifested by temporal modalities at the front of beliefs. Then, for example, there could be a belief of the form $●^2 B_j B_i\varphi$, whose intuitive meaning is 'at the second last time, agent j believed that agent i believed φ'. (Here, $●^2$ is a shorthand for $●●$.)

The following schema can be used as a global assumption.

$$(\square_i \mathbf{s}\ \mathbf{t}) = \square_i(\mathbf{s}\ \mathbf{t}),$$

where $\mathbf{s}$ is a syntactical variable ranging over terms of type $\alpha \to \beta$ and $\mathbf{t}$ is a syntactical variable ranging over *rigid* terms of type α. (A term is rigid iff every constant in it is rigid.) This schema also holds for the dual modality ◆ (when β is Ω). Thus, under the rigidity assumption on $\mathbf{t}$, the schemas

$$(B_i \mathbf{s}\ \mathbf{t}) = B_i(\mathbf{s}\ \mathbf{t})$$
$$(◆\mathbf{s}\ \mathbf{t}) = ◆(\mathbf{s}\ \mathbf{t})$$

are global assumptions. Assumptions like these are often used in evaluating predicates generated by predicate rewrite systems.

2.2   Predicate Rewrite Systems

In this subsection, we extend the predicate rewrite systems defined in [5] to the modal case. Predicates are built up by composing basic functions called transformations. Composition is handled by the (reverse) composition function

$$\circ : (a \to b) \to (b \to c) \to (a \to c)$$

defined by $((f \circ g)\ x) = (g\ (f\ x))$.

Definition 4. *A transformation f is a function having a signature of the form*

$$f : (\varrho_1 \to \Omega) \to \cdots \to (\varrho_k \to \Omega) \to \mu \to \sigma,$$

where any parameters in $\varrho_1, \ldots, \varrho_k$ and σ appear in μ, and $k \geq 0$. The type σ is called the target *of the transformation. The number k is called the* rank *of the transformation.*

Example 1. The transformation $\wedge_n : (a \to \Omega) \to \cdots \to (a \to \Omega) \to a \to \Omega$ defined by $\wedge_n \ p_1 \ldots p_n \ x = (p_1 \ x) \wedge \cdots \wedge (p_n \ x)$, where $n \geq 2$, provides the 'conjunction' of n predicates. Disjunction $(\vee_n)$ of predicates can be defined in a similar fashion.

The transformation $\neg : (a \to \Omega) \to a \to \Omega$ defined by

$$\neg p \ x = \neg(p \ x),$$

provides the negation of a predicate.

Consider the transformation $setExists_1 : (a \to \Omega) \to \{a\} \to \Omega$ defined by

$$setExists_1 \ p \ t = \exists x.((p \ x) \wedge (x \in t)).$$

The function $(setExists_1 \ p)$ checks whether a set has an element that satisfies p.

The transformation $top : a \to \Omega$ is defined by $top \ x = \top$, for each x. The transformation $bottom : a \to \Omega$ is defined by $bottom \ x = \bot$, for each x.

Many more transformations are given in [5].

Next the definition of the class of predicates formed by composing transformations is presented. In the following definition, it is assumed that some (possibly infinite) class of transformations is given and all transformations considered are taken from this class. A standard predicate is defined by induction on the number of (occurrences of) transformations it contains as follows. Let $\square$ denote a (possibly empty) sequence of modalities $\square_{j_1} \cdots \square_{j_r}$.

Definition 5. *A standard predicate is a term of the form*

$$\square_1(f_1 \ p_{1,1} \ldots p_{1,k_1}) \circ \cdots \circ \square_n(f_n \ p_{n,1} \ldots p_{n,k_n}),$$

where f_i is a transformation of rank k_i $(i = 1, \ldots, n)$, the target of f_n is Ω, $\square_i$ is a sequence of modalities $(i = 1, \ldots, n)$, p_{i,j_i} is a standard predicate $(i = 1, \ldots, n, \ j_i = 1, \ldots, k_i)$, $k_i \geq 0$ $(i = 1, \ldots, n)$ and $n \geq 1$.

Definition 5 extends that of a (non-modal) standard predicate in [5] precisely in that the definition here allows modalities to appear.

Example 2. Let p and q be transformations of type $\sigma \to \Omega$. Then

$$\boldsymbol{B}_i(setExists_1 \ (\wedge_2 \ \bullet\boldsymbol{B}_j p \ \blacklozenge\boldsymbol{B}_j q))$$

is a standard predicate of type $\{\sigma\} \to \Omega$. If t is a (rigid) set of elements of type σ, then

$$(\boldsymbol{B}_i(setExists_1 \ (\wedge_2 \ \bullet\boldsymbol{B}_j p \ \blacklozenge\boldsymbol{B}_j q)) \ t)$$

simplifies to

$$B_i \exists x.((\bullet B_j(p\ x) \wedge \blacklozenge B_j(q\ x)) \wedge (x \in t)),$$

which is true iff agent i believes that there is an element x in t satisfying the property that at the last time agent j believed that x satisfied p and at some time in the past agent j believed that x satisfied q.

Now we can informally define a predicate rewrite system. A predicate rewrite is an expression of the form $p \rightarrowtail q$, where p and q are standard predicates. The predicate p is called the *head* and q is the *body* of the rewrite. A predicate rewrite system is a finite set of predicate rewrites. One should think of a predicate rewrite system as a kind of grammar for generating a particular class of predicates. Roughly speaking, this works as follows. Starting from the weakest predicate *top*, all predicate rewrites that have *top* (of the appropriate type) in the head are selected to make up child predicates that consist of the bodies of these predicate rewrites. Then, for each child predicate and each redex in that predicate, all child predicates are generated by replacing each redex by the body of the predicate rewrite whose head is identical to the redex. This generation of predicates continues to produce the entire space of predicates given by the predicate rewrite system. The details of the (non-modal) version of this can be found in [5]; the modal version works in a similar fashion.

Example 3. Consider the following predicate rewrite system.

$$top \rightarrowtail B_i(setExists_1\ (\wedge_2\ top\ top))$$
$$top \rightarrowtail \bullet B_j top$$
$$top \rightarrowtail \blacklozenge B_j top$$
$$top \rightarrowtail p$$
$$top \rightarrowtail q$$
$$top \rightarrowtail r.$$

The following is a path in the predicate space defined by the rewrite system.

$$top \rightsquigarrow B_i(setExists_1\ (\wedge_2\ top\ top)) \rightsquigarrow B_i(setExists_1\ (\wedge_2\ \bullet B_j top\ top))$$
$$\rightsquigarrow B_i(setExists_1\ (\wedge_2\ \bullet B_j p\ top))$$
$$\rightsquigarrow \cdots \rightsquigarrow B_i(setExists_1\ (\wedge_2\ \bullet B_j p\ \blacklozenge B_j q)).$$

The set $P_{\rightarrowtail}$ of predicates that can be generated from a predicate rewrite system $\rightarrowtail$ is called a *predicate language*. Given some predicate language, it remains to specify the *hypothesis language*, that is, the form of learned theories that employ predicates in the predicate language. There are many possibilities. For the purpose of this paper, we can restrict attention to the class of decision lists [7] that can be formed. Each internal node in such a decision list would be made up of a predicate in the predicate language. For learning, we can employ standard rule-learning algorithms.

3   Illustrations

This section contains two illustrations of the usefulness of learning modal theories for agent applications.

3.1   Majordomo Agent

Consider a majordomo agent that manages a household. There are many tasks for such an agent to carry out including keeping track of occupants, turning appliances on and off, ordering food for the refrigerator, and so on.

Here we concentrate on one small aspect of the majordomo's tasks which is to recommend television programs for viewing by the occupants of the house. (See http://www.netflixprize.com for a related industrial problem.) Suppose the current occupants are Alice, Bob, and Cathy, and that the agent knows the television preferences of each of them. Methods for learning these preferences were studied in [2]. Suppose that each occupant has a personal agent that has learned (amongst many other functions) the function $likes : Program \rightarrow \Omega$, where $likes$ is true for a program iff the person likes the program. We also suppose that the majordomo has access to the definitions of this function for each occupant, for the present time and for some suitable period into the past. Let B_m be the belief modality for the majordomo agent, B_a the belief modality for Alice, B_b the belief modality for Bob, and B_c the belief modality for Cathy. Thus part of the majordomo's belief base has the following form:

$$B_m B_a \, \forall x.((likes \, x) = \varphi_0)$$
$$\bullet B_m B_a \, \forall x.((likes \, x) = \varphi_1)$$

$$\vdots$$

$$\bullet^{n-1} B_m B_a \, \forall x.((likes \, x) = \varphi_{n-1})$$
$$\bullet^n B_m \forall x.(\blacklozenge B_a (likes \, x) = \bot)$$

$$B_m B_b \, \forall x.((likes \, x) = \psi_0)$$
$$\bullet B_m B_b \, \forall x.((likes \, x) = \psi_1)$$

$$\vdots$$

$$\bullet^{k-1} B_m B_b \, \forall x.((likes \, x) = \psi_{k-1})$$
$$\bullet^k B_m \forall x.(\blacklozenge B_b (likes \, x) = \bot)$$

$$B_m B_c \, \forall x.((likes \, x) = \xi_0)$$
$$\bullet B_m B_c \, \forall x.((likes \, x) = \xi_1)$$

$$\vdots$$

$$\bullet^{l-1} B_m B_c \, \forall x.((likes \, x) = \xi_{l-1})$$
$$\bullet^l B_m \forall x.(\blacklozenge B_c (likes \, x) = \bot),$$

for suitable φ_i, ψ_i, and ξ_i. The form these can take is explained in [2].

In the beginning, the belief base contains the formula

$$\boldsymbol{B}_m \forall x.(\blacklozenge \boldsymbol{B}_a(likes \; x) = \bot),$$

whose purpose is to prevent runaway computations into the infinite past for certain formulas of the form $\blacklozenge \varphi$. The meaning of this formula is "the agent believes that for all programs it is not true that at some time in the past Alice likes the program". After n time steps, this formula has been transformed into

$$\bullet^n \boldsymbol{B}_m \forall x.(\blacklozenge \boldsymbol{B}_a(likes \; x) = \bot).$$

In general, at each time step, the beliefs about *likes* at the previous time steps each have another $\bullet$ placed at their front to push them one step further back into the past, and a new current belief about *likes* is acquired.

Based on these beliefs about the occupant preferences for TV programs, the task for the agent is to recommend programs that all three occupants would be interested in watching together. The simplest idea is that the agent should only recommend programs that all three occupants currently like. But it is possible that less stringent conditions might also be acceptable; for example, it might be sufficient that two of the occupants currently like a program but that the third has liked the program in the past (even if they do not like it at the present time). Here is a (simplified) predicate rewrite system suitable for such a learning task.

$$top \rightarrowtail \wedge_3 \; top \; top \; top$$
$$top \rightarrowtail \vee_2 \; top \; top$$
$$top \rightarrowtail \boldsymbol{B}_i likes \quad \% \text{ for each } i \in \{a, b, c\}$$
$$top \rightarrowtail \blacklozenge \boldsymbol{B}_i likes \quad \% \text{ for each } i \in \{a, b, c\}.$$

Let *group_likes* : *Program* $\rightarrow \Omega$ be the function that the agent needs to learn. Thus the informal meaning of *group_likes* is that it is true for a program iff the occupants collectively like the program. (This may involve a degree of compromise by some of the occupants.) Training examples for this task look like

$$\boldsymbol{B}_m((group\_likes \; P_1) = \top)$$
$$\boldsymbol{B}_m((group\_likes \; P_2) = \bot),$$

where P_1 and P_2 are particular programs. The definition of a typical function that might be learned from training examples and the hypothesis language given by the above predicate rewrite system is as follows.

$$\boldsymbol{B}_m \forall x. \, ((group\_likes \; x) =$$
$$\quad if \, ((\wedge_3 \; \blacklozenge \boldsymbol{B}_a likes \; \boldsymbol{B}_b likes \; \boldsymbol{B}_c likes) \; x) \; then \; \top$$
$$\quad else \; if \, ((\wedge_3 \; \boldsymbol{B}_c likes \; (\vee_2 \; \boldsymbol{B}_a likes \; \boldsymbol{B}_b likes) \; top) \; x) \; then \; \top$$
$$\quad else \; \bot).$$

Now let P be some specific program. In Figure 1, we show the computation of $(group\_likes \; P)$. The redex selected is underlined at each step in the computation.

The computation makes use of standard boolean functions defined in [5, Chap. 5] and axiom schemas like $\bullet B_i\, \varphi \longrightarrow B_i \bullet\, \varphi$ and $\blacklozenge\varphi = \varphi \vee \bullet\blacklozenge\, \varphi$. The former is used to prove that formulas of the form

$$B_m \bullet^i B_a\ \forall x.((\textit{likes }x) = \varphi_i)$$

are theorems of the belief base. These theorems are then used to simplify the (*likes P*) terms located in different modal contexts in the computation. It follows from the computation shown in Figure 1 that $B_m((\textit{group\_likes }P) = \bot)$ is a consequence of the belief base of the agent. On this basis, the agent will presumably not recommend to the occupants that they watch program P together.

In practice, one would use a richer hypothesis language for this problem. For example, the majordomo can also make use of beliefs held by the personal diary agents of Alice, Bob and Cathy in the hypothesis language. To recommend a program for common viewing, it is important, for example, that all three are free at the program time slot. Other relevant information can be included.

3.2 Learning by Revising Past Beliefs

For agents, learning is usually a continual life-long affair. For example, a recommender agent for television programs needs to track the changing preferences of its user over a life time. Similarly, to achieve optimal performance, an adaptive traffic-light control agent needs to monitor the traffic at regular intervals to keep its beliefs about current conditions updated. This section presents a general framework for incremental belief revision.

We will start by considering the following simplified form of the general problem. We want to track a function $f : \sigma \rightarrow \tau$ that changes slowly over time. We have access to the previous acquired definition $\bullet B\, (f = \lambda x.\varphi)$ in the belief base. (B is the belief modality of the relevant agent.) A new training set arrives and now a new definition for f needs to be acquired. How do we proceed?

Obviously, in computing the current definition for f, we would like to reuse those parts of the previous definition that are still valid in the light of new evidence. One way to achieve that is to define an hypothesis language that captures the different ways the old definition can be changed, or perturbed, in small ways. We will show in stages how this can be done, starting with the description of a variant of the standard decision-list learning algorithm that will be needed.

The standard decision-list algorithm is a greedy algorithm. A set of examples is covered at every step, and an element of $\mathfrak{B}_\tau$ is used to label the leaf node constructed, the exact choice being determined by the majority class of the covered examples. This is equivalent to using a constant function to make predictions in the covered subregion. We extend the algorithm to use more complex functions for this purpose. In the new algorithm, a *label language* L is specified, in addition to a predicate language P. Learning proceeds via greedy search in the usual fashion. At every step, we seek $\arg\max_{p\in P} s(S_p)$, where S_p is the subset of the current set of examples covered by p and $s(S)$ is defined to be $\max_{l\in L} |\{(x,y) \in S\ :\ (l\ x) = y\}|$. The maximising label function l^* for

$(group\_likes\ P)$

$if\ ((\wedge_3\ \blacklozenge\boldsymbol{B}_a likes\ \boldsymbol{B}_b likes\ \boldsymbol{B}_c likes)\ P)\ then\ \top\ else\ \dots$

$if\ (\blacklozenge\boldsymbol{B}_a likes\ P)\wedge(\boldsymbol{B}_b likes\ P)\wedge(\boldsymbol{B}_c\ likes\ P)\ then\ \top\ else\ \dots$

$if\ \blacklozenge(\boldsymbol{B}_a likes\ P)\wedge(\boldsymbol{B}_b likes\ P)\wedge(\boldsymbol{B}_c likes\ P)\ then\ \top\ else\ \dots$

$if\ \blacklozenge\boldsymbol{B}_a(likes\ P)\wedge(\boldsymbol{B}_b likes\ P)\wedge(\boldsymbol{B}_c likes\ P)\ then\ \top\ else\ \dots$

$if\ (\boldsymbol{B}_a(likes\ P)\vee\bullet\blacklozenge\boldsymbol{B}_a(likes\ P))\wedge(\boldsymbol{B}_b likes\ P)\wedge(\boldsymbol{B}_c likes\ P)\ then\ \top\ else\ \dots$

$\vdots$

$if\ (\boldsymbol{B}_a\bot\vee\bullet\blacklozenge\boldsymbol{B}_a(likes\ P))\wedge(\boldsymbol{B}_b likes\ P)\wedge(\boldsymbol{B}_c likes\ P)\ then\ \top\ else\ \dots$

$if\ (\bot\vee\bullet\blacklozenge\boldsymbol{B}_a(likes\ P))\wedge(\boldsymbol{B}_b likes\ P)\wedge(\boldsymbol{B}_c likes\ P)\ then\ \top\ else\ \dots$

$if\ \bullet\blacklozenge\boldsymbol{B}_a(likes\ P)\wedge(\boldsymbol{B}_b likes\ P)\wedge(\boldsymbol{B}_c likes\ P)\ then\ \top\ else\ \dots$

$if\ \bullet(\boldsymbol{B}_a(likes\ P)\vee\bullet\blacklozenge\boldsymbol{B}_a(likes\ P))\wedge(\boldsymbol{B}_b likes\ P)\wedge(\boldsymbol{B}_c likes\ P)\ then\ \top\ else\ \dots$

$if\ (\bullet\boldsymbol{B}_a(likes\ P)\vee\bullet^2\blacklozenge\boldsymbol{B}_a(likes\ P))\wedge(\boldsymbol{B}_b likes\ P)\wedge(\boldsymbol{B}_c likes\ P)\ then\ \top\ else\ \dots$

$\vdots$

$if\ (\bullet\boldsymbol{B}_a\bot\vee\bullet^2\blacklozenge\boldsymbol{B}_a(likes\ P))\wedge(\boldsymbol{B}_b likes\ P)\wedge(\boldsymbol{B}_c likes\ P)\ then\ \top\ else\ \dots$

$if\ (\boldsymbol{B}_a\bot\vee\bullet^2\blacklozenge\boldsymbol{B}_a(likes\ P))\wedge(\boldsymbol{B}_b likes\ P)\wedge(\boldsymbol{B}_c likes\ P)\ then\ \top\ else\ \dots$

$if\ (\bot\vee\bullet^2\blacklozenge\boldsymbol{B}_a(likes\ P))\wedge(\boldsymbol{B}_b likes\ P)\wedge(\boldsymbol{B}_c likes\ P)\ then\ \top\ else\ \dots$

$if\ \bullet^2\blacklozenge\boldsymbol{B}_a(likes\ P)\wedge(\boldsymbol{B}_b likes\ P)\wedge(\boldsymbol{B}_c likes\ P)\ then\ \top\ else\ \dots$

$\vdots$

$if\ \bullet^n\blacklozenge\boldsymbol{B}_a(likes\ P)\wedge(\boldsymbol{B}_b likes\ P)\wedge(\boldsymbol{B}_c likes\ P)\ then\ \top\ else\ \dots$

$if\ \bullet^n\bot\wedge(\boldsymbol{B}_b likes\ P)\wedge(\boldsymbol{B}_c likes\ P)\ then\ \top\ else\ \dots$

$\vdots$

$if\ \bot\wedge(\boldsymbol{B}_b likes\ P)\wedge(\boldsymbol{B}_c likes\ P)\ then\ \top\ else\ \dots$

$if\ \bot\wedge(\boldsymbol{B}_c likes\ P)\ then\ \top\ else\ \dots$

$if\ \bot\ then\ \top\ else\ \dots$

$\vdots$

$\bot$

Fig. 1. Computation using $\boldsymbol{B}_m$ of $(group\_likes\ P)$

the maximising predicate p^* is then used to label S_{p^*}. Accuracy is used as the heuristic function here; other measures can be used instead, of course.

We have described the algorithm. The next step is to define a suitable predicate language for use with it. In doing that, first we have to consider the structure of a decision list, which has the following general form:

$$\lambda x. if \ (p_1 \ x) \ then \ v_1 \ else \ if \ (p_2 \ x) \ then \ v_2 \ \ldots \ else \ if \ (p_n \ x) \ then \ v_n \ else \ v_0. \quad (1)$$

Writing q_{p_i} for $\wedge_i \neg p_1 \ \ldots \ \neg p_{i-1} \ p_i$ (where $q_{p_1} = p_1$ in the base case), this term is equivalent to

$$\lambda x. if \ (q_{p_1} \ x) \ then \ v_1 \ else \ if \ (q_{p_2} \ x) \ then \ v_2 \ \ldots \ else \ if \ (q_{p_n} \ x) \ then \ v_n \ else \ v_0,$$

which we will call the *expanded form* of (1). We will effectively work with the expanded form of a decision list in designing a suitable predicate language. (This is done implicitly; expanded forms of decision lists are never explicitly constructed.)

We now proceed with the definition of a predicate language. The following transformation plays a key role.

$$covered : Int \rightarrow Int \rightarrow (a \rightarrow b) \rightarrow (a \rightarrow \Omega)$$
$$covered \ i \ j \ \lambda x. if \ (p_1 \ x) \ then \ v_1 \ else$$
$$if \ (p_2 \ x) \ then \ v_2 \ \ldots \ else \ if \ (p_n \ x) \ then \ v_n \ else \ v_0$$
$$= if \ (i = 1) \ then \ (\vee_j \ p_1 \ \ldots \ p_j) \ else \ (\wedge_i \ \neg p_1 \ \ldots \ \neg p_{i-1} \ (\vee_{j-i+1} \ p_i \ \ldots \ p_j)).$$

Thus, given a decision list f, $((covered \ i \ j \ f) \ x)$ evaluates to true iff the individual x falls into one of the nodes between the ith and jth nodes inclusively. Let $\longmapsto$ be the original predicate rewrite system used to acquire the previous definition for f. The desired hypothesis predicate language is obtained by adding to $\longmapsto$ the following predicate rewrites:

$$top \ \longmapsto \ (covered \ i \ j \ \bullet\! f) \quad \% \ \text{for each} \ i, j \in \{1, \ldots, N\}, i \leq j,$$

where N is the number of nodes in the previous definition for f.

We have specified the predicate language $P_\longmapsto$. It remains to specify a suitable label language. For that, the set $\mathfrak{B}_\tau \cup \{ (\bullet\! f \ x) \}$ is adopted.

We now show that the space of functions defined by the given decision-list algorithm in conjunction with the specified predicate and label languages contains most of the ways we might want to modify an existing decision list. For convenience, we write $\langle (p_1, v_1), (p_2, v_2), \ldots, (p_n, v_n), (top, v_0) \rangle$ as a notational shorthand for a term having the form of (1) in the following. Suppose we have the following formula in the belief base:

$$\bullet\! B \ (f = \langle (p_1, v_1), (p_2, v_2), \ldots, (p_{99}, v_{99}), (top, v_0) \rangle). \quad (2)$$

The following examples show how local surgery on (the expanded form of) the decision list can be realised using the hypothesis language defined. More complex operations can be achieved in a similar fashion.

Example 4. The operation of adding a node (r, v), where $r \in P_\longmapsto$, to the front of (2) can be realised by the definition

$$B \ (f = \lambda x. if \ (r \ x) \ then \ v \ else \ (\bullet\! f \ x)).$$

Example 5. The operation of adding a node (r, v), where $r \in P_{\rightarrowtail}$, to the end of (2) can be realised by the definition

$$\boldsymbol{B}\,(f = \lambda x.if\ ((covered\ 1\ 99\ \bullet f)\ x)\ then\ (\bullet f\ x)\ else\ if\ (r\ x)\ then\ v\ else\ v_0),$$

which is equivalent to $\boldsymbol{B}\,(f = \langle (q_{p_1}, v_1), (q_{p_2}, v_2), \ldots, (q_{p_{99}}, v_{99}), (r, v), (top, v_0)\rangle)$.

Example 6. Consider the expanded form of (2). The operation of adding a node (r, v), where $r \in P_{\rightarrowtail}$, between $(q_{p_{29}}, v_{29})$ and $(q_{p_{30}}, v_{30})$ and removing the node $(q_{p_{77}}, v_{77})$ can be realised using

$$\boldsymbol{B}\,(f = \lambda x.if\ ((covered\ 1\ 29\ \bullet f)\ x)\ then\ (\bullet f\ x)$$
$$else\ if\ (r\ x)\ then\ v$$
$$else\ if\ ((covered\ 30\ 76\ \bullet f)\ x)\ then\ (\bullet f\ x)$$
$$else\ if\ ((covered\ 78\ 99\ \bullet f)\ x)\ then\ (\bullet f\ x)\ else\ v_0),$$

which can be unfolded into the following equivalent definition:

$$\boldsymbol{B}\,(f = \langle (q_{p_1}, v_1), (q_{p_2}, v_2), \ldots, (q_{p_{29}}, v_{29}), (r, v), (q_{p_{30}}, v_{30}),$$
$$(q_{p_{31}}, v_{31}), \ldots, (q_{p_{76}}, v_{76}), (q_{p_{78}}, v_{78}), \ldots, (q_{p_{99}}, v_{99}), (top, v_0)\rangle).$$

Extensions to the Basic Setup We now consider some extensions to the basic setup. To begin with, we will record all past definitions for f in the belief base. Thus our belief base will contain, among other things, the following formulas:

$$\bullet\,\boldsymbol{B}\,(f = \lambda x.\varphi_1)$$
$$\vdots$$
$$\bullet^{n-1}\,\boldsymbol{B}\,(f = \lambda x.\varphi_{n-1})$$
$$\bullet^{n}\,\blacksquare\,\boldsymbol{B}\,(f = \lambda x.\varphi_n).$$

We can add the following predicate rewrites to our rewrite system to pick out parts of any old definition previously learned.

$$top \rightarrowtail (covered\ j\ k\ \bullet^i f)\quad \%\ \text{for suitable values of } i, j \text{ and } k.$$

If desired, one can also enrich the predicate rewrite system with predicate rewrites that capture conditions that have occurred at least once in the past or in the recent past, or those that have always held in the past.

Example 7. Assume the function f changes in a cyclical manner. If we already have a good definition for each phase of the cycle, the algorithm should return

$$\boldsymbol{B}\,(f = \lambda x.if\ (top\ x)\ then\ (\bullet^i f\ x)\ else\ v_0),$$

for some i, as the current definition.

Example 8. We can piece together parts from definitions obtained at different times to form the current definition. For instance, we can have

$$\boldsymbol{B}\,(f = \lambda x.if\ ((covered\ 2\ 8\ \bullet^2 f)\ x)\ then\ (\bullet^2 f\ x)$$
$$else\ if\ ((covered\ 6\ 9\ \bullet^4 f)\ x)\ then\ (\bullet^4 f\ x)\ else\ v_0).$$

4   Conclusions

This paper has introduced some key ideas needed to learn theories that are modal. The first contribution is machinery for specifying modal hypothesis languages that extends the higher-order logic learning setting in [5]. Modalities have obvious usefulness as a language feature; the general setup introduced here shows a good way to incorporate them into the learning process. We would expect that the more traditional ILP settings [8] can be 'upgraded' in an analogous fashion.

The two illustrations given constitute the second contribution of this paper. Together they illustrate the kind of new possibilities opened up by having modalities in the hypothesis language. The multi-agent-learning paradigm exemplified by the majordomo agent is novel in ILP and has a lot of potential. The theory revision example provides a fresh perspective on an old ILP problem. Its relation to existing techniques is discussed below. A common thread that ties the two illustrations together is *learning from multiple sources of knowledge*.

The technologies introduced here are new and more work needs to be done. We have a prototype implementation of what is described here. The next step is to carry out substantial experiments to confirm the effectiveness of the approach. The complexity of learning modal theories can be analysed in the framework given in [9]. We expect results, both positive and negative, similar to those established in the non-modal setting to continue to hold in the modal setting. In other words, modalities do not come at a significant cost.

Related work. Description logic can be regarded as a form of modal logic [4]. Related work can be found in the literature on learning theories in description logic. (See [10] and [11], for example, and the references therein.)

Incremental theory revision has long been studied in ILP following [12] and [13]. The framework introduced here allows the new definition to be obtained by revising previously acquired definitions going back multiple steps. Existing frameworks are restricted to the revision of *one* previous definition. The other noteworthy difference is that admissible revision operations are captured in the hypothesis language in our framework, *not* in the actual theory revision algorithm used as in existing setups.

There is an extensive literature on belief revision much of which was inspired by [14]. In these works, if modal logic is employed at all it is usually as a logical meta-language for the belief revision process itself, rather than the logic in which the beliefs are expressed (which is usually propositional). We are not aware of any works on belief revision in which the logic of the beliefs is as rich as modal higher-order logic. Also existing belief revision frameworks do not consider *generalisation*, which is a key aspect of learning and, we would argue, an essential component of any process by which a reasonably sophisticated agent might acquire new beliefs. On the other hand, we have not explicitly addressed here the important issue of inconsistency as frameworks for belief revision do.

References

1. Lloyd, J., Sears, T.: An architecture for rational agents. In: Baldoni, M., Endriss, U., Omicini, A., Torroni, P., et al. (eds.) DALT 2005. LNCS (LNAI), vol. 3904, pp. 51–71. Springer, Heidelberg (2006)
2. Cole, J., Gray, M., Lloyd, J., Ng, K.: Personalisation for user agents. In: Dignum, F., et al. (eds.) 4th Int. Conference on Autonomous Agents and Multiagent Systems (AAMAS 05), pp. 603–610 (2005)
3. Fagin, R., Halpern, J., Moses, Y., Vardi, M.: Reasoning about Knowledge. MIT Press, Cambridge (1995)
4. Gabbay, D., Kurucz, A., Wolter, F., Zakharyaschev, M.: Many-Dimensional Modal Logics: Theory and Applications. Studies in Logic and The Foundations of Mathematics, vol. 148. Elsevier, Amsterdam (2003)
5. Lloyd, J.: Logic for Learning. Springer, Heidelberg (2003)
6. Lloyd, J.: Knowledge representation and reasoning in modal higher-order logic 2006 (submitted for publication) http://csl.anu.edu.au/~jwl
7. Rivest, R.: Learning decision lists. Machine Learning 2, 229–246 (1987)
8. De Raedt, L.: Logical settings for concept learning. Artificial Intelligence 95, 187–201 (1997)
9. Ng, K. (Agnostic) PAC learning concepts in higher-order logic. In: Fürnkranz, J., Scheffer, T., Spiliopoulou, M. (eds.) ECML 2006. LNCS (LNAI), vol. 4212, pp. 711–718. Springer, Heidelberg (2006)
10. Kietz, J.U.: Learnability of description logic programs. In: Matwin, S., Sammut, C. (eds.) ILP 2002. LNCS (LNAI), vol. 2583, pp. 117–132. Springer, Heidelberg (2003)
11. Badea, L., Nienhuys-Cheng, S.H.: A refinement operator for description logics. In: Cussens, J., Frisch, A.M. (eds.) ILP 2000. LNCS (LNAI), vol. 1866, pp. 40–59. Springer, Heidelberg (2000)
12. Sammut, C.: Learning Concepts by Performing Experiments. University of New South Wales, Australia (1981)
13. De Raedt, L.: Interactive Theory Revision: An Inductive Logic Programming Approach. Academic Press, London (1992)
14. Alchourrón, C., Gärdenfors, P., Makinson, D.: On the logic of theory change: Partial meet contraction and revision functions. Journal of Symbolic Logic 50, 510–530 (1985)

A Mining Algorithm Using Property Items Extracted from Sampled Examples

Jun-Ichi Motoyama, Shinpei Urazawa,
Tomofumi Nakano, and Nobuhiro Inuzuka

Nagoya Institute of Technology, Gokiso-cho Showa, Nagoya 466-8555, Japan
{ha8bu3,shin1008}@phaser.elcom,
{tomofumi.nakano,inuzuka}@nitech.ac.jp

Abstract. This paper proposes a mining algorithm for relational frequent patterns based on a bottom-up property extraction from examples. The extracted properties, called property items, are used to construct patterns by a level-wise way like Apriori. The property items are assumed to have a special form, which is defined in terms of mode declaration of predicates. The algorithm produces frequent itemsets as patterns without duplication in the sense of logical equivalence. It is implemented as a system called MAPIX and is evaluated with four different datasets with comparison to WARMR. MAPIX had large advantage in runtime.

1 Introduction

Association rule mining algorithms (e.g. Apriori[1]) construct association rules on a finite set of items. An object is identified with a set of items or an attribute-value vector. With the first-order representation or the multi-relational DB setting, there will be infinitely many different objects and their representations need infinitely many attributes.

WARMR[2,3,4], a successful relational association rule miner, treats first-order items. In the classification with the first-order representation the problem of infinite attributes is solved by a top-down search and incremental construction of rules. Rules classifying interesting objects from others are explored by generating infinite different attributes incrementally. WARMR also generates candidate patterns (queries) in top-down way from simple to complex in level-wise. It efficiently cuts down unnecessary patterns using a saved infrequent query set. The set has a similar function to the principle of Apriori.

If we can prepare frequent items in advance we may directly apply Apriori to multi-relational mining. We propose a concept of first order item called a property item which can be prepared from examples in a bottom-up way. Itemsets (called property itemsets) are also defined from a set of property items and a simple composition. Then we may say that the concept of property items is a kind of propositionalization but they are defined dynamically from data. A set of examples satisfied by an itemset is an intersection of cover sets of belonging items. Therefore Apriori algorithm can be fully applied.

S. Muggleton, R. Otero, and A. Tamaddoni-Nezhad (Eds.): ILP 2006, LNAI 4455, pp. 335–350, 2007.

The following section introduces preliminary definitions and an outline of the method. Then concepts of property items and itemsets are given in Section 3. Section 4 describes MAPIX algorithm and its correctness. In Section 5 MAPIX is evaluated on four different datasets comparing with WARMR.

2 Preparations and an Outline

We assume familiarity on logic programming. MAPIX uses Datalog, a Prolog without functors, to represent data and patterns. Datalog formulae are of the form $\forall(h \leftarrow b_1 \wedge \ldots \wedge b_n)$ (called a clause), where $\forall F$ means all variables in F are universally quantified and $\forall$ is omitted when understood from context. Here, $h, b_1, \ldots, b_n$ are logical atoms without functors, that is, a predicate symbol followed by a designated number of terms which are constants or variables. For $c = h \leftarrow b_1 \wedge \ldots \wedge b_n$, head(c) denotes the head atom h and body(c) denotes the body conjunction $b_1 \wedge \ldots \wedge b_n$. A fact is a clause without body. We use substitutions, described by $\theta = \{v_1/t_1, \ldots, v_n/t_n\}$, where v_i's are variables and t_i's are terms. $P\theta$ for a formula P means replacing every variable v_i with t_i.

For our mining task a Datalog DB $\boldsymbol{R}$ is given. A predicate corresponds to a relation. A predicate p is extensional when every formula whose head uses p is a ground (no variable) fact in $\boldsymbol{R}$, otherwise intensional. One of extensional relations is specified for a *target* (It is called as *key* for WARMR). A fact of the target relation is called a *target instance*.

A *query* is a clause without head $\leftarrow b_1 \wedge \ldots \wedge b_n$, equivalently an existentially quantified conjunction $\exists(b_1 \wedge \ldots \wedge b_n)$, where $\exists Q$ for a formula Q means that all variables in Q are existentially quantified. When a formula is clearly meant to be a query the $\exists$ is dropped. A query q is said to succeed wrt $\boldsymbol{R}$ when $\boldsymbol{R} \models \exists q$.

The following gives patterns, among which a mining algorithm outputs frequent patterns. Some definitions are brought from [3] with slight modification.

Definition 1 (pattern). *A pattern is a Datalog formula whose head is of the target predicate. For a target instance e and a pattern P, $P(e)$ denotes a query $\exists(body(P)\theta)$ where θ is the mgu (most general unifier) of e and head(P). The substitution θ is called a* target instantiation *of e to P. When $P(e)$ succeeds we say that e* possesses P.

Definition 2 (frequent pattern). *The frequency of P is the number of target instances which possess P. P is frequent if its frequency exceeds $sup_{min} \cdot N$, where sup_{min} is a given minimal support and N is the number of all target instances.*

Example 1. Let us consider a DB $\boldsymbol{R}_{fam}$ on a family, illustrated in Fig. 1. Here we consider four relations, parent(x, y) meaning x is a parent of y and drawn by a line in the figure, female(x) meaning x is female, marked $*$, male(x) for male x, names without $*$, and grandfather(x) meaning x is someone's grandfather, not indicated explicitly. We choose grandfather as a target, including five instances.

Then, for example the following formula is a pattern.

$$P = \mathsf{grandfather}(A) \leftarrow \mathsf{male}(A) \wedge \mathsf{parent}(A, B) \wedge \mathsf{male}(B)$$

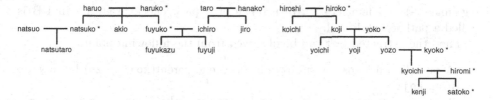

Fig. 1. A family example

Then for a target instance $e = $ grandfather(haruo), $P(e)$ means a query,

$$P(e) = \exists((\mathsf{male}(A) \wedge \mathsf{parent}(A, B) \wedge \mathsf{male}(B))\theta)$$
$$= \exists(\mathsf{male}(\mathtt{haruo}) \wedge \mathsf{parent}(\mathtt{haruo}, B) \wedge \mathsf{male}(B))$$

where θ is the target instantiation of e to P, i.e. the mgu of e and the head of P. The query $P(e)$ succeeds by a variable assignment $\{B \mapsto \mathtt{akio}\}$ then e possesses P. Actually all five target instances possess P and then its frequency is five. □

This paper assumes that useful patterns have a special form. We call such patterns *property items*, discussed in Section 3. Property items can be extracted from given target instances in a bottom-up way. The proposing algorithm MAPIX, a mining algorithm using property items extracted from examples, automatically collects property items from a given DB. We only give a frequent pattern miner and leave a part giving association rules. The outline of MAPIX is as follows:

1. It samples target instances from a target relation.
2. For each sampled target instance it collects facts (property) hold on DB.
3. By generalizing the facts it generates first-order items, called property items.
4. It executes Apriori-like level-wise frequent pattern mining algorithm by regarding the satisfaction of a property item as possession of an item.

3   Property Items and Extraction from Examples

For an instance grandfather(koji), we may find some facts on it, for example,

$$\mathsf{parent}(\mathtt{koji}, \mathtt{yozo}) \wedge \mathsf{parent}(\mathtt{yozo}, \mathtt{kyoichi}) \wedge \mathsf{male}(\mathtt{kyoichi}).$$

We may read it that koji has a grandson. We call the fact a property of grandfather(koji). By replacing terms by variables and affixing a head we have a pattern, grandfather$(A) \leftarrow \mathsf{parent}(A, B) \wedge \mathsf{parent}(B, C) \wedge \mathsf{male}(C)$.

Many ILP algorithms use execution modes and types of predicates. The above fact on koji will be analysed by a mode theory. Here we give modes to the predicates as parent$(+, -)$, male$(+)$, and female$(+)$, where $+/-$ means an input/output mode argument ($\langle + \rangle/\langle - \rangle$-arg. in short). We do not give mode for target predicate. By using mode we distinct two different classes of predicates obeying [7]. A predicate with at least one $\langle - \rangle$-arg. is called a path predicate, e.g. parent$(+, -)$. A predicate without $\langle - \rangle$-arg. is called a check predicate, e.g. male(+) and female(+). An instance of a path/check predicate in DB is called a path/check literal.

Then the extracted fact can be observed from the following points.

- A path literal leads a term from a term, e.g. parent(koji, yozo) leads yozo from koji.
- Terms lead from a term in a target instance make a chain, e.g. koji, yozo, and kyoichi, and it stops by a check literal, e.g. male(kyoichi).

Although we may imagine facts breaking this form, the observation suggests a general form of properties found in multi-relational DB. A chain of path literals has a function referring an object (an attribute) of a target instance, and a check literal describes its character (an attribute value). We assume all interesting facts have this *two-part* (a *referential part* and a *description part*) *form*.

Similar idea to the property appeared in contexts of propositionalization. The concept of first-order features used in LINUS[8] and 1BC[6] is an example. The idea of bottom-up construction of property is related to pathfinding[11] to solve the local plateau problem for top-down induction.

Formally a property of a target instance is defined by the following definition.

Definition 3 (property). *A property of a target instance e on a check literal c wrt DB R is a minimal set P of ground atoms in R that satisfies*

1. *P includes exactly the one check literal c, and*
2. *P can be given a linear order where a term in $\langle+\rangle$-arg. of a literal $l \in P$ is occurred in some precedent literals in the order or the target instance e.*

Aimed special patterns are given by variblizing properties.

Definition 4 (variablization). *For a ground formula α a formula β is a variablization of α when*

1. *β does not include any ground term, and*
2. *there exists a substitution $\theta = \{v_1/t_1, \cdots, v_n/t_n\}$ that satisfies*
   (a) $\alpha = \beta\theta$ and (b) $t_1, \ldots, t_n$ in θ are all different terms appeared in α.

Definition 5 (property item). *Let $P = \{l_1, \cdots, l_m\}$ is a property of a target instance e wrt DB R, where the linear order for P is given as l_1 to l_m. Then the variablization of the clause $e \leftarrow l_1 \wedge \ldots \wedge l_m$ is called a property item (or simply, an item in short) of the target.*

Note that a property item is a pattern, and then possessing a property item I by e and a query $I(e)$ are used as in Definition 1.

Example 2. With the DB given in Example 1 the set

$$\{\text{parent(koji, yozo)}, \text{parent(yozo, kyoichi)}, \text{male(kyoichi)}\}$$

is a property of a target instance grandfather(koji) on the check literal male (kyoichi). They satisfy the condition by the linear order written in the line.

The following clause is made from the property with the target instance,

grandfather(koji) ← parent(koji, yozo)∧parent(yozo, kyoichi)∧male(kyoichi)

and is variablized to

$$\text{item1} = \text{grandfather}(A) \leftarrow \text{parent}(A, B) \land \text{parent}(B, C) \land \text{male}(C)$$

which is an item. Naturally grandfather(koji) possesses it since the query

$$\begin{aligned}\text{item1}(\text{grandfather(koji)}) &= \exists(\text{parent}(A, B)\theta \land \text{parent}(B, C)\theta \land \text{male}(C)\theta) \\ &= \exists(\text{parent}(\text{koji}, B) \land \text{parent}(B, C) \land \text{male}(C))\end{aligned}$$

succeeds wrt $\boldsymbol{R}_{\text{fam}}$, where $\theta = \{A/\text{koji}\}$ is the target instantiation of grandfather(koji) to item1.   □

Lemma 1. *If I is an item of e then e possesses I.*

Proof. The substitution used in the variablization to have the item from a property of e gives the variable assignment for the query $I(e)$.   □

The converse does not hold however. Let us think predicates $p(+, -), q(+, +)$ in DB $\boldsymbol{R} = \{r(a), r(c), p(a, b), p(c, d), p(c, e), q(b, b), q(d, e)\}$ and $r(\cdot)$ for a target. For a target instance $r(a)$, $\{p(a, b), q(b, b)\}$ is a property of it and then $I = r(A) \leftarrow p(A, B) \land q(B, B)$ will be an item of $r(a)$. Of course $r(a)$ possesses I. Another item $J = r(C) \leftarrow p(C, D) \land p(C, E) \land q(D, E)$ can be got from $r(c)$. $r(a)$ possesses J because $\exists(p(a, D) \land p(a, E) \land q(D, E))$ succeeds by a variable assignment $\{D \mapsto b, E \mapsto b\}$. However J is not an item of $r(a)$.

As itemsets of market basket DB we treat a set of property items as a pattern.

Definition 6 (property itemset). *A set of property items of a target is called a* property itemset *(or an* itemset *in short). For a property itemset $IS = \{I_1, \ldots, I_n\}$, where we assume an item share no variables with others, it is identified with a clause (pattern) which is also denoted by IS and is defined as,*

$$head(IS) = head(I_1)\rho \quad and \quad body(IS) = body(I_1)\rho \land \ldots \land body(I_n)\rho,$$

where ρ, called a head unification, is the mgu unifying $head(I_1)\rho = \ldots = head(I_n)\rho$. When IS is a subset of the whole set $\mathcal{U}$ of items we say that IS is on $\mathcal{U}$.

Example 3. The following line also gives an item.

$$\text{item2} = \text{grandfather}(D) \leftarrow \text{parent}(D, E) \land \text{female}(E),$$

This and item1 of Example 2 make an itemset $IS = \{\text{item1}, \text{item2}\}$, representing

$IS = \text{grandfather}(A) \leftarrow \text{parent}(A,B)\land\text{parent}(B,C)\land\text{male}(C)\land\text{parent}(A,E)\land\text{female}(E)$.

For $e = \text{grandfather}(\text{koji})$,

$IS(e) = \exists(\text{parent}(\text{koji}, B)\land\text{parent}(B, C)\land\text{male}(C)\land\text{parent}(\text{koji}, E)\land\text{female}(E))$,

which does not succeeds, and then e does not possess IS.   □

The following lemma is important to apply Apriori for property item mining.

Lemma 2. *Let T be a set of target instances, I_1 and I_2 items, and $IS = \{I_1, I_2\}$ an itemset of them. Then the following equation holds.*

$$\{e \in E \mid e \text{ possesses } IS\} = \{e \in T \mid e \text{ possesses } I_1\} \cap \{e \in T \mid e \text{ possesses } I_2\}$$

Proof. When e possesses IS, $IS(e) = \exists(\mathrm{body}(IS)\theta)$ succeeds for target instantiation θ of e to IS. Because $\mathrm{body}(IS) = \mathrm{body}(I_1)\rho \wedge \mathrm{body}(I_2)\rho$ for the head unification ρ, $IS(e) = \exists(\mathrm{body}(I_1)\rho\theta \wedge \mathrm{body}(I_2)\rho\theta)$. The variable assignment for $IS(e)$ also lets $\exists(\mathrm{body}(I_1)\rho\theta)$ and $\exists(\mathrm{body}(I_2)\rho\theta)$ succeed. Noting ρ only renames variables, it means $I_1(e)$ and $I_2(e)$ succeed. Then e also possesses I_1 and I_2.

Conversely let e possess I_1 and I_2, i.e. $I_1(e) = \exists(\mathrm{body}(I_1)\theta_1)$ and $I_2(e) = \exists(\mathrm{body}(I_2)\theta_2)$ succeed. As I_1 and I_2 share no variables, θ_1 and θ_2 are composed to θ by simple merger. The θ is a unifier of $\mathrm{head}(I_1)$ and $\mathrm{head}(I_2)$ and the head unification ρ for IS is the mgu between them. Then there is σ s.t. $\theta = \rho\sigma$, and σ is the target instantiation to IS, i.e.,

$$IS(e) = \exists(\mathrm{body}(IS)\sigma) = \exists((\mathrm{body}(I_1)\rho \wedge \mathrm{body}(I_2)\rho)\sigma)$$
$$= \exists(\mathrm{body}(I_1)\theta \wedge \mathrm{body}(I_2)\theta) = \exists(\mathrm{body}(I_1)\theta_1) \wedge \exists(\mathrm{body}(I_2)\theta_2).$$

This query succeeds and then e possesses IS.   □

4   PIX and MAPIX Algorithm

This section shows the miner MAPIX, and PIX to collect property items.

Table 1 shows PIX, which takes a target instance e and outputs all its items. PIX first generates a saturation clause[12] of e for efficiency in the following steps. The saturation clause is made of the instance e added to its body all of relevant ground facts in DB. Thereafter PROPGEN is invoked with each c of check literals to collect all properties whose description part is c. Collected properties are variablized to items and checked its minimality and duplication.

Patterns outputted by a mining algorithm should have no duplication in the sense of logical implication. Although implication is undecidable generally, it is equivalent to θ-subsumption when recursion is not included.

Definition 7. *Let $\exists C$ and $\exists D$ be queries, i.e. C and D are conjunctions and are regarded as sets of conjunct atoms. When $C \supseteq D\theta$, we say that C subsumes D which is denoted by $C \preceq D$. If $C \preceq D$ and $D \preceq C$, then we say that C and D is subsumption-equivalent and write $C \sim D$.*

PROPGEN recursively grows partial property (*path*) from a given check literal. It chooses a possible literal to add *path* and stops when a property is completed. The following lemmata give the correctness of PIX algorithm.

Lemma 3. *With a target instance e and a check literal c in its saturation, PROPGEN returns PIX all properties of e on c.*

Table 1. An algorithm PIX, extracting property items from an example

---

PIX(e):

input $e = r(t_1, \ldots, t_m)$: a target instance;

output   *Items* : the set of property items extracted from e;

1. $S_e :=$ the set of body literals of the saturation of e;
2.   *Items* $:= \emptyset$;
3.   **For each** check literal $c \in S_e$ **do**
4.   NewProps $:=$ PROPGEN($c, \emptyset, \emptyset, \{t_1, \ldots, t_m\}, S_e$);
5.   **For each** $P \in$ NewProps **do**
6. $I :=$ variablization of P;
7.   **If** I is minimal and $\forall I' \in$ *Items*, $I \not\sim I'$ **then** *Items* $:=$ *Items* $\cup \{I\}$;
8.   **return** *Items*;

PROPGEN($\ell_{\text{add}}, paths, T_{\text{open}}, T_{\text{head}}, S$):

input ℓ_{add} : a literal;
                  paths : a partial property;
                  T_{open} : the set of terms that is not connected to the head;
                  T_{head} : the set of terms used in target instance;
                  S : a subset of S_e, where used literals are removed;

output   *Props* : the set of all properties of e that are superset of the *paths*
                  and is made from S;

1. $T_{\text{open}} := T_{\text{open}} - \{t | t$ is in $\langle - \rangle$-arg. of $\ell_{\text{add}}\} \cup \{t | t$ is in $\langle + \rangle$-arg. of $\ell_{\text{add}}\}$;
2.   **If** $T_{\text{open}} - T_{\text{head}} = \emptyset$ **then** *Props* $:= \{paths \cup \{\ell_{\text{add}}\}\}$
3.   **else if** $S = \emptyset$ **then** *Prop* $:= \emptyset$
4.   **else** *Props* $:= \emptyset$;
5. $C := \{\ell \in S | \ell$ is a path literal and has at least one term
                  in $T_{\text{open}} - T_{\text{head}}$ in its $\langle - \rangle$-arg.$\}$;
6.   **For each** literal $\ell \in C$ **do**
7.   *Props* $:=$ *Props* $\cup$ PROPGEN($\ell, paths \cup \{\ell_{\text{add}}\}, T_{\text{open}}, T_{\text{head}}, S - \{\ell\}$);
8.   **Return** *Props*;

Proof. For any property P of a target instance e on c we need prove that PROPGEN generates P from e. In order to prove this we need confirm the following proposition. Here we assume an order satisfying the condition in Definition 3.

1. When *paths* is a partial property of P, containing c, a certain literal l in P and literals laying between c and l by the order, PROPGEN tries a literal ℓ to add to *path* where ℓ is the immediate precedent literal of l in the order.
2. When *paths* becomes a complete property PROPGEN quits the recursion and outputs including *path*.

The first proposition is true because such ℓ is always in C of line 5 of PROPGEN. Every term in $\langle + \rangle$-arg. of literals in *paths* has to appear in some precedent literals. Then ℓ has some term in its $\langle - \rangle$-arg., the term which appears in a $\langle + \rangle$-arg. of a literal in *paths* and does not appear in any $\langle - \rangle$-arg. of precedent literals in *paths*. This is the condition of literals in C in line 5 of PROPGEN. Unless ℓ is such literal it is unnecessary by the minimality of property.

The second is obvious by line 2 of PROPGEN.   □

Lemma 4. PROPGEN *always terminates for the call from* PIX *and when it terminates every return to* PIX *satisfies the conditions 1 and 2 of Definition 3 without minimality.*

Proof. PROPGEN terminates because every recursive call consumes a literal from finite S. Obviously the return of PROPGEN satisfies the conditions.   □

Lemma 5. *For a target instance e* PIX *always terminates and generates all and the only property items of e, which include no duplication in the sense of* $\sim$.

Proof. PIX collects all properties of e containing each check literal using PROPGEN, which has the required properties because of Lemmata 3 and 4. PIX simply checks the minimality and duplication.   □

Table 2 gives MAPIX algorithm, which simply obeys the outline. It first samples target instances and collects all of their items by PIX. After the frequencies are counted all singleton itemsets consisting of each frequent item are generated. Then it goes to an Apriori-like level-wise mining step, where CANDIDATE prepares the next level itemsets of which every sub-itemset is frequent. There are two difference from the original Apriori. One is in line 7, where items possessed by all instances are deleted. We call such items *tautologyish*. Any itemset combining frequent itemsets and tautologyish items is frequent. Then all combination of tautologyish items are annoyingly produced. This is optional in case of need leaving tautologyish items when we want all frequent itemsets.

Another difference is in line 5 of CANDIDATE. It prohibits two-item itemsets in which one subsumes the other. As in higher level itemsets all sub-itemsets have to be included in frequent itemsets, all itemsets consequently do not include a pair in which one subsumes the other. This is used for correctness.

Lemma 6. *Every item has no literal which only includes variables of head variables in its body when it has at least one path literal.*

Proof. If an item I that has at least one path literal has a body literal l with only variables of its head, then $I - \{l\}$ is still an item. This is because l has no effect to connect input and output variables. This breaks the minimality.   □

Lemma 7. *If* $IS_1 \preceq IS_2$ *for itemsets* IS_1 *and* IS_2, $IS_1 \preceq I$ *for any* $I \in IS_2$.

Proof. The head unification ρ for IS_2 and θ for $IS_1 \supseteq IS_2\theta$ makes $IS_1 \supseteq I\rho\theta$.   □

Lemma 8. *If* $IS \preceq J$ *for an itemset* IS *and an item* J, $I \preceq J$ *for some* $I \in IS$.

Proof. Let $G(I)$ (similarly, $G(IS)$) be a directed graph corresponding to an item I (an itemset IS, resp.). Nodes of $G(I)$ are literals of I, and an edge lies from l_1 to l_2 when a variable at an $\langle - \rangle$-arg. of l_1 appears in l_2 for $\langle + \rangle$-arg.

In $G(J)$ any two nodes connect to a node corresponding the check literal of J. Also we see that in $G(IS)$ two nodes corresponding literals in different items connect to no common node unless either literal includes only variables of head.

Besides $IS \preceq J$ makes a homomorphism from $G(J)$ to $G(IS)$. Then if in $G(J)$ two nodes connecting to a common node are mapped to nodes in $G(IS)$, the

Table 2. An algorithm MAPIX, mining relational frequent patterns using PIX

MAPIX(R, T, sup$_{min}$):
input R : a DB;
                 T : the target relation, the set of ground instances of the relation;
                 sup$_{min}$: the minimum support threshold;
output   *Freq* : the set of itemsets whose supports are larger than sup$_{min}$
1. **Select** an appropriate size of subset $T' \subseteq T$;
2. $\mathcal{U} := \emptyset$; *Freq* $:= \emptyset$;
3. **For each** $e \in T'$ **do** $\mathcal{U} := \mathcal{U} \cup$ PIX(e);
4. **For each** $I \in \mathcal{U}$ and $e \in T$ **do**
5.   **If** query $I(e)$ succeeds **then** *cover*$[I, e] := 1$ **else** *cover*$[I, e] := 0$;
6. $\mathcal{F} := \{ I \in \mathcal{U} \mid \sum_{e \in T}$ *cover*$[I, e] \geq$ sup$_{min} \cdot$ size(T)$\}$;
7. Delete items which hold $\sum_{e \in T}$ *cover*$[I, e] =$ size(T') from $\mathcal{F}$;   # optional
8. Give a linear order to items in $\mathcal{F}$;
9. $k := 1$; $\mathcal{F}_1 := \{\langle I \rangle \mid I \in \mathcal{F}\}$
10. **while** $\mathcal{F}_k \neq \emptyset$ **do**
11. $\mathcal{C}_{k+1} :=$ CANDIDATE($\mathcal{F}_k$);
12. $\mathcal{F}_{k+1} := \{ IS \in \mathcal{C}_{k+1} \mid \sum_{e \in T} \left(\prod_{I \in IS}$ *cover*$[I, e] \right) \geq$ sup$_{min} \cdot$ size(T)$\}$;
13.   *Freq* $:=$ *Freq* $\cup \mathcal{F}_{k+1}$; $k := k + 1$;
14. **Return** *Freq*;

CANDIDATE($\mathcal{F}$):
input $\mathcal{F}$: set of frequent itemsets of a level;
output $\mathcal{C}$: the set of candidate itemsets of the next level;
1. $\mathcal{C} := \emptyset$
2. **For each** pair $(\langle I_1, \ldots, I_k \rangle, \langle I'_1, \ldots, I'_k \rangle)$ of itemsets in $\mathcal{F}$
       where $I_1 = I'_1, \ldots, I_{k-1} = I'_{k-1}$, and $I_k < I'_k$ **do**
3. $\mathcal{C} := \mathcal{C} \cup \{\langle I_1, \ldots, I_{k-1}, I_k, I'_k \rangle\}$;
4. **For each** $IS \in \mathcal{C}$ **do**
5.   **If** $k = 1$ and ($I \preceq I'$ or $I' \preceq I$), where $IS = \langle I, I' \rangle$ **then** delete IS from $\mathcal{C}$;
6.   **For each** $I \in IS$ **do if** $IS - \{I\} \notin \mathcal{F}$ **then** delete IS from $\mathcal{C}$;
7. **Return** $\mathcal{C}$;

---

mapped nodes also have to connect to a certain common node. Then it must be $I \preceq J$ for some $I \in IS$ unless IS include literal which has only head variables.

Consider the case IS has a literal l including only head variables and l is mapped from a literal of J. If J does not include any path literal, $I \preceq J$ for the item I which l belongs to. J can not include other literal because of lemma 6. $\square$

Lemma 9. *Let $\mathcal{U}$ be a set of items, of which every pair are not subsumption equivalent, IS_1 and IS_2 any itemsets on $\mathcal{U}$ in which for every pair of items one does not subsume the other. Then $IS_1 \not\sim IS_2$ unless $IS_1 = IS_2$.*

Proof. Wolg we assume $IS_1 - IS_2 \neq \emptyset$ and $I \in IS_1 - IS_2$. Then from $IS_1 \sim IS_2$ try to yield a contradiction. $IS_1 \sim IS_2$ means (a)$IS_1 \preceq IS_2$ and (b)$IS_2 \preceq IS_1$.

(b) yields $IS_2 \preceq I$ by Lemma 7, then $J \preceq I$ for some $J \in IS_2$ by Lemma 8. Another derivation from J results $I' \preceq J$ for some $I' \in IS_1$ by (a) and Lemmata 7 and 8.

Table 3. The fair numbers $N_{\sup_{\min},\delta}$ of examples for $\delta = 1\%$

$\sup_{\min}$	50%	30%	10%	5%	3%	1%	0.5%	0.3%	0.1%
$N_{\sup_{\min},\delta}$	7	13	44	90	152	458	919	1533	4603

$I \neq I'$. Otherwise, $J \preceq I$ and $I = I' \preceq J$ yields $I \sim J$. With the premise of lemma that any pair of items in $\mathcal{U}$ are not subsumption-equivalent we have to say that $I = J$, which against the way of choosing I. Even for $I \neq I'$, we have $I' \preceq I$ because of transitivity of $\preceq$ and it is also another contradiction to the premise that no pair of items in IS_1 has subsumption relationship.   □

Theorem 10. *Let $\mathcal{U}$ be the set of all property items of target instances and $\sup_{min}$ a given minimum support. When MAPIX uses all instances as property item extraction, MAPIX enumerates all frequent property itemsets on $\mathcal{U}$ without duplication in the sense of subsumption equivalence.*

Proof.   This is direct from the preceding lemmata and the correctness of Apriori[1]. By Lemma 5 MAPIX collects $\mathcal{U}$ using all target instances. After MAPIX generates all frequent items, i.e. level 1 itemsets, advances to search higher levels. It is done first by generating candidate of the next level (CANDIDATE routine) and check the frequency. The correctness of CANDIDATE is left to [1].

PIX does not generate subsumption-equivalent items. As already explained, all itemsets examined do not include item-pair in which one subsumes the other. These and Lemma 9 assure prohibition of duplicated patterns produced.

Frequency is counted by taking intersection of cover sets by element items. The correctness of this operation is given in Lemma 2.   □

Here we gave a note on the equivalence. A mining algorithm C-armr[5] treats another kind of equivalence, which is relative to a given bakground knowledge. MAPIX treats the equivalence of patterns themselves and may output duplications if some background knowledge are considered.

We may observe that a frequent item is extracted from randomly chosen examples in a probability more than or equal to $\sup_{\min}$. Unfortunately this is not true generally, because possessing an item I by a target instance e is not equivalent to being able to extract I from e, which was seen in Lemma 1 and the following paragraph. However likely these two coincide. In that case if MAPIX has enough large number of target instances sampled, it likely produces all frequent itemsets. Let $N_{\sup_{\min},\delta}$ denote the minimum integer satisfying $(1 - \sup_{\min})^N < \delta$. Then, when MAPIX samples $N_{\sup_{\min},\delta}$ instances for item extraction, output of MAPIX includes an arbitrary frequent itemset in a probability $\geq 1 - \delta$. We call the number $N_{\sup_{\min},\delta}$ a *fair number* of examples. Table 3 shows the numbers.

5   Applying to Datasets and Results

For evaluating MAPIX we used four datasets, of which Table 4 gives a summary. We also respect WARMR as a standard for comparison. All experiments were

Table 4. Relations and their mode in four datasets

Bongard target=bongard(pic)
relations: triangle(+pic,-*obj) and 3 other figure rels. : both,
config(+pic,+obj,#conf) : check.

east-west train target=east(train)
relations: has_car(+train,-car) : path, infront(+train,+car,+car) : check,
shape(+car,#shape) and 6 other train feature rels. : check.

mutagenesis target=active(drug)
relations: bond(+drug,-*atomid,-*atomid,#int) : both,
atm(+drug,#atomid,#element,#int,#charge) : path,
lumo(+drug,#energy) and one another : check,
benzene(+drug,-*ring) and 11 other structural rels. : both,
member(#ring,+ringlist) : check,
anthracene(+drug,-*ringlist) and one another : both.

English target=english(node)
relations: adjp(+node,-node) and 26 other syntactic tag relations : path,
word(+node,-word) : path, nn(+word) and 41 other POS tag rels. : check.

---

done by an implementation of MAPIX using SWI-Prolog Ver.5.4.7 for Windows on PC of CPU Xeon 2.8GHz 2GB Memory.

Bongard. This is a general discrimination problem developed by M. Bongard. It consists of 1000 records of figure configuration. We used a dataset prepared for WARMR with only modification to fit the bias declaration.

East-West train. This is dataset originally from East-West challenge competition[10]. We used 120 trains without class labels.

Mutagenesis. This is a well used dataset as ILP classification and mining problem, which is prepared in [13]. It includes record for 188 molecules, of which 125 are positive for high mutagenic character, however we did not use the data for classification and used the all 188 records together.

English corpus. This includes English corpus, which is originally from Wall Street Journal and Penn Treebank project[9] gave POS tags and syntactic analysis. Information is merged to Datalog format as shown in Table 5. 1000 sentences are used for mining. This dataset is not prepared for WARMR.

We admit another two mode types # (constant) and * (open). The definition of check/path literal is not changed, which only depends on $\langle - \rangle$-args. These affect the condition of properties and variablization. In a property terms at # or * need not appear in precedent literals in an order. Then it is useless that a term in $\langle + \rangle$-arg. appears at precedent $\langle \# \rangle$- or $\langle * \rangle$-args. On variablizing, they work differently. A term at $\langle \# \rangle$-arg. is left ground even if the same terms are variablized in the other places. A term at $\langle * \rangle$-arg. is variablized with a new variable and it is not used in the other place even for args. placed by the same term.

Table 6 shows the numbers of candidate and frequent itemsets for the datasets. We see that train and mutagenesis are complex in the aspect of items compared with the other two. English corpus has large number of items but is sparse. As a sample all frequent items of English corpus for $\sup_{min} = 10\%$ are in Table 7.

Table 5. A example of sentence in English corpus dataset

(a) Original sentence: `Japan ranks as only the fourth largest foreign investor in Mexico, with 5% of the total investments.`

(b) POS tag knowledge:

np(t11_japan) vbz(t11_ranks)
in(t11_as)   rb(t11_only) dt(t11_the)
jj(t11_fourth) jjs(t11_largest) $\cdots$

(c) Syntactic tag knowledge:

np(t11_1, t11_2) word(t11_2, t11_japan)
vp(t11_1, t11_3) word(t11_3, t11_ranks)
pp(t11_3, t11_4) word(t11_4, t11_as)
np(t11_4, t11_5) word(t11_5, t11_only)
word(t11_5, t11_the) adjp(t11_5, t11_6)
word(t11_6, t11_fourth)
word(t11_6, t11_largest) $\cdots$

(d) A graphical representation:

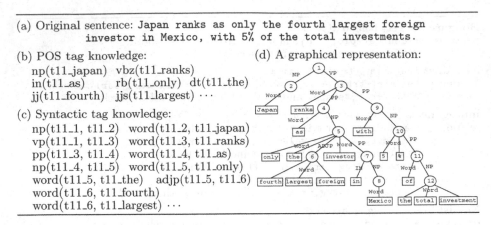

Table 6. Numbers of candidate and frequent itemsets produced by MAPIX on levels

Bongard 10%						higher level $\longrightarrow$					total
candidate	14	53	29	9	1						106
frequent	12	29	22	5	0						68

Train 10% (including no tautologyish items)

candidate	29	231	527	1060	1381	1198	654	207	31	1 0	5319
frequent	22	145	495	1030	1380	1198	654	207	31	1 0	5163

Train 10% (including tautologyish items)

candidate	29	299	1006	2835	5461	7398	7008	4565	1960	508 65 2 0	31136
frequent	25	213	974	2805	5460	7398	7008	4565	1960	508 65 2 0	30983

Mutagenesis 10% (including no tautologyish items)

candidate	56	134	99	76	29	4	0				398
frequent	17	60	95	76	29	4	0				281

Mutagenesis 10% (including tautologyish items)

candidate	56	323	1335	4645	11441	20767	28458	29787	23860	14519	
frequent	26	249	1331	4645	11441	20767	28458	29787	23860	14519	
candidate								6591	2159	481 65 4 0	144491
frequent								6591	2159	481 65 4 0	144383

English 1%

candidate	7628	34453	2193	296	23	0					44593
frequent	263	934	758	213	23	0					2191

The next experiment (Fig. 2) examined relationship between the number of examples used and the number of frequent itemsets produced. As using random sampling, experiments were iterated ten times (Three times for English due to time limitation) and the averages were plotted. The lines grow toward whole sampling. All datasets took similar trend. The ×'s on lines show points for the case of the fair number of examples. The lines converge before the fair numbers.

Table 7. Items produced in English corpus dataset with sup$_{min}$=10%

item59: english(A)←s(A, B)∧vp(B, C)∧np(C, D)∧word(D, E)∧nn(E).	(10.1%)
item67: english(A)←np(A, B)∧word(B, C)∧nn(C).	(21.7%)
item68: english(A)←vp(A, B)∧np(B, C)∧word(C, D)∧nn(D).	(11.5%)
item70: english(A)←np(A, B)∧word(B, C)∧dt(C).	(19.0%)
item71: english(A)←np(A, B)∧word(B, C)∧nns(C).	(11.9%)
item76: english(A)←s(A, B), np(B, C)∧word(C, D)∧np(D).	(11.2%)
item77: english(A)←word(A, B)∧comma(B).	(29.4%)
item78: english(A)←pp(A, B)∧word(B, C)∧in(C).	(11.6%)
item80: english(A)←s(A, B)∧np(B, C)∧word(C, D)∧nn(D).	(12.3%)
item81: english(A)←s(A, B)∧vp(B, C)∧word(C, D)∧vbd(D).	(16.2%)
item82: english(A)←s(A, B)∧np(B, C)∧word(C, D)∧dt(D).	(11.8%)
item85: english(A)←vp(A, B)∧pp(B, C)∧word(C, D)∧in(D).	(15.0%)
item87: english(A)←np(A, B)∧word(B, C)∧np(C).	(17.8%)
item88: english(A)←vp(A, B)∧word(B, C)∧vbd(C).	(29.6%)

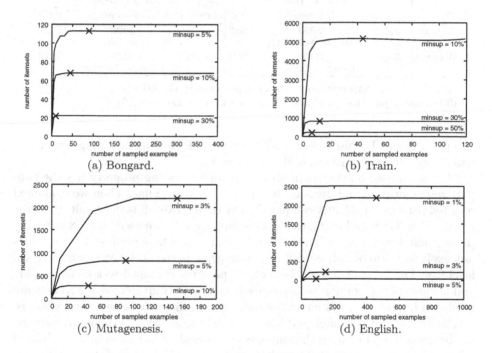

(a) Bongard.   (b) Train.

(c) Mutagenesis.   (d) English.

Fig. 2. Numbers of itemsets produced by MAPIX using sampled examples

Table 8 shows runtime of MAPIX using all/fair numbers of examples comparing WARMR. Unfortunately WARMR does not produce complete enumeration within a practical time for train and mutagenesis and we measured till level five. MAPIX performed in an enough short time. MAPIX were superior to WARMR in speed

Table 8. Run-time (sec.) of MAPIX and WARMR

	Bongard			train		
$\sup_{\min}=$	30%	10%	5%	50%	30%	10%
MAPIX (all exams.)	17.20	17.00	17.59	4.77	5.11	22.19
MAPIX (fair exams.)	2.31	6.61	12.81	1.13	2.45	17.33
WARMR	0.05	0.32	0.86	*155.41	*441.92	*3182.30
	mutagenesis			English		
$\sup_{\min}=$	30%	10%	5%	5%	3%	1%
MAPIX (all exams.)	181.20	183.38	184.91	25040	21770	22375
MAPIX (fair exams.)	29.49	75.31	140.31	3868	4482	13883
WARMR	*146.91	*500.82	*1813.96			

The numbers with * are results till level 5.

Table 9. Comparison of output patterns between MAPIX and WARMR

	East-west train			Mutagenesis		
	common	difference	total	common	difference	total
MAPIX	2732	28351 (D1:27634+D2:617)	30983	5176	139207 (D1:138696+D2:511)	144383
WARMR	3605	31199 (D1:6392+D2:24807)	34804	5176	4168 (D1:2029+D2:2138)	9343

common = patterns equivalent to some patterns in the other.
difference = patterns produced alone. (see text for D1 and D2)

except Bongard. The use of fair number of examples had an advantage especially with large datasets considering the result of Fig. 2.

MAPIX is based on the assumption that an interesting property has the two-part representation and gives up to extract other formulae. Then we examined resulted patterns by MAPIX compared to WARMR. Table 9 is the result. Patterns produced for train and mutagenesis with $\sup_{\min}=10\%$ are used. MAPIX normally prunes tautologyish items but they were left included here because WARMR does not exclude tautologyish conditions. Note that patterns by WARMR were till level five. The table shows numbers of the patterns classified to a common part and a difference. Common patterns are ones whose equivalent counterparts are produced by the other system in the sense of $\sim$. Difference is the other patterns.

The number of common patterns must be the same if systems produce no duplication. In mutagenesis the numbers are coincident but differ in train. Indeed WARMR produced duplication, such as $p(X, Y) \wedge q(Y)$ and $p(X, Y) \wedge p(X, Z) \wedge q(Z)$. This is because WARMR's top-down search has to visit such patterns. In train examples MAPIX produced total 30983 patterns and WARMR 34804. The difference was approximately 90%. While WARMR − MAPIX is resulted from the limited form of MAPIX's property itemsets, the deep level search causes MAPIX − WARMR. In mutagenesis dataset the part MAPIX − WARMR was very large, which does not include any duplication and caused by deep level.

In the table D1 and D2 are further divisions of differential part. D1 is the number of patterns which are not logically equivalent to any pattern of the other system but have the same cover set of a pattern of others and subsume or are subsumed by it. D2 is the number of other patterns, i.e. produced alone and absolutely different patterns from ones of the other.

In both datasets MAPIX had large numbers in D1 and small in D2. On the other hand WARMR had relatively large numbers in D2. This means that MAPIX had left patterns found by WARMR untouched, while WARMR could not go deep.

6   Conclusions

This paper proposed a bottom-up relational pattern mining algorithm MAPIX. It performed in a practical runtime with the four datasets. The speed-up is brought by the assumption of the two-part representation of property items and the fact that the cover set of itemsets is the intersection of items', as well as the bottom-up item extraction. In the sense of logical equivalence duplicated patterns are not produced. MAPIX uses sampled examples and the fair numbers of examples are enough to produce all frequent itemsets in large probability, although it is not theoretically assured. Although we convince the adequateness of two-part form, it need improve the other point. Itemsets are treated as independent items, and so variables in an item are not shared with other items. Bottom-up approaches to treat formulae for items sharing variables will be an important research issue.

References

1. Agrawal, R., Srikant, R.: Fast Algorithms for Mining Association Rules. In: Proc. VLDB, pp. 487–499. Morgan Kaufmann, San Francisco (1994)
2. Dehaspe, L., De Raedt, L.: Mining association rules with multiple relations. In: Džeroski, S., Lavrač, N. (eds.) Inductive Logic Programming. LNCS, vol. 1297, pp. 125–132. Springer, Heidelberg (1997)
3. Dehaspe, L.: Frequent pattern discovery in first-order logic, PhD thesis, Department of Computer Science, Katholieke Universiteit Leuven (1998)
4. Dehaspe, L., Toivonen, H.: Discovery of Relational Association Rules. In: Dzeroski, S., Lavrac, N. (eds.) Relational Data Mining, pp. 189–212. Springer, Heidelberg (2001)
5. De Raedt, L., Ramon, J.: Condensed Representations for Inductive Logic Programming. KR 2004, pp.438–446 (2004)
6. Flach, P.A., Lachiche, N.: 1BC: A first-order Bayesian classifier. In: Džeroski, S., Flach, P.A. (eds.) Inductive Logic Programming. LNCS (LNAI), vol. 1634, pp. 92–103. Springer, Heidelberg (1999)
7. Furusawa, M., Inuzuka, N., Seki, H., Itoh, H.: Induction of Logic Programs with More Than One Recursive Clause by Analysing Saturations. In: Džeroski, S., Lavrač, N. (eds.) Inductive Logic Programming. LNCS, vol. 1297, pp. 165–172. Springer, Heidelberg (1997)
8. Lavrač, N., Flach, P.A.: An extended transformation approach to inductive logic programming. ACM Trans. Computational Logic 2(4), 458–494 (2001)

9. Marcus, M.P., Santorini, B., Marcinkiewicz, M.A.: Building a large annotated corpus of english: The penn treebank. Comp. Linguistics 19(2), 313–330 (1994)
10. Michie, D., Muggleton, S., Page, D., Srinivasan, A.: Results of the new east-west challenge (1994) ftp://ftp.comlab.ox.ac.uk/pub/Packages/ILP/Trains/results.tar.Z
11. Richards, B.L., Mooney, R.J.: Learning Rlations by Pathfinding. AAAI-92, pp. 50–52 (1992)
12. Rouveirol, C.: Extensions of Inversion of Resolution Applied to Theory Completion. In: Muggleton, S. (ed.) Inductive Logic Programming, pp. 64–90. Academic Press, San Diego (1992)
13. Srinivasan, A., Muggleton, S., Sternberg, M.J.E., King, R.D.: Theories for Mutagenicity: A Study in First-Order and Feature-Based Induction. Artificial Intelligence 85(1-2), 277–299 (1996)
14. East-West Challenge: (2000) ftp://ftp.mlnet.org/ml-archive/ILP/public/data/east_west/, at MLnet: Machine Learning Online Information Service

The Complexity of Translating BLPs to RMMs

Stephen Muggleton and Niels Pahlavi

Department of Computing, Imperial College London,
180 Queen's Gate, London SW7 2BZ, UK
{shm,namdp05}@doc.ic.ac.uk

Abstract. Probabilistic Logic Learning (PLL) aims at learning probabilistic logical frameworks on the basis of data. Such frameworks combine expressive knowledge representation formalisms with reasoning mechanisms grounded in probability theory. Numerous frameworks have already addressed this issue. Therefore, there is a real need to compare these frameworks in order to be able to unify them. This paper provides a comparison of Relational Markov Models (RMMs) and Bayesian Logic Programs (BLPs). We demonstrate relations between BLPs' and RMMs' semantics, arguing that RMMs encode the same knowledge as a sub-class of BLPs. We fully describe a translation from a sub-class of BLPs into RMMs and provide complexity results which demonstrate an exponential expansion in formula size, showing that RMMs are less compact than their equivalent BLPs with respect to this translation. The authors are unaware of any more compact translation between BLPs and RMMs. A full implementation has already been realized, consisting of meta-interpreters for both BLPs and RMMs and a translation engine. The equality of BLPs' and corresponding RMMs' probability distributions has been proven on practical examples.

1 Introduction

1.1 Motivations

Probabilistic Logic Learning (PLL) [3] is considered as one of the main emerging areas in Machine Learning. This topic is particularly of interest because PLL is needed to tackle real-world learning and data mining problems in which the data are complex and heterogeneous. Gaining a deeper knowledge of the relationships between PLL formalisms is now widely considered as essential. Applying comparisons between frameworks would allow to develop general results on the expressive power, the semantics, the complexity and the efficiency of inference and learning of these frameworks. So far, the following translations have been studied ([4], [5], [15] and [17]). However, each new comparative study facilitates a more coherent view of the interrelationships between PLL formalisms.

Moreover, a practical complexity comparison of four PLL formalisms containing Bayesian Logic Programs (BLPs) and Relational Markov Models (RMMs), based on a version of the game of Blackjack, has already been made and is fully described in [10]. The same game is represented with respect to the different

S. Muggleton, R. Otero, and A. Tamaddoni-Nezhad (Eds.): ILP 2006, LNAI 4455, pp. 351–365, 2007.

frameworks. By varying several parameters of the game and analyzing the consequences on the representations, one can observe the differences of expressivity and complexity between the formalisms. Therefore, we considered it useful to determine whether the results obtained for this comparison would correspond to the implementation of a general translation and its application to several examples including the Blackjack example itself.

The choice of the two frameworks, BLPs and RMMs (described respectively in [7] and [1]) has been motivated by several arguments. Firstly, these two frameworks have been widely used by the community and have already provided significant results, as was stated in [2]. However, they are more or less efficient in terms of the applications studied. Therefore it could be useful to translate from one framework to another depending on the application. Secondly, it is convenient to consider a framework that has already been compared to other formalisms, in order to be able to directly link the findings of this study to the previous ones. In addition, it is useful to consider a formalism that has never been compared to another framework. Finally, it is of interest to consider a framework (BLP) which, as cited in [3], integrates "probabilistic models with very expressive relational representations or even logic programs" to another one (RMM), which is "typically less expressive" and to examine the validity of such a statement. The general idea is to analyse if it is possible to constitute classes of PLL formalisms with respect to their underlying representations and study if the frameworks in those classes would share the same characteristics in terms of efficiency of inference and learnability.

1.2   Outline

Section 2 consists of presenting the two PLL formalisms (BLPs and RMMs) syntax and semantics. We assume some familiarity with logic and probabilities. Section 3 is dedicated to the translation of a sub-class of BLPs, called BLP_F, to RMMs. In Sect. 4, we also prove formally that the two representations are semantically equivalent. Then, we compare the complexity of the representations and show that RMM are less compact than BLPs with respect to this translation. Section 5 presents the implementation of the previous translation. Firstly, the meta-interpreters associated with the two frameworks are presented. The translation engine itself is introduced. The translation is illustrated by the study of an example. Section 6 provides links with related works. Finally, the conclusion (Sect. 7) summarizes the results and suggests directions for future work.

2   Background

2.1   Bayesian Logic Programs (BLPs)

Syntax. This framework has been introduced in 2000 by Kersting and De Raedt in [7]. It extends both Logic Programs [9] and Bayesian nets [13]. As defined in [7], a BLP consists of 2 components: a *logical* one (which is a set of *Bayesian clauses*) and a *quantitative* one, which contains conditional probability tables (CPTs) and *combining rules*. A *Bayesian (definite) clause* is an expression of the form:

$$A \mid A_1, \ldots, A_n.$$

All the A_i are *Bayesian atoms* and are universally quantified. Bayesian atoms are assigned a finite *domain*, instead of binary values for logical atoms. Note that in Bayesian clauses "$\mid$" is employed instead of " $: -$ ". Each Bayesian clause C is associated with a conditional probability distribution $cpd(C)$ which encodes

$$\mathbf{P}(head(C) \mid body(C)) .$$

The conditional probability distributions are represented in CPTs. *Combining rules* are used when there are many clauses with the same head. They are functions which map finite sets of conditional probability distributions onto one *combined* conditional probability distribution. The *noisy-or* rule, when domains are boolean, and the *max* rule are common combining rules. Let B be a BLP. N denotes the number of clauses in the BLP. N_P denotes the number of predicates in the BLP. Considering a predicate r, D_r denotes the finite domain associated to r. We will denote the set of all random variables (i.e. parents) that directly influence a variable A by $\mathbf{Pa}(A)$.

Semantics. Let $LH(L)$ be the least Herbrand model[1] associated with the BLP. The set of ground Bayesian atoms in the least Herbrand model together with the structure defined by the set of ground instances of the Bayesian clauses and the conditional probability tables, define a global (possibly infinite) Bayesian network that can be queried like any other Bayesian net[2].

Thus the query-answering procedure actually consists of two parts: first, given a ground query and some evidence, the Bayesian network containing all *relevant* atoms is computed, using KBMC (*Knowledge Based Model Construction*). Then the resulting Bayesian network can be queried using any available inference algorithm, the results we were looking for being the probability of the initial ground query over its domain. Further details about the query-answering procedure can be found in [7]. KBMC is thoroughly detailed in [8]: from a general point of view, first-order rules with associated probabilities are used to generate Bayesian networks for particular queries. As in SLD-resolution, queries are matched to the heads of rules, but in KBMC this results in nodes representing ground facts being added to a growing (directed) Bayesian network. Once the Bayesian network is built it is then used to compute the probability that the query takes some value on its domain.

2.2   Relational Markov Models (RMMs)

Syntax. This framework has been introduced in 2002 by Anderson *et al* in [1]. It upgrades the notion of Markov Models ([16]). Let us briefly introduce

---

[1] We define the least Herbrand model of a BLP in the same way as in logic programs.

[2] Bayesian networks are formally defined only for finite sets of chance nodes; this point of view is put forward because it provides a better idea of the relations between BLPs and Bayesian nets.

the concept of (propositional) Markov Models (PMMs). As described in [1], "a *first-order Markov model* is a model" of a "discrete system that evolves by randomly moving from one state to another at each time step". This type of model "assumes the probability distribution over the next state only depends on the current state (and not the previous ones)". Formally, a first-order Markov model is a triple (Q, A, π). $Q = \{q_1, q_2, \ldots, q_n\}$ denotes a set of states. A is the *transition probability matrix*; it encodes the probabilities of transiting from one state to another. The element a_{ij} of A equals thus to $a_{ij} = P(S_t = q_j \mid S_{t-1} = q_i)$ where S_t denotes the current state of the system at the time t. Similarly to A, π is the *initial probability vector*, where $\pi_i = P(S_0 = q_i)$ is the probability that the initial state is q_i. But, in such a model, as mentioned in [1], "each state is an atomic entity and there is no notion of types of states".

In RMMs, the notion of *type* of states is added. States of the same type are grouped together. States are classified using *relations*. More formally, an RMM is a five-tuple $\langle D, R, Q, A, \pi \rangle$, for which D is a set of *domains*. A *domain* is a tree, which represents an abstraction hierarchy of values. The leafs of a tree are the ground values. R is a set of relations. Each argument of a relation takes values from the nodes of a single domain in D. Q is the set of states as for a propositional Markov model, yet each state must be a ground instance of one of the relations in R. A and π are defined exactly the same way as above. As stated in [1], "in the case of finite domains, RMMs are no more expressive than PMMs. The advantage of RMMs lies in the additional support for learning and inference that the relational structure provides".

Semantics. Given an RMM, the probability of observing a sequence of states $(st_0, st_1, \ldots, st_{I-1})$ is $P(St_0 = st_0, \ldots, St_{I-1} = st_{I-1}) = P(St_0 = st_0) \times \prod_{t=1}^{I-1} P(St_t = st_t \mid St_{t-1} = st_{t-1})$. As stated in [1], "Given a set of observed sequences, the maximum-likelihood estimate of an initial probability π_i is the fraction of sequences that start in state q_i, and the maximum-likelihood estimate of a transition probability a_{ij} is the fraction of visits to q_i that are immediately followed by a transition to q_j".

3   Translation

In this section, we will describe a translation which takes as input any BLP belonging to a subset of BLPs called BLP_F (defined in the next subsection) and returns an equivalent RMM. The algorithm BLP2RMM (Fig. 1) implements this translation and will also be detailed. The equivalence of the two representations (and therefore the soundness of the translation) will be proven in Sect. 4.

3.1   Restrictions

Definition 1. (Acyclic) *A BLP is said to be acyclic if the influenced by relation over $LH(L)$ is acyclic.*

Definition 2. *(Acyclic Finitely Influenced) A BLP B is said to be acyclic finitely influenced if B is acyclic and each random variable in $LH(L)$ is only influenced by a finite set of random variables.*

Definition 3. *(BLP_F) $B \in BLP_F$ if B is an acyclic finitely influenced BLP and the least Herbrand model $LH(L)$ is finite.*

In the following translation, we will only consider BLPs belonging to BLP_F. This restriction is necessary for both syntactic and semantic purposes. Indeed, we cannot allow for an infinite BLP, because we consider that it could not be represented by an RMM since we consider that an infinite RMM is incompatible with the definition of an RMM given in [1].

3.2 Preliminary Results

Definition 4. *Given a BLP noted L and a subset of $LH(L)$ noted Γ. TB_L is defined as follows. $TB_L(\Gamma) = \{A\theta \mid$ there is a substitution θ and a clause $(A \mid A_1, \ldots, A_n)$ in L such that $(A\theta \mid A_1\theta, \ldots, A_n\theta)$ is ground, for all $i \in \{1, \ldots, n\}: A_i\theta \in \Gamma$, and $Pa(A\theta) \subseteq \Gamma\}$.*

TB_L will be used in the algorithm BLP2RMM.

Definition 5. *Let V be a ground atom in L. We denote by D_V the domain D_r, with r predicate from which V is obtained (i.e. $V = r(\ldots)$).*

The following proposition enables to express the joint probability density of random variables, which will be useful in Sects. 3 and 4.

Proposition 1. *Let $X_1, \ldots, X_n$ be random variables. The joint probability density of these variables can be expressed with its chain rule expression*

$$P(X_1, \ldots, X_n) = \prod_{i=1}^{n} P(V_i \mid V_1, \ldots, V_{i-1}) . \tag{1}$$

If, for all $i \in 1, \ldots, n$, there is no variable V_j, for all $j \in 1, \ldots, i-1$, that is influenced by V_i, then the following equation can be derived from (1):

$$P(X_1, \ldots, X_n) = \prod_{i=1}^{n} P(V_i \mid Pa(V_i)) . \tag{2}$$

This is namely the case if the variables are ordered with respect to when they are entailed (as it will occur during the translation).

Proposition 2. *We have the following result:*

$$P(V_1, \ldots, V_M, V_{M+1}, \ldots, V_{M+N_n} \mid V_1, \ldots, V_M) = \prod_{i=1}^{N_n} P(V_{M+i} \mid Pa(V_{M+i})) . \tag{3}$$

If the parents of a random variable V_{M+i} come from more than one Bayesian clause, we use the combining rule associated with the predicate from which is obtained the random variable.

Proof.

$$\mathbf{P}(V_1, \ldots, V_M, V_{M+1}, \ldots, V_{M+N_n} \mid V_1, \ldots, V_M) =$$

$$\frac{\mathbf{P}(V_1, \ldots, V_M, V_{M+1}, \ldots, V_{M+N_n}, V_1, \ldots, V_M)}{\mathbf{P}(V_1, \ldots, V_M)} =$$

$$\frac{\mathbf{P}(V_1, \ldots, V_M, V_{M+1}, \ldots, V_{M+N_n})}{\mathbf{P}(V_1, \ldots, V_{N_M})} =$$

$$\frac{\left(\prod_{i=1}^{N_n} \mathbf{P}(V_{M+i} \mid V_1, \ldots, V_{M+i-1})\right) \times \mathbf{P}(V_1, \ldots, V_M)}{\mathbf{P}(V_1, \ldots, V_M)} =$$

$$\prod_{i=1}^{N_n} \mathbf{P}(V_{M+i} \mid V_1, \ldots, V_{M+i-1}) =$$

$$\prod_{i=1}^{N_n} \mathbf{P}(V_{M+i} \mid \mathbf{Pa}(V_{M+i})) \ .$$

$\square$

3.3   Translation Algorithm

The translation algorithm BLP2RMM is presented in Fig. 1. The general idea is to follow the calculation of the least Herbrand model and to create relevant corresponding RMM states. Each RMM state will represent exactly one interpretation of a sub-set of $LH(L)$ consisting of all the ground atoms already entailed by an operator similar to the T_P operator used for Logic Programs. Indeed, at each iteration of this operator, a set of new ground atoms is entailed and RMM states are created, each state corresponding to an interpretation of the set containing all the ground atoms already entailed by the iterations of the operator (i.e. interpretations of the new ground atoms added to the previous interpretations of the previously entailed ground atoms). Each state q created at iteration i is accessible from a unique state q' created at iteration $i - 1$ and corresponds to the interpretation of q restricted to the ground atoms defined in the $i-1$ iterations of the algorithm. The states accessible from q are all the states created in the $i+1$ iterations that corresponds to a compatible interpretation. The probabilities of the RMM are all deduced form the CPTs of the BLP. The algorithm ends when all the ground atoms of the least Herbrand model have been entailed.

The algorithm ends when the least fixpoint of TB_L is reached. At this point, all the ground atoms of $LH(L)$ have already been entailed and the corresponding RMM is complete. This means that the states created in the last step are final states (they are not the source to any state in the RMM). Let I be the number of steps necessary for the algorithm (the fixpoint is reached in an attempt to apply the operator for the $(I + 1)^{th}$ time). The following subsections refer to more detailed explanations of the translation.

Algorithm: BLP2RMM
Input: L ∈ BLP_F
Output: R ∈ RMM

1. Set $n = 0$
2. While the least fixpoint of TB_L is not reached
   (a) Define $S_n = TB_L{}^n(\emptyset)$
   (b) Define the new Bayesian atoms entailed, noted $V_{M+1}, \ldots, V_{M+N_n}$, where $M = \sum_{j=1}^{n-1} N_j$ is the number of atoms previously entailed
   (c) For each $V_{M+i}(= r_{M+i}(\ldots))$, where $i \in [1, N_n]$
       i. Define the RMM domain, $D_{V_{M+i}} = D'_{r_{M+i}}$, where $D'_{r_{M+i}}$ is a tree with a root pointing towards $|D_{r_{M+i}}|$ leafs, where $D_{r_{M+i}}$ is the predicate domain associated to r_{M+i}; each leaf being an element of $D_{r_{M+i}}$
   (d) Define the RMM relation $L_n(D_{V_1}, \ldots, D_{V_M}, D_{V_{M+1}}, \ldots, D_{V_{M+N_n}})$
   (e) Define the RMM states $L_n(v_1, \ldots, v_M, v_{M+1}, \ldots, v_{M+N_n})$, where $v_i \in D_{V_i}$ for all $i \in \{1, \ldots, M + N_n\}$
   (f) For each state $q = L_{n-1}(v_1, \ldots, v_M)$, where $v_i \in D_{V_i}$ for all $i \in \{1, \ldots, M\}$
       i. Set one transition from q towards each state $L_n(v_1, \ldots, v_M, v_{M+1}, \ldots, v_{M+N_n}), \forall (v_{M+1}, \ldots, v_{M+N_n}) \in (D_{V_{M+1}} \times \ldots \times D_{V_{M+N_n}})$, with the probability $\prod_{i=1}^{N_n} P(V_{M+i} = v_{M+i} \mid \mathbf{Pa}(V_{M+i}))$
   (g) Increment n

Fig. 1. Algorithm BLP2RMM translating any L ∈ BLP_F to an equivalent RMM

Step 1. Let us consider the set $S_1 = TB_L(\emptyset)$. We denote the variables contained in S_1 by $V_1, \ldots, V_{N_1}$. Therefore $N_1 = |S_1|$. In other words, S_1 contains the ground facts V_i for which $\mathbf{Pa}(V_i) = \emptyset$. From these variables, we create a RMM domain for each distinct predicate domain in $D_{V_1}, \ldots, D_{V_{N_1}}$. The RMM domain D' associated to a predicate domain D is a tree with a root pointing to $|D|$ leafs that are the elements of D. In addition, we create the RMM relation $L_1(D_{V_1}, \ldots, D_{V_{N_1}})$. $\prod_{i=1}^{N_1} |D_{V_i}|$ states are created. The number of states equals to the size of the cartesian product of $D_{V_1}, \ldots, D_{V_{N_1}}$. A state q obtained from this relation has the form $q = L_1(v_1, \ldots, v_{N_1})$, where $v_i \in D_{V_i}$ for all $i \in \{1, \ldots, N_1\}$.

Being in state q means that an interpretation of the N_1 first entailed variables of $LH(L)$ is set and is as follows. $V_1 = v_1, \ldots, V_{N_1} = v_{N_1}$. These states are the only possible initial states in the RMM with the following probabilities:

$$P_\pi(St_0 = L_1(v_1, \ldots, v_{N_1})) = P(V_1 = v_1, \ldots, V_{N_1} = v_{N_1})$$

$$= \prod_{i=1}^{N_1} P(V_i = v_i \mid V_1 = v_1, \ldots, V_{i-1} = v_{i-1})$$

$$= \prod_{i=1}^{N_1} P(V_i = v_i \mid \mathbf{Pa}(V_i) \ \textit{assigned like above})$$

$$= V \prod_{i=1}^{N_1} P(V_i = v_i) \ .$$

Thus, the RMM initial probability vector π is defined as follows.

$$\pi_{L_1(v_1,\ldots,v_{N_1})} = \prod_{i=1}^{N_1} P(V_i = v_i), \forall (v_1,\ldots,v_{N_1}) \in D_{V_1} \times \ldots \times D_{V_{N_1}}$$

$$\pi_q = 0 \ else \ .$$

Step n. We continue to apply the TB_L operator in order to entail new ground atoms and consequently to create new domains, new relations, new states and new transitions between states created during the last two steps. We now present the additions made to the current RMM during Step n. Let M be $\sum_{j=1}^{n-1} N_j$. Let us consider the set $S_n = TB_L(S_{n-1})$. We denote the variables contained in S_n by $V_{M+1}, \ldots, V_{M+N_n}$. Therefore $N_n = |S_n| - |S_{n-1}|$. From the new variables, we create a RMM domain for each new distinct predicate domain (with respect to the domains already defined) in $D_{V_{M+1}}, \ldots, D_{V_{M+N_n}}$. The associated RMM domains are created in the same fashion as in the previous steps. We create the RMM relation $L_n(D_{V_1}, \ldots, D_{V_M}, D_{V_{M+1}}, \ldots, D_{V_{M+N_n}})$. A state q obtained from this relation L_n has the form $q = L_n(v_1, \ldots, v_M, v_{M+1}, \ldots, v_{M+N_n})$, where $v_i \in D_{V_i}$ for all $i \in \{1, \ldots, M + N_n\}$. Being in this state q means that an interpretation of the $M + N_n$ first entailed variables (i.e. ground atoms) of $LH(L)$ is set and is as follows. $V_1 = v_1, \ldots, V_M = v_M, V_{M+1} = v_{M+1}, \ldots, V_{M+N_n} = v_{M+N_n}$. The state q is only accessible from $q' = L_{n-1}(v_1, \ldots, v_M)$. Semantically, it means, that if we have set an interpretation for the first M variables, this "sub-interpretation" cannot be modified and we can subsume this interpretation by assigning values to the N_n new entailed variables. Therefore, a state created in Step $n-1$, for instance q', is now pointing towards $\prod_{i=1}^{N_n} |D_{V_{M+i}}|$ states (of the form $L_n(v_1, \ldots, v_M, v_{M+1}, \ldots, v_{M+N_n})$ for all $(v_{M+1}, \ldots, v_{M+N_n}) \in D_{V_{M+1}} \times \ldots \times D_{V_{M+N_n}}$). By applying Proposition 2, the probabilities of the translations defined above are

$$P(St_{n-1} = L_n(v_1, \ldots, v_M, v_{M+1}, \ldots, v_{M+N_n}) \mid St_{n-2} = L_{n-1}(v_1, \ldots, v_M)) =$$

$$\prod_{i=1}^{N_n} P(V_{M+i} = v_{M+i} \mid \mathbf{Pa}(V_{M+i}) \ assigned \ accordingly) \ .$$

We can now continue the construction of the transition probability matrix A. $\forall (v_1, \ldots, v_M) \in D_{V_1} \times \ldots \times D_{V_M}$, the following states are created (with $q_{n-1} = L_{n-1}(v_1, \ldots, v_M)$ and $q_n = L_n(v_1, \ldots, v_M, v_{M+1}, \ldots, v_{M+N_n})$):

$$a_{q_{n-1}q_{n-2}} = \prod_{i=1}^{N_n} P(V_{M+i} = v_{M+i} \mid \mathbf{Pa}(V_{M+i}) \ assigned \ accordingly),$$

$$\forall (v_{M+1}, \ldots, v_{M+N_n}) \in D_{V_{M+1}} \times \ldots \times D_{V_{M+N_n}} \ .$$

The states created in Step $n-1$ will point towards no other further states created in the algorithm.

4   Results

4.1   Semantics

Theorem 1. (Equivalence) *Let $B \in BLP_F$ and $R \in RMM$ obtained by applying the algorithm BLP2RMM defined in Sect. 3 to B. The probability distributions over two corresponding representations are equivalent. We have, for every RMM State and every BLP joint state:*

$$P(St_0 = st_0, \ldots, St_{I-1} = st_{I-1}) = \prod_{i=1}^{|LH(L)|} P(V_i = v_i \mid Pa(V_i)) . \quad (4)$$

Proof. Each state in the RMM represents an interpretation of a subset of $LH(L)$. Therefore, the final states represent all the possible interpretations of $LH(L)$ (assignment of values to the random variables in $LH(L)$). The final states are of the form $L_I(v_1, \ldots, v_{|LH(L)|}), \forall (v_1, \ldots, v_{|LH(L)|}) \in D_{V_1} \times \ldots \times D_{V_{|LH(L)|}}$. According to [1], "the probability of observing a sequence of states $(st_0, st_1, \ldots, st_T)$ is $P(St_0 = st_0, St_1 = st_1, \ldots, St_T = st_T) = P(St_0 = st_0) \prod_{t=1}^{T} P(St_t = st_t \mid St_{t-1} = st_{t-1})$". In this case, for $T = (I - 1)$, the probability of observing such a sequence should be the probability of having the interpretation of $LH(L)$ induced by st_I. And, in our RMM, the elements in such a sequence are not independent one to each other ($st_{(I-1)}$ induces the values of all the other v_i, for $1 \leq i \leq (I - 2)$). Let us verify that these two semantical probabilities are the same. That would prove that the BLP and the associated RMM have the same semantics over the interpretations of $LH(L)$. Let $st_{I-1} = L_I(v_1, \ldots, v_{|LH(L)|})$,

$$P(St_0 = st_0, \ldots, St_{I-1} = st_{I-1}) =$$

$$P(St_0 = st_0) \prod_{t=1}^{I-1} P(St_t = st_t \mid St_{t-1} = st_{t-1}) =$$

$$P(S_0 = L_1(v_1, \ldots, v_{N_1})) \times$$

$$\times \prod_{i=2}^{I} P\left(L_i\left(v_1, \ldots, v_{\left(\sum_{j=1}^{I} N_j\right)}\right) \mid L_{i-1}\left(v_1, \ldots, v_{\left(\sum_{j=1}^{I-1} N_j\right)}\right)\right) =$$

$$\left(\prod_{i=1}^{N_1} P(V_i = v_i)\right) \left(\prod_{i=2}^{I} \left(\prod_{j=1}^{N_i} \mathbf{P}\left(V_{\left(\sum_{k=1}^{i-1} N_k + j\right)} \mid \mathbf{Pa}(V_{\left(\sum_{k=1}^{i-1} N_k + j\right)})\right)\right)\right) .$$

In the last expression, all the $\mathbf{Pa}\left(V_{\left(\sum_{k=1}^{i-1} N_k + j\right)}\right)$ are assigned according to the previous expressions and namely to the assignment in st_{I-1}. Eventually, the following equation is obtained:

$$P(St_0 = st_0, \ldots, St_{I-1} = st_{I-1}) = \prod_{i=1}^{|LH(L)|} P(V_i = v_i \mid Pa(V_i)) .$$

(The $Pa(V_i)$ are assigned according to the previous expressions $\forall 1 \leq i \leq |LH(L)|$). $\qquad \square$

4.2   Complexity

In this subsection, we will try to compare the size of the two equivalent representations of a same problem in terms of relevant parameters of these representations. The following theorem emphasizes the exponential explosion in terms of parameters of the representation that occurs when translating BLP_F to RMMs. The proof of this theorem is fully described in [11].

Definition 6. *(Minimal RMM)* Let $Min_{RMM}(L)$ *be the minimum number of parameters in any RMM representation of a BLP L. By definition,*

$$Min_{RMM}(L) \leq Par_{RMM}(L) \ . \tag{5}$$

Theorem 2. *(Complexity)* Let L be a BLP_F and M be the RMM obtained by applying the translation detailed in Sect. 3 to L. Let N be the number of clauses of L. Let $D_{max} = \max_r |D_r|$, where r is a predicate and D_r its associated domain. Let $Par_{BLP}(L)$ be the number of parameters in the CPTs of L. Let $Par_{RMM}(M)$ be the number of parameters in the transition matrix and vector of M. We have:

$$Par_{BLP}(L) = O(N \ D_{max}) \ , \tag{6}$$

$$Par_{RMM}(M) = O\left(N^2 \times \left((D_{max})^{(2|LH(L)|\times N)}\right)\right) \ , \ and \tag{7}$$

$$Min_{RMM}(L) \leq O\left(N^2 \times \left((D_{max})^{(2|LH(L)|\times N)}\right)\right) \ . \tag{8}$$

Proof. N is the number of clauses and of CPTs and N_P is the number of predicates. For each Bayesian clause $A \mid A_1, \ldots, A_n$, there is one CPT of size $D_A \times D_{A_1} \times \ldots \times D_{A_n}$. Therefore the total number of parameters in the CPTs is

$$Par_{BLP} = \sum_{i=1}^{N} (|D_A| \times |D_{A_1}| \times \ldots \times |D_{A_n}|) \ .$$

There are I relations, N_P domains of the size of the BLP domains D_r, $\forall$ predicate r. According to Sect. 3, the number of states is

$$N_{St} = \sum_{i=1}^{I} \left(\prod_{j=1}^{i} \left(\prod_{k=1}^{N_j} |D_{V_{N_{(j-1)+k}}}| \right) \right) \ .$$

Therefore π has N_{St} parameters and A has $(N_{St})^2$ parameters. The total number of parameters in the matrix and vector is

$$Par_{RMM} = (N_{St} + (N_{St})^2) \ .$$

Here, we try to find upper bounds of Par_{BLP} and Par_{RMM} with respect to the same variables. We choose N as our variable to obtain upper bounds. Let $D_{max} = \max_{r \ predicate} |D_r|$. We can state that $N_P = O(N)$ since, for each predicate, there exists at least one clause in which this predicate is present in the clause's head. Concerning the BLP representation, the following result is straightforward:

$$Par_{BLP} = O(N\ D_{max})\ .$$

Concerning the RMM representation, we have $I = O(N)$, because at each iteration of TB_L we use at least one Bayesian clause to entail new ground atoms. Let us obtain an upper bound for Par_{RMM}:

$$
\begin{aligned}
Par_{RMM} &= \left(N_{St} + (N_{St})^2\right) \\
&= O\left((N_{St})^2\right) \\
&= O\left(\left(\sum_{i=1}^{N}\left(\prod_{j=1}^{i}\left(\prod_{k=1}^{|LH(L)|}|D_{V_{N_{(j-1)+k}}}|\right)\right)\right)^2\right) \\
&= O\left(\left(\sum_{i=1}^{N}\left(\prod_{j=1}^{N}\left(\prod_{k=1}^{|LH(L)|}D_{max}\right)\right)\right)^2\right) \\
&= O\left(\left(\sum_{i=1}^{N}\left(\prod_{j=1}^{N}(D_{max})^{|LH(L)|}\right)\right)^2\right) \\
&= O\left(\left(\sum_{i=1}^{N}(D_{max})^{(|LH(L)|\times N)}\right)^2\right) \\
&= O\left(\left(N\times\left((D_{max})^{|(LH(L)|\times N)}\right)\right)^2\right) \\
&= O\left(N^2\times\left((D_{max})^{(2|LH(L)|\times N)}\right)\right)\ .
\end{aligned}
$$

Eventually,

$$Par_{RMM} = O\left(N^2\times\left((D_{max})^{(2|LH(L)|\times N)}\right)\right)\ .$$

□

5 Implementations

After having studied the translation theoretically in Sects. 3 and 4, we will now present an implementation of this translation. Firstly, the meta-interpreters associated with the two frameworks whose role is to infer the probability associated to a query are described. Then we will introduce the translation engine itself. The equality of the probability distributions of the two equivalent representations is also stated.

5.1 BLP Meta-interpreter

This subsection is dedicated to the BLP formalism. It is necessary to be able to
query BLPs in order to check the results. The KBMC is straightforward, thus it
is not necessary to implement this stage. To query the resulting Bayesian net,
we use free softwares such as Microsoft Belief Network. BLPs will be represented
using a Prolog formalism. We will use a simplification of the *alarm* example to
illustrate this formalism - this example can be found in [14].

```
blp_clause(1, alarm(X),[burglary(X),tornado(X)]).
blp_clause(2,burglary(Y),[neighborhood(Y)]).
blp_clause(3,neighborhood(_),[]).
blp_clause(4, tornado(_),[]).


blp_cpt(    1,
    [yes,no],[[yes,yes],[yes,no],[no,yes],[no,no]],
    [[0.99,0.8,0.9,0.05],[0.01,0.2,0.1,0.95]]).
blp_cpt(    2,
    [yes,no],[[bad],[avg],[good]],
    [[0.4,0.2,0.1],[0.6,0.8,0.9]]).
blp_cpt(    3,
    [bad,avg,good],[],
    [0.3,0.4,0.3]).
blp_cpt(    4,
    [yes,no],[],
    [0.01,0.99]).
```

A BLP can also be defined with the use of combining rules, in which case the
following type of predicate may be added at the end of the program:

```
blp_cr(alarm,max).
```

where the first argument is the predicate which is defined with a combining rule
and the second is the combining rule itself. We assume that every combining rule
used to define a BLP is already defined in the translation engine. The Bayesian
clauses are defined with the atoms whose predicate symbol is *blp_clause*. The
first argument is a unique identifier of the clause, the second is the head and the
third is the body of the Bayesian clause. The associated conditional probability
tables are defined by the *blp_cpt* atoms: the first argument is the number of
the associated clause, the second lists the domain (i.e. the possible values) of
the head, the third lists the possible sets of values that the body can take.
Eventually, the values of the probabilities are represented by a list of lists: for
each possible value of the head, there is a list of conditional probabilities given
the set of values that the body can take.

5.2 RMM Meta-interpreter

This subsection is dedicated to the RMM framework. An RMM has the following semantics. Given an RMM, the probability of observing a sequence of

states $(st_0, st_1, \ldots, st_{I-1})$ is $P(St_0 = st_0, \ldots, St_{I-1} = st_{I-1}) = P(St_0 = st_0) \times \prod_{t=1}^{I-1} P(St_t = st_t \mid St_{t-1} = st_{t-1})$. The Prolog representation of any RMM will be as follows. An RMM is constituted by a set of RMM states

```
rmm_state(1,l(1,(neighbourhood(james),bad),(tornado(james),yes))).
rmm_state(2,l(1,(neighbourhood(james),bad),(tornado(james),no))).
...
```

where the first argument is the unique identifier of the state, and the second is the usual definition of an RMM state; a set of predicates defining the initial probability vector

```
rmm_init_vector(1,0.002). rmm_init_vector(2,0.198).
...
```

where the first argument is the identifier of an RMM state and the second argument is the probability that this state is the initial state; and finally, a set of transitions defining the transition probability matrix.

```
rmm_trans_matrix(1,7,0.6). rmm_trans_matrix(1,8,0.4).
...
```

where the first argument is the identifier of an RMM state, the second argument is the identifier of an other state and the third argument is the probability that, being in the first state, the system evolves into the second at the next step.
    The meta-interpreter is then deduces quite intuitively:

```
rmm_proba([Initial_State],P):-
  rmm_init_vector(Initial_State,P).

rmm_proba([Last_State|[New_Last_State|Rest_of_Sequence]],P) :-
  rmm_proba_matrix(New_Last_State,Last_State,P1),
  rmm_proba([New_Last_State|Rest_of_Sequence],P2),
  P is P1*P2.
```

5.3   Translation Engine

The translation itself is implemented in the translation engine. Every combining rule has to be implemented in the translation engine in order to simplify the BLPs representations which only have to mention the combining rules to be used. The full implementation of the translation defined in Sect. 3 is described in [12].

5.4   Practical Equality of the Distributions

With respect to the examples we have studied to test the translation engine so far, the theoretical equality of the distributions has been confirmed by the meta-interpreters of the two equivalent representations.

6   Related Works

As already mentioned, other relationships between PLL frameworks have been investigated in [4], [5], [15] and [17]. Moreover, [6] "proposes the outlines of a general, robust framework for comparing" probabilistic-logical (pl) models, in order to "establish a general, robust framework for comparing pl-languages", which is an essential aim. Our findings could easily be adapted in order to be part of the first few results that are mentioned in [6] and could increase the rapidity of potential further results. The result at aim is that BLPs are as least as expressive as RMMs. Again, it would be very interesting to analyse the links between the underlying representations of a PLL formalism and its expressivity and learnability.

7   Conclusion and Future Work

In this paper, we have established a translation from the sub-class of BLP_F to RMMs. We have demonstrated that BLP_F and RMMs could encode the same knowledge. The complexity results have shown that RMMs are less compact than BLP_F with respect to this translation. The authors are unaware of any more compact general translation. A full implementation has already been realized. So far, all the complexity and expressivity results obtained are intuitive with respect to the underlying representations of the PLL formalisms studied.

In the future, we would like to apply this translation to other examples such as a game of poker. We could also try to optimize the implementation of the translation engine. It would be very useful to obtain general complexity results (independent of the translation utilized). We would then have to generalize the comparison. It would also be of interest to adapt our results to the expressivity frameworks described in [6].

More generally, we would like to continue to apply comparisons between frameworks. It would be interesting to examine if a classification of PLL formalisms with respect to their underlying representations would correspond to a classification in terms of expressivity and learnability. If it were the case, we could then state for instance that the learnability of the formulaes of a PLL representation would depend on the complexity of its formulaes. It would allow us to set up general results on the expressive power, the complexity and the efficiency of inference and learning. Even more generally, we would like to develop an integrated theory of Probabilistic Logic Learning.

Acknowledgements. This work was supported by the Esprit IST project "Application of Probabilistic Inductive Logic Programming II (APRIL II)".

References

1. Anderson, C., et al.: Relational Markov models and their application to adaptive Web navigation. In: 8th Intl. Conf. on Knowledge Discovery and Data Mining (2002)
2. April2 Blackforest Workshop 2006 (2006),
   palermo.informatik.uni-freiburg.de/ bfw/

3. de Raedt, L., et al.: Probabilistic logic learning. ACM-SIGKDD Explorations (2004)
4. Getoor, L., et al.: PRL: A Probabilistic relational language. Machine Learning (2006)
5. Jaeger, M.: Importance sampling on relational bayesian networks. In: Dagstuhl Seminar Proceeding 05051 (2006)
6. Jaeger, M.: Expressivity Analysis for PL-Languages. In: Online Proceedings of the ICML06 Workshop on Statistical Relational Learning (2006)
7. Kersting, K., et al.: Bayesian Logic Programs. In: Proceedings of the Work-in-Progress Track at the 10th INtl. Conf. on Inductive Logic Programming (2000)
8. Koller, D., Pfeffer, A.: Learning Probabilities for Noisy First-Order Rules. IJCAI (1997)
9. Lloyd, J.W.: Foundations of Logic Programming, 2nd edn. Springer, Heidelberg (1987)
10. Pahlavi, N.: Probabilistic Logic Learning, A Comparative Study. Technical Report. Imperial College London (2005)
11. Pahlavi, N.: Comparing RMMs with SLPs and BLPs. Technical Report. Imperial College London (2006)
12. Pahlavi, N.: The Complexity of Translating BLPs to RMMs. Technical Report. Imperial College London (2006)
13. Pearl, J.: Probabilistic Reasoning in Intelligent Systems: Networks of Plausible Inference. Morgan Kaufmann, San Francisco (1988)
14. Pearl, J.: Probabilistic Reasoning in Intelligent Systems: Networks of plausible Inference. Morgan Kaufmann, San Francisco (1988)
15. Puech, A., Muggleton, S.H.: A Comparison of Stochastic Logic Programs and Bayesian Logic Programs. IJCAI03 Workshop on Learning Statistical Models from Relational Data (2003)
16. Rabiner, L.R.: A tutorial on Hidden Markov Models and selected applications in speech recognition. In: Proceedings of the IEEE, IEEE Computer Society Press, Los Alamitos (1989)
17. Vennekens, J., et al.: A general view on probabilistic logic programming. In: Proceedings of BNAIC-03 (2003)

Inferring Regulatory Networks from Time Series Expression Data and Relational Data Via Inductive Logic Programming

Irene M. Ong[1,2], Scott E. Topper[3], David Page[2,1], and Vítor Santos Costa[4]

[1] Department of Computer Sciences,
[2] Department of Biostatistics and Medical Informatics,
[3] Department of Genetics,
University of Wisconsin – Madison, WI 53706 USA
[4] COPPE/Sistemas, UFRJ Centro de Tecnologia, Bloco H-319, Cx. Postal 68511
Rio de Janeiro, Brasil

Abstract. Determining the underlying regulatory mechanism of genetic networks is one of the central challenges of computational biology. Numerous methods have been developed and applied to the important but complex task of reverse engineering regulatory networks from high-throughput gene expression data. However, many challenges remain. In this paper, we are interested in learning rules that will reveal the causal genes for the expression variation from various relational data sources in addition to gene expression data. Following our previous work where we showed that time series gene expression data could potentially uncover causal effects, we describe an application of an inductive logic programming (ILP) system, to the task of identifying important regulatory relationships from discretized time series gene expression data, protein-protein interaction, protein phosphorylation and transcription factor data about the organism. Specifically, we learn rules for predicting gene expression levels at the next time step based on the available relational data and then generalize the learned theory to visualize a pruned network of important interactions. We evaluate and present experimental results on microarray experiments from Gasch *et al* on *Saccharomyces cerevisiae*.

1 Introduction and Motivation

Gaining insight into the underlying regulation of genes within organisms is important not just for understanding the cause of diseases but also for developing treatments. Viruses have been shown to cause cancer by affecting normal regulation in cells, and gaining an understanding of the factors that determine the ability of embryonic stem cells to maintain their self-renewal and pluripotency can significantly advance developmental biology and stem cell research.

For nearly a decade now, DNA microarray technology has enabled the simultaneous measurement of mRNA abundance of genes in an organism under normal conditions or under various treatments or perturbations. However, microarray

S. Muggleton, R. Otero, and A. Tamaddoni-Nezhad (Eds.): ILP 2006, LNAI 4455, pp. 366–378, 2007.

experiments still have many sources of error: sample preparation, hybridization, scanning, image processing, normalization, etc. Because samples for microarray data are usually obtained by pooling extracts from a population of cells rather than a single cell, in addition to experimental variables and limitations of the technology, the measurements obtained can be noisy. Noisy data inherently makes it more difficult to reverse engineer the underlying regulatory network.

Despite the difficulty of deciphering genetic regulatory networks from microarray data, numerous approaches to the task have been quite successful. Friedman *et al.* [5] were the first to address the task of determining properties of the transcriptional program of *S. cerevisiae* (yeast) by using Bayesian networks (BNs) to analyze gene expression data. Pe'er *et al.* [18] followed up that work by using BNs to learn master regulator sets. Other approaches include Boolean networks (Akutsu *et al.* [1], Ideker *et al.* [11]) and other graphical approaches (Tanay and Shamir [26], Chrisman *et al.* [3]).

The methods above can represent the dependence between interacting genes, but they cannot capture causal relationships. Pe'er *et al.* [19] ingeniously proposed the use of microarray experiments in which specific genes have been deleted (*knockout*) in yeast to obtain causality. The use of perturbations such as gene deletion mutants can allow the BN learning algorithm to learn a directed edge that suggests direct causal influence. This approach of combining observational and interventional data delivered promising results. Unfortunately, a complete library of gene knockouts are not yet available for organisms other than yeast. The advent of small interfering RNA (siRNA) can be used to reduce the expression of a specific gene in organisms other than yeast, however, siRNA does not guarantee complete silencing of the gene. In our previous work [16], we proposed that the analysis of time series gene expression microarray data using Dynamic Bayesian networks (DBNs) could allow us to learn potential causal relationships (Figure 1).

DBN learning can provide more insight into causality than ordinary BNs. An induced arc from gene X_1 to gene X_2 in an ordinary BN simply means that the expression of gene X_1 is a good predictor of the expression of gene X_2 *at the same time* (Figure 2a). While this good prediction may be because expression of gene X_1 influences expression of gene X_2, it could just as easily be because expression of gene X_2 influences expression of gene X_1 or expression of both gene X_1 and gene X_2 are influenced by expression of another gene X_3 (Figure 2b). On the other hand, an induced arc from gene X_1 to gene X_2 in a DBN implies that expression of gene X_1 at one time slice is a consistently good predictor of gene X_2 at *the next time slice*. This good prediction is unlikely to be because expression of gene X_2 influences expression of gene X_1; intuitively, it seems likely to be because expression of gene X_1 influences expression of gene X_2.[1]

---

[1] An arc in a DBN does not establish causality definitively. Nevertheless, if a learned DBN contains arcs that imply novel potential causal relationships, in some cases biologists can test these novel relationships with additional, more focused (and time-consuming) experiments.

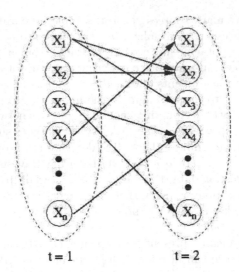

t = 1   t = 2

Fig. 1. Simple DBN model. Labeled circles within a dotted oval represent our variables in one time slice. Formally, arcs connecting variables from one time slice to variables in the next have the same meaning as in a BN, but they intuitively carry a stronger implication of causality. We note that in a DBN with more time slices, the arcs are always the same, e.g., the arc from X_1 at time slice 1 to X_2 at time slice 2 is also present from time slice t to time slice $t+1$ for all $1 \leq t < T$ where T is the last time slice in the model. This constancy of the arcs is justified by an assumption that the process being modeled is *stationary* though not static. While values of variables may change over time, the manner in which the value of one variable influences the value of a variable at the next time step (i.e., the parents and the conditional probability distribution for the latter variable) will not change.

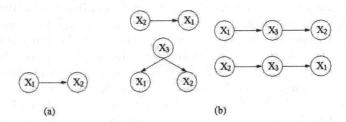

Fig. 2. (a) X_1 may be a good predictor of X_2, but is X_1 regulating X_2? (b) Ground truth might be any one of these or a more complicated variant

While temporal gene expression data contains causal information in the temporal data sequence, the dependence on the appropriate sampling rate, the small sample size, the large number of variables, and the presence of many hidden (signaling and other molecular interactions for which we do not have measurements) variables make it difficult for learning algorithms to completely determine the network.

In this paper, our goal is to utilize the abundant information available from many years of low-throughput as well as recent high-throughput research that are currently available in public databases to infer new relationships that cannot be learned from expression data alone. We are interested in discovering whether ILP is able to infer theories for particular pathways from time series microarray data and use other known relational information about the organism to refine what is already known about that pathway. Specifically, we formulate the learning in the same way as a DBN by learning theories of gene expression that are good predictors of the expression of particular genes at the next time step.

Regulatory sequences control gene expression temporally as well as spatially by *cis*-acting elements and *trans*-acting factors. *Cis*-acting elements are DNA sequences in the vicinity of the target gene, usually within 200 base pairs upstream of the transcription start site. *Trans*-acting factors, bind to the *cis*-acting sequences to control gene expression in several ways: the factor may (1) be expressed temporally (specific times in life cycle), (2) be expressed spatially (in a specific location), (3) require modification (phosphorylation), (4) be activated by ligand binding, (5) be sequestered until an environmental signal allows it to interact with the nuclear DNA. Hence, by integrating temporal gene expression data with additional information such as protein-protein interaction, transcription factor and kinase-substrate (phosphorylation) information, we believe we can capture some of these causal relationships and underlying mechanisms.

2   Related Work

Our goal in this paper is similar to that of Tu *et al.* [28]. We are interested in determining whether ILP can learn the pathway links between causal genes and target genes that explain the regulatory relationships between them. In the past few years, we have seen an increase in the use of inductive logic programming (ILP) methods for learning functional genomics [24,13,2,20], metabolic networks [25] and also predicting gene expression levels [17]. Papatheodorou *et al.* [17] used Abductive logic programming (ALP) to learn rules that would explain how gene interactions can cause changes in gene expression levels.

Recently, Fröhler and Kramer [6], applied ILP to the task of predicting up- and down-regulation of gene expression in *S. cerevisiae* under different environmental stress conditions [8] with the use of additional information. Fröhler and Kramer used the data from Middendorf *at al.* [14], where the presence of transcription factor binding sites (pruned list of 354 after removing redundant and rare sites) in the gene's regulatory region and the expression levels of regulators (selected list of 53, 50 of which were top ranking regulators identified by Segal *et al.* [21]) are used to predict gene regulation.

Following Middendorf, Fröhler and Kramer consider 3 classes of gene activity: up-regulation (> 1.2), down-regulation (< -1.2), and no change. The up- and down-regulated genes consist of 5% of all the data points since 95% of the expression were unstimulated. Their results report on discriminating between up- and down-regulation, with excellent results, although the original work from

Middendorf's showed that discriminating between the 3 classes is a much harder task. We similarly discretize into 3 classes to reduce noise, but our up- and down-regulated classes are about 20% of the total number of examples, so one would expect the discrimination task in our case to be harder.

Our work differs from that of Fröhler and Kramer in four ways. First, we learn rules to predict the up-regulation of a gene based on the activity and expression of genes from the *previous time step* as in a DBN since we are interested in learning causal relationships from the data. Secondly, we discretize the gene expression data by comparing two consecutive time series measurements under the same experimental condition and determining whether the change in expression was up, down or same based on a threshold of greater than 0.3, less than -0.3, or in between. Thirdly, we use information on transcription factors rather than transcription factor binding sites and we do not restrict the transcription factor or regulator set as our goal is to learn possible new players in the network. Finally, we use Aleph instead of Tilde.

3   ILP and Aleph

Inductive logic programming (ILP) is a popular approach for learning first-order, multi-relational concepts between data instances. ILP uses logic to induce hypotheses from observations (positive and negative examples) and background (prior) knowledge by finding a logical description of the underlying data model that differentiates between the positive and negative examples. The learned description is a set of easily interpretable rules or clauses.

There are many ILP systems available, but we chose to use Aleph [22] because it has been shown to perform well even on fairly large datasets. This is because Aleph implements the Progol algorithm [15], which learns rules from a pruned space of candidate solutions. The Progol algorithm structures and limits the search space in two steps. Initially, it selects a positive instance to serve as the seed example and searches the background knowledge for the facts known to be true about the seed example - the combination of these facts form the example's most specific or saturated clause. Then, Aleph defines the search space to be clauses that generalize a seed example's saturated clause, and performs a general to specific search over this space. The key insight of the Progol algorithm is that some of these facts explain the seed example's classification, thus generalizations of those facts could apply to other examples.

4   Data and Methodology

To test our hypotheses, we use time series gene expression data of environmental stress response experiments, including DNA-damaging agents from Gasch *et al.* [8,7]. We chose to use this dataset on yeast because yeast is a model organism used for studying many basic cellular processes and there exists many publicly accessible databases containing various sources of data from many years of research. We focused our study on the DNA damage checkpoint pathway because it is an important pathway that has been widely studied. There are about 6500 genes in yeast, 19 of which are considered to be in the "DNA damage checkpoint" pathway based on a recent review by Harrison and Haber [10].

It is well known that a common problem with current microarray data is the small number of sample points and the large number of features or genes. Nevertheless, it is hoped that discretization as well as other sources of information will permit useful results to be obtained. We determined the relative change in expression from one time step to the next by comparing the expression levels between two consecutive time series measurements. The time series data were discretized into one of three possible discrete values by comparing two consecutive time series measurements: if the change increased by 0.3, we consider the expression to be up-regulated, if the change decreased by 0.3, we consider the expression to be down-regulated, otherwise we say the expression stayed the same.

As alluded to earlier, there are many other spatial and molecular interactions that are not captured by expression data. Known transcription factors for specific genes can allow the learning algorithm to focus on specific proteins that are known to interact with the DNA of the target gene. The learning algorithm could also potentially discover combinations of transcription factors (pairs, trios, etc.) required to trigger a change in expression of a particular set of genes. Because transcription factors can also interact with other proteins or metabolites on their way to activating gene expression, background knowledge of proteins that are known to interact with each other can allow for the discovery of novel proteins in the pathway. Furthermore, an estimated 30% of proteins need to be phosphorylated in order to trigger a change in the protein's function, activity, localization and stability [12]. Thus, background knowledge about a large number of protein phosphorylation in yeast was also included [4].

Recent technological advances have produced more high-throughput data that capture different types of interactions. ChIP-chip (chromatin immunoprecipitation, a well-established procedure to investigate interactions between proteins and DNA, coupled with whole-genome DNA microarrays), technology allows one to determine the entire spectrum of in vivo DNA binding sites for any given transcription factor or protein. Mass spectrometry, large-scale two-hybrid screens, single-cell analysis of flow cytometry, and protein microarrays have all been used to generate high-throughput measurements of certain types of molecules such as proteins, metabolites, protein-protein interactions and also signaling events such as phosphorylation within cells. Most of these data are also known to be noisy especially those obtained through high-throughput methods that were conducted in vitro (outside the organism). High-throughput protein-protein interaction and phosphorylation data are especially noisy because the conditions under which the data are collected differs quite significantly from that in a cell, i.e. detecting interactions that would not actually occur in vivo (inside the organism) or missing interactions that actually take place.

We aim to link known interactions with gene expression activity to possibly learn new mechanisms. We do this by associating the up- or down-regulation of specific genes from the previous time step with its transcription factor, a protein

Table 1. Cross validation accuracies

Fold	0	1	2	3	4	5	6	7	8	9	Average across all folds
Accuracy	0.73	0.87	0.81	0.72	0.83	0.84	0.73	0.79	0.75	0.78	0.79

it might interact with, or a phosphorylation event. We assume that an event in the previous time step will contribute to the change in expression at the current time. This assumption does not necessarily hold for all biological activity but a similar assumption, that of using a gene's expression level to approximate the activity of other genes within the same pathway, have been used by others [29].

The MIPS Comprehensive Yeast Genome Database (CYGD) [9] provided much of the information regarding yeast genes, their function, location, phenotype and disruption. We obtained protein-protein interaction data from BioGRID [23], transcription factor data from the YEASTRACT database [27], and over 4000 yeast phosphorylation events from Ptacek *et al.* [4]. The ILP system, Aleph [22], was used to learn rules from the data.

We first learn rules using inductive logic programming (ILP) to predict the discretized gene expression level at the *next time step* as in a DBN. Then we use the learned theory to generate a pruned network or graph that show interactions corresponding to proofs for the rules.

5   Experiments and Results

We performed ten-fold cross validation experiments to learn theories for predicting held-out gene expression values for genes in the DNA damage checkpoint pathway at the *next time step*. The discretized microarray experiments were divided into ten folds, grouping replicate experiments together to avoid bias, based on the different experimental conditions.

We obtained an accuracy of 79% on predicting up-regulated examples averaged over ten folds of the cross-validation procedure (see Table 1).

Examples of some of the rules learned across the folds are:

Rule 1 up(GeneA,Time,Expt) :-
    previous(Time,Time1), down(GeneA,Time1,Expt), interaction(tof1,GeneA), up(tof1,Time1,Expt), function(GeneA,'CELL CYCLE AND DNA PROCESSING:cell cycle:mitotic cell cycle and cell cycle control:cell cycle arrest').

Rule 2 up(GeneA,Time,Expt) :-
    previous(Time,Time1), down(GeneA,Time1,Expt),
    phosphorylates(GeneA,GeneE), up(GeneE,Time1,Expt),
    transcriptionfactor(GeneF,GeneE), down(GeneF,Time1,Expt),
    transcriptionfactor(GeneF,cdc20), down(cdc20,Time1,Expt).

Rule 3 up(GeneA,Time,Expt) :-
    previous(Time,Time1), down(GeneA,Time1,Expt),

interaction(GeneE,GeneA), down(GeneE,Time1,Expt),
interaction(GeneE,mms4), down(mms4,Time1,Expt),
function(GeneA,'METABOLISM').

These rules all specify the activity of specific genes involved in the larger DNA damage pathway. Tof1 is a subunit of a replication-pausing checkpoint complex (Tof1p-Mrc1p-Csm3p) that acts at the stalled replication fork to promote sister chromatid cohesion after DNA damage, facilitating gap repair of damaged DNA. Cdc20, which is regulated by cell-cycle genes, is an activator of anaphase-promoting complex/cyclosome (APC/C), which is required for metaphase/anaphase transition. It is part of the DNA damage checkpoint pathway and directs ubiquitination of mitotic cyclins, Pds1p, and other anaphase inhibitors. Finally, Mms4 is a subunit of the structure-specific Mms4p-Mus81p endonuclease that cleaves branched DNA and is involved in recombination and DNA repair.

The learned rules prove examples, and proofs generate paths between genes, so using the theories in all the folds, we further generated graphs. The graphs only show links that can be used in proofs for at least 5 examples (train+test). The width of a line in the graph is an indication of the proportion of examples used in the proof. Note that the graph only displays literals that were used in successful proofs. Hence, paths in the graph correspond to proofs and the nodes are examples of literals which were used to prove the rules. The learned graph of interactions amongst the 19 genes in the DNA damage checkpoint pathway are shown in Figure 3. A more detailed graph showing interactions amongst the genes in the DNA damage checkpoint pathway as well as transcription factors and phosphorylators can be seen in Figure 4.

6   Discussion

The DNA damage checkpoint monitors genome integrity, and ensures that damage is corrected before cell division occurs. When DNA damage is detected, the checkpoint network transmits signals that stall the progression of the cell cycle and mobilize repair mechanisms. The graph resulting from our analysis recapitulates many of the central aspects of this signaling network, and connects that network temporally to the normal progression through the cell cycle.

DNA damage (often in the form of a double strand break) is first recognized by MRX, a protein complex consisting of Mre11, Rad50 and Xrs2. These proteins are shown to interact together slightly to the left of the middle of Figure 4, with Mre11 linked to both Xrs2 and Rad50. The MRX complex coordinates the restructuring of the damaged region. MRX stimulates the phosphorylation of histones, H2A, in the region adjacent to the DNA double strand break (via Tel1) and recruits an exonuclease to generate a stretch of single stranded DNA. Our graph does not include physical interactions between Tel1 and the MRX complex, however both are connected through Mec1 and through the DNA binding protein Rap1.Rap1 can act as an inducer or a repressor, and is active in many disparate elements of cell biology, including ribosome synthesis and telomere preservation.

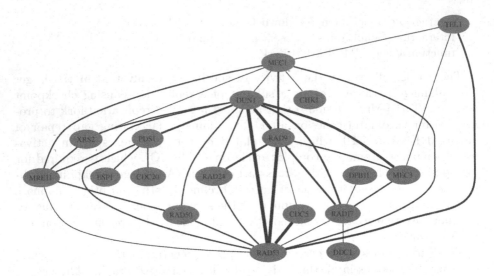

Fig. 3. Learned graph of interactions from successful proofs amongst the 19 genes in DNA damage checkpoint pathway from Harrison and Haber [10]. Straight edges represent protein-protein interactions. The width of a line in the graph is an indication of the number of examples that used this interaction in a proof.

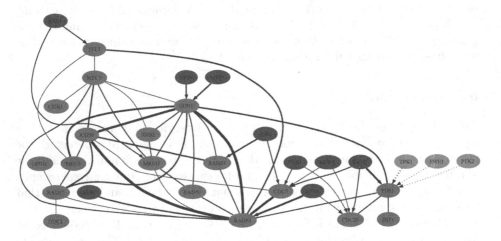

Fig. 4. Learned graph of interactions from successful proofs for the DNA damage checkpoint pathway. Red nodes indicate one of the 19 genes in DNA damage checkpoint pathway from Harrison and Haber [10], blue nodes indicate transcription factors and green nodes kinases. Straight edges represent protein-protein interactions, solid lined arrows represent transcription factor to target gene interaction, and dotted arcs represent kinase to substrate phosphorylation. The width of a line in the graph is an indication of the number of examples that used this interaction in a proof. A larger figure can be found at: http://www.biostat.wisc.edu/~ong/new2a.ps

Once single stranded DNA is generated, it is bound by the heterotrimer replication protein A (RPA) and two things occur. First, Mec1/Ddc2 binds and activates the signaling cascade. Mec1 phosphorylates Rad9 (shown as physical interaction in the graph), which in turn recruits Rad53. Ddc2 is conspicuously absent from this graph due to the requirement that only links that can be used in proofs for a certain number of examples are displayed. Next, the 9-1-1 clamp, which consists of three proteins Rad17, Mec3 and Ddc1, binds and demarcates the ssDNA/dsDNA junction, and facilitates some of the interactions described above. The 9-1-1 clamp components are grouped at the left side of the graph, linked by protein-protein interactions.

At the heart of the signaling network is Rad53, a well-connected, essential yeast kinase. Rad53 phosphorylates Dun1, a kinase whose activity ultimately controls much of the transcriptional response to DNA damage. Dun1 is also a very central protein in this network, demonstrating interactions with the 9-1-1 clamp, Rad24, the MRX complex, Rad53 and Pds1, a cell cycle control gene. Finally, Rad53 signals cell cycle arrest through Pds1 (via Cdc20), and Cdc5. Pds1 governs entry into mitosis, and Cdc5 controls exit from mitosis. All of these interactions are present in our results.

DNA damage is an inevitable consequence of DNA synthesis, and the graph reveals that the expression of the gene responsible for signaling the induction of DNA repair genes (Dun1) is coordinated by two transcription factors (Swi4 and Mbp1) that are active in the period just before DNA synthesis begins. Likewise, the transcription factors Mcm1, Fhk1 and Fkh2 are known to control the transition from G2 to mitosis, and in our graph these TFs are linked to Cdc5, Cdc20 and Pds1, which govern this transition.

At a broader level, the results shown in Figure 4 illustrates the centrality of Rad9, Rad53 and Dun1. These genes are instrumental in coordinating the various aspects of this response: detection of damage, cell cycle arrest, and mobilization of repair mechanisms.

7   Conclusions and Future Work

As a first step, we concentrated our experiments on learning the DNA damage checkpoint pathway because it is a very important pathway that have been implicated in cancer and aging, and because it has been very well studied. This pathway plays an important role by responding to single and double-stranded DNA breaks, and is therefore often activated in stressful environments. Hence, it involves a lot of signaling kinases that phosphorylates proteins that are already present within the cell or that only require molecular amounts to trigger a response.

After performing our analysis, we found that the phosphorylation dataset from Ptacek et al. [4] did not specifically include any phosphorylation relationships for the kinase and substrates in the DNA damage checkpoint pathway. The results we obtained show that our method is quite good at learning important pathway interactions and regulators despite the fact that the data may be noisy or incomplete. This further emphasizes the utility of integrating different data types, since many potential interactions, including those that were not evident from single data sources were identified.

A possible next step will be to perform a comparison with DBNs. We could also explore the larger network of genes that are connected with the core DNA damage checkpoint genes by including more specific background knowledge. This set is likely to include known targets of Dun1 activation, and genes that coordinate the biological processes involved in cell division. It may also include genes heretofore un-implicated in this process, and may provide good starting points for future wet lab experimentation.

In the future, we also plan to study other pathways and organisms, incorporate other sources of relational data including knockout data, and integrate these networks with probabilistic models.

Acknowledgments

We gratefully thank Audrey Gasch for useful discussions. Irene Ong is supported by the BACTER institute (DOE-GTL award DE-FG02-04ER25627), support for Scott Topper was provided by the Predoctoral Training Program in Genetics, 5 T32 GM07133 and Vítor Santos Costa is supported by CNPq.

References

1. Akutsu, T., Kuhara, S., Maruyama, O., Miyano, S.: Identification of gene regulatory networks by strategic gene disruptions and gene overexpressions. In: Proc. the 9th Annual ACM-SIAM Symposium on Discrete Algorithms, pp. 695–702. ACM Press, New York (1998)
2. Bryant, C.H., Muggleton, S.H., Oliver, S.G., Kell, D.B., Reiser, P.G.K., King, R.D.: Combining inductive logic programming, active learning, and robotics to discover the function of genes. Electronic Transactions in Artificial Intelligence 6, 1–36 (2001)
3. Chrisman, L., Langley, P., Bay, S., Pohorille, A.: Incorporating biological knowledge into evaluation of causal regulatory hypotheses. In: Pacific Symposium on Biocomputing (PSB) (January 2003)
4. Ptacek, J., et al.: Global analysis of protein phosphorylation in yeast. Nature 438, 679–684 (2005)
5. Friedman, N., Linial, M., Nachman, I., Pe'er, D.: Using Bayesian networks to analyze expression data. Journal of Computational Biology 7(3/4), 601–620 (2000)
6. Fröhler, S., Kramer, S.: Inductive logic programming for gene regulation prediction. In: Proceedings of the 16th International Conference on Inductive Logic Programming, Santiago de Compostela, Spain, pp. 83–85. University of Corunna (2006)
7. Gasch, A.P., Huang, M., Metzner, S., Botstein, D., Elledge, S.J., Brown, P.O.: Genomic expression responses to DNA-damaging agents and the regulatory role of the yeast ATR homolog Mec1p. Mol. Biol. Cell 12, 2987–3003 (2001)
8. Gasch, A.P., Spellman, P.T., Kao, C.M., Carmel-Harel, O., Eisen, M.B., Storz, G., Botstein, D., Brown, P.O.: Genomic expression programs in the response of yeast cells to environmental changes. Mol. Biol. Cell 11, 4241–4257 (2000)

9. Güldener, U., Münsterkötter, M., Kastenmüller, G., Strack, N., van Helden, J., Lemer, C., Richelles, J., Wodak, S.J., Garcia-Martinez, J., Perez-Ortin, J.E., Michael, H., Kaps, A., Talla, E., Dujon, B., Andre, B., Souciet, J.L., De Montigny, J., Bon, E., Gaillardin, C., Mewes, H.W.: CYGD: the Comprehensive Yeast Genome Database. Nucleic Acids Research 33, D364–368 (2005)
10. Harrison, J.C., Haber, J.E.: Surviving the breakup: The DNA damage checkpoint. Annu. Rev. Genet. 40, 209–235 (2006)
11. Ideker, T.E., Thorsson, V., Karp, R.M.: Discovery of regulatory interactions through perturbation: Inference and experimental design. In: Pacific Symposium on Biocomputing, pp. 302–313 (2000)
12. J., P., M., S.: Charging it up: global analysis of protein phosphorylation. Trends in Genetics 22, 545–554 (2006)
13. King, R.D., Whelan, K.E., Jones, F.M., Reiser, P.J.K., Bryant, C.H., Muggleton, S., Kell, D.B., Oliver, S.: Functional genomic hypothesis generation and experimentation by a robot scientist. Nature 427, 247–252 (2004)
14. Middendorf, M., Kundaje, A., Wiggins, C., Freund, Y., Leslie, C.: Predicting genetic regulatory response using classification. Bioinformatics 20, 232–240 (2004)
15. Muggleton, S.: Inverse entailment and Progol. New Generation Computing, Special issue on Inductive Logic Programming 13(3-4), 245–286 (1995)
16. Ong, I.M., Glasner, J.D., Page, D.: Modelling regulatory pathways in *Escherichia coli* from time series expression profiles. Bioinformatics 18, S241–S248 (2002)
17. Papatheodorou, I., Kakas, A., Sergot, M.: Inference of gene relations from microarray data by abduction. In: Baral, C., Greco, G., Leone, N., Terracina, G. (eds.) LPNMR 2005. LNCS (LNAI), vol. 3662, pp. 389–393. Springer, Heidelberg (2005)
18. Pe'er, D., Regev, A., Elidan, G., Friedman, N.: Inferring subnetworks from perturbed expression profiles. In: Proceedings of the 9th International Conference on Intelligent Systems for Molecular Biology, pp. 215–224. Oxford University Press, Oxford (2001)
19. Pe'er, D., Regev, A., Tanay, A.: Minreg: Inferring an active regulator set. In: Proceedings of the 10th International Conference on Intelligent Systems for Molecular Biology, pp. S258–S267. Oxford University Press, Oxford (2002)
20. Reiser, P.G.K., King, R.D., Kell, D.B., Muggleton, S.H., Bryant, C.H., Oliver, S.G: Developing a logical model of yeast metabolism. Electronic Transactions in Artificial Intelligence 5, 223–244 (2001)
21. Segal, E., Shapira, M., Regev, A., Pe'er, D., Botstein, D., Koller, D., Friedman, N.: Module networks: identifying regulatory modules and their condition specific regulators from gene expression data. Nature Genetics 34, 166–176 (2003)
22. Srinivasan, A.: The Aleph Manual. University of Oxford, Oxford (2001)
23. Stark, C., Breitkreutz, B.J., Reguly, T., Boucher, L., Breitkreutz, A., Tyers, M.: BioGRID: a general repository for interaction datasets. Nucleic Acids Research 34, D535–539 (2006)
24. Struyf, J., Dzeroski, S., Blockeel, H., Clare, A.: Hierarchical multi-classification with predictive clustering trees in functional genomics. In: Progress in Artificial Intelligence: 12th Portugese Conference on Artificial Intelligence, pp. 272–283. Springer, Heidelberg (2005)
25. Tamaddoni-Nezhad, A., Chaleil, R., Kakas, A., Muggleton, S.H.: Application of abductive ILP to learning metabolic network inhibition from temporal data. Machine Learning 64, 209–230 (2006)
26. Tanay, A., Shamir, R.: Computational expansion of genetic networks. Bioinformatics, 17 (2001)

27. Teixeira, M.C., Monteiro, P., Jain, P., Tenreiro, S., Fernandes, A.R., Mira, N.P., Alenquer, M., Freitas, A.T., Oliveira, A.L.: The YEASTRACT database: a tool for the analysis of transcription regulatory associations in *Saccharomyces cerevisiae*. Nucleic Acids Research 34, D446–451 (2006)
28. Tu, Z., Wang, L., Arbeitman, M.N., Chen, T., Sun, F.: An integrative approach for causal gene identification and gene regulatory pathway inference. Bioinformatics , e489–e496 (2006)
29. Zien, A., Kuffner, R., Zimmer, R., Lengauer, T.: Analysis of gene expression data with pathway scores. Proc. Int. Conf. Intell. Syst. Mol. Biol. 8, 407–417 (2000)

ILP Through Propositionalization and Stochastic k-Term DNF Learning

Aline Paes[1], Filip Železný[2], Gerson Zaverucha[1], David Page[3], and Ashwin Srinivasan[4]

[1] Dept. of Systems Engineering and Computer Science - COPPE
Federal University of Rio de Janeiro (UFRJ)
{ampaes, gerson}@cos.ufrj.br
[2] Dept. of Cybernetics - School of Electrical Engineering
Czech Institute of Technology in Prague
zelezny@fel.cvut.cz
[3] Dept. of Biostatistics and Medical Informatics and
Dept. of Computer Sciences
University of Wisconsin
page@biostat.wisc.edu
[4] IBM India Research Laboratory and
Dept of CSE and Centre for Health Informatics
University of New South Wales, Sydney, Australia
ashwin@cse.iitd.ernet.in

Abstract. One promising family of search strategies to alleviate runtime and storage requirements of ILP systems is that of stochastic local search methods, which have been successfully applied to hard propositional tasks such as satisfiability. Stochastic local search algorithms for propositional satisfiability benefit from the ability to quickly test whether a truth assignment satisfies a formula. Because of that many possible solutions can be tested and scored in a short time. In contrast, testing whether a clause covers an example in ILP takes much longer, so that far fewer possible solutions can be tested in the same time. Therefore in this paper we investigate stochastic local search in ILP using a relational propositionalized problem instead of directly use the first-order clauses space of solutions.

1 Introduction

ILP has been successfully applied to a variety of tasks [12], [6]. Nevertheless, ILP systems have huge time and storage requirements, owing to a large search space of possible clauses. Therefore, clever search strategies are needed [13]. One promising family of search strategies is that of stochastic local search methods. These methods have been successfully applied to propositional tasks, such as satisfiability, substantially improving their efficiency. Following the success of such methods, a promising research direction is to employ stochastic local search within ILP, to accelerate the runtime of the learning process. An investigation in that direction was recently performed within ILP [22].

S. Muggleton, R. Otero, and A. Tamaddoni-Nezhad (Eds.): ILP 2006, LNAI 4455, pp. 379–393, 2007.

Stochastic local search algorithms for propositional satisfiability benefit from the ability to quickly test whether a truth assignment satisfies a formula. As a result, many possible solutions (assignments) can be tested and scored in a short time. In contrast, the analogous test within ILP—testing whether a clause covers an example—takes much longer, so that far fewer possible solutions can be tested in the same time. Therefore, motivated by both the success and limitations of the previous work, we also apply stochastic local search to ILP but in a different manner. Instead of directly applying stochastic local search to the space of first-order Horn clauses, we use a propositionalization approach that transforms the ILP task into an attribute-value learning task. In this alternative search space, we can take advantage of fast testing as in propositional satisfiability. Our primary aim in this paper is to reduce ILP run-time.

The standard greedy covering algorithm employed by most ILP systems is another shortcoming of typical ILP search. There is no guarantee that greedy covering will yield the globally optimal hypothesis; consequently, greedy covering often gives rise to problems such as unnecessarily long hypothesis with too many clauses. To overcome the limitations of greedy covering, the search can be performed in the space of entire theories rather than clauses. A strong argument against this larger search is the combinatorial complexity, giving us another reason to transform the relational domains into propositional ones and to use stochastic local search in the resulting, simpler search space. Therefore, our secondary aim in this work is to verify the benefits of a non-covering approach to perform search in ILP systems.

In a recent work, a novel stochastic local search algorithm (SLS) was presented to induce k-term DNF formulae. The SLS algorithm performs refinements on an entire hypothesis rather than a single rule. A detailed analysis of SLS performance compared to WalkSAT shows the advantages of using SLS to learn a hypothesis as short as possible [15]. In this work we specifically investigate the relevance of that SLS algorithm to learn k-term DNF formulae in relational domains through propositionalization.

The outline of the paper is as follows. First, some background knowledge related to propositionalization and Stochastic Local Search are reviewed in Sections 2 and 3, respectively. Then the proposal of this paper, SLS in ILP through propositionalization and k-term DNF learning, is devised in Section 3.4. Before concluding, some experimental results which validate our method are shown in section 4.

2   Propositionalization

Propositionalization can be understood as a transformation method, where a relational learning problem is compiled to an attribute-value problem, which one can solve using propositional learners [9,7]. During propositionalization *features* are constructed from the background knowledge and structural properties of individuals. Each feature is defined as a clause in the form $f_i(X) := Lit_{i,1}, ..., Lit_{i,n}$ where the literals in the body are derived from the background knowledge and the argument in clause's head refers to an individual as an example identifier. The features are the attributes which form the basis for columns in single-table (propositional) representations of the data. If such a clause defining a feature is called for a particular individual and this call succeeds, the feature is set to "true" in the corresponding column of the given example; otherwise it is set to "false". Recently several propositionalization systems have been proposed. Examples include: RSD [21] and SINUS [8] among others. In the next section we briefly review RSD since it is the propositionalization system used in the experiments of our approach.

2.1   RSD

RSD is a system that uses propositionalization through first-order feature construction for discovering statistically interesting relational subgroups in a population of individuals [21][1]. RSD performs the following three stages in order to propositionalize data: (1) identifies all first-order literal conjunctions that by definition form a first-order feature, and at the same time comply to user-defined mode-language constraints. Such features do not contain any constants and the task can be completed independently of the input data; (2) employs constants by copying certain features several times with some variables substituted to constants chosen from the input data. In this step irrelevant features are also detected and eliminated; (3) generates a propositionalized representation of the input data using the generated feature set. Such representation is a table consisting of truth values of the first-order features computed for each example.

First-order feature construction. The feature language declarations accepted to RSD are very similar to those used by Aleph [19] and Progol [11]. Thus, in the declaration section the predicates that can appear in a feature are listed. A type and a mode are assigned to each argument of these predicates. If two arguments have different types they can not hold the same variable. A mode is either input or output. Input arguments are labelled by the + sign, and output variables by the − sign. Every variable in an input argument of a literal must appear in an output argument of some preceding literal in the same feature. Others setting parameters such as the maximum length of a feature (number of contained literals), maximum variable depth [11], maximum number of occurrences of a given predicate symbol among others, can be specified or acquire a default value.

RSD generates an exhaustive set of features satisfying the language declarations. A connectivity requirement, which stipulates that no feature may be decomposable into a conjunction of two or more features, must also be satisfied.

RSD implements several pruning techniques to reduce the number of examined expressions, while preserving the exhaustiveness of the resulting feature set. Such techniques may often drastically decrease the run times needed to achieve the feature set.

Employing constants and filtering features. In this step RSD substitutes selected variables in the features with constants extracted from the input data

---

[1] RSD is publicly available at http://labe.felk.cvut.cz/~zelezny/rsd

using the declared predicate *instantiate/1*. When such predicate appears in a feature having a variable as its arguments it means that all occurrences of that variable should be eventually substituted with a constant. In case of multiple instantiate/1 predicates appear in a single feature with different variables, a number of features are generated , each one corresponding to a possible combination of grounding of the indicated variables. Only those groundings which make the feature true for at least a pre-specified number of individuals are considered.

The feature filtering is performed during the feature construction process described above. Therefore, RSD discard features considering three constraints: (a) no feature should have the same Boolean value for all the examples, (b) no two features should have the same Boolean values for all the examples and (c) no feature should be true for less than a minimum prescribed number of examples.

Generating a propositional representation. After constructing an appropriate set of features RSD can use such features and the examples to generate a single relational table using an attribute-value representation. For more details about RSD we refer the reader to [21].

3 Stochastic Local Search

Stochastic Local Search (SLS) algorithms have been used to solve hard combinatorial problems such as satisfiability. SLS algorithms are characterised by the following properties [14]: (a) they are search algorithms, i.e. given a problem P they search through an instance space S_P for instances $i_P \in S_P$ which might be solutions; (b) They perform a local search. That means during their search they only consider instances which are direct neighbors of the current instance according to a neighborhood relation $R \subseteq S_P \times S_P$; (c) they use a global scoring function $score_P : S_P \times S_P \mapsto R$. The decision on which instance should be examined next depends – at least partially – on the scoring function.

SLS algorithms such as GSAT [18] and WalkSAT [17] have been successfully used to solve challenging satisfiability problems. They have also been applied on propositional tasks encoded as a satisfiability problem, substantially improving their efficiency [2]. Next section brings a brief review of these algorithms.

3.1 GSAT and WalkSAT Algorithms

GSAT is based on a hill-climbing procedure with a stochastic component. It searches for a truth assignment which satisfies a set of propositional clauses. The basic GSAT algorithm starts with a randomly generated assignment and then repeatedly changes ("flips") the assignment of a single variable that leads to the largest decrease in the number of unsatisfied clauses. These flips continue until either a satisfying assignment is found or a pre-specified maximum number of flips is reached. GSAT can easily become trapped in local minima and the only way employed to it to escape from them is restart with a new randomly generated assignment after reaching the maximum number of flips. The process is repeated until a pre set number of tries is reached.

Another mechanism for escaping from local minima is to randomly alternate between greedy minimizing moves and stochastic moves, randomly selected from the variables which appears in unsatisfied clauses. Therefore, GSAT with Random Walk [16], with probability p, takes a random variable from an unsatisfied clause and flips its value and with probability $1 - p$ follows the schema of GSAT, changing the value of the variable which minimizes the number of unsatisfied clauses the most.

WalkSAT is derived from GSAT with Random Walk, but including significant modifications. Different from the later, which maintains a list of variables appearing on unsatisfied clauses and picks a variable at random from that list, WalkSAT employs a two-steps random process: first, it picks randomly a clause not satisfied by the current assignment and then it picks a variable, at random or using a greedy heuristic, within that clause to flip. Another modification is related to the scoring function. Instead of considering the overall decrease of unsatisfied clauses, it counts the number of clauses which will become unsatisfied if each variable in the clause chosen at random is flipped.

3.2 Stochastic Local Search in k-Term DNF Learning

The aim in k-term DNF learning is to induce a formula of k terms in disjunctive normal form, where each term is a conjunction of literals. Formally, the k-term DNF learning can be defined in the following way [5]:
   Given:

- a set of Boolean variables *Var*,
- a set *Pos* of truth value assignments $p_i : Var \rightarrow 0, 1$,
- a set *Neg* of truth value assignments $n_i : Var \rightarrow 0, 1$ and
- a natural number k

Find:

- a DNF formula with k terms
- that evaluates to 1(true) for all variable assignments in *Pos*
- and evaluates to 0 (false) for all variable assignments in *Neg*.

k-term DNF learning is a NP-hard problem of combinatorial search. Therefore, SLS algorithms can be applied to solve it, sacrificing completeness for better runtime behavior. A novel SLS algorithm was designed in [15] to solve k-term DNF learning and it is reproduced here in Fig. 1.

The algorithm starts generating randomly a hypothesis, i.e., a DNF formula with k-terms and then refines this hypothesis in the following manner. First, it picks a misclassified example at random. If this example is a positive one the hypothesis must be generalized. To do so, a literal has to be removed from a term of the hypothesis. Now, with probability p_{g1} and p_{g2} respectively, the term and a literal in this term are chosen at random. Otherwise the term in the hypothesis which differs in the smallest number of literals from the misclassified example and the literal whose removal from the term decreases the score the most are chosen. On the other hand, if the example is a negative one, it means that the hypothesis must be specified. Therefore, a literal has to be added in a term. The term is chosen at random from those ones which cover the misclassified negative example. In a similar way to the last case, either with probability p_s the literal to be added in this term is chosen at random or a random literal which decreases the score the most is taken. This iterative process continues until the score is equal to zero or the algorithm reaches a maximum number of modifications. All the procedure is repeated a pre-specified number of times.

$search(k, maxTries, maxSteps)$: Given integer numbers $k, maxTries$ and $maxSteps$; probability parameters p_{g1}, p_{g2} and p_s; a set of Examples E, returns a k-term DNF formulae

1. **for** $i \leftarrow 1$ to $maxTries$ **do**
2. $H \leftarrow$ a randomly generated k-term DNF formula;
3. $steps \leftarrow 0$;
4.   **while** $steps < maxSteps$ **and** $score_L(H) \neq 0$ **do**
5. $steps \leftarrow steps + 1$;
6. $ex \leftarrow$ a random example $\in E$ that is misclassified by H;
7.   **if** ex is a positive example
8.   with probability p_{g1}: $t \leftarrow$ a random term in H;
9.   otherwise: $t \leftarrow$ the term in H that differs in the smallest number of literals from ex
10.   with probability p_{g2}: $l \leftarrow$ a random literal in t;
11.   otherwise: $l \leftarrow$ the literal in t whose removal decreases $score_L(H)$ most;
12. $H \leftarrow H$ with l removed from t
13.   **else if** ex is a negative example
14. $t \leftarrow$ a (random) term in H that covers ex;
15.   with probability p_S: $l \leftarrow$ a random literal m so that $t \wedge m$ does not cover ex;
16.   otherwise: $l \leftarrow$ a literal whose addition to t decreases $score_L(H)$ most
17. $H \leftarrow H$ with l added to t
18.   **end if**
19.   **end while**
20. **end for**

Fig. 1. An SLS algorithm for k-term DNF learning [15]

It is important to mention that SLS algorithm performs refinements of an entire hypothesis rather than a single rule. A detailed analysis of SLS performance compared to WalkSAT shows the advantages of using SLS to learn a hypothesis as short as possible [15].

3.3 Stochastic Local Search in ILP

The recent study in [22] compared the performance of several randomized strategies (GSAT, WalkSAT, Randomized General to Specific, Rapid Random Restarts) to search the ILP subsumption lattice. All these methods can be viewed

$search(B, H, E, s^{suf}, c^{all}, \gamma)$: Given background knowledge B; a set of clauses H; a training sequence $E = E^+, E^-$ (i.e. positive and negative examples); a sufficient clause score s^{suf} $(-\infty \leq s^{suf} \leq \infty)$; the maximum number of clauses the algorithm can evaluate c^{all}, $(0 < c^{all} < \infty)$; and the maximum number of clauses evaluated on any single restart or the 'cutoff' value γ $(0 < \gamma \leq \infty)$, returns a clause D such that $B \cup H \cup \{D\}$ entails at least one element e of E^+. If fewer than c^{all} clauses are evaluated in the search, then the score of D is at least s^{suf}.

1. $S := -\infty$; $C := 0$; $N := 0$
2. repeat
3.   **Select** e^{sat} from E^+
4.   **Select** D_0 such that $D_0 \succeq_\theta \bot(e^{sat}, B)$
5. $Active = \emptyset$; $Ref = \{D_0\}$
6.   repeat
7. $S^* = \max_{D_i \in Ref} \underline{eval}_{B,H}(D_i)$; $D^* := \arg\max_{D_i \in Ref} \underline{eval}_{B,H}(D_i)$
8.   if $S^* > S$ then $S := S^*$; $D := D^*$
9. $N := N + |Ref|$
10. $Active := \textbf{UpdateActiveList}(Active, Ref)$
11. $Prune := \textbf{Prune}(Active, S^*)$
12. $Active := Active \setminus Prune$
13.   **Select** D^{curr} from $Active$; $Active := Active \setminus D^{curr}$
14. $Ref := \textbf{Refine}_{B,H,(\gamma-N)}(D^{curr})$
15.   until $S \geq s^{suf}$ or $C + N \geq c^{all}$ or $N = \gamma$
16. $C := C + N$; $N := 0$
17. until $S \geq s^{suf}$ or $C \geq c^{all}$
18. if $S = -\infty$ then return e^{sat} else return D^*.

Fig. 2. A general skeleton of a search procedure—possibly randomized and/or restarted—in the clause subsumption lattice bounded by the clause $\bot(e^{sat}, B)$. This clause is derived using the saturant e^{sat} and the background knowledge B. In Step 4, $\succeq_\theta$ denotes Plotkin's (theta) subsumption between a pair of Horn clauses. Individual strategies considered in this paper are obtained by different implementations of the bold-typed commands. Clauses are scored by a finite evaluation function $\underline{eval}$. Although in the formal notation in Step 7 the function appears twice, it is assumed that the 'max' and 'arg max' operators are computed simultaneously. In Step 11 **Prune** returns all elements of $Active$ that cannot possibly be refined to have a better score than S^*. If the number of refinements of the current clause is greater than $(\gamma - N)$, **Refine** returns only the first $(\gamma - N)$ computed refinements, to guarantee that no more than γ clauses are evaluated between restarts. The search is terminated when score s^{suf} is reached or c^{all} clauses have been evaluated, and restarted (from Step 3) when γ clauses have been evaluated since the last restart. If all **Select** commands are deterministic then restarting (setting $\gamma < c^{all}$) results in mere repetitions of the identical search.

as variations of the basic skeleton in Fig. 2, by instantiating the bold-faced commands.

It was observed that if a near-to-optimal value of the cutoff parameter (the number of clauses examined before the search is restarted) is used, then the mean search cost (measured by the total number of clauses explored rather than by cpu time) may be decreased by several orders of magnitude compared to a deterministic non-restarted search. It was also observed that differences between the tested randomized methods were rather insignificant. In the present study we accept the GSAT strategy for sakes of comparison. In terms of the algorithm in Fig. 2, GSAT has the following properties: randomized saturant (example seed) and start clause selection, greedy updating of the active list (only the best scoring neighbor state is retained), deterministic next state selection (determined by the scoring function), no pruning, and bidirectional refinement (combining specialization and generalization).

A limitation of the study in [22] was that the stochastic strategies were framed in a single clause search algorithm. One consequence of this is that the statistically assessed performance ranking of individual strategies may not be representative of their performance when used for an incremental entire-theory construction due to the statistical dependence between the successive clause search procedures. Thus in the present study we compare performance measured for entire-theory construction processes.

3.4   Stochastic Local Search in ILP Through Propositionalization

In this work we investigate the relevance of using stochastic local search to learn k-term DNF formulae in relational domains and to do so we have to proposition-alize the relational problem. Therefore, we implemented a k-term DNF formulae inducer using the SLS algorithm joined to the first-order feature construction part of the RSD system. We compare the run-time when performing stochastic local search through propositionalization with the run-time when doing stochas-tic search or enumerative heuristic search directly in the relational space.

4   Experiments

4.1   Data and Methods Tested

The goals discussed before in this paper are experimentally evaluated using two ILP benchmarks: the East-West Trains [10] and Mutagenesis Data [20].
Methods:

- **Aleph** [19]. Working in its default mode, with the following exceptions. For the Mutagenesis data set, negative examples were allowed to be covered by the constructed theory while the minimum accuracy of each rule included in the theory was set to 0.7. For both data sets, the total number of nodes searched within each rule-search procedure was not limited by a constant. It was rather determined by setting the maximum number of literals in each rule (the *clauselength* parameter), ranging from 3 to 7 in Mutagenesis and 3 to 12 in East-West Trains.

- **Aleph/SLS.** This method uses the GSAT [22] stochastic local search procedure implemented in Aleph. The same settings as for the previous method were applied and additionally, the number of *tries* (randomly initiated local searches) was set to 10 and the number of *moves* (clauses explored in each local search) was set to 100.
- **DNF/SLS.** This method first propositionalizes the relational data with RSD [21] using the same language declarations as used in Aleph [2] and then applies the stochastic k-term DNF search procedure as described in [15] onto the propositional representation of the data.
- **Propositional algorithms.** In order to observe the behavior of stochastic local search in relational problems through propositionalization when the search is performed in the whole theory instead of individual clauses, we also compared DNF/SLS with two popular rule learner algorithms which use the covering approach, Part [4] and Ripper [3] with pruning disabled since we are interested in decreasing the runtime.

4.2   Experimental Procedure

The aim of the experiments was to determine the statistical dependencies between three random variables:

- N: the number of rules contained in the resulting theory (the compression achieved)
- T: the cpu time consumed by the search
- A: the estimated predictive accuracy of the resulting theory

We specifically model the two dependencies N vs. T and N vs. A.

We first split both datasets into 10 cross-validation folds, and for all methods, A was estimated on the independent test data part in each fold.

For Aleph and Aleph/SLS, all the three variables acquire different values as a result of:

- applying the method on each of the 10 cross-validation folds
- within each fold, varying the maximum *clauselength* parameter within its limits as mentioned above.

The DNF/SLS method allows to directly specify k, the number of rules (i.e. the number of DNF terms) in the constructed theory. Also Part and Ripper were modified to allow a specified maximum number of rules in the theory. Upon executing the Aleph and Aleph/SLS experiments, we extracted the

---

[2] Despite the same declarations, the theory spaces explored by the two approaches are necessarily different. On one hand, only a fraction of clauses explored by Aleph form a correct feature (as defined e.g. in [21]). On the other hand, the Aleph setting of maximum number of literals in a rule here translates into the maximum number of literals in a feature; however, in the subsequent k-DNF search, the features are combined in conjunctions and the total length of a single rule thus is unbounded.

range of the values of N from the set of resulting theories and executed repeatedly the DNF/SLS method with k acquiring all values in the detected range. This procedure was further repeated for each of the 10 cross-validation folds.

4.3   Results

Figures 3 and 4 present the empirical N vs. T dependency by plotting the mean cpu-time (on logarithmic scale) consumed by search executions resulting in a theory containing a given number of rules. This is shown for both data sets and all three methods. For DNF/SLS, we separately plot the k-DNF learning time excluding/including time consumed by propositionalization.

Figures 5 and 6 present the empirical N vs. A dependency by plotting the mean estimated predictive accuracy achieved by search executions resulting in a theory containing a given number of rules. This is shown for both data sets and all three methods.

4.4   Principal Trends

The results indicate the following trends. DNF/SLS performs faster w.r.t. all other tested methods when it comes to short theories (in number of rules). This results change when allowing an increasing number of rules in the theory, with standard Aleph being ultimately the fastest algorithm if propositionalization time is taken into account for DNF/SLS. Comparing to relational methods, the performance gap is significantly large (in orders of magnitude), while corresponding predictive accuracy do not favor either SLS/DNF or the relational methods. Comparing to the propositional methods, this performance gap is much smaller, while SLS/DNF's short theories exhibit slight superiority in terms of predictive accuracy. Note however, that e.g. in the East-West Trains domain, each 9-rule theory produced by standard Aleph is a trivial list of the positive examples[3], which is not the case for the other two methods (This fact can be verified from Fig. 5 where Aleph's 9-rule theories achieves accuracy 0.5. in the East-West Trains domain.)

In general, the size of theories (in the number of rules contained) does not demonstrate any significant influence onto their predictive accuracy. This is not surprising for the East-West trains data set, where the small number of examples (10 of each class) renders all theories almost random fits of the training data. For Mutagenesis, an 'Occam's razor' intuition would suggest that higher accuracy should be expected from a theory with fewer rules, given the same required performance on the training data. A possible explanation of the observation is that this classification problem is well modelled by a theory with a large number of short rules (few literals). Our next experiments will thus address classification problems requiring complex rules (such as the graph classification challenge described in [22]) and where stochastic search have shown to play an important role as in relational phase transition benchmarks [1].

---

[3] 9 of the 10 positive examples fall in the training split in each cross-validation fold.

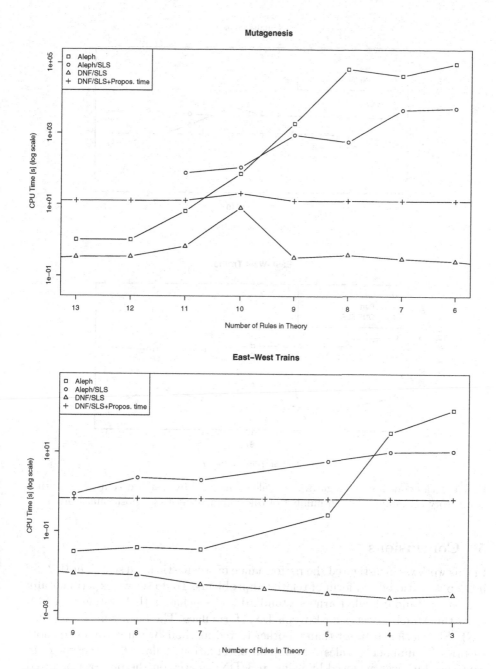

Fig. 3. Mean cpu-time (on logarithmic scale) consumed by search executions resulting in a theory containing a given number of rules: comparing to relational learners

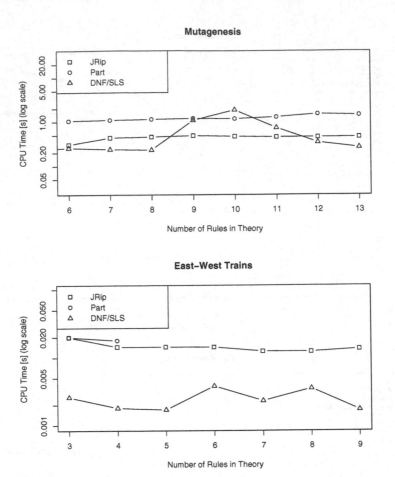

Fig. 4. Mean cpu-time (on logarithmic scale) consumed by search executions resulting in a theory containing a given number of rules: comparing to propositional learners

5   Conclusions

In this work we investigated the performance of stochastic local search in ILP using a propositionalized form of relational problems. To do so, we experimentally compared standard rule learners, standard and stochastic ILP system to a SLS algorithm which searches for k-terms DNF formulaes. The results indicated that DNF/SLS performs faster than all other tested methods when it comes to short theories (in number of rules). Two main observations follow: (1) a very significant speed-up was achieved by using SLS/DNF search on the propositionalized form of the learning data, as compared to the default enumerative search conducted by Aleph, (2) the k-term SLS run-time distribution exhibits a rapid decay, unlike the heavy-tailed clause-search run-time distributions we observed in the relational domain [22]. When comparing to standard propositional rule learners the gap performance is much smaller. Therefore our future work will extend

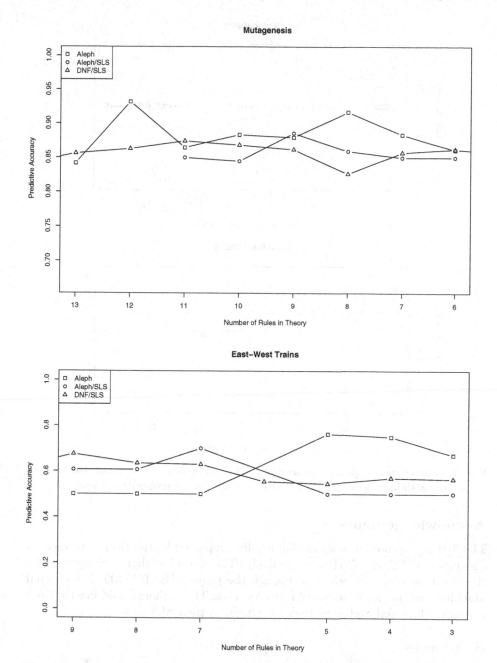

Fig. 5. Mean estimated predictive accuracy achieved by search executions resulting in a theory containing a given number of rules: : comparing to a relational learner

experiments to a larger set of ILP benchmarks and relational phase transition datasets [1] to achieve a more conclusive ranking between the DNF and greedy strategies in the propositionalized domain.

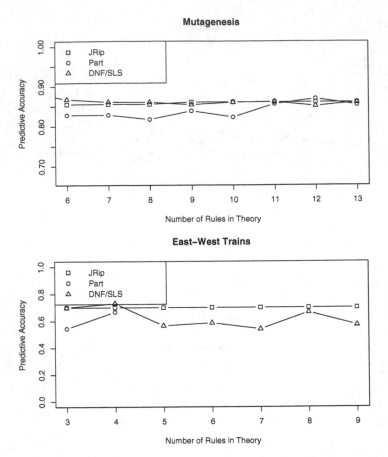

Fig. 6. Mean estimated predictive accuracy achieved by search executions resulting in a theory containing a given number of rules: comparing to propositional learners

Acknowledgements

The first and second authors are financially supported by the Brazilian research agencies CAPES and CNPq, respectively. The second author is Supported by the Czech Academy of Sciences through the project 1ET101210513 Relational Machine Learning for Biomedical Data Analysis. The authors would like to thank Ulrich Rückert and Stefan Kramer for giving us their SLS code.

References

1. Botta, M., Giordana, A., Saitta, L., Sebag, M.: Relational learning as search in a critical region. J. Mach. Learn. Res. 4, 431–463 (2003)
2. Chisholm, M., Tadepalli, P.: Learning decision rules by randomized iterative local search. In: Proc. of the 19th ICML, pp. 75–82 (2002)
3. Cohen, W.W.: Fast effective rule induction. In: Proc. of 12th ICML, pp. 115–123. Morgan Kaufmann, San Francisco (1995)

4. Frank, E., Witten, I.H.: Generating accurate rule sets without global optimization. In: Proc. of 15th ICML, pp. 144–151. Morgan Kaufmann, San Francisco (1998)
5. Kearns, M.J., Vazirani, U V.: An Introduction to Computational Learning Theory. Cambridge, Massachusetts (1994)
6. King, R.D., Whelan, K.E., Jones, F.M., Reiser, P.K.G., Bryant, C.H., Muggleton, S.H., Kell, D.B., Oliver, S.G.: Functional genomic hypothesis generation and experimentation by a robot scientist. Nature 427, 247–252 (2004)
7. Krogel, M.-A., Rawles, S., Železný, F., Flach, P.A., Lavrac, N., Wrobel, S.: Comparative evaluation of approaches to propositionalization. In: Horváth, T., Yamamoto, A. (eds.) ILP 2003. LNCS (LNAI), vol. 2835, pp. 197–214. Springer, Heidelberg (2003)
8. Lavrač, N., Džeroski, S.: Inductive Logic Programming: Techniques and Applications. Ellis Horwood (1994)
9. Lavrač, N., Flach, P.A: An extended transformation approach to inductive logic programming. ACM Trans. on Comp. Logic 2(4), 458–494 (2001)
10. Michalski, R., Larson, J.B.: Inductive inference of vl decision rules. Workshop in pattern-Directed Inference Systems, SIGART Newsletter 63, 38–44 (1977)
11. Muggleton, S.: Inverse entailment and progol. New Generation Computing Journal 13, 245–286 (1995)
12. Muggleton, S.: Scientific knowledge discovery using inductive logic programming. Communications of the ACM 42(11), 42–46 (1999)
13. Page, D., Srinivasan, A.: Ilp: A short look back and a longer look forward. Journal of Machine Learning Research 4, 415–430 (2003)
14. U. Rückert. Machine learning in the phase transition framework. Master's thesis, Albert-Ludwigs-Universität Freiburg (2002)
15. Rückert, U., Kramer, S.: Stochastic local search in k-term dnf learning. In: Proc. of the 20th ICML, pp. 648–655 (2003)
16. Selman, B., Kautz, H.A.: Domain-independent extensions to gsat: Solving large structured satisfiability problems. In: Proc. of the 13th IJCAI, pp. 290–295 (1993)
17. Selman, B., Kautz, H.A., Cohen, B.: Local search strategies for satisfiability testing. In: Cliques, Coloring, and Satisfiability: Second DIMACS Implementation Challenge, October 11-13, 1993. DIMACS Series in Discrete Mathematics and Theoretical Computer Science, vol. 26, pp. 521–532 (1996)
18. Selman, B., Levesque, H.J., Mitchell, D.G.: A new method for solving hard satisfiability problems. In: Proc. of the 10th AAAI, pp. 440–446 (1992)
19. Srinivasan, A.: The Aleph Manual (2001), http://web.comlab.ox.ac.uk/oucl/research/areas/machlearn/Aleph/aleph.html
20. Srinivasan, A., Muggleton, S., Sternberg, M.J.E., King, R.D.: Theories for mutagenicity: A study in first-order and feature-based induction. Artificial Intelligence 85(1-2), 277–299 (1996)
21. Železný, F., Lavrac, N.: Propositionalization-based relational subgroup discovery with RSD. Machine Learning 62(1–2), 33–63 (2006)
22. Železný, F., Srinivasan, A., Page, D.: A monte carlo study of randomised restarted search in ILP. In: Camacho, R., King, R., Srinivasan, A. (eds.) ILP 2004. LNCS (LNAI), vol. 3194, Springer, Heidelberg (2004)

θ-Subsumption Based on Object Context

Olga Skvortsova

International Center for Computational Logic, Technische Universität Dresden
skvortsova@iccl.tu-dresden.de

Abstract. We propose a novel method for efficient θ-subsumption. Our solution is based on the idea of object context which embody the contextual information in a clause and is given by occurrences of identical objects or chains of such occurrences. Efficient θ-subsumption is crucial for AI planning approaches that rely on lifted first-order reasoning. We incorporate our object context-based method for θ-subsumption within one approach for lifted first-order planning under uncertainty, referred to as LIFT-UP, and compare it with several related techniques.

1 Introduction

Planning under uncertainty currently represents a modern trend in the area of AI Planning because it allows to model and reason in environments, where actions may have uncertain outcomes and an agent does not necessarily acquire complete information about its internal state. In many approaches, Markov Decision Processes, MDPs for short, have been chosen as a de-facto standard representational and computational model for planning under uncertainty [1, 2, 3]. The solution to a planning task in an uncertain and dynamic environment, which is represented as an MDP, is an optimal policy, i.e., a function that delivers for each state an optimal action. Due to the uncertain and dynamic nature of the environment the solution can no longer be represented as a plain sequence of actions as in the case of classical AI Planning, because can not be guaranteed that an action will lead to a state which you expect it to.

Recently, there have been designed several efficient techniques for solving MDPs [1,4]. Among others, one could emphasize an approach, referred to as SPUDD [4], which has been used to solve MDPs with hundreds of millions of states optimally. This work demonstrates that large MDPs, described in a logical fashion, can often be solved optimally by exploiting the logical structure of the problem. In another vein, approaches, like, e.g., real-time dynamic programming (RTDP) [2] or symbolic LAO* [3], employ heuristic search that restricts the computation to those states that are reachable from the initial state.

Meanwhile, many realistic planning problems are best represented in first-order terms. In this respect, existing planning systems for solving first-order MDPs can be divided into two clusters. The first cluster is represented by propositionalization-based approaches which have performed extraordinary well on 2004 and 2006 International Planning Competitions. The second cluster, which is substantially smaller, contains a few propositionalization-free systems which currently outperform the state-of-the-art methods from the first cluster only on a certain class of problems [5]. In comparison to the

S. Muggleton, R. Otero, and A. Tamaddoni-Nezhad (Eds.): ILP 2006, LNAI 4455, pp. 394–408, 2007.

former systems, which perform inferences on grounded propositions, the latter ones operate on the lifted level, namely reason with first-order constructions.

Although propositionalization-based planning methods demonstrate a favourable computational behaviour on a wide range of benchmark problems, they suffer from one important shortcoming. Namely, once a domain of interest becomes incompletely specified or even infinite,[1] they fail to accomplish the domain propositionalization. Another reason in favour of propositionalization-free techniques is that lifted reasoning reflects the spirit and beauty of the logic-based planning which has almost vanished and which we would like to revive on the AI planning market. Therefore, our ultimate goal is to develop a competitive planning system based on the lifted reasoning that would be able to outperform its propositionalization-based opponents on a considerably larger fraction of benchmark problems.

Recently, we have developed a lifted approach, referred to as LIFT-UP, for solving first-order MDPs [6]. In order to evaluate the LIFT-UP method, we have designed a domain-dependent implementation, referred to as FLUCAP [5].

In the meantime, we have concentrated on developing efficient domain-independent inference procedures that operate on the first-order level thereby avoiding problem propositionalization. One very important inference procedure is θ-subsumption that arises at several occassions within the LIFT-UP approach. First, θ-subsumption is used as a consequence relation for the decision of whether an initial state covers preconditions of an action and, if an action is applicable, for computing the complete set of all successors of an initial state. Second, θ-subsumption is realized as a normalization test for detecting which states can be removed from the state space. Third, if a goal statement is fully specified, θ-subsumption is employed for computing all predecessors of a goal.

In general, θ-subsumption is NP-complete [7]. There have been recently proposed several approaches to cope with the NP-completeness of θ-subsumption. They include deterministic subsumption [8], constraint-based techniques, e.g., Django [9], and context-based methods, e.g., LITCON [10]. In practice, there may be only few literals, or none at all, that can be matched deterministically. Django has been initially designed as a θ-subsumption checker: It delivers only yes/no answer to the problem. Since in the LIFT-UP system we require all successors of an initial state, it remains to estimate the effort of extending Django to deliver all solutions to the subsumption problem. In comparison to the previous two methods, context-based approaches to θ-subsumption seem to provide a very flexible framework which can be naturally extended towards computing all solutions.

However, as it was shown in [11], LITCON [10] does not scale very well up to large context depth. Because in some planning problems, the size of state descriptions can be relatively large, it might be necessary to compute the contextual information for large values of the depth parameter. Therefore, we are strongly interested in a technique that scales better than LITCON. In this paper, we present an approach, referred to as object context, or OBJCON, for short, which demonstrates better computational behaviour.

---

[1] However, the construction of a realistic infinite planning domain requires substantial effort.

2 First-Order Markov Decision Processes

A *Markov decision process*, is a tuple $(\mathcal{Z}, \mathcal{A}, \mathcal{P}, \mathcal{R}, \mathcal{C})$, where $\mathcal{Z}$ is a finite set of states, $\mathcal{A}$ is a finite set of actions, and $\mathcal{P} : \mathcal{Z} \times \mathcal{Z} \times \mathcal{A} \to [0, 1]$, written $\mathcal{P}(z'|z, a)$, specifies transition probabilities. In particular, $\mathcal{P}(z'|z, a)$ denotes the probability of ending up at state z' given that the agent was in state z and action a was executed. $\mathcal{R} : \mathcal{Z} \to \mathbb{R}$ is a real-valued reward function associating with each state z its immediate utility $\mathcal{R}(z)$. $\mathcal{C} : \mathcal{A} \to \mathbb{R}$ is a real-valued cost function associating a cost $\mathcal{C}(a)$ with each action a. A *sequential decision problem* consists of a Markov decision process and is the problem of finding a policy $\pi : \mathcal{Z} \to \mathcal{A}$ that maximizes the total expected discounted reward received when executing the policy π over an infinite (or indefinite) horizon. A Markov decision process is said to be *first-order* if the expressions used to define $\mathcal{Z}$, $\mathcal{A}$ and $\mathcal{P}$ are first-order.

The *value* $V_\pi(z)$ of a state z with respect to the policy π is defined as

$$V_\pi(z) = \mathcal{R}(z) + \mathcal{C}(\pi(z)) + \gamma \sum_{z' \in \mathcal{Z}} \mathcal{P}(z'|z, \pi(z)) V_\pi(z'),$$

where $0 \leq \gamma \leq 1$ is a discount factor. We take γ equal to 1 for indefinite-horizon problems only, i. e. when a goal is reached the system enters an absorbing state in which no further rewards or costs are accrued. A value function V is set to be *optimal* if it satisfies

$$\mathcal{R}(z) + \max_{a \in \mathcal{A}} \{ \mathcal{C}(a) + \gamma \sum_{z' \in \mathcal{Z}} \mathcal{P}(z'|z, a) V^*(z') \},$$

for each $z \in \mathcal{Z}$; in this case the value function is usually denoted by $V^*(z)$. The optimal policy is extracted from the optimal value function.

3 Probabilistic Fluent Calculus

States, actions, transition probabilities, cost and reward function are specified in a probabilistic and sorted extension of the fluent calculus [12, 13].

Fluents and States. Let Σ denote a set of function symbols containing the binary function symbol $\circ$ and the nullary function symbol 1. $\circ$ is an AC1-symbol with 1 as unit element. Let $\Sigma^- = \Sigma \backslash \{\circ, 1\}$. Non-variable Σ^--terms are called *fluents*. Let $f(t_1, \ldots, t_n)$ be a fluent. The terms t_i, $1 \leq i \leq n$ are called *objects*. A *state* is a finite set of ground fluents. Let $\mathcal{D}$ be the set of all states.

Fluent Terms and Abstract States. Fluent terms are defined inductively as follows: 1 is a fluent term; each fluent is a fluent term; if G_1 and G_2 are fluent terms, then so is $G_1 \circ G_2$. Let $\mathcal{F}$ be the set of all fluent terms. We assume that each fluent term obeys the *singularity condition*: each fluent may occur at most once in a fluent term. Because of the latter, there is a bijection $\cdot^M$ between ground fluent terms and states. Some care must be taken when instantiating a non-ground fluent term F by a substitution θ because $F\theta$ may violate the singularity condition. A substitution θ is *allowed* for fluent term F if $F\theta$ meets the singularity condition.

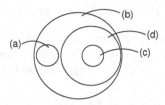

Fig. 1. The interpretations of the abstract states (a) $Z_1 = on(X_1, a) \circ on(a, table)$, (b) $Z_2 = on(X_2, a) \circ on(a, table) \circ Y_2$, (c) $Z_3 = on(X_3, a) \circ on(a, table) \circ clear(X_3)$ and (d) $Z_4 = on(X_4, a) \circ on(a, table) \circ clear(X_4) \circ Y_4$, where a is an object denoting a block, $table$ is an object denoting a table, X_1, X_2, X_3 and X_4 are variables of sort object, Y_2 and Y_4 are variables of sort fluent term, $on(X_i, a)$, $i = 1 \ldots 4$, is a fluent denoting that some block X_i is on a and $clear(X_i)$, $i = 3, 4$, is a fluent denoting that block X_i is clear.

Abstract states are expressions of the form F or $F \circ X$, where F is a fluent term and X is a variable of sort fluent term. Let $\mathcal{S}$ denote the set of abstract states. Abstract states denote sets of states as defined by the mapping $\cdot^I : \mathcal{S} \to 2^{\mathcal{D}}$: Let Z be an abstract state. Then

$$[Z]^I = \{[Z\theta]^M \mid \theta \text{ is an allowed grounding substitution for } Z\}.$$

This is illustrated in Figure 1. In other words, abstract states are characterized by means of positive conditions that must hold in each ground instance thereof and, thus, they represent clusters of states. In this way, abstract states embody a form of state space abstraction, which is called *first-order state abstraction*.

As a running example, we consider problems taken from the colored Blocksworld scenario, which is an extension of the classical Blocksworld scenario in the sense that along with the unique identifier, each block is now assigned a specific color. Thus, a state description provides an arrangement of colors instead of an arrangement of blocks. For example, a state Z defined as a fluent term:

$$Z = red(X_0) \circ green(X_1) \circ blue(X_2) \circ red(X_3) \circ red(X_4) \circ$$
$$red(X_5) \circ green(X_6) \circ green(X_7) \circ Tower(X_0, \ldots, X_7),$$

specifies a tower that is comprised of eigth colored blocks.

Subsumption. Let Z_1 and Z_2 be abstract states. Then Z_1 is *subsumed* by Z_2, in symbols $Z_1 \sqsubseteq Z_2$, if there exists an allowed substitution θ such that $Z_2\theta =_{AC1} Z_1$. Intuitively, Z_1 is subsumed by Z_2 iff $Z_1^I \subseteq Z_2^I$. In the LIFT-UP system we are often concerned with the problem of finding a complete set of allowed substitutions solving the AC1-matching problem $Z_2\theta =_{AC1} Z_1$. For example, consider the abstract states mentioned in Figure 1. Then, $Z_1 \sqsubseteq Z_2$ with $\theta = \{X_2 \mapsto X_1, Y_2 \mapsto 1\}$, $Z_3 \sqsubseteq Z_2$ with $\theta = \{X_2 \mapsto X_3, Y_2 \mapsto clear(X_3)\}$. However, $Z_1 \not\sqsubseteq Z_3$ and $Z_3 \not\sqsubseteq Z_1$.

Actions. Let Σ_a denote a set of action names, where $\Sigma_a \cap \Sigma = \emptyset$. An *action space* $\mathcal{A}$ is a set of expressions of the form $(a(X_1, \ldots, X_n), C, E)$, where $a \in \Sigma_a$, X_i, $1 \le i \le n$, are variables or constants, $C \in \mathcal{F}$ called *precondition* and $E \in \mathcal{F}$ called *effect* of the action $a(X_1, \ldots, X_n)$. E.g., a pickup-action in the blockworld can be specified by

$$(pickup\,(X,Y),\ on(X,Y) \circ clear(X) \circ empty,\ holding(X) \circ clear(Y)),$$

where $empty$ denotes that the robot arm is empty and $holding(X)$ that the block X is in the gripper. For simplicity, we will often supress parameters, preconditions and effects of an action $(a(X_1,\ldots,X_n),C,E)$ and refer to it as a instead.

Nature's Choice and Probabilities. In analogy to the approach in [14] stochastic actions are decomposed into deterministic primitives under nature's control, referred to as *nature's choices*. It can be modelled with the help of a binary relation symbol *choice* as follows: Consider the action $pickup\,(X,Y)$:

$$choice\,(pickup\,(X,Y),a) \leftrightarrow (a = pickupS\,(X,Y) \vee a = pickupF\,(X,Y)),$$

where $pickupS$ and $pickupF$ define two nature's choices for action $pickup$, viz., that it succeeds or fails. For simplicity, we denote the set of nature's choices of an action a as $Ch\,(a) := \{a_j | choice\,(a,a_j)\}$.

For each of nature's choices a_j associated with an action a we define the probability $prob\,(a_j,a,Z)$ denoting the probability with which one of nature's choices a_j is chosen in a state Z. For example,

$$prob\,(pickupS\,(X,Y),pickup\,(X,Y),Z) = .75$$

states that the probability for the successful execution of the $pickup$ action in state Z is .75. We require that for each action the probabilities of all its nature's choices sum up to 1.

Rewards and Costs. Reward and cost functions are defined for abstract states using the unary relation symbols *reward* and *cost*. For example, we might want to give a reward of 500 to all states in which some block X is on block a and 0, otherwise:

$$reward\,(Z) = 500 \leftrightarrow Z \sqsubseteq (on(X,a),\emptyset),$$
$$reward\,(Z) = 0 \quad \leftrightarrow Z \not\sqsubseteq (on(X,a),\emptyset).$$

In other words, the state space is divided into two abstract states depending on whether or not, a block X is on block a. Likewise, value functions can be specified with respect to the abstract states only. Action costs can be analogously defined. E. g., with

$$cost(pickup\,(X,Y)) = 3$$

the execution of the $pickup$-action is penalized with 3.

Forward and Backward Application of Actions. An action $(a(X_1,\ldots,X_n),C,E)$ is *forward applicable with* θ to an abstract state $Z \in S$, denoted as $forward\,(Z,a,\theta)$, if $(C \circ U)\theta =_{AC1} Z$, where U is a new variable of sort fluent term and θ is an allowed substitution. If applicable, then the action *progresses to* or *yields* the state $(E \circ U)\theta$. In this case, $(E \circ U)\theta$ is called *successor state* of Z and denoted as $succ(Z,a,\theta)$.

An action $(a(X_1,\ldots,X_n),C,E)$ is *backward applicable with* θ to an abstract state $Z \in S$, denoted as $backward\,(Z,a,\theta)$, if $(E \circ U)\theta =_{AC1} Z$, where U is a new variable of sort fluent term and θ is an allowed substitution. If applicable, then the action *regresses to* the state $(C \circ U)\theta$. In this case, $(C \circ U)\theta$ is called *predecessor state* of Z and denoted as $pred(Z, a, \theta)$. One should observe that the AC1-matching problems involved in the application of actions are subsumption problems, viz. $Z \sqsubseteq (C \circ U)$ and $Z \sqsubseteq (E \circ U)$. Moreover, in order to determine all possible successor or predecessor states of some state with respect to some action we have to compute complete sets of allowed substitutions solving the corresponding subsumption problems.

4 LIFT-UP Algorithm

In order to solve first-order MDPs, we have developed a new algorithm that combines heuristic search and first-order state abstraction techniques. Our algorithm, referred to as LIFT-UP, can be seen as a generalization of the symbolic LAO* algorithm by [3]. Given an initial state, LIFT-UP uses an admissible heuristic to focus computation on the parts of the state space that are reachable from the initial state. Moreover, it specifies MDP components, value functions, policies, and admissible heuristics using a first-order language of the Probabilistic Fluent Calculus. This allows LIFT-UP to manipulate abstract states instead of individual states. The algorithm itself is presented in Figure 2.

As symbolic LAO*, LIFT-UP has two phases that alternate until a complete solution is found, which is guaranteed to be optimal. First, it expands the best partial policy and evaluates the states on its fringe using an admissible heuristic function. Then it performs dynamic programming on the states visited by the best partial policy, to update their values and possibly revise the current best partial policy. We note that we focus on partial policies that map a subcollection of states into actions.

In the policy expansion step, we perform reachability analysis to find the set F of states that have not yet been expanded, but are reachable from the set S^0 of initial states by following the partial policy π. The set of states G contains states that have been expanded so far. By expanding a partial policy we mean that it will be defined for a larger set of states in the dynamic programming step. In symbolic LAO*, reachability analysis is performed on propositional algebraic decision diagrams (ADDs). Therefore, an additional preprocessing of a first-order MDP is required at the outset of any solution attempt. This preprocessing involves propositionalization of the first-order structure of an MDP, viz., instantiation of the MDP components with all possible combinations of domain objects. Whereas, LIFT-UP relies on the lifted first-order reasoning, that is, computations are kept on the first-order level avoiding propositionalization. In particular, action applicability check and computation of successors as well as predecessors are accomplished on abstract states directly.

In the dynamic programming step of LIFT-UP, we employ a modified first-order value iteration algorithm (FOVI) that computes the value only on those states which are reachable from the initial states. More precisely, we call FOVI on the set E of states that are visited by the best current partial policy. In this way, we improve the efficiency of the original FOVI algorithm by [15] by using symbolic dynamic programming together with reachability analysis. Given a first-order MDP and a value function represented in PFC, FOVI returns the best partial value function V, the best partial policy π and the residual r. In order to update the values of the states Z in E, we assign the values from the current value function to the successors of Z. We compute successors with respect to all nature's choices a_j. The residual r is computed as the absolute value of the largest difference between the current and the newly computed value functions V' and V, respectively. We note that the newly computed value function V is taken in its normalized form, i.e., as a result of the *normalize* procedure. Extraction of a best partial policy π is straightforward: One simply needs to extract the maximizing actions from the best partial value function V.

As with symbolic LAO*, LIFT-UP converges to an ε-optimal policy when three conditions are met: (1) its current policy does not have any unexpanded states, (2) the residual r is less than the predefined threshold ε, and (3) the value function is initialized with an admissible heuristic. When calling LIFT-UP, we initialize the value function with an admissible heuristic function h that focuses the search on a subset of reachable states. A simple way to create an admissible heuristic is to use dynamic programming to compute an approximate value function. Therefore, in order to obtain an admissible heuristic h in LIFT-UP, we perform several iterations of the original FOVI. We start the algorithm on an initial value function that is admissible. Since each step of FOVI preserves admissibility, the resulting value function is admissible as well. The initial value function assigns the goal reward to each state thereby overestimating the optimal value, since the goal reward is the maximal possible reward.

5   Efficient Domain-Independent θ-Subsumption

To evaluate the LIFT-UP approach we have developed a domain-dependent implementation called FLUCAP [5]. It can solve probabilistic Blocksworld problems as they appeared, for example, in the colored Blocksworld domain of the 2004 International Planning Competition [16]. In the meantime, we have concentrated on developing efficient domain-independent inference procedures that operate on the first-order level thereby circumventing problem propositionalization. One very important inference procedure is θ-subsumption that arises at several occassions within the LIFT-UP approach. First, θ-subsumption is used at the policy expansion step for computing all successors of an initial state. Second, θ-subsumption underlies the normalization procedure at the dynamic programming step, where the FOVI algorithm is called. Third, if a goal statement is fully specified, θ-subsumption is employed for computing the heuristic function h. However, in most competition benchmark problems, goal statements are only partially defined. In this cases, an extended θ-subsumption, where subsumee is partially specified, is required.

Let F_1 and F_2 be fluent terms under singularity condition. Then $\widehat{F}_1$ and $\widehat{F}_2$ are clause representations of F_1 and F_2, respectively. The clause representation $\widehat{F}$ of a fluent term F is defined as follows.

$$\widehat{F} = \begin{cases} \{\} & F = 1 \\ \{F\} & F \text{ is a fluent} \\ \widehat{G}_1 \cup \widehat{G}_2 & F = G_1 \circ G_2 \end{cases}$$

Then AC1-matching problem of whether there exists an allowed substitution θ such that $(F_1 \circ U)\theta =_{AC1} F_2$, where U is a new variable of sort fluent term, is equivalent to the θ-subsumption problem of whether there exists a substitution θ such that $\widehat{F}_1\theta \subseteq \widehat{F}_2$,

```
policyExpansion(π, S⁰, G)
    E := F := ∅ and from := S⁰
    repeat
        to :=    ⋃       ⋃      {succ(Z, aⱼ, θ)},
              Z∈from  aⱼ∈Ch(a)
        where (a, θ) := π(Z)
        F := F ∪ (to − G) and E := E ∪ from
        from := to ∩ G − E
    until (from = ∅)
    E := E ∪ F and G := G ∪ F
    return (E, F, G)

FOVI(E, 𝒜, prob, reward, cost, γ, V)
    repeat
        V' := V
        loop for each Z ∈ E
            loop for each a ∈ 𝒜
                loop for each θ such that forward (Z, a, θ)
                    Q(Z, a, θ) := reward(Z) + cost(a)+
                                γ  ∑     prob(aⱼ, a, Z) · V'(succ(Z, aⱼ, θ))
                                 aⱼ∈Ch(a)
            end loop
        end loop
        V(Z) := max  Q(Z, a, θ)
                (a,θ)
    end loop
    V := normalize(V)
    r := ||V − V'||
    until stopping criterion
    π := extractPolicy(V)
    return (V, π, r)

LIFT-UP(𝒜, prob, reward, cost, γ, S⁰, h, ε)
    V := h and G := ∅
    For each Z ∈ S⁰, initialize π with an arbitrary action
    repeat
        (E, F, G) := policyExpansion(π, S⁰, G)
        (V, π, r) := FOVI(E, 𝒜, prob, reward, cost, γ, V)
    until (F = ∅) and r ≤ ε
    return (π, V)
```

Fig. 2. LIFT-UP algorithm

where $\widehat{F}_1$, $\widehat{F}_2$ are clause representations of F_1 and F_2, respectively. A clause represents a set of literals.

5.1 Existing Techniques

In general, θ-subsumption is NP-complete [7] One approach to cope with the NP-completeness of θ-subsumption is deterministic subsumption. A clause is said to be determinate if there is an ordering of literals, such that in each step there is a literal which has exactly one match that is consistent with the previously matched literals [8]. However, in practice, there may be only few literals, or none at all, that can be matched deterministically. Recently, in [10], it was developed another approach, which we refer to as literal context, LITCON, for short, to cope with the complexity of θ-subsumption. The authors propose to reduce the number of matching candidates for each literal by using the contextual information. The method is based on the idea that literals may only be matched to those literals that possess the same relations up to an arbitrary depth in a clause. As a result, a certain superset of determinate clauses can be tested for subsumption in polynomial time.

Unfortunately, as it was shown in [11], LITCON does not scale very well up to large depth. Because in some planning problems, the size of state descriptions can be relatively large, it might be necessary to compute the contextual information for large values of the depth parameter. Therefore, we are strongly interested in a technique that scales better than LITCON. In this section, we present an approach, referred to as object context, OBJCON, for short, which demonstrates better computational behaviour than LITCON. Based on the idea of OBJCON, we develop a new θ-subsumption algorithm and compare it with the LITCON-based approach.

We should pinpoint a very efficient constraint-based approach for solving the θ-subsumption problem, referred to as Django [9]. Django is nowadays the fastest θ-subsumption checker that delivers only yes/no answers. In subsequent sections, we present a comparison analysis of our OBJCON -based reasoner with Django on the normalization problems, viz., problems that require only yes/no answers in order to decide whether a state can be effortlessly removed from the state space.

5.2 Object Context

In general, a literal f in a clause C can be matched with several literals in a clause D, that are referred to as matching candidates of f. LITCON is based on the idea that literals in C can be only matched to those literals in D, the context of which include the context of the literals in C [10]. The context is given by occurrences of identical objects (variables $Vars\,(C)$ and constants $Const\,(C)$) or chains of such occurrences and is defined up to some fixed depth. In effect, matching candidates that do not meet the above context condition can be effortlessly pruned. In most cases, such pruning results in deterministic subsumption, thereby considerably extending the tractable class of clauses.

The computation of the context itself is dramatically affected by the depth parameter: The larger the depth is, the longer the chains of objects' occurrences are, and thus, more effort should be devoted to build them. For example, consider a clause

$$C = \{on(X, Y), on(Y, table), red(X), blue(Y), heavy(X), wet(X),$$
$$fragile(X), fragile(Y), light(Y), dry(Y)\}$$

that can be informally read as: A block X is on the block Y which is on the table, and both blocks enjoy various properties.

In LITCON, the context should be computed for ten literals in order to keep track of all occurrences of identical objects. What if we were to compute the context for each object instead? In our running example, we would need to perform computations only three times, in this case. Herein, we propose a more efficient approach, referred to as OBJCON, for computing the contextual information with respect to objects instead of literals. More formally, we build the object occurrence graph $\mathcal{G}_C = (V, E, \ell)$ for a clause C, where vertices are objects of C, denoted as $Obj\,(C)$, and edges $E = \{(o_1, \pi_1, f, \pi_2, o_2) \mid f(t_1, \ldots, t_n) \in C$ and $o_1 = t_{\pi_1}$ and $o_2 = t_{\pi_2}\}$ with $o_1, o_2 \in Obj\,(C)$, $f(t_1, \ldots, t_n)$ being a literal and π_1, π_2 being positions of objects o_1, o_2 in f. The labeling function $\ell(o) = \{f \mid f(o) \in C\}$ associates each object o with

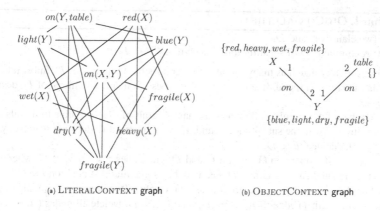

(a) LITERALCONTEXT graph   (b) OBJECTCONTEXT graph

Fig. 3. Literal (a) and object (b) occurrence graphs for the clause C

a unary literal name f, this object belongs to. Figure 3b presents the object occurrence graph for the clause C from our running example which contains three vertices X, Y and $table$ with labels $\{red, heavy, wet, fragile\}$, $\{blue, light, dry, fragile\}$ and $\{\}$, resp., and two edges $(X, 1, on, 2, Y)$ and $(Y, 1, on, 2, table)$. For comparison, the literal occurrence graph is depicted on Figure 3a and contains ten vertices and twenty four edges.

Definition 1. *Let C be a clause, $o \in Obj(C)$ and $d > 0$. The object context, denoted as* OBJCON(o, C, d), *of depth d is defined as the set of chains of labels:*

$$\ell(o) \xrightarrow{\pi_1^1 \cdot f^1 \cdot \pi_2^1} \ell(o_1) \xrightarrow{\pi_1^2 \cdot f^2 \cdot \pi_2^2} \ldots \xrightarrow{\pi_1^d \cdot f^d \cdot \pi_2^d} \ell(o_d) \in \text{OBJCON}(o, C, d)$$

iff

$$o \xrightarrow{\pi_1^1 \cdot f^1 \cdot \pi_2^1} o_1 \xrightarrow{\pi_1^2 \cdot f^2 \cdot \pi_2^2} \ldots \xrightarrow{\pi_1^d \cdot f^d \cdot \pi_2^d} o_d$$

is a path in $\mathcal{G}_C$ of length d starting at o.

In our running example, OBJCON$(X, C, 1)$ of depth 1 of the variable X in C contains one chain $\{red, heavy, wet, fragile\} \xrightarrow{1 \cdot on \cdot 2} \{blue, light, dry, fragile\}$.

Following the ideas of [10], we define the embedding of object contexts for clauses C and D, which serves as a pruning condition for reducing the space of matching candidates for C and D. Briefly, let $OC_1 = $OBJCON$(o_1, C, d)$, $OC_2 = $OBJCON$(o_2, D, d)$. Then OC_1 is embedded in OC_2, written $OC_1 \preccurlyeq OC_2$, iff for every chain of labels in OC_1 there exists a chain of labels in OC_2 which preserves the positions of objects in literals and the labels for each object in OC_1 are included in the respective labels in OC_2 up to the depth d.

Proposition 1 (Pruning). *Let C and D be clauses, $X \in Vars(C)$, $o \in Obj(D)$, and $d > 0$. Let $X\mu = o$, where μ is a matching substitution. If* OBJCON$(X, C, d) \not\preccurlyeq$ OBJCON(o, D, d) *then there exists no θ such that $C\mu\theta \subseteq D$.*

Algorithm 1. OBJCON-ALLTHETA

Input: Two clauses C and D.
Output: A complete set of substitutitons θ such that $C\theta \subseteq D$.

1. Deterministically match as many literals of C as possible to literals of D. Substitute C with the substitution found. If some literal of C does not match any literal of D, decide $C\theta \not\subseteq D$.
2. OBJCON-based deterministically match as many literals of C as possible to literals of D. Substitute C with the substitution found. If some literal of C does not match any literal of D, decide $C\theta \not\subseteq D$.
3. Build the substitution graph (V, E) for C and D with nodes $v = (\mu, i) \in V$, where μ is a matching candidate for C and D, i.e., matches some literal at position i in C to some literal in D and $i \geq 1$ is referred to as a layer of v. Two nodes (μ_1, i_1) and (μ_2, i_2) are connected with an edge iff $\mu_1\mu_2 = \mu_2\mu_1$ and $i_1 \neq i_2$. Delete all nodes (μ, i) such that $X\mu = o$ for some $X \in Vars(C)$ and $o \in Obj(D)$, and OBJCON$(X, C, d) \not\preceq$ OBJCON(o, D, d) for some d. Find all cliques of size $|C|$ in (V, E).

In other words, a variable X in C cannot be matched against an object o in D within a globally consistent match, if the variable's context cannot be embedded in the object's context. Therefore, the substitutions that meet the above condition can be effortlessly pruned from the search space. For any context depth $d > 0$, the context inclusion is an additional condition that reduces the number of candidates, and hence there exists more often at most one remaining matching candidate.

Based on the idea of the object context, we describe a θ-subsumption algorithm in Algorithm 1. Please note that this algorithm provides a complete set of all allowed substitutions which is used later on for determining the set of all possible successors or predecessors of some abstract state with respect to some action. Due to the lack of space, we omit the algorithm for computing all cliques in a substitution graph. However, it can be found along with other clarifications in [11].

5.3 Experimental Evaluation

All results presented in this section were obtained using RedHat Linux running on a 2.4GHz Pentium IV machine with 2GB of RAM.

Literal Context Versus Object Context. Figure 4 depicts the comparison timing results for the LITCON-based subsumption reasoner, referred to as LITCON-ALLTHETA, and its OBJCON-based opponent, referred to as OBJCON-ALLTHETA. We note that both reasoners deliver a complete set of *all* possible solutions for the θ-subsumption problem between preconditions of an action and a state.

We demonstrate the advantages of exploiting the object-based context information on problems that stem from the colored Blocksworld and Pipesworld planning scenarios. The colored Blocksworld has been defined in Section 3. The Pipesworld domain models the flow of oil-derivative liquids through pipeline segments connecting areas, and is inspired by applications in the oil industry. Liquids are modeled as batches of a certain unit size. A segment must always contain a certain number of batches (i.e., it

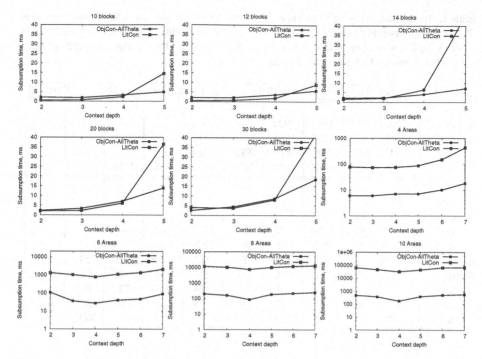

Fig. 4. Comparison timing results for OBJCON-ALLTHETA and LITCON-ALLTHETA. The results present the average time needed for one subsumption test. Please note that the plots for Pipesworld are shown in logscale. Therefore small differences in the plot may indicate a substantial difference on runtimes.

must always be full). Batches can be pushed into pipelines from either side, leading to the batch at the opposite end "falling" into the incident area. Batches have associated product types, and batches of certain types may never be adjacent to each other in a pipeline.

For each problem, there have been done 1000 subsumption tests. The time limit of 100 minutes has been allocated. The results show that OBJCON-ALLTHETA scales better than LITCON-ALLTHETA. It is best to observe on the problems of fourteen-, twenty-, and thirty-blocks. As empirical results demonstrate, the optimal value of the depth parameter for Blocksworld and Pipesworld is four. Moreover, on the Pipesworld problems, OBJCON-ALLTHETA requires two orders of magnitude less time than LITCON-ALLTHETA.

The main reason for the computational gain of OBJCON-ALLTHETA is that it is less sensitive to the growth of the depth parameter. Under the condition that the number of objects in a clause is strictly less than the number of literals and other parameters are fixed, the amount of object context information is strictly less than the amount of the literal context information.

Table 1 depicts the comparison timing results between LITCON-ALLTHETA and OBJCON-ALLTHETA on larger instances of the colored Blocksworld problems. Both reasoners attempt to solve the normalization task of whether one state subsumes

Table 1. Representative timing results in milliseconds for one subsumption teston large instances of colored Blocksworld problems for LITCON-ALLTHETA and OBJCON-ALLTHETA. BWX, where X stands for the number of blocks in a problem. A dash means that the algorithm did not finish within 100 minutes. The best results are marked in bold.

algorithm	BW100	BW125	BW150	BW175	BW200	BW250	BW300	BW350	BW400	BW450
LITCON										
d=2	2085	2951	4745	3921	–	–	–	–	–	–
d=3	365	611	1285	834	1815	3513	–	–	–	–
d=4	**117**	**162**	**320**	**172**	**597**	**1264**	5791	–	–	–
d=5	589	713	1015	1050	3421	5182	**2783**	**3914**	–	–
OBJCON										
d=2	54	490	–	–	–	–	–	–	–	–
d=3	13	15	5391	3718	–	–	–	–	–	–
d=4	4	83	1768	972	4236	5017	–	–	–	–
d=5	**3**	**5**	362	11	981	1249	3769	5351	–	–
d=6	**3**	6	**19**	**10**	**28**	713	1115	2018	2517	–
d=7	5	7	22	14	37	**59**	553	942	**102**	–
d=8	12	15	40	25	78	115	**94**	**71**	163	–
d=9	35	40	99	69	255	395	145	186	605	**618**
d=10	148	124	365	254	1053	–	516	770	3445	4529

another one. The reasoners deliver yes/no answer. For each problem, there have been done 1000 subsumption tests. The time limit of 100 minutes has been allocated. The results show that OBJCON-ALLTHETA scales better than LITCON-ALLTHETA on large problems. E.g., LITCON-ALLTHETA could solve problems of size up to 350 blocks only. Whereas OBJCON-ALLTHETA easily scales further.

Object Context Versus Django. Django has been initially designed as a θ-subsumption checker: It delivers only yes/no answer to the problem. Therefore, we could perform comparison on the normalization tasks only. Our main question in this part was to figure out whether we could use Django for solving normalization tasks. The outcome of our preliminary investigations is that on Blocksworld problems OBJCON-ALLTHETA is two times faster than Django. Please refer to Figure 5. Whereas, on Pipesworld problems, Django considerably outperforms our reasoner. Therefore, on the normalization tasks that arise at the dynamic programming step of the LIFT-UP approach, it is advisable to employ Django than an OBJCON-based reasoner.

However, we argue that for computing all successors of an initial state at the policy expansion step in LIFT-UP it is desirable to use OBJCON-based solver. We present several justifications. If we aim at applying Django for computing all solutions of the θ-subsumption problem, a substantial effort is required to extract a solution under current dual constraint representation of a problem. The graph that represents a problem in Django is substantially 'lighter' than the object occurrence graph in the sense that it does not contain enough information to efficiently extract the substitution itself as soon as it is required. More precisely, the graph under dual representation does not store the list of pairs $(\{f/f'\}, \{g/g'\})$, where f and g (resp., f' and g') belong to C (resp., D),

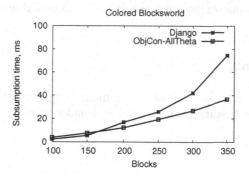

Fig. 5. Comparison timing results for OBJCON-ALLTHETA and Django on colored Blocksworld problems

such that assignment $\{f/f', g/g'\}$ is consistent. Instead, the local consistency check is implemented as a function checking for each pair f' and g' in the domain of Y_f and Y_g, resp., whether assignment $\{f/f', g/g'\}$ is consistent.

Moreover, in cases, where an extended θ-subsumption is required (e.g., where clauses are partially specified), it remains to investigate how the current dual constraint representation can be extended towards solving this extended θ-subsumption problem. In case of the OBJCON -based approach, we propose to extend the algorithm for finding all cliques in the substitution graph in the following way. Instead of searching for all cliques of size $|C|$ in a substitution graph G, find all cliques of any size in the extended substitution graph $\widehat{G}$, where the vertices are unifying substitutions and the compatibility condition is defined on the unifying substitutions.

6   Related Work

Some related approaches are known. For example, Django [9] is, nowadays, the fastest θ-subsumption checker that is based on the constraint satisfaction. Yet, it returns a binary answer 'yes/no' only and provides no solutions, even in the positive case. The system Fasϑ [17] can be applied to compute all solutions of the θ-subsumption problem. It was recently shown that LITCON-ALLTHETA is substantially faster than Fasϑ [11]. In the ReBel approach, authors employ a θ-subsumption algorithm that delivers a set of all solutions for the θ-subsumption problem [18]. For this, a generalized θ-subsumption framework is applied.

7   Conclusions

We have proposed a novel approach for efficient θ-subsumption that is based on the idea of object context. We have motivated our method by applying it for several reasoning tasks in a planning system LIFT-UP. Our method demonstrates an advantageous computational behaviour on problems of finding all possible solutions of the θ-subsumption problem. On most normalization tasks, except for Blocksworld problems, it is outperformed by Django.

Acknowledgements

We thank anonymous reviewers for useful comments. Olga Skvortsova was supported by the grant from the Graduate School GRK 334 under auspices of the German Research Foundation.

References

1. Boutilier, C., Dean, T., Hanks, S.: Decision-theoretic planning: Structural assumptions and computational leverage. JAIR 11, 1–94 (1999)
2. Barto, A.G., Bradtke, S.J., Singh, S.P.: Learning to act using real-time dynamic programming. AI 72(1-2), 81–138 (1995)
3. Feng, Z., Hansen, E.: Symbolic heuristic search for factored Markov Decision Processes. In: AAAI (2002)
4. Hoey, J., St-Aubin, R., Hu, A., Boutilier, C.: SPUDD: Stochastic Planning using Decision Diagrams. In: UAI (1999)
5. Hölldobler, S., Karabaev, E., Skvortsova, O.: FluCaP: A heuristic search planner for first-order MDPs. JAIR 2006 (to appear)
6. Hölldobler, S., Skvortsova, O.: LIFT-UP: Lifted first-order planning under unceainty. In: IWIL 2006 (to appear)
7. Kapur, D., Narendran, P.: NP-completeness of the set unification and matching problems. In: Siekmann, J.H. (ed.) 8th International Conference on Automated Deduction. LNCS, vol. 230, Springer, Heidelberg (1986)
8. Kietz, J.-U., Lübbe, M.: An efficient subsumption algorithm for inductive logic programming. In: ICML (1994)
9. Maloberti, J., Sebag, M.: Fast theta-subsumption with constraint satisfaction algorithms. ML 55(2) (2004)
10. Scheffer, T., Herbrich, R., Wysotzki, F.: Efficient θ-subsumption based on graph algorithms. In: Inductive Logic Programming. LNCS, vol. 1314, Springer, Heidelberg (1997)
11. Karabaev, E., Rammé, G., Skvortsova, O.: Efficient symbolic reasoning for first-order MDPs. In: PLMUDW (2006)
12. Hölldobler, S., Schneeberger, J.: A new deductive approach to planning. New Generation Computing 8, 225–244 (1990)
13. Thielscher, M.: Introduction to the fluent calculus. ETAI (1998)
14. Boutilier, C., Reiter, R., Price, B.: Symbolic Dynamic Programming for First-Order MDPs. In: IJCAI (2001)
15. Hölldobler, S., Skvortsova, O.: A Logic-Based Approach to Dynamic Programming. In: AAAI Workshop (2004)
16. Younes, H.L.S., Littman, M.L., Weissman, D., Asmuth, J.: The first probabilistic track of the International Planning Competition. JAIR 24, 851–887 (2005)
17. Di Mauro, N., Basile, T.M.A., Ferilli, S., Esposito, F., Fanizzi, N.: An exhaustive matching procedure for the improvement of learning efficiency. In: Horváth, T., Yamamoto, A. (eds.) ILP 2003. LNCS (LNAI), vol. 2835, Springer, Heidelberg (2003)
18. Kersting, K., van Otterlo, M., de Raedt, L.: Bellman goes relational. In: ICML (2004)

Word Sense Disambiguation Using Inductive Logic Programming

Lucia Specia[1], Ashwin Srinivasan[2,3], Ganesh Ramakrishnan[2],
and Maria das Graças Volpe Nunes[1]

[1] ICMC - University of São Paulo, Trabalhador São-Carlense, 400,
São Carlos, 13560-970, Brazil
{lspecia, gracan}@icmc.usp.br
[2] IBM India Research Laboratory, Block 1, Indian Institute of Technology,
New Delhi 110016, India
[3] Dept. of Computer Science and Engineering & Centre for Health Informatics,
University of New South Wales,
Sydney, Australia
{ashwin.srinivasan, ganramkr}@in.ibm.com

Abstract. The identification of the correct sense of a word is necessary for many tasks in automatic natural language processing like machine translation, information retrieval, speech and text processing. Automatic Word Sense Disambiguation (WSD) is difficult and accuracies
with state-of-the art methods are substantially lower than in other areas
of text understanding like part-of-speech tagging. One shortcoming of
these methods is that they do not utilize substantial sources of background knowledge, such as semantic taxonomies and dictionaries, which
are now available in electronic form (the methods largely use shallow
syntactic features). Empirical results from the use of Inductive Logic
Programming (ILP) have repeatedly shown the ability of ILP systems to
use diverse sources of background knowledge. In this paper we investigate
the use of ILP for WSD in two different ways: (a) as a stand-alone constructor of models for WSD; and (b) to build interesting features, which
can then be used by standard model-builders such as SVM. In our experiments we examine a monolingual WSD task using the 32 English verbs
contained in the SENSEVAL-3 benchmark data; and a bilingual WSD
task using 7 highly ambiguous verbs in machine translation from English to Portuguese. Background knowledge available is from eight sources
that provide a wide range of syntactic and semantic information. For both
WSD tasks, experimental results show that ILP-constructed models and
models built using ILP-generated features have higher accuracies than
those obtained using a state-of-the art feature-based technique equipped
with shallow syntactic features. This suggests that the use of ILP with
diverse sources of background knowledge can provide one way for making
substantial progress in the field of automatic WSD.

S. Muggleton, R. Otero, and A. Tamaddoni-Nezhad (Eds.): ILP 2006, LNAI 4455, pp. 409–423, 2007.
© Springer-Verlag Berlin Heidelberg 2007

1 Introduction

Word Sense Disambiguation (WSD) aims to identify the correct sense of an ambiguous word in a sentence. Usually described as an "intermediate task"—that is, not an end in itself—it is necessary in most natural language tasks like machine translation, information retrieval, speech and text processing, and so on. That it is extremely difficult, possibly impractical, to completely solve WSD is a long-standing view [2] and accuracies with state-of-the art methods are substantially lower than in other areas of text understanding. Part-of-speech tagging accuracies, for example, are now over 95%; in contrast, the best WSD results are still below 80%.

The principal approach adopted for the automatic construction of WSD models is a "shallow" one. In this, sample data consisting of sentences with the ambiguous words and their correct sense are represented using features capturing some limited context around the ambiguous words in each sentence. For example, features may denote two to three words on either side of an ambiguous word and the part-of-speech tags of those words. Sample data represented in this manner are then used by a statistical model constructor to build a general predictive model for disambiguating words. Results from the literature on benchmark data like those provided under the various SENSEVAL competitions[1] suggest that support vector machines (SVMs) yield models with one of the highest accuracies. Despite some improvements made in the accuracy of predictions, it is generally thought that significant progress in automatic WSD would require a "deep" approach in which access to substantial body of linguistic and world knowledge could assist in resolving ambiguities. However, the incorporation of large amounts of domain knowledge has been hampered by the following: (a) access to such information in electronic form suitable for constructing models; and (b) modeling techniques capable of utilizing diverse sources of domain knowledge. The first of these difficulties is now greatly alleviated by the availability in electronic form of very large semantic lexicons like WordNet [14], dictionaries, parsers, grammars and so on. In addition, there are now very large amounts of "shallow" data in the form of electronic text corpora from which statistical information can be readily extracted. Using these diverse sources of information is, however, beyond the capabilities of existing general-purpose statistical methods that have been used for WSD. Arguably, Inductive Logic Programming (ILP) systems provide the most general-purpose framework for dealing with such data: there are explicit provisions made for the inclusion of background knowledge of any form; the representation language is powerful enough to capture the contextual relationships that arise; and modeling is not restricted to being of a particular form (for example, classification only).

In this paper, we investigate the use of ILP for WSD in two different ways: (a) the construction of models that can be used directly to disambiguate words; and (b) the construction of interesting features that can be used by standard feature-based algorithms such as SVMs to build models to disambiguate verbs. We call

---

[1] see: http://www.senseval.org

the two different kinds of models "ILP models" and "ILP-assisted models". In each case, background knowledge is from eight different sources that provide syntactic and semantic information that could be useful for disambiguation. The purpose of our investigation is to examine whether using an ILP system equipped with these diverse sources of background information can substantially improve the predictive accuracy of WSD models. Our investigation is in the form of an empirical evaluation of ILP models and ILP-assisted models on WSD data arising from two different tasks: (1) monolingual disambiguation of 32 English verbs contained in SENSEVAL-3; and (2) bilingual disambiguation of the Portuguese sense of 7 highly ambiguous English verbs in a translation task.

The rest of the paper is organized as follows. In Section 2 we present some related work on WSD. The specification of ILP implementations that construct ILP models and features for use in ILP-assisted models is in Section 3. The experimental evaluation comprising our investigation is described in Section 4. This includes materials (Section 4.1) and methods (Section 4.2). Results are presented in Section 5. Section 6 concludes the paper.

2   Models for Word Sense Disambiguation

The earliest computer-executable models for WSD are manually constructed, capturing specific aspects of human disambiguation expertise in symbolic structures like semantic networks [23] and semantic frames [5,6,12]. Early reports also exist of sub-symbolic neural networks [4]. Most of these techniques have suffered from the important difficulty in manual acquisition of expert knowledge identified by Feigenbaum (and somewhat anticipated, in the WSD context [2]), resulting in their application being limited to very small subsets of the languages.

The development of machine readable resources like lexical databases, dictionaries and thesauri has provided a turning point in automatic processing of natural language, enabling the development of techniques that used information extracted automatically from these resources [11,25,1,32]. While the resources provided ready access to large bodies of knowledge, the actual disambiguation models continued to be manually codified. This changed with the use of statistical and machine-learning techniques for constructing models. The characteristic of these methods is the use of a corpus of examples of disambiguation to automatically construct disambiguation models. The most common of these "corpus-based" techniques employ statistical methods that build models based on features representing frequencies estimated from a corpus, for example, frequencies of some words on either side of the ambiguous word [33,16,26,21]. While techniques using such "shallow" features referring to the local context of the ambiguous word have yielded the best models so far, the accuracies obtained are low, and significant improvements do not appear to be forthcoming.

More sophisticated corpus-based approaches such as [31] try to incorporate deeper knowledge using machine readable resources. These are special-purpose methods aimed at specific tasks and it is not clear how they could be scaled-up for use across a wide range of WSD tasks. ILP provides a general-purpose approach that can be tailored to a variety of NLP tasks by the incorporation of appropriate background knowledge. To date, [28] is the only work dealing with the use of ILP for WSD. The work here extends this substantially in terms of experimental results; and in exploring alternate ways of using ILP for WSD.

3   Inductive Logic Programming

Functionally, Inductive Logic Programming (ILP) can bee largely characterised by two classes of programs. The first, predictive ILP, has been concerned with constructing models (sets of rules; or first-order variants of classification or regression trees) for discriminating accurately amongst two sets of examples ("positive" and "negative"). The partial specifications provided by [17] have formed the basis for deriving programs in this class. We refer the reader to [19] for definitions of the logical terms used below:

- B is background knowledge consisting of a finite set of clauses $= \{C_1, C_2, \ldots\}$
- E is a finite set of examples $= E^+ \cup E^-$ where:
  - *Positive Examples.* $E^+ = \{e_1, e_2, \ldots\}$ is a non-empty set of definite clauses;
  - *Negative Examples.* $E^- = \{\overline{f_1}, \overline{f_2} \ldots\}$ is a set of Horn clauses (this may be empty)
- H, the output of the algorithm given B and E is acceptable if the following conditions are met:
  - *Prior Satisfiability.* $B \cup E^- \not\models \square$
  - *Posterior Satisfiability.* $B \cup H \cup E^- \not\models \square$;
  - *Prior Necessity.* $B \not\models E^+$
  - *Posterior Sufficiency.* $B \cup H \models e_1 \wedge e_2 \wedge \ldots$

The second category of ILP programs, descriptive ILP, has been concerned with identifying relationships that hold amongst the background knowledge and examples, without a view of discrimination. The partial specifications for programs in this class are based on the description in [18]:

- B is background knowledge consisting of a finite set of clauses $= \{C_1, C_2, \ldots\}$
- E is a finite set of examples (this may be empty)
- H, the output of the algorithm given B and E is acceptable if the following condition is met:
  - *Posterior Sufficiency.* $B \cup H \cup E \not\models \square$

The idea of using a feature-based model constructor that uses first-order features can be traced back at least to the LINUS program [10]. More recently, the task of identifying good features using a first-order logic representation has been the province of programs developed under the umbrella of "propositionalization" (see [8] for a review). Programs in this class are not easily characterised as either predictive or descriptive ILP and we have not found explicit specifications for them within the ILP literature. Conceptually, solutions involve two steps: (1) a feature-construction step that identifies (within computational reason) all the features that are consistent with the constraints provided by the background knowledge. This is characteristic of a descriptive ILP program; and (2) a feature-selection step that retains some of the features based on their utility in classifying the examples. This is characteristic of a predictive ILP program. To this extent, we present partial specifications for feature construction that reflect a combination of the two dominant categories of ILP programs:

- B is background knowledge consisting of a finite set of clauses $= \{C_1, C_2, \ldots\}$
- E is a finite set of examples $= E^+ \cup E^-$ where:
  - *Positive Examples.* $E^+ = \{e_1, e_2, \ldots\}$ is a non-empty set of definite clauses;
  - *Negative Examples.* $E^- = \{\overline{f_1}, \overline{f_2} \ldots\}$ is a set of Horn clauses (this may be empty)
- $\mathcal{H}$ is the set of definite clauses, constructible with predicates, functions and constants in $B \cup E$; $\mathcal{F}$ the set of features constructible using a set of individuals and B; and $\tau : \mathcal{H} \mapsto \mathcal{F}$ a function that maps a definite clause $h \in \mathcal{H}$ to a feature $f \in \mathcal{F}$.
- $F = \{f_1, f_2, \ldots\} \subseteq \mathcal{F}$, the output of the algorithm given B and E is acceptable for any set $H = \{h_1, h_2, \ldots\} \subseteq \mathcal{H}$ if the following conditions are met:
  - *Posterior Sufficiency.* $B \cup \{h_i\} \models e_1 \vee e_2 \vee \ldots$, where $\{e_1, e_2, \ldots\} \subseteq E^+$
  - $f_i = \tau(h_i)$

The reader would have noted the principal differences in the 3 Posterior Sufficiency constraints. For feature construction—for the purposes of this paper—clauses identified are required to entail at least one positive example given B. Obviously more would be better, but this specification is a minimal one. This is not the case for descriptive ILP, and clearly insufficient for the predictive case.

We still need to clarify the meanings of $\mathcal{F}$, $\mathcal{H}$ and τ. For the purposes of this paper, we will assume that the boolean values $FALSE$ and $TRUE$ are represented by 0 and 1; the features f_i are functions of the form $f_i : \mathcal{X} \mapsto \{0, 1\}$; and examples E are some subset of the binary relation $\mathcal{X} \times \mathcal{Y}$, where $\mathcal{X}$ denotes the set of individuals and $\mathcal{Y}$ some finite set of classes. Positive and negative examples are represented by the predicate $class : \mathcal{X} \times \mathcal{Y} \mapsto \{0, 1\}$ and we will take each $h_i \in \mathcal{H}$ to be a definite clause $class(X, y_k) \leftarrow cp_i(X)$, where X is a variable and y_k is some class in $\mathcal{Y}$. Here, adopting terminology from [24], $cp_i : \mathcal{X} \mapsto \{0, 1\}$ is a "context predicate" and corresponds to a conjunction of literals that evaluates to true or false for any particular individual x. With these preliminaries in place, given $h_i : class(X, y_k) \leftarrow cp_i(X)$, $f_i(x) = \tau(h_i) = 1$ iff $cp_i(x) = 1$ (and 0 otherwise).

Given a set of examples represented by individuals and their classes, a program for feature construction that minimally satisfies this specification would proceed as follows. First, a set of clauses H is identified for the individuals. Each clause in this set entails at least one positive example, given the background knowledge B. Next, each clause h_i in H is converted into a boolean feature f_i that takes the value 1 (or 0) for any individual for which the body of the clause is true (if the body is false). Thus, the set of clauses H gives rise to a boolean vector for each individual in the set of examples. Examples in the WSD context are shown in Figure 1.

Clause:

h_1 : $class(X, voltar) : -has\_expression(X, \text{'come back '}, voltar)$
                    $has\_pos(X, pcwr\_4, nn)$

Feature:

$$f_1(X) = \begin{cases} 1 & has\_expression(X, \text{'come back '}, voltar) \wedge has\_pos(X, pcwr\_4, n) = 1 \\ 0 & \text{otherwise} \end{cases}$$

Fig. 1. Example of a boolean feature constructed from a clause for WSD. The clause in Prolog syntax identifies the Portuguese sense of the English verb 'to come'. The meanings of $has\_expression$ and has_pos are explained in Section 4.

4   Empirical Evaluation

Our objectives are to evaluate empirically the use of ILP in constructing models for WSD. Specifically, we intend to investigate the performance of two kinds of models:

1. *ILP models*. These are models constructed by an ILP system for predicting the correct sense of a word, by an implementation conforming to the specification for predictive ILP systems in Section 3.
2. *ILP-assisted models*. These are models for predicting the correct sense of a word that, in addition to existing shallow features, use features constructed by an ILP system. They are constructed by an implementation conforming to the specification for feature construction in Section 3.

4.1   Materials

Data

Monolingual task. Data consist of the 32 verbs from the SENSEVAL-3 competition. SENSEVAL[2] is a joint evaluation effort for WSD and related tasks. We use all the verbs of the English lexical sample task from the third and last edition of the competition: *activate, add, appear, ask, begin, climb, decide, eat, encounter, expect, express, hear, lose, mean, miss, note, operate, play, produce, provide, receive, remain, rule, smell, suspend, talk, treat, use, wash, watch, win,* and *write.* The number of examples for each verb varies from 40 to 398 (average of 186). The number of senses varies from 3 to 12 (average of 7). The average accuracy of the majority class is about 55%. We refer the reader to [13] for more information about the SENSEVAL-3 data.

---

[2] http://www.senseval.org

Bilingual task. Data consist of 7 highly frequent and ambiguous verbs: *come,*
get, give, go, look, make, and *take.* The sample corpus comprises around 200
English sentences for each verb extracted from a corpus of fiction books,
with the verb translation automatically annotated [29]. In that corpus, the
number of translations varies from 5 to 17, with an average of 11 translations.
The average accuracy of the majority class is about 54%.

Background Knowledge. To achieve accurate disambiguation is believed to
require a variety of syntactic and semantic information. In what follows, we
describe the background knowledge available for the tasks and illustrate it using
the following sentence (assuming that we want to disambiguate 'coming'):

"If there is such a thing as reincarnation, I would not mind coming back
as a squirrel".

B0. *Shallow features.* Features corresponding to the predicates in B1-B5, con-
veying the same information, but represented by attribute-value vectors.

B1. *Bag-of-words.* The 5 words to the right and left of the verb, extracted
from the corpus and represented using definitions of the form *has_bag*
(*sentence, word*):

$$has\_bag(snt1, mind).$$
$$has\_bag(snt1, not). \ldots$$

B2. *Narrow context.* Lemmas of 5 content words to the right and left of the verb,
extracted from the corpus, previously lemmatized. These are represented
using definitions of the form *has_narrow(sentence, wordposition, word)*:

$$has\_narrow(snt1, first\_content\_word\_left, mind).$$
$$has\_narrow(snt1, first\_content\_word\_right, back). \ldots$$

B3. *Part-of-speech tags.* Part-of-speech (POS) tags of 5 content words to the
right and left of the verb, obtained using MXPOST [24] and represented
using definitions of the form: *has_pos(sentence, wordposition, pos)*:

$$has\_pos(snt1, first\_content\_word\_left, nn).$$
$$has\_pos(snt1, first\_content\_word\_right, rb). \ldots$$

B4. *Subject-Object relations.* Subject and object syntactic relations with respect
to the verb. These were obtained from parsing sentences using MINIPAR
and represented using definitions of the form *has_rel(sentence, type, word)*:

$$has\_rel(snt1, subject, i).$$
$$has\_rel(snt1, object, nil). \ldots$$

B5. *Word collocations.* 11 collocations with respect to the verb: 1st preposition
to the right, 1st and 2nd words to the left and right, 1st noun, 1st adjective,
and 1st verb to the left and right. These are represented by definitions of
the form *has_collocation(sentence, collocation_type, collocation)*:

$$has\_collocation(snt1, first\_word\_right, back).$$
$$has\_collocation(snt1, first\_word\_left, mind). \dots$$

B6. *Verb restrictions*. Selectional restrictions of the verbs, defined in terms of the semantic features of their arguments in the sentence, extracted from LDOCE [22]. A hierarchy of feature types and WordNet relations are used to make the process more comprehensive. These are represented by definitions of the form $satisfy\_restrictions(sentence, rest\_subject, rest\_object)$:

$$satisfy\_restrictions(snt1, [human], nil).$$
$$satisfy\_restrictions(snt1, [animal, human], nil).$$

B7. *Dictionary definitions*. A relative count of the overlapping words in dictionary definitions of each of the possible translations of the verb (from [20]) and the words surrounding it in the sentence. These are represented by facts of the form $has\_highest\_overlap(sentence, translation)$:

$$has\_highest\_overlap(snt1, voltar).$$

B8. *Phrasal verbs*. Phrasal verbs possibly occurring in a sentence, according to the list of phrasal verbs given by dictionaries and the context of the verb (5 surrounding words). These are represented by definitions of the form $has\_expression(sentence, verbal\_expression)$:

$$has\_expression(snt1, 'come\ back').$$

Of these definitions, B0 is intended for use by a feature-based model constructor. B1–B8 are intended for use by an ILP system. The ILP implementation we use is capable of exploring intensional definitions of each of B1–B8. However, it is more efficient to represent the definitions in an extensional form (that is, as a set of ground facts). The background knowledge B1–B8 amount to about $204,000$ ground facts for the monolingual task and $24,000$ for the bilingual task.

Algorithms. We use implementations within the ILP system Aleph [30] to construct disambiguation models and to construct features. Feature-based model construction is performed by a linear SVM (the implementation provided in WEKA called SMO[3]). For convenience, we will call the Aleph implementation the "ILP learner" and the SVM implementation the "feature-based learner."

4.2   Method

We adopt the following method:

For each verb in each task (that is, 32 verbs in the monolingual task and 7 verbs in the bilingual task):

---

[3] http://www.cs.waikato.ac.nz/~ml/weka/

1. Obtain the best possible model using the feature-based learner and the features in B0. Call this the "baseline model"[4].
2. Obtain the best possible model using the ILP learner, equipped with background knowledge definitions B1–B8. Call this the "ILP model".
3. Construct at most k features using the ILP learner, equipped with background knowledge definitions B1–B8. Call these features "B9".
4. Obtain the best model possible using the feature-based learner with features in B0 and B9. Call this the "ILP-assisted model".
5. Compare the performance of the baseline model against that of the ILP model and the ILP-assisted model.

The following details are relevant:

(a) The SENSEVAL-3 benchmark specifies 34% of the data that are to be used to estimate the performance of disambiguation models. For uniformity, we randomly use 34% of the bilingual data for evaluation (the test set). The remaining 66% in each task is available for model construction (the training set). Performance will be measured by the accuracy of prediction on the test set (i.e., the percentage of test examples whose sense is predicted correctly).

(b) The ILP learner constructs a set of clauses in line with the specifications for predictive ILP as described in Section 3. Positive examples for the ILP learner are provided by the correct sense of the verb in a sentence. Negative examples are generated automatically using all other senses. The specifications do not, however, describe how the clauses constructed are to be used to predict the sense or translation of verbs in the test data. Clauses are evaluated in order of their identification by the ILP learner and the class of an example is determined by the first clause for which literals in the body are satisfied by the example. If no such clause exists, then the example is assigned the majority class, as computed on the training data.

(c) For each verb and task, constructing the "best possible model" requires determining optimal values for some parameters of the feature-based or ILP learner. We estimate these values using an instance of the method proposed in [7]: first, we decide on the relevant parameters. Second, we obtain, using the training set only, unbiased estimates of the predictive accuracy of the models for each verb arising from systematic variation across some small number of values for these parameters. Values that yielded the best average predictive accuracy across all verbs are taken to be optimal ones.

(d) The principal parameter for the feature-based learners concerns the extent of feature-selection to be performed. Values experimented with were: selecting 50, 100, 150, 200, 250, 500 or all features. For the monolingual task the best average accuracy for baseline models was obtained with 150 features; and with 250 features for the ILP-assisted case. For the bilingual task, the best

---

[4] The term "baseline" is not used in a pejorative sense: models constructed with shallow features of the form in B0 in fact represent the state-of-the-art, and any other techniques would have to perform at least as well as these.

average accuracy for baseline models used all features. The ILP-assisted models case required 500 features. For the ILP-learner, the principal parameters selected were: the choice between a greedy and non-greedy rule construction strategy (`induce` and `induce_max` in Aleph); the maximal length of clauses; and the minimum accuracy of clauses. For both tasks, the best average accuracies were obtained with the non-greedy strategy, in conjunction with a maximal clause length of 8 literals. The best minimal clause accuracy was 1.0 for the monolingual task, and 0.8 for the bilingual task.

(e) In all cases, the value of k (the number of features constructed) is 5000.

(f) Comparison of performance is done using the Wilcoxon signed-rank test [27]. This is a non-parametric test of the null hypothesis that there is no significant difference between the median performance of a pair of algorithms. The test works by ranking the absolute value of the differences observed in performance of the pair of algorithms. Ties are discarded and the ranks are then given signs depending on whether the performance of the first algorithm is higher or lower than that of the second. If the null hypothesis holds, the sum of the signed ranks should be approximately 0. The probabilities of observing the actual signed rank sum can be obtained by an exact calculation (if the number of entries is less than 10), or by using a normal approximation.

5   Results and Discussion

Figures 2 and 3 tabulate the performance of baseline, ILP, and ILP-assisted models—these two collectively termed ILP-based models—on the two disambiguation tasks. It is also standard practice to include the performance of a classifier that simply predicts the most frequent sense of the verb. The principal details in these tabulations are these: (1) The "majority class" classifier clearly performs poorest; (2) For both tasks, the accuracies of the baseline models are usually lower than the ILP-based models. Discarding ties, the baseline model has the highest accuracy only for 5 of the 32 verbs in the monolingual task and for 0 of the 7 verbs in the bilingual task; (3) ILP models and ILP-assisted models appear to be comparable in their performance in the monolingual task, while ILP models are uniformly better than ILP-assisted models for the bilingual task.

We turn now to the question of whether the differences observed between the models are in fact significant. The probabilities calculated by using the Wilcoxon test are shown in Fig. 4. The tabulations suggest that one or the other of the ILP-based models perform substantially better than the baseline or majority class models. However, they also suggest that a simple choice between ILP and ILP-assisted models is not evident: ILP-assisted models appear to be the best choice for the monolingual task and it is evident that ILP models are uniformly best for the bilingual task.

It is curious that the two ILP-based approaches are comparable on the monolingual task and are completely incommensurate on the bilingual task. Closer study of the performance of the ILP model reveals the substantial role of the default rule predicting the majority class (as described in Section 4.2). Removal

Verb	Senses	Accuracy			
		Majority class	Baseline	ILP	ILP-assisted
activate	5	82.46±3.56	**85.09±3.34**	52.63±4.68	83.33±3.49
add	6	45.80±4.35	**82.44±3.32**	73.28±3.87	**82.44±3.32**
appear	3	44.70±4.33	68.18±4.05	**87.88±2.84**	71.21±3.94
ask	6	27.78±3.99	**53.17±4.45**	40.48±4.37	50.00±4.45
begin	4	59.74±5.59	57.14±5.64	55.84±5.66	**74.03±5.00**
climb	5	55.22±6.08	71.64±5.51	59.70±5.99	**83.58±4.53**
decide	4	67.74±5.94	**77.42±5.31**	**77.42±5.31**	**77.42±5.31**
eat	7	**88.37±3.46**	**88.37±3.46**	83.72±3.98	87.21±3.60
encounter	4	50.77±6.20	**73.85±5.45**	67.69±5.80	72.31±5.55
expect	3	74.36±4.94	75.64±4.86	79.49±4.57	**92.31±3.02**
express	4	69.09±6.23	67.27±6.33	70.91±6.12	**72.73±6.01**
hear	7	46.88±8.82	53.13±8.82	65.62±8.40	**65.63±8.40**
lose	9	52.78±8.32	**58.33±8.22**	55.56±8.28	**58.33±8.22**
mean	7	52.50±7.90	**77.50±6.60**	55.00±7.87	70.00±7.25
miss	8	33.33±8.61	36.67±8.80	**56.67±9.05**	33.33±8.61
note	3	38.81±5.95	58.21±6.03	82.09±4.68	**88.06±3.96**
operate	5	16.67±8.78	72.22±10.56	**83.33±8.78**	77.78±9.80
play	12	46.15±6.91	**53.85±6.91**	46.15±6.91	**53.85±6.91**
produce	6	52.13±5.15	63.83±4.96	**75.53±4.43**	67.02±4.85
provide	6	85.51±4.24	**89.86±3.63**	88.41±3.85	**89.86±3.63**
receive	9	88.89±6.05	88.89±6.05	**92.59±5.04**	88.89±6.05
remain	3	78.57±4.90	84.29±4.35	80.00±4.78	**87.14±4.00**
rule	5	50.00±9.13	66.67±8.61	**86.67±6.21**	83.33±6.80
smell	7	40.74±6.69	**79.63±5.48**	68.52±6.32	77.78±5.66
suspend	7	35.94±6.00	**60.94±6.10**	**60.94±6.10**	57.81±6.17
talk	9	72.60±5.22	**73.97±5.14**	**73.97±5.14**	**73.97±5.14**
treat	9	28.07±5.95	40.35±6.50	**57.89±6.54**	47.37±6.61
use	5	71.43±12.07	85.71±9.35	**92.86±6.88**	**92.86±6.88**
wash	12	67.65±8.02	70.59±7.81	61.76±8.33	**73.53±7.57**
watch	7	74.51±6.10	74.51±6.10	**76.47±5.94**	74.51±6.10
win	7	44.74±8.07	52.63±8.10	47.37±8.10	**60.53±7.93**
write	8	26.09±9.16	52.17±10.42	**56.52±10.34**	34.78±9.93
Mean	7	55.31	68.56	69.15	71.97
Median	6	52.31	71.11	69.71	74.03

Fig. 2. Estimates of accuracies of disambiguation models on the monolingual task. "Senses" refers to the numbers of possible senses of each verb. "Majority class" gives the accuracy of models that simply predict the most common sense of each verb. The entries in boldface represent the highest accuracy obtained for a verb.

of this rule lowers the ILP column's median accuracy by about 11% for the monolingual task and 8% for the bilingual task (the two ILP-based methods are then comparable on the bilingual task). Since it is not evident that the use of the default rule will always yield such beneficial results to the ILP model,

Verb	Translations	Accuracy			
		Majority class	Baseline	ILP	ILP-assisted
come	11	50.30±7.62	67.44±7.15	**86.67±5.07**	76.74±6.44
get	17	21.00±6.70	32.43±7.70	**51.28±8.00**	40.54±8.07
give	5	88.80±4.81	97.67±2.30	**97.78±2.20**	95.35±3.21
go	11	68.50±6.78	72.34±6.52	**85.71±5.00**	78.72±5.97
look	7	50.30±7.45	77.78±6.20	**82.98±5.48**	82.22±5.70
make	11	70.00±7.25	75.00±6.85	**76.19±6.57**	75.00±6.85
take	13	28.50±8.24	46.67±9.11	**62.50±8.56**	60.00±8.94
Mean	11	53.91	67.05	77.59	72.65
Median	11	50.30	72.34	82.98	76.74

Fig. 3. Estimates of accuracies of disambiguation models on the bilingual task. "Translations" refers to the numbers of possible translations of each verb into Portuguese.

	Majority class	Baseline	ILP
Baseline	< 0.001, 0.020	–	–
ILP	< 0.001, 0.020	0.849, 0.020	–
ILP-assisted	< 0.001, 0.020	0.037, 0.075	0.134, 0.020

Fig. 4. Probablities of observing the differences in accuracies for the monolingual and bilingual tasks, under the assumption that median accuracies of the pair of algorithms being compared are equal. Each entry consists of a pair of probability estimates, corresponding to the mono and bilingual tasks.

and ILP-assisted models do not require such a rule, the ILP-assisted approach probably represent a more reliable route for constructing WSD models.

For the monolingual task, we are also able to compare the performance of ILP-based models to those of models produced by the best supervised techniques for the same data. SENSEVAL's evaluation software provides estimates on the performance of the systems according to two different levels of sense distinction: fine and coarse-grained. The former comprises average accuracies in the normally understood sense. Comparative results with the best systems from the various sites which participated in SENSEVAL's lexical sample subtask are shown in Fig. 5. Syntalex-3 [15] is based on an ensemble of bagged decision trees with narrow context part-of-speech features and bigrams. CLaC1 [9] uses a Naive Bayes algorithm with a dynamically adjusted context window around the target word. Finally, MC-WSD [3] is a multi-class averaged perceptron classifier using syntactic and narrow context features, with one component trained on the data provided by Senseval and other trained on WordNet glosses. As we can see, among all the approaches, ILP-based models are outperformed only by MC-WSD and therefore it is evident that these models are comparable to the state-of-the-art in the field. In practice, we believe that all these methods would be able to use features constructed by an ILP system. With that, improvements in their performance similar to those seen from the baseline classifier could follow.

Models	Accuracy
MC-WSD	72.50
ILP-assisted	71.97
ILP	69.15
Syntalex-3	67.60
CLaC1	67.00

Fig. 5. Comparative average fine-grained accuracies of the best models reported for the SENSEVAL-3 competition

6   Concluding Remarks

Word sense disambiguation, a necessary component for a variety of natural language processing tasks, remains amongst the hardest to model adequately. It is of course possible that the vagaries of natural language may place a limit on the accuracy with which a model could identify correctly the sense of an ambiguous word, but it is not clear that this limit has been reached with the modelling techniques that constitute the current state-of-the-art. The performance of these techniques depends largely on the adequacy of the features used to represent the problem. As it stands, these features are usually hand-crafted and largely of a syntactic nature. For substantial, scalable progress it is believed that knowledge that accounts for more elaborate semantic information needs to be incorporated: however, no adequate general-purpose techniques have been forthcoming. In this paper, we have investigated the use of Inductive Logic Programming as a mechanism for incorporating multiple sources of syntactic and semantic information into the construction of models for WSD. The investigation has been in the form of empirical studies of using ILP to construct models for monolingual and bilingual WSD tasks and the results suggest that the use of ILP can improve predictive accuracies. These studies represent the first extensive application of ILP to the task of constructing WSD models.

We believe much of the gains observed with ILP stems from the use of substantial amounts of background knowledge. This knowledge has been obtained by translations of information in standard corpora or electronic lexical resources. This is promising, as it suggests that these translators, in conjunction with ILP, may provide a set of tools for the automatic incorporation of deep knowledge into the construction of general WSD models. Turning specifically to the tasks addressed here, further improvements could be achieved with the inclusion of other kinds of background knowledge. For example, for the bilingual task, the "translation context" for a verb may help greatly. This refers to the translations into the target language of the words forming the context of the verb.

On the basis of results achieved here there is little to chose between ILP-models and ILP-assisted models, although we believe that the latter may provide a more reliable approach for constructing WSD models. There does not appear to be any inherent limitation in using a feature-based representation for verb disambiguation: a finding that may extend to other WSD tasks. The key is to get a good set of features, and results here suggest that ILP could provide a reliable method of identifying these.

References

1. Agirre, E., Rigau, G.: Word Sense Disambiguation Using Conceptual Density. In: 16th International Conference on Computational Linguistics, Copenhagen (1996)
2. Bar-Hillel, Y.: Automatic Translation of Languages. In: Alt, F., Booth, D., Meagher, R.E. (eds.) Advances in Computers, Academic Press, New York (1960)
3. Ciaramita, M., Johnson, M.: Multi-component Word Sense Disambiguation. In: SENSEVAL-3: 3rd International Workshop on the Evaluation of Systems for the Semantic Analysis of Text, Barcelona, pp. 97–100 (2004)
4. Cottrell, G.W.: A Connectionist Approach to Word Sense Disambiguation. Research Notes in Artificial Intelligence. Morgan Kaufmann, San Mateo (1989)
5. Hayes, P.J.: A Process to Implement Some Word Sense Disambiguation. Institut pour les Etudes Semantiques et Cognitives, Geneve (1976)
6. Hirst, G.: Semantic Intepretation and the Resolution of Ambiguity. Natural Language Processing. Cambridge Universisty Press, Studies in (1987)
7. Kohavi, R., John, G.H.: Automatic Parameter Selection by Minimizing Estimated Error. In: 12th Int. Conference on Machine Learning, San Francisco (1995)
8. Kramer, S., Lavrac, N., Flach, P.: Propositionalization Approaches to Relational Data Mining, pp. 262–291. Springer, Heidelberg (2001)
9. Lamjiri, A., Demerdash, O., Kosseim, F.: Simple features for statistical Word Sense Disambiguation. In: SENSEVAL-3: 3rd International Workshop on the Evaluation of Systems for the Semantic Analysis of Text, Barcelona, pp. 133–136 (2004)
10. Lavrac, N., Dzeroski, S., Grobelnik, M.: Learning nonrecursive definitions of relations with LINUS. Technical report, Jozef Stefan Institute (1990)
11. Lesk, M.: Automated Sense Disambiguation Using Machine-readable Dictionaries: How to Tell a Pine Cone from an Ice Cream Cone. In: SIGDOC Conference, Toronto, pp. 24–26 (1986)
12. McRoy, S.: Using Multiple Knowledge Sources for Word Sense Discrimination. Computational Linguistics 18(1), 1–30 (1992)
13. Mihalcea, R., Chklovski, T., Kilgariff, A.: The SENSEVAL-3 English Lexical Sample Task. In: SENSEVAL-3: 3rd International Workshop on the Evaluation of Systems for Semantic Analysis of Text, Barcelona, pp. 25–28 (2004)
14. Fellbaum, C.: WordNet. An Electronic Lexical Database and some if its Applications. MIT Press, Massachusetts and London (1998)
15. Mohammad, S., Pedersen, T.: Complementarity of Lexical and Simple Syntactic Features: The SyntaLex Approach to SENSEVAL-3. In: SENSEVAL-3: 3rd International Workshop on the Evaluation of Systems for the Semantic Analysis of Text, Barcelona, pp. 159–162 (2004)
16. Mooney, R.J.: Inductive Logic Programming for Natural Language Processing. In: Inductive Logic Programming. LNCS, vol. 1314, pp. 3–24. Springer, Heidelberg (1997)
17. Muggleton, S.: Inductive Logic Programming: derivations, successes and shortcomings. SIGART Bulletin 5(1), 5–11 (1994)
18. Muggleton, S., Raedt, L.D.: Inductive logic programming: Theory and methods. Journal of Logic Programming 19,20, 629–679 (1994)

19. Nienhuys-Cheng, S., de Wolf, R.: Foundations of Inductive Logic Programming. Springer, Heidelberg (1997)
20. Parker, J., Stahel, M.: Password: English Dictionary for Speakers of Portuguese. Martins Fontes, São Paulo (1998)
21. Pedersen, T.A: Baseline Methodology for Word Sense Disambiguation. In: 3rd International Conference on Intelligent Text Processing and Computational Linguistics, Mexico City (2002)
22. Procter, P. (ed.): Longman Dictionary of Contemporary English. Longman Group, Essex (1978)
23. Quillian, M.R.: A Design for an Understanding Machine, Colloquium of semantic problems in natural language. Cambridge University, Cambridge (1961)
24. Ratnaparkhi, A.: A Maximum Entropy Part-Of-Speech Tagger. In: Empirical Methods in NLP Conference, University of Pennsylvania (1996)
25. Resnik, P.: Disambiguating Noun Groupings with Respect to WordNet Senses. In: 3rd Workshop on Very Large Corpora. Cambridge, pp. 54–68 (1995)
26. Schutze, H.: Automatic Word Sense Discrimination. Computational Linguistics 24(1), 97–124 (1998)
27. Siegel, S.: Nonparametric Statistics for the Behavioural Sciences. McGraw-Hill, New York (1956)
28. Specia, L.: A Hybrid Relational Approach for WSD - First Results. In: Student Research Workshop at Coling-ACL, Sydney, pp. 55–60 (2006)
29. Specia, L., Nunes, M.G.V., Stevenson, M.: Exploiting Parallel Texts to Produce a Multilingual Sense-tagged Corpus for Word Sense Disambiguation. In: RANLP-05, Borovets, pp. 525–531 (2005)
30. Srinivasan, A.: The Aleph Manual (1999) Available at http://www.comlab.ox.ac.uk/oucl/research/areas/machlearn/Aleph/
31. Stevenson, M., Wilks, Y.: The Interaction of Knowledge Sources for Word Sense Disambiguation. Computational Linguistics 27(3), 321–349 (2001)
32. Wilks, Y., Stevenson, M.: Combining Independent Knowledge Sources for Word Sense Disambiguation. In: 3rd Conference on Recent Advances in Natural Language Processing, Tzigov Chark, pp. 1–7 (1997)
33. Yarowsky, D.: Unsupervised Word Sense Disambiguation Rivaling Supervised Methods. In: 33rd Annual Meeting of the Association for Computational Linguistics, Cambridge, pp. 189–196 (1995)

ReMauve: A Relational Model Tree Learner

Celine Vens, Jan Ramon, and Hendrik Blockeel

Katholieke Universiteit Leuven - Department of Computer Science,
Celestijnenlaan 200 A, 3001 Leuven, Belgium
{celine.vens,jan.ramon,hendrik.blockeel}@cs.kuleuven.be

Abstract. Model trees are a special case of regression trees in which linear regression models are constructed in the leaves. Little attention has been paid to model trees in relational learning, mainly because the task of learning linear regression equations in this context involves dealing with non-determinacy of predictive attributes. Whereas existing approaches handle this non-determinacy issue either by selecting a single value or by aggregating over all values, in this paper we present a model tree learning system that combines both.

1 Introduction

Model trees are regression trees that contain some non-trivial, usually linear, model in their leaves. In the propositional case, they have been shown to be able to increase predictive performance compared to regression trees that predict the same constant value for each example falling into the same leaf [1,2,3,4,5,6].

In this paper we investigate the use of model trees in ILP (inductive logic programming, [7]). While classification and regression trees have been around in ILP for several years now [8,9,10], less can be said about model trees. This may be due to the issues arising when learning a linear regression function in the relational context. Since individuals are related to other objects via one-to-many or many-to-many relationships, the predictive attributes to be included in a regression function may be non-determinate: there may be several instances of them related to the target value. We distinguish a number of approaches to handle non-determinate predictive attributes in regression functions:

1. do not use non-determinate attributes [10]
2. assume one of the instances is relevant
   (a) and it can be specified with conditions [11]
   (b) and it can not be specified [12,13]
3. summarize the instances
   (a) using simple aggregate functions defined in advance [14]
   (b) using complex aggregate functions

Complex aggregate functions [15,16] are expressed as $\mathcal{F}(\sigma_C(R))$ in relational algebra, with $\mathcal{F}$ an aggregate function (e.g., exists, max, min, count, ...), $\sigma_C(R)$ a selection function based on a condition C, and R a set of tuples somehow connected to the tuple we want to classify. They are thus a combination of

S. Muggleton, R. Otero, and A. Tamaddoni-Nezhad (Eds.): ILP 2006, LNAI 4455, pp. 424–438, 2007.

aggregates and selections and therefore approach 3(b) generalizes approaches 2(a) and 3(a). For example, $min\{A|child(P,Ch),age(Ch,A),blue\_eyes(Ch)\}$ is a complex aggregate which takes the minimum age of a person's children that have blue eyes. In this aggregate, $blue\_eyes(Ch)$ is the selection condition C.

It has been studied how complex aggregates can be efficiently learned to be included in the condition part of a hypothesis [17]. In that work, complex aggregate conditions are learned general-to-specific, subsequently reducing the coverage of the hypothesis. It is still an open problem how complex aggregates can be learned in the conclusion part of a hypothesis (e.g., when the conclusion part is a regression function).

In this paper, we present a model tree system that constructs regression functions with complex aggregates in the leaves. These complex aggregates are not learned at the leaves, but are included in the regression model of a leaf if a linear effect with the target was shown on the path from the root to the leaf. It has been shown [3,6] that model tree learners produce good results if their heuristic function takes linear models into consideration. Most (propositional and relational) systems that use such a heuristic are quadratic [1] or cubic [2,3,14] in the number of numeric attributes. Since we want to include complex aggregates in the search, the number of numeric attributes can become very large, which renders existing systems infeasible to use. Therefore, an important requirement for our system is an efficient heuristic function.

In Sect. 2 we present some related work. Section 3 presents our system in detail. Section 4 presents experimental results. In Sect. 5 we conclude.

2   Related Work

The task of relational regression was formalized by Džeroski [18] in the normal ILP framework. This work presents the transformation based system DINUS, which is the first ILP system to address the task of relational regression. The induction is delegated to a propositional learner. Using a model tree learner as RETIS [2], linear regression is used in the model output by DINUS.

FORS [11] is the first system able to predict numbers with non-determinate background knowledge. It is a sequential covering approach that learns rules that contain linear regression models. Non-determinacy among the predictive attributes is handled by testing for the existence of a specific instance giving a number of conditions. If the conditions succeed for more than one instance, the value of the first of these instances is taken.

TILDE [8] and SRT [9] are first order regression tree learners. S-CART [10], the successor of SRT, is capable of including linear models in the leaves. The use of non-determinate predictors in these linear models is not supported. The model trees induced by S-CART are built by first constructing a normal regression tree (using a standard variance reduction heuristic), and afterwards replacing the constant predictions by linear models. This heuristic has been shown to produce sub-optimal model trees in the sense that it tends to split the data set in the wrong places and results in trees that are larger than necessary [3,6,19].

Appice et al. [14] present a system called MR-SMOTI which is a relational upgrade of their propositional SMOTI model tree algorithm [3]. The SMOTI algorithm is different from most model tree inducers in the sense that the multiple linear model that is associated with the leaves is built incrementally from simple linear regression models. These models are introduced by so-called regression nodes occurring in the tree. Each regression node thus adds one term to the multiple regression model and requires updating the target value and other continuous attributes in order to remove the linear effect of the introduced term. To determine the coefficients of a simple linear regression model in a regression node, the problem is locally transformed into a propositional problem by joining the tables from the underlying relational database structure, and normal least squares is applied on this flattened table. Note that this propositionalisation step gives examples that have a higher number of related objects more weight in the least squares procedure. The predicted value for unseen examples is the average prediction for all instances in the propositional representation of the example. Contrary to the efficient methods as S-CART, the systems SMOTI and MR-SMOTI have a high computational complexity. This is due to the heuristic function, which takes into account the fact that linear models are built. It is discussed in more detail further in the paper.

3   ReMauve

In this section we present a relational model tree system that is more efficient than MR-SMOTI, but still uses a heuristic function that takes into account the fact that linear models are constructed at the leaves. Moreover, these models may contain complex aggregates. The system is a relational upgrade of the propositional system MAUVE [6], and is called REMAUVE (RElational MAUVE).

3.1   Mauve: A Propositional Model Tree Learner

MAUVE [6] is a model tree inducer that operates on a single table. It takes as input a number of training examples e_i ($i = 1..n$) of the form $(x_{i1}, x_{i2}, ..., x_{im}, y_i)$, where each x_{ij} denotes the value for the j-th independent attribute X_j ($j = 1..m$), and y_i is the value for the dependent (target) attribute Y. Y is numeric, while the X_j can be numeric or nominal. The system outputs a model tree where each leaf contains a multiple linear regression model that predicts the target in relation to all numeric independent attributes in the table. MAUVE is a TDIDT approach, thus the model tree is built top-down, recursively splitting the training examples according to some condition on the independent attributes.

To estimate the quality of a candidate split, MAUVE proceeds as follows. If the split contains a nominal attribute, the heuristic function is the same as in normal regression trees: the weighted average of the standard deviations in both child nodes, i.e.,

$$heur\_nom(T) = \frac{|E_l|}{|E|} SD(E_l) + \frac{|E_r|}{|E|} SD(E_r),$$

where E denotes the set of examples at node T, E_l and E_r denote the subsets of E associated with the left and right child node of T, and $SD(E_m) = \sqrt{\sum_{e_i \in E_m}(y_i - \overline{y_m})^2/|E_m|}$, with $\overline{y_m}$ the sample mean of the target attribute in the examples E_m. If the split concerns a numeric attribute, instead of taking the standard deviation, the *residual* standard deviation is used, i.e., the root of the mean squared errors calculated w.r.t. a simple linear regression line constructed in the target attribute. The predictive attribute used in the simple regression function is the attribute used in the split. The heuristic of a numeric split at node T is thus

$$heur\_num(T) = \frac{|E_l|}{|E|}RSD(E_l) + \frac{|E_r|}{|E|}RSD(E_r),$$

with $RSD(E_m) = \sqrt{\sum_{e_i \in E_m}(y_i - (\alpha_m x_{ik} + \beta_m))^2/|E_m|}$, where α_m and β_m are estimated using least squares and X_k is the split attribute at T, i.e., the split takes the form $X_k \leq V$ or $X_k \geq V$ with V some value in the domain of X_k. The split that minimizes this heuristic function ($heur\_nom(T)$ or $heur\_num(T)$, respectively) is chosen to split T.

3.2   Upgrading Mauve to Relational Learning

In this section we discuss how MAUVE is upgraded to a relational model tree learner. We first describe the relational regression tree learning system that we start from and afterwards discuss several aspects of the algorithm.

Tilde-RT: A Relational Regression Tree Learner. TILDE [8] is a relational top-down induction of decision trees (TDIDT) instantiation, and outputs a first order decision tree, i.e., a decision tree that contains a first order query in the internal nodes. The algorithm is included in the ACE-ilProlog data mining system [20]. TILDE learns both classification and regression trees. The regression tree subsystem is usually denoted by TILDE-RT.

TILDE-RT's procedure to grow a tree is given in Table 1. It takes as input the training examples E and a query Q that corresponds to the empty query. In the recursive calls of the algorithm, Q will represent the conjunction of all succeeding tests from the root of the tree to the node being split. This query will be referred to as the *current query*. The procedure to grow a node T is as follows. First, a refinement operator generates the set of candidate splits. This set is determined by the language bias given by the user, and by the variables occurring in the current query at T. The refinement operator typically operates under θ-subsumption [21] and generates candidates by extending the current query with a number of new literals. Next, the OPTIMAL_SPLIT procedure executes all candidates on the set of examples E, estimating the quality of each candidate, and returns the best candidate Q_b. The quality of a candidate is calculated using a simple heuristic function, similar to MAUVE's $heur\_nom$[1]. The candidate Q_b

---

[1] In fact, the sum of squared errors is used instead of standard deviation, and an F-test is used to decide whether an improvement is obtained w.r.t. the parent node.

Table 1. TILDE-RT algorithm for first order logical regression tree induction [8]

---
procedure GROW_TREE (E: **examples**, Q: **query**):
    $candidates := \rho(\leftarrow Q)$
    $\leftarrow Q_b :=$ OPTIMAL_SPLIT($candidates, E$)
    if STOP_CRIT ($\leftarrow Q_b, E$)
    then
        $K :=$ PREDICT(E)
        return leaf(K)
    else
        $conj := Q_b - Q$
        $E_1 := \{e \in E | \leftarrow Q_b \text{ succeeds in } e \wedge Background\}$
        $E_2 := \{e \in E | \leftarrow Q_b \text{ fails in } e \wedge Background\}$
        $left :=$ GROW_TREE (E_1, Q_b)
        $right :=$ GROW_TREE (E_2, Q)
        return node($conj, left, right$)

---

is chosen to split the examples. The conjunction put in the node T consists of $Q_b - Q$, i.e., the literals that have been added to Q in order to produce Q_b. In the left branch, Q_b will be further refined, while in the right branch Q is to be refined. When the stop criterion holds (typically, this is when a predefined minimum number of examples is reached), a leaf is built. The PREDICT procedure returns the mean target value of the examples E.

Van Assche et al. [16] described how to add (complex) aggregates to the set of candidate splits generated by the refinement operator. This may result in a very large refinement space and it was shown by Vens et al. [17] how the aggregate conditions can be efficiently executed on the examples.

Adapting Tilde-RT's Heuristic Function. We replaced TILDE-RT's heuristic function by Mauve's *heur_nom* for nominal, and *heur_num* for numeric splits.

For the *heur_num* function, an important issue to deal with concerns the multivaluedness of the numeric split attribute to be introduced in the regression functions for the *RSD* calculations. An attribute is determinate if it has exactly one value for each example. It is non-determinate if it may have 0, 1, or more values for each example. For example, the age of a person is determinate, whereas the age of a person's children is non-determinate. Non-determinacy or multivaluedness occurs when an example is related to a set of objects via one-to-many or many-to-many relationships in the relational dataset. In general, two approaches exist to deal with multi-valuedness. ILP systems usually test for the existence of a specific element, thus, a split condition $child(P, C), age(C, A), A < 18$ corresponds to testing the existence of a child with age smaller than 18. Other approaches [22,23,24] use aggregate functions (such as *max, min, avg, sum,...*) to summarize the set of values. The following lemma shows that an ILP test is semantically equivalent to an aggregate function [25]:

Lemma 1. *Let B be a bag of real numbers, and t some real value, then*
$\exists v \in B : v \geq t$ *iff* $max(B) \geq t$, *and*
$\exists v \in B : v \leq t$ *iff* $min(B) \leq t$.

Using this lemma, every numeric attribute results for each example in one deterministic value to feed to the simple linear regression models. The previous nondeterminate numeric attribute would become $min\{A|child(P, C), age(C, A)\}$.

Adapting Tilde-RT's Predictive Function. In MAUVE the leaves contain a multiple linear regression function using *all* numeric attributes as predictors. Adopting this strategy in REMAUVE is not feasible: in relational learning the number of numeric attributes becomes very high, especially when complex aggregate conditions are taken into account. Therefore, we include a numeric attribute in the predictive model of a leaf if it was chosen at a node on the path[2] from the root to the leaf. The underlying idea is that an attribute would not have been chosen to split the dataset if it did not result in a linear relation with the target in the child nodes.

Dealing with Global Effects. Consider an attribute that has a global linear effect on the target. Sooner or later in the tree building process this attribute will give rise to a best split, with the same linear effect in both child nodes and will thus generate a superfluous split in the model tree. While the split is redundant, we do want to take into account this attribute in the predictive models at the leaves. Therefore, when the best test for a node N is determined and is found to be a numeric split, the RSD is also calculated for all examples at node N. If an F-test considers this RSD equal to the heuristic value of the split, then we know that the linear effect between the split attribute and the target holds in the complete set of examples at N, thus it should be introduced in the predictive models in the leaves under N without splitting the data at N. To deal with such global linear effects, we introduce unary regression nodes that do not split the data, but only serve to introduce an extra predictor in the linear regression function. The regression nodes contain numeric attributes (without the $>$ or $<$ equation) and pass all examples down to their unique child node. As for split nodes, variables occurring in the attribute of a regression node can be used further down the tree.

In relational learning, especially when aggregates are used, correlation between attributes often comes into play, either true or apparent [26]. For example, in the task of predicting a person's income, the income may increase with the number of children. However, the number of children is correlated with the number of daughters or with the sum of the ages of the children. In our system, if the number of children is an attribute occurring in a regression node, the probability of having an other regression node with the

---

[2] Note that we use the numeric attributes on the complete path from the root to the leaf, not only those from the current query which correspond only to the succeeding tests.

number of daughters is high. To avoid this, the linear effect of numeric attributes occurring in the tree needs to be accounted for. Therefore, after introducing a regression node or a numeric split node, we remove the linear effect of the involved attribute A from the target, i.e., we pass on the residuals $y_i - \hat{y}_i$ with $\hat{y}_i = \alpha * A + \beta$ to the child node(s). In fact, the linear effect should also be removed from all other numeric attributes that can still be used in the model. Given the large number of such attributes, this is not feasible, and instead, when building a regression node N we check whether the involved numeric attribute A has a significant correlation with an attribute in a split or regression node on the path from the root to N. If this is the case a leaf is built.

By introducing regression nodes, the analogy with MR-SMOTI increases. A comparison between the two systems is given further in this section.

Stop Criterion. We implemented several stop criteria. The first one concerns the minimal number of examples a leaf has to cover. Building a linear model in k attributes in the leaves requires at least $k + 1$ examples. Therefore, after refining a node T, we check whether each child node of T contains at least $m + 1$ examples, where m is the number of numeric attributes occurring on the path from the root to T. If this is not the case, T is made a leaf. The second stop criterion calculates the SD of the target values, before they are updated to reflect the linear effect of the best test. If this falls below a certain percentage (default 5%) of the original SD at the root node, a leaf is constructed. As a last stop criterion, if the best test turns out to be nominal, an f-test checks whether the corresponding SD value is significantly better than the SD value of the parent node. If not, a leaf node is built. As stated before, for numeric tests, a regression node is built in that case.

The pseudo code of the most important procedures of the algorithm is presented in Table 2.

Undefined Attributes. An issue that has not been mentioned in the description of the algorithm is what happens if an attribute is undefined for an example. For example, the age of a person's children is undefined for a person that has no children, or the maximum age of a person's sons is undefined if a person only has daughters. Undefined attributes often occur when using complex aggregates: the selection condition on the set to aggregate over can become so complex that the aggregate is defined only for a few examples. In our system, in order to not violate the monotonicity assumptions assumed by our refinement operator [17], examples for which a split condition is undefined go to the right (failing) branch of the tree. However, this is not sufficient: the heuristic function needs to have a numeric value for each example in the node to be split (also for those going to the right branch) and the linear equations in the leaves need to be able to provide a prediction for each example. Therefore, whenever an explicit value for an undefined attribute is needed (i.e., to calculate the heuristics or to build the regression functions or make predictions in the leaves), we make use of a default value. There are several possibilities for choosing a default value. We decided to use a value that reduces as much as possible the influence of examples for which the attribute is undefined. The exact values are:

- $F(\emptyset) = avg(F(S_1), F(S_2), ..., F(S_n))$ for $F \in \{max, min, avg, sum\}$
- $mode(\emptyset) = mode(mode(S_1), mode(S_2), ..., mode(S_n))$

where S_i is the set of values observed for the attribute for the i-th example and n is the number of training examples at the node under consideration for which the attribute is defined.

Table 2. ReMauve algorithm for first order logical model tree induction

---

procedure GROW_TREE (E: **examples**, T: **targets**, Q: **query**, P: **path**):
    $candidates := \rho(\leftarrow Q)$
    $\leftarrow Q_b :=$ OPTIMAL_REFINEMENT$(candidates, E, T)$
    $conj := Q_b - Q$
    $P_{new} := P + conj$
    if STOP_CRIT $(conj, P_{new}, E)$
    then
        $K :=$ PREDICT(E, P)
        return leaf(K)
    else
        if SPLIT_COND $(conj)$
        then
            $E_l := \{e \in E | \leftarrow Q_b$ succeeds in $e \wedge Background\}$
            $E_r := \{e \in E | \leftarrow Q_b$ fails in $e \wedge Background\}$
            $T_l :=$ REMOVE_LINEAR_EFFECT $(E_l, T, conj)$
            $T_r :=$ REMOVE_LINEAR_EFFECT $(E_r, T, conj)$
            $left :=$ GROW_TREE (E_l, T_l, Q_b, P_{new})
            $right :=$ GROW_TREE (E_r, T_r, Q, P_{new})
            return split node$(conj, left, right)$
        else
            $T_{ch} :=$ REMOVE_LINEAR_EFFECT $(E, T, conj)$
            $child :=$ GROW_TREE $(E, T_{ch}, Q_b, P_{new})$
            return regression node$(conj, child)$

procedure OPTIMAL_REFINEMENT (Qs: **queries**, E: **examples**, T:**targets**):
    for all $Q \in Qs$
        EXECUTE(Q, E)
        if (NOMINAL (Q))
        then $Heur(Q) := \frac{|E_l|}{|E|}SD(E_l) + \frac{|E_r|}{|E|}SD(E_r)$
        else $Heur(Q) := \frac{|E_l|}{|E|}RSD(E_l, Q) + \frac{|E_r|}{|E|}RSD(E_r, Q)$
    $Q_b := arg\ min_Q Heur(Q)$
    if (NOMINAL (Q_b))
    then return Q_b
    else
        $Heur_p(Q_b) := RSD(E, Q_b)$
        if $(Heur_p(Q_b) \leq Heur(Q_b))$
        then return EXTRACT_NUMERIC_ATTR(Q_b)
        else return Q_b

Comparison with Mr-Smoti. By introducing regression nodes into our system, the resemblance with MR-SMOTI increases. In the remainder of this section, we discuss the most important differences between both systems.

Complexity of finding the best split node. In REMAUVE the evaluation of a numeric split requires the calculation of two simple linear regression functions: one for each child node. In MR-SMOTI a similar, but more complex heuristic function is used: in each child node simple linear regression models are constructed with each numeric attribute used as the predictive attribute. The best regression is chosen independently for the two children and the heuristic value associated with the split under consideration is the weighted average of the RSD of the best regression lines of left and right child. Finding the best numeric split amongst all predictors therefore has complexity $O(m)$ for REMAUVE and $O(m^2)$ for MR-SMOTI, with m the number of numeric predictors. In the propositional setting of both algorithms the more complex heuristic of SMOTI did not outperform MAUVE on predictive performance [6].

Complexity of introducing regression nodes. In our system, introducing a regression node requires almost no computation: after the best split condition is obtained and is found to be numeric, the global linear effect of the attribute in the split is tested. This requires only one extra RSD to be computed. In MR-SMOTI the best regression node is searched for independently of the best split node and requires a lookahead step, in the sense that the best split is searched after the new attribute is included in the multiple model. This renders the whole node selection procedure for MR-SMOTI cubic in the number of predictors.

Removing the linear effect of attributes. In MR-SMOTI regression nodes were introduced in order to incrementally build the multiple regression models in the leaves of the model tree. Therefore, next to updating the target values, the linear effect of an introduced numeric attribute also has to be removed from all other numeric predictors that may be used later in the tree. In REMAUVE it is not possible to update all numeric attributes in the dataset, because these attributes are generated on-the-fly at each node. It would not be feasible to do this updating during refinement generation (requiring another RSD calculation for each refinement and each numeric attribute on the path from the root to the node) given the huge search spaces that may be dealt with by introducing complex aggregates. Therefore, in REMAUVE, the final multiple regression model in the leaves is built from scratch.

Overall complexity. The observations above lead to the following overall complexity results. For MR-SMOTI, the inner node refinement procedure has complexity $O(m^3)$, with m the number of numeric attributes. In a leaf, however, the predictive regression model is obtained by composing the models on the path from the root to the leaf, and thus, can be performed in constant time. A model tree with k inner nodes contains at most $k+1$ leaves, thus the overall complexity for building a model tree with MR-SMOTI is $k \times O(m^3) + (k+1) \times O(1)$.

For REMAUVE the node refinement process has complexity $O(m)$. Constructing a leaf requires $O(p^3)$, where p is the number of numeric attributes on the path from the root to the leaf. This results in an overall complexity of $k \times O(m) + (k + 1) \times O(p^3)$. Given the fact that $p << m$, especially when using complex aggregates, the REMAUVE system is more efficient for the applications we target.

Representational formalism. A last important difference between both systems concerns their representational formalism. Whereas REMAUVE is an ILP system, MR-SMOTI operates on a relational database, using selection graphs [27] to represent nodes of the model tree.

4   Experiments

In this experiments section, we address two questions:

1. How do model trees that predict functions with complex aggregates perform compared to model trees that do not predict aggregates?
2. How does REMAUVE compare to other systems as TILDE-RT or MR-SMOTI?

We have performed experiments on two biological datasets: *Mutagenesis* [28] and *MassSpectrogram* [29]. Given the scarceness of publicly available relational regression datasets with numeric attributes, we also constructed two synthetic datasets.

In *Mutagenesis*, the task is to predict the mutagenicity level of 230 nitro-aromatic compounds. Of these 230 compounds, 188 are known to be well predicted by linear regression methods. In our experiments we use both the regression friendly subset and the full dataset. Several descriptions of the compounds have been proposed [30]. We use the backgrounds B2 (atoms and bonds, including partial charge of atoms) and B3 (B2 extended with the *Lumo* and *LogP* properties). In the *MassSpectrogram* dataset, the task is to predict the weight of a molecule based on its mass spectrogram. A mass spectrogram is a graph of the mass-to-charge ratio of the different fragments versus the frequency. The dataset contains 873 molecules.

For the synthetic datasets the true target function is a model tree that contains aggregates. They both contain 1000 examples. The first dataset (*Artificial1*) contains two predictive attributes: $x(X)$ (determinate) and $y(Y)$ (non-determinate). Each example contains 8 y literals, for which the value can be aggregated. All numeric values are random values, uniformly distributed between 0 and 10. The target function for this dataset is shown in Fig. 1(a). It requires two regression nodes in REMAUVE. The second dataset (*Artificial2*) includes three predictive attributes: $x(X)$, $y(C, Y)$, and $z(Z)$, of which y is non-determinate and has 15 values for each example. Again the numeric values for x, y, and z are uniformly distributed between 0 and 10. The C variable in the y literal is a boolean value. The target function is shown in Fig. 1(b). This dataset also requires two regression nodes, one of which involves a complex aggregate using the boolean condition. For the two datasets, we added Gaussian distributed noise to the target value.

As explained in Sect. 3, REMAUVE is able to learn complex aggregate conditions. In order to address the first question defined above and to allow for a comparison with MR-SMOTI, we also performed the experiments without the ability to learn aggregates.

$x(X), X < 5$?
+yes: $max\{Y|y(Y)\} < 9$?
| +yes: $4x(X) + 6avg\{Y|y(Y)\}$
| +no: $3max\{Y|y(Y)\} + 1$
+no: $avg\{Y|y(Y)\} < 4$?
| +yes: $3x(X) + 4$
| +no: $x(X) - 2max\{Y|y(Y)\} + 3avg\{Y|y(Y)\}$

(a)

$x(X), X < 6$?
+yes: $min\{Y|y(\_, Y)\} < 1$?
| +yes: $2x(X) + 3max\{Y|y(true, Y) + 3\}$
| +no: $2x(X) + 5min\{Y|y(\_, Y)\}$
+no: $-2x(X) + z(Z)$?

(b)

Fig. 1. Target function for two synthetic datasets. (a) The *Artificial1* dataset. (b) The *Artificial2* dataset.

The results are presented in Tables 3 and 4. Predictive performance is obtained by taking the average MSE (mean squared error) of five tenfold crossvalidations. Model size is measured as the number of leaves and the number of regression nodes (the latter only for REMAUVE and MR-SMOTI). Induction times are difficult to compare, since TILDE-RT and REMAUVE were run on a different platform than MR-SMOTI.

The first question is dealt with by comparing REMAUVE's predictive performance when learning complex aggregates to when not learning them. For *MassSpectrogram* and the artificial datasets, a clear predictive performance improvement is obtained when complex aggregates are considered. Moreover, the improvement holds for both REMAUVE and TILDE-RT. Part of the resulting tree for *MassSpectrogram* is shown in Fig. 2. For *Mutagenesis*, the result is less obvious. Both for REMAUVE and TILDE-RT the error tends to increase when learning aggregates. Whereas in the classification setting complex aggregates turned out to be beneficial for this task, to our knowledge, complex aggregates have not been used before to predict the numeric mutagenicity level of molecules, thus we can not compare this result to other results in the literature.

The second question is answered by comparing REMAUVE to TILDE-RT and MR-SMOTI w.r.t. predictive performance and model complexity. When comparing REMAUVE to TILDE-RT, we see that in the aggregate settings (i.e., in the context of many numeric attributes), an improvement in both predictive accuracy and model complexity is obtained. Also, for the artificial datasets, where the target concept involves linear regressions, a clear improvement is obtained,

$\max\{Ratio|\text{ms}(Mol, Ratio, Freq)\} < 199.0$?

+yes: $\text{avg}\{Ratio|\text{ms}(Mol, Ratio, Freq), Ratio < 83.0\} < 51.0$?

| +yes: $\max\{Ratio|\text{ms}(Mol, Ratio, Freq), Freq < 2.3\} < 119.0$?

| | +yes: $0.84 * \max\{Ratio|\text{ms}(Mol, Ratio, Freq)\}+$

| | $0.85 * \text{avg}\{Ratio|\text{ms}(Mol, Ratio, Freq), Ratio < 83.0\}+$

| | $0.06 * \max\{Ratio|\text{ms}(Mol, Ratio, Freq), Freq < 2.3\} - 19.08$

| | . . .

+no: $\text{avg}\{Freq|\text{ms}(Mol, Ratio, Freq)\} < 8.0$?

| +yes: $\text{avg}\{Freq|\text{ms}(Mol, Ratio, Freq), Ratio < 60.0\}$

| | +--: $0.95 * \max\{Ratio|\text{ms}(Mol, Ratio, Freq)\}+$

| | $-13.30 * \text{avg}\{Freq|\text{ms}(Mol, Ratio, Freq)\}+$

| | $5.50 * \text{avg}\{Freq|\text{ms}(Mol, Ratio, Freq), Ratio < 60.0\} + 97.91$

| . . .

Fig. 2. Resulting tree for the *MassSpectrogram* dataset

Table 3. Comparing ReMauve's predictive performance and tree size to Tilde-RT and Mr-Smoti for the *Mutagenesis* dataset

	Mutagenesis					
	Regression friendly subset			Full dataset		
	B2	B3	B3	B2	B3	B3
	no agg.	no agg.	agg.	no agg.	no agg.	agg.
Avg. MSE						
ReMauve	1.98 (0.1)	1.45 (0.5)	1.43 (0.4)	4.01 (0.2)	3.50 (0.6)	3.70 (0.6)
Tilde-RT	1.96 (0.1)	1.57 (0.1)	1.85 (0.2)	3.67 (0.2)	3.44 (0.2)	3.94 (0.4)
Mr-Smoti	3.02 (0.1)	1.14 (0.2)	-	32.68 (28.1)	3.32 (0.2)	-
Regr. nodes						
ReMauve	1	2	8	2	1	6
Mr-Smoti	8	5	-	8	15	-
Leaves						
ReMauve	7	3	5	11	8	5
Tilde-RT	14	16	28	11	23	28
Mr-Smoti	10	7	-	9	15	-

both with and without aggregates. In the other settings, while generally resulting in smaller models, the comparison in predictive performance is less clear. When comparing ReMauve to Mr-Smoti, a first observation is that ReMauve tends to build shorter trees. Only on the *Artificial2* dataset is the model built by Mr-Smoti simpler. Regarding predictive performance, we see clear winners for ReMauve on the artificial datasets. On the *MassSpectrogram* dataset, Mr-Smoti outperforms ReMauve. However, when learning complex aggregates, ReMauve reduces Mr-Smoti's MSE with a factor 3.6. On the *Mutagenesis* datasets, the results are divided: two winners for each system. (The high MSE of 32.68 for Mr-Smoti on the full dataset with background B2 is due to two particular test examples. Removing them from the test sets yields an average MSE of 4.79 (0.12).)

Table 4. Comparing REMAUVE's predictive performance and tree size to TILDE-RT and MR-SMOTI for the *MassSpectrogram* and artificial datasets

	MassSpectrogram		Artificial1		Artificial2	
	no agg.	agg.	no agg.	agg.	no agg.	agg.
Avg. MSE						
REMAUVE	8144 (65)	1289 (101)	30.84 (0.2)	1.08 (0.0)	1.64 (0.1)	0.97 (0.0)
TILDE-RT	8132 (24)	2401 (146)	35.18 (0.3)	3.94 (0.1)	2.55 (0.0)	2.06 (0.1)
MR-SMOTI	4583 (221)	-	60.58 (2.0)	-	12.08 (0.7)	-
Regr. nodes						
REMAUVE	1	9	1	2	2	3
MR-SMOTI	6	-	10	-	0	-
Leaves						
REMAUVE	3	10	5	4	3	3
TILDE-RT	3	222	30	58	44	64
MR-SMOTI	8	-	14	-	3	-

5 Conclusion

We have presented a relational model tree learner, REMAUVE, that is able to construct regression functions with complex aggregates in the leaves. These complex aggregates occur in the leaves if they have shown a linear relation with the target during the tree building process. The system uses a heuristic function that takes into account the fact that linear models are built in the leaves, while having a time complexity linear in the number of numeric attributes. This differs only a constant factor with the most efficient heuristics, which have been shown to produce sub-optimal model trees. The efficiency is necessary when considering complex aggregates, since the number of numeric attributes becomes very high.

Experimental results demonstrate that, if many numeric attributes occur in the dataset (e.g., in the context of learning aggregates), our system outperforms normal regression tree learners. When comparing to a model tree learner that uses a more complex heuristic function, the comparison in predictive performance is less obvious, while our system in general produces shorter trees.

Acknowledgements

CV is supported by the GOA 2003/8 project and by the Fund for Scientific Research (FWO) of Flanders. JR and HB are post-doctoral fellows of the Fund for Scientific Research (FWO) of Flanders. The authors thank Bart Demoen for some useful discussions on implementation details and Pieter-Jan Drouillon for providing us with the *MassSpectrogram* dataset.

References

1. Alexander, W., Grimshaw, S.: Treed regression. Journal of Computational and Graphical Statistics 5, 156–175 (1996)
2. Karalic, A.: Employing linear regression in regression tree leaves. In: European Conference on Artificial Intelligence, pp. 440–441 (1992)
3. Malerba, D., Esposito, F., Ceci, M., Appice, A.: Top-down induction of model trees with regression and splitting nodes. IEEE Transactions on Pattern Analysis and Machine Intelligence 26(5), 612–625 (2004)
4. Quinlan, J.: Learning with continuous classes. In: Proc. of the 5th Australian Joint Conference on Artificial Intelligence, pp. 343–348. World Scientific, Singapore (1992)
5. Torgo, L.: Functional models for regression tree leaves. In: Proceedings of the 14th International Conference on Machine Learning, pp. 385–393. Morgan Kaufmann, San Francisco (1997)
6. Vens, C., Blockeel, H.: A simple regression based heuristic for learning model trees. Intelligent Data Analysis 10(3), 215–236 (2006)
7. Muggleton, S. (ed.): Inductive Logic Programming. Academic Press, London (1992)
8. Blockeel, H., De Raedt, L.: Top-down induction of first order logical decision trees. Artificial Intelligence 101(1-2), 285–297 (1998)
9. Kramer, S.: Structural regression trees. In: Proceedings of the Thirteenth National Conference on Artificial Intelligence, Cambridge/Menlo Park, AAAI Press/MIT Press, pp. 812–819 (1996)
10. Kramer, S., Widmer, G.: Inducing classification and regression trees in first order logic. In: Džeroski, S., Lavrač, N. (eds.) Relational Data Mining, pp. 140–159. Springer, Heidelberg (2001)
11. Karalič, A., Bratko, I.: First order regression. Machine Learning 26, 147–176 (1997)
12. Ray, S., Page, D.: Multiple instance regression. In: Proceedings of the 18th International Conference on Machine Learning, pp. 425–432. Morgan Kaufmann, San Francisco (2001)
13. Srinivasan, A.: Note on the use of statistical procedures as background predicates in ilp. Technical Report PRG-RR-03-09, Oxford University Computing Lab (2003)
14. Appice, A., Ceci, M., Malerba, D.: Mining model trees: a multi-relational approach. In: Horváth, T., Yamamoto, A. (eds.) ILP 2003. LNCS (LNAI), vol. 2835, pp. 4–21. Springer, Heidelberg (2003)
15. Knobbe, A., Siebes, A., Marseille, B.: Involving aggregate functions in multi-relational search. In: Elomaa, T., Mannila, H., Toivonen, H. (eds.) PKDD 2002. LNCS (LNAI), vol. 2431, pp. 287–298. Springer, Heidelberg (2002)
16. Van Assche, A., Vens, C., Blockeel, H., Džeroski, S.: First order random forests: Learning relational classifiers with complex aggregates. Machine Learning 64(1-3), 149–182 (2006)
17. Vens, C., Ramon, J., Blockeel, H.: Refining aggregate conditions in relational learning. In: Fürnkranz, J., Scheffer, T., Spiliopoulou, M. (eds.) PKDD 2006. LNCS (LNAI), vol. 4213, pp. 383–394. Springer, Heidelberg (2006)
18. Džeroski, S.: Numerical constraints and learnability in inductive logic programming. PhD thesis, University of Ljubljana (Slovenia) (1995)
19. Torgo, L.: Computationally efficient linear regression trees. In: Proc. of the 8th Conf. of the International Federation of Classification Societies, Springer, Heidelberg (2002)

20. Blockeel, H., Dehaspe, L., Ramon, J., Struyf, J., Van Assche, A., Vens, C., Fierens, D.: The ace data mining system: User's manual (2006), http://www.cs.kuleuven.be/dtai/ACE
21. Plotkin, G.: A note on inductive generalization. Machine Intelligence 5, 153–163 (1969)
22. Koller, D.: Probabilistic relational models. In: Džeroski, S., Flach, P.A. (eds.) Inductive Logic Programming. LNCS (LNAI), vol. 1634, pp. 3–13. Springer, Heidelberg (1999)
23. Neville, J., Jensen, D., Friedland, L., Hay, M.: Learning relational probability trees. In: Proceedings of the 9th ACM SIGKDD International Conference on Knowledge Discovery and Data Mining, ACM Press, New York (2003)
24. Krogel, M.A., Wrobel, S.: Facets of aggregation approaches to propositionalization. In: Horváth, T., Yamamoto, A. (eds.) Proceedings of the Work-in-Progress Track at the 13th International Conference on Inductive Logic Programming, pp. 30–39 (2003)
25. Knobbe, A., Ho, E.: Numbers in multi-relational data mining. In: Jorge, A.M., Torgo, L., Brazdil, P.B., Camacho, R., Gama, J. (eds.) PKDD 2005. LNCS (LNAI), vol. 3721, pp. 544–551. Springer, Heidelberg (2005)
26. Jensen, D., Neville, J., Hay, M.: Avoiding bias when aggregating relational data with degree disparity. In: Proceedings of the 20th International Conference on Machine Learning (2003)
27. Knobbe, A., Siebes, A., van der Wallen, D.: Multi-relational decision tree induction. In: Żytkow, J.M., Rauch, J. (eds.) Principles of Data Mining and Knowledge Discovery. LNCS (LNAI), vol. 1704, pp. 378–383. Springer, Heidelberg (1999)
28. Srinivasan, A., Muggleton, S., Sternberg, M., King, R.: Theories for mutagenicity: A study in first-order and feature-based induction. Artificial Intelligence 85(1,2), 277–299 (1996)
29. MassSpectrogram dataset: SDBS, National Institute of Advanced Industrial Science and Technology, Japan http://www.aist.go.jp
30. Srinivasan, A., Muggleton, S., King, R.: Comparing the use of background knowledge by inductive logic programming systems. In: De Raedt, L. (ed.) Proc. of the 5th International Workshop on Inductive Logic Programming, Leuven, pp. 199–230 (1995)

Relational Data Mining Applied to Virtual Engineering of Product Designs

Monika Žáková[1], Filip Železný[1], Javier A. Garcia-Sedano[2],
Cyril Masia Tissot[2], Nada Lavrač[3,4], Petr Křemen[1], and Javier Molina[5]

[1] Czech Technical University, Prague, Czech Republic
[2] Semantic Systems, Av. Del Txoriherri 9, Derio, Spain
[3] Jožef Stefan Institute, Jamova 39, Ljubljana, Slovenia
[4] University of Nova Gorica, Nova Gorica, Slovenia
[5] Fundiciones del Estanda, Beasain (Gipuzkoa), Spain

Abstract. Contemporary product design based on 3D CAD tools aims at improved efficiency using integrated engineering environments with access to databases of existing designs, associated documents and enterprise resource planning. The ultimate goal of this work is to achieve design process improvements by applying state-of-the-art ILP systems for relational data mining of past designs, utilizing commonly agreed design ontologies as background knowledge. This paper demonstrates the utility of relational data mining for virtual engineering of product designs through the detection of frequent design patterns, enabled by the proposed baseline integration of hierarchical background knowledge (a CAD ontology) using sorted refinements.

1 Introduction

Despite considerable successes of ILP in various knowledge discovery problems such as in bioinformatics [7], industrial applications of ILP have been relatively rare. Although the usefulness of ILP has been demonstrated in areas such as finite element mesh design [4], we are not aware of industrial software employing ILP technologies in regular real-life practice. Engineering, as a knowledge-intensive activity, has great potential for ILP. Consider product engineering which involves diverse knowledge types including CAD structures, technical specifications, and standards. In addition, knowledge about the electrical, mechanical, thermodynamic and chemical behavior may be made available, supported by means of empirical data and simulation models. The abundance of data and knowledge motivates the application of ILP to solving numerous relational data mining tasks. For example, discovering design substructures frequently occurring in a corporate CAD repository would allow to establish their easily invocable templates, with a potential of eliminating repetitive designing work.

This paper reports on the approach developed in the SEVENPRO[1] project which aims at developing a semantic virtual engineering environment for product

---

[1] SEVENPRO, Semantic Virtual Engineering Environment for Product Design, is the project IST-027473 (2006-2008) funded under the 6th Framework Programme of the European Commission. The authors acknowledge the support by this project.

S. Muggleton, R. Otero, and A. Tamaddoni-Nezhad (Eds.): ILP 2006, LNAI 4455, pp. 439–453, 2007.
© Springer-Verlag Berlin Heidelberg 2007

design, extending traditional CAD tools with semantic web, virtual reality and relational data mining (RDM) technologies. In one of the tasks the aim is to improve the effectiveness of the search for typical patterns stored in design command chains[2]—conducted for a product of a certain class—thus making explicit the tacit knowledge of an experienced engineer. Other objectives like relational classification, clustering or outlier detection are also motivated in this domain, including rather unorthodox tasks such as learning to match between a formalized product requirement set with an appropriate product design, where both the requirements and designs are represented in relational database formalisms.

The information available in CAD files, associated documents, enterprise resource planning (ERP) and other data sources can be formalized and combined by means of a semantically enriched layer of meta-information (i.e., semantic annotation) based on ontologies. Semantic annotations of CAD designs can be generated automatically from commands histories available via an API of a CAD tool, based on a CAD ontology. These annotations, including the ontology of CAD items, typically encoded in the RDF format, can be automatically transformed to Prolog files containing an ontology of CAD items, axioms and data.

There are three main challenges for ILP due to the use of ontologies in the background knowledge, corresponding to hierarchies of concepts, hierarchies of relations and representation conversion (between Prolog and other knowledge representation languages). *SubclassOf* is a core ontological relation corresponding to taxonomy on terms. Therefore an efficient handling of term taxonomies has to be integrated into the employed RDM systems. The RDF formalism also allows to define hierarchies on relations by means of the *subpropertyOf* relation. To exploit the subproperty relation directly, RDM systems would have to deal with taxonomies of predicates.

Motivated by the virtual engineering of product designs application domain, this work focuses both on what ILP can offer to SEVENPRO problem solving, but also on foundational ILP research challenges motivated by SEVENPRO engineering problems. One of these ILP challenges is the effective use of term/predicate taxonomies which have been, to the best of our knowledge, not commonly addressed in ILP. This work therefore focuses on the technique of taxonomy-exploiting search space structuring, which underlies most other specific SEVENPRO RDM tasks such as frequent pattern mining, classification, feature construction, and design clustering.

This paper is organized as follows. Section 2 provides background for our work by introducing the application domain. Section 3 outlines the role of RDM in the SEVENPRO project and then deals more specifically with RDM of CAD data. In section 4 we describe integration of taxonomies into ILP techniques. Section 5 describes experiments that we conducted and their results. The last section contains conclusions and future work.

---

[2] A design is obtained by successive applications of CAD commands, such as *extrusion, rotation*, etc., which are mutually parametrically related. Various command sequences may lead to the same design, while differing greatly in quality respects, such as complexity, reusability, etc.

2   Background

This section first introduces the application domain, followed by the state-of-the-art in ILP.

2.1   Semantic Virtual Engineering for Product Design Environments

Engineering is one of the most knowledge-intensive activities that exist. More specifically, product engineering has been a key to the development of a strong and specialized manufacturing industry in Europe, organized in RTD departments and technical offices. Product engineering deals with very specific knowledge types, like product structures, CAD designs, technical specifications, standards, and homologations. Moreover, specific electrical, mechanical, thermodynamic and chemical knowledge may include empirical data, simulation models and Computer-aided engineering analysis (CAE) tools that serve to optimise relevant features of the design. The result is rich and complex knowledge stored in many heterogeneous formats, of which probably CAD, documentation and ERP/database are the most frequently found, and which constitute the focus of the SEVENPRO project. The project addresses the most important problem encountered by engineering teams: the effective reuse of knowledge and past designs.

Most engineering teams currently have to access heterogeneous information sources from different tools which, in most cases, do not interoperate. The development of a new product, or a product order with high level of customization, requires a new engineering approach. During the development process, engineering staff works out new product item designs by means of CAD tools. CAD designs contain vast amounts of implicit knowledge about the way experienced engineers design very specialized parts. Efficient reuse of knowledge depends on appropriate organization of information and the capability of retrieving it for later use. Engineering teams still have to spend lots of time trying to find existing designs from a vast CAD repository; in many occasions, they design again and again items very similar to others already existing. Moreover, the different types of knowledge described are supported by different systems, which are used separately and have no communication with each other, like CAD tools, ERP systems, documents and spreadsheets, etc. This situation is illustrated in Figure 1(left).

To efficiently retrieve information, it is necessary to be able to carry out complex searches, combining geometrical, technical and managerial aspects. This would allow the engineer, for example, to query about "parts of type clamp [itemFamily], with more than 6 holes [Geometry], set in order later than November/2004 [Management], compliant with ISO-23013 [Documentation]". This is not possible with current information systems, unless an expensive and complex Product Lifecycle Management (PLM) system is set up, whose maintenance in terms of information updates is burdensome for every company and simply unaffordable in terms of cost for SMEs. The only feasible approach to this is by using semantic-knowledge technologies and a well automated semantic-annotation

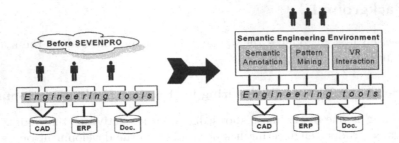

Fig. 1. Engineering heterogeneous information sources before and after SEVENPRO

system from the different information sources, able to extract from them all the knowledge that is useful for the engineering activity. In order to achieve this, an integrated architecture is required, able to extract and maintain a layer of semantic annotations from the different information sources targeted, namely ERP, CAD and Document repositories. As shown in Figure 1(right), a novel semantic virtual engineering product design scenario aims at a better integration and reuse of design knowledge.

2.2   ILP Background: Relational Data Mining by RSD

The RSD relational data mining system [16] enables the discovery of interesting relational subgroups from data (facts) and relational background knowledge. In the engineering design context, an example of a relational subgroup description is e.g.: "a structure containing two co-centric cylinders" (here two substructures of a structure with the mutual relation of co-centricity). A subgroup is then a set of all designs complying with the above description. An interesting subgroup is one that is sufficiently large and in which the distribution of values of a chosen attribute of interest substantially differs from the distribution in the entire data set. For example, the attribute of interest may be the functional category of the design. Similar to Aleph [12], RSD is controlled through command line and accepts data and background knowledge in the Prolog syntax. A distinguishing point of RSD is that it tackles the relational mining task by an (approximate) conversion into a non-relational (propositional) data mining task by constructing a set of truth-valued relational features. The technique (known as propositionalization) implemented in RSD is not limited to the task of subgroup discovery and can be used to transform relational design descriptions into forms that can be used as input to other data mining techniques (e.g. those in WEKA [15]), whose outputs can then be back-converted and interpreted as relational non-recursive patterns/models.

The task addressed in this work is discovery of interesting design patterns describing detected groups of frequent design sequences. Such discovery is made from stored designs and background knowledge in the form of a CAD ontology.

The patterns are also converted to Boolean features using method of propositionalization described in [16] and used for classification by propositional methods.

The usefulness of ILP-generated patterns as attributes for propositional methods has been described e.g. in [14], where ILP-generated attributes were used in addition to expert attributes for regression. The background knowledge used in this work does not contain any hierarchical information. Since in our work we are using only function-free Horn clauses, the generating relational patterns in our work is similar to discovery of frequent patterns in DATALOG described in [3]. This work deals with hierarchical background knowledge by means of is_a predicate, providing it in form of facts e.g. is_a(1001,BSC_disturbance), is_a(BSC_disturbance,BSC_alarm). The hierarchy does not distinguish between "subclass" and "member of" relations. The level-wise algorithm for frequent pattern discovery is used. Expressing class hierarchy using is_a predicate also appears in [2]. Ceci and Appice compare classification using multi-level association with propositional classification using association rules having only class label in the head converted into Boolean attributes. We are adopting a similar approach to propositional classification, however we are extending the used hierarchical background knowledge to hierarchy on predicates.

3 Relational Data Mining Applied to the Discovery of Product Design Patterns

This section first outlines the role of RDM in the SEVENPRO project. Then a more detailed description of data from CAD designs is provided.

3.1 Overall RDM Role in the SEVENPRO Project

The discovery of patterns from engineering knowledge repositories is expected to be an important facility for reusing engineering knowledge. The amount of data and its availability through the use of several independent tools has always been an obstacle for such reuse. Coupling a unified view of the available knowledge through commonly agreed ontologies with the capabilities of mining the information gathered in various engineering resources will broaden the range of actually reusable engineering knowledge. In particular, it is foreseen that the sequences of CAD design operations (design features) can be exploited to obtain from them abstract design patterns. These patterns (after human revision) can be reused as corporate design standards or recommendations

- to support the work of engineers (reusability),
- to check pattern compliance of new designs (quality checking), and
- to teach novel engineers on how to design specific parts (training).

Engineering designs capturing implicit expert knowledge have a relational nature: they cannot be efficiently described by attribute tuples. Rather, flexible-size structural descriptions are needed, specifying various numbers of primitive objects as well as relations between them. To discover and explicitly define knowledge from such data by means of relational patterns, RDM algorithms are needed.

The status of the current SEVENPRO developments is presented in Sections 4 and 5 of this paper.

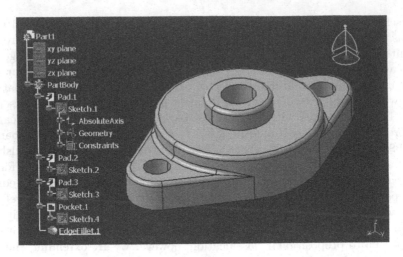

Fig. 2. Example of a CAD design including commands history

3.2 CAD Data Used for Relational Data Mining

The SEVENPRO ontologies and the corresponding annotations cover a large spectrum of engineering concepts (items, orders, norms, problems, versioning, among many others). As mentioned, this allows for complex queries across the available knowledge. An important facet of this knowledge is the CAD design information. Engineering departments generate a large amount of CAD files. Such files can be 3D part-definition files, 3D assembly definition files or 2D drafting files. In addition, relevant information ranges from textual data (like block, operation or part names) and generic document structure (like assembly structure), to detailed design information in the case of 3D parts. In the later case, the shape of a 3D part is the result of sequence of operations specified by the designer. This sequence of design operations (design features) is where most of the designer's knowledge resides, as it is a reflection of the designer's experience.

Figure 2 represents a simple mechanical part, a two bolt flange. Notice the command history (at the left-hand side of the figure) leading to the particular virtually designed object. In command histories the basic operations are "creating" matter (e.g., a pad, a stiffener) and "removing" matter (e.g., a chamfer, an edgeFillet).

This design history conveys the higher level information on how the object was designed as well as high level dimensional information, as the commands have parameters associated to them (like the height of an extrusion or the radius of a fillet). This information would be more difficult to determine using only the final shape of the part. Having it associated to the operation not only makes it easily accessible but also keeps its real meaning. The design history, presented at the left-hand side of Figure 2, is depicted in the annotation layer as a design sequence in terms of ontology classes and instances, as shown in Figure 3.

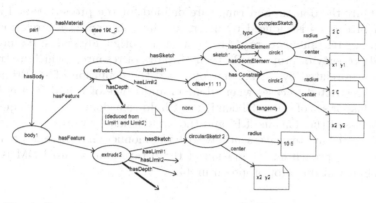

Fig. 3. Part of a semantic annotation of the design shown in Figure 2

This kind of highly relational data exists for all the annotated files, and is the input to a RDM algorithm. The generated instance schema is simplified with respect to the internal CAD representation. For example, if a sketch does not belong to any predefined category, it is identified as a complexSketch and it is not further elaborated. The schema also contains some properties derived from other properties, e.g. property hasDepth of extrude is derived from the two limits. In SEVENPRO, this representation has been converted into Prolog facts, more suitable as input for the RDM algorithms. An example of Prolog facts describing part of CAD design is presented below.

```
hasCADEntity('eItemT_BA1341',part_183260395_10554).
typeOf('eItemT_BA1341', eItemT).
typeOf(part_183260395_10554, cADPart).
hasBody(part_183260395_10554,body_183260395_10555).
typeOf(body_183260395_10555, body).
hasFeature(body_183260395_10555,extrude_183260395_10556).
typeOf(extrude_183260395_10556, extrude).
hasSketch(extrude_183260395_10556,complexSketch_183260395_10557).
typeOf(complexSketch_183260395_10557, complexSketch).
hasGeomElem(complexSketch_183260395_10557,circle_183260395_10558).
typeOf(circle_183260395_10558, circle).
hasDepth(extrude_183260395_10556,0).
```

4   ILP Advances: Integration of Taxonomies

The ontological background knowledge currently available in the described CAD domain is represented in the RDF formalism [11]. The ontology can be represented by an acyclic directed graph (DAG). Concepts are defined only by means of declaring class and its place in the class hierarchy. No set operators or restrictions commonly used in OWL are present in the background knowledge and dataset. Only the domain and range are defined for the properties and a hierarchy on properties is induced by means of the subpropertyOf relation. The definition of rdfs:subPropertyOf relation in [11] originally states: If a property P is a subproperty of property P', then all pairs of resources which are related by P are also related by P'. For our purposes the definition of subPropertyOf relation is restricted to cases where domain and range of P and P' are defined by some class or set of classes. Then it must hold that domain of P is equivalent to or subclass of the domain of P' and the same holds for range.

Therefore we have to deal essentially with taxonomies on terms and predicates. Our baseline approach for integration of these taxonomies into RDM is based on the refinement operator proposed in [6].

4.1   Sorted Downward Refinement

The background knowledge built into this refinement is based on sorted logic, which encodes the taxonomies. Sorted logic contains in addition to predicate and function symbols also a disjoint set of sort symbols. A sort symbol denotes a subset of the domain called a sort [6]. A sorted variable is a pair, $x : \tau$, where x is a variable name and τ is a sort symbol. Semantically, a sorted variable ranges over only the subset of the domain denoted by its sort symbol. The semantics of universally-quantified sorted sentences can be defined in terms of their equivalence to ordinary sentences: $\forall x : \tau\phi$ is logically equivalent to $\forall x : \neg\tau(x) \vee \phi'$ where ϕ' is the result of substituting x for all free occurrences of $x : \tau \in \phi$.

The background knowledge that is to be built into the instantiation, subsumption and refinement of sorted clauses is known as a sort theory. A sort theory is a finite set of sentences that express relationships among the sorts and the sortal behavior of the functions. Sentences of the sort theory are constructed like ordinary sentences of first-order predicate calculus except that they contain no ordinary predicate symbols; in their place are sort symbols acting as monadic predicate symbols. In [6] the form of the sort theory is restricted to two types of sentences: function sentences and subsort sentences.

Function sentence

$$\forall x_1, \ldots, x_n \tau_1(x_1) \wedge \ldots \wedge \tau_n(x_n) \to \tau(f(x_1, \ldots, x_n))$$

Subsort sentence

$$\forall x \tau_1(x) \to \tau_2(x).$$

Graph of the sort theory has to be acyclic and singly rooted. In our task we are not dealing with functions, therefore the only type of sort theory is restricted to subsort sentences. As was stated above the background knowledge is acyclic and since no multiple inheritance is used, graph of the background knowledge is a DAG, graphs for the individual sorts are trees. For the sort theory special substitution is defined [6]:

Definition 1. *Sorted substitution θ is a Σ-substitution if for every variable $x : \tau$, it holds that $\Sigma \models \bar{\forall}\tau(t)$ where t is $(x : \tau)\theta$.*

In [6] it was proved there that the sorted downward refinement is finite for finite set of predicate symbols and that it is correct and complete.

4.2   Extending θ-Subsumption with Σ-Substitution

We have extended the traditional θ-subsumption with Σ-substitution obtaining a refinement operator with three substitution rules:

1. specialization through changing the type of a variable to its direct subclass (based on Σ-substitution),
2. specialization through adding a literal (traditional θ-substitution),
3. specialization through replacing predicate P by a predicate P', where it holds subPropertyOf(P',P).

In addition to the two new specialization rules, specialization through adding a literal was extended, so that the types of input variables of a literal to be added can be supertypes of some already used variables. This was done to accommodate for situation similar to the following example: Conjunction created so far is hasCADEntity(X1:cADFileRevision,X2:cADPart),hasBody(X2:cADPart, X3:body),hasFeature(X3:body,X4:extrude),hasDepth(X4:extrude, X5:length), the literal to be added is defined by hasValue(+literalValue, -float) (i.e. by predicate hasValue with input argument of type literalValue and output argument of type float). In the background knowledge it is stated that length is a subclass of literalValue. Therefore the predicate hasValue can be added to the conjunction, creating new conjunction: hasCADEntity(X1:cADFileRevision,X2:cADPart),hasBody(X2:cADPart, X3:body),hasFeature(X3:body,X4:extrude),hasDepth(X4:extrude, X5:length),hasValue(X5:length,X6:float). We have not included substitution of variables by constants so far, since in data mining from CAD designs we are currently focusing on the structure of similar designs, not on numeric values of parameters.

4.3   Pattern Discovery

The pattern discovery task using the sorted refinement operator is approached through constructing first-order features. An overview of the system is shown in Figure 4. The ILP system generates features with user-defined maximal length and minimal support. The generated features are connected subgraphs of generalizations of the graphs describing the individual examples. Since the graphs describing the examples are not trees and there are relations connecting variables at the same variable depth, reuse of variables within the features is necessary, i.e. one variable can be used either as input or output variable of several predicates within one feature. An example of relation connecting variables at the same variable depth is appliesTo(fillet, cADFeature) in the following example

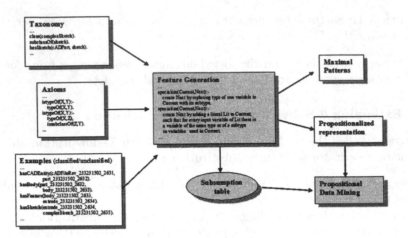

Fig. 4. An overview of the RDM system

hasCADEntity(X1:cADFileRevision,X2:cADPart),hasBody(X2:cADPart,X3:
body), hasFeature(X3:body,X4:cADFeature), next(X3:body,X5:fillet),
appliesTo(X5:fillet,X4:cADFeature).

Depth-first search is used to generate the features. To prevent generation of irrelevant features, the coverage of each feature is computed immediately after the feature is generated. Features with coverage lower than the minimal required support are pruned and not refined further. To prevent generating features that are permutations of features already generated, an explicit order on predicates and concept types is defined and enforced in each feature. Ordering of predicates is checked for the set of literals with the same variable depth of input variables. Moreover, in case of multiple use of the same predicate with same input variables and output variables of the same type, subtree rooted at each occurrence of the predicate has to be smaller than subtree rooted at previous occurrences of this predicate. Total order on the subtrees is induced by order defined on predicates. Therefore the search is complete even with ordering.

An example of a discovered feature, which was the single most important feature for description of the class `itemFamilyLiner`, can be seen below. It contains variables of types at different levels of granularity e.g. `cADFeature` is 2 levels higher in the hierarchy of features than `fillet`.

f(X1:eItemT):- hasCADEntity(X1:eItemT,X2:cADPart), hasBody(X2:
cADPart,X3:body), hasFeature(X3:body,X4:pocket), hasSketch(X4:
pocket,X5:complexSketch), hasGeomElement(X5:complexSketch,X6:
circle), next(X4:pocket,X7:fillet), next(X7:fillet,X8:cADFeature)

During the feature generation, a table of feature subsumption pointing to all ancestors of the feature is maintained. This is similar to the approach employed in SPADA [1]. This subsumption table is exploited for pruning of features for propositionalization. The subsumption is also exploited in propositional pattern search, which prunes any conjunctions of a subsumer with its subsumee and

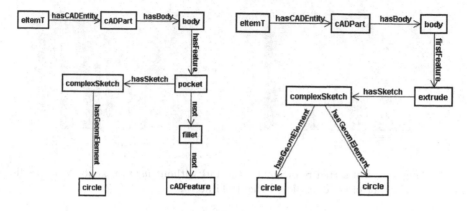

Fig. 5. Examples of discovered features

specializes a conjunction not only by extending it, but also by replacing an included feature with its subsumee.

4.4 Feature Visualization

To improve RDM usability both for users and for developers, graphical visualization of features is useful. A tool based on the JGraph library has been developed. As the input data schema for RDM contains only unary and binary predicates, we can restrict our attention to oriented directed acyclic graphs (DAGs). Nodes in such a DAG represent undistinguished variables labeled by sort atoms, while edges represent binary predicate atoms.

In Figure 5 an example of discovered patterns is shown. The two patterns in the figure simultaneously cover 44 of 62 instances classified as itemFamilyLiner, while they also cover 3 other (non-itemFamilyLiner) instances. Accordingly, the class itemFamilyLiner can be well described as a set of instances having as a starting feature a two circle extrusion, while having also another feature – a circled pocket followed by a fillet and another feature.

5   Experimental Results

Experiments were performed on a dataset containing 160 examples of CAD design drawings provided by a metal casting company that participates in the project: Fundiciones del Estanda. Two main types of experiments were run:

- searching for relational patterns present in all examples of a given class, to compare efficiency of the sorted refinement enriched RDM to a baseline ILP system, and
- classification based on constructing propositional features to evaluate the predictive accuracy of the propositionalisation approach to classification.

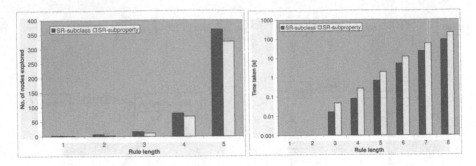

Fig. 6. Comparison of sorted refinement with and without using taxonomy on predicates. Left: Number of nodes explored Right: Time taken.

5.1 Comparison of Sorted Refinement with Aleph

We conducted experiments to compare the efficiency of RDM including sorted refinement (SR) on one hand and a standard ILP system on the other hand. The baseline ILP system chosen for comparison was Aleph. The specific goal of the experiment was to determine the volumes of search space traversed by the respective systems in order to find patterns covering all of the provided positive examples.

The majority class of examples is considered as positive. For the sake of this experiment, no negative examples are needed. There were 57 examples, where each example contained a description of one CAD design drawing. Around 100 predicates were used to describe each example.

The tests were performed for pattern length from 1 to 8. For pattern length greater than 7, pattern generation was no longer tractable for Aleph. In the first set of experiments only term subsumption was used in our system. It can be seen that the number of expanded nodes is decreased very significantly. In the second set of experiments, predicate subsumption was used in our system as well. Results of these experiments can be seen in Figures 6 and 7. Figure 6 shows results of using sorted refinement with and without predicate subsumption. Figure 7 shows results of both our approaches compared to Aleph. The time taken for evaluation roughly doubles w.r.t. experiments using term subsumption only. The number of explored nodes decreases, however the decrease is not very significant. This is due to the fact that the subproperty relation hierarchy that was used has only two levels and includes around 10 predicates. Our system can be used for pattern sizes, which are intractable in Aleph. This is important, because it has been discovered that patterns with length less than 7 do not provide information sufficient for classification.

5.2 Classification Based on Propositional Features

For the data set containing 160 design drawings their classification was provided. Examples were classified into 4 proper classes describing families of designs and

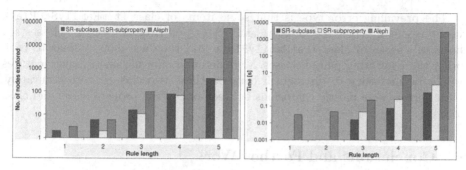

Fig. 7. Comparison of sorted refinement and Aleph. Left: Nodes explored Right: Time taken.

57 examples that did not belong to any of the 4 classes were classified as 'other'. By consultation with the users it was found out that the first feature used is important and also relative order of the features is important. Therefore properties describing the order of CAD features were added to background knowledge and to annotations e.g. `next(+cADFeature,-cADFeature)`, `sequenceStart` and `firstFeature(+body,-cADFeature)`. The following relations were also added to the background knowledge:
`subpropertyOf(firstFeature,hasFeature)`, `subpropertyOf(hasFeature,`
`sequenceStart)`. Special treatment of relations that are subproperties of `next` and `sequenceStart` was implemented. Subproperties of `sequenceStart` can occur only once in a pattern and for subproperties of `next` order on the level of arguments is not checked.

Our system was used to generate a set of features of length 7. The feature set was then pruned by excluding features covering all examples. Also in case a feature covered the same examples as some of its children, the feature was excluded. More general features are pruned rather than more specific ones, since concepts that are leaves of the class hierarchy are mapped to specific design operations available in CAD systems and therefore are more interesting for the user. Propositional algorithm J48 implemented in WEKA [15] was then used for classification using generated features as attributes. For testing 10 fold cross-validation was used. Results of the classification are summarized in Table 1.

Table 1. Results of classification using the J48 algorithm

Class	TP Rate	FP Rate	Precision	Recall	F-Measure	ROC Area
itemFamilyTT	0.826	0.036	0.792	0.826	0.809	0.9
itemFamilyLiner	0.895	0.068	0.879	0.895	0.887	0.927
itemFamilyStdPlate	0.5	0.02	0.571	0.5	0.533	0.834
itemFamilySlottedPlate	0.8	0.02	0.727	0.8	0.762	0.883
other	0.855	0.071	0.883	0.855	0.869	0.897

The prevailing error type is that some items of class `itemFamilyStdPlate` were incorrectly classified as `itemFamilySlottedPlate`. These two classes are both subclasses of class `itemFamilyPlate` and they are more similar to each other than any other pair of classes. More detailed information or longer features would be necessary to distinguish between these two classes more accurately. Other errors were mostly confusions between one of the proper classes and class 'other'.

6 Conclusions and Further Work

In this paper we have described semantic virtual engineering for product design in engineering environments, which integrates information from heterogeneous sources by means of a semantic layer, and identified the role of relational data mining in this application. As a case study, semantic annotation and RDM on CAD designs was chosen, since CAD designs are challenging from the ILP point of view due to the various length and structure of the description of each example combined with taxonomical background knowledge. We have proposed a baseline approach for integrating taxonomical background knowledge into an ILP system by implementing sorted refinement operator and extending it to include taxonomies on predicates.

The efficiency of our approach was demonstrated by comparing it to standard ILP system Aleph without any support for integration of hierarchical background knowledge. The results were strongly convincing in favor of the former. In terms of the volume of search spaced traversed to find a set of frequent patterns, the 'hierarchy-blind' search conducted by Aleph maintains a roughly exponential overhead w.r.t. the ontology-aware refinement, as the maximum pattern size is being increased. This has a strong consequence in this application domain: working in spaces of patterns of length greater than 7 literals becomes intractable for Aleph, while such and longer patterns are important for capturing common design sequences as exemplified earlier in the text. More experiments comparing frequent patterns discovered with different types of hierarchies will be performed, when the CAD design ontology becomes more fine grained. Then also tests of scalability will be conducted.

Features generated by our system were also used for classification of CAD designs. Generally speaking, the accuracies obtained through cross-validation were surprisingly high, which can be ascribed both to the noise-free character of the data and to the sufficient expressivity of the features our system constructed. Analyzing the prevailing classification error type, it was discovered that the order of CAD design features was important for classification, and thus predicates and rules describing the order of predicates were established.

In future work we will consider a more principled approach of integrating more complex ontological background knowledge, including recursive definitions and multiple inheritance, and the order on predicates. The first approach we will consider in future work is using a hybrid language integrating description logics and Horn logic similar to $\mathcal{AL}$-log [9] and CARIN [8]. Another approach is using a more expressive formalism such as F logic. We will also closely collaborate with the end users to restrict the form of features.

References

1. Appice, A., Ceci, M., Lanca, A., Lisi, F.A., Malerba, D.: Discovery of spatial association rules in geo-referenced census data: A relational mining approach. Intelligent Data Analysis 7, 541–566 (2003)
2. Ceci, M., Appice, A.: Spatial Associative Classification: Propositional vs. Structural approach. In: Proceedings of the ECML/PKDD 04 Workshop on Mining Spatio temporal Data (2004)
3. Dehaspe, L., Toivonen, H.: Discovery of frequent DATALOG patterns. Data Mining and Knowledge Discovery 3(1), 7–36 (1999)
4. Dolšak, B., et al.: Finite element mesh design: An engineering domain for ILP application. In: Proc. of ILP 1994, GMD-Studien, vol. 237, pp. 305–320 (1994)
5. Donini, F.M., Lenzerini, et al.: AL-log: Integrating Datalog and Description Logics. Journal of Intelligent Information Systems 10(3), 227–252 (1998)
6. Frisch, A.: Sorted downward refinement: Building background knowledge into a refinement operator for ILP. In: Džeroski, S., Flach, P.A. (eds.) Inductive Logic Programming. LNCS (LNAI), vol. 1634, Springer, Heidelberg (1999)
7. King, R.D., et al.: Functional genomic hypothesis generation and experimentation by a robot scientist. Nature 427, 247–252 (2004)
8. Levy, A., Rousset, M.-C.: Combining Horn rules and description logics in CARIN. Artificial Intelligence 104, 165–209 (1998)
9. Lisi, F.A., Malerba, D.: Ideal Refinement of Descriptions in AL-Log. In: Horváth, T., Yamamoto, A. (eds.) ILP 2003. LNCS (LNAI), vol. 2835, pp. 215–232. Springer, Heidelberg (2003)
10. McGuinness, D.L., van Harmelen, F. (eds.): OWL Web Ontology Language Overview. W3C Recommendation (February 10, 2004) Available online at http://www.w3.org/TR/owl-features/
11. RDF Vocabulary Description Language 1.0: RDF Schema. W3C Recommendation (February 10, 2004) Available at http://www.w3.org/TR/rdf-schema/
12. Srinivasan, A.: The Aleph manual version 4 (2003) (June 7, 2006) Available online at http://web.comlab.ox.ac.uk/oucl/research/areas/machlearn/Aleph/
13. Srinivasan, A., Muggleton, S., et al.: Theories for mutagenicity: A study in first-order and feature-based induction. Artificial Intelligence 85(1-2), 277–299 (1996)
14. Srinivasan, A., King, R.: Feature construction with ILP: A study of quantitative predictions of biological activity aided by structural attributes. In: ILP 1996. LNCS, vol. 1314, pp. 352–367. Springer, Heidelberg (1997)
15. Witten, I.H., Frank, E.: Data Mining: Practical machine learning tools and techniques, 2nd edn. Morgan Kaufmann, San Francisco (2005)
16. Železný, F., Lavrač, N.: Propositionalization-based relational subgroup discovery with RSD. Machine Learning 62, 33–63 (2006)

Author Index

Lecture Notes in Artificial Intelligence (LNAI)

Vol. 4371: K. Inoue, K. Satoh, F. Toni (Eds.), Computational Logic in Multi-Agent Systems. X, 315 pages. 2007.

Vol. 4369: M. Umeda, A. Wolf, O. Bartenstein, U. Geske, D. Seipel, O. Takata (Eds.), Declarative Programming for Knowledge Management. X, 229 pages. 2006.

Vol. 4342: H. de Swart, E. Orłowska, G. Schmidt, M. Roubens (Eds.), Theory and Applications of Relational Structures as Knowledge Instruments II. X, 373 pages. 2006.

Vol. 4335: S.A. Brueckner, S. Hassas, M. Jelasity, D. Yamins (Eds.), Engineering Self-Organising Systems. XII, 212 pages. 2007.

Vol. 4334: B. Beckert, R. Hähnle, P.H. Schmitt (Eds.), Verification of Object-Oriented Software. XXIX, 658 pages. 2007.

Vol. 4333: U. Reimer, D. Karagiannis (Eds.), Practical Aspects of Knowledge Management. XII, 338 pages. 2006.

Vol. 4327: M. Baldoni, U. Endriss (Eds.), Declarative Agent Languages and Technologies IV. VIII, 257 pages. 2006.

Vol. 4314: C. Freksa, M. Kohlhase, K. Schill (Eds.), KI 2006: Advances in Artificial Intelligence. XII, 458 pages. 2007.

Vol. 4304: A. Sattar, B.-h. Kang (Eds.), AI 2006: Advances in Artificial Intelligence. XXVII, 1303 pages. 2006.

Vol. 4303: A. Hoffmann, B.-h. Kang, D. Richards, S. Tsumoto (Eds.), Advances in Knowledge Acquisition and Management. XI, 259 pages. 2006.

Vol. 4293: A. Gelbukh, C.A. Reyes-Garcia (Eds.), MICAI 2006: Advances in Artificial Intelligence. XXVIII, 1232 pages. 2006.

Vol. 4289: M. Ackermann, B. Berendt, M. Grobelnik, A. Hotho, D. Mladenič, G. Semeraro, M. Spiliopoulou, G. Stumme, V. Svátek, M. van Someren (Eds.), Semantics, Web and Mining. X, 197 pages. 2006.

Vol. 4285: Y. Matsumoto, R.W. Sproat, K.-F. Wong, M. Zhang (Eds.), Computer Processing of Oriental Languages. XVII, 544 pages. 2006.

Vol. 4274: Q. Huo, B. Ma, E.-S. Chng, H. Li (Eds.), Chinese Spoken Language Processing. XXIV, 805 pages. 2006.

Vol. 4265: L. Todorovski, N. Lavrač, K.P. Jantke (Eds.), Discovery Science. XIV, 384 pages. 2006.

Vol. 4264: J.L. Balcázar, P.M. Long, F. Stephan (Eds.), Algorithmic Learning Theory. XIII, 393 pages. 2006.

Vol. 4259: S. Greco, Y. Hata, S. Hirano, M. Inuiguchi, S. Miyamoto, H.S. Nguyen, R. Słowiński (Eds.), Rough Sets and Current Trends in Computing. XXII, 951 pages. 2006.

Vol. 4253: B. Gabrys, R.J. Howlett, L.C. Jain (Eds.), Knowledge-Based Intelligent Information and Engineering Systems, Part III. XXXII, 1301 pages. 2006.

Vol. 4252: B. Gabrys, R.J. Howlett, L.C. Jain (Eds.), Knowledge-Based Intelligent Information and Engineering Systems, Part II. XXXIII, 1335 pages. 2006.

Vol. 4251: B. Gabrys, R.J. Howlett, L.C. Jain (Eds.), Knowledge-Based Intelligent Information and Engineering Systems, Part I. LXVI, 1297 pages. 2006.

Vol. 4248: S. Staab, V. Svátek (Eds.), Managing Knowledge in a World of Networks. XIV, 400 pages. 2006.

Vol. 4246: M. Hermann, A. Voronkov (Eds.), Logic for Programming, Artificial Intelligence, and Reasoning. XIII, 588 pages. 2006.

Vol. 4223: L. Wang, L. Jiao, G. Shi, X. Li, J. Liu (Eds.), Fuzzy Systems and Knowledge Discovery. XXVIII, 1335 pages. 2006.

Vol. 4213: J. Fürnkranz, T. Scheffer, M. Spiliopoulou (Eds.), Knowledge Discovery in Databases: PKDD 2006. XXII, 660 pages. 2006.

Vol. 4212: J. Fürnkranz, T. Scheffer, M. Spiliopoulou (Eds.), Machine Learning: ECML 2006. XXIII, 851 pages. 2006.

Vol. 4211: P. Vogt, Y. Sugita, E. Tuci, C.L. Nehaniv (Eds.), Symbol Grounding and Beyond. VIII, 237 pages. 2006.

Vol. 4203: F. Esposito, Z.W. Raś, D. Malerba, G. Semeraro (Eds.), Foundations of Intelligent Systems. XVIII, 767 pages. 2006.

Vol. 4201: Y. Sakakibara, S. Kobayashi, K. Sato, T. Nishino, E. Tomita (Eds.), Grammatical Inference: Algorithms and Applications. XII, 359 pages. 2006.

Vol. 4200: I.F.C. Smith (Ed.), Intelligent Computing in Engineering and Architecture. XIII, 692 pages. 2006.

Vol. 4198: O. Nasraoui, O. Zaïane, M. Spiliopoulou, B. Mobasher, B. Masand, P.S. Yu (Eds.), Advances in Web Mining and Web Usage Analysis. IX, 177 pages. 2006.

Vol. 4196: K. Fischer, I.J. Timm, E. André, N. Zhong (Eds.), Multiagent System Technologies. X, 185 pages. 2006.

Vol. 4188: P. Sojka, I. Kopeček, K. Pala (Eds.), Text, Speech and Dialogue. XV, 721 pages. 2006.

Vol. 4183: J. Euzenat, J. Domingue (Eds.), Artificial Intelligence: Methodology, Systems, and Applications. XIII, 291 pages. 2006.

Vol. 4180: M. Kohlhase, OMDoc – An Open Markup Format for Mathematical Documents [version 1.2]. XIX, 428 pages. 2006.

Vol. 4177: R. Marín, E. Onaindía, A. Bugarín, J. Santos (Eds.), Current Topics in Artificial Intelligence. XV, 482 pages. 2006.

Vol. 4160: M. Fisher, W. van der Hoek, B. Konev, A. Lisitsa (Eds.), Logics in Artificial Intelligence. XII, 516 pages. 2006.

Vol. 4155: O. Stock, M. Schaerf (Eds.), Reasoning, Action and Interaction in AI Theories and Systems. XVIII, 343 pages. 2006.

Vol. 4149: M. Klusch, M. Rovatsos, T.R. Payne (Eds.), Cooperative Information Agents X. XII, 477 pages. 2006.

Vol. 4140: J.S. Sichman, H. Coelho, S.O. Rezende (Eds.), Advances in Artificial Intelligence - IBERAMIA-SBIA 2006. XXIII, 635 pages. 2006.